LANGUAGE
LOYALTIES

LANGUAGE LOYALTIES

A Source

Book on

the Official

English

Controversy

Edited by
James Crawford

With an Afterword by
Geoffrey Nunberg

The University of Chicago Press / Chicago and London

JAMES CRAWFORD is author of *Bilingual Education: History, Politics, Theory, and Practice* (1989) and *Hold Your Tongue: Bilingualism and the Politics of "English Only"* (in press). An independent writer, he is the former Washington editor of *Education Week*.

The University of Chicago Press, Chicago 60637
The University of Chicago Press, Ltd., London
© 1992 by The University of Chicago
All rights reserved. Published 1992
Printed in the United States of America

00 99 98 97 96 95 94 93 92   5 4 3 2 1

ISBN (cloth) 0-226-12015-5
ISBN (paper) 0-226-12016-3

Library of Congress Cataloging-in-Publication Data

Language loyalties : a source book on the official English controversy
  / edited by James Crawford : with an afterword by Geoffrey Nunberg.
       p.   cm.
Includes bibliographical references and index.
   1. Language policy—United States.   2. English language—Political
aspects—United States.   I. Crawford, James, 1949–
P119.32.U6L36   1992
306.4'4973—dc20   91-29445

⊗ The paper used in this publication meets
the minimum requirements of the American National
Standard for Information Sciences—Permanence of
Paper for Printed Library Materials, ANSI Z39.48-1984.

Contents

Editor's Introduction

By James Crawford

Official English caught most Americans by surprise. When the campaign emerged in the early 1980s, language was an unlikely political issue for the United States. The matter of our national tongue had long since been settled—or so it seemed. At first, we paid little attention to warnings about creeping bilingualism and the endangered status of English. This sounded like nothing more than the buzzing of gadflies. Or perhaps, as one New York Congressman suggested, it was "another of the crazy California movements" with an apocalyptic vision to espouse. Who else would claim that English needed "legal protection" in a country where, according to the 1980 census, it was spoken by all but 2 percent of residents above the age of four and where only 11 percent were regular speakers of another tongue?[1] A new Babel hardly seemed imminent. Americans have seldom fought over language, precisely because we have taken the dominance of English for granted. As late as 1987, two-thirds of respondents to a national survey assumed that the Constitution already designated English as the official language of the United States.[2]

In fact, the framers were silent on the question. No one had even thought to broach it in Congress until Senator S. I. Hayakawa did so in 1981. A critic of bilingual education and bilingual voting rights, Hayakawa introduced a constitutional amendment to make English official. That seemed innocuous enough, a ceremonial gesture to ratify the obvious—except that it went further. The measure would also prohibit federal and state "laws, ordinances, regulations, orders, programs, and policies" from requiring the use of other languages (see p. 112). Its thrust was not only *for* English, but *against* bilingualism. If adopted, Hayakawa's proposal would reverse a trend begun in the late 1960s toward accommodating the needs of linguistic minorities. But the English Language Amendment was largely ignored, and it died without a hearing in the 97th Congress.

1. The latter figure is probably overstated; 11 percent of U.S. residents above the age of four *lived in households* where a language other than English was spoken, while 98 percent reported that they spoke English "well" or "very well"; U.S. Bureau of the Census, *United States Summary, General Social and Economic Characteristics* (1980), table 99, p. 68.

2. Hearst Corp. survey on the Constitution reported in "Survey: Most Think English Is Official U.S. Language," Associated Press, Feb. 14, 1987.

Then, shortly after retiring in 1983, the senator helped to found U.S. English, a lobbying effort that generated national attention. Its program—"In Defense of Our Common Language"—was greeted as a curiosity by journalists. "The Mother Tongue Has a Movement," announced *The New York Times*.[3] A spectrum of luminaries including Alistair Cooke, Saul Bellow, Walter Cronkite, Norman Cousins, Gore Vidal, Norman Podhoretz, and Arnold Schwarzenegger signed up for the U.S. English "advisory board," lending their prestige to its letterhead and direct-mail fundraising. (Later, several would resign in embarrassment.) Official English now became fodder for right-of-center pundits. In a Fourth of July column, George F. Will pontificated on "the connection between the English language and American liberty." William F. Buckley, Jr., citing the "Canadian Frog" nuisance, endorsed Hayakawa's approach for quelling our own "militant Spanish-speaking minority." Another boost came when Phil Donahue featured the English Language Amendment on his syndicated talk show, staged before thousands of screaming guests in a Miami stadium.[4] "I ♥ English" bumper stickers began to appear in Florida and other areas feeling the impact of Hispanic and Asian immigration. Within five years U.S. English mushroomed into a 400,000-member organization with a $6 million annual budget.

Legislators, always on the lookout for novel issues, began to climb aboard. Thirty-seven state houses considered Official English in 1987 alone. It was also a hit with the voters. U.S. English passed ballot initiatives in California and other Sunbelt states, usually by large margins; elsewhere, opinion polls showed support ranging from 60 to 90 percent. More than a dozen versions of the English Language Amendment have appeared in Congress since Hayakawa's original proposal, attracting scores of cosponsors, although none has yet come to a vote. The campaign has fared better in the states. By 1990 seventeen had adopted statutes or constitutional amendments declaring English their official tongue *(for a detailed chronology, see pp. 89–94)*.

Despite the groundswell, however, Official English has become a polarizing issue, revealing an enormous gap in perceptions. For supporters, the case is obvious: English has always been our common language, a means of resolving conflicts in a nation of diverse racial, ethnic, and religious groups. Reaffirming the preeminence of English means reaffirming a unifying force in American life. Moreover, En-

3. June 3, 1984, sec. 4, p. 8.

4. George F. Will, "In Defense of the Mother Tongue," *Newsweek*, July 8, 1985, p. 78; William F. Buckley, Jr., "Avoiding Canada's Problem," *National Review*, Oct. 18, 1985, pp. 62–63; Lourdes Meluza, "Donahue Touches Bilingual Nerve in Show's Finale," *Miami Herald*, Feb. 8, 1986, p. 1B.

glish is an essential tool of social mobility and economic advancement. The English Language Amendment would "send a message" to immigrants, encouraging them to join in rather than remain apart, and to government, cautioning against policies that might retard English acquisition.

For opponents, Official English is synonymous with English Only: a mean-spirited attempt to coerce Anglo-conformity by terminating essential services in other languages. The amendment poses a threat to civil rights, educational opportunities, and free speech, even in the private sector. It is an insult to the heritage of cultural minorities, including groups whose roots in this country go deeper than English speakers': Mexican Americans, Puerto Ricans, and American Indians. Worst of all, the English Only movement serves to justify racist and nativist biases under the cover of American patriotism.

Sorting out the arguments and counterarguments is no easy task. This has been especially true for voters encountering the English Language Amendment for the first time. Because Americans lack a tradition of language politics—that is to say, a history in which language predominated as a symbol, weapon, and stake of ethnic conflict— there is little information or experience to apply. And yet, amending the Constitution is no casual enterprise. It would be rash to go forward without answering a number of pertinent questions:

• If declaring English the official U.S. language is a good idea, why didn't it occur to anyone in the previous two hundred years? What language legislation was adopted by Americans in the past and what were the results?

• Are today's immigrants learning English more slowly or more rapidly than their predecessors? Do bilingual programs discourage assimilation by serving as a crutch, or promote it by easing newcomers' passage into the mainstream?

• What would happen if government suddenly terminated its use of languages other than English? Who would be affected and how?

• Is our situation comparable to Canada's, a bilingual federation that may face dissolution because of ethnic and linguistic tensions? Or Australia's, an English-dominant society where immigrant and indigenous languages are conserved as national assets?

Serious discussion of these points has been limited. The factual vacuum, however, seems to have done nothing to inhibit opinionated bickering over Official English.

My first encounter with the campaign occurred in the mid–1980s as a reporter for *Education Week*. William J. Bennett, then secretary of education, had recently delivered a speech attacking the federal Bilingual Education Act as "a failed path, a bankrupt course," and a waste of $1.7 billion of the taxpayers' money *(see p. 361)*. This caused an uproar in education circles. But Bennett's office announced it was receiving hundreds of letters from the public, which were running more than five to one in support of his views. As a newcomer to the bilingual education beat, I thought it might be instructive to stop by and read the secretary's mail (along with public comments on new regulations he had proposed for bilingual programs).

To my surprise, most of the "supporting" letters had less to do with schooling for non-English-speaking students than with illegal aliens on welfare, communities being "overrun" by Asians and Hispanics, "macho-oriented" foreigners trying to impose their culture on Americans, and—a special concern—the out-of-control birthrates of linguistic minorities. Some writers singled out particular groups for abuse: "Today's Hispanics, on the whole, lack the motivation of earlier immigrants." Others worried that they would be "forced to learn a foreign language" (i.e., Spanish) or that the interests of "the English-speaking majority" would be sacrificed on the altar of affirmative action. Several charged that providing bilingual education and bilingual ballots was "an insult to the memory of my non-English-speaking ancestors," who allegedly had struggled to learn the language without any special help. Many correspondents ended with calls for Official English: "WHOSE AMERICA IS THIS? ONE FLAG. ONE LANGUAGE."[5]

Obviously, a lot more was happening here than an arcane debate over instructional methodologies. Bilingual education had become a lightning rod for tensions about demographic and cultural change, increased immigration from the Third World, reforms in civil rights, and the political empowerment of minorities. Secretary Bennett's fans were in no mood to be distracted by evidence and analysis. They were offended by *the idea* of spending tax dollars to perpetuate foreign tongues, rather than requiring immigrants to learn our language from the outset; of catering to newcomers, who should be grateful to be here instead of demanding government handouts; of creating rights and privileges for foreigners never granted to U.S. citizens abroad; of subsidizing ethnic cultures, formerly a private matter, rather than revering the public tradition of the melting pot; of devaluing English and the American way of life. Amid all the outrage over symbols, there was little awareness of the practicalities of bilingual education—

5. For more samples of these letters, see "'Supporting' Comments Reveal Animosity toward Ethnic Groups," *Education Week*, Feb. 12, 1986, and my book, *Bilingual Education: History, Politics, Theory, and Practice* 2d ed. (Los Angeles: Bilingual Educational Services, 1991), pp. 12–13, 55–56.

for example, its role in teaching English (which is demonstrably superior to the brutal, sink-or-swim methods of the past) or its potential to nurture vital skills in other languages (which is seldom realized, to the country's misfortune).

This, in microcosm, is the state of the Official English controversy. A mythic struggle is raging over models of Americanism, preconceptions about immigrants and their place in the pecking order, shibboleths of belonging and exclusion, and loyalties to tribal gods and national icons. Meanwhile, back in the real world, linguistic diversity is increasing and posing challenges for the United States.

To cite just one example: During the past decade the enrollment of limited-English-proficient (LEP) children nearly tripled in California's public schools, far outpacing the state's ability to train or recruit bilingual and English-as-a-second-language (E.S.L.) teachers. Understandably, the state is scrambling to serve speakers of the fastest growing language groups: Cambodian, Hmong, Lao, Pilipino, Farsi, and Armenian. In raw numbers, however, the shortage of qualified teachers is greatest for the 75 percent of California's LEP students who speak Spanish.[6] According to the U.S. Supreme Court in *Lau v. Nichols,* children who receive no help in overcoming language barriers "are effectively foreclosed from any meaningful education" *(see p. 253).* Yet this is the fate of many California pupils who sit in classrooms unable to understand what their teachers are saying. Such instruction as they receive is provided by uncertified teacher aides and itinerant E.S.L. specialists. Ironically, a state that has pioneered innovative bilingual programs is failing to meet the demand for them, in part because of budget constraints, in part because of ideological resistance. English Only fervor, culminating in the passage of Proposition 63, frustrated attempts to extend California's bilingual education law after it expired in 1987. Now there is uncertainty about school districts' obligations toward language-minority students, more of whom arrive each year. What is to be done?

It is time that Americans had a constructive discussion about language policy, indeed, *that we had a language policy,* consciously planned and national in scope. The question of Official English, which has focused public attention on these problems for the first time in many years, could supply the impetus. But not without a more informed debate. While numerous excellent articles have appeared in recent

6. The state's language census identified more than 743,000 LEP students in 1989, up from 288,000 in 1979. By 1990 California faced a shortfall of approximately 11,000 bilingual teachers; see Assembly Bill 4308 (March 2, 1990); California State Department of Education, Bilingual Education Office, *BEOutreach,* Jan. 1990, p. 1.

years, no single volume has been available to offer a multidimensional view of the issues.

This *Source Book* was conceived at the Conference on Language Rights and Public Policy on April 16–17, 1988, organized by the Stanford University Department of Linguistics and Californians United against Proposition 63. As its title and sponsorship suggest, the conference brought together academics and activists (as well as language educators, civil rights lawyers, business representatives, and public officials) who oppose Official English and seek alternatives. One important goal of the conference was to broaden the public discussion. Policy choices involving language are asserting themselves in the schools, social service agencies, courtrooms, voting booths, government licensing bureaus, places of employment, and the consumer marketplace. Such decisions are far more complex than an up-or-down vote on whether we should, in the words of Proposition 63, "take all steps necessary to insure that the role of English as the common language . . . is preserved and enhanced" *(see p. 134)*. Whatever that may mean. Debates over Official English tend to focus narrowly (and inconclusively) on the legislation's likely effects, intended or otherwise, and on the motives of supporters and opponents. More substantive matters tend to be neglected.

Nevertheless, the Official English controversy is exerting a strong influence on policymakers—which makes public education crucial. The issue cannot be understood out of context, through fiery slogans and thirty-second television spots. An intelligent position requires some knowledge of (1) the historic role of English in American identity and our past responses to minority tongues; (2) the array of arguments for and against Official English as they have developed in Congress and state campaigns; (3) the sociological significance of language conflicts, for example, their impact in various U.S. communities; (4) legal precedents on language and civil liberties, as well as the constitutional questions raised by Official English; (5) implications of linguistic diversity for American schools, in particular the contention surrounding bilingual education; and (6) other nations' experiences in grappling with language as a political problem and an exploitable resource.

These topics of interest formed the agenda of the Stanford conference, and they define this anthology as well. The goal of the *Source Book* is to provide a comprehensive guide to today's language policy debates. It is intended to aid advocates, educators, policymakers, scholars, and citizens seeking to join this fascinating and important discussion. Besides reprinting what I regard to be the strongest existing articles in each subject area, I have solicited original contributions from conference participants and other experts. Also, I have collected relevant primary documents: court decisions, legislation, historical writings, and Congressional testimony. Finally, I have included samples of advocacy on both sides of the Official English question.

The intent here is not to offer "equal time" to opposing views, but to elaborate and clarify the central arguments. My own bias, and the bias of those who have supported this project, should be stated clearly: Adopting English as the official language would be a backward step for this country. The English Only campaign offers at best a simplistic answer to our language problems, at worst a vehicle for xenophobia. This, I believe, is good reason to portray it accurately for purposes of analyzing and responding to its claims. At the same time, I would emphasize that the *Source Book* reflects a variety of opinion about many issues apart from Official English.

A note on terminology: No attempt has been made to standardize usage. Except in minor matters of spelling and punctuation, each author retains full responsibility for his or her words. This includes the labeling of Anglos, Americans, Anglo-Americans, non-Hispanic whites, Chicanos, Latinos, Cubans, blacks, African Americans, Asians, Chinese Americans, Indians, Native Americans, and similar political decisions. Also, the reader will notice that the terms *Official English* and *English Only* often appear as synonyms, a usage that warrants some explanation. Supporters of Official English have objected to equating their position with English Only, arguing that they are concerned solely with the language of government, not of private speech. They neglect to acknowledge, however, that it was U.S. English that first popularized the label during a 1984 California initiative, entitled "Voting Materials in English Only." More important for opponents, English Only highlights the restrictionist face of Official English: its attempt not merely to recognize one language, but to limit the use of others in government and other domains. The dispute over terms has become a feature of the larger debate, and I see no reason to restrict anyone's freedom of speech in the matter.

In the interest of readability, I have chosen articles for their brevity or, failing in that, have abridged longer selections. Where documents of a legal or historical nature have been excerpted, the omissions are marked with elipses. For readers who prefer to skip around rather than read straight through, there are frequent cross-references to related articles and documents.

I want to acknowledge the generous support of the National Education Association and, in particular, Mary Sosa, Wilbur Luna, and Gloria Barajas of the N.E.A.'s Human and Civil Rights Division, who provided encouragement and resources that made this volume possible. Additional support came from Californians United against Proposition 63 through the auspices and financial management of the

Japanese American Citizens League. Edward Chen and Geoffrey Nunberg of Californians United supplied invaluable advice at every stage of the project, from conception through final editing. I am also indebted to the numerous authors who allowed me to reprint their work, and especially to those who contributed original articles to fill gaps in the literature. Finally, I want to thank Mary Carol Combs, former director of the English Plus Information Clearinghouse and unequaled resource on the Official English controversy, who first brought to my attention many of the materials collected here.

PART ONE

Historical Roots of U.S. Language Policy

Why has the United States never designated an official language? A common assumption is that we have been an essentially monolingual nation. Because the vast majority of citizens spoke English as their native language, or learned to speak English soon after immigrating here, there was no serious competition from other tongues. Ethnic languages survived in private schools, homes, churches, and clubs, but before the 1960s no one expected the taxpayers to subsidize their maintenance. Without demands for bilingual services, the language of government was not at issue. Therefore, there was no need to consider language legislation.

Neat as this explanation appears, it is merely a projection of today's concerns onto an unexamined past. Such fallacies are widely accepted because the linguistic dimension of American history remains relatively unexplored. There is little awareness of the bilingualism—or more accurately, the *multilingualism*—that prevailed from earliest times. Diego Castellanos describes this remarkable diversity: the numerous Indian and European languages spoken in the original thirteen states even before territorial expansion and immigration swelled the number of non-English-speaking Americans.

Sometimes there was a backlash against minority language groups. In the 1750s Benjamin Franklin expressed alarm over the Pennsylvania Germans' alleged refusal to speak English. His complaints about bilingual street signs anticipated a contemporary target of English Only wrath. Similarly, his exasperation with the Germans, whom he once described as "Palatine Boors," revealed more than a little ethnic resentment. Perhaps this had something to do with Franklin's own failed attempt to publish a German-language newspaper. It was certainly related to his political feuds with the Germans, for example, over their pacifist disinclination to fight the Indians.

A more common response was that of Benjamin Rush, who also encouraged the Germans to assimilate, but through the voluntary means of a bilingual college. As Shirley Brice Heath explains, the Continental Congress saw a need to broaden the appeal of the Revolutionary cause by translating key documents into German and French. The ideas of political liberty were universal, after all, and there was no reason to restrict their expression to English. In that era

9

the major language question was whether to set official standards for American English, as proposed by John Adams in his call for a language academy. A majority of early leaders rejected this idea, believing that government had no business mandating the people's language choices. Their reliance on private efforts like Noah Webster's speller and dictionary amounted to a deliberate "policy not to have a policy," Heath argues. In the main, English was regarded as a practical instrument rather than a symbolic unifier.

To the extent that language played a nationalistic role in our history, it usually involved the competition between British and American English. The young Webster hoped to foster differences between the two, believing that "as an independent nation, our honor requires us to have a system of our own, in language as well as government." Dennis Baron reports that after the Revolution there was even some idle talk about getting rid of English in favor of German, French, Greek, or Hebrew as the national tongue. The legend, however, that German failed by one vote to become our official language is just that—a tall tale popularized by aficionados of German culture. In 1923 Washington J. McCormick, a Montana congressman, introduced the first official language proposal ever considered at the federal level: a bill to enshrine "American" in the place of English. As is generally the case, this language dispute was a symptom of underlying political tensions—Westerners versus New Englanders, and in some areas, Irish Americans versus the British Empire.

Similar forces governed policies toward minority languages, which varied considerably. Bilingual education is not a recent invention, but originated in the colonial era. During the nineteenth century, German-English schooling was authorized by law in several states and flourished unofficially elsewhere. Other European tongues were also taught (sometimes as the language of instruction and sometimes as a subject) in response to pressure from immigrant communities.[1] But libertarian attitudes did not extend to indigenous languages, as Jon Reyhner demonstrates. Anglicizing the Indian was regarded as a "civilizing" device, an alternative to military measures in pacifying warlike tribes. Children were removed from their reservations, often forcibly, and shipped to faraway boarding schools, where they were punished if caught speaking their native tongues. J. D. C. Atkins, federal Indian commissioner in the 1880s, describes the policy of eradicating students' "barbarous dialects," along with every other remnant of Indian-ness.

Intolerance also characterized policies toward conquered peoples,

1. For a detailed account, see Heinz Kloss, *The American Bilingual Tradition* (Rowley, Mass.: Newbury House, 1977).

notably Spanish speakers in the Southwest and Puerto Rico. The 1848 Treaty of Guadalupe Hidalgo, which ended the Mexican-American War, made various guarantees to the inhabitants of the annexed territory. While there was no explicit mention of language and cultural rights, many believed that these were implicit in the treaty—as illustrated by the debate over California's 1879 constitution. In practice, Spanish language rights were seldom observed except in New Mexico, where English speakers were greatly outnumbered before the twentieth century. As detailed by the U.S. Commission on Civil Rights, New Mexico waged a long struggle for statehood against a Congress reluctant to grant self-rule to a non-English-speaking majority. When finally admitted in 1912, the state adopted a constitution with protections for Spanish speakers, for example, the bilingual publication of official documents.

On the other hand, "bilingualism" as promoted by the United States in Puerto Rico had nothing to do with upholding language rights. It was an attempt to impose English on an island that was almost totally Spanish-speaking when it became a U.S. colony in 1898. As recounted by the Language Policy Task Force, Puerto Rican schools became a battleground over Americanization, a policy that for half a century insisted on English as the language of instruction.

Meanwhile, measures to assimilate immigrants became increasingly coercive after the turn of the twentieth century. An Americanization campaign arose in response to fears that the "new immigrants" from eastern and southern Europe were resisting English (among other unsavory practices), as compared with the Germans and Scandinavians who had preceded them. For the first time a popular link was made between Anglo-conformity and political loyalty to the United States. John Higham describes the evolution of Americanization from social work in urban slums, to an effort to combat labor organizing, to wartime hysteria against Germans (and foreign language speakers generally), to an instrument of the Big Red Scare. Theodore Roosevelt's concerns in 1917 have a familiar ring today: bilingualism as a basis for divided loyalties versus English as a patriotic symbol. Enthusiasm for forced assimilation waned quickly, however, as Congress addressed cultural and linguistic diversity in another way. In 1924 it enacted the strictest immigration quotas in U.S. history, which remained in effect until 1965.

A Polyglot Nation

Diego Castellanos, New Jersey's state director of bilingual education programs in the 1970s, is a television producer in Philadelphia. This article is excerpted from his book, *The Best of Two Worlds: Bilingual-Bicultural Education in the U.S.* (Trenton, N.J.: New Jersey State Department of Education, 1983), pp. 1–9.

In the beginning the Western Hemisphere offered its bounty to the brave, the strong, the curious, and the lucky, whatever their national origin, social status, or motivation for coming here. Willing pioneers came from Spain, France, England, and other countries of the world. Scholars believe that the first Americans simply wandered in from Asia, crossing the Bering Strait from Siberia to Alaska. Although these prehistoric nomads preceded the Europeans by thousands of years, they—the ancestors of the "native" Americans—were migrants nonetheless. It is believed that at the time of the first European arrivals, there were more than a million natives living in what is today the contiguous United States. Spreading out over their new continent, they formed new nations. The Apache and Navajo would eventually settle in the southwestern deserts; the Kickapoo in the central prairies; the Cheyenne, Pawnee, and Crow in the northern plains; the Comanche in the southern plains; the Washo in the Great Basin; the Natchez and Arawak along the Gulf Coast; the Taino and Carib in the Caribbean Basin; the Chickasaw, Choctaw, Cherokee, Creek, and Shawnee in the southeastern woodlands; the Lenni Lenape along the mideastern seaboard; the Mohegan, Ottawa, Cayuga, Mohawk, Delaware, and Seneca in the northeastern woodlands; and others—all having their own peculiar rituals, culture, and language or dialect. Prior to the arrival of the Europeans, more than five hundred languages were spoken in North America.[2]

The first part of (what is today) the United States to be settled by the Europeans was Puerto Rico. The island was colonized by Juan Ponce de León in 1508, fifteen years after it had been visited by Christopher Columbus. After serving as Puerto Rico's first governor, Ponce de León migrated toward the North American continent, reaching its

2. Gay Lawrence, "Indian Education: Why Bilingual-Bicultural?" *Education and Urban Society* 10, no. 3 (May 1978): 314.

southern peninsula in 1513. He explored the area, named it Florida, resettled there, and became its first governor. The lands discovered by Ponce de León and Juan de Garay were given in 1527 to Pánfilo de Narváez by the king of Spain. Ponce de León was followed by Alonso de Pineda, who reached the mouth of the Mississippi River in 1519. The Spanish established a colony (which did not survive) in the Carolinas in 1526, sixty years before Sir Walter Raleigh made a similar unsuccessful attempt. Around 1529, when he was governor of Florida, Narváez visited Louisiana with Alvar Núñez Cabeza de Vaca. In 1536 Hernando Cortés visited California and Cabeza de Vaca explored Texas. In 1539 Hernando de Soto visited Georgia and Tennessee, García López de Cárdenas discovered the Grand Canyon of Colorado, General Francisco Vásquez de Coronado explored New Mexico and Kansas, and Hernando Alarcón discovered the Colorado River. In 1541 de Soto discovered the Mississippi River near Memphis. The following year, twenty years before French colonizers reached the New World, Juan Rodríguez Cabrillo, a Portuguese, became the first European to set foot on the Pacific Coast, by the San Diego harbor.

The first permanent European settlement on this continent was Spanish-speaking, St. Augustine, established in 1565 by Pedro Menéndez de Aviles (later governor of Florida) on a site where French Huguenots had failed two years earlier. The colony remained Spanish for more than two and a half centuries. In 1566 the colony of Santa Elena was founded at the site of today's Parris Island marine base in South Carolina. The settlement, which lasted twenty-one years, had sixty houses and reached a population of four hundred. It served as the capital of Spanish Florida. In 1573 Pedro Márquez discovered the Chesapeake Bay, and in 1582—five years before the first attempt to establish an English colony there (which failed)—Antonio de Espejo explored and named New Mexico. Sixteen years later Juan de Oñate led four hundred soldiers and their cattle into New Mexico and settled in the territory.

Spaniards held a virtual monopoly over the southern half of this country for one entire century before the arrival of other Europeans. They conducted extensive explorations, discovering and naming many of our national landmarks and spreading the gospel among the natives. Jesuits accompanying these pioneers used the autochthonous dialects of Florida, as well as Spanish, to teach Christianity to the natives. A similar bilingual approach was used by Franciscan missionaries in the Southwest by Dominicans elsewhere. Spain's domain in the Western Hemisphere between the early sixteenth and nineteenth centuries extended southward to include Mexico, all of Central and South America except Brazil, and most of the Caribbean Islands. It seemed possible during the sixteenth century that Spanish would become not only the language of the Western Hemisphere, but of the entire world. That possibility was terminated by the defeat of the Spanish Armada by the British in 1588, as well as by further Spanish defeats by the French, who in the mid-seventeenth century became the leading power in Europe.

The French came to the New World in 1534, and by the end of the sixteenth century, France had established colonies in the St. Lawrence Valley, the region around Lake Superior, and the northern part of the Ohio Valley. In 1605 they settled Arcadia, off the coast of Canada. Not until 1607, 115 years after Columbus's first voyage, did the first permanent English colony in the New World appear, in Jamestown, Virginia. A dozen years later West Africans were brought to Jamestown as indentured servants. In 1620 another permanent colony was founded in Plymouth, Massachusetts, by a group of Pilgrims.

The first group of permanent Dutch settlers came to New Netherland (New York State) in 1624, when their country was still under Spanish rule. Two years later Peter Minuit purchased Manhattan from the natives. Spanish-Portuguese Jews, the Sephardim, arrived around the mid-seventeenth century. Meanwhile, Huguenots were settling in Charleston, South Carolina. Minuit brought a shipload of Finns and Swedes to the Delaware River Valley in 1638. William Penn, a Quaker, came to this area in 1682, and in October of the following year, the ship *Concord* brought thirteen Quaker and Mennonite families from the German town of Krefeld to Philadelphia. Led by Fritz Daniel Pastorius, a thirty-year-old lawyer from Franconia, they founded the community of Germantown.

It became obvious very early that the British would be the dominant nationality and that English would be the predominant language in the central portion of North America. Because of the many nationalities represented in Anglo-America, along with the many Indian nations that existed here, knowledge of two or more languages became a decided advantage for trading, scouting, teaching, and spreading the gospel, as well as for diplomacy. Anthony Sadowski, a Pole who came to America in the first decade of the eighteenth century, became one of many interpreters of Latin languages. Linguists performed other essential functions as some schools, churches, and other institutions offered bilingual services. The Protestant missionary schools established by these northwestern European settlers to "introduce Indians to civilization and Christianity" were—of necessity—also bilingual. While the efforts of missionaries to maintain the native tongues of the aborigines were not encouraged, they were tolerated by the powers that be.

Settlers from almost every northern and western European nation continued to arrive in the Americas during the seventeenth century.

The immigration traffic was so diverse that eighteen different languages were being spoken by people of twenty different nationalities in New Amsterdam (Manhattan Island) in 1664 when it was captured from the Dutch by the English.[3]

By 1763 England had succeeded in gaining total control over Franco-America, thus ending a hundred years of French sovereignty in that area. This conquest began the process of Anglicizing the land that was to become Canada, as British expansion extended Anglo-America to include the northern as well as the central regions of North America. In the mid-eighteenth century the British rulers of Nova Scotia expelled four thousand Acadians when they refused to pledge their loyalty to the British Empire. The outcasts ended up years later among other French speakers in Louisiana, where their descendants became known as the Cajuns. They settled in the bayou country of the Mississippi Delta and retained French as their primary language.

Around 1719 Scotch-Irish constituted one-fourth of the population of New York, New Jersey, and Pennsylvania. In 1736 Moravians, a German sect, arrived in Georgia and eventually migrated on to Pennsylvania. A great deal of conflict—having little to do with linguistic differences—was generated among the various nationalities of the New World. For example, in Pennsylvania the Scotch-Irish, who seemed more inclined toward belligerence, and the Quakers, who were devoted to nonviolence, disagreed on such issues as Indian relations.

It was around this time that the Germans, the most important group in the early history of bilingual education, were coming to Anglo-America. From Pennsylvania they followed the mountain valleys leading southward into the back country of Maryland, Virginia, and the Carolinas. By the mid-eighteenth century they had moved north into the Mohawk Valley of New York and east into New England. Settling in relatively unpopulated frontier areas, the Germans were often unnoticed, even when they were in the majority. In these farming districts the Germans initially had no teachers at their disposal who were familiar with English. In reality, there was little need for a command of English either for communicating with each other, raising their livestock, or harvesting their crops. The Germans' strong desire to perpetuate their culture in the new land and the relative unimportance of English in their early settlements—combined with the fact that they were unimpressed with Anglo-American schooling—led

3. John F. Kennedy, *A Nation of Immigrants* (New York: Harper & Row, 1964), p. 11; and Clarence Senior, *Strangers—Then Neighbors: From Pilgrims to Puerto Ricans* (New York: Freedom Books, 1971), p. 1.

the Germans to establish their own private parochial schools to inculcate their ethnic traditions and to preserve their language.[4]

In 1753 Benjamin Franklin voiced the fear that the Germans "will
soon so out number us that all the advantages we have will not, in My
Opinion, be able to preserve our language" (see p. 19). With Franklin's
help a systematic attempt to introduce English schools into the
German-speaking areas of Pennsylvania was made by the London-
based Society for the Propagation of Christian Knowledge. The effort
failed when Pennsylvania Germans became aware that the plan was
ethnolingual in its aims, and not religious, as the name of the society
implied.[5] A quarter of a million strong, Germans constituted the largest non-English-background group during the Revolutionary period.
Although they were distributed more uniformly throughout Anglo-
America than most other immigrant groups, one-third of the German
population resided in Pennsylvania. There were smaller but significant German enclaves in each of the other twelve colonies, as well as
along the Mississippi River and in the Northwest Territory.

Some of the other ethnic minorities in the United States at the time
of its independence included large settlements of Scotch-Irish on the
frontier (Virginia, Pennsylvania, and the Carolinas); Irish below the
Mason-Dixon line; Scottish in North Carolina, New York, and Georgia; Dutch in Manhattan, Staten Island, and Long Island, as well as
along the Hudson River and on the coastlines of New Jersey and Connecticut; French in Maine and Charleston; Huguenots in Manhattan;
French Catholics in Louisiana; Swedes in the Delaware Valley; Jews in
Manhattan and Rhode Island; Danes in New York; and Welsh in New
England and Pennsylvania. The demographic registers circa 1776 officially listed the country's white population as 61 percent English, 10
percent Irish (mostly from Ulster), 9 percent German, 8 percent Scottish, 3 percent Dutch, 2 percent French, 1 percent Swedish, and 6
percent other.[6]

Twenty percent of the total population of Anglo-America was believed to be black, most of whom lived in the South. Although these
Africans brought scores of languages with them, slave traders' prac-

---

4. Arnold B. Faust, *The German Element in the United States* (Salem, N.H.: Arno Press,
1969), p. 204; George S. Clark, "The Germans," in *The New Jersey Ethnic Experience*, ed.
Barbara Cunningham (Union City, N.J.: William H. Wise, 1977), p. 224; and Gerald D.
Kanoon, "The Four Phases of Bilingual Education in the United States," *TESOL Newsletter* 12 (Apr. 1978), p. 1.

5. Heinz Kloss, *American Bilingual Tradition* (Rowley, Mass.: Newbury House, 1977),
p. 148.

6. *Reports of the Committee on Linguistic and National Stocks in the Population of the United
States* (Washington, D.C.: American Council of Learned Societies, 1932).

tice of dispersing speakers of the same tongue, and the resulting development of pidgins and creoles, prevented any West African languages from surviving in North America.

Just months after the Revolution was won, in 1782, French-American writer Hector St. John de Crèvecoeur said of his adopted land: "Individuals of all nations are melted into a new race of men."[7] In line with this melting pot ideal, English came to assume a greater importance, although non-English-language instruction continued in many schools founded by immigrants. In some schools English was taught as the main language, while the native language was offered as a school subject and used for part of the instruction. The languages most frequently taught were German, Dutch, Polish, and French. Spanish was used exclusively in the Southwest, of course, but that area was not yet part of the United States.

During the eighteenth century, the German Lutheran and Reformed churches built a comprehensive private elementary school system, which at times received public funds. By the beginning of the Revolutionary War, 78 Reformed and 40 Lutheran parochial schools were thriving, and the total number (in both denominations) increased to 254 by 1800.[8] As the number of Germans increased, public schools began to adjust their programs to the needs of these children. Instruction in several districts in Pennsylvania, Maryland, Virginia, the Carolinas, and later Wisconsin was given in German—often to the exclusion of English. It is quite obvious that this nation was born multilingual and multicultural, despite the indisputable fact that English became accepted as a lingua franca.

The German Language in Pennsylvania

By Benjamin Franklin

This passage is from Franklin's letter to Peter Collinson, a British member of Parliament, dated May 9, 1753, in *Papers*, ed. Leonard W. Labaree (New Haven: Yale University Press, 1961), vol. 4, p. 234. Several variant copies of the

7. *Letters from an American Farmer*; for excerpts, see Oscar Handlin, ed., *This Was America: As Recorded by European Travelers in the Eighteenth, Nineteenth, and Twentieth Centuries* (New York: Harper Torchbooks, 1964), pp. 36–59.
8. Kloss, *American Bilingual Tradition*, p. 147.

letter exist, none in Franklin's own hand; this version is from the Hardwick Papers, New York Public Library.

Those [Germans] who come hither are generally the most ignorant Stupid Sort of their own Nation, and as Ignorance is often attended with Credulity when Knavery would mislead it, and with Suspicion when Honesty would set it right; and as few of the English understand the German Language, and so cannot address them either from the Press or Pulpit, 'tis almost impossible to remove any prejudices they once entertain. Their own Clergy have very little influence over the people; who seem to take an uncommon pleasure in abusing and discharging the Minister on every trivial occasion. Not being used to Liberty, they know not how to make a modest use of it. . . .

I remember when they modestly declined intermeddling in our Elections, but now they come in droves, and carry all before them, except in one or two Counties; Few of their children in the Country learn English; they import many Books from Germany; and of the six printing houses in the Province, two are entirely German, two half German half English, and but two entirely English; They have one German News-paper and one half-German.[9] Advertisements, intended to be general are now printed in Dutch [German] and English; the Signs in our Streets have inscriptions in both languages, and in some places only German: They begin of late to make all their Bonds and other legal Writings in their own Language, which (though I think it ought not to be) are allowed good in our Courts, where the German Business so increases that there is continued need of Interpreters; and I suppose in a few years they will also be necessary in the Assembly, to tell one half of our Legislators what the other half say; In short, unless the stream of their importation could be turned from this to other Colonies, as you very judiciously propose, they will soon so out number us, that all the advantages we have will not, in My Opinion, be able to preserve our language, and even our government will become precarious.

9. Editor's note: In 1732 Franklin founded the *Philadelphische Zeitung*, the first German-language newspaper in the New World, but it failed after two issues. Also, in his early years as a printer, he published a number of German books, notably for a pietist religious sect. But a better-qualified German printer soon cornered this market, to Franklin's annoyance. See Glenn Weaver, "Benjamin Franklin and the Pennsylvania Germans," in Leonard Dinnerstein and Frederick Jaher, eds., *The Aliens: A History of Ethnic Minorities in America* (New York: Appleton-Century-Crofts, 1970).

Why No Official Tongue?

By Shirley Brice Heath

Shirley Brice Heath is professor of linguistics at Stanford
University, author of numerous works on language policy
and planning, and coeditor of *Language in the USA* (1981).
This article is excerpted from "A National Language Acad-
emy? Debate in the New Nation," *International Journal of the
Sociology of Language* 11 (1976): 9–43.

The United States of America was born among speakers of many dialects and languages, and until well past its "critical age," the new nation had neither institutions nor processes designed to choose or promote a single linguistic norm as appropriate for identification with
the national character. The colonial legacy of the United States did not
include official selection of a specific language to be encouraged
among the indigenous or a linguistic standard to be maintained
among the settlers. The absence of a designation of official status for
the English language within the colonies reflected both the notions of
language which the peculiar historical events of the sixteenth and
seventeenth centuries shaped for England and the diversity of settlement motivations which drew widely differing social, linguistic, and
ethnic groups to America.

Unlike other colonial powers, which attempted to determine both
language choice and processes of change for group unification and
cultural assimilation, England's policymakers did not consider language problems in their determination of policies for their New World
colonies. Moreover, most settlers of the colonies came to pursue their
own interests, not to transplant either Christianization to indigenous
peoples or to extend Old World political systems to the New. Therefore, they brought with them neither the institutional sponsorship
nor the techniques of linguistic unification and change which were so
prominent among French and Castilian colonizers.[10] Hence, at the
founding of the United States, there were no colonial language policies or programs to build upon.

At the political decision-making level of the new nation, focus on

10. See Shirley Brice Heath, *Telling Tongues: Language Policy in Mexico, Colony to Nation*
(New York: Teachers College Press, 1972), and "Colonial Language Status Achievement: Mexico, Peru, and the United States," in *Language in Sociology*, ed. Albert Veroodt
and Rolf Kjolseth (Louvain, Belgium: Editions Peeters, 1976).

political theory was all-pervasive and crucial. Acutely self-conscious about their role in adjusting and adapting European political theories to a newly independent nation, the founders of early U.S. national policy first considered issues in the context of particular systems or theories with which these topics had formerly been associated. Often, political decision-makers faced with suggestions related to language choice and standardization identified supranational language decisions with monarchies. The language academies of Spain and France, well known to many U.S. leaders, provoked images of crowned heads and royal courts dictating cultural norms. Antimonarchical forces in the United States, therefore, viewed negatively any national polity–sponsored manipulation of language.

From 1770 to 1820, when policies related to either language choice or standardization were proposed, they were debated for their potential to meet pragmatic and universal aims consonant with those of the American political system. When political leaders recognized language as a problem, they did so most consistently in the institutional contexts of law and learning, and here they saw language as a pragmatic tool—not as an ideal or as an ideological symbol.[11] Recognition of the potential of a standard language of wide communication as an instrument of access to codes of law, institutions, and written sources of learning (particularly in science and literature) was common among the nation's elite. In addition, the political leaders of the new nation yearned for universal extension of American achievements in government and science. Extension had to be preceded by, or at least coordinate with, both standardization of the code and legitimatization through a national literature. The results of France's standardization program and that nation's coordinate rise to fame in literature and science in the eighteenth century particularly underscored this need to many political leaders in the United States. However, the ideals of the political system supported by many of these same men could not include a centralized agency designed to designate and control language choices. What alternatives existed?

During the early national period, those most frequently labeled "the founding fathers" discussed language problems in various contexts and proposed diverse solutions. However, the choice of a single language as the official communication mode was never made.[12] Multiple languages played critical roles in the political and social life of the nation during this period. Cultural and ethnic pluralities

---

11. See, e.g., Thomas Jefferson's recommendations on language and law and his margin notes to the Declaration of Independence, cited in Saul K. Padover, *The Complete Jefferson* (New York: Duell, Sloan & Pearce, 1943), p. 856.

12. Editor's note: Nevertheless, there have been various rumors about alternatives to English being considered. *See* Dennis Baron, "Federal English," *pp. 36–40.*

abounded both in the clusters of representatives of different nationalities which had come during the colonial period and in the se-
quences of diverse groups which entered the new nation during the
years 1770–1820.[13] German and French armed forces played important roles during the Revolution; many of those who remained after
the War became economically, politically, and socially prominent,
while retaining their native tongues. Refugees from the French Revolution arrived in large numbers between 1790 and 1800, and these
émigrés were allowed to assume positions of power and support in
business and politics. Even their establishment of little colonies
within the United States and their support of land companies went
undisturbed, an indication that English speakers held no great fears
of their using different languages to build separate power bases or
promote animosities.[14]

Many churches offered services in different languages. Acceptance
of and support for separate schools, newspapers, and societies for
French and German speakers occurred in both northern and southern
cities. Benevolent societies of French and German speakers, which
held as a prerequisite for membership the speaking of French or German, provided libraries, and either sponsored schools or provided
tutors for both their own children and English speakers'. These societies provided not only cultural and social security to immigrants, but
of their own volition, these institutions often became havens for the
learning of English, as well.[15]

In the main, the use of languages other than English was encouraged and looked upon with favor by national leaders, because of both
practical advantages and opportunities for the expansion of knowledge that different languages offered. Thomas Jefferson advised his
daughters and young correspondents to learn French and Spanish—
French not only for its obvious importance in diplomatic affairs, but
also for the access it provided to publications presenting recent ad-
vancements in science. He recommended Spanish because of the in-

13. Marcus Lee Hansen, *The Atlantic Migration, 1607–1860*, ed. Arthur M. Schlesinger
(Cambridge, Mass.: Harvard University Press, 1940), chap. 3.

14. Frances Sergeant Childs, *French Refugee Life in the United States, 1790–1800: An
American Chapter of the French Revolution* (Baltimore: Johns Hopkins University Press,
1940).

15. Representative of those who advocated the acceptance of diverse languages was
Benjamin Rush, whose "Information to Europeans Who Are Disposed to Migrate to the
United States" was published in Philadelphia in 1790. Rush saw the maintenance of
various languages and institutions which promoted the assemblages of former fellow
countrymen as an appeal to potential European immigrants; L. H. Butterfield, ed., *Letters of Benjamin Rush* (Princeton, N.J.: Princeton University Press, 1951) 1:549–62. See
also Arthur Henry Hirsch, *The Huguenots of South Carolina* (Hamden, Ct.: Archon Books,
1962), pp. 259ff.

creasing diplomatic importance Spain would presumably hold in U.S. foreign relations. Jefferson admitted that modern languages were not well taught in the United States, and he encouraged the importation of modern language professors from abroad and recommended that French be learned in Canada.

Benjamin Rush, a member of the Continental Congress and a signer of the Declaration of Independence, urged that German and French be taught in America's "English Schools." A strong proponent of the retention and spread of modern languages in the United States, Rush expressed his concern that "narrow-minded people," fearful of retention of the German language among Pennsylvania's citizens, would not recognize the benefits a German college might provide the nation. The spread of learning among citizens, no matter what their native tongues, was crucial to the cause of the government. Rush noted:

> What Pennsylvanian of British or Irish extraction would not prefer [German speakers] as fellow citizens learned in the arts and sciences than in a state of ignorance of them all? A man who is learned in the dialect of a Mohawk Indian is more fit for a legislator than a man who is ignorant even in the language of the learned Greeks. The German language has existed for fifty years in Pennsylvania. It never can be lost while German churches and schools exist in it. A German college will serve to preserve it, but it will preserve it, not in its present state, but in its original force and purity.[16]

Members of the Continental Congress also agreed that any and all languages could be used as instruments for spreading communication necessary to legitimate the political system within the new nation. The Congress issued critical documents in French and German in local areas where members recognized a need for spreading information to promote loyalty to the cause of Independence.[17] The use of multiple languages, moreover, would help preserve the fragile democracy. Rush summed up the view of many of his contemporaries: "Wherever learning is confined to *one* society, or to a *few* men, the government of that country will always be an *aristocracy*, whether the prevailing party be composed of rich or poor. It is by diffusing learn-

---

16. *Letters of Benjamin Rush*, 1:365–66.

17. The printed *Journals of the Continental Congress* note publications in both German and French. For example, "Extracts from Votes and Proceedings of the Congress" (1774), "Declaration of Articles Setting Forth Causes of Taking up Arms" (1775), and "Resolves of Congress" (1776) were printed in German; the Articles of Confederation (1777) and various memorials were printed in French.

ing that we shall destroy aristocratic juntos of all parties, and establish a true commonwealth." [18]

Leaders throughout the nation repeatedly pleaded for recognition—not restriction or promotion—of local, regional, or special interests. The same theory applied to linguistic minorities; if a national government should legally pressure groups to abandon their native languages, the repression of these tongues and separate unities could provoke resistance. Instead, if leaders recognized the potential of plural languages to spread the ideas of the new government, the citizens would become capable of helping legitimate the new government. Recognizing that forces which cause one to change his language or add to it must be internally motivated, leaders reasoned that linguistic minorities would not become separate and distinct peoples within the nation so long as no legal force proscribed the use of their languages. Moreover, wider use of the majority language would come without coercion. On behalf of a German College, Rush pointed out: "It will open the eyes of the Germans to a sense of the importance, and utility of the English language and become perhaps *the only possible means*, consistent with their liberty, of spreading a knowledge of the English language among them." [19]

Coexisting with the ideological climate favoring linguistic diversity in the new nation was the view that some type of standard English might be necessary. Two different standards were, however, urged: speakers of the English tongue should *either* retain the purity of their speech according to the standard of England *or* define and refine a new speech—an American version of English. Just as Rush had advocated that the Germans of Pennsylvania use their college to preserve German "in its original force and purity," so others would argue that native English speakers should have a national institution to do the same for their tongue. Some believed the English tongue to be the only legacy from British rule which should be held by citizens of the new nation. [20] Others argued that a politically independent nation needed and deserved to add its own features and its own processes of change to English. A uniquely standardized English could spread with news of the political system and national achievements of the United States. English in America should therefore be "improved and perfected" for its native speakers as well as for those speakers of other tongues who wished to acquire English. [21]

18. *Letters of Benjamin Rush*, 1:368; italics in original.

19. Ibid., 1:366; italics in original.

20. See, e.g., Samuel Lorenzo Knapp, *Lectures on American Literature, with Remarks on Some Passages of American History* (New York, 1829).

21. "An Enquiry into the Utility of the Greek and Latin Languages," *The American Museum or Repository* 5 (1789): 532, American Periodical Series, Reel 4.

In nations such as Italy, France, and Spain, academies prepared an official dictionary, grammars, and regulated literary works which served as authorities for other institutions and for national elites. Academy members believed that their own national languages were superior to others and were necessary as national symbols. They appealed to traditions of civilizations and well-established national literatures. Associated with classical traditions of maintaining stability in language, these institutions linked language use primarily with literary forms rather than with spoken varieties. Leaders of the academies were elites in nations with highly stratified societies, and the position of intellectuals gave them particular responsibilities for preserving not so much a model in language and behavior for all classes as a standard by which elites could measure themselves or toward which aspiring elites could set their goals.

The first proposal for an academy of standardization in the American colonies represented a rejection of European models, not in form, but in purpose and practice. In addition, this proposal foreshadowed the two major themes in language policy of the early national years—pragmatism and universalism. In 1774 an anonymous contributor to the *Royal American Magazine* provided two basic reasons for an American Society of Language: the advantages to science and the example which the establishment of such an institution in a *"land* of light and freedom" would provide the rest of the world. To be sure, the institution would "correct, enrich, and refine" the language, but in so doing, the members would promote new ideas in science while "perfecting" and extending the English language as Great Britain had not been able to do.[22]

This proposal showed a recognition of the pragmatic value of English as a tool and the universal appeal of English propagated by the United States. American scientists recognized the value of using the English language to spread their scientific findings abroad to learned societies and individuals eager for knowledge from the New World. Furthermore, as the scientific accomplishments of the United States were extended, so would be news of its political system, which many believed also had universal appeal. By 1774 many intellectuals were self-assured about the contribution of the American colonies to the world of science. The United States could capitalize on the curiosity of Old World intellectuals about the New World to spread its language. French and Latin had dominated the world of science in the period prior to the founding of the United States; the English of America now had a chance to move into prominence.

22. The writer has most frequently been identified as John Adams; see Daniel J. Boorstin, *The Americans: The Colonial Experience* (New York: Random House, 1958), p. 282. However, this is unlikely, since Adams's diaries and personal letters indicate little interest in language standardization until after his trip abroad in 1778.

John Adams, strongly influenced by his recognition of the power of language as a pragmatic tool and by a desire to promote the universal thrust of the new nation's achievements, urged that America extend English and help elevate it as a world language. In 1780 Adams proposed to the Continental Congress the establishment of a "public institution for refining, correcting, improving, and ascertaining the English language" *(see p. 32).* He viewed the promotion of the language as an opening for the dissemination of American views of "liberty, prosperity, and glory." Citing Athens and Rome as examples, Adams argued that furtherance of English models of eloquent speech throughout the United States and around the world through "universal connection and correspondence with all nations" would contribute to a reputable status for the American nation. An heir of Puritan forefathers who had come to Massachusetts to establish "a city upon a hill" whose citizens would set examples "with the eyes of all people upon us,"[23] Adams carried a commitment to extend the influence of the United States in as many spheres as possible; language was not to be an exception.

Fresh from the Continental Congress's struggles to draft the Articles of Confederation, Adams had gone to Europe in 1778 on a diplomatic mission. Convictions drawn from his experiences among foreign tongues in foreign lands (by a man who confessed to great difficulties in learning French) lay behind Adams's proposal for an American academy of language. His diary reveals a fascination with the multilingualism of Europeans and the diplomatic and political implications for those nations which chose not only to preserve but also to promote their national tongues. While in Amsterdam attempting to negotiate a loan from Holland, Adams had dinner on the evening of August 28, 1780, with a Dutch minister and a lawyer, both of whom seemed favorable to the advancement of the United States. The lawyer observed that the United States would be responsible for expanding English in the nineteenth century, enabling it to take the place that Latin had held in the seventeenth century and French had assumed in the eighteenth.[24] Within a few weeks Adams developed the idea of an academy of language for the United States. He wrote the Contintental Congress and proposed both the organization of an academy and the establishment of a library containing writings concerning "languages of every Sort, ancient and modern."

In Adams's plan, language was an instrument, a tool of communication available for and in need of manipulation by the State for prop-

23. Page Smith, *As a City upon a Hill: The Town in American History* (New York: Alfred A. Knopf, 1966).

24. L. H. Butterfield, ed., *Diary and Bibliography of John Adams,* (Cambridge, Mass.: Harvard University Press, 1961), 2:446–48.

agating ideals embedded within the nation itself. Political rules of a nation should be laid out clearly for use and adoption by its citizens and for consideration by other nations. In service within public institutions, language became a public institution; as such it should be determined, promoted, and put forward as an indication of the "unconquerability" of the nation. Adams carried the conviction of many of his European contemporaries that "tongues, like governments, have a natural tendency to degeneration."[25] Therefore, Adams saw the need for American language *and* government to be codified for presentation and expansion to other nations at the elemental point of creation.

Apparently sensing that some members of the Continental Congress would think he was proposing that the academy establish a new language, Adams reasserted his allegiance to the English tongue: "We have not made war against the English Language, any more than against the old English character. An Academy instituted by the Authority of Congress, for correcting, improving, and fixing the English language would strike all the World with Admiration and great Britain with Envy."[26] Aware that England had failed to establish a language academy, Adams insisted that if the United States did so, the new nation could then have the responsibility for expanding English as a world tongue. In addition, while America promoted the English language, it could assert its own views and cultural confidence as well: "England will never have any more honor, excepting now and then that of imitating the Americans."[27]

However, as Adams had feared, the Continental Congress was not convinced of the importance of the academy to American goals; the proposal was sent to committee, from which it never emerged. With the temporary resolution of the European crisis and the acquisition of a loan from Holland, members of Congress did not consider Adams's arguments that the academy of language could help solve current problems. Furthermore, nationally sponsored cultural institutions faced severe obstacles during the early years of the Republic. Adams himself was often termed a monarchist, and his proposal for a cen-

25. This view, cited by Samuel Johnson in the preface to his 1755 *Dictionary*, was common among eighteenth-century intellectuals. Nevertheless, Johnson himself opposed a language academy as contrary to "the spirit of English liberty." Moreover, he rejected as futile the idea of "embalming" a language and suggested that neither academies nor lexicographers could prescribe or prevent linguistic change. Still, Johnson felt that a dictionary based on etymological studies and guided in usage by authors whose works represented "the wells of English undefiled" might slow down the tendency of languages to "degeneration" and help conserve "constancy and stability."

26. Adams to Huntington, *Papers of the Continental Congress*, Sept. 25, 1780, item 84.

27. Adams to Jennings, Sept. 23, 1780, in *Life and Works of John Adams* (Boston: Little, Brown, 1856), 9:510.

tralized language academy must have seemed to many republicans further "proof" of his monarchical leanings. Adams's view of language as an instrument critical to a particular task—and the consequent need for the national government to shape, mend, and maintain that tool—could not overcome the ideological blocks of other early leaders to an American academy of language and the hints of monarchialism it carried.

In no plan for the elevation and extension of a standard English could there be a program for coercing speakers. Benjamin Rush's concern with means "consistent with liberty" applied not only to extension of the English language, but also to its elevation or standardization among native speakers. Furthermore, the United States could appeal neither to established traditions and literary pursuits nor to maintenance of class structure and elite norms—ever-present associations with academies in the minds of republicans. For liberals of the early nation, both the goals and the processes of state-imposed uniformity through standardized cultural norms seemed far too elitist for a democracy founded on the promise of equality of opportunities for all citizens.

Haunted by the assumption that great nations past and present had produced widely recognized national literatures, many in the United States felt the nation's claim to international acceptance depended on the spread of a national literature which would promote "moral and political research" within and beyond the nation.[28] Some leaders suggested the establishment of a university or union of learned societies under national patronage to further a literature which would provide written models of standards of usage for American English. However, all such plans failed to meet Congress's approval. Samuel Mitchill, a congressman from New York who supported proposals for a national university, wrote Noah Webster that without federal promotion of literature, "individuals must continue to labour on as well as they can under all the disadvantages of solitary efforts."[29]

Solitary efforts and the resulting disadvantages were not unfamiliar to Webster or to other individuals who had in the past two decades proposed alternatives to a national institution of language standardization. Webster, whose name is synonymous with standardization in the modern period, had begun peddling his *Grammatical Institute of the English Language*, which included a speller, grammar, and readers,

28. Joel Barlow, *Prospectus of a National Institution to Be Established in the United States* (Washington City, 1806).
29. Jan. 7, 1807, Noah Webster Manuscripts Collection, New York Public Library.

as early as 1783. Prior to 1800 individual contributors to periodicals frequently argued for instruction of English grammar in "English schools" in the United States. Skills in writing and speaking the mother tongue were emphasized as necessary to the improvement of individuals and the nation. Webster capitalized on this often-expressed ideal. He urged linguistic independence for the United States and proposed that this be accomplished through dissemination of written materials on the language which could be taken up by individuals independently choosing to further their education and to advance their social position. However, individual efforts toward standardization of the language were comparatively unsuccessful at that time in American history. Webster's *American Dictionary of the English Language*, published in 1828, sold only 2,500 copies. He was forced to mortgage his home to bring out a second edition. Neither this work nor others previously published on language provided enough support to prevent Webster from being almost constantly in debt, and his work drew relatively little praise during his lifetime.[30]

Nevertheless, in practical consequences if not in philosophy, Webster's work came to substitute for a national language academy. Along with the continuing insistence on the absence of national restraints on cultural habits, the nation's literate population increasingly stressed the *"naturalness"* of language learning, but the *need for training* in the skills of oratory and writing. The young learned language from their associates in the earliest years; until age eight a young student learned through hearing correct models and reading books "written in a simple and correct style."[31]

In the preface to his 1828 dictionary, Webster insisted that language was the pragmatic instrument of the people, and as such, would be molded by them in accordance with their choice for adoption and adaptation of grammars, spellers, dictionaries, or the emulation of models in public usage. Webster admitted that there could be no nationally designated final authority in language. Written sources of standardization fit the democratic scheme of the early Republic; learning and achievement of "correctness in language" could thus be available to a wide spectrum of society. Dictionaries, grammars, and written handbooks representing different scholars' views provided a wider access among the population to language choice and change than did academies' approaches. Furthermore, there was an increasing recognition that a standard in usage had to be sought not just in literary works, but in the speech of the public—speech that would

30. Henry R. Warfel, *Noah Webster: Schoolmaster to America* (New York: Macmillan, 1936).

31. "Plan of a Liberal English Education," *The American Museum* 5:533.

continue to change and could never be stabilized. Webster's philosophy held that flexibility and effectiveness, particularly with regard to science, technology, and new-found geographic and cultural items, had to be primary characteristics of a living, changing language in a young, growing Republic.

Language choice was considered an individual matter in the new nation, as were the direction and advancement of literature. Individuals were free to choose guidance through available written authorities or alliance with particular societies, which directed standardization in language according to their special interests: literary, scientific, religious, or business. The American ambiguity about whether limits upon government derived from the written text of constitutions or from an antecedent body of unwritten natural law applied also to language. Americans sought authorities, some in an academy, others in written sources or public models; yet others felt too that language was somehow "natural" in the Rousseauian sense and was governed by its own internal rules. A national language academy had proved too monarchical, too rigid for citizens whose colonial experiences had convinced them that language and other cultural items should not be matters of national dictate.

Moreover, language was not yet a national ideological symbol, although it could serve such goals as the stimulation of European applause for things American. Language was, indeed, a pragmatic instrument. The effectiveness of language as a tool had ultimately to be determined by those individuals or groups using the tool. Motivations for language choice, change, and use had to derive from estimations of local group identity, special-interest allegiance, or personal advancement. National intervention in choosing one form of English over an alternate form had the potential to eradicate familiar distinctions, regional, social, and ethnic, which made the daily world comprehensible to unlike-minded men in a fluctuating, developing, plural society.

Some have maintained that an American language standard is part of the heritage of the founding fathers and is somehow mystically bound up with patriotism and nationalism. Such folk notions have blocked or deflected efforts to provide for bilingual-bicultural individuals and groups through educational programs and legal decisions. Yet during the founding period of 1780–1820, the national elite recognized the plural nature of American society, as well as the need to strike a balance between the absence of restraint on the number and kind of languages to be spoken and the need and ability of the citizenry to belong to a common entity. During this period leaders rejected national institutions designed to determine either a uniform process of Anglicization or a consistent pattern of Americanization in language and culture. Diversification in language choice, change, and use not only prevailed, but was purposefully left unrestrained by leaders' repeated failure to provide a national language academy.

Proposal for an American Language Academy

By John Adams

John Adams penned this proposal while on a diplomatic mission to Europe during the Revolutionary War. Formally entitled "A Letter to the President of Congress," it was dispatched from Amsterdam on September 5, 1780. Along with other correspondence on the same issue, it appears in *The Works of John Adams*, ed. Charles Francis Adams (Boston: Little, Brown, 1852), 7:249–51.

As eloquence is cultivated with more care in free republics than in other governments, it has been found by constant experience that such republics have produced the greatest purity, copiousness, and perfection of language. It is not to be disputed that the form of government has an influence upon language, and language in its turn influences not only the form of government, but the temper, the sentiments, and manners of the people. The admirable models which have been transmitted through the world, and continued down to these days, so as to form an essential part of the education of mankind from generation to generation, by those two ancient towns, Athens and Rome, would be sufficient, without any other argument, to show the United States the importance to their liberty, prosperity, and glory, of an early attention to the subject of eloquence and language.

Most of the nations of Europe have thought it necessary to establish by public authority institutions for fixing and improving their proper languages. I need not mention the academies in France, Spain, and Italy, their learned labors, nor their great success. But it is very remarkable, that although many learned and ingenious men in England have from age to age projected similar institutions for correcting and improving the English tongue, yet the government have never found time to interpose in any manner; so that to this day there is no gram-

mar nor dictionary extant of the English language which has the least
public authority; and it is only very lately, that a tolerable dictionary
has been published, even by a private person, and there is not yet a
passable grammar enterprised by any individual.

The honor of forming the first public institution for refining, correcting, improving, and ascertaining the English language, I hope is
reserved for congress; they have every motive that can possibly influence a public assembly to undertake it. It will have a happy effect
upon the union of the States to have a public standard for all persons
in every part of the continent to appeal to, both for the signification
and pronunciation of the language. The constitutions of all the States
in the Union are so democratical that eloquence will become the instrument for recommending men to their fellow-citizens, and the
principal means of advancement through the various ranks and offices of society.

In the last century, Latin was the universal language of Europe.
Correspondence among the learned, and indeed among merchants
and men of business, and the conversation of strangers and travel-
lers, was generally carried on in that dead language. In the present
century, Latin has been generally laid aside, and French has been sub-
stituted in its place, but has not yet become universally established,
and, according to present appearances, it is not probable that it will.
English is destined to be in the next and succeeding centuries more
generally the language of the world than Latin was in the last or
French is in the present age. The reason of this is obvious, because
the increasing population in America, and their universal connection
and correspondence with all nations will, aided by the influence of
England in the world, whether great or small, force their language
into general use, in spite of all the obstacles that may be thrown in
their way, if any such there should be.

It is not necessary to enlarge further, to show the motives which
the people of America have to turn their thoughts early to this subject;
they will naturally occur to congress in a much greater detail than I
have time to hint at. I would therefore submit to the consideration of
congress the expediency and policy of erecting by their authority a
society under the name of "the American Academy for refining, improving, and ascertaining the English Language." The authority of
congress is necessary to give such a society reputation, influence, and
authority through all the States and with other nations. The number
of members of which it shall consist, the manner of appointing those
members, whether each State shall have a certain number of members
and the power of appointing them, or whether congress shall have a
certain number of members and the power of appointing them, or
whether congress shall appoint them, whether after the first appoint-

ment the society itself shall fill up vacancies, these and other questions will easily be determined by congress.

It will be necessary that the society should have a library consisting of a complete collection of all writings concerning languages of every sort, ancient and modern. They must have some officers and some other expenses which will make some small funds indispensably necessary. Upon a recommendation from congress, there is no doubt but the legislature of every State in the confederation would readily pass a law making such a society a body politic, enable it to sue and be sued, and to hold an estate, real or personal, of a limited value in that State.

Declaration of Linguistic Independence

By Noah Webster

Noah Webster, the preeminent authority on language for generations of schoolchildren, is best remembered for his *American Spelling Book* (1783) and *American Dictionary of the English Language* (1828). The following ramblings on the need for a linguistic standard are excerpted from *Dissertations on the English Language: With Notes, Historical and Critical* (Boston: Isaiah Thomas, 1789; rpt. Meniston, England: Scolar Press, 1967), pp. 18–23, 35–36.

The English tongue, tho later in its progress towards perfection, has attained to a considerable degree of purity, strength and elegance, and been employed, by an active and scientific nation, to record almost all the events and discoveries of ancient and modern times.

This language is the inheritance which the Americans have received from their British parents. To cultivate and adorn it, is a talk reserved for men who shall understand the connection between language and logic, and form an adequate idea of the influence which a uniformity of speech may have on national attachments.

It will be readily admitted that the pleasures of reading and conversing, the advantage of accuracy in business, the necessity of clearness and precision in communicating ideas, require us to be able to speak and write our own tongue with ease and correctness. But there are more important reasons, why the language of this country should be reduced to such fixed principles, as may give its pronunciation and construction all the certainty and uniformity which any living tongue is capable of receiving.

The United States were settled by emigrants from different parts of Europe. But their descendants mostly speak the same tongue; and the intercourse among the learned of the different States, which the revolution has begun, and an American Court will perpetuate, must gradually destroy the differences of dialect which our ancestors brought from their native countries. This approximation of dialects will be certain; but without the operation of other causes than an intercourse at Court, it will be slow and partial. The body of the people, governed by habit, will still retain their respective peculiarities of speaking; and for want of schools and proper books, fall into many inaccuracies, which, incorporating with the language of the state where they live, may imperceptibly corrupt the national language. Nothing but the establishment of schools and some uniformity in the use of books, can annihilate differences in speaking and preserve the purity of the American tongue. A sameness of pronunciation is of considerable consequence in a political view; for provincial accents are disagreeable to strangers and sometimes have an unhappy effect upon the social affections. All men have local attachments, which lead them to believe their own practice to be the least exceptionable. Pride and prejudice incline men to treat the practice of their neighbors with some degree of contempt. Thus small differences in pronunciation at first excite ridicule—a habit of laughing at the singularities of strangers is followed by disrespect—and without respect friendship is a name, and social intercourse a mere ceremony.

These remarks hold equally true, with respect to individuals, to small societies and to large communities. Small causes, such as a nickname, or a vulgar tone in speaking, have actually created a dissocial spirit between the inhabitants of the different states, which is often discoverable in private business and public deliberations. Our political harmony is therefore concerned in a uniformity of language.

As an independent nation, our honor requires us to have a system of our own, in language as well as government. Great Britain, whose children we are, and whose language we speak, should no longer be *our* standard; for the taste of her writers is already corrupted, and her language on the decline. But if it were not so, she is at too great a distance to be our model, and to instruct us in the principles of our own tongue.

It must be considered further, that the English is the common root or stock from which our national language will be derived. All others will gradually waste away—and within a century and a half, North America will be peopled with a hundred millions of men, *all speaking the same language*. Place this idea in comparison with the present and possible future bounds of the language in Europe—consider the Eastern Continent as inhabited by nations, whose knowledge and intercourse are embarrassed by differences of language; then anticipate the period when the people of one quarter of the world, will be able to associate and converse together like children of the same family.[32] Compare this prospect, which is not visionary, with the state of the English language in Europe, almost confined to an Island and to a few millions of people; then let reason and reputation decide, how far America should be dependent on a transatlantic nation, for her standard and improvements in language.[33]

Let me add, that whatever predilection the Americans may have for their native European tongues, and particularly the British descendants for the English, yet several circumstances render a future separation of the American tongue from the English, necessary and unavoidable. The vicinity of the European nations, with the uninterrupted communication in peace, and the changes of dominion in war, are gradually assimilating their respective languages. The English with others is suffering continual alterations. America, placed at a distance from those nations, will feel, in a much less degree, the influence of the assimilating causes; at the same time, numerous local causes, such as a new country, new associations of people, new combinations of ideas in arts and science, and some intercourse with tribes wholly unknown in Europe, will introduce new words into the American tongue. These causes will produce, in a course of time, a language in North America, as different from the future language of England, as the modern Dutch, Danish and Swedish are from the German, or from one another: Like remote branches of a tree springing from the same stock; or rays of light, shot from the same center, and diverging from each other, in proportion to their distance from the point of separation. . . .

Rapid changes of language proceed from violent causes; but these causes cannot be supposed to exist in North America. It is contrary to all rational calculation, that the United States will ever be conquered

32. Even supposing that a number of republics, kingdoms or empires, should within a century arise and divide this vast territory, still the subjects of all will speak the same language, and the consequence of this uniformity will be an intimacy of social intercourse hitherto unknown, and a boundless diffusion of knowledge.

33. Editor's note: It is important to bear in mind that these views represent the early Webster. By the 1830s, his linguistic nationalism had cooled, as attested by the following: "Our language is the *English* and it is desirable that the language of the United States and Great Britain should continue to be the same, except so far as local circumstances, laws and institutions shall require a few particularities in each country"; Letter "from Dr N. Webster to a gentleman of this town," n.d., Library of Congress, Misc. Manuscripts Collection, cited in Richard N. Rollins, *The Long Journey of Noah Webster* (Philadelphia: University of Pennsylvania Press, 1980), p. 127.

by any one nation, speaking a different language from that of the country. Removed from the danger of corruption by conquest, our language can change only with the slow operation of the causes before-mentioned and the progress of arts and sciences, unless the folly of imitating our parent country should continue to govern us, and lead us into endless innovation. This folly however will lose its influence gradually, as our particular habits of respect for that country shall wear away, and our *amor patriae* acquire strength and inspire us with a suitable respect for our own national character.

We have therefore the fairest opportunity of establishing a national language, and of giving it uniformity and perspicuity, in North America, that ever presented itself to mankind. Now is the time to begin the plan. The minds of the Americans are roused by the events of a revolution; the necessity of organizing the political body and of forming constitutions of government that shall secure freedom and property, has called all the faculties of the mind into exertion; and the danger of losing the benefits of independence, has disposed every man to embrace any scheme that shall tend, in its future operation, to reconcile the people of America to each other, and weaken the prejudices which oppose a cordial union.

Federal English

By Dennis Baron

Dennis Baron is professor of English at the University of Illinois at Champaign-Urbana and author of *The English-Only Question: An Official Language for Americans?* (1990) and *Grammar and Good Taste* (1982). This article is excerpted from *Brandeis Review,* Spring 1987, pp. 18–21.

For a little more than two hundred years, the United States of America has gotten by without an official language. The founders of the United States chose not to designate English as the national language either in the Constitution or in subsequent federal law. American legislators have generally steered clear of such attempts to direct the course of English through the establishment of a language academy or the designation of approved dictionaries and grammars of our speech. But this reluctance to privilege or mold English does not mean that on the occasions when official American policy tolerates or promotes minority languages, it does so out of any sympathy for cultural pluralism. It was always clear to our leaders that national and linguistic unity went hand in hand. The United States was never envisioned as permanently multilingual.

Practically speaking, though, we had to recognize—sometimes officially, sometimes unofficially—the presence of large numbers of non-English speakers on American soil, granting them certain linguistic and cultural rights while at the same time integrating them into the mainstream of American society. The presence of non-English-speaking populations has often promoted official tolerance in the interests of producing an informed citizenry, maintaining efficient communication, and assuring public safety. Nonetheless, English has always been the de facto standard in the United States as a whole. Public policy has dealt with bilingualism as a temporary, transitional facet of assimilation.

From the outset, the colonization of the New World spurred language competition. Europeans did what they could to eradicate Native American languages (along with Native Americans), but in the United States, English speakers learned to cope with large monolingual populations of other Europeans. While early settlers never doubted the domination of English on the North American continent, they were careful in areas of mixed settlement to assure that non-English speakers be included in the systems of education and government and that English speakers be protected from the occasional non-English majority. This attitude prompted policies of bilingual or multilingual tolerance alternating with an intolerant, English-only approach on the part of local, state, and federal governments.

In the early days of the Republic, questions of language were fairly prominent, and they centered not only on the status of English vis-à-vis other languages, but on which kind of English—British or American—should become standard in the New World. Anti-British sentiment after the Revolutionary War led to suggestions that the newly emerging nation speak a different language than English. Some reformers advocated Hebrew, felt by many eighteenth-century language experts to be the original, Edenic language. Other anti-English patriots suggested Greek, the language of the world's first democracy, or French, considered to be the language of pure rationality. The impracticality of converting Americans to any new language was always clear, however. One revolutionary wag advised that we retain English for ourselves and instead force the British to learn Greek.

More popular than giving up English altogether was the insistence by Noah Webster, among others, that we rename our speech *American* rather than *English*. In 1789 Webster was so pro-American that he urged his compatriots to reject British linguistic standards simply because of their association with colonial oppression, even when those standards were demonstrably correct. Webster argued that it was in our national interest to foster the continued divergence of American, or "Federal English," as he sometimes called it, from British English. In the same vein, John Adams predicted that our republican form of government would produce linguistic as well as social perfection, while the British monarchy and British English would continue to decay.

At the start of his language career, Webster envisioned creating a uniform American standard language, free of dialect variation or foreign (particularly French) impurities, and rational in spelling and grammar. To this end, he wrote a series of textbooks—a speller, a grammar, and a reader—using American spellings, place names, and authors instead of British, and published at home rather than overseas. Webster campaigned to have his series adopted in all the states and endorsed by Congress and the universities.

Although he does not allude to the situation in Europe, Webster may have been influenced by French attempts at linguistic centralization as much as by his anti-British fervor. The French Academy had been authorized to produce official language texts, including a dictionary, a grammar, and a guide to usage. It attacked this mission with renewed vigor after the French Revolution, partly out of a new national spirit, but also as a means of distancing itself from the *ancien régime,* and did produce a new edition of its dictionary in the year VII, with an appropriately revolutionary preface. The Academy's grammar did not appear until the 1930s, however, and never ever achieved the universality intended for it. Webster also failed in his grandiose scheme to establish a uniform set of approved textbooks. Competition from other texts, both British and American, was simply too stiff. Also, the country did not pursue the kind of national, educational, and linguistic uniformity that Webster supported.

Of course, not all Americans were so hostile to the mother country. Joseph Emerson Worcester, Noah Webster's arch-rival in lexicography, believed that the only practical English standard was that of London and the royal court. Many nineteenth-century language commentators on both sides of the Atlantic rejected the notion of a separate, Federal English, emphasizing instead the common heritage of the two tongues. Nonetheless, Winston Churchill's comment that England and America were two countries separated by a common language aptly summarized popular attitudes, as each national group continued to decry the linguistic barbarities perpetrated by its transatlantic cousin.

Even Webster's radical position on British English eventually softened. He named his great lexicon of 1828 *An American Dictionary of the*

English Language and during a trip to England to promote his publications, Webster claimed that the few differences between the two varieties of English were trivial and superficial. Despite Webster's change of heart, sentiment for an American rather than an English language surfaced sporadically in the nineteenth and twentieth centuries. There were American grammars and Columbian grammars, American spellers (including Webster's own blue-backed speller, originally entitled *An American Spelling Book*), even an *American Primer*, written by Walt Whitman.

In 1923 Representative Washington J. McCormick of Montana introduced a bill in Congress to make American the nation's official tongue and to amend all Congressional acts and government regulations, substituting American for English in references to language. McCormick's anglophobia is reminiscent of Webster's. Not only did he advocate dropping all references to the English language, but he urged Americans to do away with any usage that suggested British influence *(see pp. 40–41).*

McCormick's bill died in committee, but American English was clearly in the air in 1923, and similar bills appeared in a number of state legislatures that year. All but one failed. Illinois state senator Frank Ryan did manage to push through a law making American, and not English, the official language of his state. In its initial version Ryan's bill was virulently anti-British. Its *whereases* attacked those American Tories "who have never become reconciled to our republican institutions and have ever clung to the tradition of King and Empire." According to Ryan, such anglophiles foster racism and defeat the attempts of American patriots "to weld the racial units into a solid American nation." The bill as finally worded was toned down considerably, though its original sentiment was clearly unaltered. The Brit-bashing clauses were replaced by a paean to America as the world's welcoming haven. A final clause justified changing the official nomenclature to bring it into line with common practice because immigrants to the United States considered our institutions and language to be American. Despite its passage, the Illinois law produced no sweeping changes in usage in the state, where English rather than American continued to be taught in the public schools. It was quietly repealed in 1969, when English once again became the official state language.

Although English has always been the unofficial language of government and public communications throughout the United States, American politicians have sensed the advantages of communicating in the various languages of their constituents. From the outset, important documents like the Articles of Confederation, and a good number of our laws, have been translated into minority languages by federal, state, and territorial governments. The early proceedings of the Continental Congress were published in German, for example, and in French as well, possibly with a view toward attracting the Québecois as future fellow citizens. In 1795 a proposal in Congress to print all federal laws in German as well as English lost by only one vote. This event, known as the "Muhlenberg Vote" after the Speaker of the House, a Pennsylvania German who reportedly stepped down from the chair to cast the deciding negative, has been transmuted by folk tradition into a myth that German came close to replacing English as our national language.[34]

The English-only movement has been around in one form or another in the United States for some time. While English-only rhetoric is often cloaked in the rationality of language unification, it has frequently been associated either with crackpot linguistic schemes or xenophobia, or sometimes both. For many proponents its real purpose has been to oppose the immigration and naturalization of non-English speakers, whether French, Spanish, German, Scandinavian, Central European, African, or Asian.

That the framers of the Constitution, who were well aware of the same problems of multilingualism that face us today, chose not to adopt an English-only stance is instructive. Their attitude should lead us to question the necessity of an Official English amendment today whose purpose seems not linguistic, but culturally and politically isolationist in its thrust.

"American" as the Official Language of the United States

By Washington J. McCormick

In 1923 Washington J. McCormick, a Republican congressman from Montana, proposed to replace English with "American." Apparently, this was the first official-language measure ever considered by the U.S. Congress. The bill died in committee, although it was adopted later that year

---

34. Editor's note: Historians disagree on this incident, which is clouded by poor record-keeping in the Third Congress. See Robert A. Feer, "Official Use of the German Language in Pennsylvania," *Pennsylvania Magazine of History and Biography* 76 (1952): 394–405; and Heinz Kloss, *The American Bilingual Tradition* (Rowley, Mass.: Newbury House, 1977), pp. 28–29.

by the state of Illinois. McCormick's rationale for the change was quoted in "Language by Legislation," *Nation* 116 (April 11, 1923): 408.

I might say I would supplement the political emancipation of '76 by the mental emancipation of '23. America has lost much in literature by not thinking its own thoughts and speaking them boldly in a language unadorned with gold braid. It was only when Cooper, Irving, Mark Twain, Whitman, and O. Henry dropped the Order of the Garter and began to write American that their wings of immortality sprouted. Had Noah Webster, instead of styling his monumental work the *American Dictionary of the English Language*, written a "Dictionary of the American Language," he would have become a founder instead of a compiler. Let our writers drop their top-coats, spats, and swagger-sticks, and assume occasionally their buckskin, moccasins, and tomahawks.

Policies toward American Indian Languages: A Historical Sketch

By Jon Reyhner

Jon Reyhner is associate professor of curriculum and instruction at Eastern Montana College. This article, which he wrote for the *Source Book*, is adapted from *A History of Indian Education*, coauthored with Jeanne Eder (Billings: Eastern Montana College, 1989).

The repression of American Indian languages began with the arrival of the first Europeans on this continent. Even before reaching these shores, the colonists had absorbed images of the savage nature of America's native inhabitants.[35] Along with these ethnocentric biases, early European colonists held strong religious convictions and saw Indian religions as works of the devil. The colonists set out to "civilize" and Christianize the Indians, forcing them to accept Western civilization and to speak English. Often, however, the unintended con-

---

35. V. J. Vogel, *This Country Was Ours: A Documentary History of the American Indian* (New York: Harper & Row, 1972).

sequence was cultural disintegration, a legacy that is associated today with Indian poverty, alcoholism, and educational failure.

When the British government tried to slow down the colonists' encroachment upon Indians and to make the colonists pay for their own defense, they rebelled. After the American Revolution, however, Indian wars started by settlers eager to acquire Indian lands became a major expense to the new government. Civilizing the Indian through education came to be seen as a cheaper way to pacify the frontier. Money was appropriated, beginning in 1802, for missionaries to establish schools among the Indians. Teachers in these schools were expected to promote government policies by convincing their students that reducing the size of their land holdings and moving farther west were in the Indians' best interest.

Nevertheless, because of their close contact with Indians, missionaries sometimes identified with Indian interests, even to the point of going to jail, as Samuel Worcester did in the Cherokees' fight against removal. Dictionaries written by missionaries such as Stephen R. Riggs's *Grammar and Dictionary of the Dakota Language*, published in 1852, actually helped preserve Indian languages. But government policy was made in the East by people who, unlike the missionaries, had usually never lived among Indians. As the U.S. government became militarily stronger, it became more dictatorial in its dealing with Indians, and in 1871 Congress ended all treaty-making with tribes. This action marked a shift in government plans for the Indian, from relocation to the unsettled West to assimilation into the general population. With this change in policy, the federal government became more involved in the direct operation of Indian schools.

The popular attitude toward Indians was reflected in schoolbooks that portrayed them as "destitute of all that constitutes civilization." [36] The 1878 report of the Commissioner of Indian Affairs declared that "education of their children" was the quickest way to civilize Indians and that education could only be provided "to children removed from the examples of their parents and the influence of the camps and kept in boarding schools." The report quoted Lieutenant Richard Pratt as saying the students would be "hostages for good behavior of [their] parents." [37] Meanwhile, the parents themselves were, in the words of an aide-de-camp to General Sherman, "held on reservations, actually prisoners of war." [38] To leave they were required to have passes signed

36. William Swinton, *A Condensed School History of the United States* (New York: Ivison, Blakeman & Taylor, 1875), p. 21.

37. *Annual Report of the Commissioner of Indian Affairs to the Secretary of the Interior* (Washington, D.C.: U.S. Government Printing Office, 1878), pp. xxv–xxvi, 174.

38. Richard Irving Dodge, *Our Wild Indians: Thirty-three Years' Personal Experience among the Red Men of the Great West* (1882; rpt. New York: Archer House, 1959), p. 644.

by the Indian agent; in turn, non-Indians needed permission to visit reservations, requirements which continued into the twentieth century.

In 1878 Pratt brought seventeen adult Indian prisoners of war from Florida to the Hampton Institute, a private nondenominational boarding school for black children in Hampton, Virginia. He recruited another forty boys and nine girls from Dakota Territory. Encouraged by the success of the students at Hampton but believing Indians should be educated separately from black students, Pratt got government approval to start a school exclusively for Indian students at Carlisle, Pennsylvania. In a burst of optimism, the government built twenty-five boarding schools between 1879 and 1902 with an enrollment of 9,736 students in 1905. The school superintendent for the Bureau of Indian Affairs (B.I.A.) predicted that "if there were a sufficient number of reservation boarding-school-buildings to accommodate all the Indian children of school age, and these buildings could be filled and kept filled with Indian pupils, the Indian problem would be solved within the school age of the Indian child now six years old."[39]

At these boarding schools, students were forbidden to speak their native languages. One of the first students at Carlisle, Luther Standing Bear, a Sioux, remembered "how hard it was to forgo the consolation of speech" when he and his fellow students were told to speak only English.[40] Enforcement of the English-only rule was usually strict. Lawrence Horn, a Blackfeet who attended the government school at Heart Butte, Montana, recalled students getting a stroke of a leather strap every time they spoke Indian languages.[41]

It was expected that upon graduation students would blend into the general population. In fact, few did. Most returned to their reservations, where they found themselves ill-fitted to live in their tribal culture. For those remaining in white America, racial prejudice usually excluded them from all but the most menial jobs.

In contrast to the government's approach, some mission schools instructed children in their native languages. A correspondent who visited schools with Secretary of the Interior Carl Schurz reported in 1880 that the educational facilities of the Santee Sioux in Nebraska "are perhaps better than those of any other of the northern tribes." At the American Mission boarding school, the Dakota dialect was

---

39. John H. Oberly, "Report of the Indian School Superintendent," in *Annual Report of the Commissioner of Indian Affairs to the Secretary of the Interior* (Washington, D.C.: U.S. Government Printing Office, 1885), p. cxiii.

40. Luther Standing Bear, *My People, the Sioux*, ed. E. A. Brininstool (Boston: Houghton Mifflin, 1928), pp. 16, 242.

41. Jackie Parsons, *The Educational Movement of the Blackfeet Indians, 1840–1979* (Browning, Mont.: Blackfeet Heritage Program, [1980]).

taught, and all elementary school books and the Bible were in Dakota. After the children learned to read in Dakota, they were given a bilingual book with illustrations. Stephen Riggs felt that first teaching "children to read and write in their own language enables them to master English with more ease when they take up that study. . . . [A] child beginning a four years' course with the study of Dakota would be further advanced in English at the end of the term than one who had not been instructed in Dakota." [42]

Despite Riggs's success, Secretary Schurz issued regulations in 1880 that "all instruction must be in English" in both mission and government schools, under threat of loss of federal funding.[43] Similar orders followed. J. D. C. Atkins, commissioner of Indian Affairs from 1885 to 1888, wrote a long condemnation of the use of native languages in schools and on the importance of English (see pp. 47–51). But in spite of such policies emanating from Washington, observers in the field such as General Oliver O. Howard reported that successful missionary teachers learned the tribal language so that they could understand the children and the children could understand them.[44]

Luther Standing Bear started teaching in 1884. He described using illustrated primers: "I would have the children read a line of English, and if they did not understand all they had read, I would explain it to them in Sioux. This made the studies very interesting." He felt that the civil service exam was not necessary for primary teachers, observing that his students did better than those of white teachers who got all their knowledge from books, "but outside of that, they knew nothing." Standing Bear believed that "the Indian children should have been taught how to translate the Sioux tongue into English properly; but the English teachers only taught them the English language, like a bunch of parrots. While they could read all the words placed before them, they did not know the proper use of them; their meaning was a puzzle."[45]

Teacher, disciplinarian, and Indian agent Albert H. Kneale found the lessons monotonous in the Oklahoma boarding school where he worked at the turn of the century:

> Few of the students had any desire to learn to read, for there was nothing to read in their homes nor in the camp; there seemed little incentive to learn English, for there was

42. *Report of the Board of Indian Commissioners* (Washington, D.C.: U.S. Government Printing Office, 1880), p. 77.

43. Francis Paul Prucha, ed., *Americanizing the American Indians* (Cambridge, Mass.: Harvard University Press, 1973), p. 199.

44. Oliver O. Howard, *My Life and Experiences among Our Hostile Indians* (Hartford: A. T. Worthington, 1907; rpt. New York: DeCapo, 1972).

45. Standing Bear, *My People*, pp. 193, 239.

no opportunity to use it, there seemed to be nothing gained through knowing that "c-a-t" spells cat; arithmetic offered no attraction; not one was interested in knowing the name of the capital of New York. . . .

[The B.I.A.] went on the assumption that any Indian custom was, per se, objectionable, whereas the customs of whites were the ways of civilization. . . . [Students] were taught to despise every custom of their fore-fathers, including religion, language, songs, dress, ideas, methods of living.[46]

For the vast majority of Indians, however, boarding schools did not erase their Indian-ness. Another teacher, Gertrude Golden, found that the tribes she worked with had an "aversion to speaking English . . . the tongue of their despised conquerors."[47]

The B.I.A.'s approach came under sharp criticism in a government-sponsored investigation conducted in 1927. It concluded: "The philosophy underlying the establishment of Indian boarding schools, that the way to 'civilize' the Indian is to take Indian children, even very young children, as completely as possible away from their home and family life, is at variance with modern views of education and social work, which regard the home and family as essential social institutions from which it is generally undesirable to uproot children."[48]

John Collier, appointed commissioner of Indian Affairs in 1933, shared these objections to forced assimilation. Modern society, he wrote, had "lost that passion and reverence for human personality and for the web of life and the earth which the American Indians have tended as a central sacred fire."[49] Collier revolutionized B.I.A. schools, for the first time placing an emphasis on teaching Indian cultures and languages; the B.I.A. even produced a few textbooks in Indian tongues.

Polingaysi Qoyawayma, a Hopi teacher, has described the difference that Collier's new policies made in her teaching environment. Previously, her supervisors had forbidden her to speak Hopi to her students. In her own mind she had questioned such directives, as well as the curriculum she was asked to teach: "What do these white-man stories mean to a Hopi child? What is a 'choo-choo' to these little ones who have never seen a train? No! I will not begin with the out-

46. Albert H. Kneale, *Indian Agent* (Caldwell, Idaho: Caxton, 1950), pp. 41, 52, 168.

47. Gertrude Golden, *Red Moon Called Me: Memoirs of a Schoolteacher in the Government Indian Service*, ed. Cecil Dryden (San Antonio: Naylor, 1954), p. 10.

48. Lewis Meriam, ed., *The Problem of Indian Administration* (Baltimore: Johns Hopkins University Press, 1928), p. 403.

49. John Collier, *The Indians of the Americas: The Long Hope* (New York: W. W. Norton, 1947), p. 17.

side world of which they have no knowledge. I shall begin with the familiar. The everyday things. The things of home and family." So, in defiance of her supervisors, Qoyawayma continued to substitute familiar Hopi legends, songs, and stories for Little Red Riding Hood. Despite complaints, she persevered in trying to help her students "blend the best of the Hopi tradition with the best of the white culture, retaining the essence of good, whatever its source." When Collier changed B.I.A. policies, Qoyawayma found her teaching methods supported "overnight" to the "consternation" of her older colleagues.[50]

After World War II the old assimilationist ideas again became predominant in a conservative Congress. The proposed solution to the problem of the Indian was to "set the Indian free" by terminating the "socialistic" reservations. Small gains made in bilingual education under John Collier were largely reversed. During U.S. Civil Rights Commission hearings on the Navajo Reservation in 1973, parents described their limited say in their children's education and the curriculum's neglect of the Navajo language and culture.[51] One Navajo teacher testified that she had been reprimanded by her public school principal and accused of violating Arizona state law because she used some Navajo words with her kindergarten students. Indian children's school achievement continued to be two to three years behind that of white students of the same age.[52]

However, a new era of bilingual-bicultural instruction was beginning in tribally operated facilities like the Rough Rock Demonstration School. After 1968 the federal Bilingual Education Act funded a growing number of Indian bilingual programs; also, it supported centers to produce bilingual materials in a number of Indian languages. In 1984 the Northern Ute Tribal Business Committee proclaimed the Ute language as the official language of the Northern Ute Nation. A year later the Navajo Tribal Council declared Navajo to be "an essential element of the life, culture and identity of the Navajo people." Both tribes now require that their language be taught in reservation schools.[53]

50. Polingaysi Qoyawayma [Elizabeth Q. White], *No Turning Back: A Hopi Indian Woman's Struggle to Live in Two Worlds,* as told to Vada F. Carlson (Albuquerque: University of New Mexico Press, 1964), p. 125.

51. U.S. Commission on Civil Rights, *The Navajo Nation: An American Colony* (Washington, D.C.: U.S. Commission on Civil Rights, 1975), p. 127.

52. U.S. Senate, Select Committee on Indian Education, *Indian Education: A National Tragedy, A National Challenge* (Washington, D.C.: U.S. Government Printing Office, 1969), p. ix.

53. Northern Ute Tribal Business Committee, "Ute Language Policy," *Cultural Survival Quarterly* 9, no. 2 (1985): 16–19; *Navajo Nation: Educational Policies* (Window Rock, Ariz.: Navajo Division of Education, 1985).

Despite the progress made in the last twenty years in the new era of Indian self-determination, a legacy of linguistic and cultural repression remains. Some Indian parents object to modern bilingual education for their children, having internalized the old boarding-school attitude that any time spent on ancestral languages is time wasted, while others are resentful and suspicious of any program sponsored by the U.S. government. Today, however, when the United States is publicly supporting basic human rights of minorities to retain their ancestral languages, religions, and cultures in Eastern Europe and the rest of the world, the time has come for an equal recognition of the basic human rights of America's first inhabitants. The negative results of past assimilationist policies toward Native Americans will take many years to erase; for some groups who no longer speak their ancestral languages, there is probably no going back. Still, there is hope in the policy of "English Plus," endorsed by groups like the National Education Association, which encourages parents and students to maintain their native languages and cultures as they learn to work with mainstream America.

"Barbarous Dialects Should Be Blotted Out . . . "

By J. D. C. Atkins

J. D. C. Atkins was federal commissioner of Indian affairs during the first Grover Cleveland administration. This policy statement is excerpted from his annual report for 1887.[54]

In the report of this office for 1885, incidental allusion was made to the importance of teaching Indians the English language, the paragraph being as follows:

A wider and better knowledge of the English language among them is essential to their comprehension of the duties and obligations of citizenship. At this time but few of the adult population can speak a word of English, but with the efforts now being made by the Government and by re-

54. Washington, D.C.: U.S. Government Printing Office, 1887, pp. xx–xxiv.

ligious and philanthropic associations and individuals, especially in the Eastern States, with the missionary and the
schoolmaster industriously in the field everywhere among
the tribes, it is to be hoped, and it is confidently believed,
that among the next generation of Indians the English language will be sufficiently spoken and used to enable them
to become acquainted with the laws, customs, and institutions of our country.

The idea was not a new one. As far back as 1868 the commission
known as the "Peace Commission," composed of Generals Sherman,
Harney, Sanborn, and Terry, and Messrs. Taylor (then Commissioner
of Indian Affairs), Henderson, Tappan, and Augur, embodied in the
report of their investigations into the condition of Indian tribes their
matured and pronounced views on this subject, from which I make
the following extracts:

> The white and Indian must mingle together and jointly oc-
> cupy the country, or one of them must abandon it. . . .
> What prevented their living together? . . . Third. The dif-
> ference in language, which in a great measure barred inter-
> course and a proper understanding each of the other's mo-
> tives and intentions. Now, by educating the children of
> these tribes in the English language these differences
> would have disappeared, and civilization would have fol-
> lowed at once. Nothing then would have been left but the
> antipathy of race, and that, too, is always softened in the
> beams of a higher civilization. . . . Through sameness of
> language is produced sameness of sentiment, and
> thought; customs and habits are moulded and assimilated
> in the same way, and thus in process of time the differences
> producing trouble would have been gradually obliterated.
> By civilizing one tribe others would have followed. Indians
> of different tribes associate with each other on terms of
> equality; they have not the Bible, but their religion, which
> we call superstition, teaches them that the Great Spirit
> made us all. In the difference of language to-day lies two-
> thirds of our trouble. . . . Schools should be established,
> which children should be required to attend; their barba-
> rous dialects should be blotted out and the English lan-
> guage substituted. . . . The object of greatest solicitude
> should be to break down the prejudices of tribe among the
> Indians; to blot out the boundary lines which divide them
> into distinct nations, and fuse them into one homogeneous
> mass. Uniformity of language will do this—nothing else
> will.

In the regulations of the Indian Bureau issued by the Indian Office
in 1880, for the guidance of Indian agents, occurs this paragraph: "All

instruction must be in English, except in so far as the native language of the pupils shall be a necessary medium for conveying the knowledge of English, and the conversation of and communications between the pupils and with the teacher must be, as far as practicable, in English."

In 1884 the following order was issued by the Department to the office, being called out by the report that in one of the schools instruction was being given in both Dakota and English: "You will please inform the authorities of this school that the English language only must be taught the Indian youth placed there for educational and industrial training at the expense of the Government. If Dakota or any other language is taught such children, they will be taken away and their support by the Government will be withdrawn from the school."

In my report for 1886 I reiterated the thought of my previous report, and clearly outlining my attitude and policy I said:

> In my first report I expressed very decidedly the idea that Indians should be taught the English language only. From that position I believe, so far as I am advised, there is no dissent either among the law-makers or the executive agents who are selected under the law to do the work. There is not an Indian pupil whose tuition and maintenance is paid for by the United States Government who is permitted to study any other language than our own vernacular—the language of the greatest, most powerful, and enterprising nationalities beneath the sun. The English language as taught in America is good enough for all her people of all races.

Longer and closer consideration of the subject has only deepened my conviction that it is a matter not only of importance, but of necessity that the Indians acquire the English language as rapidly as possible. The Government has entered upon the great work of educating and citizenizing the Indians and establishing them upon homesteads. The adults are expected to assume the role of citizens, and of course the rising generation will be expected and required more nearly to fill the measure of citizenship, and the main purpose of educating them is to enable them to read, write, and speak the English language and to transact business with English-speaking people. When they take upon themselves the responsibilities and privileges of citizenship their vernacular will be of no advantage. Only through the medium of the English tongue can they acquire a knowledge of the Constitution of the country and their rights and duties thereunder.

Every nation is jealous of its own language, and no nation ought to be more so than ours, which approaches nearer than any other nationality to the perfect protection of its people. True Americans all feel that the Constitution, laws, and institutions of the United States, in their adaptation to the wants and requirements of man, are superior to those of any other country; and they should understand that by the spread of the English language will these laws and institutions be more firmly established and widely disseminated. Nothing so surely and perfectly stamps upon an individual a national characteristic as language. So manifest and important is this that nations the world over, in both ancient and modern times, have ever imposed the strictest requirements upon their public schools as to the teaching of the national tongue. Only English has been allowed to be taught in the public schools in the territory acquired by this country from Spain, Mexico, and Russia, although the native populations spoke another tongue.[55] All are familiar with the recent prohibitory order of the German Empire forbidding the teaching of the French language in either public or private schools in Alsace and Lorraine. Although the population is almost universally opposed to German rule, they are firmly held to German political allegiance by the military hand of the Iron Chancellor. If the Indians were in Germany or France or any other civilized country, they should be instructed in the language there used. As they are in an English-speaking country, they must be taught the language which they must use in transacting business with the people of this country. No unity or community of feeling can be established among different peoples unless they are brought to speak the same language, and thus become imbued with like ideas of duty.

Deeming it for the very best interest of the Indian, both as an individual and as an embryo citizen, to have this policy strictly enforced among the various schools on Indian reservations, orders have been issued accordingly to Indian agents, and the text of the orders and of some explanations made thereof are given below:

> December 14, 1886
>
> In all schools conducted by missionary organizations it is required that all instructions shall be given in the English language.

> February 2, 1887
>
> In reply I have to advise you that the rule applies to all schools on Indian reservations, whether they be Government or mission schools. The instruction of the Indians in

---

55. Editor's note: This was untrue in the case of California from 1849–1855 and in New Mexico as the commissioner spoke. See Arnold H. Leibowitz, "Educational Policy and Political Acceptance: The Imposition of English as the Language of Instruction in American Schools" (Washington, D.C.: ERIC Clearinghouse for Linguistics, [1971]), pp. 45–54; rpt. in U.S. House Committee on the Judiciary, Subcommittee on Civil and Constitutional Rights, *English Language Constitutional Amendments: Hearing on H.J. Res. 13, H.J. Res. 33, H.J. Res. 60, and H.J. Res. 83*, 100th Cong., 2d sess., 1988.

the vernacular is not only of no use to them, but is detrimental to the cause of their education and civilization, and no school will be permitted on the reservation in which the English language is not exclusively taught. . . .

To teach Indian school children their native tongue is practically to exclude English, and to prevent them from acquiring it. This language, which is good enough for a white man and a black man, ought to be good enough for the red man. It is also believed that teaching an Indian youth in his own barbarous dialect is a positive detriment to him. The first step to be taken toward civilization, toward teaching the Indians the mischief and folly of continuing in their barbarous practices, is to teach them the English language. The impracticability, if not impossibility, of civilizing the Indians of this country in any other tongue than our own would seem to be obvious, especially in view of the fact that the number of Indian vernaculars is even greater than the number of tribes. . . .

But it has been suggested that this order, being mandatory, gives a cruel blow to the sacred rights of the Indians. Is it cruelty to the Indian to force him to give up his scalping-knife and tomahawk? Is it cruelty to force him to abandon the vicious and barbarous sun dance, where he lacerates his flesh, and dances and tortures himself even unto death? Is it cruelty to the Indian to force him to have his daughters educated and married under the laws of the land, instead of selling them at a tender age for a stipulated price into concubinage to gratify the brutal lusts of ignorance and barbarism?

Spanish Language Rights in California: Constitutional Debates

By the time California's first constitution was drafted in 1849, the Gold Rush had already transformed the state's Spanish speakers into a minority (13,000 of nearly 100,000 residents).[56] Without opposition, however, delegates to the constitutional convention approved an important recognition of Spanish language rights: "All laws, decrees, regulations, and provisions emanating from any of the three supreme powers of this State, which from their nature

---

56. Rodolfo Acuña, *Occupied America: The Chicano's Struggle toward Liberation* (San Francisco: Canfield Press, 1972), p. 104.

require publication, shall be published in English and Spanish." To some, this step seemed legally required by the Treaty of Guadalupe Hidalgo (1848), in which Mexico had ceded nearly half its territory to the United States. Although the treaty made no explicit reference to language rights, Article IX guaranteed, among other things, that Mexicans who chose to remain on the conquered lands would enjoy "all the rights of citizens of the United States . . . and in the mean time shall be maintained and protected in the free enjoyment of their liberty and property, and secured in the free exercise of their religion without restriction."

By 1878, however, when Californians met to revise their state constitution, support for minority language rights had waned. Not a single delegate to the convention came from a Spanish-language background. Moreover, the assembly was dominated by the nativist Workingmen's Party, which pushed through a number of draconian measures aimed at Chinese immigrants. In this climate the delegates not only eliminated the 1849 guarantee for Spanish-language publications, but also limited all official proceedings to English (a restriction that remained in effect until 1966), making California the nation's first "English only" state. The debate on this provision, and on an unsuccessful attempt to amend it, is excerpted from *Debates and Proceedings of the Constitutional Convention of the State of California, 1878–1879* (Sacramento, 1880–81), 2:801–2.

Mr. SMITH of Santa Clara. I wish to offer an amendment to that section [of Article IV].

The SECRETARY read: "Amend section twenty-four by adding 'and all laws of the State of California, and all official writings, and the executive, legislative, and judicial proceedings shall be conducted, preserved, and published in no other than the English language.'"

Mr. ROLFE. Mr. Chairman: I understand that refers to all judicial proceedings. I hardly think that it is necessary, and in some instances it would work injury. We have a provision in our present Constitution requiring laws to be translated and published in Spanish; that, I think is entirely unnecessary, and should be rescinded. We have statutes, however, passed for the purpose of meeting exigencies in some parts of this State, allowing, in some kind of proceedings—judicial proceedings in the Courts—to be conducted either in the English or Spanish language. Now, while I would not make that mandatory, and while I would say nothing about it in the Constitution, I would leave it in the discretion of the Legislature to make that same provision, for I can assure this Convention that there are Justices of the Peace in my county [San Bernardino], and their proceedings are judicial proceedings, who are intelligent men, and very able Justices of the Peace, who have no knowledge of the English language. There are settlements in that county, in certain localities and townships, in which the English language is scarcely spoken, the population being made up, almost entirely, of people who use the Spanish language. Now, in this instance, it would work a very great injury. . . . Therefore I think that in these townships where almost the entire population is made up of a Spanish-speaking people, there would be no harm done in allowing the judicial proceedings of the Justices' Courts to be conducted in the Spanish language. . . .

Mr. TINNIN. Mr. Chairman: I hope this amendment will be adopted. There was a day when such proceedings were necessary— in the early days of this State—but I contend that day has now passed. Thirty years have elapsed since this portion of the country became a portion of the Government of the United States, and the different residents who were here at that time have had ample time to be conversant with the English language if they desired to do so. This is an English-speaking Government, and persons who are incapable of speaking the English language certainly are not competent to discharge public duties. We have here in the Capitol now tons and tons of documents published in Spanish for the benefit of foreigners.

Mr. ROLFE. Do you call the native population of this State foreigners?

Mr. TINNIN. They had ample time to learn the language.

Mr. AYERS. . . . In the section of the State which I represent [Los Angeles County] there are large portions of it which are entirely populated by a Spanish-American population, not a foreign population, but a population who were here before we were here, and I wish to say that almost without an exceptional instance these natives of California, who were adults at the time this State was ceded to the United States by Mexico, are still in the same condition, as far as their knowledge of English is concerned. There are but very few of them, if any, who understand our language at all, and, if I am not mistaken, in the treaty of Guadalupe Hidalgo there was an assurance that the natives should continue to enjoy the rights and privileges they did under their former Government, and there was an implied contract that they should be governed as they were before. It was in this spirit that the laws were printed in Spanish. As Judge Rolfe says, there are townships in Southern California which are entirely Spanish, or Spanish-American. . . . [I]t would be wrong, it seems to me, for this Convention to prevent these people from transacting their local business in their own language. It does no harm to Americans, and I think they should be permitted to do so. . . .

Mr. BEERSTECHER. Mr. Chairman and gentlemen of the committee: As has been aptly stated by the gentleman from Los Angeles, Mr. Ayers, there was an implied contract in the treaty of peace with Mexico that the Mexican citizen should enjoy the same privileges and immunities under the American rule as they enjoy it under the Mexican rule. And among these privileges and immunities was the right of having laws of this State printed in Spanish, and having the judicial proceedings of this State, at least in certain districts, . . . conducted in the Spanish language. And the Codes of this State, to-day, contain a special provision that in certain counties of this State the proceedings may be in the Spanish language. . . . Now, it is not the policy of any State in the Union to publish exclusively in the English language. In the State of Michigan, where I resided for eight years, our public documents were published in the English, the German, and the French languages. In the State of Wisconsin the public documents are printed in the English, German, and Norwegian languages. In Pennsylvania, in English and German; and it is the policy of the Western States, generally, with their cosmopolitan population, to publish State documents in more than one language. Be this proper, or be it improper, it is a matter that ought to rest in the discretion of the Legislature, and we ought not to put any Know-Nothing clause into the Constitution. . . . I hope that the Spaniards will have their rights, as they have them to-day, and if the Legislature can assist them by having documents published in their language, I hope they will do so.

Mr. TINNIN. Where do you find in the treaty of Hidalgo any such contract? . . .

Mr. AYERS. I say the treaty implied that.

Mr. BEERSTECHER. It says that they should have the same privileges and immunities.

Mr. SCHELL. If we are to be so exceedingly cosmopolitan, would it not be equally reasonable that our laws should be published in German and French?

Mr. INMAN. And Chinese.

Mr. SCHELL. And every other language that we have here.

Mr. BEERSTECHER. I do not say that our laws ought to be published in any but the English language; but I do say that there should not be any inhibition contained in the Constitution that would prevent the Legislature from publishing official documents in any other language, if it was desirable to do so. I do not see why the Governor's messages should not be published in German and French, and any other language, if it is desirable. . . .

Mr. SCHELL. How many voters are there that speak the Spanish language down there that can also speak the English language?

Mr. BLACKMER. There are a great many, but there are a great many who are able to speak the English language who cannot read it.

Mr. GREGG. Can they read the Spanish?

Mr. BLACKMER. Most of them can.

Mr. HEISKELL. I demand the previous question.

The main question was ordered. . . .

The amendment was adopted, on a division, by a vote of 46 ayes to 39 noes.

Mr. ROLFE. Mr. Chairman: I offer an amendment to the last amendment.

The SECRETARY read: "Add to the last amendment to section twenty-four the following: 'Provided, that the Legislature may, by law, authorize judicial or other official proceedings in any designated counties or other localities, to be conducted in the English or Spanish language.'" . . .

Mr. ROLFE. This amendment which I propose now does not interfere with the laws of this State, proclamations of the Governor, or anything of a State nature. It only refers to proceedings of a local nature, and then, unless the Legislature specifically authorizes that to be done, these local proceedings must be conducted in the English language. But I do say that, in localities in this State, where the population are almost universally of the Spanish-speaking people, it is unjust to them to compel them to conduct their proceedings in the English language. . . . There are some English-speaking people there, it is true, but most of them understand the Spanish language. They conduct their business and all their proceedings in Spanish. They make their contracts in Spanish. Although a man may be very well-educated in Spanish, and may have a very ordinary knowledge of the English language, it may still be very inconvenient for him to conduct his proceedings in English. . . . He will make mistakes in language which will be injurious to litigants before his Court. . . .

Now, I say that we should take into consideration the fact that the American, or English-speaking people, of this State are the new comers. We settled this State and took it from these people when the Spanish was universally the mother tongue of the people. . . . Now, I say when we take their country and the people, too, and make American citizens of them, we must take them as they are and give them an equal show with us whether it was so contracted in the treaty or not. I say it is nothing but just, as long as there is one township in the State which is populated mostly by these people. . . .

Mr. WEST. Mr. Chairman: I have as high regard, sir, as any man for the foreign element of citizens of this State who have come here and identified themselves with the institutions of this country, and assim-

ilated, they and their families, with its institutions; but I have no regard for that demagogism that panders to this foreign element, that
follows it for years and years for the sake of the votes it affords on
election days. I speak whereof I know when I say that hundreds of
those who pretend to be citizens of California are recent immigrants
from Sonora and other portions of Mexico, some of them bandits, cut-
throats, and robbers, that come in and are placed on the Great Register, and vote . . . while the Dutchman, and the Irishman, and the
Frenchman must be naturalized and come in, in the regular way. It is
an abuse, it is an outrage upon the institutions of our country. On
election day they are corralled and voted, when they have not been in
the State five days. . . .

We have opened the doors of our public schools to them and their
children, and attempted to educate them under the general influence
of our schools, and if thirty years will not do it, I think we had better
send missionaries into the county from which the gentleman from
San Bernardino comes. I do not know that these gentlemen spoken of
are competent to perform the duties of Justices of the Peace or any
other position, but I am satisfied that the Spanish element do not ask
it. It is the demagogues who ask it, and not the educated, thinking,
and reading part of that population. I respect that population, where
they are bona fide citizens, as much as any member of this Convention, but I want a period placed where the importation of Mexicans into this country and the collecting of them at the polls shall
cease. . . .

Mr. AYERS. Mr. Chairman: This is not a question of demagogism, or
partisanism; it is a question of right. Now, I know that in Southern
California there are districts and communities that are so entirely
Spanish that if you deprive them of the right to continue their proceedings in Justices' Courts in Spanish, you will deprive them of justice. I do not see what it has to do with this case, whether people are
run in, in bands, from Mexico, and put upon the Great Register, or
not. That is a question for the Courts. If they are run in, in that way,
and falsely placed on the Register, it ought to be stopped; but even if
that was the case, it is no reason for taking away the rights of any
portion of this people. It is only five years since the Mayor of Los
Angeles could not speak the English language, and he was a very
efficient Mayor. . . . I hope that the amendment of the gentleman
from San Bernardino will be adopted on the ground that it is right
and just. It is all well enough for us here, who are strong, to stand up
and denounce them because they are weak. We have taken from them
their patrimony and their lands and now we are kicking them when
they are down.

Mr. OVERTON. Mr. Chairman: I am not in favor of the amendment;

neither do I care for this sympathetic appeal. We have done it, it is true. We have done it honorably, and we have lived up to their contract. We have protected them for thirty years, and if they have not learned to conduct their business in English, I think it is about time they did learn. I do not think, Mr. President, that there is a township in this State that there is not some Americans, or some foreigners, who do not speak the Spanish language, and we are doing them an injustice if we allow proceedings to be carried on in a language they do not understand. These cases are subject to appeal, and if the proceedings of that Court is had in Spanish, there is not a County Court in this State the proceedings of which are conducted in Spanish, and therefore you cannot appeal. If you are going to permit one township to have it in Spanish, there is just as much reason why another would have it in Swiss and another in Italian.

Mr. AYERS. Mr. Chairman: I would like to ask the gentleman whether the Swiss and Italians came here from other countries, or were born here, or whether they were found here?

Mr. OVERTON. They came here under a treaty, and have got just as much right as those under the Hidalgo treaty. These people sold us their country, and we have paid them the money. I am not in favor of printing laws in Spanish. Our County Court House has a room that is occupied by statutes published in Spanish, and there they remain to-day by the ton, and they are not worth anything. This State has paid out thousands and thousands of dollars—thrown it away—for the purpose of publishing books in Spanish, and we have got them there now, and no one ever has any use for them.

Mr. ROLFE. We do not ask the laws to be published in Spanish.

Mr. AYERS. Does the gentleman know that there are tons and tons of English literature in this building too?

Mr. OVERTON. Yes, I know there are. We can read it too. When it comes to publishing laws in Spanish, I hold that it is useless. There is not a nationality in this State that has not got papers that publish them, and they can read them there. . . .

Mr. BLACKMER. Mr. Chairman: I do believe that these people have some rights that we ought to respect. I do not believe, because we are stronger, because we outnumber them and are continually increasing the ratio, that we should entirely ignore the rights that these people ought to have under a free government. It is a simple question whether we will do right because it is right, or whether we will do wrong because we have the power to do it. I look upon it in that light. I say that it is but simple justice that the Legislature be given the authority to allow, in certain localities, these Courts to conduct their business in that language, and, if necessary, that they may also publish in that language. . . .

Mr. WICKES. Mr. Chairman: In addition to what has been said, I think it very good policy to give some official recognition to the Spanish language. It is a noble language, spoken by millions of people upon the American continent. . . .

The CHAIRMAN. The question is on the adoption of the amendment offered by the gentleman from San Bernardino, Mr. Rolfe.

The amendment was lost on a division, by a vote of 27 ayes to 55 noes.

Language Rights and New Mexico Statehood

By the U.S. Commission on Civil Rights

This article is excerpted from *The Excluded Student: Educational Practices Affecting Mexican Americans in the Southwest*, Mexican American Education Study, Report III (Washington, D.C.: U.S. Government Printing Office, 1972), pp. 76–82.

Before the United States achieved independence, Spanish soldiers and colonists from Mexico had established settlements in California, Arizona, and Texas, as well as New Mexico. When Mexico ceded these lands to the United States following the war of 1846–48, an estimated 75,000 Spanish-speaking people lived in the Southwest: 60,000 in New Mexico, 7,500 in California, 5,000 in Texas, 1,000 or so in Arizona, and 1,500 in Colorado.[57] Spanish was the dominant language and a combination of Spanish-Mexican-Indian culture dominated the region's life-style.

The Treaty of Guadalupe Hidalgo, signed on February 2, 1848 and ratified three months later, gave U.S. citizenship to all Mexican nationals who remained in the ceded territory. Only a few—less than 2,000—left. The treaty also guaranteed certain civil, political, and religious rights to the Spanish-speaking colonists and attempted to protect their culture and language.

With the California Gold Rush as the principal impetus, streams of

57. Editor's note: These estimates, which first appeared in Carey McWilliams, *North from Mexico: The Spanish-Speaking People of the United States* (Philadephia: J. P. Lippincott, 1949), p. 52, are now considered conservative.

Anglos began flowing West. As they achieved sufficient population majorities, the treaty's guarantees, explicit or implied, were sometimes circumvented or totally ignored. With two cultures in conflict and new political powers at stake, a series of legal actions started which to this day affects the treatment Mexican Americans receive from our institutions of law and learning.

In 1850 the Territory of New Mexico (which included the present state of Arizona) was added to the union. Thirteen years later New Mexico and Arizona were separated as territories, but in 1906 the U.S. Congress passed a joint statehood bill for them, stipulating that rejection of joint statehood by the voters of either territory would prevent it from taking place. New Mexico was roughly 50 percent Spanish-speaking, while estimates of Arizona's Indian and Mexican American population ranged from 5 percent to nearly 20 percent.

After introduction of a similar bill the year before, the Arizona legislature had passed a resolution of protest, stating that joint statehood "would subject us to the domination of another commonwealth of different traditions, customs and aspirations."[58] The Arizona Territorial Teachers Association passed a resolution opposing joint statehood. Arizona schools taught all classes in English; New Mexico schools used interpreters. The resolution warned that the union of New Mexico and Arizona would disrupt the Arizona school system. Arizonans' fears were summarized in a Protest against Union of Arizona with New Mexico presented to Congress on February 12, 1906, which cited

> the decided racial difference between the people of New Mexico, who are not only different in race and largely in language, but have entirely different customs, laws and ideals and would have but little prospect of successful amalgamation . . . [and] the objection of the people of Arizona, 95 percent of whom are Americans, to the probability of the control of public affairs by people of a different race, many of whom do not speak the English language, and who outnumber the people of Arizona two to one.[59]

Further in the document the delegates explained that the New Mexico courts and legislature were conducted through interpreters; that New Mexico published its statutes in two languages; that New Mexico derived its law from the civil law system, while Arizona law stemmed from the common law system; and that the Spanish-speaking New Mexicans would not consent to the loss of their right to serve on juries. The proposed statehood bill gave sixty-six votes in the constitutional convention to New Mexico and forty-four votes to

58. Peplow, *History of Arizona* (New York: Lewis Historical Publishing, 1958), 2:2, 12.

Arizona. The protest prophesied that New Mexico would control the constitutional convention and impose her dual language conditions on Arizona.[60] Joint statehood won in New Mexico, 26,195 to 14,735. It lost in Arizona, 16,265 to 3,141.

In 1910 the Senate Committee on Territories considered separate statehood for Arizona and New Mexico. An Arizona delegate sought to amend the statehood bill by inserting a provision that "nothing in this Act shall preclude the teaching of other languages" in public schools. He was opposed by the committee chairman, Senator Albert Beveridge of Indiana, and other senators. Beveridge declared:

> The purpose of that provision, both with reference to New Mexico and Arizona, and particularly to the former is to continue the thing that has kept back the speaking of English and the learning of English, to wit: that because they may conduct the schools in other languages, in many of those Spanish-speaking communities, particularly in New Mexico, they will do so. . . . [61]
>
> Everybody knows . . . one of the difficulties down there . . . [is] the curious continuance of the solidarity of the Spanish-speaking people. It would be well . . . if at least the men who make the laws could speak the language which all the rest of us speak.[62]

On June 10, 1910, Congress passed an enabling act which provided for the calling of constitutional conventions. The act required the Arizona and New Mexico state constitutions to include two provisions which would limit the use of the Spanish language as an official language. First, the public schools must be conducted in English: "That provisions shall be made for the establishment and maintenance of a system of public schools, which shall be open to all children of said state and free from sectarian control, and that said schools shall always be conducted in English."[63]

Second, knowledge of the English language was a prerequisite for holding state offices and positions in the legislature: "That said State shall never enact any law restricting or abridging the right of suffrage on account of race, color, or previous conditions of servitude, and that ability to read, write, speak, and understand the English language sufficiently well to conduct the duties of the office without the

59. U.S. Senate Document 216, 59th Cong., 1st sess., Feb. 12, 1906, pp. 1–2.
60. Ibid., pp. 14–15.
61. *Congressional Record*, 61st Cong., 2d sess., 1910, p. 109.
62. Ibid., p. 8225.
63. Arizona and New Mexico Enabling Act of 1910, ch. 310, 36 Stat. §§2(4), 20(4).

aid of an interpreter shall be necessary qualification for all State officers and members of the State legislature."[64]

Nevertheless, the draft of the New Mexico constitution, completed on November 21, 1911, contained three provisions which protected the rights of the Spanish-speaking. One related to voting:

> *Sec. 3. Religious and racial equality protected; restrictions on amendments.* The right of any citizen of the state to vote, hold office, or sit upon juries, shall never be restricted, abridged, or impaired on account of religion, race, language or color, or inability to speak, read or write the English or Spanish languages as may be otherwise provided in this Constitution; and the provisions of this section and of section one of this article shall never be amended except upon the vote of the people of this state in an election at which at least three-fourths of the electors in the whole state, and at least two-thirds of those voting in each county of the state, shall vote for such amendment.[65]

The other two related to education:

> *Sec. 8. Teachers to learn English and Spanish.* The legislature shall provide for the training of teachers in the normal schools or otherwise so that they may become proficient in both the English and Spanish languages, to qualify them to teach Spanish-speaking pupils and students in the public schools and educational institutions of the State, and shall provide proper means and methods to facilitate the teaching of the English language and other branches of learning to such pupils and students.
>
> *Sec. 10. Educational rights of children of Spanish descent.* Children of Spanish descent in the State of New Mexico shall never be denied the right and privilege of admission and attendance in the public schools or other public educational institutions of the State, and they shall never be classed in separate schools, but shall forever enjoy perfect equality with other children in all public schools and educational institutions of the State, and the legislature shall provide penalties for the violation of this section. This section shall never be amended except upon a vote of the people of this State, in an election at which at least three-fourths of the electors voting in the whole state and at least two-thirds of those voting in each county in the State shall vote for such amendment.[66]

64. Ibid., §§2(5), 20(5).
65. New Mexico Constitution, Art. VII §3 (1912).
66. Ibid., Art. XII §§8, 10.

The Constitution also preserves all rights granted under the Treaty of Guadalupe Hidalgo: "The rights, privileges and immunities, civil, political and religious, granted to the people of New Mexico by the Treaty of Guadalupe Hidalgo shall be preserved inviolate."

On January 12, 1911, New Mexico ratified a constitution and forwarded it to President Taft, who approved it on February 24, 1911. The Senate, however, did not approve the constitution because of the provision which made amendments far too difficult. Arizona also ratified its constitution, but it was rejected by the President. A resolution was adopted by Congress requiring New Mexico to resubmit to the electors a less restrictive provision for constitutional amendments, and Arizona to resubmit an amendment on recall of officers. This resolution also deleted the provision of the enabling act which required state officers and legislators of New Mexico to have a comprehensive knowledge of the English language. Representative Legare said:

> These people come to us from New Mexico, both Republicans and Democrats, and say that in the Enabling Act passed last year we have taken them by the throat and told them that they must enact an irrevocable ordinance whereby no Spanish-speaking person can hold office in their State. They tell us, both factions, that some of the best people of their State and some of their most brilliant men are Spanish-speaking people.[67]

On November 7, 1911, the electors of New Mexico approved a substitute provision on the amendment process. On January 6, 1912, President Taft signed the Statehood Proclamation.

The Mexican Americans of New Mexico succeeded in protecting their heritage by inserting provisions in their constitution which made Spanish an official language, equal to the English language. The constitution also provided that, for the following twenty years, all laws passed by the legislature be published in both Spanish and English, and thereafter as the legislature should provide.[68] Prior to 1967, notices of statewide and county elections were required to be printed in English and "may be printed in Spanish." Additionally, many legal notices today are required to be published in both English and Spanish.

In 1925 the legislature provided that "in every high school with fifty (50) or more pupils, one (1) special teacher, in addition to those already provided for, may be employed providing that such teacher is qualified to teach both Spanish and English and does teach classes in

67. *Congressional Record*, 78th Cong., 2d sess., 1911, p. 1251.
68. New Mexico Constitution, Art. XX §12 (1912).

Spanish."[69] This law was repealed in 1962. In 1943 the position of State Supervisor of Spanish was created "to bring about an improvement in the teaching of Spanish in the schools of the State, and in order to insure the retainment and the development of the Spanish language, with a view of future Inter-American relations."[70] This law was repealed in 1967.

A 1941 act required all public grade schools of the state—rural or municipal—having at least three teachers and a daily attendance of ninety pupils to teach Spanish in the fifth to the eighth grades, except where the governing board of education by resolution relieves a school from teaching Spanish during any scholastic year.[71] In 1969 the legislature authorized any school district to establish in any level of instruction a bilingual and bicultural study involving a culture in which a language other than English is spoken in the home.[72]

English and Colonialism in Puerto Rico

By the Language Policy Task Force

This article is excerpted from "Language Policy and the Puerto Rican Community," *Bilingual Review/La Revista Bilingüe* 5, nos. 1–2 (1978): 1–39, an essay that emerged from many discussions and drafts by members of the Centro de Estudios Puertorriqueños of the City University of New York. The Language Policy Task Force includes Ana Celia Zentella, Pedro Pedraza, Jr., Emilio González Atiles, Frank Bonilla, Ricardo Campos, Dagmaris Cabezas, and Juan Flores. This final version was written by John J. Attinasi.

Language policy directly influences education and the maintenance of dominated national cultures in a multiethnic setting. At the same time it should be understood that language is often only the symbol, battleground, and visible tip of the iceberg reflecting deeper conflicts. These conflicts are political and economic in nature. Population

69. N. Mex. Stat. Ann. 73–12–7 (1953).
70. Ibid., 73–4–1 to 73–4–7.
71. Ibid., 73–17–2.
72. N. Mex. Stat. Ann. 77–11–12 (1969).

movements, patterns of labor-force use, and the needs of capitalism underlie the debate over official languages, bilingualism, and multicultural education.

Two major colonial regimes and their languages have dominated Puerto Rico. The Puerto Rican community in the United States was created by the sweep of American imperialism through the Caribbean. There has been extensive population exchange and language interaction, resulting in a class-stratified command of bilingual skills, as well as differing attitudes toward use of the two languages, Spanish and English. Puerto Rico has been used as a military stronghold for the Caribbean and Latin America, as a site for industrial expansion and economic investment, as a market for commodities and agricultural surplus, as a source for mineral resources and tropical agricultural products, as a playland for the wealthy, and as a source of human labor. Millions of Puerto Ricans, during the course of this relationship, have been catapulted into cities in Puerto Rico and across the United States. These population movements, which reached their peak in the early 1950s and are still taking place, plunged Puerto Ricans into a web of racial prejudice, urban ghettos, and economic exploitation. In the last decade there has been a growth of return migration to Puerto Rico, adding to the complexity of the situation.[73]

On October 18, 1898, the United States established a military government which was to administer and "Americanize" its new possession with a fierce policy of economic and cultural domination. A report written by the office of the colonial school system sums up the view of Puerto Rico's language problems:

> Their language is a patois almost unintelligible to the native of Barcelona and Madrid. It possesses no literature and has little value as an intellectual medium. There is a bare possibility that it will be nearly as easy to educate this people out of their patois into English as it will be to educate them into the elegant tongue of Castile. Only from the very small intellectual minority in Puerto Rico trained in Europe and imbued with European ideals of education and government, have we to anticipate any active resistance to the introduction of the American school system and the English language.[74]

Political callousness and linguistic chauvinism of this type served as the basis for policy throughout the next fifty years. Time and again,

73. Centro de Estudios Puertorriqueños, *Cuaderno de Migración* (New York: Research Foundation of the City University of New York, 1975).
74. Quoted in Juan José Osuna, *A History of Education in Puerto Rico* (Río Piedras: Universidad de Puerto Rico, 1949), p. 342.

pedagogical principles, cultural realities, and political rights were brutalized for the sake of creating a colony whose people spoke English and were loyal to the United States.

The U.S. government during this time had complete control of the state apparatus of Puerto Rico by way of the Foraker Act of 1900, which had created a civilian regime overseen by the War Department. The President of the United States had the power to appoint the Commissioner of Education, and indeed all major government officials. Despite this absolute power, the open drive to convert the population to the English language failed calamitously. Every educational administrator found himself unable to sustain English as the only language of instruction in the schools. Every colonial administration found it necessary to reorganize, rearrange, restructure, and shift policies in an attempt to overcome the resistance of the Puerto Rican people.

The first education commissioner (1900–1901), Martin G. Brumbaugh, began by using English as the primary language of instruction in all subjects in the schools. When this failed, he instituted Spanish as the vernacular in the primary grades (1–8), but retained English in the secondary grades (9–12). Toward the end of his one-year term, he introduced English as a mandatory and privileged subject in the primary grades.[75]

Brumbaugh foreshadowed subsequent administrators by bringing in American teachers and supervisors and opting for a policy of benevolent "bilingualism." During the administration of Roland P. Falkner (1904–7), English was reinstated as the primary language of instruction in all grades, and for all subjects. By 1912 it was officially reported that 98 percent of all schoolchildren were receiving their instruction in English.[76] During the administrations of Paul G. Miller (1916–21) and Juan B. Huyke (1921–30), a new policy was established: Spanish in grades 1–4, and English in grades 6–8 (grade 5 was a transitional year). This period was filled with great political tension over the language question. In 1915, in the Puerto Rican House of Delegates, a bill was introduced to make Spanish the compulsory language of instruction. It also required that Spanish be used in all judicial proceedings. At the Central High School a student strike was triggered by the expulsion of a student collecting signatures in support of the bill. The strike ended in the creation of a private school which would teach in Spanish. Commissioner Miller nevertheless pressed forward with the imposition of English, upgrading the professional staff through summer workshops for English teachers and

75. Aída Negrón de Montilla, *Americanization in Puerto Rico and the Public School System, 1900–1930* (Río Piedras: Editorial Edil, 1971), pp. 35–60.

76. Michael Bernard Gorman, "Language Policy in Puerto Rican Education" (Ph.D. diss., American University, 1973), p. 48.

increasing the number of basic English texts from two to four. When the policy of bilingual education was attacked by the Puerto Rican Teachers Association in 1919, Miller defended his position thus: "As citizens of the United States the children of Porto Rico possess an inalienable right to learn the English language."[77]

Throughout this period the colonial intent of the United States remained constant while varying programs of instruction were implemented. Administrators had to use Spanish in order to accomplish even a minimal level of instruction. José Padín was the first to undertake a pedagogically oriented analysis of the problem. As general superintendent of schools, he had conducted studies that led him, as early as 1915, to recommend the comparative approach, emphasizing what is common to both languages, attending to difficulties where Spanish and English diverge, and emphasizing conversation. Even these sensible and mild pedagogical approaches were rejected.

It was not until 1925 that a full-scale study of Puerto Rican education was commissioned. Conducted by the International Institute of Teachers College, Columbia University, it found that more than 80 percent of Puerto Rican students were dropping out of school without meeting the standards for either English or Spanish. The results of this study remained essentially unused until the appointment of Padín as Commissioner of Education. In 1934 he combined his own findings with those of Teachers College and reinstated a policy of Spanish as the medium of instruction in grades 1–8, retaining English in grades 9–12. English was to be studied in the elementary grades for two class periods a day. While English instruction continued to be a prime goal, it was to be achieved through special pedagogical methods instead of by fiat alone. This pedagogically sensitive policy was short-lived. The realities of colonialism soon overtook and crushed Padín's efforts.

In 1935 the Massacre of Río Piedras left several students and activists dead. Over the issue of language of instruction, a journalistic polemic flared and lives were lost, including that of Colonel Francis E. Riggs, whose assassination ushered in a period of open repression on every level of Puerto Rican society. In 1937, after the Massacre of Ponce, the U.S. Congress retrenched on the language issue, and Commissioner Padín was forced to leave his post only two years after reinstating Spanish instruction. President Franklin D. Roosevelt appointed a new commissioner, José M. Gallardo, and reemphasized the United States' resolve to make Puerto Rico an English-speaking territory. Roosevelt wrote to Gallardo that Puerto Ricans should profit from "the unique historical circumstance which has brought them the

77. Negrón de Montilla, *Americanization*, p. 160.

blessing of American citizenship by becoming bilingual." But English dominance underlay this concept of "bilingualism," which "will be achieved . . . only if the teaching of English throughout the insular educational system is entered into at once with vigor, purposeful- ness, and devotion, and with the understanding that English is the official language [sic] of our country."[78] These bureaucratic directives were ineffectual, however, thanks to the resistance of the Puerto Ri- can people. Gallardo was soon forced to gradually reinstate Spanish in much the same manner as his predecessors. This retreat from Roo- sevelt's directive finally forced his resignation in 1945, and the post of education commissioner was virtually vacant until 1948.

Starting in 1898 with English as the sole medium of instruction in all grades, the language of instruction had alternated periodically from English to Spanish and back again. This vacillation went on for fifty years, creating extreme chaos and prompting Adrian Hull, the last director of Puerto Rico's English program, to comment that every conceivable policy had been tried except English and Spanish on al- ternate days.[79] Despite the programmatic confusion of the years 1898–1948, some gains had been registered in English competence. In 1910 Puerto Rico had a population of about one million and only 3.6 percent of Puerto Ricans over the age of ten spoke English. By 1940 the population had risen to 1.8 million and the proportion of English speakers had increased to 27.8 percent.[80]

During this period the language struggle solidified along several dimensions: (1) the contention over language was seen by many as a political struggle between U.S. imperialism and independence forces; (2) resistance was also directed against "bilingualism" as a covert pol- icy for imposing English; (3) the failure of English instruction pro- grams forced the United States–dominated school system to resort to repeated upgradings of teacher-training programs, curriculum, and textbooks; (4) this same failure moved the school system to use in- creasingly more Spanish and less English in order to achieve even minimal levels of learning.

By 1944, the beginning of political dominance by the Partido Popu- lar Democrático (P.P.D.), the United States had changed its policy. In- struction in English alone would not work in Puerto Rico. And so, the P.P.D. adopted the method tried by Padín, namely that English com- petence is advanced as one teaches in Spanish. English could come to dominance only through its being taught as a second language.

78. Osuna, History of Education, p. 391.

79. Jean C. Nye, "The Teaching of English as a Second Language in the Junior High Schools of Puerto Rico" (Ph.D. diss., University of Toledo, 1972), p. 18.

80. Commonwealth of Puerto Rico, Department of Education, Yesterday, Today, and Tomorrow (Hato Rey, P.R.: Commonwealth Department of Education, 1968), pp. 3–4.

By increasing its regional support among *campesinos* in the 1930s and early 1940s, the P.P.D. became a strong political force by the end of the Second World War. It built a populist coalition between the working class and the new professionals and technocrats. By this time the capitalist plantation system in Puerto Rico had completely collapsed, giving way to medium-scale industrial development. Once in power, the Populares nationalized certain public utilities, embarked on a modest campaign of agrarian reform, and adopted a policy of stimulating growth through the attraction of foreign capital.

Just as the economic program was portrayed as a path to eventual autonomy through "bootstrap" self-help, the political program was encapsulated in the concept of "commonwealth." This proposal shaped Puerto Rico in the image of a nation-state while maintaining political, juridical, and economic ties to United States colonialism. Similarly, there were deep unresolved conflicts over the question of language. In 1946, President Truman vetoed a bill passed by the Puerto Rican Senate in defiance of the U.S. Congress which legislated the establishment of Spanish as the language of instruction, with English as a compulsory subject. This tension and conflict was reflected in the Commonwealth Constitution, which finally in 1948 decreed the use of Spanish as the language of instruction in Puerto Rico. The Populares, riding the winds of nationalism, made a great show of defending the national language and culture of Puerto Rico. They created the Instituto de Cultura and officially supported the Ateneo, two institutions of "popular" culture whose purposes were to preserve, enrich, and spread the values of Puerto Rican nationality.

Behind this rhetoric, however, the machinery of neocolonialism began to turn. In 1948 Columbia University was once again commissioned to study the failures of the educational system, especially with respect to language instruction. As a result of the study, English was developed as a priority and a special subject. Spanish was used as the language of instruction throughout all grades, English was introduced orally in grades 1–2, reading and writing skills were developed in English beginning in grade 3, and so on. English instruction programs were enhanced by the utilization of audio-visual equipment, after-school English clubs, and teacher-training programs.[81]

Teachers from the United States were assigned to Puerto Rico in large numbers. Many of them did not speak Spanish, though they received rigorous drilling in the techniques of teaching English as a second language and in applied linguistics. Technical support came from the curriculum materials developed during the Second World War by Charles C. Fries, of the English Language Institute at the Uni-

81. Ibid., p. 52.

versity of Michigan, for use in military foreign-language programs. This mobilization of resources was directed at English, while Spanish instruction was neglected. Pauline M. Rojas, director of the English program in the Department of Education, spoke quite candidly in 1954 about the amount of support given to English and its growing importance on the island: "Education costs money; the best available education will necessitate additional funds. However, you can be assured that of the money that is today utilized in Puerto Rico for public instruction, English is receiving more than its share."[82] The assumption underlying this educational policy was that the continuation of Spanish in Puerto Rico could be accomplished for free in the homes and streets of the colony. Because the English language training programs were technically and pedagogically more efficient than Spanish programs, an emerging assumption was reinforced: quality education means instruction in the English language.

The 1968 elections took place amid political turmoil that reflected a worsening economic situation (in 1967 there were forty-nine strikes in Puerto Rico; in 1968 there were seventy-three). The Partido Independentista (P.I.P.) had been weakened by internal reorganizations, and the Populares had been discredited by corruption and factionalism. The Partido Nuevo Progresista (P.N.P.), headed by the industrialist Luis Ferré, won by a plurality, accumulating 44 percent of the votes cast. This party, representing a pro-American and pro-statehood position, was an offshoot of the old Republican Party. Its ranks were expanded by new professionals and by sectors of the working class that saw their interests as tied to the United States.

During the years preceding the P.N.P. victory, a fresh issue had arisen which again revealed many of the contradictions in Puerto Rican society: the question of English instruction in private schools. Throughout the 1960s private schools, both secular and religious, began to grow in number. These schools used English as the primary language of instruction. (In 1959 the United States had declared English to be a foreign language in Puerto Rico, so as to increase the flow of funding to English programs via the National Defense Education Act.) In 1945 private schools had enrolled 4.1 percent of the school-age population; by 1951 this proportion had risen to 5.2 percent, and by 1960 to 8.4 percent. In 1975 they accounted for 16.9 percent of the student population, and it is estimated that by the end of 1980, this figure may be as high as 25 percent.[83]

The Populares had initially attacked these schools, only to retreat in

82. *Sobre la enseñanza de inglés en Puerto Rico* (Hato Rey, P.R.: Editorial del Departamento de Instrucción Pública, 1954), p. 10.
83. Gorman, "Language Policy," p. 121.

the face of pressures exerted by U.S. Congressmen, educators, the Catholic Church, supporters of statehood, and many P.P.D. members who had graduated from private schools. Their party platform stated their linguistic policy:

> We submit that teaching in public schools should be done basically in Spanish, the mother tongue of Puerto Ricans, and that English be used as much as necessary, following the new educational precepts, so that Puerto Ricans may have a perfect mastery of it. . . . Private or parochial schools have the constitutional right to teach in the language of their preference within educational experience.[84]

The position of the P.N.P. was based legally on the individual's right to equal education, but overlooked the political reality that equal access to majority-language education is more easily attained than educational equality for minority languages. It is clearly a case of some language rights being more equal than others.

The debate over private vs. public education prompted the Department of Public Instruction in 1960 to conduct a series of studies which revealed controversial linkages between language, class, and national identity. The studies showed that public-school children had no Spanish language superiority over children taught in English private schools.[85] Further, they revealed little perceived connection, among either student population, between language and cultural identity, whether Latin American, North American, or Puerto Rican. But a strange result was that twice as many public-school as private-school pupils felt it was necessary for Puerto Ricans to become more Americanized, and voiced a desire for increased English instruction. Students said their contact with English had not jeopardized or changed their feelings of national identity.[86] The English language was perceived as a valuable political, intellectual, and economic resource.

Privileged class sectors in colonial nations frequently move toward a command of the language and culture of the colonial power. This need not threaten their loyalty to the national language. As the power of the colonial language becomes manifest, other classes begin to demand access to the same economic and educational privileges. To do otherwise implies political resistance against strong economic odds. In the Puerto Rican case, as elsewhere, anticolonial forces must make

---

84. Ibid., p. 146.

85. It must be remembered that the private schools serve a particular sector of Puerto Rican society. The median income of private-school families is attained by only 10 percent of families of children in public schools.

86. Cited in Erwin H. Epstein, ed., *Politics and Education in Puerto Rico* (Metuchen, N.J.: Scarecrow Press, 1970), p. 152.

the difficult choice between defending the national language and the democratic demand that everyone share the economic and pedagogical benefits of bilingualism. Multifunctional bilingualism is clearly the best choice in such a situation; it offers links to both family and traditional culture and to the resources of the economically more powerful language. The threat to such bilingualism lies in the fact that poorer classes, seeking individual advancement and lacking progressive leadership, may see English and Americanization as expedient (as did many European immigrant groups in the United States). Also, the wealthy sectors, as well as return migrants from the continent, may claim legal rights to English instruction. As a result of these forces, English may gain a new foothold as an optional first language of instruction, a backward move toward the pre–1944 policy.

In colonial settings and Third World nations, these choices have deep historical implications. Short-term economic benefits for working-class sectors must be balanced against the possible permanent loss of the national language. On the other hand, a stubborn defense of the national language may mean relinquishing access to intellectually, politically, and economically powerful languages, eventually weakening the position of the progressive forces. In Puerto Rico, these issues were raised again in the 1960s and 1970s by the return migration.

The number of United States–born Puerto Ricans, mainly young and of working-class background, is growing in almost every region of the island, renewing the controversy over language and national identity: Are these English-dominant people Puerto Rican? Do they have a right to be taught in English and maintain its use as a second language? The Commonwealth government has begun bilingual programs in every district, but the need is far greater than the resources allotted. The P.P.D. and P.N.P. do not want Puerto Ricans from the United States to return. They have declared an ability to provide bilingual instruction to only 2,000 of the 25,000 English-dominant children. Dominance in Spanish, rather than stable and multifunctional bilingualism, seems to be the practical goal of education. The lack of initiative in dealing with the problem reflects the fact that colonialism devised the migration to ease the contradictions of the colony, and now the contradictions have come home.

Crusade for Americanization

By John Higham

John Higham is professor of history at Johns Hopkins University and author of numerous works on immigrants and their reception in the United States. What follows are excerpts of a chapter from *Strangers in the Land: Patterns of American Nativism, 1860–1925,* 2d ed. (New Brunswick, N.J.: Rutgers University Press, 1988), pp. 234–63.

Until the twentieth century, native Americans had not supposed that national homogeneity depended, necessarily or desirably, on special pressures to assimilate the immigrants. Surely, assimilation would follow readily enough from the general institutions and atmosphere of American society, unless of course an especially vicious immigration appeared on the scene; and in that case America could restrict its entry or influence. Thus virtually the whole American response to foreign minorities was contained in two general attitudes: on the one hand, rejection and withdrawal; on the other, a confident faith in the natural, easy melting of many peoples into one. When fearful of disruptive influences, the Americans sought to brake the incoming current or to inhibit its political power; otherwise they trusted in the ordinary processes of a free society.

In contrast, some of the multinational states of Europe had adopted a third approach to unity. In Russia and in Hungary, for example, dominant nationalities tried to force or stimulate absorption of entrenched minorities. Drives to impose a unitary national culture by repressing minority languages, churches, and names created storms and stresses from which the United States long and happily escaped. Part of the difference was due to the more fluid character of America's ethnic groups. In Europe most minorities were fixed in place and rooted in the soil of an ancient culture they were determined to preserve. But immigration brought the United States uprooted peoples who wanted to share in large degree in the new national life; cohesion developed without coercion. Equally important, nineteenth-century Americans did not really demand a high level of national solidarity. Their country had achieved its own loose kind of homogeneity in the very course of accepting a variety of peoples and institutions. And since the American concept of freedom sanctioned a various and flexible ethnic pattern, a large measure of diversity was taken for granted.

Yet America did not forever avoid a version of the European experience. When neither a preventive nativism nor the natural health of a free society seemed sufficient to cope with disunity, a conscious drive to hasten the assimilative process, to heat and stir the melting pot, emerged. From its tiny beginnings at the end of the nineteenth century to its height during World War I, the movement for Americanization was another indication of the growing urgency of the nationalist impulse. Americanization brought new methods for dealing with the immigrants; it significantly altered the traditions of both nativism and confidence. At the same time, the movement embraced the underlying spirit of both traditions. Within the crusade for Americanization, the struggle between nativistic and democratic instincts persisted.

The institution, above all others, on which nineteenth-century Americans relied to further such ethnic unity as they required was the common school. "Education," declared a New York high school principal with characteristically American faith in that commodity, "will solve every problem of our national life, even that of assimilating our foreign element."[87] The education to which he referred, however, consisted of the standard regimen applied to all children alike. The schools made almost no effort to single out the immigrants for special attention. Although a few eastern cities in the latter part of the century opened special night school classes in English, and sometimes civics, for foreigners, such programs functioned on a very modest scale.[88] As an organized, articulate movement, Americanization did not receive its primary impetus from educators. The impulse came from two civic-minded groups who had little in common with one another except a felt need for closer social unity. From different points of view, both groups reacted to the stresses of urban, industrial conditions, which were forcing America's peoples into increasing interdependence.

The social settlements faced the problem from a humane perspective. There a whole generation of humanitarians discovered how deep was the cultural gulf dividing the people of the slums from the rest of society. Beginning in the 1890s, the settlements undertook the first practical efforts toward social integration of the new immigrant nationalities with the older America. Yet places like Hull House and

87. John T. Buchanan, "How to Assimilate the Foreign Element in Our Population," *Forum* 32 (1902): 691. See also Lawrence A. Cremin, *The American Common School: An Historic Conception* (New York, 1951).

88. New York City, which undoubtedly had the most extensive program, was teaching 1,376 foreign students in special evening classes in 1879 and 36,000 in 1905; Gustave Straubenmueller, "The Work of the New York Schools for the Immigrant Class," *Journal of Social Science* 44 (1906): 177.

the University Settlement aimed at Americanization only in the loosest sense of the term. They laid no special emphasis on English or civics classes. They tried to bind together and complete a neighborhood, not to make a nation. On the whole, they did more to sustain the immigrant's respect for his old culture than to urge him forward into the new one. One of the greater lessons the settlements discovered was that the normal, assimilative influences in America often worked too harshly. Immigrant families were divided; the children developed a brassy, swaggering Americanism in their yearning for acceptance. The settlements, therefore, sought to temper as well as improve the ordinary course of assimilation by providing a receptive environment for Old World heritages. Preaching the doctrine of immigrant gifts, Jane Addams and her fellow workers concentrated less on changing the newcomers than on offering them a home.[89]

A second, and closer, approach to Americanization came from another side of the 1890s: not from its hopes of reform, but from its nationalist anxieties. Since the whole Americanization movement reflected a demand for a more tightly knit nation, it was characteristic that the campaign got its essential start from the new patriotic hereditary societies.

Led by the Daughters of the American Revolution, several of these societies embarked on programs of patriotic education designed to indoctrinate the adult foreigner with loyalty to America. In 1898 the Buffalo chapter of the D.A.R. prepared lectures on American history and government to be delivered in foreign languages to men who would soon be voting. Other chapters joined in the work of teaching the "spirit of Americanism," some directing their attention to immigrant children. The Society of Colonial Dames in 1904 launched a somewhat more extensive program, including scholarships to train experts for such patriotic educational work, the sponsorship of lectures and civics classes, and the preparation of appropriate literature. The Sons of the American Revolution, stirred into action by the assassination of President McKinley, soon outdid the ladies' groups. By 1907 the S.A.R. was devoting half of its income to the job of making aliens into good citizens.[90]

Throughout their Americanizing efforts, the patriotic societies preached a loyalty that consisted essentially of willing submissive-

89. University Settlement Society, *Report*, 1896, p. 26; 1898, pp. 27–28; *Hull-House Bulletin* 1 (Oct. 15, 1896): 1–2, 7; Hale House, *Eleventh Annual Report*, 1908, p. 10.

90. *Report of the National Society of the Daughters of the American Revolution*, 1898–1900, pp. 156–57, 196–97, 213; and 1905–6, p. 23; Edward G. Hartmann, *The Movement to Americanize the Immigrant* (New York, 1948), pp. 31–36; *Immigrants in America Review* 1 (1915): 63; Records of the Immigration and Naturalization Service, Americanization Section, File 2761–1828 (National Archives).

ness. Above all, in the words of the D.A.R., they "taught obedience to law, which is the groundwork of true citizenship." The main object of such self-constituted champions of America was to combat the danger of immigrant radicalism or discontent; their chief motive, fear. The settlements, on the other hand, had acted in response to a human need, rather than a political or economic threat; their gentler kind of assimilation arose from sympathy, not from dread. One program drew support from nativistic groups and emotions, the other from the tolerant, cosmopolitan traditions of American democracy.

These were the two sides of the Americanization movement. The impulse of fear and the impulse of love ran throughout its whole course, clashing in principle though in practice sometimes strangely blended. One current tended to soften the movement, orienting it toward the welfare of the immigrant; the other steeled it to an imperious demand for conformity. Out of fear, the Americanization movement fostered a militant nationalism, and by this means it eventually made its widest, most fervent appeal to the native-born public. But Americanization worked most successfully upon the immigrants through love. It was part of the paradox of the movement that the side which evoked the most ardent American response produced the slightest positive results.

Perhaps the most successful of these efforts came from the Young Men's Christian Association, which during those years was turning from missionary work to a program of social service. Under the direction of Peter Roberts, a trained sociologist, the "Y" began in 1907 to organize evening classes in English and civics for foreigners. Roberts developed his own system for teaching practical English conversation to foreign-born adults, and by 1914 his volunteer instructors had some thirty thousand students.[91]

To Roberts, as to many of the humanitarian Americanizers, the immigrant seemed a blessing if redeemed and uplifted, but a danger if left alone. A call to preserve American ideals was fairly commonly interwoven into pleas for service to mankind. In fact, the individual who emerged in the last years of the Progressive Era as the presiding genius of the still amorphous movement for Americanization combined to a unique degree the reformer's passion for social improvement with the nationalist's insistence on a single loyalty. Frances A. Kellor, half reformer, half nationalist, represented both sides of the Americanization movement. Always an apostle of industrial efficiency, she abhorred the chaos and waste of laissez-faire. Through social research and national planning, she hoped to organize and emancipate America's human resources, to rationalize opportunity,

---

91. Hartmann, *Movement*, pp. 28–29; *Immigrants in America Review* 1 (1915): 18–23.

and to build a more unified nation. In one breath she preached social welfare and national discipline.[92]

Like any American with a cause, Miss Kellor needed an organization. It happened that one was at hand. In 1908 a group of public-spirited New England businessmen had launched in Boston the North American Civic League for Immigrants. Its founders, though not unmoved by sympathy, were chiefly concerned with protecting the status quo from the menace of ignorant, incendiary foreigners without resorting to immigration restriction. The league, therefore, combined aid with propaganda; it hired agents who advised new arrivals about jobs, housing, and transportation, and it sponsored widely publicized patriotic lectures in foreign languages in the evening schools. Frances Kellor, supported by a group of wealthy New Yorkers, organized a New York branch of the N.A.C.L. in December 1909.

But the branch and its parent soon parted ways. The New Yorkers developed a much broader, more imaginative program under Miss Kellor's direction. They employed all sorts of ingenious devices to stimulate education for immigrants and, most important, exerted constant pressure on the mid-Atlantic states for protective legislation. While the New York effort followed a liberal direction, emphasizing state-supported social welfare, the parent league became increasingly reactionary. After the Lawrence textile strike of 1912, the Boston group, subsidized by New England industrialists, concentrated on sending agents into foreign communities to act as industrial spies and leaders of antistrike movements. Early in 1914, therefore, the New Yorkers broke away completely to form the Committee for Immigrants in America, with Frances Kellor as vice-chairman and guiding spirit.[93]

Meanwhile, Pennsylvania, New Jersey, Massachusetts, Rhode Island, and California undertook investigations into immigrant life on the model of the original New York inquiry, and some of those states followed through with permanent agencies. At the same time the larger American cities were expanding their evening school classes in English for immigrants; by 1915 Chicago had 13 percent of its total non-English-speaking population enrolled in school.[94]

Nevertheless, these uncoordinated local, state, and voluntary efforts left Frances Kellor unsatisfied. Her new Committee for Immi-

92. Among Kellor's early writings, see especially "New Spirit in Party Organization," *North American Review* 199 (1914): 879–92; "Who Is Responsible for the Immigrants?" *Outlook* 106 (1914): 912–17; and *Straight America: A Call to National Service* (New York, 1916).

93. N.A.C.L., *Annual Report*, 1912–13, p. 6; 1913–14, p. 4; and 1914–15, pp. 9–10, 16; *Immigrants in America Review* 1 (1915): 16–17.

94. Immigrants' Protective League, *Annual Report*, 1916, p. 10.

grants in America set itself up as a central clearinghouse to aid, advise, and unify all public and private agencies interested in the problem throughout the country. It sought both "a national policy . . . to make of all these people one nation" and a federal bureau to lead the way. At the moment, the best Miss Kellor could get from the federal government was the enthusiastic interest of the Bureau of Education, which had little power and scant appropriations. Undaunted, the Committee for Immigrants persuaded its own well-to-do backers to put up the money for establishing a Division of Immigrant Education within the Bureau of Education to publicize the need for Americanization. Throughout its five-year life, the Division of Immigrant Education remained the subsidized creature of Miss Kellor's private pressure group.[95]

Molded by the social conscience and the growing national aspirations of the Progressive Era, the Americanization movement took definite form. It developed a broad program and a vigorous leadership. In a small way it was undoubtedly beginning to have some effect on the immigrants. What it lacked chiefly was followers. It failed signally to awaken a mass response in the American people. Then the war transformed it. In a few months Americanization blossomed into a great popular crusade. And it swelled on the waves of wartime sentiment, the character of the movement subtly but profoundly changed. "With startling suddenness," wrote one authority in 1916,

> the effects flowing out of the war have brought to public attention aspects of immigration that heretofore have been regarded with unruffled complacency. It has consciously become all of a sudden of the very greatest importance to us as a nation that the immigrants whom we have welcomed into our society . . . should be an integral part of that society and not foreign to it. We have found that our forces for assimilating this foreign element have not been working. . . . We have suddenly been made to realize that . . . many of these . . . are not strangers to the hand that stabs in the dark or the lips that betray with a kiss.[96]

Spurred by fear of the "hyphen," the drive for national solidarity, the deepest force underlying Americanization, now reached far beyond its earlier demands.

Americanization pushed dramatically into the public eye in the

95. *Immigrants in America Review* 1 (1915): 3–4, 15; Frances Kellor and Joseph Mayper, *Recommendations for a Federal Bureau of Distribution, Department of Labor* (New York, [1914]); Hartmann, *Movement*, pp. 97–101.

96. Frank Julian Warne, *The Tide of Immigration* (New York: Appleton-Century-Crofts, 1916).

spring and summer of 1915. The U.S. Bureau of Naturalization, set up in 1906 to supervise and standardize the admission of aliens to citizenship, had already begun before the European war to consider ways to encourage civic education for aspiring citizens and to make naturalization ceremonies more impressive. As a publicity device, the bureau persuaded the city fathers of Philadelphia to hold a great public reception for thousands of newly naturalized citizens on May 10, 1915. President Wilson came to the city of brotherly love for the occasion and delivered an important neutrality speech containing one of his noblest affirmations of the cosmopolitan sources of American nationality. The event caused so much interest that the Committee for Immigrants in America eagerly seized upon the idea. It established an auxiliary, the National Americanization Day Committee, which organized similar receptions throughout the country on the Fourth of July, which 107 cities celebrated as "Americanization Day."

The tone was still liberal, and the emphasis still rested on social welfare; but the impulse behind the new interest in Americanization was fear of divided loyalties. The National Americanization Day Committee dropped the "Day" out of its title and largely absorbed the functions of the Committee for Immigrants. Still led by Frances Kellor, the group never entirely abandoned a humanitarian sympathy for the alien. But after the summer of 1915, it shifted its emphasis to a program of stimulating naturalization, breaking the immigrant's ties with the Old World, and teaching him an American culture. The earlier social objectives faded into the background. Loyalty was contrasted with "dual citizenship." Its slogan, "Many Peoples, But One Nation," gave way to a new one: "America First."

Also, the National Americanization Committee deliberately tried to link its own objectives to the more powerful preparedness movement by interpreting Americanization as the civilian side of national defense. Miss Kellor appeared before the National Security League to warn of the internal peril from foreign influences.[97] In the same year, 1916, her most breathless book, *Straight America*, pleaded for military preparedness, industrial mobilization, universal service, and Americanization as coessential to a more vital nationalism.

The Americanizers were now gaining fresh recruits daily. The General Federation of Women's Clubs put its maternal shoulder to the wheel; the D.A.R. girded itself for more strenuous efforts; fraternal organizations saw an opportunity for patriotic service; educators, under pressure both from the Bureau of Naturalization and the Bu-

97. Hartmann, *Movement*, pp. 124–29; National Security League, *Proceedings of the National Security Congress*, 1916, p. 202.

reau of Education, revised their teaching methods and expanded their classes. Significant support came from business organizations. The Detroit Board of Commerce showed the way in 1915 with a massive civic campaign to get non-English-speaking foreigners into the night schools. Henry Ford, who was just then launching a spectacular experiment in welfare capitalism, set up his own Ford English School and compelled his foreign employees to attend it before and after work two days a week. Both the National Association of Manufacturers and the U.S. Chamber of Commerce then commended Americanization to their members. As a result, a good many businessmen inaugurated factory classes, distributed civics lessons in pay envelopes, and even subsidized public evening schools. A substantial segment of employers regarded these operations as quixotic, but those who did participate in them commonly thought that Americanization paid dividends in productivity and morale.

America's entry into the war keyed up the whole agitation which had been developing over the preceding two years to a more intense and frantic pitch. Since victory itself might depend on the loyalty of the vast foreign population, a note of urgency and a plea for haste sharpened the entreaties for national solidarity. Furthermore, the crusade provided an outlet for civilian America's tremendous hunger to "do something" to help win the war. In a global encounter which touched off the most strenuous appeals for "service," Americanization took its place along with Liberty Bond campaigns, food conservation, Red Cross work, the detection of disloyalty, and a dozen other voluntary drives as a way of enlisting on the home front. In some ways, Americanizing the alien was perhaps more satisfying than merely spying upon him because success seemed to depend on the same type of moral exhortation which sustained so much of the war effort. To a nation charged with evangelical impulses, Americanization was a mission of redemption; to a country of salesmen, it offered an adventure in high-pressure salesmanship.

The movement had now grown too large and chaotic to conform to any central leadership. Although the National Americanization Committee kept issuing directives and recommendations and continued to exert much influence, enthusiasm overflowed the bounds of all authority or direction. Thousands of agencies were in some measure engaged: schools, churches, fraternal orders, patriotic societies, civic organizations, chambers of commerce, philanthropies, railroads, industries, and—to a limited degree—trade unions. There was much duplication, overlapping, and pawing of the air. Many harassed their local school superintendents; others deluged the foreign-born with patriotic leaflets. Now that the preparedness movement was past, the

National Security League and the American Defense Society developed a program of war propaganda which included public meetings in immigrant neighborhoods.

The war carried much further the shift from sympathy to fear, from cosmopolitan democracy to jealous nationalism, which had displayed itself in the preparedness period. In large measure the Americanizers were swept up in the current of "100 Percent Americanism." Most of them gave themselves over to more or less the whole range of 100 Percent ideas: the insistence on a conformist loyalty intolerant of any values not functional to it; the demand for a high sense of duty toward the nation; the faith in a drumfire of exhortation and propaganda to accomplish desired social objectives; and the ultimate reliance on coercion and punishment. In short, by threat and rhetoric, 100 Percent Americanizers opened a frontal assault on foreign influence in American life. They set about to stampede immigrants into citizenship, into adoption of the English language, and into an unquestioning reverence for existing American institutions. They bade them abandon entirely their Old World loyalties, customs, and memories. They cajoled and they commanded.

The drillmasters of Americanization made an appearance as early as the preparedness period. There was some talk of applying economic compulsions to naturalization by giving job preferences to citizens, and Henry Ford's compulsory English School represented a pioneering attempt to apply the 100 Percent philosophy to education. The first thing that foreign-speaking employees learned in the Ford school was how to say, "I am a good American." Later the students acted out a pantomime which admirably symbolized the spirit of the enterprise. In this performance a great melting pot (labeled as such) occupied the middle of the stage. A long column of immigrant students descended into the pot from backstage, clad in outlandish garb and flaunting signs proclaiming their fatherlands. Simultaneously from either side of the pot, another stream of men emerged, each prosperously dressed in identical suits of clothes and each carrying a little American flag.[98]

With America's entry into the war, of course, 100 Percent Americanization picked up momentum. Various official and semiofficial agencies foisted patriotic articles on foreign-language newspapers. Schoolteachers in New York City made use of the immigrants' children to circulate loyalty pledges for the signature of their parents. The Cincinnati city council closed down poolrooms operated by aliens, on the theory that such establishments kept foreigners apart from American influences. The governor of Iowa issued a proclamation banning

98. Gregory Mason, "'Americans First,'" *Outlook* 114 (1916): 193–201.

any language except English in all schools, church services, and conversations in public places or over the telephone.[99]

Nothing better illustrated the drift of wartime Americanization than the views of Frances Kellor and her National Americanization Committee, still the chief claimants for leadership of the movement. Already pulled partway from its original course by the anxious militancy of the preparedness period, the committee in 1917 embraced much of the 100 Percent philosophy. So far had Miss Kellor and her wealthy associates swung from their early emphasis on reform that now they stressed the protection of the economic status quo.

Above all, the N.A.C. now urged the suppression of unrest and disloyalty, the elimination of conditions under which "anti-American" influences flourished, and the dissolution of minority cultures. To prevent strikes or other disaffection, the committee recommended a constant surveillance of aliens by means of a semiannual registration of the whole population. "Let us insist frankly," the committee warned, "that a man born on another soil has to *prove* himself for America." It demanded internment wherever proof of "anti-American sympathy" existed. And it proposed requiring all aliens to learn English and apply for citizenship within three years or face deportation.[100] A note of sympathy remained, strangely blended with the sense of menace: the committee still criticized social discriminations and barbaric working conditions. But against an ounce of accommodation, it balanced a pound of coercion.

By the time the war ended and the specter of Bolshevism came to the fore, Miss Kellor was looking much more to business than to government for national unity and protection. Her National Americanization Committee's longstanding subsidization of the U.S. Bureau of Education ceased in March 1919, following passage of a statute prohibiting the federal government from accepting financial aid from private organizations. But Miss Kellor was already absorbed in a new project. To replace the N.A.C., she was organizing a new society of, by, and for American industry. In late November 1918, addressing fifty of the biggest employers of foreign-born labor, she warned that Americanization had thus far had little success and that they would now face great unrest, with minority nationalism sucking many for-

99. Arthur D. Dean, *Our Schools in War Time—and After* (Boston, 1918), p. 22; *The Survey* 42 (1919): 279; George Creel, *Rebel at Large: Recollections of Fifty Crowded Years* (New York: G. P. Putnam's Sons, 1947), pp. 198–99.

100. N.A.C., *Memorandum to the Advisory Commission of the Council of National Defense Concerning a War Policy for Aliens* (New York, 1917), pp. 20–22; Memo from N.A.C., Jan. 7, 1918, in Theodore Roosevelt Papers, Box 272; Frances Kellor, *Neighborhood Americanization* (New York, 1918).

eign workers back to their homelands and Bolshevism spreading among those who remained. She proposed a somewhat oblique propaganda campaign by which industry might strengthen its grip on its labor force and "break up the nationalistic, racial groups by combining their members for America." With an initial subscription of $100,000, Miss Kellor launched the Inter-Racial Council, and soon enlisted the support of hundreds of industrial corporations.

While furnishing its members with pro-American films and advice on their labor problems, the council gave its main attention to dominating the foreign-language press. A unique opportunity arose in December 1918. Some of the leading backers of the Inter-Racial Council seized the occasion to buy Louis Hammerling's American Association of Foreign Language Newspapers and to install Frances Kellor as its new president. The association, which handled practically all of the national advertising in the immigrant press, then became the organ of the Inter-Racial Council. The association's stranglehold on national advertising enabled it to flood immigrant editors' columns with patriotic articles, admonitions against emigration to Europe, and antiradical propaganda.[101]

A sustained campaign for broad federal support of Americanization began in 1918 and extended into 1920. The Bureau of Naturalization sponsored one bill, the Bureau of Education another and more extensive one. The latter measure provided for substantial federal aid to the states, on a dollar-matching basis, to finance the teaching of English to aliens and native illiterates. In behalf of this plan, Franklin K. Lane, secretary of the interior, organized national conferences and bombarded Congress with pleas for a common language as imperative to national self-protection. After the war there was much sentiment for making such a program of educational Americanization compulsory for all aliens. When the bill finally came before the Senate in January 1920, it offered a federal grant only to those states which would require all adult aliens under forty-five to attend the course.[102] Congress, however, was in no mood to embark on new expenditures or to invest the federal government with new powers. The Bureau of Education had to withdraw from Americanization after its subsidy from the Kellor groups ended, leaving the Bureau of Naturalization the sole federal agency still active. The latter continued, on a progressively reduced scale, its customary supervision of citizenship classes in the public schools.

Without federal aid, the states in 1919–20 rushed in to press the

101. Robert E. Park, *The Immigrant Press and Its Control* (New York, 1922), pp. 451–57.
102. *Congressional Record*, 66th Cong., 2d sess., pp. 1650–51; U.S. Senate Committee on Education and Labor, *Hearings: Americanization Bill*, 1919; Hartmann, *Movement*, pp. 229–32.

crusade for Americanization. A deluge of legislation designed to counteract Bolshevism with nationalism poured out of state legislatures. As always, the principal effort centered on immigrant education. More than a score of states passed laws authorizing or strengthening night-school classes in English for foreigners. Some gave local governments considerable financial support for such work; some also took over the propaganda activities which the state councils of defense had conducted among the foreign-born. At least two states, Idaho and Utah, yielded to the coercive spirit by requiring non-English-speaking aliens to attend Americanization classes. Others went further along the path of 100 Percentism, accompanying their educational laws with certain legislative inhibitions on foreign influences. In 1919 fifteen states decreed that English must be the sole language of instruction in all primary schools, public and private. Several states followed the lead of New York in insisting that all public schoolteachers be citizens. Nebraska extended the same requirement to private schools and also stipulated that all meetings except religious or lodge meetings must be conducted in English. Oregon, in the interest of Americanization, came close to outlawing the foreign-language press by requiring that all foreign-language publications display prominently a literal English translation of their entire contents.[103]

With these statutes the Americanization movement reached and passed its zenith. As a workaday endeavor to teach English and civics to foreigners in the public evening schools, the program had taken permanent root, and it endured. There, in the schools, it had its major institutional impact, and its most lasting effect was to give a powerful stimulus to all phases of adult education. But as a major expression of American nationalism, Americanization faded swiftly in the latter part of 1920 and in 1921.

Two events—the onset of economic depression and the passing of the Red Scare—delivered the coup de grace. The Depression cut off much of the financial support. During the war and postwar boom, businessmen, by organizing factory classes, subsidizing propaganda campaigns, and contributing to the largest Americanization societies, had invested heavily in a movement that promised them a more efficient as well as a more American labor force. Now, however, as production levels slumped, as labor shortages eased and unemployment soared, Americanization no longer seemed worth the expense or effort. Factory classes folded up; even Henry Ford stopped stirring the melting pot. The rich income of the Inter-Racial Council dwindled

103. Hartmann, *Movement*, pp. 233–52; Harry Rider, "Americanization," *American Political Science Review* 14 (1920): 111–14; *Laws of the State of New York*, 1918, p. 749; *New Republic* 22 (1920): 262.

and after 1920 it disappeared from sight, bringing to a close Frances Kellor's long career as chaperon of the immigrants. Yet funds were less basic to the vigor of the Americanization movement than were the fears. Above all, the crusade came to an end because the collapse of the Big Red Scare dried up its emotional wellsprings. Once the specter of an imminent Bolshevik revolution dissolved, the crusade lost all urgency, lost, in fact, its whole immediate and pressing object.

The dissolution of the movement left 100 Percenters with a sense of failure and disillusion. Had they not tried their best to bring the great mass of newcomers into the fold? Did not the experiment prove the incorrigibly unassimilable nature of the material on which they had worked? America's task, 100 Percenters now realized, was much simpler. Instead of struggling to transform the foreign-born, nationalists must concentrate on keeping them out. Thus, while the movement for the redemption of the alien ebbed in 1920, the old drive for the rejection of the immigrant passed all previous bounds.

One Flag, One Language

By Theodore Roosevelt

Former president Theodore Roosevelt drafted this wartime appeal in September 1917. Entitled "The Children of the Crucible," the statement was signed by thirty-eight other prominent citizens, including several from language-minority backgrounds. A complete version is reprinted in *Annals of America*, vol. 14, *1916–1928* (Chicago: Encyclopedia Britannica, 1968), pp. 129–31.

We Americans are the children of the crucible. It has been our boast that out of the crucible, the melting pot of life in this free land, all the men and women of all the nations who come hither emerge as Americans and as nothing else. . . .

The crucible must melt all who are cast in it; it must turn them out in one American mold; and this must be the mold shaped 140 years ago by the men who under Washington founded this as a free nation, separate from all others. Even at that time, true Americans were of many different race strains; Paul Revere and Charles Carroll, Marion, Herkimer, Sullivan, Schuyler, and Muhlenberg stood on an equality of service and achieved respect with "Lighthorse Harry" Lee and Israel Putnam. But the majority of the leaders and of their followers were of English blood. They did not, because of this, hesitate to resist and antagonize Great Britain when Great Britain wronged this nation. . . .

All Americans of other race origin must act toward the countries from which their ancestors severally sprang as Washington and his associates in their day acted. Otherwise they are traitors to America. This applies especially today to all Americans of German blood who directly or indirectly in any manner support Germany as against the United States and the allies of the United States. . . .

We must have but one flag. We must also have but one language. That must be the language of the Declaration of Independence, of Washington's Farewell address, of Lincoln's Gettysburg speech and second inaugural. We cannot tolerate any attempt to oppose or supplant the language and culture that has come down to us from the builders of this Republic with the language and culture of any European country. The greatness of this nation depends on the swift assimilation of the aliens she welcomes to her shores. Any force which attempts to retard that assimilative process is a force hostile to the highest interests of our country. . . .

Whatever may have been our judgment in normal times, we are convinced that today our most dangerous foe is the foreign-language press and every similar agency, such as the German-American Alliance, which holds the alien to his former associations and through them to his former allegiance. We call upon all loyal and unadulterated Americans to man the trenches against the enemy within our gates.

PART TWO

The Debate over Official English

What is at issue in the Official English debate? A consensus has been elusive, because to define the terms of the argument is to gain a decisive advantage. While supporters and opponents frame the controversy in various ways, they tend toward two distinct outlooks.

Viewed in one way, this is a discussion about national identity: what it means to be an American in the late twentieth century and what will hold Americans together during a time of bewildering change. It is about how much diversity a nation can tolerate, even a nation of immigrants. Should cultural pluralism extend to language if that means Americans will be less able to communicate with each other? Are we ready to discard the ideal of a common language, which has kept the melting pot simmering for so long? Can't we respect ethnic traditions without accepting a "salad bowl" mentality that emphasizes what divides rather than what unites us as a people? If government allows immigrants to cast ballots and go to school in their native tongues, won't this reduce their incentives to learn English? By legitimizing bilingualism, are we not we asking for a future of linguistic strife and perhaps separatism *à la Québec*?

Viewed from another perspective, this is a conflict over rights: equal access to education and government—for immigrants and other Americans who face language barriers—and freedom of speech in the language of one's choice. It is also a clash of attitudes: nativist bias versus tolerance toward newcomers, Anglo-conformity versus an appreciation of diversity. Should we bow to ethnic fears and resentments, imposing a cultural tyranny of the majority? Can we allow language to be used as a weapon of race prejudice, an instrument to discriminate against unpopular minorities? Shall we deny citizens the right to vote or children the opportunity to learn, canceling bilingual programs because some zealots perceive a symbolic threat to English? Can we live with an English Only amendment that usurps local discretion to offer needed services in other tongues? Are Americans willing to submit to government language restrictions, perhaps enforced by language police *à la Québec*?

Both positions are plausible and internally consistent. The question is, what relation do they bear to the material world? A number of claims cry out for factual documentation, for example:

- the "erosion of English" in the United States;
- draconian effects of an English Language Amendment;

- linguistic uniformity or democratic principles as the key unifier of Americans;
  - separatist inclinations among language minorities;
  - immigrant resistance to learning English;
  - the anti-immigrant agenda of English Only proponents;
  - analogies to language conflicts elsewhere.

The commentaries that follow include speeches by Congressional sponsors and opponents of Official English, newspaper columns and editorials, miscellaneous articles, and organizational statements, pro and con. In addition, there are documents relevant in assessing these opinions: versions of the English Language Amendment, state Official English laws, and legislative alternatives, including resolutions endorsing "English Plus" and Native American language rights. To put these writings in perspective, this section begins with a chronology detailing the progress of the English Only movement and related skirmishes over language issues.

A further complication in the debate over Official English is the fact that many Americans have trouble taking it seriously. It has inspired not only rancor, but a good deal of frivolity—perhaps for similar reasons. Language is inescapable, bound up not only with our politics, but also with our most personal experience. It conveys status, intellect, group loyalties, and a myriad of impressions about our fellow humans, justified and otherwise. Though it is a social institution, language defies social control, capriciously changing at the whim of individuals. It evokes anger, pride, humor, and ridicule, in varying proportions. Some Americans become incensed over the latest neologism, while others are fascinated with dialect differences or amused by language snobbery.

Often, when introduced in state legislatures, Official English has meant a break from the dreary routine of public business—not an insignificant factor in its success. Mississippi declared English official following "debate" over various tongue-in-cheek amendments. One would have required legislators to pass a remedial English course before the law could take effect. Another declared: "The following words and terms will no longer be recognized in this state, since said terms are either incomprehensible or are not of pure English extraction: *Y'all; hominy; canoe; up-air; down-nair; and yonder.*" In Tennessee, when one wag proposed an amendment to recognize "Southern English," the sponsor of Official English legislation cut short the clowning, explaining that bilingualism was "no laughing matter." Whereupon his chastened colleagues passed the bill with a single dissenting vote.[1]

1. Raymond Tatalovich, "English Language Statutes in Six Midwestern States: A Comparative Analysis," paper presented at the Western Political Science Association meeting, Newport Beach, Calif., March 22–24, 1990.

A Chronology of the Official English Movement

By Jamie B. Draper and Martha Jiménez

Jamie B. Draper is assistant director of the Joint National Committee for Languages, and Martha Jiménez is a former legislative attorney for the Mexican American Legal Defense and Educational Fund. Both have served on the steering committee of the English Plus Information Clearinghouse. This article is adapted from "Language Debates in the United States: A Decade in Review," *EPIC Events* 2, no. 5 (1990): 1, 4, 7.

Not since the beginning of this century has language received as much attention in the United States. Like the language battles of the early 1900s, those of the 1980s were rife with appeals to patriotism and unity, casting language minorities in the role of outsiders who deliberately "chose" not to learn the English language. But unlike the earlier period, when these issues were confined primarily to local and state arenas, the 1980s featured a campaign orchestrated at the national level by a powerful and highly funded lobby, U.S. English. Ostensibly, the whole purpose of this organization is to establish English as the official language of the United States, but its connections to immigration restriction groups suggest a more far-reaching agenda. The irony of the appearance of the English Only movement in the 1980s is that it advocates a return to a mythic era of English monolingualism in the face of growing demands for multilingual abilities in the world marketplace.

At the beginning of the decade, states already had measures on the books declaring English to be their sole official language. Nebraska's constitutional amendment dated back to 1920, when the country was experiencing a wave of anti-German sentiment because of World War I. An Illinois statute, passed in 1969, amended a 1923 law which had declared "American" the state's official language. A third state, Hawaii, adopted a constitutional amendment in 1978 designating both English and Native Hawaiian as its official languages *(for the texts of these and other Official English laws, see pp. 132–35).*

In 1979 the President's Commission on Foreign Language and International Studies released its report on Americans' "scandalous" lack of foreign language ability. Not one state had foreign language requirements for high-school graduation, and many did not even require schools to offer foreign language instruction. Meanwhile, bilingual education was coming under close scrutiny. Under the Bilingual Education Act of 1968, federal funding had been available for programs that maintained and developed languages other than English. But in 1978 Congress amended the law to emphasize the goal of competence in the English language and restricting support to *transitional* programs only; no funds would be available for language maintenance. At the same time, federal civil rights authorities were aggressively enforcing the *Lau v. Nichols* ruling of the U.S. Supreme Court, which established the right of limited-English-proficient students to special help in overcoming language barriers *(see pp. 251–55)*. Still, many school districts resented the federal insistence on bilingual instruction. The stage was set for a decade of debate on language in American society.

1980

• Dade County, Florida, voters approve an "anti-bilingual ordinance" prohibiting the expenditure of public funds on the use of languages other than English *(see p. 131)*. Fire safety information pamphlets in Spanish are prohibited, Spanish marriage ceremonies are halted, and public transportation signs in Spanish are removed.

1981

• Senator S. I. Hayakawa, Republican of California, introduces a constitutional English Language Amendment (S.J. Res. 72), the first proposal to declare English the nation's official language *(see p. 112)*. The bill dies without Congressional action.

• The Virginia legislature declares English the state's official language and makes English the language of public instruction.

1982

• Senator Alan Simpson, Republican of Wyoming, introduces the first version of the Immigration Reform and Control Act (later known as the Simpson-Rodino bill). The measure would provide amnesty to illegal immigrants who have resided in the United States for a period of time and provide sanctions against employers who hire the undocumented. It passes the Senate, but goes nowhere in the House.

1983

• U.S. English is founded by Senator Hayakawa and Dr. John Tanton, a Michigan ophthalmologist who also heads the Federation for American Immigration Reform.

• The California Committee for Ballots in English sponsors Proposition O in San Francisco, calling for an end to bilingual ballots. The measure passes with 63 percent of the vote.

1984

• New York State passes sweeping educational reforms, including foreign language requirements for all students. Nonnative English speakers may receive credit for proficiency in their native language.

• Indiana and Kentucky adopt English as their official state language; these measures amend sections of the law code dealing with state emblems.

• Tennessee declares English the "official and legal" language of the state. The statute further requires all official documents; communications, including ballots; and public instruction to be in English.

• An immigration bill passed by the U.S. House of Representatives requires a "minimal understanding of ordinary English" to qualify for permanent residency under the amnesty program. The House and Senate fail to agree, however, on a final version of the legislation.

• The Senate Subcommittee on the Constitution holds hearings on S.J. Res. 167 (see p. 113), an English Language Amendment sponsored by Senator Walter Huddleston, Democrat of Kentucky. Congress takes no further action on the measure.

• The Education for Economic Security Act becomes law, authorizing federal funding for the improvement of foreign language instruction.

• In extending the Bilingual Education Act through 1988, Congress creates several new programs. *Developmental* bilingual programs offer students an opportunity to maintain their native tongues after learning English; *academic excellence* programs replicate successful approaches in bilingual education; and *family English literacy* programs involve parents of limited-English-proficient children. A limited amount of funding (4 to 10 percent of program grants) is allowed for "special alternative instructional programs," or nonbilingual programs in which students' native language is not used.

• California voters approve Proposition 38, "Voting Materials in English Only," sponsored by Senator Hayakawa and other leaders of U.S. English. The measure places California on record in opposition to the bilingual ballot provisions of the federal Voting Rights Act.

1985

• Secretary of Education William J. Bennett delivers a speech questioning the effectiveness of bilingual education over other methods, including the "sink or swim" approach (see pp. 358–63). He calls for eliminating the requirement that schools use native-language instruction to qualify for most grants under the Bilingual Education Act.

• Responding to Bennett's speech, the Spanish-American League Against Discrimination coins the term "English Plus" in describing the goals and benefits of bilingual education (see pp. 216–24).

• In a Miami survey, 98 percent of Hispanic parents say it is "essential for their children to read and write English perfectly" (as compared with 94 percent of Anglo parents). A Rand Corporation study reports that more than 90 percent of U.S.–born Mexican Americans are proficient in English and more than half of their children are monolingual in English.

1986

• Two more lobbies for Official English are organized. English First, a project of the Committee to Protect the Family, is founded by Larry Pratt, a former Virginia state representative and president of Gun Owners of America. Lou Zaeske, of Bryan, Texas, organizes the American Ethnic Coalition "to prevent the division of America along language or ethnic lines."

• Congress finally passes the Immigration Reform and Control Act, including the English proficiency requirements for amnesty. Before final passage, a Senate-approved "sense of Congress" resolution declaring English to be the nation's official language is removed.

• Proposition 63 passes in California with 73 percent of the vote, the first Official English measure passed by ballot initiative. Included is a provision allowing anyone living or doing business in the state to sue state or local governments for actions that diminish or ignore "the role of English as the common language of the State of California" *(see p. 134).*

• Norman Cousins resigns from the U.S. English advisory board on learning that 40,000 people in Los Angeles are on waiting lists for English-as-a-second-language (E.S.L.) classes. He criticizes the "negative symbolic significance" of Proposition 63 and warns it could lead to discrimination against language minorities.

• The Georgia legislature passes a nonbinding resolution declaring English to be the state language.

1987

• Official English measures are considered in thirty-seven state legislatures. They pass in five: Arkansas, Mississippi, North Carolina, North Dakota, and South Carolina.

• North Carolina mandates foreign language instruction for all students in kindergarten through the fifth grade.

• A Cultural Rights Amendment to the U.S. Constitution, recognizing "the right of the people to preserve, foster, and promote their respective historic, linguistic, and cultural origins," is proposed by Senator John Breaux and Representative Jimmy Hayes (both Lousiana Democrats). Congress takes no action.

• Linda Chávez, former staff director of the U.S. Commission on Civil Rights and director of public liaison in the Reagan White House, is hired as president of U.S. English.

• The English Plus Information Clearinghouse (EPIC) is established in Washington, D.C. A coalition of education, civil rights, and ethnic advocacy organizations, EPIC seeks to centralize information on the Official English/English Only movement and respond to efforts to restrict language rights *(see pp. 151–53).*

1988

• In *Gutiérrez v. Municipal Court*, a case striking down English-only rules in the workplace, the 9th U.S. Circuit Court of Appeals declares Proposition 63 to be "primarily symbolic" *(see p. 280)*.

• The House Subcommittee on Civil and Constitutional Rights holds hearings on five English Language Amendments proposed in the 100th Congress, but takes no further action.

• Congress passes an omnibus bill affecting elementary, secondary, and adult education. It increases to 25 percent the portion of Bilingual Education Act funds available for "alternative," nonbilingual programs. The new law authorizes aid for model foreign language programs at the elementary and secondary level and creates the English Literacy Grants Program to support adult E.S.L. instruction.

• An internal memorandum by Dr. John Tanton, the chairman of U.S. English, surfaces in the press. It warns that Hispanic immigrants could be importing unwanted traits: "the tradition of the *mordida* (bribe)"; "low educability"; Catholicism, which could "pitch out the separation of church and state"; and high birthrates. Further investigation links Tanton's funding to a eugenics foundation and a distributor of nativist propaganda *(see pp. 171–77)*. These revelations prompt the resignations of Tanton and Linda Chávez as leaders of U.S. English, and Walter Cronkite as a member of the group's advisory board.

• Voters pass Official English amendments to their state constitutions in Arizona (50.5 to 49.5 percent), Colorado (61 to 39 percent), and Florida (84 to 16 percent). Afterward, a rise in incidents of discrimination against minority language speakers is reported.

1989

• New Mexico becomes the first state to endorse the policy of English Plus *(see p. 154)*. Washington and Oregon will soon follow suit with their own English Plus resolutions.

• Voters in Lowell, Massachusetts, approve a nonbinding resolution requesting their state legislature and the U.S. Congress to declare English the official language.

• Defying a well-financed lobbying campaign by U.S. English, the New York State Board of Regents votes to extend eligibility for bilingual education by raising the "exit criteria" for graduation from bilingual programs from the 23d to the 40th percentile in English proficiency.

1990

• U.S. District Judge Paul Rosenblatt strikes down Arizona's Official English amendment as unconstitutional. The measure's requirement that state officers and employees "act in English and no other language" is ruled to violate free speech guarantees under the First Amendment *(see pp. 287–91)*.

• Alabama voters, by a margin of 89 percent to 11 percent, adopt English as their official language. Official English measures have now passed in a total of seventeen states.

The Case for Official English

By Senator S. I. Hayakawa

S. I. Hayakawa, a California Republican, served as U.S. senator from 1977 to 1983 following his retirement from the academic world. A semanticist, he is the author of a widely used college text, *Language in Thought and Action*. After sponsoring the original version of the English Language Amendment in 1981, Hayakawa helped to establish a lobby to promote it, U.S. English, and remains the organization's honorary chairman. This article is excerpted from a speech, reprinted as *One Nation . . . Indivisible? The English Language Amendment* (Washington, D.C.: Washington Institute for Values in Public Policy, 1985), pp. 6–18.

What is it that has made a society out of the hodgepodge of nationalities, races, and colors represented in the immigrant hordes that people our nation? It is language, of course, that has made communication among all these elements possible. It is with a common language that we have dissolved distrust and fear. It is with language that we have drawn up the understandings and agreements and social contracts that make a society possible.

But while language is a necessary cause of our oneness as a society, it is not a sufficient cause. A foreigner cannot, by speaking faultless English, become an Englishman. Paul Theroux, a contemporary novelist and travel writer, has commented on this fact: "Foreigners are always aliens in England. No one becomes English. It's a very tribal society. . . . No one becomes Japanese. . . . No one becomes Nigerian. But Nigerians, Japanese, and English become Americans."[2]

One need not speak faultless American English to become an American. Indeed, one may continue to speak English with an appalling foreign accent. This is true of some of my friends, but they are

---

2. Interviewed by James T. Yenchel, *Washington Times*, Dec. 30, 1984.

seen as fully American because of the warmth and enthusiasm with which they enter into the life of the communities in which they live.

Even as the American nation was coming into being, it had become obvious that the American experience was creating a new kind of human being. Among the first to comment on this fact was Thomas Paine, who wrote:

> If there is a country in the world where concord, according to common calculation, would be least expected, it is America. Made up, as it is, of people from different nations . . . speaking different languages, and more different in their modes of worship, it would appear that the union of such a people was impracticable. But by the simple operation of constructing government on the principles of society and the rights of man, every difficulty retires, and the parts are brought into cordial unison.[3]

Hector St. John de Crèvecoeur, in *Letters from an American Farmer*, wrote in 1782:

> What then is the American, this new man? . . . I would point out to you a family whose grandfather was an Englishman, whose wife was Dutch, whose son married a French woman, and whose present four sons have four wives of different nations. *He* is an American who, leaving behind him all his ancient prejudices and manners, receives new ones from the new mode of life he has embraced. . . . The Americans were once scattered all over Europe. Here they are incorporated into one of the finest systems of population which has ever appeared. . . . The American ought therefore to love his country much better than that wherein he or his forebears were born. Here the rewards of his industry follow with equal steps in the progress of his labor.[4]

Herman Melville, in *Redburn*, published in 1849, wrote: "You cannot spill a drop of American blood without spilling the blood of the whole world. . . . We are not a narrow tribe of men. No: our blood is the flood of the Amazon, made up of a thousand noble currents all pouring into one. We are not a nation, so much as a world."[5]

Despite the exclusion of the Chinese after 1882, the idea of immigration as "a thousand noble currents all pouring into one" continued

---

3. Quoted in J. A. Parker and Allan C. Brownfield, "The Jackson Campaign and the Myth of a Black-Jewish Split," *Lincoln Review* (Summer 1984): 21–22.
4. Ibid.
5. Ibid.

to haunt the American imagination: Israel Zangwill's play *The Melting Pot* opened in New York in 1908 to enthusiastic popular acclaim, and its title, as Nathan Glazer and Daniel P. Moynihan remark, "was seized upon as a concise evocation of a profoundly significant American fact." In the play David Quixano, the Russian Jewish immigrant—"a pogrom orphan"—has escaped to New York, and he exclaims:

> Here you stand, good folk, think I, when I see them at Ellis Island . . . in your fifty groups with your fifty languages and histories, and your fifty blood hatreds and rivalries, but you won't be long like that, brothers, for these are the fires of God you've come to. . . . A fig for your feuds and vendettas! German and Frenchman, Irishman and Englishman, Jews and Russians—into the Crucible with you all! God is making the American.[6]

In the past several years, strong resistance to the "melting pot" idea has arisen, especially for those who claim to speak for the Hispanic peoples. Instead of a melting pot, they say, the national ideal should be a "salad bowl," in which different elements are thrown together but not "melted," so that the original ingredients retain their distinctive character. In addition to the increasing size of the Spanish-speaking population in our nation, two legislative actions have released this outburst of effort on behalf of the Spanish language and Hispanic culture.

First, there was the so-called "bilingual ballot" mandated in 1975 in an amendment to the Voting Rights Act, which required foreign language ballots when voters of selected language groups reached 5 percent or more in any voting district. The groups chosen to be so favored were Asian-Americans (Chinese, Filipino, Japanese, Korean), American Indians, Alaskan Natives, and "peoples of Spanish heritage," that is, Puerto Ricans, Cubans, and Mexican Americans.

Sensitive as Americans have been to racism, especially since the days of the civil rights movement, no one seems to have noticed the profound racism expressed in the amendment that created the bilingual ballot. Brown people, like Mexicans and Puerto Ricans, red people, like American Indians, and yellow people, like the Japanese and Chinese, are assumed not to be smart enough to learn English. No provision is made, however, for non-English-speaking French-Canadians in Maine or Vermont, or for the Hebrew-speaking Hasidic Jews in Brooklyn, who are white and are presumed to be able to learn English without difficulty. Voters in San Francisco encountered ballots

---

6. Quoted in Nathan Glazer and Daniel P. Moynihan, *Beyond the Melting Pot* (Cambridge, Mass.: M.I.T. Press, 1963), p. 289.

in Spanish and Chinese for the first time in the elections of 1980, much to their surprise, since authorizing legislation had been passed by Congress with almost no debate, no roll-call vote, and no public discussion. Naturalized Americans, who had taken the trouble to learn English to become citizens, were especially angry and remain so.

Furthermore, there was the *Lau* decision of the U.S. Supreme Court *(see pp. 251–55)*, in response to a suit brought by a Chinese of San Francisco who complained that his children were not being taught English adequately in the public schools they were attending. Justice William O. Douglas, delivering the opinion of the court, wrote: "No specific remedy is urged upon us. Teaching English to the students of Chinese ancestry who do not speak the language is one choice. Giving instructions to this group in Chinese is another. There may be others. Petitioner asks only that the Board of Education be directed to apply its expertise to the problem and rectify the situation." Justice Douglas's decision, concurred in by the entire court, granted the *Lau* petition. Because the *Lau* decision did not specify the method by which English was to be taught, it turned out to be a go-ahead for amazing educational developments, not so much for the Chinese as for Hispanics, who appropriated the decision and took it to apply especially to themselves.

The new U.S. Department of Education, established during the Carter administration, was eager to make its presence known by expanding its bureaucracy and its influence. The department quickly announced a vast program with federal funding for bilingual education, which led to the hiring of Spanish-speaking teachers by the thousands. The department furthermore issued what were known as the Lau Regulations, which required under the threat of withdrawal of federal funds that (1) non-English-speaking pupils be taught English, and that (2) academic subjects be taught in the pupils' own language. The contradiction between these two regulations seems not to have occurred to the educational theorists in the Department of Education. Nor does it seem to trouble, to this day, the huge membership of the National Association for Bilingual Education.[7]

Bilingual education rapidly became a growth industry, requiring more and more teachers. Complaints began to arise from citizens that "bilingual education" was not bilingual at all, since many Spanish-speaking teachers hired for the program were found not to be able to speak English. Despite the ministrations of the Department of Edu-

7. Editor's note: At the time Hayakawa spoke, this professional organization had fewer than 2,000 members and an annual budget of less than $250,000, according to its executive director, James J. Lyons.

cation, or perhaps because of them, Hispanic students to a shocking degree drop out of school, educated neither in Hispanic nor in American language and culture. "Hispanics are the least educated minority in America, according to a report by the American Council on Education," writes Earl Byrd. "The report says 50 percent of all Hispanic youths in America drop out of high school, and only 7 percent finish college. Twelve percent of black youths and 23 percent of whites finish college. Eighteen percent of all Hispanics in America who are 25 or older are classified as functional illiterates, compared to 10 percent for blacks and 3 percent for whites."[8]

I welcome the Hispanic—and as a Californian, I welcome especially the Mexican—influence on our culture. My wife was wise enough to insist that both our son and daughter learn Spanish as children and to keep reading Spanish as they were growing up. Consequently, my son, a newspaperman, was able to work for six months as an exchange writer for a newspaper in Costa Rica, while a Costa Rican reporter took my son's place in Oregon. My daughter, a graduate of the University of California at Santa Cruz, speaks Spanish, French, and after a year in Monterey Language School, Japanese.

The ethnic chauvinism of the present Hispanic leadership is an unhealthy trend in present-day America. It threatens a division perhaps more ominous in the long run than the division between blacks and whites. Blacks and whites have problems enough with each other, to be sure, but they quarrel with each other in one language. Even Malcolm X, in his fiery denunciations of the racial situation in America, wrote excellent and eloquent English. But the present politically ambitious "Hispanic Caucus" looks forward to a destiny for Spanish-speaking Americans separate from that of Anglo-, Italian-, Polish-, Greek-, Lebanese-, Chinese-, and Afro-Americans, and all the rest of us who rejoice in our ethnic diversity, which gives us our richness as a culture, and the English language, which keeps us in communication with each other to create a unique and vibrant culture.

The advocates of Spanish language and Hispanic culture are not at all unhappy about the fact that "bilingual education," originally instituted as the best way to teach English, often results in no English being taught at all. Nor does Hispanic leadership seem to be alarmed that large populations of Mexican Americans, Cubans, and Puerto Ricans do not speak English and have no intention of learning. Hispanic spokesmen rejoice when still another concession is made to the Spanish-speaking public, such as the Spanish-language Yellow Pages telephone directory now available in Los Angeles.

8. *Washington Times*, July 3, 1984.

"Let's face it. We're not going to be a totally English-speaking country any more," says Aurora Helton of the governor of Oklahoma's Hispanic Advisory Committee. "Spanish should be included in commercials shown throughout America. Every American child ought to be taught both English and Spanish," says Mario Obledo, president of the League of United Latin American Citizens, which was founded more than a half-century ago to help Hispanics learn English and enter the American mainstream. "Citizenship is what makes us all American. Nowhere does the Constitution say that English is our language," says Maurice Ferré, mayor of Miami, Florida.

"Nowhere does the Constitution say that English is our language." It was to correct this omission that I introduced in April 1981 a constitutional amendment which read as follows: "The English language shall be the official language of the United States" *(see p. 112)*. Although there were ten cosponsors to this resolution, and some speeches were given on the Senate floor, it died without being acted upon in the 97th Congress.

But the movement to make English the official language of the nation is clearly gaining momentum. It is likely to suffer an occasional setback in state legislatures because of the doctrinaire liberals' assumption that every demand made by an ethnic minority must be yielded to. But whenever the question of English as the official language has been submitted to a popular referendum or ballot initiative, it has won by a majority of 70 percent or better.

It is not without significance that pressure against English language legislation does not come from any immigrant group other than the Hispanic: not from the Chinese or Koreans or Filipinos or Vietnamese; nor from immigrant Iranians, Turks, Greeks, East Indians, Ghanaians, Ethiopians, Italians, or Swedes. The only people who have any quarrel with the English language are the Hispanics—at least the Hispanic politicians and "bilingual" teachers and lobbying organizations. One wonders about the Hispanic rank and file. Are they all in agreement with their leadership? And what does it profit the Hispanic leadership if it gains power and fame, while 50 percent of the boys and girls of their communities, speaking little or no English, cannot make it through high school?

For the first time in our history, our nation is faced with the possibility of the kind of linguistic division that has torn apart Canada in recent years; that has been a major feature of the unhappy history of Belgium, split into speakers of French and Flemish; that is at this very moment a bloody division between the Sinhalese and Tamil populations of Sri Lanka. None of these divisions is simply a quarrel about language. But in each case political differences become hardened and made immeasurably more difficult to resolve when they are accompanied by differences of language—and therefore conflicts of ethnic pride.

The aggressive movement on the part of Hispanics to reject assimilation and to seek to maintain—and give official status to—a foreign language within our borders is an unhealthy development. This foreign language and culture are to be maintained not through private endeavors such as those of the *Alliance française*, which tries to preserve French language and culture, but by federal and state legislation and funding. The energetic lobbying of the National Association for Bilingual Education and the Congressional Hispanic Caucus has led to sizable allocations for bilingual education in the Department of Education: $142 million in fiscal 1985, of which the lion's share goes to Hispanic programs. The purpose of this allocation at the federal level is to prepare administrators and teachers for bilingual education at the state level—which means additional large sums of money allocated for this purpose by state governments. In brief, the basic directive of the *Lau* decision has been, for all intents and purposes, diverted from its original purpose of teaching English.

One official language and one only, so that we can unite as a nation. This is what President Theodore Roosevelt also perceived when he said: "We have room for but one language here, and that is the English language, for we intend to see that the crucible turns our people out as Americans, of American nationality, and not as dwellers in a polyglot boarding house." Let me quote in conclusion a remark from the distinguished American novelist, Saul Bellow, when he agreed to serve on the advisory board of our national organization, U.S. English: "Melting pot, yes. Tower of Babel, no!"[9]

9. Editor's note: Through his literary agent, Saul Bellow has denied any involvement with U.S. English. But the organization, claiming to "have a letter on file" from the author, has continued to use his name in its fundraising; William Trombley, "Norman Cousins Drops His Support of Prop. 63," *Los Angeles Times*, Oct. 16, 1986, Pt. I, p. 3.

Official English: Another Americanization Campaign?

By Joseph Leibowicz

Joseph Leibowicz is a lawyer in New Haven, Connecticut. This article is excerpted from "The Proposed English Language Amendment: Sword or Shield?" *Yale Law and Policy Review* 3, no. 2 (Spring 1985): 519–50.

Supporters of the English Language Amendment (E.L.A.) and other measures to protect the English language in the United States base their proposals on a venerable idea, one reaching back at least to biblical times: A common language is a strong bond of nationhood. The Select Committee on Immigration and Refugee Policy based its recommendations for continuing the language requirement for naturalization on this idea, simply quoting Noah Webster's famous dictum that "a *national language* is a band of *national union*."[10] In justifying the additional burden of a requirement that illegal aliens seeking amnesty study English, Representative Jim Wright admitted that this demand was inconsistent with the policy of other federal programs, but stated that such a requirement was necessary to reverse a national trend toward "balkanization" because "language is the thread, the common thread, that ties us all together."[11] In supporting inclusion in the Immigration Reform and Control Act of a nonbinding declaration that English is the official language of the United States, the Senate Judiciary Committee warned: "If language and cultural separatism rise above a certain level, the unity and political stability of the nation will—in time—be seriously diminished."[12] During hearings on the E.L.A., Gerda Bikales, the executive director of U.S. English, an organization formed to combat the displacement of the English language from official life, described how general cultural and political fragmentation has created a situation in which "English is no longer *a* bond, but *the* bond between all of us."[13]

10. Select Commission on Immigrant and Refugee Policy, *U.S. Immigration Policy and the National Interest*, Final Report, March 1, 1981, p. 289.

11. *Congressional Record*, 98th Cong., 2d sess., 1984, p. H6066.

12. Senate Rep. no. 62, 98th Cong., 1st sess., 1983, p. 7.

13. U.S. Senate, Committee on the Judiciary, Subcommittee on the Constitution, *The English Language Amendment: Hearing on S.J. Res. 167*, 98th Cong., 2d sess., June 12, 1984, p. 6.

As these statements show, an acceptance of the language-nationhood link can lead to the conclusion that threats to the hegemony of English in the United States may strike at the very heart of our political and cultural institutions. The urgency with which proposals to protect English are being pressed in turn reflects a belief that other national bonds have already been weakened to such an extent that language is our last hope, or that language usage is itself such a powerful determinant of national identity that other national bonds are ineffective without a national language. In an era in which "old-fashioned" patriotism is popular again, prospects of significant immigration reform are rapidly receding, and monolingual English speakers often feel like aliens in their own land, the argument that difficult problems can be eased or solved simply by granting English the constitutional protection it "obviously" deserves is quite seductive. Unfortunately, the assumptions, arguments, conclusions, and in some cases, the motives of the E.L.A.'s supporters are highly suspect.

First, the statistical arguments made by the amendment's proponents are flawed and unpersuasive. For example, there is serious doubt whether a problem of the kind or magnitude described by the proponents of the E.L.A. actually exists. Some researchers contend that Spanish speakers are following the traditional pattern of English acquisition, only at a pace slowed somewhat by the continual influx of large numbers of Spanish speakers. Calvin Veltman, a sociolinguist who has studied Spanish-speaking communities in the United States *(see pp. 317–22),* concludes that "Hispanics will survive as an ethnic identity, but not as a language group. If the border closed, Spanish would fade out."[14] If Veltman is correct, then the problem is much smaller than imagined and is more a result of migration patterns than language policy. Attempting to solve the problem with a constitutional amendment aimed solely at language usage would seem to be inappropriate at best, and at worst, counterproductive.

Second, even accepting the idea that language and nationhood are linked, it does not follow that language is not just *a,* but *the* most important bonding force of a people. Language is only one of a multiplicity of factors that can bind or rend a people, a fact that was manifestly apparent to the Founders. It is true that the Enlightenment theory that lay behind the birth of the United States explicitly embraced the idea that a common language was essential for successful nations. But other forces in our early history led in another direction. The core notions of individual liberty and tolerance upon which the new nation was based (and which arguably justified its very exis-

14. Quoted in Marshall Ingwerson, "A Tale of Two Languages: For Hispanic Immigrants, Shift to English Is Slow, But Sure," *Christian Science Monitor,* Aug. 22, 1983, p. 1.

tence), as well as the obvious supremacy of the English language in national life, militated against any inclination to grant English official status or special protection. Also, the fact that the United States was breaking away from a nation that spoke the same language tended to undermine some aspects of the argument for the link between language and nationhood, even leading to some strained attempts to distinguish English from the American language (see pp. 40–41).

The political scientist Karl Deutsch provides a vivid anecdotal confirmation that language is neither the only nor the most important bond of a people. A prominent German-Swiss editor reported the following experience:

> I found that my German was more closely akin to the French of my [French-Swiss] friend than to the likewise German (Ebenfallsdeutsch) of the foreigner. . . . The French-Swiss and I were using different words for the same concepts, but we understood each other. The man from Vienna and I were using the same words for different concepts, and thus we did not understand each other in the least.

Deutsch explains this counterintuitive outcome in this way:

> The Swiss may speak four different languages and still act as one people, for each of them has enough learned habits, preferences, symbols, memories, patterns of landholding and social stratification, events in history, and personal associations, all of which together permit him to communicate more effectively with other Swiss than with the speakers of his own language who belong to other peoples.[15]

Supporters of the E.L.A. seem to be making precisely the mistake of equating the obviousness of language usage with its importance to national unity. Of course, they do not claim that language is the only bond of the American people, but the ease with which they dismiss other elements of national unity and their eagerness to elevate English to a role as the primary (if not the only) guardian of the American way of life reveal that their allusions to cultural diversity are little more than perfunctory.

Admittedly, foreign language use is the most striking symbol of foreignness itself. There is little doubt that acquisition of a nation's language audibly manifests an immigrant's desire to join the mainstream of society, while at the same time removing the veil of incomprehension that appears to threaten both sides. It is not so clear, however, that a mastery of English is a prerequisite for commitment to Ameri-

---

15. Karl Deutsch, *Nationalism and Social Communication* (New York: Wiley, 1953), p. 97.

can ideals or that speaking English assures loyalty to American values. Yet this fact is easily lost when forced to compete with the immediate symbolic impact of language use.

Just as supporters of the E.L.A. feel it is unnecessary to delve deeply into their sociolinguistic assumptions and empirical data, they casually depict a nightmarish vision of separatist Quebec as the inevitable future of the United States if we fail to protect English now. Once again, however, the purveyors of these warnings rely completely on their "obvious" correctness and immediate emotional impact, without any careful examination of the cultural, political, historical, religious, and linguistic differences between Canada and the United States. Veltman completely rejects any linguistic comparison between the French-speaking population in Quebec and Spanish speakers in the United States, noting that in Quebec only 2 percent of native speakers of French become primarily English speakers, while in the American Southwest, 60 percent of the Spanish speakers adopt English as their usual language.[16]

Lawrence H. Fuchs identifies five factors whose different roles in the two societies make Mexican American separatism of the Quebec sort extremely unlikely in the United States: (1) *language*—unlike the French-speaking Québecois, Mexican American leaders strongly favor the acquisition of English even while promoting cultural maintenance; (2) *memory and geography*—most Mexican Americans in the United States are immigrants or descendants of immigrants who feel no historic sense of defeat and loss; at the same time they do not constitute the majority in any state or region of the United States; (3) *religion*—the Catholic Church in the United States is national and assimilationist, unlike that in Quebec; (4) *politics*—American politics is integrationist, not separatist; and (5) *founding myths*—Canada is seen as a union between two nations, each with its own separate language, culture, and religion; the United States is premised on individuals forming a nation to protect their liberties, free from group controls. Considering all of these factors, Fuchs concludes that fears of Mexican American separatism comparable to the movement in Quebec "appear to be groundless."[17]

A potentially destructive irony may also lurk in the reliance on the prospect of a Quebec-like future to promote the E.L.A. According to Maxwell Yalden, the commissioner of official languages for Canada:

16. Ingwerson, "Tale," p. 13.
17. Lawrence H. Fuchs, "Immigration, Pluralism, and Public Policy: The Challenge of Pluribus to the Unum," in *U.S. Immigration and Refugee Policy,* ed. Mary M. Kritz (Lexington, Mass.: Lexington Books, 1983), pp. 289, 308–10.

"We do not have the separatist problem in Canada because we have two languages. We have the problem because we refuse to give status to the other [French] language."[18] If Yalden is correct, supporters of the E.L.A. may be playing the role of characters in a Greek tragedy who bring about their fate through their efforts to avoid it.

Language diversity did not become a major issue in American life until the beginning of the twentieth century, when massive waves of immigrants from southeastern Europe began landing on our shores and crowding our cities. The reaction to these newcomers was far from uniform. Some welcomed them and were genuinely concerned for their well-being; others feared and detested them for racial or other xenophobic reasons and hoped to be rid of them, or at least "neutralize" their effect on American society as quickly as possible. All agreed, however, that the new immigrants already here must be "Americanized"—for their own good, for America's good, or both. From this morass of contradictory impulses and assumptions, the Americanization movement was born with a single goal: making Americans out of foreigners as quickly as possible.

Though in theory it was only one of several elements in the definition of an assimilated American, language became in practice the major, if somewhat schizophrenic, focus of the Americanization movement. English language education emerged as the chief goal (and perhaps the only lasting product) of its positive program, while the exclusion of the new immigrants from American society through the use of onerous English language requirements for entry, employment, and political participation was a major part of its nativist and restrictionist agenda.[19]

Nativists rejected the contention that one could keep one's mother tongue, yet still be a good citizen of the United States. Learning English was not enough—committed immigrants had to cast off their alien tongues along with their alien status. Some immigrant groups, however, resisted the idea that deracination was a prerequisite for good citizenship. German speakers, in particular, had a long tradition of mother-tongue maintenance and bilingual education in the United States, a fact not unnoticed by nativists and Know-Nothings as far back as the middle of the nineteenth century. The coming of World War I reawakened hostility toward the teaching of German and other foreign languages, and by 1923 thirty-four states had passed legisla-

18. Quoted in Gary Turbak, "Bilingualism: Terrible Time Bomb?" *Kiwanis Magazine* (June–July 1984), pp. 22–23.

19. Edward G. Hartmann, *The Movement to Americanize the Immigrant* (New York: Columbia University Press, 1948), pp. 24ff.

tion installing English as the sole language of instruction in all public and private schools.[20]

States also used more direct language restrictions to exclude foreigners from economic and political participation in American life. As early as 1897, Pennsylvania imposed residency and English-language requirements on miners. In 1918 New York passed a law requiring foreign language speakers to be enrolled in educational programs as a condition of continued employment. Other states had similar laws. In a particularly venal move, a Republican administration fearful of Jewish votes amended the New York State constitution to include an English literacy requirement whose purpose was to disenfranchise over one million Yiddish-speaking citizens. Once again, neither New York's goal nor its method was unique.[21]

In the areas of language requirements for employment and voting, the states had often followed the lead of the federal government, which had exclusive control over qualifications for immigration and naturalization. Unfortunately, much federal action was guided by the report of the U.S. Immigration Commission (better known as the Dillingham Commission), issued in forty-two volumes in 1911. Beginning with restrictionist presumptions and ignoring or distorting much of its own data, the commission concluded that the new immigrants were inferior intellectually, racially, and educationally; were not learning English, assimilating, or naturalizing quickly enough; and were criminally inclined.

Literacy tests for admission to the United States became a goal of immigration restrictionists, who openly admitted that their purpose was to decrease immigration by 25 percent, specifically that 25 percent which came from eastern and southern Europe. Some proponents of the literacy test wanted to base admissibility to the United States on knowledge of English itself, but the legislation that emerged merely required literacy in the prospective immigrant's own language. First introduced in 1895, the literacy test was not enacted into law until 1917, when wartime enthusiasm enabled Congress to override President Wilson's veto.

The English language requirement for naturalization had a much easier birth. Recommended by the U.S. Commission on Naturalization in 1905, this requirement was included in the Naturalization Act

---

20. Arnold H. Leibowitz, "English Literacy: Legal Sanction for Discrimination," *Notre Dame Lawyer* 45 (Fall 1969): 42.

21. Ibid., pp. 34–35; John Higham, "Crusade for Americanization," in *Strangers in the Land: Patterns of American Nativism, 1860–1925* (New Brunswick, N.J.: Rutgers University Press, 1955), p. 72; Susan S. Forbes and Peter Lemos, "History of American Language Policy," in Select Commission on Immigrant and Refugee Policy, *U.S. Immigration and the National Interest*, Staff Report, April 30, 1981, Appendix A, p. 53.

of 1906. Under the act's provisions an applicant for citizenship had to be able to sign his name and speak English to the satisfaction of a naturalization examiner. Even the nativists' opponents regarded these requirements as the minimum necessary to assure the maintenance of American culture and political institutions.[22]

In specifically linguistic terms, however, the new immigrants' acquisition of English depended more on economic realities and their own motivation than on the impositions of the Americanization movement. This is not to say that the educational programs that grew out of the movement were ineffective or negative, but it is clear that the Founders' initial reliance on the natural dominance of English in American life was more realistic than the elaborate programs of the Americanizers.

The Americanization movement is an example of the use of language not just as a shield, but also as an offensive weapon against hidden, nonlinguistic targets. This is because language not only uses symbols but is symbolic itself. The apparent solicitude for the national language exhibited by many of the Americanizers was a mask for racial, economic, and political hostility toward users of other tongues. Because language issues can easily be loaded with otherwise unsavory or unacceptable agendas, elements of the Americanization movement were able to transform language from a shield against linguistic chaos into a sword against supposed *nonlinguistic* differences as well—even when those supposed differences were arguably beyond the reach of legitimate public debate.

The Americanization movement's strident defense of threatened American institutions from alien influences raises questions about how accurately such threats were gauged. Even more intriguing is the possibility that the real threat to American institutions in this period arose more from the Americanizers themselves than from any alien hordes. Of course, mere reference to the mistakes of the Americanizers answers no questions about the merit of present claims concerning the status of English in the United States and its role in protecting American institutions and values. But the first important lesson of the Americanization movement must be that attempts to use language for "patriotic ends" must be subjected to the strictest sort of scrutiny, and that elements of jingoism, racism, and xenophobia hiding behind expressed concern for linguistic unity must be identified and rooted out of the debate before proposals to impose English on our official and unofficial life are given any serious consideration.

The second lesson to be derived from the Americanization movement and the responses it provoked is that the debate over the protection of English in the United States can be viewed as a major battle in

22. Forbes and Lemos, "History," p. 123.

the ongoing struggle between two normative visions of American society: *Anglo-conformity* and *cultural pluralism*. According to Milton Gordon, the ideal of Anglo-conformity, of "maintaining English institutions (as modified by the American Revolution), the English language, and English-oriented cultural patterns as dominant in American life," has dominated our history until very recently.[23] During the heyday of the Americanization movement, its requirement that immigrants must completely shed their prior identity was accepted by both reformers and nativists alike.

Yet the narrowness of the Anglo-conformist vision underlying the Americanization movement never commanded complete unanimity, and its harsh prescriptions stimulated the search for more tolerant outlooks. There arose an intellectually well-developed alternative model of American society which has come to be known as cultural pluralism. Beginning in 1915, Horace Kallen began to develop this vision of an America in which cultural and linguistic diversity were not a threat to be avoided, but the strength and genius of American democracy. While recognizing the importance of English as the common language of the United States, Kallen sought to promote the maintenance of mother tongues and ethnic identity as the best way to realize American democratic ideals.[24]

Like the systems of thought with which it competes, cultural pluralism raises problems of definition and historical accuracy. Nevertheless, as a normative vision of American society, it offers a clear alternative to Anglo-conformity and drives policy in a radically different direction. Proponents of cultural pluralism accept the basic proposition that a common language provides social cohesion, but given the ease with which arbitrary language requirements can be used to discriminate, they argue that society should encourage mother-tongue maintenance and individual choice in language usage.[25]

In the decades since the end of the Americanization movement, cultural pluralism has come to dominate most of the rhetoric and much of the political action of our society. This change in outlook has many complex sources, but among the major ones must be included the repudiation of the suspect sociology and race-science which served to legitimate many of the harsher prescriptions of Anglo-conformity, the horrific lessons of World War II about the conse-

23. Milton Gordon, *Assimilation in American Life: The Role of Race, Religion, and National Origins* (New York: Oxford University Press, 1964), p. 89.

24. Horace Kallen, *Culture and Democracy in the United States* (New York: Boni & Liveright, 1924); *Cultural Pluralism and the American Idea* (Philadelphia: University of Pennsylvania Press, 1956). For a summary of Kallen's ideas, see Gordon, *Assimilation*, pp. 141ff.

25. See, e.g., Joshua A. Fishman et al., *Language Loyalty in the United States* (The Hague: Mouton, 1966).

quences of obsessive drives for national unity and purity, the flowering of the civil rights movement, and the growing awareness among later generations of Americans of the price paid for their assimilation.[26]

This change in the normative model of American society has been accompanied by an equally dramatic change in our conception of the role of the national government. Despite federal control over immigration policy, the essentially conservative, traditionalist thrust of the Americanizers militated against the national government's playing a dominant role in the Americanization movement. Instead, their attempt to realize the ideal of Anglo-conformity played itself out in areas largely under the control of private individuals and local governments, primarily employment and education. In contrast, cultural pluralism's emphasis on assuring the cultural and linguistic rights of minorities seems to require the active assistance of the federal government. It is, therefore, not surprising that the national government has not only entered traditionally local and private areas of American life, but has also created such programs as bilingual education, multilingual ballots, and translation services in an attempt to promote a culturally pluralistic society.

Once again, however, the pendulum seems to have swung. Just as the theoretical and political excesses of the Americanization movement stimulated a contrary response, the perception that well-intentioned government programs for minority groups may actually be exacerbating the problems they were intended to solve has undermined some of the basic assumptions of the cultural pluralism model of American society and has made notions of Anglo-conformity attractive again.

Although as a matter of political necessity they speak the language of cultural pluralism, there is no doubt that most proponents of the E.L.A. embrace an astonishingly pure form of Anglo-conformity. Sadly, it appears that in doing so, some supporters also have an affinity for using language issues as a weapon against those who are already the objects of cultural or racial prejudice. Where the Americanizers were afraid of Slavic or Mediterranean hordes, supporters of the E.L.A. are afraid of Spanish and the people who speak it. It is almost as if we had traveled back in time seventy-five years; once again the United States is facing unprecedented numbers of non-English speakers, seemingly unassimilable, and possibly hostile to American ideals and institutions. In ominous echoes of the Americanizers, the supporters of the E.L.A. not only insist that the problem posed by Span-

26. Fuchs, "Immigration," pp. 302-4.

ish speakers is unique; they also view this new situation exactly as their predecessors viewed the coming of the new immigrants at the turn of the century—as a threat, not as an opportunity or a challenge.

According to an E.L.A. sponsor, Senator Walter Huddleston: "For the last fifteen years, we have experienced a growing resistance to the acceptance of our historic language. Increasingly, we have been subjected to an antagonistic questioning of the melting pot philosophy that has traditionally helped speed newcomers into the American mainstream" *(see p. 115).* He goes on to quote Theodore White's proposition that "some Hispanics have . . . made a demand never voiced by immigrants before: that the United States, in effect, officially recognize itself as a bicultural, bilingual nation."[27] In remarks placed in the *Congressional Record* and mailed to his constituents in North Dakota, Senator Quentin Burdick finds it unnecessary even to mention Spanish by name, referring to it as "that language."[28] Former senator S. I. Hayakawa contrasts the eagerness of other immigrant groups to learn English and assimilate with the alleged failure of Hispanics to do so. In apportioning the blame, Hayakawa disavows any prejudice or hostility toward Hispanics, blaming the current state of affairs on Hispanic political leaders, not Spanish speakers themselves.[29] Such rhetoric is disconcerting in an age where blatant racism and xenophobia are unacceptable in public debate, but language issues remain susceptible to use as barely disguised carriers of covert messages.

Given that passing a constitutional amendment is no easy task, and that a successful drive for the E.L.A. may not even bring about some of its supporters' major goals, there must be some other reason that the constitutional route has become so attractive to opponents of specific, nonconstitutionally mandated government language programs. One possibility is that passage of the E.L.A. is not the true goal of many of its erstwhile supporters. They may be using the *idea* of the amendment as simply one part of an attack on despised programs and emergent Hispanic political power.

Supporters of the E.L.A. often depict bilingual education as largely Hispanic porkbarreling, a means of providing jobs and influence to the Hispanic population, particularly its political leaders. Faced with what seems to them to be pure self-interest masquerading as part of the civil rights movement, the opponents of such programs may hope to trump Hispanic political power by linking their own position to an even more powerful, self-evident, patriotic imperative. Wrapping their primary goals in the mantle of support for the English language in the United States changes the terms of the political argument in a

27. *E.L.A. Hearing*, pp. 15–16.
28. *Congressional Record*, 98th Cong., 2d sess., 1984, p. S385.
29. *E.L.A. Hearing*, pp. 52–54.

way that "naturally" favors their position. Cast in these new terms, the argument is no longer about assuring the civil rights of a minority, but rather about protecting the fabric of American society from linguistic and cultural fragmentation. From this perspective, actual passage of the E.L.A. may be largely irrelevant. Just waging the battle—recasting the terms of the political debate in a way that puts opponents on the defensive against a seemingly obvious, patriotic position—may constitute winning it.

There is, however, a deep irony underlying such a symbolic strategy. The explicit claim of the E.L.A.'s supporters is that Spanish speakers are failing to enter the American mainstream and that this failure threatens our political and cultural institutions. But supporters of the E.L.A. seem to have chosen the constitutional route for precisely the opposite reason: Hispanic political power is too strong for their liking, that is, too successful in getting what it wants out of the American political system. Is the problem really bloc voting rather than not voting?[30] If it is, if Hispanics are voting "self-interest," why is the exercise of Hispanic political power in traditional American ways threatening to the integrity of the American political system? One can understand the impulses behind the movement for official protection of the English language, and one can sympathize with the fears felt by those concerned for our country's future. Nevertheless, passage of the E.L.A. would be a major mistake.

The goal of a unified citizenry committed to democratic ideals is an admirable one, and universal acquisition of the English language by all residents of the United States would no doubt further that goal. But the means by which we promote English should not in themselves run counter to our democratic tradition. Imposing English upon Spanish speakers through a constitutional amendment would likely exclude many from political participation, sacrifice equal justice in the courtroom, narrowly restrict educational alternatives on the basis of political criteria, and mark linguistic minorities as "un-American" in the eyes of the rest of society. Based on undocumented fears of separatism and cultural fragmentation, passage of the E.L.A. would insult and alienate a significant portion of our society in the name of national unity.

30. Senator Huddleston seems to imply this; *E.L.A. Hearing*, p. 20.

Proposed Official English Amendments to the U.S. Constitution

Sixteen English Language Amendments were introduced in the U.S. Congress between 1981 and 1990, in addition to various statutes and "sense of Congress" resolutions. There are two basic versions of the amendment: the *one-liner*, which simply establishes English as the nation's official language and leaves the interpretation to Congress and the federal courts, and the *English Only mandate*, which outlaws uses of other languages by federal, state, and local governments, with a few exceptions specified (e.g., emergency situations and foreign language classrooms). Although the Senate convened hearings on Official English in 1984 and the House in 1988, the English Language Amendment has never come to a Congressional vote, even in committee. Ratification would require approval by two-thirds of each house of Congress and three-quarters of state legislatures.

S.J. Res. 72 (1981)[31]

Section 1. The English language shall be the official language of the United States.

Section 2. Neither the United States nor any State shall make or enforce any law which requires the use of any language other than English.

Section 3. This article shall apply to laws, ordinances, regulations, orders, programs, and policies.

Section 4. No order or decree shall be issued by any court of the United States or of any State requiring that any proceedings, or matters to which this article applies, be in any language other than English.

Section 5. This article shall not prohibit educational instruction in a language other than English as required as a transitional method of making students who use a language other than English proficient in English.

Section 6. The Congress and the States shall have power to enforce this article by appropriate legislation.

31. Sponsored by Senator S. I. Hayakawa (R-Calif.)

S.J. Res 167 (1983)[32]

Section 1. The English language shall be the official language of the United States.

Section 2. The Congress shall have the power to enforce this article by appropriate legislation.

H.J. Res. 13 (1987)[33]

Section 1. The English language shall be the official language of the United States.

Section 2. Neither the United States nor any State shall require, by law, ordinance, regulation, order, decree, program, or policy, the use in the United States of any language other than English.

Section 3. This article shall not prohibit any law, ordinance, regulation, order, decree, program, or policy requiring educational instruction in a language other than English for the purpose of making students who use a language other than English proficient in English.

Section 4. The Congress and the States may enforce this article by appropriate legislation.

H.J. Res. 81 (1989)[34]

Section 1. The English language shall be the official language of the United States.

Section 2. Neither the United States nor any State shall require, by law, ordinance, regulation, order, decree, program, or policy, the use in the United States of any language other than English.

Section 3. This article shall not prohibit any law, ordinance, regulation, order, decree, program, or policy—

(1) to provide educational instruction in a language other than English for the purpose of making students who use a language other than English proficient in English,

(2) to teach a foreign language to students who are already proficient in English,

(3) to protect public health and safety, or

(4) to allow translators for litigants, defendants, or witnesses in court cases.

Section 4. The Congress and the States may enforce this article by appropriate legislation.

32. Sponsored by Senators Walter Huddleston (D-Ky.) and Steve Symms (R-Idaho).
33. Sponsored by Representative William Broomfield (R-Mich.).
34. Sponsored by Representative Norman Shumway (R-Calif.).

The Misdirected Policy of Bilingualism

By Senator Walter Huddleston

Walter Huddleston, a Kentucky Democrat, served as U.S.
senator from to 1973 to 1985. He explains his reasons for
sponsoring an English Language Amendment in the following speech, as excerpted from the *Congressional Record*,
98th Congress, 1st session, Sept. 21, 1983, pp. S12640–43.

The remarks I am about to make will be readily understood by my
distinguished colleagues in the Congress. They will be understood by
my constituents in Kentucky. They will be understood by the journalists in the press gallery, and by most of their readers across the country. No simultaneous interpreters will be needed for those in this
chamber, and no translators will be needed for most of those who will
be reading these words in the *Congressional Record*. In order to guarantee that this current state of affairs endures, as it has for over two
hundred years, I am introducing today a constitutional amendment
(S.J. Res. 167) to make English the official language of the United
States *(see p. 113)*.

The amendment addresses something so basic, so very fundamental to our sense of identity as Americans, that some who are in full
agreement with the objectives of this amendment, will nevertheless
question the necessity for it. So widely held is the assumption that
English is already our national language that the notion of stating this
in our national charter may seem like restating the obvious. However,
I can assure my colleagues that this is not the case and that the need
for a constitutional amendment grows stronger every day.

Almost alone among the world's very large and populous nations,
the United States enjoys the blessings of one primary language, spoken and understood by most of its citizens. The previously unquestioned acceptance of this language by immigrants from every linguistic and cultural background has enabled us to come together as one
people. It has allowed us to discuss our differences, to argue about
our problems, and to compromise on solutions. It has allowed us to
develop a stable and cohesive society that is the envy of many fractured ones, without imposing any strict standards of homogeneity, or
even bothering to designate the language, which is ours by custom,
as the nation's official one.

As a nation of immigrants, our great strength has been drawn from our ability to assimilate vast numbers of people from many different cultures and ethnic groups into a nation of people that can work together with cooperation and understanding. This process was often referred to as the melting pot and in the past it has been seen as an almost magical concept that helped to make the United States the greatest nation on earth. But for the last fifteen years, we have experienced a growing resistance to the acceptance of our historic language, an antagonistic questioning of the melting pot philosophy that has traditionally helped speed newcomers into the American mainstream.

Initially, the demands to make things easier for the newcomers seemed modest enough; and a generous people, appreciative of cultural diversity, was willing to make some allowances. For example, the English language requirements for naturalization were removed for elderly immigrants living here for twenty years who were still unable to meet them; and the use of a child's home language was encouraged, in a well-intentioned attempt to soften the pain of adjustment from the home to the English-speaking society that the school represents.

However, the demands have sharply escalated, and so has the tone in which they are presented. Bilingual education has gradually lost its role as a transitional way of teaching English, and now mandates a bicultural component. This mandate has been primarily shaped by the federal government. The unfortunate result is that thousands of immigrant and nonimmigrant children are languishing in near-permanent bilingual-bicultural programs, kept in a state of prolonged confusion, suspended between two worlds, and not understanding what is expected of them. They and their parents are given false hopes that their cultural traditions can be fully maintained in this country, and that the mastery of English is not so important, after all.

This misdirected public policy of bilingualism has been created primarily by the federal government, at the insistence of special interest groups, and it continues today because elected officials do not want to run the risk of taking a position that could, in some way, offend these groups. Over the last few years the federal government has spent approximately $1 billion on the bilingual education program. What we have bought with this money is a program that strives to keep separate cultural identities rather than a program that strives to teach English. It is a program which ignores the basic fact that in order to learn another language the student must talk, read, and use that language on a regular basis. Even though the bilingual education program has received failing marks by many reputable educators, it still survives because it is a political issue rather than an educational issue. What this means is that we will continue to finance an expensive bilingual program that does more to preserve cultural identities than it does to teach children to speak English.

In the area of voting rights, we have also formulated a national policy that encourages voting citizens not to learn to speak English. The Voting Rights Act, which was reauthorized in 1982, requires bilingual ballots if more than 5 percent of the citizens of voting age in a jurisdiction are of specified language minority groups and the illiteracy rate is higher than the national rate. As a result, bilingual ballots are required by federal law to be provided in thirty states—even if there is no demand for them. The wisdom of this policy is clearly lacking when you consider that the vast bulk of political debate, whether it is in the printed press or the electronic media, is conducted in English. By failing to provide a positive incentive for voting citizens to learn English, we are actually denying them full participation in the political process. Instead, we are making them dependent upon a few interpreters or go-betweens for information as to how they should vote. Although this process helps to preserve minority voting blocs, it seriously undercuts the democratic concept that every voting individual should be as fully informed as possible about the issues and the candidates.

There are other less prominent provisions of federal law which now require the use of foreign languages; for example, the use of interpreters in federal civil and criminal proceedings for parties whose primary language is other than English; and the use of foreign language personnel in connection with federally funded migrant health centers and alcohol-abuse treatment programs. Although I can understand that this kind of assistance is helpful, the fact that it must be legislated strongly indicates that we are failing miserably in our efforts to teach immigrants and many of our native born how to speak, read, and write English.

These federal laws are only the tip of the iceberg. I recently sent a request to all of the state governors and the major federal agencies asking for information regarding non-English forms and publications that their offices produce which are intended for use in this country. Although my staff is still in the process of reviewing the data, and I have not yet received responses to all of my letters, we know that hundreds of different, non-English forms and publications are now being printed and distributed on a wide scale throughout the United States. These publications cover a broad spectrum and range from White House press releases in Spanish to National Labor Relations Board notices in thirty-two languages. The non-English materials which I have received are in a stack that is about three feet high, and we are adding to it almost daily. I am told that if copies of all bilingual educational materials were sent, we could fill a large room. While distribution of these materials may be seen as providing just another government service, it can also be seen as reducing the incentive to learn English. It demonstrates a growing nationwide problem.

At the nongovernmental level there is a great deal of emphasis being placed on the use of non-English languages. In some major metropolitan areas, English is the second language; minorities who speak only English are being told that they must learn a foreign language to be eligible for a job; in many stores non-English languages are the only ones used to conduct business. It is not uncommon to find areas in this country where individuals can live all of their lives having all their social, commercial, and intellectual needs met without the use of English.

If this situation were static and merely a reflection of the large-scale legal and illegal immigration the United States has been experiencing over the last few years—in 1980 more immigrants entered the United States than at any time other than the peak years at the turn of the century—there would not be cause for concern. However, what we are seeing is a decrease in the use of English and a widely accepted attitude that it is not necessary to learn English. The United States is presently at a crucial juncture. We can either continue down the same path we have walked for the last two hundred years, using the melting pot philosophy to forge a strong and united nation, or we can take the new path that leads in the direction of another Tower of Babel.

National unity does not require that each person think and act like everyone else. However, it does require that there be some common threads that run throughout our society and hold us together. One of these threads is our common belief and support of a democratic form of government, and the right of every person to fully participate in it. Unfortunately, this right of full participation means very little if each individual does not possess the means of exercising it. This participation requires the ability to obtain information and to communicate our beliefs and concerns to others. Undoubtedly, this process is greatly hindered without the existence of a commonly accepted and used language.

In essence, what a policy of bilingualism-biculturalism does is to segregate minorities from the mainstream of our politics, economy, and society because we are not making it possible for them to freely enter into that mainstream. We are pushing them aside into their own communities, and we are denying them the tools with which to break out. I have always been against segregation of any kind, and by not assuring that every person in this country can speak and understand English, we are still practicing segregation. It was wrong when we segregated blacks because of their color, and it is just as wrong when we create a system which segregates any group of people by language.

As Americans we are a unique people, and one of the things that makes us uniquely American is our common language—English. My proposed constitutional amendment would assure that anyone in this country can fully take part in the American dream and that future generations also will have this privilege.

Viva la Roja, Blanca y Azul

By Delegate Baltasar Corrada

Baltasar Corrada, a member of the New Progressive Party, served as Resident Commissioner of Puerto Rico, the commonwealth's nonvoting delegate in the U.S. House of Representatives, from 1977 to 1985. His remarks in opposition to Official English are excerpted from testimony before the U.S. Senate, Committee on the Judiciary, Subcommittee on the Constitution, *The English Language Amendment: Hearing on S.J. Res. 167*, 98th Congress, 2d session, June 12, 1984, pp. 79–82.

There are some people who believe that minority languages pose a threat to dethrone English as the language of the vast majority of our people and of our government. I submit that the people of the United States believe in freedom and not in government imposition of language or culture. English is the language of the United States, and it is so because of a cultural and social phenomenon, because that is the people's choice and not because the Constitution mandates it.

The freedom we enjoy here allows us to make the choice every single day to speak whichever language we prefer, and for over two hundred years, overwhelmingly, we have decided to communicate in English. Immigrants or migrants to the United States have historically been eager to learn English. Even the 3.2 million American citizens residing in Puerto Rico, where Spanish is the language used in government, in state courts, in business, and in all facets of daily living, strive to improve our proficiency in English.

I, for instance, was born and raised in Puerto Rico and educated there and developed in an academic environment where Spanish is the vehicle of public education. Throughout my college years and my law studies in Puerto Rico, Spanish was the language of my education. I never resided in the U.S. mainland until the people of Puerto Rico elected me to Congress in 1977. Yet I sit before you this morning conversing in English, even though Spanish is my vernacular. I cherish both languages. They, I believe, make me a better educated person and better-suited to understand the people and the world I live in.

I fail to see how a constitutional amendment establishing English as the official language of the United States would, in the balance, yield a positive impact on our social, economic, and political life. The United States is composed of different cultures which have allowed us to rapidly and effectively expand our international horizons. Our economic and political ties with foreign countries have been strengthened, thanks to the enlightening contributions based on first-hand knowledge and understanding of foreign cultures immigrants have brought to our country.

Because of the economic dominance of the United States in recent decades, English has become the standard language in business and diplomacy throughout the world, and Americans have become comfortable in their knowledge that all others will accommodate to them. As our world becomes smaller, through transportation and communication, and as economic strength becomes more evenly distributed among nations, we must raise ourselves from this false sense of security and begin to recognize and reward cultural and linguistic differences as an asset rather than a detriment to our national power.

Let me point out that in the year 1917 Congress passed the Jones Act, granting American citizenship to all residents of Puerto Rico, regardless of whether they spoke English or not. It would be unfair, now that we may be moving closer to the point where we may ask to join the union, as the fifty-first or fifty-second state, to require that English be the sole official language in Puerto Rico. I believe that we ought to have the opportunity to have Spanish as well as English, and that this essentially is a matter for each state to decide, rather than having the federal government imposing to each of the political bodies that comprise this great nation a mandatory use of English as the official language.

Puerto Rico, being a neighbor of Latin American countries and possessing similar language, culture, and idiosyncrasy, would afford the United States the catalyst it needs to improve and develop currently strained relations with some of those countries. The admission of Puerto Rico into the union as an Hispanic state would send a clear message to the countries in the region that the United States does not look down on Hispanics, but rather, welcomes them on an equal footing.

Yes, we in Puerto Rico want to learn English, as I and my children and many others on the island have—not as an imposition, but as a matter of practicality and choice. Any attempt to impose the English language on me or anybody would be a frontal attack on the right to freedom of speech provided in the First Amendment to the Constitution. To try to impose the English language on the states' official business would be contrary to the states' rights, protected under the Tenth Amendment, to manage their internal affairs however they see fit.

Freedom of speech and the right to vote are the cornerstones of our democracy. Any effort to undermine either one weakens our democracy. We cannot backtrack in our efforts to bring equality of access to the polls and to ensure full participation for all in our democratic and electoral process. For instance, the bilingual ballot provisions under the Voting Rights Act are a prime example of how we are responding to the need to give a greater meaning to democracy in our country. It is also a fine example of the negative impact of a constitutional amendment establishing English as the official language. The right to vote is the key to all freedoms we enjoy in the United States. It assures our citizens participation in the decision-making process regarding issues which affect our daily lives and give direction to our society. By imposing a language barrier to the right to vote, we would deny many citizens in our nation access to the most basic and important tool of democracy. Language minority groups should not be alienated or obstructed from participating in the political process, but rather, encouraged to do so by facilitating their understanding of that process. In that way, we truly bring them into the mainstream.

It might be easy for the English-speaking majority of our country to attempt to impose English on our linguistic minorities. I would not doubt it for a moment, that perhaps you could garner the majority of the members of Congress to vote for this. But what would it do? The adoption of such a measure, in my view, would accomplish nothing save a straining of relations between the diverse cultures that nurture the greatness of our nation.

No one is arguing against the need for all Americans to attain proficiency in English in order to participate in all levels of our society. No one is suggesting that any other language should replace English as the vehicle for interaction in our society. That is the way it is; that is the way it should be. But we do not need the Constitution to mandate this, just as we do not need the Constitution to mandate that we have to love our mother and our father, or that we have to be patriotic. This is part of the responsibility of citizenship that does not have to be imposed upon us.

America is great not because we speak one language or the other, but because we are united by the fundamental principles than bind our people together: freedom, justice, equal opportunity for all, fairness, democracy. To say that we make our country stronger because we make it "U.S. English" is like saying that we would make it stronger by making it "U.S. white." It is as insidious to base the strength or unity of the United States in one language as it is to base that strength or unity in one race.

When Jimmy López was held hostage in Iran for more than a year, together with other Americans, he wrote an inscription in his cell that the Iranians could not understand: "Viva la Roja, Blanca y Azul." It meant: "Long Live the Red, White, and Blue." He was fully American and fully patriotic even though he wrote that inscription in Spanish, and it remained there while his captors wanted to restrain his freedom.

Today, as a Puerto Rican and as an American, proud of being a Puerto Rican and proud of being an American, I repeat here: Viva la Roja, Blanca y Azul.

Preserve the Primacy of English

By Representative Norman Shumway

Norman Shumway, a California Republican, served as a member of the U.S. House of Representatives from 1979 to 1991. He has sponsored several versions of the English Language Amendment. The following testimony is excerpted from U.S. House Committee on the Judiciary, Subcommittee on Civil and Constitutional Rights, *English Language Constitutional Amendments: Hearing on H.J. Res. 13, H.J. Res. 33, H.J. Res. 60, and H.J. Res. 83,* 100th Congress, 2d session, May 11, 1988, pp. 36–44.

English has been the common language of the United States as a result of historical custom, not legal designation. That common language has been the "glue" which has held us together, forging strength and unity from our rich cultural diversity. From our earliest days, despite our melting pot inheritance, English has been the language in which we expressed the goals, objectives, ideals, principles, and duties of our form of government. It is the language in which the Declaration of Independence and the Constitution are written. It is the language in which the welcome at the base of the Statue of Liberty is written. And in my view, it is the primary language in which our government should continue to function. However, without that missing measure of legal protection, I believe that the primacy of English is being threatened, and that we are moving toward the status of a bilingual society.

That drift towards bilingualism may be unwitting. One reason I am involved in this effort to have English designated our official language is to call attention to that fact, and to focus on the phenomenon *now*. If we want to *be* a bilingual, replicating Canada and all the problems inherent with that nation's language divisiveness, all we need to do is stay on our present course. Frankly, I believe that would be a mistake, and a tragic one if it happens unintentionally. Nonetheless, we have taken some steps down the road to bilingualism; the time is ripe for us to step back a few paces, review our present policies, and make a conscious decision about our language future.

I am continually amazed by the intense degree of emotionalism which opponents to this effort display. Contrary to their allegations, those of us who endorse the English Language Amendment—and there are more than sixty sponsors of my bill alone—are not a group of wild-eyed reactionaries bent on demanding "English Only."

Equally amazing is the seeming lack of substance to opponents' arguments. The only objections which have been voiced to me over the years that I have sponsored this measure reflect an extrapolation of facts, resulting in unreasonable and erroneous conclusions. For example, some opponents allege that designating English our official language will deny emergency services, basic civil rights, and human dignity to language minorities. To me, those conclusions are absurd. The United States has always been in the vanguard when it comes to personal liberty and civil rights. We have refined our perspective considerably over the past few decades, but even as a newly born nation, we were the symbol of hope, freedom, and opportunity for all the world. Our status as that symbol is unlikely to undergo drastic change simply because we designate English our official language.

Some who protest the measure claim that it will prevent other languages from being used by those who know them, and deny students the opportunity to learn a second language. Again, there is no validity to that argument. I would never endorse a measure that could result in such restriction. In a world growing ever smaller as a result of technology and increasing sophistication, I believe everyone should try to master another tongue. And certainly those who emigrate from their native lands should be free to maintain the language which reflects their cultural and ethnic heritage. Semanticist and former senator S. I. Hayakawa, the first sponsor of the English Language Amendment and the founder of U.S. English, summed up the situation very aptly: "We are all free to use whatever language we choose at the dinner table, but English is the language of the marketplace." This is not an effort to stifle private freedom; it is an effort to clarify public policy.

The most specious argument against the English Language Amendment is that it is "xenophobic" or, worse, that it seeks to discriminate against those of certain backgrounds. In my view, existing government policies are discriminatory, by keeping language minorities forever on the fringes of our society. Those who cannot communicate fluently in our common language cannot possibly avail themselves of America's many opportunities. We are fostering policies which discourage language minorities from learning English, and we are sending conflicting and confusing signals to those language minorities. For example, we expect all those under the age of fifty seeking naturalization to demonstrate competence in English as a condition of citizenship. However, in 375 jurisdictions in 21 states, the federal government still requires that ballots be printed in languages other than English. How can we require English knowledge on the one hand, then turn around and encourage dependency on other languages with the other?

Bilingual education is another such policy. It originally was developed to be a transitional, temporary program enabling children with limited English proficiency to acquire our language while keeping up with their schoolwork in other basic subjects. The theory was a good one; in some cases its implementation was effective—but not in all. No one is advocating that we turn our backs on *Lau v. Nichols (see pp. 251–55)*; we must provide limited-English-proficient children with every opportunity to learn English. In many cases, however, bilingual education may be counterproductive by fostering continued reliance on the student's native language. More basically, I believe that educators and parents, not lawmakers and bureaucrats, should determine appropriate means of teaching English.

While there is no controversy about the need to provide *some* type of assistance to those with limited English proficiency, there is a great deal of debate concerning the most effective instructional approach. No doubt each argument is correct in some situations. The arguments for and against the success of bilingual education are as many and varied as the diversity of limited-English-proficient students throughout America. They are also beside the point. The point is that school districts should be free to decide how they will teach their students.

The most commonly asked question about the English Language Amendment is: "Why do we need it?" We need it to provide English with legal protection as our national language, thereby continuing our heritage as a unilingual nation. We need it to end conflicting government policies and signals being sent to language minorities. We need it to prevent the divisiveness that is bound to result from a plurality of official languages. We need it to ensure that our government continues to function primarily in English. And there is one more reason, perhaps the most important reason of all.

The key to being successful as a newcomer to America is to learn the language. Fluency in English is in turn the door to opportunity. By discouraging newcomers from mastering English and being assimilated into our society, we are denying them opportunity.

I don't believe in "English Only." I *do* believe in English *primarily*, and certainly I believe it is incumbent upon the government, which is today debating in that language, to take steps to protect that primacy. I cherish our cultural diversity, but I also cherish our common bond of language.

Official English: A Concession to Nativism

By Representative Stephen J. Solarz

Stephen J. Solarz, a New York Democrat, has been a member of the U.S. House of Representatives since 1975. His testimony is excerpted from U.S. House Committee on the Judiciary, Subcommittee on Civil and Constitutional Rights, *English Language Constitutional Amendments: Hearing on H.J. Res. 13, H.J. Res. 33, H.J. Res. 60, and H.J. Res. 83,* 100th Congress, 2d session, May 11, 1988, pp. 67–70.

On the face of it, the establishment of English as our official language seems to be an innocuous endeavor—free of controversy and devoid of any real dangers. However, like the metaphorical patch of quicksand, once you step into the issues surrounding this proposal, the severe problems that accompany this initiative become readily apparent.

We are not in danger of becoming another Quebec, or the national equivalent of the Tower of Babel, as some of my colleagues have suggested. Census data reveal there are fewer non-English-speaking citizens in the United States today than there were in 1900. A 1985 Rand Corporation survey of Mexican Americans, a community often cited during discussions of these amendments, reported that 95 percent of those individuals who were born in the United States are English-proficient. There is nobody more cognizant of the disability of non-English proficiency than the individual who is struggling to make it in this country without being able to speak English. I see no reason, therefore, to enact legislation that would only punish a huge segment of a society for a disability that they themselves are earnestly trying to correct.

I believe that the proposals that have been offered here this morning are unnecessary and unwise. They are unnecessary because it is clear that English is unquestionably our primary language, and I see no evidence that its position, as such, is in danger. They are unwise for two reasons. First, there is the potential that an English Language Amendment could pose significant threats to the civil and constitutional rights of citizens with little or no English proficiency. Second, the proposals represent a concession to nativist instincts and are incompatible with the cultural diversity and ethnic pluralism that constitute fundamental strengths of our nation.

If this amendment were adopted, it is entirely conceivable, if not certain, that the courts of our country could subsequently rule unconstitutional a whole series of legislative measures designed to provide linguistic assistance and relief to those limited number of Americans who are not able to read or converse fluently in English. It is my understanding that the sponsors of these amendments would like to see fewer government programs in languages other than English. I respectfully disagree. On the federal level, several critical statutes could be threatened, including the bilingual ballot provisions of the Voting Rights Act, the Court Interpreters Act, and statutes mandating language services at federally funded migrant-health and substance-abuse centers. Other routine federal services could also be seriously jeopardized, among them the Surgeon General's enlightened policy of sending out his groundbreaking AIDS information mailing in Spanish. The Internal Revenue Service currently uses forms and materials in other languages, as does the Department of Commerce in conducting the census.

The possible consequences of the proposed constitutional amendments are disturbing and, in my view, are not worth risking. There is too real a danger that court rulings and legislation in the wake of such an amendment could undermine the civil rights of millions of Americans. But even if an English Language Amendment were purely symbolic, I would oppose it. Such an amendment would have the perverse effect of making huge segments of our society feel unwanted and *not wanted*, strangers and not citizens. In my view, this amendment would have the very opposite effect than that intended by its authors, by serving to hinder the assimilation of non-English-speaking Americans into the mainstream of our society.

The time-worn cliché dictates that America is a "melting pot." This is no longer an apt description. We are instead a tapestry of many races, creeds, religions, and ethnic backgrounds—each independent, but all interwoven with one another. Like no other country in the world, this diversity creates not a clash of cultures, but a nation in which each culture leaves its own imprint and enriches us all.

I am proud to say that during a walk through my district, one would hear my constituents speaking over a dozen languages, including Yiddish, Russian, Hebrew, Greek, Arabic, Farsi, Polish, Hungarian, German, Spanish, Italian, Haitian Creole, Korean, and Chinese. The glue that bonds these diverse communities together is not commonality of language, but a commitment to the democratic ideals on which our country was founded. Among these principles are freedom of speech, equality of opportunity, and tolerance for minorities.

Proponents of the English Language Amendment have often claimed that the use of other languages in any official capacity dilutes American unity and prevents ethnic groups from participating in the mainstream of our country's economic and political pursuits. I believe that just the opposite is true. During the Second World War, at a time when the very survival of our nation was at stake, when our capacity to defeat the fascist foe depended on our ability to muster all of the resources at our command, the Office of War Information sent out publications in seventeen different languages—Baltic, Chinese, Czechoslovakian, Filipino, Finnish, French, German, Greek, Hungarian, Italian, Japanese, Polish, Portuguese, Scandinavian, Spanish, Serbo-Croatian, and Yiddish. Did anybody say then, at the height of the Second World War with the *Wehrmacht* on the loose, the Japanese Imperial Army rampaging through Asia and the Pacific, that we didn't want the contributions of these Americans in a war effort that would bring us to victory? Of course not. But if there had been an English Language Amendment to the Constitution at that time, we might not have been able to reach out to those people.

Let me give you a more contemporary example. I happen to have in my district in Brooklyn probably the largest number of Russian immigrants in America. Most of them have moved into a neighborhood called Brighton Beach, which they have renamed Odessa-by-the-Sea. Some of them already have become citizens. They are trying to learn English, all of them without exception, but many, particularly the older folks, still can't speak it or read it that well, so they have to rely on Russian. I recently sent out a Congressional newsletter to these people printed in the Cyrillic script because a newsletter in English would not have been understandable to them. In this newsletter I spoke about problems facing those Russian Jews who were still not able to get out of the Soviet Union, and I asked them to let me know of examples of people living in the Soviet Union who had been denied permission to emigrate. Dozens of Soviet Jewish families responded to this newsletter. In their letters to me—most of them also written in Russian—I learned of many *refusenik* cases of which I was previously unaware. I was then able to contact Soviet officials in an effort to expedite their emigration requests.

I believe that this newsletter is a perfect example of why the English Language Amendment—however well-intentioned—is not in the best interests of our nation. I think it passing strange that many of my colleagues in Congress who have joined me in condemning the Soviet Union for stifling expressions of ethnic diversity would support an initiative that could have a similar effect here in the United States. My Russian-speaking constituents have finally arrived in a country that respects pluralism and human rights. They are actively trying to learn English. They are as patriotic as any ethnic group in our nation and are actively involved in our political process. To prevent these individuals—and any other immigrant group—from being able to use their native language a part of any governmental activity would make it harder, not easier, for them to enter the American mainstream. The Congress would commit a grave error if it amended the Constitution in a way that would circumvent the very purposes for which that document was written.

U.S. English

By Guy Wright

Guy Wright is a columnist for the *San Francisco Examiner*, in which this article first appeared on March 28, 1983. A reprint has been widely circulated by U.S. English as part of its direct-mail fundraising appeals (although the passages that appear in italics were deleted from recent reprints).

At last we have a national organization to combat the misnamed bilingual movement. U.S. English, nonprofit and tax-deductible, has opened shop at 1424 16th St., N.W., Washington, D.C. 20036, and welcomes to membership "all who agree that English is and must remain the only official language of the people of the United States."

Or, to put it another way, it will try to speak for those who don't want to see this English-speaking nation turned into a poly-lingual Babel.

Former senator S. I. Hayakawa, who fought this battle almost alone while in Congress, is honorary chairman of U.S. English.

Chairman is Dr. John Tanton, a Michigan physician whose years of concern about population trends and immigration—he founded the Federation for American Immigration Reform—led him to embrace this kindred cause. "With an organizational structure in place, we may at last be able to gain some ground," he said.

It is none too soon. Although there is virtually no public support for the proposition that this country should conduct its affairs in foreign languages for the convenience of those who don't want to learn English, the ethnic leaders pressing that demand are highly organized and single-minded, and they have won every skirmish so far against the disorganized opposition of a general public with many other worries.

Until a few years ago there was no problem. It was taken for granted that everyone who wanted to share in the benefits of American citizenship should learn English. Even today most immigrants realize the value of knowing English and are eager to learn—witness the packed newcomer classes.

The resistance comes from leaders of ethnic blocs, mostly Hispanic, who reject the melting-pot concept, resist assimilation as a betrayal of their ancestral culture, and demand government funding to maintain their ethnic institutions.

We have seen the fruits of their victories. Laws now require multilingual ballots and voting aids, and tax money pays for voter registration campaigns aimed solely at those who will vote in a foreign language.

As for bilingual education, it has fallen into the hands of people less interested in building a bridge to help immigrant children learn English than in building a bridgehead within the school system for foreign-language pressure groups.

This anti-assimilation movement (a more accurate name than bilingualism) comes at a time when the United States is receiving the largest wave of immigration in its history. This influx strains our facilities for assimilation and provides fertile ground for those who would like to turn language minorities into permanent power blocs.

To combat these forces, U.S. English offers this program:

• Adopt a constitutional amendment to establish English as the official language of the United States.

• Repeal laws mandating multilingual ballots and voting materials.

• Restrict government funding for bilingual education to short-term transitional programs only.

• *Control immigration so that it does not reinforce trends toward language segregation.*

U.S. English is no refuge for red-necked chauvinists. Among its guiding principles, it says: "The study of foreign languages should be encouraged," and "the rights of individuals and groups to use other languages must be respected."

But it also says: "In a pluralistic nation such as ours, government should foster the similarities that unite us, rather than the differences that separate us."

Amen.

"Ohio English": A Modest But More Specific and Patriotic Proposal Than the One Offered Recently by U.S. English

By Roger Shuy

Roger Shuy is chairman of the Department of Linguistics at the Georgetown University School of Languages and Linguistics. This rejoinder to Guy Wright is reprinted from *EPIC Events* 1, no. 4 (Sept.–Oct. 1988): 3, 10.

At last we have a national organization to combat the misuses of English within the United States. Dialect variation has run rampant far too long, and it is now under pressure to cease and desist. Ohio English, nonprofit and tax-deductible, has opened shop in Washington, D.C., and welcomes to membership "all who agree that the variety of English spoken in Ohio is the only official dialect of the people of the United States." Or, to put it another way, it will try to speak for those who don't want to see this nation turned into a poly-dialectal Babel.

Although there is virtually no public support for the proposition that this country should conduct its affairs in a wide range of dialects simply for the convenience of those who don't want to learn Ohio English (formerly called General American), the regional leaders pressing for that demand are highly organized and single-minded.

They have attempted to give credence to dialects called Southern, New England, New York Urban, Ozark, Appalachian, Northern, Midland, and even Baltimorese. So far they have won every battle.

Until a few years ago there was no problem. It was taken for granted that anyone who wanted to share in the benefits of American citizenship should learn to talk like Ohioans. The resistance comes mostly from leaders of ethnic blocs, such as the Minnesota Language Institute, the Southern Speech Association, and others, who reject the melting-pot concept, resist assimilation as a betrayal of their ancestral culture, and demand government funding to maintain their ethnic and regional institutions, such as "Prairie Home Companion."

We have seen the fruits of their victories. Commercials on television now are conducted in various regional dialects. Politicians now adjust their speech to the local pronunciations and vocabulary. Of the last six presidents, five have committed regional dialect publicly, the only exception being President Reagan, whose words, spoken without any accent, go largely unnoticed by the public.

The anti-assimilation movement comes at a time when the United States is experiencing the latest wave of migration in the country. Easterners are moving South in particular, learning even worse language habits than before. This influx strains our facilities for assimilation and provides fertile ground for those who would like to turn language minorities into power blocs.

To combat this program, Ohio English offers this program:

• Adopt a constitutional amendment to establish the Ohio dialect as the official dialect of the United States.

• Restrict television commercials that glorify regionalism in speech.

• Require politicians to campaign and serve, if elected, using only good general American Ohio speech.

• Insist that all American teachers spend a semester in Ohio, take remedial courses in Ohio English, and pass the national Ohio English Teacher's Examination.

Ohio English is no refuge for red-necked chauvinists. Among its guiding principles, it says: "The study of dialects should be encouraged. Just as biologists study germs and agronomists carry out research on weeds, so speech variation must be thoroughly understood in order to be effectively wiped out. Meanwhile, Ohio English believes in fair-minded tolerance. Teachers should tolerate regional dialects on the playground, where seriousness is not central. Likewise, regional speech may be permitted in the home, at least for now."

But Ohio English also says: "In a pluralistic nation such as ours, government should foster sameness, the similarities that unite us, rather than the differences that separate us."

Holy Toledo.

Dade County "Antibilingual" Ordinance

Passed by citizen initiative in 1980 (by a vote of 59 to 41 percent), Dade County's is the most restrictive Official English measure ever passed in the United States. It repealed a 1973 resolution declaring the county to be "bilingual and bicultural," and terminated a variety of county services in other languages—from bus schedules to prenatal-care brochures to signs at the Dade Metrozoo. The ordinance was amended in 1984 to permit county expenditures to safeguard public health, cope with emergencies, and promote tourism.

ORDINANCE NO. 80–128. ORDINANCE PROHIBITING THE EXPENDITURE OF COUNTY FUNDS FOR THE PURPOSE OF UTILIZING ANY LANGUAGE OTHER THAN ENGLISH, OR PROMOTING ANY CULTURE OTHER THAN THAT OF THE UNITED STATES; PROVIDING FOR GOVERNMENTAL MEETINGS AND PUBLICATIONS TO BE IN THE ENGLISH LANGUAGE; PROVIDING EXCEPTION; PROVIDING SEVERABILITY, INCLUSION IN THE CODE, AND AN EFFECTIVE DATE.

Be it ordained by the people of Dade County, Florida:

Section 1. The expenditure of county funds for the purpose of utilizing any language other than English, or promoting any culture other than that of the United States, is prohibited.

Section 2. All county governmental meetings, hearings, and publications shall be in the English language only.

Section 3. The provisions of this ordinance shall not apply where a translation is mandated by state or federal law.

Section 4. If any section, subsection, sentence, clause, phrase, words or provision of this ordinance is held invalid or unconstitutional, the remainder of this ordinance shall not be affected by said holding.

Section 5. It is the intention of the people of Dade County, Florida, that the provisions of this ordinance shall become and be made a part of the code of Metropolitan Dade County, Florida.

Section 6. This ordinance shall take effect on the day after the election approving this ordinance, November 5, 1980.

PASSED AND ADOPTED: NOVEMBER 4, 1980.

State Official Language Statutes and Constitutional Amendments

At the state level, Official English has taken the form of both one-liners and more proscriptive legislation. Seventeen such measures had been adopted by 1990 (all but two of which were passed since 1980). Most of these were statutes (Arkansas, Illinois, Indiana, Kentucky, Mississippi, North Carolina, North Dakota, South Carolina, Tennessee, and Virginia), while six were constitutional amendments (Alabama, Arizona, California, Colorado, Florida, and Nebraska), and one was a nonbinding resolution (Georgia). Hawaii, sometimes erroneously counted as an Official English state, declared itself officially bilingual in 1978.

Arizona State Constitution (1988)[35]

Article XXVIII

Section 1. English as the Official Language; Applicability

(1) The English language is the official language of the State of Arizona.

(2) As the official language of this State, the English language is the language of the ballot, the public schools, and all government functions and actions.

(3) (a) This Article applies to:

(i) the legislative, executive, and judicial branches of government;

(ii) all political subdivisions, departments, agencies, organizations, and instrumentalities of this State, including local governments and municipalities;

(iii) all statutes, ordinances, rules, orders, programs, and policies;

(iv) all government officials and employees during the performance of government business.

(b) As used in this Article, the phrase "This State and all political subdivisions of this State" shall include every entity, person, action, or item described in this Section, as appropriate to the circumstances.

Section 2. Requiring This State to Preserve, Protect, and Enhance English

This State and all political subdivisions of this State shall take all reasonable steps to preserve, protect, and enhance the role of the En-

---

35. Adopted by voter initiative on Nov. 8, 1988, this amendment was struck down as unconstitutional by a federal judge on Feb. 6, 1990 *(see pp. 287–91).*

glish language as the sole official language of the State of Arizona.

Section 3. Prohibiting This State from Using or Requiring the Use of Languages Other Than English; Exceptions

(1) Except as provided in Subsection (2):

(a) This State and all political subdivisions of this state shall act in English and no other language.

(b) No entity to which this Article applies shall make or enforce a law, order, decree, or policy which requires the use of a language other than English.

(c) No governmental document shall be valid or enforceable unless it is in the English language.

(2) This State and all political subdivisions of this State may act in a language other than English under any of the following circumstances:

(a) to assist students who are not proficient in the English language, to the extent necessary to comply with federal law, by giving educational instruction in a language other than English to provide as rapid as possible a transition to English;

(b) to comply with other federal laws;

(c) to teach a student a foreign language as part of a required or voluntary educational curriculum;

(d) to protect public health or safety;

(e) to protect the rights of criminal defendants or victims of crime.

Section 4. Enforcement; Standing

A person who resides in or does business in this State shall have standing to bring suit to enforce this Article in a court of record of the State. The Legislature may enact reasonable limitations on the time and manner of bringing suit under this subsection.

Arkansas Annotated Code (1987)

Section 1–4–117

(a) The English language shall be the official language of the State of Arkansas.

(b) This section shall not prohibit the public schools from performing their duty to provide equal educational opportunities to all children.

California State Constitution (1986)

Article III, Section 6

(a) *Purpose*

English is the common language of the people of the United States of America and the State of California. This section is intended to preserve, protect and strengthen the English language, and not to supersede any of the rights guaranteed to the people by this Constitution.

(b) *English as the Official Language of California*

English is the official language of the State of California.

(c) *Enforcement*

The Legislature shall enforce this section by appropriate legislation. The Legislature and officials of the State of California shall take all steps necessary to insure that the role of English as the common language of the State of California is preserved and enhanced. The Legislature shall make no law which diminishes or ignores the role of English as the common language of the State of California.

(d) *Personal Right of Action and Jurisdiction of Courts*

Any person who is a resident of or doing business in the State of California shall have standing to sue the State of California to enforce this section, and the Courts of record of the State of California shall have jurisdiction to hear cases brought to enforce this section. The Legislature may provide reasonable and appropriate limitations on the time and manner of suits brought under this section.

Colorado State Constitution (1988)

Article II, Section 30

The English language is the official language of the State of Colorado. This section is self-executing; however, the General Assembly may enact laws to implement this section.

Florida State Constitution (1988)

Article II, Section 9

(a) English is the official language of the State of Florida.

(b) The Legislature shall have the power to enforce this section by appropriate legislation.

Hawaii State Constitution (1978)

Article XV, Section 4

English and Hawaiian shall be the official languages of Hawaii, except that Hawaiian shall be required for public acts and transactions only as provided by law.

Illinois Annotated Statutes (1969)[36]

Chapter 1, Section 3005
The official language of the State of Illinois is English.

Nebraska State Constitution (1920)

Article I, Section 27
The English Language is hereby declared to be the official language of this State, and all official proceedings, records and publications shall be in such language, and the common school branches shall be taught in said language in public, private, denominational and parochial schools.

Code of Virginia (1981)

Section 22.1–212.1
English shall be designated as the Official Language of the Commonwealth of Virginia. School boards shall have no obligation to teach the standard curriculum, except courses in foreign languages, in a language other than English. School boards shall endeavor to provide instruction in the English language which shall be designed to promote the education of students for whom English is a second language.

Prop. 63 Deserves Approval

San Francisco Examiner, October 24, 1986

There is a curious aspect to the battle over Proposition 63, the proposal to designate English as the official state language. This is supposed to be one of the high-voltage issues on the ballot, as suggested by the emotional heat being generated in arguments for and against. But the heat is altogether on the peripheries; the public is, from all indications, unaffected by the noisy debate. This is because the public

---

36. This statute, which repealed a 1923 law declaring "American" to be the state's official language, was ruled to have no legal impact on bilingual voting materials in *PROPA v. Kusper (see pp. 267–68).*

for once has its mind made up. On November 4 the voters will—and should, we think—approve this proposition.

The polls show an overwhelming support; there is no stopping Proposition 63. Nor, after the returns are in, and through the months and years ahead, will the dark prophecies of the opponents ever materialize. This measure will not become, as they say now, an implement of racism, a tool for discrimination along ethnic lines. To the contrary, it will work to the vast benefit of immigrants and others in our society whose prospects for livelihood too often are crippled by deficiency in the language that propels this country's economic life and its major activities otherwise.

This state constitutional amendment will serve to disabuse anyone of the nonsense, which otherwise might arise in future years, that multilingualism is a credible option in the larger affairs of California. The unforgettable message from the public majority—engraved as state policy—will be that people who want to succeed need to learn the common language, quickly and thoroughly. It is a message of practicality, not of ethnocentricity. The majority that favors this proposition is not racist or xenophobic, but simply realistic. We think the California majority wants to *help* immigrants to assimilate and succeed, rather than to raise a barrier against them. This is a law to help improve the melting pot, not interfere with it.

True enough, a large majority of immigrants is learning English rapidly and has a passion to do so, but some newcomers are neglecting this imperative. And while there is no push for a legal division of languages, there is some pressure to insert legal concessions to linguistic division (as on juries).

Proposition 63 requires state government to take "all steps necessary to insure that the role of English as the common language of the State of California is preserved and enhanced." It rules out any law "which diminishes or ignores" that role *(see pp. 133–34)*. Actually, the measure does not reduce anyone's constitutional rights, or forbid the teaching of foreign languages. Nor do we think it would, as some people charge, eliminate bilingual education in public schools. Rather, it could be a spur to more intensive and effective bilingual education, of the kind that gets quicker results in the teaching of English to newcomers than do some of the slow-motion bilingual curricula. No one should look upon Proposition 63 as an insult to ethnic identity: anyone can retain such identity. This initiative just asserts the obvious—that the citizen who does not become proficient in English is lost in the competition for higher achievement in this state.

Also, it expresses the conviction that the common language is the glue that helps to hold a society together. The frightful problems of some nations that are divided linguistically attest to the wisdom of the common-language thesis, even though some immigrants may feel that such a common designation denigrates their original languages. It does not. The long-term practicalities of national cohesion and the advancement of immigrants in American life, through linguistic assimilation, need to take precedence over temporary emotional responses. Proposition 63 should be given a strong "yes" vote.

Language Purity

Bangor Daily News, November 14, 1986

Frightened by Spanish-speaking immigrants flowing across its border, California last week became the eighth state to declare English its official language. Whatever that means will be left up to the state's legislature. Supporters of the measure hope to use their success to launch a nationwide drive.

Untouched by the southern border's hysteria over Hispanic-speaking immigrants, Mainers are in a better position to coolly assess the need for such a declaration. Despite a large French-speaking population, English remains the language of choice here. You can still hear French spoken on the streets of Madawaska, Lewiston, and a few other communities, but English is overwhelmingly dominant. The vast majority of younger Franco-Americans today are either bilingual or have lost their ability to speak French. The assimilation occurred for a simple reason: In order to enter the economic mainstream in the United States, people need a working knowledge of the English language.

Mainers might be tempted to vote for such an official English-language dictum with a shrug of the shoulders. They should pause a moment, however, and remember the atmosphere that existed in this state caused apparently by the kinds of fears infecting states like California. A state law until recently prohibited teaching in public schools any language but English (except in foreign language classes). In effect, it banned even bilingual educational programs aimed at helping students learn English! In some school systems in the St. John River Valley, the law was interpreted as a ban on speaking French on school property altogether. French-speaking children actually were punished.

Mainers are more tolerant today. Most people would want to avoid the excesses of the past that bordered on xenophobia—the fear or hatred of anything foreign. Telling children they couldn't speak their language on school property, or discouraging them from maintaining their proficiency, was an insult and an overreaction. The irony is that Maine is all the poorer for the loss of this bilingual, bicultural aspect of its population. One of the main problems facing America and its educational system today is not too many different languages, but too many people who only speak one language.

Legislating Language

Denver Post, January 6, 1987

At first glance, the "English only" bill to be put before the Colorado legislature this month looks like a celebration of the obvious. To declare that English is "the official language of the state of Colorado," as the one-sentence bill proposes, would seem akin to proclaiming the Denver Broncos the city's official football team. It's such a dominant force that it hardly needs an imprimatur.

But many supporters of the "official language" concept aren't really concerned about English per se. They're worried about the flood of immigration from Latin America, and the threat this may pose to the nation's cultural integrity. Specifically, they fear that the growth of Hispanic ghettos in cities like Los Angeles and Miami—where Spanish-speaking aliens may live for years without ever learning English—eventually may fracture the body politic in the same way that French speakers in Quebec have weakened the sense of national unity in Canada. In addition, concerned politicians like Governor Dick Lamm have argued that immigrants who fail to learn English and assimilate in the society are a "social time bomb," composed of millions of ill-educated, poverty-stricken, and alienated foreigners on American soil.

It seems to us that one self-evident fact of life in the U.S.—to get ahead, you have to be fluent in English—should give anyone a pretty strong incentive to learn the language. But even if today's immigrants don't turn out to realize this, as previous generations of newcomers have, will an "English only" rule do the trick? Most likely not. If anything, scrapping the bilingual approach will make it even harder for the hordes of new arrivals to assimilate. One way of picking up the mother tongue, after all, is to see Spanish and English side by side—on everything from ballots to utility bills.

More important, the strident rhetoric of the "official language" folks conveys a discouraging air of cultural arrogance that can easily be interpreted as racism by those for whom English is a second language. By inviting the state to say "shut up"—presumably in a foreign language, so it can be understood—to anyone who walks in the door speaking a foreign language, it offers a phony solution to an exaggerated problem.

In a year when there are so many constructive challenges facing lawmakers, this divisive legislation would only waste valuable time and create needless tension. The legislature should give this ill-conceived bill a deaf ear.

English-Only a Mistake: Amendment Sends Wrong Message to Tourists

Palm Beach Post, September 4, 1988

It is good that opponents of the English-language amendment to the state constitution are gearing up to tell their side of the story. Unless the voters understand what a terrible mistake such an amendment would be, they might be talked into doing something that could cripple both tourism and foreign trade.

A lot of Floridians appear to be uncomfortable with the growing Hispanic presence in the state. In particular, they believe a large proportion of Hispanics are not learning to speak English. That is not true—when people are heard speaking Spanish on the street, it usually means simply that they are more comfortable in their native language—but it is widely believed nonetheless.

The proposed solution to this nonproblem is a constitutional amendment declaring English to be the state's official language. Proponents of the measure, which will be on the November ballot, insist that it does nothing except encourage people to learn English. Is that all? What about the sentence that says, "The Legislature shall have the power to enforce this section by appropriate legislation" (see p. 134)? What does that mean?

Can the legislature forbid the use of bilingual or multilingual signs in airports or cruise-ship terminals? What about hospital emergency rooms? What happens to someone who disobeys the law?

The answer is that, in terms of the law, the effect probably will be minimal at worst. The legislature is unlikely to pass any draconian laws and, if it did, the laws would be vetoed. This last is especially true as long as Bob Martínez, a man of Hispanic ancestry who opposes the amendment, sits in the governor's office.

Where the amendment *will* hurt is in sending a message that Florida doesn't like people who don't speak English. Coming atop the bad press the state already has received for its lax gun laws, that can only do more damage to an economy dependent in large part on tourism.

A briefing paper put out by opponents of the amendment notes that two million foreign tourists spent more than $1 billion in Florida last year, while the state exported more than $11 billion in goods, mostly to Venezuela, Colombia, Brazil, and the Dominican Republic. That's a lot of economic activity to jeopardize, especially based on a misconception.

Vote No on Bigotry

Tempe Daily News Tribune, October 22, 1988

Politics is often a realm of nuance, compromise, grays, and maybes. It is a world rarely populated by things that are clearly good and clearly bad. Arizona has been treated to an exception to the rule in the form of Proposition 106. Without ifs, buts, or maybes, this proposal is bad stuff, to be clearly and simply rejected by the voters of this state on November 8.

Critics of the measure produce volumes of problems with the proposition. They name grief after grief that would be visited upon the state under such a jingoistic and draconian amendment to the constitution. Adults seeking to learn English would be turned away because the amendment would forbid the use of foreign languages by government entities. Those facing civil court proceedings, such as divorce, liability, accident damage, would not be eligible for a state-supplied translator. So the poor who don't speak English would simply be out of luck in trying to pursue their rights in civil court. The use of foreign languages in tourism and economic development efforts by the state might well be banned under the amendment. There is every reason to believe that an Arizona governor on an official mission to Mexico could not give a speech in Spanish, much less have her paid staff produce the speech.

Proponents of the proposition give a standard rebuttal to all of these criticisms and more. They say that the amendment would really have no effect at all. So why bother? Why all the efforts, all the money spent to promote the Official English measure? Why hire people and pay them as much as $1 per signature to circulate petitions to put the measure on the ballot?

The Proposition 106 proponents' rebuttal of the criticisms is disingenuous. They know exactly what it will do. It will set up a two-tiered social and legal system in Arizona. Instead of encouraging non-English-speaking people to learn English and move into the mainstream of social, economic, and political life in this state, the amendment will force those people to hide their language deficiency, make them into second-class citizens. Above all, and this is most important to the most zealous supporters of this proposition, it will make it clear just who's boss around here. It will codify racial and cultural bias. It will steep in constitutional legitimacy the illegitimate notion that personal worth is based upon the color of one's skin, the place of one's birth, and the language one speaks.

The promoters of this mean-spirited proposition don't want those who don't speak English to learn the language. They want them to go back home. They want them to leave or, at the very least, they want others like them to stay home and not come here in the first place.

The intentions behind this national campaign—and make no mistake, that's exactly what this is, not some home-grown, grassroots exercise in democracy—have been laid bare by recent revelations and resignations at the very top of the organization promulgating this institutionalized bigotry. The resignations of Walter Cronkite from the advisory board of U.S. English, of organization president Linda Chávez, and finally, of founder John Tanton document how fast this house of cards has crumbled under scrutiny. Tanton's bigoted paranoia about "those with their pants up being caught by those with their pants down" is sufficient evidence that this proposition is no warm-hearted effort to keep America's melting pot perking along.

It's rare that citizens get such a clear-cut opportunity to strike a blow against xenophobia, bigotry, and elitism. They can strike that blow with a resounding "no" on Proposition 106 November 8.

Ruling Upholds Need to Respect Free Speech

San Antonio Light, February 9, 1990

"Official English" efforts pushed by groups who are uncomfortable with the bilingual nature of the Southwest United States always have had a troubling undertone. These groups have sought to plant the suspicion that something is not quite right about people who speak a language other than English in their everyday lives. Aside from ignoring the historical fact that Spanish has been spoken in the Southwest for more than 400 years, the Official English groups are a divisive element in a region where Hispanic traditions and culture are cherished and nurtured.

Now a federal judge in Arizona has added another element to the debate over language usage. U.S. District Judge Paul Rosenblatt ruled this week that Arizona's Official English law is unconstitutional. Rosenblatt said the imposition of such a law violates the U.S. Constitution's First Amendment guarantees of free speech *(see pp. 287–91).*

The impact of Rosenblatt's ruling is hard to foresee. Sixteen other states have some sort of Official English laws, and generally, these measures are probably harmless, even if they are unnecessary. But in states like Texas, California, and Arizona, where growing Hispanic populations are gaining new power and influence, Official English measures are politically explosive matters better left in the domain of usually well-meaning but misguided English-advocacy groups.

In Texas, there are periodic efforts to bring forth Official English laws. Discussions of these proposed measures invariably find their way into political campaigns. Kent Hance, a Texas Republican running for governor, this week deflected criticism that he is for an "English Only" law, but did say he supports a proposal to designate English as the "official" language of the state. The line of difference between these two positions appears to be very narrow indeed. We hope Judge Rosenblatt's ruling will discourage the efforts of Hance and others who seek to impose an antagonistic language mandate in a state where the Spanish language is not only used as a means to conduct business and commerce, but is a badge of cultural pride as well.

There can be no argument about whether English is the language of this state and nation. It is the language that binds us together, the language every American must learn to succeed and prosper. It is not, despite what the English Only groups contend, a language under siege, but rather the dominant language in regions like the Southwest that are a blend of different cultures and influences. English will endure as this nation's language because of its acknowledged place as the voice by which all Americans can communicate with each other. No law is needed to tell us the obvious, and there is most certainly no need for language laws that would insult so many citizens who speak a second language.

Judge Rosenblatt's ruling should be a reminder not only of the constitutional values Americans hold so dear, but also of the wonderful diversity inherent in this nation. Both of these American cornerstones should be honored and respected with tolerance and understanding.

In Defense of Our Common Language . . .

By U.S. English

U.S. English, the largest and oldest lobby promoting Official English, describes itself as "a national, nonprofit, nonpartisan organization . . . founded to defend the public interest in the growing debate on bilingualism and biculturalism." It used the following text as its basic fundraising brochure from 1984 until 1988.

English, Our Common Bond

Throughout its history, the United States has been enriched by the cultural contributions of immigrants from many traditions, but blessed with one common language that has united a diverse nation and fostered harmony among its people.

As much by accident as by design, that language is English. Given our country's history of immigration and the geography of immigrant settlements, it might have been Dutch, or Spanish, or German; or it might have been two languages, as is the case in Canada, our neighbor to the North.

But English prevailed, and it has served us well. Its eloquence shines in our Declaration of Independence and in our Constitution. It is the living carrier of our democratic ideals.

English is a world language which we share with many other nations. It is the most popular medium of international communication.

The Spread of Language Segregation

The United States has been spared the bitter conflicts that plague so many countries whose citizens do not share a common tongue. Historic forces made English the language of all Americans, though nothing in our laws designated it the official language of the nation.

But now English is under attack, and we must take affirmative steps to guarantee that it continues to be our common heritage. Failure to do so may well lead to institutionalized language segregation and a gradual loss of national unity.

The erosion of English and the rise of other languages in public life have several causes:

• Some spokesmen for ethnic groups reject the "melting pot" ideal; they label assimilation a betrayal of their native cultures and demand government funding to maintain separate ethnic institutions.

• Well-intentioned but unproven theories have led to extensive government-funded bilingual education programs, ranging from preschool through college.

• New civil rights assertions have yielded bilingual and multilingual ballots, voting instructions, election site counselors, and government-funded voter registration campaigns aimed solely at speakers of foreign languages.

• Record immigration, concentrated in fewer language groups, is reinforcing language segregation and retarding language assimilation.

• The availability of foreign language electronic media, with a full range of news and entertainment, is a new disincentive to the learning of English.

U.S. English: A Timely Public Response

In 1981, Senator S. I. Hayakawa, himself an immigrant and distinguished scholar of semantics, proposed a constitutional amendment designating English as the official language of the United States. Senator Hayakawa helped found U.S. English in 1983 to organize and support a citizens' movement to maintain our common linguistic heritage.

U.S. English is committed to promoting the use of English in the political, economic, and intellectual life of the nation. It operates squarely within the American political mainstream, and rejects all manifestations of cultural or linguistic chauvinism.

Our Guiding Principles

Our goal is to maintain the blessing of a common language—English—for the people of the United States. These principles guide us:

• In a pluralistic nation such as ours, government should foster the similarities that unite us rather than the differences that separate us.
• The nation's public schools have a special responsibility to help students who don't speak English to learn the language as quickly as possible.
• Quality teaching of English should be part of every student's curriculum, at every academic level.
• The study of foreign languages should be strongly encouraged, both as an academic discipline and for practical, economic, and foreign policy considerations.
• *All* candidates for U.S. citizenship should be required to demonstrate the ability to understand, speak, read, and write simple English, and demonstrate basic understanding of our system of government.
• The rights of individuals and groups to use other languages and to establish *privately funded* institutions for the maintenance of diverse languages and cultures must be respected in a pluralistic society.

Our Action Program

U.S. English actively works to reverse the spread of foreign language usage in the nation's official life. Our program calls for:

• Adoption of a constitutional amendment to establish English as the official language of the United States.
• Repeal of laws mandating multilingual ballots and voting materials.
• Restriction of government funding for bilingual education to short-term transitional programs only.
• Universal enforcement of the English language and civics requirement for naturalization.
• Expansion of opportunities for learning English.

Towards these ends, U.S. English serves as a national center for consultation and cooperation on ways to defend English as the sole official language of the United States. It directs its efforts to leading a public discussion on the best language policies for our multiethnic society; educating opinion leaders on the long-term implications of language segregation; encouraging research on improved methods of teaching English; and promoting effective programs of English language instruction.

We Need Your Help

U.S. English welcomes to membership all who are concerned about the prospect of entrenched language segregation and the possibility of losing our strongest national bond.

We hope that you will join us and defend our common language against misguided policies that threaten our national unity.

What Others Are Saying

"We have room for but one language here and that is the English language, for we intend to see that the crucible turns our people out as American, of American nationality, and not as dwellers in a polyglot boarding house."

Theodore Roosevelt

"People can live with language differences, as Switzerland has shown. But if these differences are politicized, as for example in Belgium, Canada, and Sri Lanka, a nation can be torn apart. Sri Lanka has decided on English as a national language, so that speakers of Sinhalese and Tamil can communicate with one another and with the world outside. Can we not be warned by the experience of other nations? Can we not unite on English as our national language by law as well as by custom, so that our nation shall not be torn asunder in the decades and centuries to come?"

S. I. Hayakawa

"A new bilingualism and biculturalism is being promulgated that would deliberately fragment the nation into separate, unassimilated groups . . . The new metaphor is not the melting pot but the salad bowl, with each element distinct. The biculturalists seek to use public services, particularly schools, not to Americanize the young but to heighten their consciousness of belonging to another heritage.

William A. Henry III
Time, June 13, 1983

". . . the valid historical basis and modern rationale for conducting governmental affairs in English is clear: the national language of the United States is English."

Judge Edward R. Neaher
U.S. District Court
Eastern District of New York

"You can be born here in a Cuban hospital, be baptized by a Cuban priest, buy all your food from a Cuban grocer, take your insurance from a Cuban bank. You can get all the news in Spanish—read the Spanish daily paper, watch Spanish TV, listen to Spanish radio. You can go through life without having to speak English at all. . . . It works because citizenship is what makes us all American. Language is not necessary to the system. Nowhere does the Constitution say that English is our language."

Mayor Maurice Ferré of Miami
Esquire, May 1983

"Look! They are one people and there is one language for them all. . . . Come now! Let us go down there and confuse their language that they may not listen to one another's language."

The Tower of Babel, Genesis 11:6–7

U.S. English[37]

Board of Directors

Senator S. I. Hayakawa, Honorary Chairman
John H. Tanton, M.D., Chairman
Linda Chávez, President

Gerda Bikales
Stanley Diamond
Leo Sorensen

Board of Advisors

Walter Annenberg
Clarence Barnhart
Jacques Barzun
Saul Bellow
Bruno Bettelheim
Alistair Cooke
Denton Cooley
Joseph V. Corcoran
Walter Cronkite
Angier Biddle Duke

André Emmerich
George Gilder
Sidney Hook
Barbara Mujica
Mrs. Eugene Ormandy
Norman Podhoretz
Karl Shapiro
Arnold Schwarzenegger
W. Clement Stone
Rosalyn Yalow

U.S. English is a project of U.S., a voluntary association of public interest groups sharing overhead and organizational skills for greater cost effectiveness. All contributions to U.S. English are fully tax deductible.

37. Editor's note: John Tanton, Linda Chávez, and Walter Cronkite resigned in Oct. 1988 (*see pp. 171–77*).

Resolution on Language Rights

By the Teachers of English to Speakers of Other Languages

This statement in opposition to Official English was adopted on April 24, 1987, by the Teachers of English to Speakers of Other Languages (TESOL), which describes itself as "an international professional organization for those concerned with the teaching of English as a second or foreign language and of Standard English as a second dialect."

WHEREAS TESOL is an organization which promotes programs that provide for speakers of other languages the opportunity to learn English; and

WHEREAS TESOL supports the study of other languages for native English speakers; and

WHEREAS, in recognition of the rights of all individuals to preserve and foster their linguistic and cultural origins, TESOL also supports learners of English maintaining their native tongues during and after their learning of English; and

WHEREAS these rights have been affirmed by such international organizations as UNESCO and the European Economic Community and in such international treaties as the Helsinki Accord; and

WHEREAS several states within the United States of America have enacted and other states and the U.S. Congress are considering legislative measures which could be used to deny these basic language rights; and

WHEREAS the considerable resources being spent to promote and implement English Only policies in the United States of America could be allocated more effectively for language instruction, including English as a second language, at all educational levels and within all educational settings;

THEREFORE BE IT RESOLVED that TESOL support measures which protect the right of all individuals to preserve and foster their linguistic and cultural origins;

BE IT FURTHER RESOLVED that TESOL oppose all measures declaring English the official language of the United States of America or of any legally constituted part thereof; and

FINALLY BE IT RESOLVED that TESOL circulate this resolution to its affiliates and interest sections, to other professional organizations, and to appropriate public officials, especially those officials in localities where policies counter to the principles established in this resolution are being considered.

WE IN TESOL STRONGLY BELIEVE THAT THIS RESOLUTION REAFFIRMS THE HIGHEST IDEALS AND TRADITIONS OF OUR PROFESSION AS TEACHERS OF ENGLISH TO SPEAKERS OF OTHER LANGUAGES—NAMELY THAT ALL INDIVIDUALS HAVE THE OPPORTUNITY TO ACQUIRE PROFICIENCY IN ENGLISH WHILE MAINTAINING THEIR OWN LANGUAGE AND CULTURE.

Resolution Opposing Official English/ English Only Measures

By the Mexican American Legal Defense and Educational Fund

This resolution was adopted on April 28, 1989, by the board of the Mexican American Legal Defense and Educational Fund (MALDEF), a national civil rights organization.

WHEREAS MALDEF was founded in 1968 as a legal advocacy organization dedicated to the protection and advancement of the civil and constitutional rights of Hispanics and other ethnic/language minorities; and

WHEREAS there is a well-organized and well-financed campaign to restrict the civil rights of Hispanics and other ethnic/language minorities by establishing English as the official language of the United States, much of which is motivated by racism and anti-immigrant sentiments; and

WHEREAS the current Official English/English Only movement has declared its intention to eliminate a full range of language assistance policies and programs that permit limited-English-proficient Americans meaningful participation in the life of this nation; and

WHEREAS the Official English/English Only movement seeks to restrict the non-English language resources of the nation at a time when language diversity is essential to the ability of the United States to compete in the global economy; and

WHEREAS this Official English/English Only movement seeks to accomplish its goal of restricting the civil and constitutional rights of ethnic/language minorities by the passage of English Only legal measures at the state and local level and as an amendment to the United States Constitution; and

WHEREAS several states have recently passed constitutional measures making English the official state language, several other states are considering such measures, and several such measures are pending in the Congress;

WHEREAS many Hispanics and other ethnic/language minorities have experienced restrictions and have been harassed in the workplace and denied access to government and to important social services as a result of such measures, including the denial of bilingual emergency services, court interpreters, fire prevention information, housing assistance, voting, and education; and

WHEREAS the burden of this discrimination falls most heavily on the Hispanic young and elderly; and

WHEREAS immigrants and refugees have consistently expressed that their first three priorities in the United States are learning English, securing employment, and obtaining housing; and

WHEREAS the Official English/English Only movement has not wholly supported the learning of English, but instead has concentrated on conditioning social and political benefits and rights on English and mandated the governmental use of English; and

WHEREAS the courts have not been consistent in recognizing and accepting language discrimination as a sufficient basis for litigation;

BE IT THEREFORE RESOLVED that the Mexican American Legal Defense and Educational Fund opposes Official English/English Only measures on the grounds that such measures:

• discriminate against ethnic and language minorities under the guise of enhancing English;

• promote and encourage fear, misunderstanding, and intolerance of persons of different cultures and ethnicities who are not yet fully proficient in English;

• create divisiveness, hostility, and resentment within communities;

• insult and belittle the contributions of Hispanics and other ethnic/language minorities to this country and by questioning their loyalty;

• effectively establish a second-class citizenship status on the basis of English language ability;

• misrepresent the multilingual and multicultural history and character of this nation by implying that this country has always been unilingual in character; and

• undermine the development of languages other than English as resources of the nation essential to international commerce, diplomacy, and national security.

BE IT FURTHER RESOLVED that MALDEF reaffirms our commitment to bilingual education, bilingual ballots, and other official or unofficial language-assistance policies and practices that maintain the integrity of our democracy by ensuring all members of society with an equal opportunity to exercise their rights and responsibilities.

BE IT FURTHER RESOLVED that MALDEF supports the learning of English for those persons in our community who do not speak it.

BE IT FURTHER RESOLVED that MALDEF affirms the following principles:

• individuals have a right to be free from discrimination based on language; and
• language is a national origin characteristic; and
• federal, state, and local governments have a shared responsibility to ensure that non-English-proficient and limited-English-proficient individuals are provided with the opportunity to become proficient in English.

BE IT FURTHER RESOLVED that MALDEF develop a comprehensive plan to address language discrimination and to defeat Official English/English Only measures on the federal, state, or local level.

The English Plus Alternative

By the English Plus Information Clearinghouse

This "Statement of Purpose" is the founding document of the English Plus Information Clearinghouse (EPIC), a coalition of more than fifty civil rights and educational organizations opposed to Official English. EPIC was established in 1987 under the auspices of the National Immigration, Refugee, and Citizenship Forum and the Joint National Committee for Languages.

The core of the strength and vitality of the United States is the diversity of our people and our constitutional commitment to equal protection under the law. Now, more than ever, our commitment to cultural and democratic pluralism is essential to enhance our competitiveness and position of international leadership. In an interdependent world, the diversity of our people provides a unique reservoir of understanding and talent. In order to sustain and strengthen these values and the national interest, the undersigned organizations[38] have come together to address more effectively the role of language in the national and international community. . . .

The English Plus concept holds that the national interest can best be served when all members of our society have full access to effective opportunities to acquire strong English language proficiency *plus* mastery of a second or multiple languages. . . . English Plus rejects the ideology and divisive character of the so-called English Only movement. English Plus holds that national unity and our constitutional values require that language assistance be made available in order to ensure equal access to essential services, education, the electoral process, and other rights and opportunities guaranteed to all members of society. . . .

In establishing EPIC, the founding member organizations have agreed to the following resolution:

WHEREAS English is and will remain the primary language of the United States, and all members of our society recognize the importance of English to national life, individual accomplishment, and personal enrichment; and

WHEREAS many U.S. citizens have native languages other than English, including many languages indigenous to this continent, and many members of our society have not had an equal opportunity to learn English; and

WHEREAS the ability to communicate in English and other languages has promoted and can further enhance American economic, political, and cultural vitality, and contributes to our nation's productivity, worldwide competitiveness, successful international diplomacy, and national security; and

---

38. Editor's note: The founding endorsers of EPIC were: the American Civil Liberties Union, American Jewish Committee, American Jewish Congress, Caribbean Education and Legal Defense Fund, Center for Applied Linguistics, Chinese for Affirmative Action, Coloradans for Language Freedom, Committee for a Multilingual New York, Conference on College Composition and Communication, Christian Church (Disciples of Christ), El Concilio de El Paso, Haitian American Anti-Defamation League, Haitian Refugee Center, Image de Denver, IRATE (Coalition of Massachusetts Trade Unions), Mexican American Legal Defense and Educational Fund, Michigan English Plus Coalition, META (Multicultural Education, Training, and Advocacy) Inc., National Association for Bilingual Education, National Coalition of Advocates for Students, National Council of La Raza, National Puerto Rican Coalition, New York Association for New Americans, Organization of Chinese Americans, Spanish-Speaking/Surnamed Political Association, Stop English Only Committee of Hostos Community College, Teachers of English to Speakers of Other Languages.

WHEREAS our fundamental values and national documents ensure tolerance and respect for diversity and guarantee all persons equal protection under the law; and

WHEREAS English Only and other restrictionist language legislation have the potential for abridging the citizen's right to vote, eroding other civil rights, fostering governmental interference in private activity and free commerce, and causing social disunity; and

WHEREAS the organizations establishing the English Plus Information Clearinghouse are committed to the principles of democratic and cultural pluralism and encourage respect for the cultural and linguistic heritages of all members of our society;

BE IT RESOLVED THAT:

1. There is a need for a vastly expanded network of facilities for comprehensive English language instruction and services to ensure all persons the ability to exercise the rights and responsibilities of full participation in society.

2. There is a need to foster multiple language skills among all of our people in order to promote our position in the world marketplace and to strengthen the conduct of foreign relations.

3. There is a need to encourage the retention and development of a person's first language, to build upon the multiple language skills of all members of our society, and to strengthen our commitment to cultural and democratic pluralism.

4. There is a need to retain and strengthen the full range of language assistance policies and programs, including bilingual assistance, in order to ensure all members of society an equal opportunity to exercise their rights and responsibilities in regard to the electoral process, education, the legal system, social services, and health care.

5. There is a need to reject the objectives and premises of English Only and promote the concept of English Plus in order to promote public civility and the fundamental values and objectives of our society.

6. There is a need to defeat any legislative initiative on the federal, state, or local level which would mandate English as the official language and thereby restrict the civil rights, civil liberties, or equal opportunities of all persons, including persons with limited English proficiency.

7. There is a need for an English Plus Information Clearinghouse to facilitate and enhance: the exchange of information, public education, advocacy, effective policies and programs, and cooperation among a wide range of communities, private organizations, and public sector entities.

English Plus Resolution

By the New Mexico Legislature

State declarations of Official English produced a counter-trend: legislative endorsement of English Plus. In March 1989, at the urging of the New Mexico State Task Force on Modern and Classical Languages, the New Mexico legislature adopted House Joint Memorial 16, a nonbinding resolution "Supporting Language Rights in the United States."

WHEREAS the people of New Mexico promote the spirit of diversity-with-harmony represented by the various cultures that make up the fabric of our state and American society; and

WHEREAS the people of New Mexico acknowledge that "English Plus" best serves the national interest since it promotes the concept that all members of our society have full access to opportunities to effectively learn English plus develop proficiency in a second or multiple languages; and

WHEREAS the people of New Mexico recognize that the position of English in the United States needs no official legislation to support it; and

WHEREAS the people of New Mexico recognize that for survival in the twenty-first century our country needs both the preservation of the cultures and languages among us and the fostering of proficiency in other languages on the part of its citizens;

Now THEREFORE BE IT RESOLVED . . . that the First Session of the Thirty-Ninth Legislature of the State of New Mexico hereby reaffirms its advocacy of the teaching of other languages in the United States and its belief that the position of English is not threatened. Proficiency on the part of our citizens in more than one language is to the economic and cultural benefit of our state and the nation, whether that proficiency derives from second language study by English speakers or from home language maintenance plus English acquisition by speakers of other languages. Proficiency in English plus other languages should be encouraged throughout the State.

Native American Language Act

A federal policy statement recognizing the language rights of American Indians, Alaskan Natives, Native Hawaiians, and Pacific Islanders living in U.S. trust territories was quietly enacted in the waning hours of the 101st Congress. Sponsored by Senator Daniel Inouye, Democrat of Hawaii, the bill passed on a voice vote in both House and Senate without hearings or vocal opposition.[39] It authorizes no new programs for Native Americans, nor additional funding for existing ones, but is expected to facilitate efforts to preserve indigenous languages. The text (omitting technical provisions) is excerpted from the *Congressional Record*, 101st Congress, 2d session (April 3, 1990), p. S3916.

Section 2. The Congress finds that—

(1) the status of the cultures and languages of Native Americans is unique and the United States has the responsibility to act together with Native Americans to ensure the survival of these unique cultures and languages;

(2) special status is accorded Native Americans in the United States, a status that recognizes distinct cultural and political rights, including the right to continue separate identities;

(3) the traditional languages of Native Americans are an integral part of their cultures and identities and form the basic medium for the transmission, and thus survival, of Native American cultures, literatures, histories, religions, political institutions, and values;

(4) there is a widespread practice of treating Native American languages as if they were anachronisms;

(5) there is a lack of clear, comprehensive, and consistent Federal policy on treatment of Native American languages which has often resulted in acts of suppression and extermination of Native American languages and cultures;

(6) there is convincing evidence that student achievement and performance, community and school pride, and educational opportunity is clearly and directly tied to respect for, and support of, the first language of the child or student;

(7) it is clearly in the interests of the United States, individual

---

39. The bill, originally known as S. 1781, was incorporated into S. 2167, a measure reauthorizing federal support for tribal community colleges. President Bush signed the measure, P.L. 101–477, on October 30, 1990.

States, and territories to encourage the full academic and human potential achievements of all students and citizens and to take steps to realize these ends;

(8) acts of suppression and extermination directed against Native American languages and cultures are in conflict with the United States policy of self-determination for Native Americans;

(9) languages are the means of communication for the full range of human experiences and are critical to the survival of cultural and political integrity of any people; and

(10) language provides a direct and powerful means of promoting international communication by people who share languages. . . .

Section 4. It is the policy of the United States to—

(1) preserve, protect, and promote the rights and freedom of Native Americans to use, practice, and develop Native American languages;

(2) allow exceptions to teacher certification requirements for Federal programs and programs funded in whole or in part by the Federal Government, for instruction in Native American languages when such teacher certification requirements hinder the employment of qualified teachers who teach in Native American languages, and to encourage State and territorial governments to make similar exceptions;

(3) encourage and support the use of Native American languages as a medium of instruction in order to encourage and support—

    (a) Native American language survival,

    (b) equal educational opportunity,

    (c) increased student success and performance,

    (d) increased student awareness and knowledge of their culture and history, and

    (e) increased student and community pride;

(4) encourage State and local education programs to work with Native American parents, educators, Indian tribes, and other Native American governing bodies in the implementation of programs to put this policy into effect;

(5) recognize the right of Indian tribes and other Native American governing bodies to use the Native American languages as a medium of instruction in all schools funded by the Secretary of the Interior;

(6) fully recognize the inherent right of Indian tribes and other Native American governing bodies, States, territories, and possessions of the United States to take action on, and give official status to, their Native American languages for the purpose of conducting their own business;

(7) support the granting of comparable proficiency achieved through course work in a Native American language the same academic credit as comparable proficiency achieved through course work

in a foreign language, with recognition of such Native American language proficiency by institutions of higher education as fulfilling foreign language entrance or degree requirements; and

(8) encourage all institutions of elementary, secondary, and higher education, where appropriate, to include Native American languages in the curriculum in the same manner as foreign languages and to grant proficiency in Native American languages the same full academic credit as proficiency in foreign languages.

Section 5. The right of Native Americans to express themselves through the use of Native American languages shall not be restricted in any public proceeding, including publicly supported education programs.

Section 6. (a) The President shall direct the heads of the various Federal departments, agencies, and instrumentalities to—

(1) evaluate their policies and procedures in consultation with Indian tribes and other Native American governing bodies as well as traditional leaders and educators in order to determine and implement changes needed to bring the policies and procedures into compliance with the provisions of this Act;

(2) give the greatest effect possible in making such evaluations, absent a clear specific Federal statutory requirement to the contrary, to the policies and procedures which will give the broadest effect to the provisions of this Act; and

(3) evaluate the laws which they administer and make recommendations to the President on amendments needed to bring such laws into compliance with the provisions of this Act.

(b) By no later than the date that is one year after the date of enactment of this Act, the President shall submit to Congress a report containing recommendations for amendments to Federal laws that are needed to bring such laws into compliance with the provisions of this Act.

Section 7. Nothing in this Act shall be construed as precluding the use of Federal funds to teach English to Native Americans.

PART THREE

Symbolic Implications of Language Conflict

Why has "bilingualism" suddenly become a burning issue in the United States? A simple answer is that linguistic diversity increased sharply in the 1980s, owing to sharply increased immigration. More immigrants and refugees entered the country during the last decade than any other except for 1901–10. The majority of newcomers no longer arrived from Europe, but from the Third World; racially and culturally, they were even more heterogeneous than the "new immigrants" that alarmed nativists three generations ago. With more contact between more language groups and with more demands on government for more bilingual services, friction was inevitable between monolingual Americans and speakers of other tongues. Language barriers created, or at least exacerbated, social tensions and thus led to political conflicts.

While there is undeniable truth in this explanation, it leaves a lot unanswered. "Irrational fear" may be a universal response to foreigners and to foreign speech, as Carlos Alberto Montaner suggests. And yet, the questions persist: Why are Americans today so eager to legislate Anglo-conformity? Why wasn't Official English a salient issue in earlier periods when ethnic diversity was at least as prevalent? Why have such measures been adopted in states like Alabama that have minuscule populations of linguistic minorities? Why is the idea so broadly appealing, attracting white Anglo-Saxon Protestants, Euro-ethnics, and to a lesser extent blacks; racial reactionaries as well as supporters of civil rights; Democrats and Republicans; liberals and conservatives? Something more is at work here than a visceral reaction to language differences.

It is ironic, notes Joshua Fishman, that the Official English campaign has appeared at a time when English is not only *not* threatened, but is becoming the preeminent world language. He analyzes English Only as a classic nativist movement, a diversion from real social problems into a mythic world of scapegoats and stereotypes. Proponents have seized upon bilingualism as a metaphor for troubling social change. "Defending" English provides a way to express anxieties that have little to do with language: the United States's slippage as a superpower, economic polarization in the Reagan era, rootlessness and the decline of community, our seeming impotence in coping with crises both foreign and domestic.

At the same time, there are rational if sometimes concealed motives that guide the Official English campaign. James Crawford unveils the intimate connections between U.S. English and the anti-immigration lobby. A single citizen-activist, Dr. John Tanton, has been the principal fundraiser, organizer, and intellectual force for both causes. His philosophy was elaborated in a confidential paper warning of the perils of changing demographics—in particular, "the Latin onslaught" from South of the Border. Widely regarded as anti-Hispanic when it surfaced during the campaigns of 1988, the memorandum created a scandal that forced the resignation of Tanton and Linda Chávez from the leadership of U.S. English. At the same time, it uncovered some surprising ideological bedfellows. While this movement has attracted ultra-conservatives like Larry Pratt, the founder of English First (as well as the Committee to Protect the Family, Gun Owners of America, and U.S. Border Control), Dr. Tanton's roots are in liberalism. His language- and immigration-restrictionist positions evolved out of, not in spite of, his environmental and population-control advocacy.

Politically, Official English fits no predictable pattern. In Texas, 92 percent of Republican voters expressed their support in a 1988 straw poll, while Democratic leaders in the legislature blocked a binding statewide referendum. And yet, the lead sponsor of Official English has been a Democrat, while the Texas Republican hierarchy, hopeful of recruiting more Hispanics, has quietly tried to sabotage the campaign. Meanwhile, Republicans in the California Assembly have united in support of English Only measures, prompting former governor George Deukmejian to veto bilingual education bills. But in Florida, following a landslide vote to adopt Official English, it was Republicans (largely Cuban Americans) who spearheaded the defeat of Democratic legislation to enforce the amendment.

As a symbolic issue, language can carry a variety of political meanings, depending on local conditions. Official English has affected no two communities in quite the same way. Miami, the birthplace of the English Only movement, illustrates the power of ethnicity to override ideology, with liberal Jews attacking language rights and conservative Cubans defending them. Max Castro analyzes the Hispanophobic inspiration for Dade County's "antibilingual ordinance"—the jealousies, cultural resentments, and status anxieties that Anglo-Miamians frankly acknowledge. In Monterey Park, California, where a similar backlash has greeted Chinese immigrants, Official English has been tied to antidevelopment activism. John Horton and José Calderón describe an attempt to navigate these waters by a con-

trolled-growth, ethnic-harmony coalition, which ultimately succeeded. Southeast Asian refugees and Latino newcomers in Lowell,
Massachusetts, have encountered a more traditional nativist reception. Camilo Peréz-Bustillo outlines the rise of English Only as an instrument to oppose bilingual, desegregated schools.

Quantitative attempts to analyze support for Official English remain at a primitive stage. One problem is that the public is confused
about the issue's implications, as revealed by opinion polls. How the
question is posed can be significant. For example, when the New York
Times/CBS News Poll asked whether government should conduct
business bilingually in areas with non-English-speaking minorities,
or only in English, respondents favored the latter by 60 percent to 36
percent. But when the question changed slightly to imply that non-
English speakers might be denied services under an English Only
policy, respondents were equally split, at 47 percent.[1] Simply asking,
"Should English be the official language?" tends to elicit overwhelming sentiment in favor. A demographic breakdown yields few significant patterns when 80 to 90 percent of voters are on the same side of
the issue.

Nevertheless, after dissecting one of the more sophisticated exit
polls on Official English, Carol Schmid ventures some conclusions.
First, ethnicity (Hispanic or Anglo) is a significant determinant of
opinions on the issue. Second, in supporters' *lack* of variation across
education and income levels, English Only departs from the traditional model of conservative social movements. Taking a more ethnographic approach, Joanne Bretzer explores the symbolic function of
language politics in Miami. She discovers links between Anglo-
conformity and nostalgia for a simpler, homogeneous community—
as if Official English could somehow turn back the clock.

If language restrictionism is not the answer, what is? Mary Carol
Combs describes the strengths and drawbacks of English Plus, the
major slogan and policy alternative advanced by opponents of English Only. Despite the ranks of educators and civil rights advocates
who have rallied behind English Plus, it has yet to capture the popular imagination.

1. On June 19–23, 1986, the question was: "In parts of this country where many
people speak a language other than English, should state and local governments conduct business in that language, as well as in English, or should they only use English?"
On May 11–14, 1987, the question was: "Would you favor or oppose an amendment to
the Constitution that requires federal, state, and local governments to conduct business
in English and not use other languages, even in places where many people don't speak
English?" The sample's margin of error was plus or minus 3 percent.

"Talk English—You Are in the United States"

By Carlos Alberto Montaner

Carlos Alberto Montaner, a native of Cuba who now re-
sides in Spain, is editorial page editor of Miami's *El Nuevo
Herald*. This article first appeared as "Why Fear Spanish?"
Miami Herald, April 25, 1988, p. 14-A.

I was walking quietly with my wife on a sidewalk in Miami Beach. We
were speaking Spanish, of course, because that is our language. Suddenly, we were accosted by a spry little old lady, wearing a baseball
cap and sneakers, who told us: "Talk English. You are in the United
States." She continued on her way at once, without stopping to see
our reaction. The expression on her face, curiously, was not that of
somebody performing a rude action, but of somebody performing a
sacred patriotic duty.

And the truth is that the lady in question was not an eccentric mad-
woman. Thousands, millions of monolingual Americans are morti-
fied that in their country there is a vast minority that constantly
speaks a language that they do not understand. It disturbs them to
hear Spanish prattle in shops, at work, in restaurants. They are irritated when conversations that they do not understand are held in
their presence. Indeed, they are upset to stumble across Spanish-
language stations on their radio or television dial, or by the fact that
the *Miami Herald* occasionally includes an unsolicited supplement in
the language of Castile.

Actually, the old lady's attitude was natural. Miami Beach is, more
or less, the United States. And the language of the United States is
English. Moreover, one of the key elements in the configuration of a
nation is its language. A monolingual American who suddenly finds
himself on Miami's Calle Ocho or in San Francisco's Chinatown has
the feeling that he is not in his own country. And when one is not in
one's own country, one feels endangered. Not faced with any danger
in particular, but subject to that diffuse and irrational fear caused by
words, expressions, and traits different from our own.

Hostility to a foreign language on our own turf generally does not
come from balanced reflection on the advantages or disadvantages of
linguistic homogeneity, but from an atavistic reaction that probably
has been part of human nature for millions of years, when the differ-

163

ences between the groups that populated the planet might result in
the death or destruction of the other. Much more recently, as far as
the Greeks were concerned, barbarity flowed from ignorance of
Greek. Since then—and, I fear, for all time—foreigners are inevitably
considered barbarians.

All right; thus far, I have confined myself to a kindly comprehension of prejudice, but there are other factors that cannot be ignored in
approaching this unhappy problem. A language is much more than a
way to communicate. By one's own language—and on this Edward
Sapir wrote much and well—one masters reality, one takes to oneself
and understands all that exists. All: history, interpersonal relations,
the most intimate and definitive emotions. For example, anybody
who learns to love in one language will never be able spontaneously
to translate his expressions of affection into a language acquired later.

We quarrel, are jealous, love, and hate with certain words, with
certain tones, with certain inflections of the voice learned in childhood and adapted to a given set of gestures that also cannot be trans-
ported into another language. And this matching of word and message comes solely in the mother tongue. "Language," said the
Spanish writer Miguel Unamuno, "is the blood of the spirit." He was
right. We cannot do without our own tongue without brutally muti-
lating our individual consciousness, without being left without
blood.

If this is so, is it reasonable to ask millions of human beings to do
without this fundamental part of their lives solely so that others are
not inconvenienced, or in order to comply with a few debatable rules
of urbanity? Is it not more sensible and less painful to explain to monolingual Americans that to live in places where various living tongues
converge can have a certain enriching enchantment, because diversity
is also an expression of cultural riches?

But, what is more, American society spends thousands of millions
of dollars every year in attempting unavailingly to get high school and
college students to learn Spanish, because it is assumed that mastery
of a second language benefits the country. If this is the rationale, then
why ask the bilingual citizens present in the nation to abandon their
use of that other language so covetously sought in educational establishments?

Fear of Spanish and the desire that only English be spoken in the
United States do not stand up to a calm analysis of reality. The United
States is and will continue to be a fundamentally English-speaking
nation, but it is a fortunate fact for the country that there are other
languages and other marginal cultures capable of enriching the powerful current of the mainstream. This can be perfectly understood by
any American, even a monolingual one, if he is capable of savoring a

Mexican taco while listening to the Miami Sound Machine's *Conga* or reading a wonderful story by Isaac Bashevis Singer written in Yiddish—very near the spot where we were berated by the irate old lady in baseball cap and sneakers.

The Displaced Anxieties of Anglo-Americans

By Joshua A. Fishman

Joshua A. Fishman, author of *Language Loyalty in the United States* and numerous related works, is research professor of social sciences at Yeshiva University's Ferkauf Graduate School of Professional Psychology. This article is an abridged version of "'English Only': Its Ghosts, Myths, and Dangers," *International Journal of the Sociology of Language* 74 (1988): 125–40.

With the adoption of the English Language Amendment in California in November 1986 and with the margin in favor of that adoption being nearly three to one, it is doubtlessly true that, for the first time in American history, a language-policy issue has come to the fore as a prominent internal issue in the United States. It was not by any means the first nor probably the last triumph for the "Official English/English Only" nativism of the 1980s, but it was a triumph in one of our most populous, economically developed, and modernistically oriented states. This triumph signaled that gone were the days when I and other language-status specialists would have trouble explaining to American academic and lay audiences why there were those among the Irish and the Welsh, the Jews and the Poles, the Flemings and the Frisians, the Catalans and the Basques, and various other "emotional nationalities that so get upset about and make such an issue over" their language, whereas Americans are too solid, secure, rational, and realistic to get involved in anything like that.

Clearly, something has happened of late in the United States to bring the status of English into controversial prominence, and I would like to ask what that is, why now, and why in the United States? In what has been referred to as the "century of English," at a time when English is the world's most prestigious, most effective, and most sought-after vehicle of communication the world over;[2] when political careers in non-English-mother-tongue countries are made or ruined partially on the basis of whether candidates for national office there can handle English effectively (in order to negotiate with George Schultz or Ronald Reagan, or appear before the American Congress—few of whose members can handle any language other than English); when English is still spreading and gaining uses and users in the entire non-English-mother-tongue world; why should a concern for its functional protection arouse so much interest in the wealthiest, most prestigious, and most powerful English-mother-tongue country of the world, a country in which fully 85 percent of the population is of English mother tongue and anywhere between 94 percent and 96 percent of the population is English-speaking?[3]

It does not seem to me that the very ubiquity of English, whether worldwide or in the United States, can be appealed to as an explanatory vehicle in answering this question. It cannot merely be that the American defenders of English, flushed by the victories of their dearly beloved tongue on a world scale, have become enraged at the "slights" to the hegemony of English in its own, American, backyard. No similar legislative effort to redress the internal insults to English, real or imaginary, have surfaced in other core countries of English, such as England, Australia, or New Zealand, all of which have substantial non-English-mother-tongue populations of their own. The general view toward non-English languages in governmental use in these countries is quite benevolent and even supportive in ways undreamed of here.[4] In all of these countries, there is at least as much concern as in the United States for the future of English in the world, for its continuation as the de facto official language of record within these countries, and for a good standard of English mastery in the schools and proper English usage thereafter as in the United States, with actual school achievement in English being at least as high and

2. Joshua A. Fishman et al., *The Spread of English* (Rowley, Mass.: Newbury House, 1977); Braj B. Kachru, *The Other Tongue: English across Cultures* (Urbana: University of Illinois Press, 1982).

3. Joshua A. Fishman et al., *The Rise and Fall of the Ethnic Revival* (Berlin: Mouton de Gruyter, 1985).

4. See Ofelia Garcia and Ricardo Otheguy, "The Education of Language-Minority Children: Impressions of London from a New York Perspective," *Primary Teaching Studies* 2 (1985): 81–94; Linguistic Minorities Project, *Linguistic Minorities in England* (London: University of London Institute of Education, 1983); Australia, Commonwealth Department of Education, *Towards a National Language Policy* (Canberra: Australian National Printing Service, 1982); Michael G. Clyne, ed., *Australia: Meeting Place of Languages* (Canberra: Australian National University, 1985); and Anne Pauwels, ed., "The Future of Ethnic Languages in Australia," *International Journal of the Sociology of Language* 72 (1988).

probably higher. Even Anglo-Canada, with all its wounded pride at the hands of a recalcitrant Quebec, is more accommodating to its language minorities, francophone and nonfrancophone alike, than would be considered either seemly or likely in the United States.[5]

No purported American self-image as the true keeper of the English flame can really hope to account for the phenomenon we are trying to explain. It is not English-centeredness itself—love of the language, mastery of its nuances, fascination with the beauty of the language per se—that seems to be the crucial variable. I have yet to hear of English Only advocates mustering votes to increase anemic budgets to expand the currently small number of TESOL[6] programs, which cannot begin to accommodate the non-English and limited-English students who are clamoring for admission.

When the Official English/English Only advocates tell us that our linguistic minorities "are getting the wrong message" when the U.S. government addresses or serves them in languages other than English, presumably a message that it is not necessary to learn English in order to live and prosper in the United States, I sense a wounded *amour propre*. Otherwise, why the paranoia about the possible inability of one part of the country to communicate with the other? Why the nightmares of bloodshed or social conflict because of language differences? Is there any internal evidence at all to confirm such fears? Aren't the comparisons to Sri Lanka or India not only farfetched and erroneous, but completely removed from the reality of the United States? And, to top things off, aren't the problems even of these countries fundamentally unrelated to linguistic homogeneity?[7]

There is a seriously wounded self-concept involved, insofar as mainstream America yearns for Official English/English Only to salvage its sense of propriety and law and order. Otherwise, why the imperviousness to the data on language maintenance and language shift with respect to our non-English-mother-tongue population? Why are facts so useless in this discussion? Why is it so irrelevant that, with the exception of isolated and self-isolated groups such as certain AmerIndians, the German-speaking Old Order Amish and Hutterites, the Russian-speaking Old Believers, and the Yiddish-

5. Stacy Churchill and Anthony Smith, "The Emerging Consensus," and Kenneth McRae and Jean-Paul L'Allier, "Youth Speaks Out," *Language and Society/Langue et société* 18 (1986): 5–19.

6. Editor's note: TESOL is a synonym for the teaching of English as a second language. It is also the acronym of the professional organization Teachers of English to Speakers of Other Languages.

7. See Joshua A. Fishman and Frank Solano, "Cross-Polity Linguistic Homogeneity/ Heterogeneity and Per-Capita Gross National Product: An Empirical Exploration," *Language Problems and Language Planning* 13, no. 2 (Summer 1989): 103–18.

speaking Hasidim (none of whom would be in the least bit affected by Official English/English Only legislation), *all other ethnolinguistic minorities in the United States lose their ethnic mother tongue fairly completely by their second or third generation of encounter with American urban life.* Not only do they become "English usually" speakers by then; they usually become "English only" speakers.[8]

Hispanics are no exception to this "iron law" as far as learning English is concerned. Their only exceptionality is a slightly longer retention of Spanish (a one-generational difference at most), due to the continued influx of monolingual Spanish speakers into their urban barrios. As a result of this influx, the concentration of Spanish speakers remains high and the economic value of Spanish remains substantial for the denizens of the barrios for one generation beyond the immigrant norm.[9] Accordingly, many second- and third-generation Hispanics who haven't learned any Spanish at home, whose parents and siblings may have stopped speaking it themselves, learn it from life in the immigrant-impacted neighborhoods.

Instead of rigidly perseverating on the linguistic behavior of recent arrivals who need governmental services in Spanish if their health, education, welfare, and political rights are to be safeguarded, Official English/English Only advocates should be asking themselves: "Why are those second- and third-generation Hispanics—who usually or only speak English by now—still living in those barrios where previously their parents and grandparents lived and where now the new immigrants concentrate?" But to ask this question would lead to yet another unknown, undesired, or rejected body of data, which shows that mastery of English is almost as inoperative with respect to Hispanics' social mobility as it is with respect to black social mobility. Twenty-five percent of Hispanics today live at or below the poverty line, a rate that is easily two or even three times as high as the proportion of Hispanics that are not English-speaking. Among the older immigrant groups, English was acquired, their immigrant cultures were destroyed, and social mobility was their payoff for the dislocation experienced. Among Hispanic, Asian, and Pacific islander immigrants of the last two decades, only the first two steps in this equation have been realized (and these have been due more to the dynamics of urban dislocation and mobility aspirations than to any governmental program whatsoever).

What signs of "getting the wrong message" are there and what

8. Calvin Veltman, *Language Shift in the United States* (Berlin: Mouton de Gruyter, 1983).

9. Shirley Brice Heath, "Language Policies: Patterns of Retention and Maintenance," in *Mexican-Americans in Comparative Perspective*, ed. Walker Connor (Washington, D.C.: Urban Institute Press, 1985).

could the wrong message be? Are there any signs of separatism, of ethnic political parties, of ethnic militancy, of anti-Americanism, of ethnic terrorism? Why does the Anglo-oriented middle bourgeoisie feel as much or more abused by government services in languages other than English than the ethnic poor and immigrants themselves feel by the rapidly diminishing scale of such services? A higher proportion of middle-class Americans have been turned off by multilingual ballots than there are non-English-mother-tongue voters who have used such ballots. More Anglo-oriented Americans have been offended by the very notion of bilingual education than there are limited-English-proficient children who have received bilingual education. The "Why should we pay for them?" syndrome, the "Why didn't my grandparents get such benefits?" syndrome, the "We only want to liberate them from their ethnic self-imprisonment" syndrome—when we follow our leaders that is "free choice," but when they follow their leaders that is capitulating to demagoguery—these all boil down to "Who's in control here, anyway? We who deserve to be, or those riffraff and upstarts?"

These attitudes are all sublimations of the sense of being abused, of being taken advantage of, of being denied one's own rightful place in the sun. And in the scheme of things, that seems to plague so much of Anglo-oriented America today. The Official English/English Only movement may largely represent the displacement of middle-class Anglo fears and anxieties from the more difficult, if not intractable, *real* causes of their fears and anxieties, to mythical and simplistic and stereotyped scapegoats. If those with these fears are successful in passing Official English amendments, this would represent another "liberation of Grenada," rather than any mature grappling with the really monumental economic, social, and political causes of conflict, unrest, and contention in either America or the world at large today.

In political parlance Official English is a "stampeder," an issue whose importance far transcends its own limits. The insecurity of the relatively secure and those who wishfully identify with them shouts out from this odd assembly of defenders of middle-class good-and-welfare. It is this insecurity that needs to be examined, more than anything else, in order to understand the Official English/English Only appeal on the current American political scene.

And why is Anglo-oriented, middle-class America particularly insecure and upset by "these foreigners" in its midst who are getting government services in languages other than English? Perhaps because America has lost more relative leverage on the world scene than any other major power during the past two score years; perhaps because the American economy has performed less glamorously than its own mythology and built-in aspirations had led its prior benefi-

ciaries to expect; perhaps because the ethnic revival led to multicultural mutterings that finally frightened more of the mutterers and
their listeners than it satisfied, gratified, or influenced in any way;
perhaps because this is the first Anglo-American generation that has
had to face the possibility that it would not rise to a station in life
higher than that of its parents. The new insecurities of mainstream
middle-class American life, combined with the widespread disappointment in the liberal promise of the Roosevelt-to-Johnson era,
have led to the Official English/English Only solution, a cheap thrill if
there ever was one.

It is the classical wrong solution to the wrong problem. Indeed,
even were English in America being threatened by other languages,
the Official English/English Only forces have failed to recognize that
such a language conflict, like all language conflicts wherever they
arise, merely represents the tip of the iceberg of interethnolinguistic
conflict based upon economic, political, and cultural grievances.
These grievances represent the real problems and not their linguistic
concomitants. If interethnolinguistic divisiveness is a real threat to
America—which I firmly believe it is not (that charge being no more
than a currently fashionable form of nativistic witch-hunting)—then
Official English/English Only advocates are wasting our time, leading
us away from real solutions to the causes of this threat and orienting
us to the pursuit of mere symptoms and byproducts. By manufacturing the myth of "giving our new arrivals the wrong message"—
which, like all myths, is shrouded in vague and unspoken mysteries
and allusions—they must wind up with an unreal solution. Myths,
as Barthes and Woolard remind us, do not simply hide the truth; they
distort it.[10]

The truth is that Official English/English Only efforts cannot hide
the fact that the power class (as well as those Anglos and non-Anglos
who aspire to join its ranks) feels insecure about its own leadership
role and its prerogatives in American society. The distortion arises
when others—those who are presumably "getting the wrong message" by thinking that they, too, deserve some power in American
life—are blamed for these insecurities and for the power class's difficulties in finding genuine solutions to them.

10. Roland Barthes, *Mythologies* (New York: Hill and Wang, 1972); Kathryn A. Woolard, "Sentences in the Language Prison: The Rhetoric of an American Language Debate," paper presented to the American Anthropological Association, Philadelphia,
1986.

What's behind Official English?

By James Crawford

James Crawford, the editor of this volume, is author of *Bilingual Education: History, Politics, Theory, and Practice* and *Hold Your Tongue: Bilingualism and the Politics of "English Only."* An earlier version of this article appeared as a three-part series of commentaries syndicated by the Hispanic Link News Service in October 1988.

Self-appointed guardians of English have always been with us. But never before have we seen a high-powered Washington lobby, complete with political action committee, pledged to "defend our common language." A group known as U.S. English has spent upwards of $18 million since 1983 to promote English as the official language of the United States.[11] It has supported Official English campaigns in more than forty states and is bankrolling ballot initiatives this fall in Arizona, Colorado, and Florida.

The question is why. Consider that 98 percent of U.S. residents over the age of four speak English "well" or "very well," according to the 1980 census. Immigrants are lining up for scarce seats in adult English classes, which operate twenty-four hours a day in cities like Los Angeles. After fifteen years in this country, three out of four Hispanic immigrants speak English on a daily basis. More than 85 percent of children from language-minority homes become dominant in English, and their children rarely speak anything else.[12]

Under these circumstances, who would assert that "English is under attack" and needs "legal protection" from the ravages of bilingualism? What is the real concern here? The proliferation of other tongues, or the people who speak them? Is the English Only campaign a new strain of nativism, as opponents have charged, a Know-Nothing movement for the 1980s?

The mystery began to unravel this week amid angry resignations by the top leaders of U.S. English. Linda Chávez, the group's presi-

11. Federal tax reforms (IRS Form 990s) and audit reports, 1984–88, for U.S., Inc. (parent organization of which U.S. English was a project until mid–1988).

12. National Center for Education Statistics, *The Retention of Minority Languages in the United States: A Seminar on the Analytic Work of Calvin J. Veltman* (Washington, D.C.: U.S. Government Printing Office, 1980), p. 4; Calvin Veltman, *The Future of the Spanish Language in the United States* (New York and Washington: Hispanic Policy Development Project, 1988); *see also pp. 317–22*.

dent, quit to protest what she called "repugnant" and "anti-Hispanic" comments by her boss, Dr. John Tanton, in a recently disclosed memorandum.[13] Tanton stepped down as chairman of U.S. English, blasting the "McCarthyite tactics" of his opponents. And Walter Cronkite, who had lent his venerable name to the group's fundraising efforts, severed his ties to the U.S. English advisory board, which he described as "embarrassing."

Since taking the helm of U.S. English in 1987, Chávez had often found herself defending the organization against charges of anti-immigrant bias. Just look at the immigrants supporting us, she would say, naming former U.S. senator S. I. Hayakawa, Alistair Cooke, and Arnold Schwarzenegger. Formerly a civil rights official in the Reagan administration, Chávez liked to stress the inclusionist potential of Official English. "Hispanics who learn English will be able to avail themselves of opportunities," she argued earlier this year. "Those who do not will be relegated to second-class citizenship. I don't want to see that happen to my people."[14]

Chávez now says she knew nothing about the links between U.S. English and organizations working to stem what Tanton calls "the Latin onslaught." According to federal tax records (which nonprofit groups must make public), until this year U.S. English was a project of U.S., Inc., a tax-exempt entity that has channeled nearly $200,000 to the Center for Immigration Studies, Californians for Population Stabilization, Americans for Border Control, and the Federation for American Immigration Reform (FAIR). John Tanton is the architect of this network. A Michigan ophthalmologist, he founded both FAIR and U.S. English, and his influence extends to more than a dozen spinoff projects, PACs, and affiliates dedicated to Official English, immigration restriction, and population control.

How are these causes connected? "The question of bilingualism grows out of U.S. immigration policy," Tanton says, because the influx of non-English speakers has overwhelmed "the assimilative capacity of the country."[15] There is no question which language group he finds most menacing. "*Gobernar es poblar* translates 'to govern is to populate,'" he writes in his 1986 memo. "In this society, will the present majority peaceably hand over its political power to a group that is simply more fertile? . . . Can *homo contraceptivus* compete with *homo progenitiva* [sic] if borders aren't controlled?"

Besides language differences, Tanton enumerates a range of cul-

13. Interview with Linda Chávez, Oct. 17, 1988; John Tanton, memorandum to "WITAN IV Attendees," Oct. 10, 1986.
14. *U.S. English Update*, Jan.–Feb. 1988, p. 1.
15. Interview with John Tanton, Sept. 20, 1988.

tural threats posed by Spanish-speaking immigrants: "the tradition of the *mordida* (bribe), the lack of involvement in public affairs"; Roman Catholicism, with its potential to "pitch out the separation of church and state"; low "educability" and high school-dropout rates; limited concern for the environment; and of course, high fertility. "Perhaps this is the first instance in which those with their pants up are going to get caught by those with their pants down," he muses. "As Whites see their power and control over their lives declining, will they simply go quietly into the night? Or will there be an explosion? . . . We are building in a deadly disunity."

Tanton's memo was written for WITAN, a private discussion group that takes its name from an Old English word meaning a member of the *witenagemot*, or council of wise men. His farfetched scenarios were never intended for publication. Among these, only the subject of language divisions is safe to broach in polite company.

It is tempting to write off the Official English campaign as a fringe movement, a haven for extremists. Certainly, these people have a penchant for the outrageous.

"The language issue could feed and guide terrorism in the U.S." by Spanish-speaking separatists, warned Rusty Butler in 1985 while serving as an aide to Senator Steve Symms, an Idaho Republican who sponsored an English Language Amendment to the U.S. Constitution. Robert Melby, as chairman of the Florida English Campaign in 1986, called for eliminating 911 emergency services in Spanish as a way to give immigrants an incentive to learn English. Hispanics must be "educated to the fact that the United States is not a mongrel nation," declared Terry Robbins, leader of Dade Americans United to Protect the English Language, in 1987. Larry Pratt, president of English First, a competing group based in Virginia, raises money through the mail with a letter that claims: "Tragically, many immigrants these days refuse to learn English! They never become productive members of American society. They remain stuck in a linguistic and economic ghetto, many living off welfare and costing working Americans millions of tax dollars every year." [16]

Such overt appeals to prejudice are usually confined to the Far Right. But not in this case. While that label may fit a few zealots, it fails to describe the movement as a whole. English Only is a political

16. R. E. Butler, *On Creating a Hispanic America: A Nation within a Nation?* (Washington, D.C.: Council for Inter-American Security, 1985); James Crawford, "Conservative Groups Take Aim at Bilingual Education Programs," *Education Week*, March 19, 1986; Terry Robbins speech at Florida International University, Oct. 8, 1987; English First fundraising letter (n.d.) signed by Texas state representative Jim Zorn.

hybrid that defies easy classification. The roots of U.S. English, the most influential group, are in two liberal causes of the 1960s: ecology and population control.

U.S. English founder Tanton describes himself as a "congenital conservationist" who came to view population growth as a serious threat to the environment.[17] An activist in the Sierra Club and Planned Parenthood, he also served as national president of Zero Population Growth in the mid–1970s. When U.S. birthrates dropped below replacement level, Tanton's interest turned to immigration restriction, and in 1978 he launched FAIR. Five years later, believing that rising numbers of non-English speakers were failing to assimilate, he joined forces with former senator Hayakawa to start U.S. English, a group that serves to highlight the cultural impact of immigration.

Tanton has worked to build a broad political base for his activities. "Analogous to Nixon's opening to China," he writes, liberals must be the ones to raise questions about ethnic diversity and its potential to create a "social and political San Andreas fault. . . . Conservatives simply can't do it without tainting the whole subject." Indeed, these are sensitive issues. In the 1980s, it is difficult to justify tight immigration quotas—as Tanton does in his unpublished memorandum—by predicting that Hispanic population growth will lead to linguistic, economic, racial, and religious "apartheid" in the United States. People might suspect that your public-spirited rhetoric is a mask for intolerance.

That conclusion became inescapable when Tanton's paper came to light. In resigning as president of U.S. English, Linda Chávez described his views as "anti-Hispanic, anti-Catholic, and not excusable," adding that she was especially upset to learn about the funding sources behind Tanton's organizational network.[18]

Since 1980, a single contributor—Mellon heiress Cordelia Scaife May—has contributed at least $3.5 million to FAIR, U.S. English, the Center for Immigration Studies, the Immigration Reform Law Institute, Population-Environment Balance, the Immigration Political Action Committee, the English Language Political Action Committee, and related organizations. Five years ago, May's Laurel Foundation financed the distribution of a futuristic novel, *The Camp of the Saints*, by Jean Raspail, in which Third World immigrants invade Europe and destroy Western civilization. Chávez said she had once reviewed this "sickening book," describing it as "racist, xenophobic, and paranoid," and had been disturbed to see a U.S. English staff member reading it.

Other donors to Tanton's network run the ideological gamut from

17. Tanton interview.
18. Chávez interview.

Warren Buffett, a billionaire financier whose other philanthropic interests include the nuclear freeze movement, to the Pioneer Fund, a little-known foundation dedicated to "racial betterment" through eugenics. Created in 1937, the Pioneer Fund worked to popularize what it called "applied genetics in present-day Germany"—that is, Adolf Hitler's massive program of forced sterilization for persons judged to be of inferior heredity. In the 1970s the foundation financed genetic research by William Shockley and Arthur Jensen purporting to prove that blacks have lower intelligence than whites. John B. Trevor, Jr., a current officer of the Pioneer Fund, in 1965 testified against repeal of racial preferences in U.S. immigration law, warning that the change would produce "a conglomeration of racial and ethnic elements" and lead to "a serious culture decline."[19] Tanton recently disclaimed any knowledge of these activities by the Pioneer Fund, although he served as chairman of FAIR from 1982 to 1987, when it received $480,000 in general support from the eugenics foundation.

To be sure, the unsavory allies and hidden agendas of U.S. English are unknown to most of its supporters. Direct-mail appeals have swelled the group's membership to 400,000 and its budget to $6 million annually. Its Official English proposals, which voters will consider in three states on November 8, are running well ahead in the polls. This is no fringe movement. Unlike eugenics or border control, the English language has acquired a broad following—which makes its defenders all the more dangerous.

It seems only logical that Official English advocates, who assert that a common language is this country's "main unifying force," would favor expanded opportunities for immigrants to learn English. Indeed, many voters assume this is an important aim of initiatives to declare English the official language of Arizona, Colorado, and Florida. Logical or not, the assumption is false.

U.S. English spent lavishly to get these measures on the ballot. Yet it declined to support legislation to create the new English Literacy Grants program, approved by Congress in the spring of 1988. The federal subsidy is modest—just $4.8 million this year—but is the first to be earmarked for adult classes in English as a second language. According to Senator John McCain, an Arizona Republican who, along with the Congressional Hispanic Caucus, led the struggle to enact the English literacy bill, the Official English lobby did nothing to help. When questioned about its position in 1986, Gerda Bikales,

19. Pioneer Fund founding documents and related correspondence on file at Group Research, Inc., Washington, D.C.; investigation by Grace Lichtenstein, "Fund Backs Controversial Study of 'Racial Betterment,'" *New York Times*, Dec. 11, 1977.

executive director of U.S. English, responded that teaching English was the "moral obligation" of Spanish-language television stations, not the federal government. Stung by charges of hypocrisy, the following year U.S. English began to aid a few private English literacy projects. Though announced with much fanfare, these grants represented less than one percent of the group's $4 million in expenditures for 1987.[20]

If not to enable newcomers to speak our language, what are the priorities of U.S. English? What does it seek to accomplish through Official English amendments to federal and state constitutions? The organization has been hard to pin down on these questions. In the past, U.S. English leaders have advocated abolition of bilingual health and emergency services, endorsed English Only rules in the workplace, petitioned to limit broadcasting in other tongues, threatened to boycott businesses that advertise in Spanish, and sought to ban telephone bills in Chinese. Today, spokesmen for the group deny taking any of these positions, insisting that they seek merely to clarify that English is our national language and to head off a hypothetical threat of official bilingualism.

One thing is clear. Rather than promote English proficiency, 99 percent of the organization's efforts go toward restricting the use of other languages. Certainly, there is nothing in Official English legislation to help anyone learn English. On the other hand, there is much to penalize those who have yet to do so.

The potential for mischief is wide-ranging. Would states be allowed to provide drivers' exams, assist voters, publish tourist information, or enforce contracts in languages other than English? Could courts supply translators in eviction, bankruptcy, divorce, or adoption proceedings? Would schools be permitted to use bilingual education to foster fluency in foreign languages? Could Indian or Hispanic legislators communicate with constituents in their native tongues? Probably not, under the more draconian Official English measures. Arizona's Proposition 106, for example, would largely forbid public employees to use other languages on the job. In any case, such questions would be litigated for years to come.

English Only is a label that has stuck, despite the protests of U.S. English, because it accurately sums up the group's logic: That people will speak English only if forced to do so. That the crutch of bilingual assistance must be yanked away or newcomers will be permanently handicapped. That immigrants are too lazy or dim-witted to accept "the primacy of English" on their own.

20. McCain statement at May 11, 1988, press conference; James Crawford, "Hispanic Lawmakers Sponsor Measure to Make $10 Million in Literacy Grants," *Education Week*, June 18, 1986; IRS 990 Form, U.S., Inc.

Dr. Tanton argues that we must act now or face upheavals like Canada's. "How will we make the transition from a dominant non-Hispanic society with a Spanish influence to a dominant Spanish society with a non-Hispanic influence?" he asks in his confidential memo. "All great empires disintegrate. We want stability." Ironically, Tanton advocates the same brand of language restrictionism that has tied Quebec in knots. In the late 1970s, when the Parti Québécois passed French Only laws to defend against the encroachments of English, they served to exacerbate ethnic tensions, not to relax them. English Only campaigns are starting to have the same effect here. Even if the United States faced a genuine crisis, with ethnic groups forming parties and preaching separatism—even if such fears amounted to more than Hispanophobia—a policy of coercion would be foolish. Legislating Anglo-conformity would produce more dissension than unity.

In 1787 German Americans represented a proportion of the population comparable to that of Hispanics today (8.6 percent versus 9.0 percent).[21] They took pride in the German language and culture, resenting Ben Franklin's efforts to "Anglify" their children. Yet the Framers declined to give English official status in our Constitution or to stop printing public documents in German. Their writings suggest this was no oversight. The prevailing view, then and throughout most of our history, was that a democratic government has no business telling the people how to talk. Now U.S. English is asking Congress to reconsider that judgment. Hoping that victories in Arizona, Colorado, and Florida will increase its clout, the group has strong-armed Representative Don Edwards, Democrat of California, into holding hearings on a Constitutional English Language Amendment. That battle is likely to heat up next year.

If U.S. English sincerely wanted to foster ethnic harmony, it would stop chastising immigrants, open its multi-million-dollar campaign chest, and join with advocates for Asians and Hispanics to remedy the scarcity of seats in adult English classes. Instead, it exploits strong feelings about language to build a new nativist movement.

21. "American Council of Learned Societies Report of the Committee on Linguistic and National Stocks in the Population of the United States," in *Annual Report of the American Historical Association for the Year 1931* (Washington, D.C.: AHA, 1932), pp. 103–441; Barbara Vobejda, "Asian, Hispanic Numbers in U.S. Soared in 1980s, Census Reveals," *Washington Post*, March 11, 1991, pp. A1, A5.

On the Curious Question of Language in Miami

By Max J. Castro

Max J. Castro, is executive director of Greater Miami United, a civil rights and social advocacy organization. A sociologist, he has authored numerous papers on inter-ethnic relations. He wrote this article for the *Source Book*.

Although more stereotyped for other vices, Miami is the birthplace of the contemporary English Only movement in the United States. On November 4, 1980, more than 59 percent of the voters in Dade County, Florida, approved an "antibilingual" ordinance.[22] Its first clause said that "the expenditure of county funds for the purpose of utilizing any language other than English, or promoting any culture other than that of the United States, is prohibited." The second clause established that "all county governmental meetings, hearings and publications shall be *in the English language only*" (emphasis added; *see p. 131*).

The Dade County vote was the first shot in the language wars of the 1980s, involving numerous campaigns to declare English the official language. It began, seemingly by spontaneous combustion, in the summer of 1980. A *Miami Herald* reporter, writing on the day after the vote, described the sequence of events:

> Marion Plunske heard Emmy Shafer on a WNWS radio talk show on July 8. The two women started their campaign the next day and the Citizens of Dade United registered as a political action group on July 21. From the start the campaign seemed to run itself.
>
> In just over four weeks the group gathered 44,166 signatures, nearly twice as many as they needed to put the ordinance on the ballot. Exulting in their strength, they brought another 25,767 signatures to the supervisor of elections on Sept. 16.
>
> "It was like giving gold away," Shafer said in late October. On one day alone she received over 300 phone calls

---

22. The vote was 251,259 in favor, 173,168 against; Fredric Tasker, "Latins Fight New Language Law in Court," *Miami Herald*, Nov. 6, 1980, p. 1-C.

from people who wanted to sign the anti-bilingualism petition.[23]

The antibilingual campaign was, first and foremost, an episode of collective behavior akin to a panic or craze. It did not emerge from any institution or pre-existing interest group, and it developed without benefit of much in the way of organization or resources. The phenomenon's appeal, however, was highly selective. Despite its impressive success, the antibilingual movement, both in terms of leadership and electoral support, was almost exclusively a creature of one ethnic sector of a triethnic community: whites of other than Hispanic descent, who voted in favor of the proposal in massive numbers. In contrast, Hispanic opposition to the ordinance was overwhelming, while a solid majority of black voters also opposed the amendment, despite what the *Herald* described as "their history of cool relations with Latins in Dade." The ethnic breakdown of the vote was[24]

	For	Against
Whites (non-Hispanic)	71%	29%
Blacks	44%	56%
Hispanics	15%	85%

Established institutions like the *Miami Herald*, fearing a worsening of ethnic tensions, came out against the ordinance, to no avail. The Greater Miami Chamber of Commerce, a key element of the white Anglo elite, spent $50,000 in opposition. In contrast, the antibilingual forces spent less than $10,000 in their successful campaign. Clearly, supporters of the ordinance were motivated by ethnic resentments and a feeling of alienation from the community in which they lived. In the exit poll cited above, more than half of the non-Hispanic whites who voted in favor said they would be pleased if the measure "would make Miami a less attractive place for Cubans and other Spanish-speaking people." More than 75 percent said they would move away from Dade County "if it were practical."[25]

The ethnic polarization seen in the antibilingual vote reflected widely diverging interpretations of the impact of Hispanics on the city. According to the exit poll, more than 85 percent of Hispanics agreed with the statement that "the Latin influence has helped this county's economy and made it a more enjoyable place to live," as com-

23. Michael Browning, "Anti-Bilingual Backers Celebrate Early," *Miami Herald*, Nov. 5, 1980, p. 11-A.

24. Ibid.

25. Fredric Tasker, "Anti-Bilingualism Measure Approved in Dade County," *Miami Herald*, Nov. 5, 1980, pp. 1-A, 11-A.

pared with only 42 percent of blacks and 39 percent of non-Hispanic whites. Also, two out of three Hispanics agreed that the vote on the antibilingual ordinance was "an insult to the Spanish-speaking residents of Dade," while only one in four non-Hispanic whites agreed.

The Dade County antibilingual campaign was a harbinger and model of future language struggles. It provided the method that would prove most effective for reversing bilingual gains and imposing official monolingualism: the citizen-initiated referendum. It provided the first test of the extent of voter sentiment against government recognition of language pluralism and thus of the potential for a national English Only movement. It showed that even in a community with a huge and empowered language minority and in the face of opposition from the local establishment, a group of political novices could push through an English Only proposition. Finally, it gave testimony to the divisive nature of the issue.

In Miami this movement can be understood as the spontaneous reaction of an alienated, white, non-Hispanic, nonelite population against the Cuban/Hispanic presence. Why did this presence arouse such a strong reaction? Why did Miami give birth to English Only? "This question of language was curious," writes Joan Didion. "The sound of spoken Spanish was common in Miami, but it was also common in Los Angeles, and Houston, and even in the cities of the northeast." The difference was that in the other cities Spanish was "the language spoken by the people who worked in the car wash and came to trim the trees and cleared the tables in restaurants. In Miami Spanish was spoken by the people who ate in the restaurants, the people who owned the cars and the trees, which made, on the socioauditory scale, a considerable difference. . . . What was so unusual about Spanish in Miami was not that it was so often spoken, but that it was so often heard."[26]

Immigrants are not supposed to be heard. Immigrants, particularly Spanish-speaking immigrants from a Caribbean island, are expected to be subordinate—numerically, economically, politically, culturally, linguistically, even psychologically. In terms of numbers, Americans expect immigrants to be a small fraction of the population. In class terms, immigrants are supposed to work for others, for established Americans, generally in low-paid and undesirable jobs. Politically, they are expected to have little or no power; immigrant status is virtually synonymous with powerlessness. Immigrant culture and language—assumed to have little prestige or usefulness in comparison with the dominant American culture and the English language—are supposed to fade away quickly as assimilation runs its course. Psy-

26. *Miami* (New York: Simon & Schuster, 1987), p. 63.

chologically, the uprooted immigrant is subject to the stigma placed by the dominant society on foreigners. By 1980 the norm of immigrant subordination was being massively violated in Miami. The English Only movement arose as one reaction of a sector of the population to that transgression.

It premiered in a city that by 1980 had the largest proportion of immigrants of any U.S. metropolitan area. Even before the middle of that year, when the Mariel Cuban boatlift and the Haitian influx would swell the numbers, Miami was far more popular than Los Angeles or New York City as a destination for newcomers. Consider the following ranking of cities in terms of population born outside the United States:[27]

Miami	35.5%
Los Angeles	22.3%
New York City	21.3%
San Francisco	15.7%
San Diego	12.7%
Total U.S.	6.2%

Miami's lead was no doubt increased when, shortly after the census was taken, tens of thousands of Cuban and Haitian boat people poured into South Florida in one of the most dramatic and traumatic episodes of U.S. immigration history.

Immigrants had transformed Miami in the 1960s and 1970s, and the nature of the demographic and cultural changes were quite specific. As a result of the arrival of hundreds of thousands of Cubans fleeing the 1959 revolution, and of smaller but still significant numbers of other Latin American immigrants, Miami underwent a lightning Latinization, an enormous cultural change in scarcely two decades. In 1960 about 5 percent of the metropolitan population was Hispanic. Just twenty years later, shortly before the Mariel boatlift, this figure had risen to 36 percent and, by the time of the November 1980 referendum, to 41 percent.

Latinization, accelerated by the sheer number of new immigrants, inevitably changed the cultural and social climate of the city from one monopolized by dominant North American norms and styles to one in which other traditions and forms competed powerfully for cultural and linguistic space. While English remained overwhelmingly the

27. U.S. Bureau of the Census, *1980 Census of Population*, vol. 1, *Characteristics of the Population*, chap. D, "Detailed Population Characteristics," pt. 6, "California," PC–80–1-D 6; pt. 11, "Florida," PC–80–1-D 11, Oct. 1983; pt. 34, "New York," PC–80–1-D 34, Nov. 1983; *World Almanac and Book of Facts, 1989* (New York: World Almanac, 1988), p. 540; Andrew Hacker, ed., *US: A Statistical Portrait of the American People* (New York: Penguin Books, 1983), p. 44.

dominant language of the area, and mainstream American culture the dominant culture, another linguistic and cultural tradition had managed to establish—in an astoundingly short time in historical scale—a significant presence. The Latin influence affected the way houses looked in Miami, how people dressed on the street, the language spoken on the bus, at the bank, and on the airwaves, and most other aspects of community life. Many people were uncomfortable with the changes, which they said made them feel like foreigners in their own country.

The English supremacy movement arose out of this alienation and the resentment it created. The language of the campaign signaled the level of fear and anger among the backers of the proposal. At the outset, a spokesman for the antibilingual forces called bilingualism "a cancer in the community." As the *Herald* observed:

> If the people who voted for the new ordinance had one thing in common it was their unhappiness, a peevish sort of impatience with their neighbors. Sizable numbers of them made it clear they are fed up with co-existing. Now they want to leave, no matter which language wins out.[28]

Indeed, the fact that three out of every four white voters who supported the antibilingual ordinance told the *Herald* that they would move out of Dade County if they could bespeaks an estrangement from the community among a huge sector of non-Hispanic Miami, and especially among the measure's core constituency, the white population. That these sentiments went beyond mere discontent with life in the city is suggested by the fact that more than half the measure's supporters hoped it would make the city less attractive to Hispanics. The essential anti-immigrant, anti-Hispanic character of the English Only movement—the full extent of which would emerge later in confidential documents by its founder, Dr. John Tanton *(see pp. 171–77)*—was already implicit in its Miami genesis.

Numbers matter, but what was unique about Miami's Spanish-speaking newcomers in 1980 was not that they were numerous, but that so many had become economically successful. The middle-class background of many of the Cuban exiles was undoubtedly the key factor in the speed of their economic success. Far from occupying the lowest rungs in the economy, Cubans were competing—often successfully—with natives in the labor market, in business, and in the professions. As one example, between 1969 and 1982 the number of Hispanic-owned businesses in Miami increased by 622 percent, from 3,447 to 24,898. The rise of Cuban enterprises in Miami provided fer-

28. Browning, "Anti-Bilingual Backers," p. 11-A.

tile ground for language maintenance and produced real and perceived interethnic economic competition, which fueled fears and resentments among Anglos that translated into support for English
Only politics. Cuban and other Latin immigration had not only
changed the demographic and cultural makeup of Miami but had also
upset expectations about class relations between immigrant and established American. It violated the expected sequence of assimilation,
then economic success.

Dade County was the site of the first bilingual education program
in a modern U.S. public school, established in 1963 at the Coral Way
elementary school. In 1973 the board of commissioners for Metropolitan Dade County passed a resolution that "declares Dade County a
bilingual and bicultural county, where Spanish language is considered the second official language." And so, Miami—which had led
the country in bilingual education and bilingual government services—in 1980 led the backlash against bilingualism. While the English Only movement aimed specifically to abolish the official recognition of other languages and cultures, many of its adherents had a
broader program: undoing institutional mechanisms like bilingual
education, through which those languages and cultures could be
maintained and transmitted.

Probably the single most resented consequence of the ethnic transformation was the increasing number of jobs in Miami that required
bilingual skills. In this arena bilingualism had real, not just symbolic,
consequences for non-Hispanic Miamians. But for many it also symbolized a reversal of the expectation that the newcomers must adjust
to the dominant language and culture. Even worse, it conferred upon
immigrants a labor market advantage based on a need that had been
created by their own presence. The issue of bilingualism in employment crystallized the symbolic and socioeconomic grievances that in-
furiated backers of the antibilingual movement. The fact that Miami's
bilingual job market had resulted from decisions by thousands of private employers made it an impossible target for an ordinance aimed
at county services. Nevertheless, resentment over the issue undoubtedly increased support for the antibilingual campaign.

Miami's antibilingual campaign arose in one sector of the formerly
dominant culture as a collective reaction to immigration, Latinization,
and Cuban economic empowerment, and seized upon the trend toward bilingualism in government, education, and the labor market.
By directly curtailing the use of Spanish and other minority languages
in a wide range of county programs, it succeeded in sending a message about power and ethnicity in Miami. Yet judged by the wider
aspirations expressed by its supporters on the day of the vote, the

antibilingual effort must be judged a failure. Far from making the city an uncomfortable place for Spanish-speaking people to live, the movement made no dent in the pace of Cuban/Latin growth or cultural, socioeconomic, and political empowerment, all of which accelerated in the 1980s.

Ten years after its electoral success, the futility of the English Only movement can be seen in the evolving practices of the *Miami Herald*, a leading corporation as well as civic presence in Dade County. In the late 1970s the newspaper created a Spanish-language edition, *El Herald*. A modest daily supplement, it had limited staff and editorial independence, but was nevertheless the first Spanish-language daily produced by a major American newspaper. In the 1980s, *after* passage of the antibilingual ordinance, the *Herald* responded to its miserable penetration of the Hispanic market by upgrading and expanding its Spanish-language edition, now known as *El Nuevo Herald*. The corporation also promoted training in the Spanish language and Latin American culture among its employees. Finally, in 1990, Roberto Suárez, a Cuban-American, was named president of the Miami Herald Publishing Company. The message is not lost on those who resent the ascendancy of Miami's newcomers. As one reader wrote in a letter to the editor:

> Well, it is finally over! Roberto Suárez's becoming president of the Miami Herald Publishing Co. kills—once and for all—any chance of Miami's ever returning to its former status as an English-speaking city located in the United States! Shortly it will be time to begin a death watch over the *Herald's* English editions. . . . To get a letter printed, you'll have to say nice things, such as how very enjoyable it is to listen to the 120-decibel level of casual Cuban conversation. . . . Well, I don't need a big pile of *El Nuevo Heralds* to fall on me—it's time to move on. Maybe I'll go back to the United States. I still remember some English. I'll get by.[29]

And yet, what is happening in Miami is quite different from the xenophobe's nightmare of a Cuban takeover. It is much more interesting and complex. Geography has made southern Florida a kind of border area, and the Cuban presence dates from the late nineteenth century, when thousands of Cubans resided in Key West and Tampa, before Miami was founded in 1896. In the late twentieth century Miami has become, among other things, the border between Latin America and the United States. Middle-class Latin Americans come to Miami to shop, invest, get medical treatment, and transact busi-

29. *Miami Herald*, July 18, 1990, p. 12-A.

ness. When they are dispossessed by revolution or threatened by instability, Miami is where they usually flee. Such groups have resources—not always material—that enable them to interact with Miami residents in ways that differ significantly from the norm of immigrant-native relations.

The same changes that created among Anglos a sense of disempowerment and loss of community had, for Cubans and other Latinos, a diametrically opposite effect. Enrique Fernández, a Cuban-American journalist who lives in New York, overstates the facts of the case, but captures the essence of the Cuban/Latino attachment to Miami:

> I keep going back to Miami, the only American city where I feel on top. I don't mean just Cuban. Miami is a Latino city, where English is virtually a second language and, most importantly, where our speech patterns, our gestures, our posture, our dress, our unsubdued Latino selves are all part of the dominant culture. . . . Miami is the one place in America where Latinos are spared the full weight of the arrogance of the empire.[30]

Cubans in Miami have been joining the mainstream and thereby transforming it, not by making Miami a Spanish-speaking, Latin American city, but rather by making it a much more multicultural, even transcultural, city. Cubans and other Hispanics have not created a Latin Miami, but a New Miami where the Latin sensibility and presence is increasingly integral—somewhat in the way that Cajun culture is a constituent part of what defines Louisiana. Spanish has hardly replaced English as the dominant language in Miami, but it has become a significant second language. Rather than existing in an isolated cultural ghetto, Cubans are becoming involved in the city's traditional institutions, from chambers of commerce and labor unions to the United Way and political parties. These institutions have not been Cubanized but have been affected in complicated and often fascinating ways. For several years the ascendant Republican Party of Dade County, which owes its success mostly to Cuban Americans, was presided over by Jeb Bush, the very Anglo son of the President of the United States. Yet the younger Bush, who is married to a Mexican immigrant, speaks nearly flawless Spanish.

Cubans have also played key roles in creating new institutions that are not Cuban as such, but reflect a process of cultural combination. The Miami Sound Machine, with its mix of Latin rhythms and American pop styles, and the Calle Ocho festival, which began under the

---

30. Enrique Fernández, "Ideological Vise Traps Some Cuban-Miamians," *Miami News*, Aug. 11, 1988, p. 9A.

name of "Open House Eight," the brainchild of Cuban yuppies (a.k.a. "yucas"[31]) in the Kiwanis Club of Little Havana, are good examples.

The Dade County antibilingual movement, which ignored these distinctions, was an attempt to legislate away the new demographic and cultural realities of Miami, which it could neither reverse nor destroy. The current crisis of the national Official English movement suggests that in this regard, too, the experience of Miami might point the way to the future.

Language Struggles in a Changing California Community

By John Horton and José Calderón

John Horton is associate professor of sociology at the University of California, Los Angeles. José Calderón is a doctoral candidate in sociology at U.C.L.A. and a community activist in Monterey Park, California. They wrote this article for the *Source Book.*

The rise of the Official English movement in the United States could well signal a growing nativism and anti-immigrant backlash. Like the nativist movements of the late nineteenth and early twentieth centuries, the campaign for Official English coincides historically with a period of massive immigration. During the 1980s about 6 million immigrants and refugees, overwhelmingly from Asia and Latin America, entered the country legally and an undetermined number came without documents. California has been a primary destination. By 1983 its foreign-born population was already estimated to be about 20 percent.[32] In this state dramatically transformed by newcomers, voters have approved Official English measures by wide margins.

Will the broad consensus behind Official English translate automatically into strong support for the restrictive legislation being proposed

---

31. Besides being a young, upscale Cuban American, the *yuca* is a starchy tuber that is a staple of the Cuban diet.

32. Thomas Muller and Thomas J. Eppenshade, *The Fourth Wave: California's Newest Immigrants* (Washington, D.C.: Urban Institute, 1985), p. 40; Alejandro Portes and Rubén G. Rumbaut, *Immigrant America: A Portrait* (Berkeley: University of California Press, 1990).

by the movement's leaders? Recent electoral studies show significant pockets of opposition behind the dominant consensus: mainstream media and public officials, liberals, the highly educated, Latinos, and (to a lesser extent) Asian Americans. Can the rest of the population—the apparent supporters—be dismissed as xenophobic, racist, or right-wing? Electoral statistics cannot provide all the answers because they touch only the surface of complex and unexamined social processes. In order to assess the significance of the Official English movement, and to locate its roots of support and opposition, we need to tap the lived experience of established residents and immigrants in their communities. We need detailed ethnographic case studies of how the forces for and against language restrictions are played out—how they are formed, reinforced, or transformed in the course of actual political struggle.

What follows is a report on one such study of politics and language in Monterey Park, California, the city widely proclaimed, and frequently denounced, as the first suburban Chinatown in the United States: "Little Taipei" or the "Chinese Beverly Hills." We trace the language struggle from an abortive attempt to declare Official English in 1986 to electoral support for Proposition 63, the state's Official English amendment later in the same year, to compromises on city codes regulating the use of Chinese business signs in 1989. It is a story of initial polarization and conflict, followed by a lessening of language struggles and accommodation to the realities of a multiethnic community.[33]

A city of 62,000 residents located just east of Los Angeles in the populous San Gabriel Valley, Monterey Park exemplifies the kinds of economic, demographic, and political changes that could fuel nativistic reactions to immigration. In 1960 the town's population was 85 percent Anglo (non-Hispanic white), 12 percent Latino, and 3 percent Asian. By 1980 the accelerated arrival of second- and third-generation Chicanos (Americans of Mexican descent), Nisei (second-generation Japanese Americans), and Asian immigrants had changed the ethnic makeup of the city to 25 percent Anglo, 39 percent Latino, and 35 percent Asian. During the 1980s these proportions continued to

33. Our research in Monterey Park began in 1986; it has focused on local issues as they affect, and are affected by, relations between established residents and immigrant newcomers within formal and informal political arenas. We have used a variety of methods and data sources appropriate to a community study: analysis of newspaper articles, pamphlets, and demographic and electoral data, interviews with community leaders, and most of all, ethnographic observation of daily events. Our research team of two sociology professors and four graduate students has been multiethnic and multilingual. Since 1988 the research has been funded by the Changing Relations Project, sponsored by the Ford Foundation, and by the Institute of American Cultures and the Asian American Studies Center of the University of California, Los Angeles.

change dramatically in response to increased Chinese immigration from Taiwan, Hong Kong, and Southeast Asia. According to the 1986 Special Test Census, between 1980 and 1986 the number of Asian residents in the city increased by 70.6 percent to become a 51 percent majority; Anglos made up 15.8 percent, Latinos 30.5 percent, and blacks 1.9 percent. If current trends continue, Asians may reach 70 percent of the population in the 1990s.

Today, Monterey Park is a town in transition from a middle-American, racially mixed suburban bedroom community to a financial and service center for a growing regional Chinese and Asian population. Chinese signs and businesses line the major commercial streets, and longtime citizens complain about having to go outside of town to find "American" stores. Mandarin is spoken downtown in most offices, banks, and shops. Just seconds away, English is the language of city hall, where every other Monday the five-person city council hotly debates the issues of the day. Monterey Park is precisely the kind of community where one expects to find a backlash against change by established residents. Throughout the 1980s city politics were dominated by battles over growth, as developers and proponents of "slow growth" fought for control over land use, mini-malls, condominiums, high-rise apartments, and traffic.

In this city where economic development has an Asian face, a related conflict developed over the questions of language and immigration. In 1985 Monterey Park received a national award for its cross-cultural programs. But a year later, after intense debate, the city council enacted an ordinance requiring signs to include an English-language description of a firm's business. In 1986 Monterey Park became the second California city (after Fillmore) to pass an ordinance declaring English its official language. The measure also denounced the concept of sanctuary and encouraged local police to cooperate with the U.S. Immigration and Naturalization Service in apprehending undocumented immigrants. It was introduced by Councilman Barry Hatch, an outspoken advocate for restrictions on language and immigration. Even before the ordinance was passed, two Anglo residents and their supporters had collected three thousand signatures of registered voters—with Asians, Latinos, and Anglos equally represented, the organizers claimed[34]—on a petition to place an Official English referendum on the ballot.

The Official English law was immediately challenged by a new group, the Coalition for Harmony in Monterey Park (CHAMP), an

34. This approximated the actual ethnic breakdown of registered voters; as recent immigrants, a large proportion of the Asian population had yet to qualify for citizenship and, thus, for voting rights.

uneasy interethnic coalition of business people and civil libertarians. Targeting the major "American" and several Chinese supermarkets, CHAMP volunteers collected five thousand signatures on a counter-petition requesting the city council to rescind the ordinance.[35] This challenge was temporarily successful. One council member of the three who had supported Official English changed his vote, and the measure was rescinded. However, when the voters had the opportunity to express their own opinions, they demonstrated their divided support for the idea. In November 1986 the citizens of Monterey Park voted 53 percent to 47 percent for Proposition 63, the statewide Official English initiative. Nevertheless, the margin was much closer than in neighboring cities in the San Gabriel Valley, with an average 73 percent "yes" vote.

The clash between opponents and proponents of Official English was not over. Several powerful Anglo and Chinese developers formed a new organization, Americans for Better Cityhood (A.B.C.), to mount an attack against the "racism" of leaders of the Official English and slow-growth movements. Mobilizing its considerable financial resources, A.B.C. collected enough signatures to hold a special election to recall two council members, Barry Hatch and Pat Reichenberger, who had strongly supported Official English legislation. But in April 1987 the Monterey Park voters rejected the recall by 62 percent—an apparent victory for both slow-growth and Official English advocates, who denied the charges of racism. The outcome, however, can also be attributed to the tactics of A.B.C., which hired Spanish speakers to try to persuade middle-class, assimilated, and English-speaking Latino residents that the city council was out to deport them to Mexico.

After the defeat of the recall movement, the stage seemed to be set for a resurgence of defensive and xenophobic politics. In the April 1988 council elections, the pro-growth candidates were defeated, attesting to the continuing strength of the slow-growth forces. But at the same time, the voters defeated an extreme advocate of language and immigration restrictions and elected a Chinese American, Judy Chu, along with Betty Couch, one of two candidates endorsed by the slow-growth movement. Chu introduced a new tendency in local politics which would have a profound impact on the course of language struggles. She combined the implicit promise of Asian representation with the explicit promise of support for managed growth within a

35. Of those who signed CHAMP's petition, 67 percent were residents (though not necessarily citizens and voters), and of these, 81 percent were Chinese, 13 percent Latinos, and 6 percent Anglos.

framework of appreciation for diversity. This formula has usually prevailed over the politics of language restrictionism.

As predicted, Councilman Hatch, the city's most vocal proponent of Official English, revived his campaign on the language issue. In 1988 he introduced an ordinance to require two-thirds English on all business signs, led a move to fire the city's independent and progressive library board, and used his office to complain about the increasing number of Chinese books in the library. In many speeches and media appearances, Hatch has advocated a temporary moratorium on all immigration. But ultimately, none of Hatch's campaigns was successful. The city's Planning Commission and Design and Review Board recommended no action on signs, and in the end a compromise ordinance was passed, requiring only slightly more English signage.[36] A federal court ordered the reinstatement of the library board, and the library continues to receive Chinese books and to cater to Chinese patrons.

The most devastating blow to Hatch and his political agenda, however, was his defeat in the April 1990 city council election, in which he received the lowest vote among six candidates. The winners for the three open seats were, in order of vote size: Samuel Kiang, a political newcomer, Chinese immigrant, engineer, and lawyer; Fred Balderrama, a Latino and president of the Monterey Park Chamber of Commerce; and Marie Purvis, an Anglo businesswoman and longtime resident. It would be wrong to attribute Hatch's defeat solely to his anti-immigrant politics. No doubt he was also a victim of the local tendency to sweep incumbents out of office and to blame them for the city's many ills. Nevertheless, voters were clearly dissatisfied with Hatch's particular brand of politics. Onetime political allies in the slow-growth movement did not endorse his candidacy. Ideological supporters of Official English told us that he was "divisive," "against everything," and that he did not "propose positive solutions to anything." These sentiments translated into lack of electoral support. Hatch not only received the fewest votes; according to our exit poll, he was the last choice among voters of every ethnic group. Kiang, the largest vote-getter, was the first choice among Chinese voters, the third choice among Latinos, and the fifth choice among Anglos.

Monterey Park now has a less white and more ethnically diverse city council—one Chinese immigrant, a Chinese American (the current mayor), two Anglos, and a Latino. Nobody on the council talks

---

36. Elsewhere in the San Gabriel Valley, Asian American business owners won a federal court suit against a Pomona city ordinance requiring at least 50 percent English on their signs; the mandate violated the First Amendment, according to Judge Robert M. Takasugi (see pp. 284–87).

about language restrictions; everyone at least gives lip service to the more important goal of managed growth. The composition of the council reflects a voter reaction against ethnically divisive politics and in favor of addressing shared problems like overdevelopment, traffic, a crumbling dam, earthquakes, and malathion spraying. While neither of these tendencies can be interpreted as a victory for tolerance over nativism, two important facts suggest that the local battle about immigration and language has died down. First, the city's most visible supporter of Official English lost his reelection (as did Reichenberger, who finished next to last). Second, at least for the moment, political discourse is colored by the language of "cultural diversity" rather than by charges against immigrants and countercharges of racism.

The story of the rise and apparent decline of language conflict in Monterey Park can be reconstructed from day-to-day political struggles wherein contradictions are exposed. It is a story of the gradual emergence of cross-ethnic politics. There is no question that the first round of language struggle was extremely divisive. The call to English language unity targeted Asians for linguistic and economic discrimination and polarized the community between established residents and new immigrants. But the actual course of battle revealed class, political, and ethnic contradictions within both groups. The Official English movement drew support from slow-growth Democrats and fiscal-conservative Republicans and contained two political currents: a populist concern with community control and planning and a reactionary attempt to restrict the cultural and political influence of new immigrants. Out of the struggle between these factions, within and across both movements, emerged a new political alliance that undercut racial polarization and pushed both developers and Official English leaders into more isolated positions.

Early in the battle, the slow-growth and Official English currents tended to coincide at the level of leadership and also probably in the minds of many Monterey Park residents. Thus Barry Hatch got slow-growth support for his election in 1986 because he spoke out strongly for community control over development. He got the same kind of support during the unsuccessful recall in 1987, when developers lumped together slow growth with Official English and labeled both as racist. It was the fight against racism that also united a disparate coalition of business people and liberals. But out of the struggle surrounding racism, Americanism, language, immigration, and land use grew an altogether new political force that cut across the old nativism/slow growth and diversity/development divisions by combining the populist issue of community control over development with a new emphasis on ethnic harmony. This realignment weakened both developers and Official English forces.

In 1988 the old opposition coalition, CHAMP, split along class lines. Local business people who opposed slow-growth restrictions on the rapid development of homes and commercial areas in Monterey Park ran their own minority and probusiness candidate, a Latino, for city council. Those within CHAMP who supported controlled growth and steps toward ethnic harmony supported Judy Chu, who refused developer contributions. The developer candidate was defeated, while Chu led the field of seven candidates, with massive support from Chinese and Japanese Americans and significant support from Latino and Anglo voters. The rise of the controlled-growth/harmony tendency also prompted slow-growth leaders to begin backing away from the Official English campaign and to stress the primacy of economic rather than language issues. Lacking non-Anglo leadership in their movement, they were beginning to see the political virtues of an alliance with progressive Asian and Latino forces on issues of controlled development. Although these former supporters of Barry Hatch stopped short of denouncing him as a racist, they began to say: "He is going too far," "He is too extreme." One leader of the Residents Association of Monterey Park (RAMP), the major slow-growth group, put this changing perspective very clearly:

> The problem with Barry is that he divides the community into "newcomers/bad guys" and "us good-old Americans." His pressing the point on these social issues and taking advantage of being mayor to gain national notoriety is harmful. We need peaceful reconciliation on all fronts.[37]

In sum, there are three reasons why ethnic polarization seems to have subsided for the moment in Monterey Park. First, the language struggle and continual charges of racism hinder the goals of the strong slow-growth movement. Second, the reality of demographic change requires established residents to come to terms with Asians. Third, the emergence of a politics of diversity and controlled growth opens up a middle ground for uniting moderates and progressives around demands for representation and diversity in the struggle for controlled development.

In Monterey Park, as elsewhere in the United States, the Official English movement has been divisive and xenophobic. It pits longtime residents against newcomers, particularly Asians and Latinos. Its declarations, written into law, seem to give legal justification for de-

37. Berkley Hudson, "Heavily Asian Town's Mayor Holds Tight to Controversial Views," *Los Angeles Times*, July 16, 1989, sec. III, p. 4.

priving immigrants of the tools they need for empowerment and mobility, while blaming them for all the complex problems brought by rapid economic and demographic change. The major lesson of our case study, however, is that this movement can be challenged and defused through political struggle around issues that cut across divisions between established residents and immigrants.

Activists interested in explaining and resisting this movement have two tasks. First, they must carefully distinguish between leaders and followers of the movement and not dismiss both as racists. There is the racism which is built into the very structure of capitalist exploitation, the racism of white supremacists who can be found in the leadership of Official English, and the scapegoating of immigrants by established residents in the working and middle classes who fear competition and displacement in increasingly internationalized workplaces and neighborhoods. Second, activists must expose the xenophobia of leaders of the Official English movement, while addressing the structural causes of ethnic conflict within a framework of genuine ethnic and cultural diversity. The followers of Official English cannot be won over through charges that they are racist or through bland sermons about respect for diversity that fail to address the genuine problems behind the current wave of nativism—economic dislocations, the declining infrastructure, massive demographic changes, and the alienation of ordinary people from the process of social planning.

For many Anglos and assimilated minorities, restrictive language legislation has offered a concrete response to insecurities caused by the rapid restructuring of community life, and especially those brought on by immigration. The nativistic reaction in Monterey Park was reinforced by the arrival of (real or imagined) high-status Asian immigrants with assets as entrepreneurs or educated professionals. Another factor in the rise of nativism has been the economic context of the new immigration. It comes at a time of uncertainty for the United States in an increasingly competitive world economy and of cutbacks in domestic social services and wages, a lack of affordable housing, and a general decline in the quality of life. While these forces most severely affect the working classes, they also extend to the middle classes, as the case of Monterey Park demonstrates.

Paradoxically, the same historical conditions that breed nativism and racism open up opportunities for greater ethnic and cultural diversity and for the emergence of ideologies that undermine the assumption that the United States will be saved through policies of linguistic and cultural subordination. The domination of English in this country has historically depended on Anglo political superiority and the weakness of ethnic communities. Today, this power balance is shifting, with the territorial and political growth of nonwhite minorities in the United States and with the rapid integration of the United States into a world economy. Under these new conditions, the appeals for popular control over community development within a framework of cultural and linguistic diversity, as expressed at the grass roots in Monterey Park, are not pie-in-the-sky idealism, but reasonable responses to local and international realities that can only be addressed through interethnic alliances.

What Happens When English Only Comes to Town?
A Case Study of Lowell, Massachusetts

By Camilo Peréz-Bustillo

Camilo Peréz-Bustillo is associate counsel for Multicultural Education, Training, and Advocacy (META), Inc., a public-interest law firm in San Francisco, California, and served as the plaintiffs' attorney in the Lowell school desegregation case. He wrote this article for the *Source Book*.

On the evening of May 6, 1987, more than one hundred Latino, Cambodian, and Laotian parents and community leaders gathered for a special hearing before the Lowell, Massachusetts, school board. They had come together out of increasing concern regarding the quality of their children's education in the city's oldest, most dilapidated, and segregated schools. Within those sites language-minority students were assigned to substandard facilities, such as basements, converted boiler rooms, bathrooms, and closets. Others were housed in temporarily rented space in the city's Y.M.C.A. and Boy's Club—sites that were literally separate from, and unequal to, those provided for white, English-proficient students.

A substantial percentage of the Latino and Southeast Asian parents had turned out that night to be heard by their elected representatives on the Lowell School Committee. All seven committee members were white Anglos—although Anglo is perhaps a misnomer in this context; most were of Greek, Irish, Polish, or Italian ancestry. As designated members of the language-minority communities prepared to speak, George Kouloheras, the school committee's senior member in both age and tenure, called the meeting to order. The sole agenda item for the public hearing was discussion of the need for a citywide desegregation plan. As Lowell's racial and ethnic minority-student population had soared—from 15 percent in 1982 to more than 40 percent in 1987—it had become concentrated in a few facilities under a long-standing "neighborhood schools" policy. The Acre, where Latinos and Southeast Asians were most numerous, was the city's poorest area, with its oldest and cheapest housing stock. Long home to the state's major Greek American community, the Acre was the neighborhood where the parents of Governor Michael Dukakis and former U.S. senator Paul Tsongas had first settled. And it remained the turf of George Kouloheras.

When Kouloheras realized that some parents intended to address the school committee in languages other than English and had brought their own interpreters to translate the discussion, he became agitated. "English is the official language of this committee," he proclaimed. "It always has been, and it always will be." Kouloheras then moved to ban the use of interpreters. When the motion failed on a tie vote among the six members present, he stood and announced he would walk out in protest. In so doing, he denied the meeting a quorum, thus preventing it from proceeding. Shouting matches erupted among Kouloheras, an opponent on the school committee, and several Latino parents. Outside the hall, in remarks widely reported by the local press, Kouloheras attacked "these bastards who speak Spanish" and added that "Hispanics are the worst of all in this city."[38] By the next morning Lowell's ethnic strains, the segregation of language-minority children, and Kouloheras's English Only stance were beginning to attract regional and national media attention.

Lowell is renowned in U.S. social history as a classic "immigrant city." One of the first planned urban communities, it was established by Boston entrepreneurs in 1821 as a textile manufacturing center. The mills first recruited New England "farm girls" as laborers and, later, successive waves of Irish, French Canadian, Portuguese, Polish, and Greek immigrants. From the beginning Lowell has been characterized by top-down development promoted by (and beholden to) outsiders, a large immigrant work force, and a tradition of community-based struggles.[39]

---

38. Nancy Costello, "Kouloheras Sparks Racial Clash at Meeting," *Lowell Sun*, May 7, 1987; Diego Ribadeneira, "School Panelist in Lowell Is Accused of Racism," *Boston Globe*, May 8, 1987. Kouloheras later denied making these statements.

39. Peter Nien-chu Kiang, "Southeast Asian Parent Empowerment in Lowell, Massachusetts," paper presented to the Sixth Annual Conference of the Association for Asian American Studies, New York City, June 1–3, 1989.

By the early 1920s, 20,000 Greeks had arrived in Lowell—the largest immigrant influx in the city's history until the 1980s—and most of them settled in the Acre. Initially, children were educated in private religious schools, for the most part, with bilingual instructional programs in the early grades. But there was a distinct shift in the Greek community's linguistic and cultural identity over time. "Some children of Greek-Americans are wholly ignorant of Greek," local historian Nicholas V. Karas wrote in 1984.

> Others speak or understand only a few basic words like a non-Greek tourist struggling to be understood. One major reason is that the majority of [second-generation] Greek-American parents don't speak Greek in their homes on a daily basis. . . . For so many Greek immigrants, their grandchildren's ignorance of Greek, shackled to their own inability to express themselves deeply in English, robs both of that 'satisfaction of the soul' that comes when grandparents and grandchildren talk to each other in words that each can understand.[40]

Increasingly, other traditions lapsed as well, such as the celebration of name days (corresponding to the Greek Orthodox saint for whom a person is christened). The erosion of the community's cultural identity was undoubtedly accelerated by its physical dispersion beyond the Acre. New Deal urban renewal efforts led to demolition of old tenements and the construction of the city's first public housing projects. The Greek community's disappearance was stemmed only by a smaller, second wave of immigration after the Greek Civil War of 1946–49.

Survival, however, remained precarious. Lowell's economy had entered a sharp decline in the 1920s, with the flight of most textile and related manufacturing firms to the nonunion South, seeking the low wage levels that had earlier made Lowell's female and immigrant labor pools so attractive. The Great Depression accelerated the process of deindustrialization, and unemployment persisted well above the national average until the late 1970s.

On April 29, 1987, Michael Dukakis announced his candidacy for the Democratic presidential nomination on the Massachusetts State House steps in Boston. He was introduced by An Wang, founder and chief executive officer of Wang Laboratories, the Lowell-based computer firm. Speaker after speaker that day cited Lowell's role in the "Massachusetts miracle," the state's economic rebirth on which Dukakis based his claims to national leadership. As Wang put it, "Lowell

---

40. *The Greek Triangle of the Acre: Then and Now* (Lowell, Mass.: Meteora Press, 1984), p. 16.

was a dying symbol of the past, but Mike Dukakis saw Lowell as a symbol of the future."[41] Two key factors in the city's recovery were a massive infusion of more than $500 million in federal, state, and private redevelopment funds in the late 1970s and the Reagan-era surge in high-technology military expenditures in the area. Also, two events in 1978 served as crucial catalysts: Wang's decision to relocate his world headquarters in Lowell (made possible by a $5 million federal grant)[42] and the designation of the city's downtown mill area as a national park (which would attract over 800,000 visitors annually by 1987).

Lowell's unemployment rate, which had reached a high of 15 percent during the 1974–75 recession, fell to 13.8 percent in 1978, 7 percent in 1982, and 3 percent in 1986.[43] As Wang's sales of computers and related products climbed from $97 million in 1977 to $2.88 billion by 1986, it became the city's largest employer; overall, high-tech jobs accounted for 24 percent of all employment in Lowell by 1982.[44] Proximity to university-based research facilities and an unusual combination of high skills and low wages made Lowell an ideal center for the new "information economy." According to economist Lester Thurow, Massachusetts had always been a high-cost place to buy low-skilled labor (which had driven away the textile mills), but a low-cost place to buy high-skilled labor (which lured back the high-tech sector).[45] Lowell's reindustrialization also manifested itself in downtown redevelopment, including a gleaming new Hilton Hotel. In 1985 and 1986, seventy-five different buildings were rehabilitated in the city center— as many as in the previous ten years. The process was assisted by $54 million in federal and $44 million in state subsidies.[46]

During this same period Lowell began to experience a rising tide of immigration greater than the Irish wave of 1846–56, the Greek wave of the early twentieth century, or the periodic Puerto Rican waves beginning in the late 1940s. The success of An Wang, himself a Chinese immigrant, lured thousands of Southeast Asians; some were refugees resettled in Lowell by the federal government, but most were second-

41. Kevin Landrigan, "Dukakis Cites Lowell Success As He Launches Campaign," *Lowell Sun*, April 30, 1987, p. 3.

42. Jonathan Kaufman, "Lowell: The Dark Side of the Boom," *Boston Globe*, Oct. 25, 1987, p. 26.

43. Ibid., pp. 1, 26; John Wilke, "Wang Had Key Role in Lowell's Economic Revival," *Boston Globe*, Nov. 9, 1987, p. 24.

44. As compared with 4 percent in the U.S. as a whole; Patricia M. Flynn, "Lowell: A High Tech Success Story," in *The Massachusetts Miracle*, ed. David R. Lampe (Cambridge, Mass.: MIT Press, 1988), p. 280.

45. *Massachusetts Miracle*, p. xi.

46. Irene Sege, "Lowell Hopeful, Apprehensive As Renewal Takes a New Focus," *Boston Globe*, April 13, 1987, p. 20; Flynn, "Lowell," p. 275.

ary migrants from other parts of the United States. Supporters of
George Kouloheras would later charge that this heavy influx, beginning in 1980, was a kind of unspoken tax for the city's enjoyment of
disproportionate federal and state aid. Others claimed that the reset-
tlement of Indochinese refugees in Massachusetts was an ironic trib-
ute to the state's prominent role in opposing the Vietnam War. For
whatever reason, by 1987 Lowell's Cambodian population had grown
to more than 20,000 (the largest in the United States after that of Long
Beach, California). Many found work at Wang Labs.

But Lowell's new prosperity was far from unblemished. As Lowell's
representative in Congress, Chester Atkins, explained:

> The Massachusetts miracle has always had two sides—a
> glittering side and a dark side. The dark side is that for
> people who don't own homes in places like Lowell, as
> property values skyrocket, they were pushed out of the
> housing market. The dark side is that for most urban fami-
> lies in this state they don't have access to good schools. . . .
> It's always been a perilous miracle.[47]

In 1987 local studies showed that rent on an average four-room apartment had increased by 278 percent in Lowell over a period in which
average income had increased by only 96 percent. The availability of
affordable housing for low- and middle-income families had never
been a priority in Lowell's redevelopment. City Planning Director Peter Aucella acknowledged that the focus had been on market-rate, un-
subsidized housing: "If we're to sustain the revitalization, we must
have people with money near our downtown."[48] The arrival of a new
professional class drawn by high-tech firms set off speculative buying
and selling of single-family homes and small apartment buildings; the
surge in home prices and rents put a devastating squeeze on the
working class, affecting whites as well as minorities.

The Acre became the major battleground in Lowell's redevelopment wars. Its immediate proximity to downtown, the old mills, and
city hall made it a natural target for developers. Only broad-based
community organizing by the Coalition for a Better Acre prevented
large-scale displacement of the traditional Greek neighborhood and
the growing number of residents from Cambodia, Laos, Vietnam,
Puerto Rico, and Central and South America. But the quality of life—
and equality of access to basic services—continued to deteriorate for
these groups.

Among Lowell's longtime residents there were sharp disparities in

47. Kaufman, "Lowell: The Dark Side," p. 26.
48. David Mehegan, "Revitalized Lowell Leaves Renters out in the Street," *Boston Globe*, Sept. 20, 1986, p. 19.

receptiveness to the new groups in the city's mosaic. Southeast Asians seemed "more welcome"—initially, at least—than Latinos. The director of the Lowell Plan, a business group instrumental in the revitalization effort, hailed the arrival of Southeast Asians as "very positive. Business owners and industry types think they're terrific. They say Asians are hardworking." An unspoken implication of such sentiments was that Latinos were less desirable as workers, neighbors, and tenants.[49] Such stereotyped comparisons were detrimental for both groups. Negative assumptions about Latino hostility toward the police were coupled with condescension regarding Asians' submissiveness; Latinos were expected to be lazy and Asians to work themselves to the bone for little pay. Hispanic children were presumed to be destined for academic failure, while Southeast Asian students were classified as a "model minority" without need of special services. The net result was that often neither group received appropriate help, while both suffered disproportionately high levels of underachievement, dropping out, and eventual unemployment.

By the mid–1980s Lowell presented an explosive combination of virulent nativism and working-class populism. For several reasons the schools became the focal point of racial and ethnic strains. To begin with, the need for an improved and equitable educational system had been largely ignored in the overall redevelopment effort. In 1987 almost half the city's functioning public school buildings had been constructed before 1925, and teaching methods were often just as antiquated. Lowell's children were being trained in a nineteenth-century school system for a twenty-first-century economy. The advent of Asian and Latino students—their numbers and their need for language services—exerted enormous pressures for change. Between 1982 and 1987 the enrollment of limited-English-proficient children quadrupled to more than 2,000 out of a total school population of 12,000. To comply with Massachusetts law, Lowell provided instruction in English and five other languages—Spanish, Portuguese, Khmer, Lao, and Vietnamese—but it did so in illegally segregated, substandard classrooms. By 1987 the controversies over bilingual education and school desegregation had become intertwined with broader conflicts over the city's changing racial and ethnic character and potential shifts in political power.

George Kouloheras, a son of Greek immigrants who learned English as a second language, had long been the Acre's champion vote-getter. Seventy-six years old and a school committeeman since 1962, he was a leading spokesman for antibusing sentiment and a vocal member of

49. Sege, "Lowell Hopeful," p. 20.

U.S. English. Perhaps the best explanation for Kouloheras's success lies in the fact that he embodied the contradictions afflicting his white ethnic constituency—once perceived as a threat, now threatened themselves by new waves of immigrants. Every time Kouloheras struck a blow for the English language, symbolically he was standing up for the traditional Greeks who had struggled to master the language and make it their own. Initially a foreign, alienating tongue, English became a vehicle for expressing the immigrant identity and culture it had supposedly buried. Kouloheras's embrace of the English Only movement, along with his strong opposition to desegregation, made a confrontation over school issues virtually inevitable.

The desegregation issue first erupted at a Lowell School Committee meeting on March 26, 1987. Led by Kouloheras, committee members defeated, five to two, a proposal to "pair" two schools—one heavily minority, the other heavily white—as a first step toward systemwide desegregation. A large turnout of white parents, enthusiastic Kouloheras supporters, helped stir him to passionate oratory in defense of the "civil liberties of the majority." Also, he vented his anger over news of a demonstration earlier that day at the State House in Boston, where more than five hundred educators, language-minority parents, and community activists had opposed legislative proposals to dismantle the state's bilingual education law and to declare English its official language. On Kouloheras's motion, the committee went on record in support of the first bill (though it declined to take a position on the second).

Reports of this meeting, along with a realization that the school board majority opposed any change for children languishing in separate and unequal facilities, jolted Lowell's language-minority parents into action. Several weeks of door-to-door organizing brought a large turnout for the May 6 hearing and laid the basis for a more extensive movement afterward. The multiethnic mobilization had been set in motion, above all, by Kouloheras himself—his pandering to a hungry gallery in a way that transformed opposition to "forced busing" into a nativist attack on newcomers. Desegregation, which up until that point had been a bureaucratic and defensive concern of state officials, became an affirmative, felt demand by minority parents.

The near-riot in response to George Kouloheras's actions and statements at the May 6 hearing touched off a period of racial and ethnic tension unprecedented in Lowell's history. A multiethnic coalition for educational equity led weeks of marches, picket lines at city hall, and demands for the resignation of Kouloheras. This pressure—combined with threats of a lawsuit both by the state's attorney general and by META, Inc.—prompted the school committee on June 11 to adopt an initial desegregation plan. The four-to-three vote to approve the plan came over vitriolic opposition by Kouloheras and his allies. Although the committee had addressed the state's immediate concerns, it failed to provide improvements in Lowell's bilingual education programs, the concern that had brought many parents to the May 6 hearing. For these parents desegregation was an empty vessel unless it was accompanied by sufficient resources for equitable programming. So in August a coalition of Puerto Rican, Cambodian, and Laotian parents and students filed suit in federal court regarding these issues.

Continuing controversy over the initial implementation of desegregation in the fall of 1987 and over the pending federal lawsuit kept interethnic tensions high. On September 21 a thirteen-year-old Cambodian boy was pushed into a canal and drowned by an eleven-year-old white boy in an incident that featured anti-Asian racial slurs. In his reelection bid on November 3, George Kouloheras led all municipal candidates in number of votes polled. Despite this personal triumph, however, a four-vote majority of the school committee continued to support desegregation and eventually reached a negotiated settlement of the parents' lawsuit in December 1988.

Ironically, this settlement, which reaffirmed the need for expanded and better-quality bilingual education, seemed to strengthen Kouloheras's resolve to continue pushing the English Only agenda. He sponsored a referendum in November 1989 declaring English to be the city's official language—and recommending an English Language Amendment to the U.S. Constitution—which Lowell voters approved by nearly three to one.

This referendum, like the abortive May 6 meeting, has had contradictory effects. On the one hand, it laid the basis for continuing coalition efforts among the city's Latinos and Southeast Asians around perceived interests in common. (Ironically, these groups held their meetings primarily in English.) Leaders from the minority communities, such as Alex Huertas, Ana Ocasio, Boran Reth, and Sambath Fennell, and organizations like the Cambodian and Laotian mutual assistance associations are more influential in city politics than ever before. On the other hand, the Official English vote highlights the deep anti-Asian and anti-Latino animosities that persist in Lowell's civic life. Following three years of strife over ethnicity and language, the resounding defeat of Michael Dukakis, and the subsequent fiscal collapse of Massachusetts, Lowell has been freed of the burden of being described as anyone's "model" or "miracle." But it remains a troubled harbinger of America's future.

The English Only Movement: Social Bases of Support and Opposition among Anglos and Latinos

By Carol Schmid

Carol Schmid is professor of sociology at Guilford Technical Community College in Jamestown, North Carolina. She
wrote this article for the *Source Book* using exit-poll data
gathered by Robert Brischetto, director of the Southwest
Voter Research Institute in San Antonio, Texas.[50]

How can we explain the recent rise of Official English/English Only
campaigns, which have gained adherents at incredible speed? Before
1981 no one had heard of the English Only movement because it did
not exist. While there are precedents for language restrictionism and
repression in American history, the claim that the nation's common
language is endangered represents a new political phenomenon. In
1986 California voters, by 73 to 27 percent, adopted a constitutional
amendment declaring English the state's official language. In 1988
Florida voters approved a similar amendment by 84 to 16 percent. So
far, voters or legislators have enacted Official English measures in
seventeen states, and nowhere has such an initiative been defeated at
the polls.

Who votes for Official English legislation, and why? Many social
scientists view the focus on language differences and opposition to
bilingualism as thinly veiled hostility toward Hispanics and other minority language groups. There has been limited research on this question, however, despite its obvious importance in testing theories of
conservative social movements. English Only campaigns conform to
the pattern of such movements in that they attempt "to maintain
structures of order, status, honor, or traditional social differences or
values."[51]

Complaints about a breakdown in the process of assimilation seem
to be especially prevalent during periods of high immigration, economic restructuring, and recession, providing fertile soil for the

50. An earlier version of this paper was presented to a meeting of the Society for the
Study of Social Problems, Berkeley, California, Aug. 8, 1989. The author gratefully acknowledges a grant from the National Science Foundation.
51. Clarence Y. H. Lo, "Countermovements and Conservative Movements in the
Contemporary U.S.," *Annual Review of Sociology* 8 (1982): 108.

growth of nativism. Several theories about status and politics have been developed to explain conservative social movements. According to the notion of status preservation, declining groups seek to maintain their eroding position by identifying with extremist causes.[52] A second approach also emphasizes status politics, arguing that supporters of Senator Joseph McCarthy, for example, were either falling in status (small-town, old Protestants) or rising in status (immigrant groups anxious to demonstrate their "Americanism.")[53] A final theory postulates that status symbolism, rather than an angry response to changes in status, is of primary importance in swelling the ranks of conservative movements. According to this view, the American temperance movement reflected identification with a threatened lifestyle, a symbolic clash between two cultures—dry, Protestant middle classes versus wet, immigrant, primarily Catholic workers.[54]

In order to answer the question of who votes for English Only measures, I examined Anglo and Hispanic exit-poll results in California and Texas in 1988.[55] These two states together account for 55 percent of the Hispanic population of the United States; Hispanics comprise

52. Seymour Martin Lipset and Earl Raab, *The Politics of Unreason* (Chicago: University of Chicago Press, 1978).

53. This approach is elaborated in Daniel Bell, *The Radical Right* (New York: Doubleday, 1964), and Richard Hofstadter, *The Paranoid Style in American Politics* (New York: Vintage Books, 1967).

54. J. R. Gusfield, *Symbolic Crusade: Status Politics and the American Temperance Movement* (Urbana: University of Illinois Press, 1963).

55. The two representative exit polls were conducted on Nov. 8, 1988, by the Southwest Voter Research Institute, employing a two-stage stratified sample of voters. In both California and Texas, the first stage of sampling involved the selection of fifty precincts with probabilities proportional to the number of Hispanic registered voters in the precinct. The second stage employed an optimum allocation design, oversampling precincts with high concentrations of Hispanic voters. All survey estimates generated from the two polls were weighted to reflect the actual distribution of Hispanic registered voters, thus correcting the oversampling in stage two; see *Southwest Voter Research Notes* 2, no. 9 (Sept.–Dec. 1988). In 19 out of 20 cases, the margin of error in the California poll of 1,716 Hispanic voters should be no more than 3 percentage points; in the Texas poll of 2,694 Hispanic voters, no more than 2 percentage points. The Anglo samples in both states are representative of the precincts sampled with 5 percent or more of Hispanic registered voters (rather than of the entire Anglo population). The exact question asked was: "Suppose that today you could have voted on the following issues. Indicate how you would vote on English as the only official language of the U.S.: Favor, Oppose, Not Sure." The exit poll was printed in both English and Spanish. Only responses that indicated support for English Only legislation are presented in this paper. Approximately 10 percent of Hispanic and Anglo voters in both California and Texas answered, "Not Sure." Those responding to the survey question in California included 1,521 Hispanics, 2,461 white Anglos, 613 blacks, 186 Asians, 144 Native Americans, and 94 others or unspecified. The corresponding breakdown in Texas was: 2,273 Hispanics, 1,815 white Anglos, 242 blacks, 14 Asians, 70 Native Americans, and 21 others or unspecified. Because of the small numbers of the other groups, only Hispanics and white Anglos were analyzed in this study.

approximately one-fourth of each state's population. Among the voter characteristics I analyzed were income, education, use of Spanish-language media and bilingual ballots, age, sex, and party and ideological identification.

To what degree are individuals with lower incomes and less education more likely to vote for Official English legislation? Are they, as Seymour Martin Lipset has argued in other contexts, more liberal or leftist on economic issues, but more conservative than their affluent neighbors when liberalism is defined in noneconomic terms, such as tolerance of linguistic differences, bilingual ballots, and bilingual education? Contrary to Lipset's prediction, the exit polls show no consistent relationship between voters' education and income and their support for Official English. Perhaps the most striking finding is the marked difference in support for this legislation between Hispanics and Anglos at all educational and income categories in both California and Texas.

Higher education does not necessarily provide a more tolerant attitude toward language legislation. Among neither California nor Texas Anglos is there a consistent relationship between more education and opposition to English Only laws. In fact, the most educated Anglos in California (those with four or more years of college) are 4.8 percentage points more likely to vote for such measures than their counterparts with less than a high school diploma *(see Table 1)*. Family income presents a similar mosaic of findings. Considerably less than half of Hispanics support this legislation, ranging in Texas from 17.4 percent of Hispanics with an annual family income between $10,000 and $20,000 to 26.0 percent of those earning over $50,000. In California, Hispanics with incomes below $10,000 are least likely to support Official English (19.9 percent), while those with incomes between $30,000 and $40,000 are most likely to do so (30.5 percent). By contrast, almost two in three Anglos support English as the sole official language; only California Anglos with incomes between $10,000 and $20,000 fall below the 50 percent mark. A simple analysis of working-class authoritarianism fails to explain these patterns.

While it was impossible to test Richard Hofstadter's notion of status politics by isolating groups that are falling or rising in status, such factors may partly explain the appeal of Official English. Moreover, Joshua Fishman has speculated that the English Language Amendment represents a simplistic response to "middle-class Anglo fears and anxieties . . . another 'liberation of Grenada,' rather than any mature grappling with the really monumental economic, social, and political causes of conflict."[56] Anglo-Americans may identify with the

---

56. "'English Only': Its Ghosts, Myths, and Dangers," *International Journal of the Sociology of Language* 74 (1988): 132.

TABLE 1   Percentage in Favor of English Only Legislation
Among California and Texas Hispanic and Anglo Voters, 1988

	CALIFORNIA		TEXAS	
	Hispanic	Anglo	Hispanic	Anglo
Education				
Some High School	25.4	62.1	25.0	68.9
High School Graduate	26.8	62.7	16.9	71.3
Some College	27.3	64.1	24.8	71.5
College Graduate +	21.5	66.9	20.6	65.2
Income				
< $10,000	19.9	67.0	22.3	62.5
$10,001–20,000	21.4	43.4	17.4	67.0
$20,001–30,000	30.5	65.8	21.1	69.0
$30,001–40,000	22.9	68.8	23.6	68.5
$40,001–50,000	27.9	63.7	24.0	72.3
> $50,000	28.2	70.1	26.0	67.7
Use of Spanish-Language TV				
Often	17.6	——	19.0	——
Some	20.0	——	14.9	——
Never	28.8	——	35.6	——
Use of Spanish-Language				
Newspapers				
Often	12.6	——	21.1	——
Some	20.2	——	14.1	——
Never	25.6	——	23.2	——
Use of English, Spanish				
or Both Ballot Versions				
English Only	25.9	——	22.0	——
Spanish Only	19.8	——	26.6	——
Both English and Spanish	17.4	——	18.9	——
Sex				
Male	30.3	65.6	21.8	70.7
Female	19.5	64.3	21.6	66.5
Age				
18–25	21.6	55.2	17.8	61.0
26–35	21.0	66.9	19.5	62.1
36–45	21.2	66.0	19.8	78.8
46–55	30.8	64.4	19.6	73.6
56–65	29.1	76.7	24.4	80.4
> 65	29.5	68.6	31.7	79.3
Party Identification				
Democrat	21.6	50.7	19.7	59.9
Republican	40.9	78.6	37.0	78.2
Independent	20.3	58.1	21.7	61.4
Ideological Identification				
Liberal	15.2	36.0	20.5	50.0
Conservative	32.3	79.6	26.1	76.8
In Between	27.0	68.1	19.8	66.5

English Only movement, as they once identified with the temperance movement, on a symbolic basis. That is, many perceive a threat to their life-style from Hispanics and other language minorities, who are increasing in numbers. The decline of American education, "better" job opportunities, health facilities, and other taxpayer-funded services have been blamed on the growing immigrant population in California.[57]

Hispanics who are rising in status present a confusing and inconsistent picture. While affluent Texas Hispanics are somewhat less likely to oppose Official English legislation than their poorer counterparts, this is not the case among California Hispanics earning above $50,000 in family income. This contradictory pattern is also evident when one analyzes the effect of higher education. Nevertheless, at least two out of three Hispanics in both states oppose Official English regardless of educational attainment—hardly a vote of support among affluent members of the group. With respect to the Official English movement, ethnicity rather than status politics appears to be the most important explanatory variable.

Assimilation, including linguistic assimilation, would seem to predict less allegiance to the Spanish language and a greater support for English Only measures. There is some evidence that this is the case among California Hispanics who never watch Spanish-language television or read a Spanish-language newspaper. Care must be taken, however, not to overgeneralize from these results. In Texas, Hispanics who use Spanish-language media only some of the time are less supportive of Official English than those who use them often. A complex trend emerges when one examines use of the ballot. Predictably, those who rely on the English ballot exclusively are slightly more supportive of Official English. But contrary to expectation, the lowest level of support in both California and Texas is among Hispanics who use both English and Spanish versions of the ballot.

Language is a potent symbol of political identity, which unifies the Hispanic community, notwithstanding minor class, educational, and linguistic differences. In societies segregated by class, race, and ethnicity, the status of one's language affects self-esteem. As Donald Horowitz observes, language is an especially salient symbolic issue because it links political claims with psychological feelings of group worth.[58]

What emerges from this study is that status and language politics interact in ways very different from those envisioned by social scien-

57. José Calderón and John Horton, "The English Only Movement: Sources of Support and Opposition in California," paper presented to the American Sociological Association, Atlanta, August 1988.

58. *Ethnic Groups in Conflict* (Berkeley: University of California Press, 1985).

tists who analyzed earlier conservative social movements. The high levels of support from Anglos of all socioeconomic and educational levels—rather than mainly from groups that are falling in status—appear related to generalized fears and anxieties about the monumental economic, social, and political problems facing Americans. In contrast, Hispanics see the English Only movement as a new means to justify discrimination, a phenomenon driven by prejudice and fear, and a threat to their ethnic community. Status considerations do play a role—Hispanics with higher income express less opposition to Official English—but their support is considerably less than 35 percent over the entire spectrum of income and education.

To what extent are these trends reinforced according to sex and age? In general, within both Hispanic and Anglo communities, females are more likely to oppose English Only laws. Among California Hispanics, for example, female support levels are 11 percentage points lower than those of males. This finding might be explained by the important role of Hispanic females in socializing the young and transmitting the Spanish language and culture, as well as their closer ties to the family. Among Hispanics in Texas, however, the sex gap is much smaller; similarly, among California Anglos the difference is insignificant. In sum, sex differences in support for Official English remain a subject for further investigation.

The generational picture also defies simple generalizations. Between the ages of 18 and 25, California Anglos are much more likely to vote against language restrictions than their Texas counterparts or than older California Anglos. Hispanics currently living in California and born after World War II (those 45 and younger) also show lower support levels than older cohorts. The Texas landscape provides an even greater contrast between the generations. Anglos over 35 overwhelmingly support English Only measures—perhaps in reaction to dramatic changes in Mexican American political empowerment during their lifetime. Among Texas Hispanics, on the other hand, except for the two oldest cohorts, the age groups cluster around the average support level of approximately 20 percent.

Many commentators and social scientists have observed the nation's swing to the right over the last decade and a half. This general trend was reflected in support levels for language legislation. For example, Republican Hispanics in both California and Texas are twice as likely to endorse Official English (although it is important to note that only 17.8 percent of Hispanics in the California sample and 8.8 percent in Texas identified themselves as Republicans).[59] Anglo voter

59. The overwhelming number of Hispanics called themselves Democrats: 72.1 percent in California and 75.2 percent in Texas. Independents and others accounted for 10.2 percent in California and 16.2 percent in Texas.

attitudes also varied with party identification, with more than three-quarters of Anglo Republicans supporting Official English—1.5 times the number of Anglo Democrats. Significantly, more Anglos identified themselves as Republicans: 46.9 percent in California and 34.5 percent in Texas.[60] Attitudes varied even more dramatically by ideological identification. The only Anglo group where the majority consistently opposed Official English was among self-reported liberals in California (and this encompasses only 22.7 percent of the Anglo voters in that state). By a large margin, conservatives favored language legislation; those who classified themselves as "in between" were much closer to the conservative than the liberal camp on this issue.

The implications of Official English are complex and often hidden behind a pseudo-patriotic veil. The likelihood that they would disenfranchise and disadvantage many Hispanics and other language minorities is apparently ignored by most Anglo voters. Early in this century a similar spirit of exclusiveness spread when a rapid influx of immigrants coincided with a major domestic and international crisis. Under these conditions a significant segment of American society felt that national unity depended on maintaining cultural homogeneity.[61]

Unlike earlier nativist movements, however, the English Only campaign is not merely a reaction against poor, working-class newcomers. It is also a reaction to wealthy professional and business-owning immigrants, who were encouraged to come by the 1965 immigration act. Antiforeigner sentiment currently cuts across class boundaries. Within the white working class, fears center on the potential undercutting of established wages and labor standards, as well as increased dependency on already pressed social services and housing. The middle and upper-middle classes feel threatened by immigrants who bring a lot of capital, bid up real-estate values, take over businesses, and succeed in the professions, and whose children will compete for prime white-collar jobs. This explanation may help account for the widespread support for the English Only movement in the 1980s and 1990s.

The major objective of this paper was to present an initial analysis of the sources of support and opposition for Official English. Because the exit polls did not ask for the motivations behind these views, my theoretical conclusions are tentative and additional analysis must await further research. Nevertheless, what stands out is a schism between the Hispanic and Anglo communities along the entire expanse

60. In California 36.5 percent of Anglos called themselves Democrats and 16.6 percent independents or others; in Texas, 30.5 percent Democrats and 35.0 percent independents or others.

61. John Higham, *Strangers in the Land: Patterns of American Nativism, 1860–1925*, 2d ed. (New Brunswick, N.J.: Rutgers University Press, 1988); *(see pp. 72–84)*.

of demographic variables. Except for the small percentage who identify themselves as liberals, a majority of Anglos in almost every educational, income, age, and sex category supports Official English legislation. Among Hispanics this trend is exactly reversed.

A second goal of the paper was to examine the adequacy of established theories in explaining the recent rise and success of the English Only movement. None of the traditional explanations adequately account for its strong appeal among the majority white population, which is not confined to individuals of low educational and income status. (Unfortunately, the exit polls were unable to test whether supporters of restrictive language legislation perceive that they are losing ground.) This overwhelming support among white Anglos makes it difficult to categorize the campaign for Official English as a conservative social movement. Unlike traditional right-wing causes, it has been successful in portraying language restrictionism as a patriotic movement whose purpose is to "protect the only common bond which holds our diverse society together." Rather than preserving feelings of community, however, this study indicates that the English Only movement is more likely to breed disharmony and intergroup tension.

Language, Power, and Identity in Multiethnic Miami

By Joanne Bretzer

Joanne Bretzer is a doctoral candidate in political science at the University of Washington, now completing a dissertation on the political discourse of the Official English movement. She wrote this article for the *Source Book*.

Up to the early sixties, according to widely shared mythology, Miami typified the neighborhood-based American community, with screen doors flapping in the breeze, unlocked; a place where the grocer knew your children by name and kept them in line, and where evenings were whiled away rocking on the porch and talking with the neighbors. One longtime resident describes that Miami and compares it to the Miami of today:

Before we had our revolution, it was laid back. You could
start out in the morning and go down to Matheson Ham-
mock [a local park], take the kids down and stop at Shorty's
on the way home. Of course, people, their language—it
was very easy to conduct your business, and I miss it, I
miss it. I have lost my city. . . . All of the places that we
used to go when the kids were growing up, all the nice
places are now entirely Cuban, with their bang-bang ra-
dios and their food all over the beach. You can't go anywhere without stepping in it. And [those places are] gone;
we don't have them anymore.

"Their language," over and over again. While interviewing non-
Hispanic whites in Greater Miami,[62] I found them returning constantly to this theme. It seemed that if only the language problem
would go away, people could dust the cobwebs off the old porch
swing, feel the gentle Miami breeze, and hear the harmonies of the
McGuire Sisters once again. To the question, "How has Miami
changed in the last thirty years?" the most common response was:
"the language." It has become a metaphor for everything from the
decline of schools to the rampaging growth of a frighteningly alien
metropolis, a sentiment captured by former senator S. I. Hayakawa
when he said, "The issue is not the Spanish vs. English languages,
but English vs. chaos."[63] Oldtime non-Hispanic white residents of
Miami describe the chaos of change, and the loss of hegemony, in
terms of the politics of language.

Scholars of contemporary language politics in the United States,
and specifically of the Official English movement, have pointed to the
symbolic function of such politics. The problem, according to this
understanding, goes beyond the use of language as a medium of communication. Language politics acts to organize and give voice to other
concerns, such as cultural identity, economic threats, and loss of political power, which can all be accommodated within the same symbolic
structure.

The discourse of language politics addresses problems ranging
from getting service or jobs when languages are not shared to allowing speakers to construct, reconstruct, and preserve their individual
and cultural identity. At the level of everyday experience, there is in-
convenience and discomfort in a newly bilingual community. For
longtime residents, identity concerns arise when such displacements

62. In this essay I will speak of Greater Miami and Dade County, Florida, inter-
changeably. Miami the city makes up only a small part of this area. Significant area
politics are conducted through the Dade County Commission, and the full multicultural
nature of the region can only be appreciated as a unit.

63. "Common Language, Common Sense," *New York Times*, Feb. 21, 1990, p. A19.

and fears, including loss of political power, become attached to clearly identifiable "others"—immigrants who presumably do not share the same culture and values, and are thus viewed as a threat. "American" identity, which the dominant majority has historically defined in terms of northern European culture, is now being challenged and altered with the loss of political, economic, and social power by American-born whites and with the large-scale immigration of non-European and nonwhite others. This challenge is especially acute in Dade County, where the grass-roots politics of language has been the focus of my research.

Greater Miami initiated the Official English movement in the United States in 1980, with a successful citizen initiative to amend the county charter; in 1988 a statewide initiative made English Florida's official language (see p. 131). But language politics is expressed on the street in ways other than electoral campaigns, ways that are instructive for understanding the movement's broad-based support. Language conflict in Miami has arisen in response to rapid and profound demographic changes in the last thirty years. These changes have meant a loss of hegemony, as well as majority status, for the non-Hispanic white population. In the words of one longtime resident: "It's the numbers that give them this foothold that lets them do this [not learn English and assimilate], and there isn't anything we can do about it."

In 1960 Dade County was a relatively homogeneous region of less than one million residents. The population was 80 percent (748,000) non-Hispanic white, 5.3 percent (50,000) Hispanic, and 14.7 percent (137,000) black. Today, no one group has a majority, and Hispanics are projected to make up a plurality of 45.4 percent in 1990. Meanwhile, the non-Hispanic white population has declined proportionally to 35 percent, and in real numbers to 658,000, as a result of white flight; it is not expected to grow for the rest of the century. The black population has grown to 21 percent, including Hispanic and Haitian newcomers, and is expected to stabilize at that level. In sum, Miami has rapidly evolved from a medium-sized, non-Hispanic white community in 1959, the year of Cuba's revolution, to a multiethnic community with a visible triethnic character—African American, Hispanic, and non-Hispanic white.[64]

The loss of non-Hispanic white hegemony in Miami has been occurring on all fronts—political, economic, and cultural. Politically, the loss has come as a result of both immigration and civil rights gains.

64. "Population Projections: Race and Hispanic Origin, Dade County, Florida, 1980–2000," Research Division, Metro-Dade County Planning Department, Miami, Florida, 1987.

Immigration and eventual naturalization has expanded the voting strength of Hispanics enormously, from virtually zero in 1960 to almost 27 percent in 1989 in the county and 41.3 percent in the city. Civil rights and voting rights laws have helped African Americans to become players, albeit limited ones, in the political arena. Hispanics, who vote in higher percentages than either blacks or non-Hispanic whites, have gained political power in Miami by virtue of their demographic strength and economic power. Within the metropolitan area Hispanics hold six mayoral seats, ten of twenty-eight positions on the state legislative delegation, and city commission majorities in Miami, Hialeah, West Miami, and Sweetwater, and now the U.S. Congressional seat long held by the late Claude Pepper.[65] Moreover, they occupy many appointed and informal positions of power, and the previously non-Hispanic power structure, for example, the *Miami Herald*, has been incorporating more Hispanics as their influence grows.[66]

The Cuban economic success story has taken on mythic proportions. For a number of reasons, Cubans in Miami have fared better than their Latino counterparts elsewhere in the United States, but less well, on average, than non-Hispanic whites.[67] It is the perception, however, of relative Cuban success that has fueled the perception of relative decline by non-Hispanic whites.

African Americans have also gained a measure of political power in Greater Miami. On both city and county commissions, there is a "black seat." African Americans have held positions on the school board, as school superintendent, as city manager for Miami, and numerous appointed positions. The city and county governments employ blacks at a higher than representative rate. Of course, ethnic seats and high numbers of low-level clerical and maintenance jobs are not the same as equitable power-sharing.[68] Still, they mark a clear di-

65. Christopher L. Warren, John G. Corbett, and John F. Stack, Jr., "Hispanic Ascendancy and Tripartite Politics in Miami," in *Racial Politics in American Cities*, ed. Rufus P. Browning, Dale R. Marshall, and David H. Tabb (New York: Longman, 1980), pp. 155–77.

66. Max J. Castro, "Miami: Newcomers and Power, Newcomers in Power," paper presented to the Latin American Studies Association, Miami, Dec. 4–7, 1989.

67. Lisandro Pérez, "Cubans in the United States," *Annals of the American Academy of Political and Social Science* 487 (Sept. 1986): 126–37. Pérez points out that while household income is relatively high among Cubans, there is a comparatively large number of workers per household. "When figures on personal income are examined . . . the income of Cubans is much closer to that of the Spanish-origin population than to that of the total U.S. population" (p. 134). Even with that qualifier, family income for Cubans in Miami was 75 percent of the average for all households. See also *Hispanic Profile, Dade County, Florida*, Research Division, Metro-Dade County Planning Department, 1986.

68. Allen Bronson Brierly and David Moon, "Ethnic Differences, Coalitions, and Metropolitan Reform in Greater Miami," paper presented at the annual meeting of the American Political Science Association, Atlanta, Aug. 30–Sept. 3, 1989.

vergence from the days of complete non-Hispanic white political hegemony.

This cultural hegemony began to dissipate in the 1970s as churches, schools, community organizations, entertainment, and media all began to reflect the multiethnic nature of Greater Miami. Two major television stations and innumerable radio stations, including the top-rated station in the area, broadcast in Spanish. At any given time, conferences, festivals, concerts, films, and theater celebrate and re-create ethnic identity, not only for Cubans, but for Haitians, Nicaraguans, Bahamians, and West Indians, among others.

Cultural, political, and economic factors reinforce one another and support the perception among remaining non-Hispanic whites that the world as they knew it, a world enunciated and circumscribed by English, has disappeared. Here is how one interviewee described the experience of driving through Miami in the late 1980s:

> I couldn't believe it. I mean, it was like a foreign country . . . a Spanish-speaking country. You won't see a sign that's in English. . . . It was Spanish; every word on every building—it was Spanish. . . . Even back in '77, it was already the Cubans. . . . I took my son down to Ecuador. . . . On the plane coming back, my friend said to me, "Well, now we're going back to another Spanish-speaking country."

While non-Hispanic whites retain their dominance of Dade County's economy and politics—and U.S. national culture, albeit with an international accent, remains dominant—they sense the gradual erosion of their position. One recent study shows that relative decline, underscored by the constant arrival of new immigrants, has led non-Hispanic whites to feel the least represented and least well-treated by government of all three major ethnic groups.[69]

The mythology of Miami's halcyon days before 1959 is rooted in the experience of non-Hispanic whites who grew up or raised families there at the time. They lived in a world in which African Americans were legally segregated in public bathrooms, department-store dressing rooms, beaches, schools, and neighborhoods. Jews were informally excluded (and in some cases still are) from private clubs, beaches, and neighborhoods. Hispanics were few, and other non-English speakers were mainly tourists who spent their money in the winter and left before spring. By the 1970s all this had changed. Civil rights demonstrations and court-mandated desegregation brought an end to whites' perverse naïveté about Miami's black population, and brought about a modest level of power-sharing. Cubans, once regarded as temporary exiles who would return to a liberated Cuba, became an economically and politically significant presence. Then

69. Ibid.

came Haitians, Central Americans, and of course, the Mariel Boatlift of 1980, with over 100,000 new Cuban exiles, including a visible minority of Afro-Cubans, gays, and criminals.

Miamians, for the most part, cannot affect the forces of international politics that influence the ebb and flow of immigration, or other changes they are experiencing, such as rapid urbanization and the resulting displacement, crime, and population density. Language politics serves as an attempt to regain stability, to define the parameters of community, and to maintain individual, group, and national identity in the face of these changes. The choice of language in Miami—and it is often a matter of choice—can be an everyday act of resistance. Many of the non-Hispanics I interviewed claimed to be proficient in Spanish, but unwilling to use it; one student even claimed that such a refusal was a favor, because it forced Spanish speakers to learn English. For these Miamians the use of English articulates a claim to some measure of power based on American identity and at the same time a resistance to the forces of cultural, political, and economic changes that seem to be engulfing them.

Still, it must be acknowledged that language differences create immediate, and salient, problems in Miami. For monolinguals it can be difficult to accomplish simple tasks, such as finding something in a grocery store or getting help from a business over the telephone. Particularly for working-class people, employment and economic advancement—even "advancement" to minimum-wage labor—may require acquisition of another language, not an easy task for those scrambling to survive. Moreover, English-speaking Miamians often feel that information is unavailable to them, by design, when it is transmitted in another language. A left-liberal political activist told me that *El Nuevo Herald*, the Spanish-language edition of the *Miami Herald*, often prints significantly different stories, and versions of stories, than those appearing in the English-language edition. He felt that non-Spanish speakers would be outraged if they knew what was being printed in *El Nuevo Herald*. In this case language seems to pose a barrier to the flow of information from one community to another, as is often perceived to be the case when bilinguals switch languages in mid-conversation. Monolinguals often feel both excluded and diminished, believing that bilingual code-switchers are drawing a verbal circle around their terrain.

The symbolic issues of identity, community, and distribution of power are linked to multiple levels of meaning. While language conflict is played out in practical arenas, the daily inconveniences give heft and substance to larger struggles over identity and hegemony. For example, a confrontation I witnessed in a Cuban restaurant between a Cuban waitress and a non-Hispanic white customer shifted from the subject of poor communication over the temperature of a steak to a broadside assault on the waitress, the restaurant, and the entire Cuban population of Miami for its "refusal" to assimilate and learn English. One interviewee linked all of Miami's woes with Hispanic immigration:

> The [Cuban] culture . . . has taken over—there is no integration. . . . If you are working someplace . . . the language is mainly Spanish; if you don't know it, you don't belong here. . . . They consider this Cuba across the water. . . . They all carry guns as part of their culture. . . . Probably 98 percent of the drug arrests are from that element. . . . They brought a lot of things we really don't need, but it is a part of their culture. . . . They have to open all the new schools. . . . Now it is up to us, with our tax money, to open schools that don't speak English.

Few of those I interviewed saw language itself as responsible for the fall of idyllic Miami; rather, they understood it as representative of the various dimensions of decline. Language, it would seem, is audible evidence of loss of power for non-Hispanic whites. The battle over language acts as a surrogate for ethnic conflict for another important reason. Almost all of the people I interviewed had internalized the post-civil-rights sensibility about public discourse over race and ethnicity. In fact, many chose to project all remaining racism in Miami onto Cubans, accusing them of being the cause of black economic displacement and of practicing more overt forms of racism. I found only one non-Hispanic white who acknowledged some level of residual racism, while most others felt that such thinking belonged to a bygone era. Language, on the other hand, is seen as a mutable quality, unlike race; language choice is something individuals can be held responsible for. So in this case, language choice replaces race as a means of defining inclusion and exclusion in the community of Americans. Language—and, by extension, ethnicity—become nonessential characteristics to be relinquished for the sake of assimilation.

In discussing assimilation, most interviewees felt that if only Cubans would give up their language, the rest would follow. Official English activist Terry Robbins put it this way:

> It is a problem of nonassimilation and holding onto one's own identity, moving away from the melting pot. What identifies a person? His language. When Cubans came to Dade County, they soon realized that they had to stay here and that they must hang onto their language for their identity as Cubans, and they have succeeded.

A University of Miami historian linked language and ethnicity so completely that he predicted that if a Cuban child were raised by English-speaking parents, he or she would have no remaining traces of Cuban ethnicity. A University of Miami student referred to Cubans who would not learn English as "lumps in the melting pot."

For these non-Hispanic whites, assimilation would seem to mean relinquishing the characteristics that distinguish "them" from "us." It would require an abdication of one's natal ethnic identity for the right of admission into the community defined and circumscribed by the use of English. It would include, by extension, the acquisition of the non-Hispanic-white culture that has historically defined "American" identity. The hope, perhaps, is that such Americanization would bring back the mythological, pre-Hispanic Miami, of tranquil nights undisturbed by the rhythm of salsa.

English Plus: Responding to English Only

By Mary Carol Combs

Mary Carol Combs formerly served as director of the English Plus Information Clearinghouse in Washington, D.C., and as director of the English Plus project of the League of United Latin American Citizens. Now a doctoral student in multicultural education at the University of Arizona, she wrote this article for the *Source Book*.

English Plus emerged from the language battles of the 1980s, a philosophy of inclusion and openness toward linguistic minority groups. While acknowledging the importance of English proficiency in this country, it advocates the preservation of other languages and cultures. As an alternative to English Only, it has attracted the attention of language educators, community leaders, politicians of varying views, business executives, and grass-roots activists. Coalitions throughout the United States have embraced English Plus as an approach to counter local, state, and national campaigns for Official English. Meanwhile, a number of states and municipalities have passed resolutions endorsing the principles of English Plus.[70]

So far, what have been the results? How effective has English Plus proved as a strategy for defeating English Only legislation? How has English Plus influenced voters' understanding of Official English ini-

---

70. These include the states of New Mexico, Oregon, and Washington, and the cities of Atlanta, Cleveland, Dallas, San Antonio, Tucson, and Washington, D.C.

tiatives? What is the future of English Plus as a viable response to the growing xenophobia in North America? This article will attempt to answer these questions, tracing the origin and evolution of English Plus, analyzing its political role, and discussing some of the issues surrounding a new and sometimes confusing concept.

English Plus, though commonly identified with opposition to the English Only movement, initially appeared in another context. It was conceived as a reaction to attacks on bilingual education by then-Secretary of Education William J. Bennett. In a September 1985 speech, Bennett declared that "we have lost sight of the goal of learning English as the key to equal educational opportunity" *(see pp. 358–63)*. Shortly thereafter, a Miami-based civil rights organization, the Spanish-American League against Discrimination (SALAD) issued a detailed response to Bennett. This document would become a blueprint for the English Plus approach to combating language restrictionism. Its authors wrote:

> We fear that Secretary Bennett has lost sight of the fact that English is *a* key to equal educational opportunity, necessary but not sufficient. English by itself is not enough. Not English Only, English *Plus!* . . .
> Bennett is wrong. We won't accept English Only for our children. We want English plus. English plus math. Plus science. Plus social studies. Plus equal educational opportunities. English plus competence in the home language. Tell Bennett to enforce bilingual education and civil rights laws you enacted, or tell the President he cannot do his job. English Plus for everyone![71]

The statement emphasized the empowering aspects of knowing a second language and celebrated the contribution that language-minority groups have made to many fields, including international commerce, diplomacy, and the military.

SALAD and the League of United Latin American Citizens began to use the term English Plus to symbolize support for bilingual education, as the Reagan administration stepped up its attacks on the program. Also, they began to promote the idea as a policy alternative to English Only—as a way to highlight the importance of second language skills for native and non-native English speakers alike. Editorial writers, professional organizations, legislators, and initially even some proponents of Official English spoke out in favor of English Plus.[72] Since 1985 activists in Pennsylvania, Michigan, Massachu-

71. "Not English Only, English Plus! Bilingual Education Issue Analysis," Oct. 15, 1985; SALAD press release, Miami, Dec. 4, 1985.

72. Gerda Bikales, the first executive director of U.S. English, reacted to the SALAD statement in the *Miami News*, Dec. 4, 1985: "When you speak of American students born

setts, Washington, Texas, and Florida have formed English Plus coalitions to promote expanded opportunities to learn English and foreign languages. Meanwhile, other coalitions have stressed the need to defend and extend minority language rights and services. Despite these differences in emphasis, these two responses share the objective of defeating English Only measures wherever they appear.

With this common goal in mind, in early 1987 a diverse group of organizations and individuals met in Washington, D.C., to discuss the need to centralize information on language rights and to develop language policy alternatives. The English Plus Information Clearinghouse (EPIC) was established in October 1987 as a coalition of approximately thirty organizations[73] under the sponsorship of the National Immigration, Refugee, and Citizenship Forum and the Joint National Committee for Languages. EPIC's goal was threefold: to foster informed debate on language policy in the United States, to produce greater public awareness of the English Only movement, and to promote positive, alternative policies. English Plus proponents were united in rejecting the divisiveness of the English Only movement and warning of its threats to civil rights and freedom of speech. They emphasized the need for limited-English-proficient populations to acquire the language as an economic and social necessity. Also, they stressed the importance of multiple language skills for the future well-being of the nation, citing their importance in international commerce, diplomacy, and national security.

Since the EPIC statement of purpose was drafted (*see pp. 151–53*), a wide variety of individuals and organizations have embraced the concept of English Plus. In the process they have defined the term to appeal to their own constituencies. Some have focused more on the *English,* and others more on the *Plus.* Stated another way, there has been a tension between the strategies of advocating expanded opportunities for second-language education and of defending language rights, for example, freedom to maintain minority cultures, equal access to public services, and guarantees against language-based discrimination. These different approaches became apparent during efforts to defeat Official English at the polls.

In November 1988 voters in Arizona, Colorado, and Florida considered state constitutional amendments to declare English their official

---

to American parents, I agree that English Plus is better than English only. But what Secretary Bennett is talking about is the student who comes to this country without knowing any English."

73. By 1990 the number had grown to fifty-six. *For a listing of the original sponsors, see p. 152.*

language (see pp. 132–34). These campaigns were aggressively waged and financed by U.S. English, the most influential national group promoting Official English. The amendments passed easily in Colorado and Florida, while Arizona's Proposition 106, the most restrictive of the three, was approved by just 11,659 votes, a margin of barely one percent. Predictably, public concern about the effect of Official English on multilingual services by government led to organized opposition in each state. Such coalitions sprang up relatively early in the Arizona and Colorado campaigns (approximately a year before the elections), and a Florida group was organized in the summer of 1988. Working primarily through EPIC, these coalitions established contact with one another and with other opponents of the English Only movement.

Leading the opposition to Proposition 106 was a coalition calling itself Arizona English (a bit confusing for an organization opposed to Official English). Composed of a cross-section of community, political, business, and cultural groups, Arizona English countered the proposed amendment with one of its own. Its ballot measure would have required the state legislature to "take the steps necessary to provide the opportunity to learn and be proficient in the English language," while guaranteeing the "right and freedom to learn and use other languages." Arizona English was the only coalition opposing English Only that adopted the counter-initiative strategy. The group explained its rationale in an early press release: "Our position is that all Arizonans should be proficient in English and our approach is a positive one to the problem of the lack of English literacy. We think Arizona's national image has suffered enough and we don't want to further that reactionary image."[74]

Also, it concentrated primarily on the need to expand opportunities for English acquisition rather than on the potential termination of bilingual services under Proposition 106. Arizona English volunteers managed to gather almost 90,000 of the 130,000 signatures needed to place the measure on the ballot. (Meanwhile, Arizonans for Official English, which received 98 percent of its budget from the U.S. English Legislative Task Force in Washington, D.C., paid professional petition circulators up to $1 for each signature.) State Representative Armando Ruiz, a leader of Arizona English, then proposed legislation to place the initiative on the ballot, but it failed by one vote in the Arizona Senate.

In the fall of 1988, Arizona English reorganized itself into the No on 106 Committee and began to focus on the punitive, discriminatory aspects of Official English. Unlike propositions in the other states,

74. State Representative Armando Ruiz, press release, Phoenix, Sept. 11, 1987.

which were vague about their intentions, the Arizona measure stated bluntly: "This State and all political subdivisions of this State shall act in English and no other language." So it was perhaps easier to convince voters about the dangers of Official English in Arizona than in Florida or Colorado. No on 106 produced some of the most hard-hitting literature of the three state campaigns, as well as a controversial television spot that compared English Only intolerance to Nazi atrocities. The committee's commentary about the xenophobic nature of the English Only movement, together with publicity about an anti-Hispanic memorandum by Dr. John Tanton, the chairman of U.S. English *(see pp. 171–77)*, contributed to the remarkably close election. Thus, organized opposition to Official English in Arizona evolved strategically, from a coalition that focused on the benefits of English proficiency into one that warned of the proposition's discriminatory potential and the hidden motives of its supporters.

Coloradans for Language Freedom and Colorado Unity formed the backbone of opposition to Official English in that state. As a multiethnic coalition of community activists and business leaders, these groups focused on the divisiveness of the initiative, Amendment One, and its threat to multilingual services:

> [It] is unnecessary to make official the language already spoken by the majority of Colorado citizens, except as a tool for furthering the goals of modern-day racism. . . .
> The real purpose of Official English legislation is to diminish human rights in a very fundamental way—by limiting language freedom. The aim of Official English proponents is to institutionalize racism and to stifle the growing economic and political power of minorities.[75]

Unlike Arizona's Proposition 106, however, Amendment One was a simple "one-liner" declaration of English as the official language that left its practical effects open to interpretation. So Colorado opponents faced a harder sell for their warnings about the initiative's impact on linguistic minorities. Although coalition leaders remained in regular contact with English Plus activists nationwide, the concept of English Plus played almost no role in the campaign. It is unclear whether an alternative campaign strategy would have resulted in a different outcome in Colorado, where Official English won with 61 percent of the vote. Opposition leaders conceded that a lack of funding and limited outreach in all areas of the state hampered efforts to run a successful campaign.

The Florida English Campaign began organizing for an Official En-

---

75. Coloradans for Language Freedom, "Defeat Official English: The Number One Menace to Human Rights" [brochure, 1988].

glish amendment in 1985. Not until a few months before the November 1988 election did opponents form an organization, known as English Plus, Inc. The nonprofit group was sponsored by Unidos, a South Florida Hispanic coalition, which put up money to hire a political consultant and executive director, develop a logo, publish briefing papers, and initiate fundraising within Miami's Cuban business community. At first, English Plus, Inc. attempted to attract a broader array of regional forces to oppose Amendment 11. But policy differences soon developed between the Hispanic board and the predominantly Anglo staff of English Plus, which wanted to portray language restrictionism as primarily an economic threat rather than an issue of anti-Hispanic prejudice. One tactic that especially angered the board was a so-called "Hispanic gag order" advocated by English Plus, that is, an effort to discourage Hispanic activists from discussing the campaign in the mainstream media. English Plus literature warned mainly of the negative effects on tourism and international business from passage of a "Language Enforcement Amendment":

> What will tourists from other states and countries think of Florida when the state legislature begins to enforce English as the official language of the state? Will international trading partners see the Florida L.E.A. as something that puts them in a poor position to bargain in, or with, this state? Will they take their business elsewhere?
>
> How many tourist and trade dollars will Florida attract in the future if the message we convey is: "Bring your business to Florida—but only if you speak English"? We cannot afford to find out.
>
> Instead of making English the official language of Florida, we should focus on foreign language proficiency to boost our ability to compete directly with other economic powers and expand markets for American products.[76]

Leaving to form a new organization, Speak Up Now (SUN) for Florida, the English Plus staff members continued this approach, emphasizing the vagueness of the proposed amendment, its unintended consequences for a variety of educational programs, and its inflationary impact on Florida taxpayers. SUN for Florida continued to downplay threats to the civil rights of language-minority groups. Late in the campaign, however, following the disclosure of the notorious Tanton memo and subsequent resignations from U.S. English, the group issued statements accusing English Only leaders of white supremacist tendencies.

76. "English Plus Briefing Paper on the Language Enforcement Amendment," July 24, 1988.

Perhaps the election would have been closer if the opponents had organized earlier and settled their internal differences. But it would be pure speculation to suggest what, if anything, could have altered the outcome: Amendment 11 passed by more than five to one (84 to 16 percent). From the beginning it was clear that the opposition faced long odds. Florida is a southern state, where voters tend to reflect traditional, conservative values. Also, statewide polls revealed that voters were generally uninformed about Official English and its implications. A strong majority favored the idea even after hearing the arguments against it, such as the following paragraph read to participants in a 1987 Mason-Dixon survey:

> Opponents of this amendment say it is a dangerous law that we can do without. They say it goes far beyond affirming that English is our official language because it requires the state to enforce language preference, which is impossible to do in practice. It will cost Florida vitally needed jobs and revenues because regulation of language will require more government bureaucracy and lead to costly lawsuits over the interpretation of language laws. Most importantly, the amendment will not get more immigrants to speak English and will only further fragment our society. If anything, it will make it more difficult for immigrants to learn to speak English.

Now asked what appeal the English Only measure had for them, some 60 percent of respondents indicated from moderate to a great deal of appeal and 24 percent indicated little or no appeal (14 percent were unsure). Obviously, threats to the state's language minority communities did not strike a sympathetic chord among many voters. A final problem was that the concept of English Plus had little name recognition in Florida. Raising money for the campaign against Official English proved to be difficult, as in Arizona and Colorado, a problem that limited the amount of media advertising.

How effective was English Plus as a campaign strategy? In Arizona (even though the term was not used) the concept of promoting English proficiency, along with the right to learn and use other languages, garnered considerable support. That, combined with a high-profile debate over the restrictionist and anti-immigrant motives behind Proposition 106, nearly resulted in a defeat for Official English. But in Colorado, where English Plus played little if any role, a hard-hitting campaign against Amendment One as racist and divisive attracted a disappointing 39 percent of the vote. In Florida, an English Plus campaign that focused heavily on the threat to tourism and international business elicited a largely "so what" response from the voters, although there are indications that this appeal simply lacked credibility. For many, it was difficult to see how anyone would be offended, much less turned away from Florida, by a symbolic declaration of Official English.

Despite the distinct character of each state campaign, some patterns stand out. First, there is a shared conviction among the public that proficiency in English is important. Second, voters appear less inclined to approve language restrictionist policies when educated about the inherent xenophobia behind the English Only movement and the civil rights violations that could result from Official English measures. This was clearly the case in Arizona and, arguably, in Colorado. Third, an alternative to English Only, whether a policy stressing the value of multiple language skills or preservation of linguistic rights, must *make sense* to a public based on its own experience, which is still limited with respect to language as a political issue. Finally, a strong organization is essential to defeat state initiatives for Official English—for example, pulling together a diverse coalition and starting early to raise funds for a major voter-education effort.

As a positive alternative to English Only, English Plus has won the endorsements of three state legislatures since 1988. In New Mexico, a nonbinding resolution supporting language rights, House Joint Memorial 16, passed in March 1989 (see p. 154). The first English Plus measure in the nation, H.J.M. 16 encouraged multilingualism as beneficial to the state's continuing economic and cultural vitality, "whether that proficiency derives from second language study by English speakers or from home language maintenance plus English acquisition by speakers of other languages." Responding to an Official English bill introduced in a previous legislative session, H.J.M. 16 disputed the idea that English is threatened by other languages and warned that an English Only policy would endanger New Mexico's multicultural tradition of "diversity with harmony." Although passed with strong support from the state's foreign-language educators, the bill contains no "legal teeth" to guarantee increased funding for language programs. At this writing it is unclear whether it has had a measurable effect on language policy in New Mexico, other than to discourage further campaigns for Official English. Meanwhile, the states of Washington and Oregon have also adopted English Plus policies.[77]

77. Washington's House Bill 2129 (1989) established an official policy "to welcome and encourage the presence of diverse cultures and the use of diverse languages in business, government, and private affairs in this state." Oregon's Senate Joint Resolution 16 (1989) resolved "to welcome, encourage and protect diverse cultures and use of diverse languages in business, government and private affairs." Both were offered as alternatives to Official English bills.

Clearly, the appeal of English Plus has increased since 1985, through the efforts of EPIC and a growing network of coalitions and activists around the country. Still, the approach is not without its critics. For one thing, there has been confusion about the term English Plus, which has sometimes been equated with English Only. In 1988 one Hispanic advocacy group adopted a resolution opposing "such groups as U.S. English and English Plus [that] have been organizing a movement to amend the U.S. Constitution to make English the official language of the country."[78] More serious reservations have come from some language-minority activists who regard English Plus as assimilationist, arguing that it fails to emphasize rights to maintain non-English languages and cultures. A desire to compromise with majority-group attitudes, they say, has no place in countering a racist and xenophobic movement that is attempting to impose English at the expense of other languages. Most important, these critics maintain, English Plus fails to acknowledge the role that minority groups themselves must play in developing language policies that affect their own communities. In response, the defenders of English Plus contend that the only way to defeat English Only is by forging the broadest possible coalition.

On balance, English Plus has provided a vehicle in several states and at the federal level to advance pluralistic language policies, and to bring together diverse groups to advance this agenda. To judge from the experience acquired in the 1988 campaigns, it can also be successful in defeating English Only efforts. Nevertheless, local coalitions must define alternative strategies based on the needs of their communities. English Plus represents one approach; there are undoubtedly others.

78. Labor Council for Latin American Advancement, Resolution No. 10, passed at its national meeting, San Antonio, Aug. 25–27, 1988.

PART FOUR

The Question of Minority Language Rights

What would be the legal impact of an English Language Amendment to the U.S. Constitution? There is no simple answer. First, there is confusion about the intent of the Official English campaign. Does it seek primarily to make a symbolic statement about the role of English as our common language or to protect the dominant status of English by outlawing all (or all but a few) public uses of other tongues? Second, there is uncertainty over potential conflicts between an English Language Amendment and the Constitution's more libertarian provisions. Broad governmental restrictions on speech or on services for linguistic minorities would likely be inconsistent with the First and Fourteenth amendments. Finally, the language rights in question are poorly defined in American law. It is hard to assess what might be lost without knowing what there is to lose. Precedents in this area are limited, as U.S. courts and legislators are only beginning to address the legal issues raised by language diversity. It was not until the 1970s that special help was mandated for language-minority students in public schools, that bilingual voting rights were established (and English literacy tests abolished), and that non-English-speaking defendants were guaranteed the services of a translator during criminal trials.

In a legal tradition oriented toward the liberties and duties of individuals, rights that flow from group membership seem anomalous to many Americans, affirmative action being the most obvious example. There is predictable resistance to granting minority language speakers an entitlement to special services. Without hesitation, federal courts have banned intentional discrimination against individuals on the basis of language when it is clearly a form of national-origin discrimination (prohibited under the Civil Rights Act of 1964). Judges have been reluctant, however, to order bilingual assistance to ensure equal access to government for broad classes of non-English speakers. The question inevitably arises: With immigrant groups speaking scores of different languages these days, how can we accommodate them all, each in their own tongue? Attempting to do so, warned one federal judge, "would virtually cause the processes of government to grind to a halt."[1] Language rights advocates have rejected this argu-

1. *Carmona v. Sheffield*, 325 F.Supp. 1341 (N.D. Cal. 1971), *aff'd*, 475 F.2d 738 (9th Cir. 1973).

ment as a red herring. The issue, they say, is whether to address the needs of a few language minorities in areas where they are concentrated—hardly a staggering burden when one considers the societal benefits of bringing newcomers into the mainstream.

Moreover, there is the question of equity for linguistic minorities who became U.S. citizens not through immigration, but through annexation of their homelands. One small recognition of such claims is embodied in the Voting Rights Act of 1965, which outlawed English literacy requirements for voters (mainly Puerto Ricans) who had been schooled in languages other than English on U.S. soil. Nevertheless, federal courts declined to extend this principle to the Social Security Administration in *Soberal-Pérez v. Heckler,* a case involving U.S.-born, Spanish-speaking citizens who were denied access to the agency's proceedings in their native tongue.

Bill Piatt details the contradictory precedents on language rights in the United States. For example, the 1970 *Negrón* decision recognized the inhumanity of trying an accused criminal in an incomprehensible tongue and mandated that an interpreter be provided for non-English-speaking defendants. But, as yet, no such right has been established for parties in civil and administrative cases—divorce, welfare, adoption, and other proceedings with consequences often as severe as criminal trials. *Meyer v. Nebraska* (1923), the earliest Supreme Court decision regarding the rights of linguistic minorities, relied on the Fourteenth Amendment's due-process clause in striking down a restriction of foreign language teaching, enacted during a period of anti-German xenophobia. The court determined the law to be an unreasonable interference with pupils' right to acquire knowledge, teachers' right to practice their profession, and parents' right to control the education of their children. Still, it carved out no firm prohibition on language-based discrimination and left intact a state mandate for English as the medium of instruction.

Regarding the "right" to bilingual education, the situation is similarly ambiguous. In *Lau v. Nichols* (1974), the Supreme Court outlawed the longstanding neglect of non-English-speaking students. Equal public education was "a mockery," wrote Justice William O. Douglas, if it meant English-only instruction for children who could not understand the language. The court ruled that such students were entitled to special assistance in learning English, although it stopped short of ordering bilingual education as the only remedy for past discrimination. In the 1970s, however, federal civil rights authorities did not hesitate to take that step with the so-called *Lau* Remedies (subsequently withdrawn by the Reagan administration). Also, as Martha Jiménez notes, some lower courts have mandated bilingual programs based on local conditions and an evolving set of legal standards.

These cases normally involved Hispanic and Asian children, but in *Martin Luther King Jr. Elementary School Children v. Ann Arbor School District*, a federal judge ordered special help for speakers of Black English.

Bilingual ballots, authorized by the 1975 amendments to the Voting Rights Act, are among the most symbolically charged fields of language rights. The idea of voting in anything other than the national tongue offends the civic assumptions of many Americans. According to the melting pot myth, immigrants have always conformed to our ways—not vice versa. But history is a poor advocate for the English-only ballot. As documented by *Castro v. State of California* and *PROPA v. Kusper*, literacy tests were long used to disenfranchise linguistic minorities, as well as Afro-Americans. The new bilingual voting rights are not an entitlement bestowed on all non-English speakers. Rather, they represent an attempt to compensate for historic patterns of discrimination, in education as well as voting, that excluded Hispanics, Asian Americans, and American Indians from the political process. John Trasviña traces the evolution of bilingual ballots and previews the debates likely to occur when the law comes up for reauthorization in 1992.

Today the growth sector for language litigation is private business. Conflicts are proliferating over "speak English only" rules in the workplace and ordinances restricting foreign-language advertising. Since 1987 the U.S. Equal Employment Opportunity Commission has prohibited arbitrary language policies on the job—that is, English-only rules that have no demonstrated business necessity—as a form of national-origin discrimination. This position was upheld by a federal appeals panel in *Gutiérrez v. Municipal Court*, although other courts have ruled differently. In *Asian American Business Group v. City of Pomona*, an attempt to regulate the use of Asian characters on business signs was ruled to violate the First Amendment. And yet, as Edward Chen explains, the case law in these areas is neither extensive nor consistent, and many constitutional questions remain to be resolved.

The constitutionality of Official English measures has long been at issue. In *Yniguez v. Mofford* a federal judge invalidated Arizona's Proposition 106, passed by voters in 1988, which required the state to "act in English and in no other language," as an infringement of free-speech rights under the First Amendment. But opponents' major avenue of attack has yet to be followed by a court: the Equal Protection Clause of the Fourteenth Amendment. A commentary by the *Harvard Law Review* analyzes this line of argument and suggests how it might be pursued successfully. Because language—like race, gender, and national origin—has previously served as a basis to exclude, harass, or exploit unpopular groups, courts should exercise added vigilance over government actions that single out non-English speakers. To the extent that Official English measures fail to further legitimate public purposes, unduly trample the rights of non-English speakers, serve as an instrument of racial and ethnic bigotry, or erect obstacles to minority participation in the political process, they may be in conflict with constitutional guarantees of equal protection.

Predicting the precise effect of Official English remains problematic. But the American Civil Liberties Union outlines what is at stake with its detailed inventory of minority language services now provided by the state of California. Although Proposition 63, the Official English initiative approved in 1986, has so far been interpreted as purely symbolic, an English Language Amendment to the U.S. Constitution might be a different story. As the A.C.L.U. survey illustrates, a surprising variety of programs could be jeopardized, affecting not only minority groups, but California's population as a whole.

The Confusing State of Minority Language Rights

By Bill Piatt

Bill Piatt is professor of law at Texas Tech University. This article is excerpted from "Toward Domestic Recognition of a Human Right to Language," *Houston Law Review* 23 (1986): 885–94. Professor Piatt expands upon these themes in his book *¿Only English? Law and Language Policy in the United States* (Albuquerque: University of New Mexico Press, 1990).

To what extent do we have the right in this country to express ourselves or receive communications in a language other than English? While there are threads of authority running through our law that appear to provide some answers to this question in several contexts, there is no clearly defined "right to language" in the United States. It is as though the threads have not been woven into the fabric of the law, but rather surface as bothersome loose ends to be plucked when convenient.

The notion that there is a constitutionally protected right to express oneself or receive communications in a language other than English is supported by federal court decisions in several contexts. In *Meyer v. Nebraska (see pp. 235–37)*, the U.S. Supreme Court reversed a conviction of Nebraska schoolteacher who had been convicted of violating a state statute which prohibited the teaching of any language other than English in any school to a child who had not passed the eighth grade. The court determined that the right to teach a language and the right of parents to engage a teacher to so instruct their children are among the liberties protected against infringement by the due process clause of the Fourteenth Amendment. On the same day, and relying upon the *Meyer* decision, the Supreme Court struck down similar statutes in Ohio and Iowa.[2]

Three years later the court again relied upon *Meyer* in declaring unconstitutional a Philippine territorial statute which required Chinese merchants to keep their books in English, Spanish, or in a local dialect, thereby prohibiting them from utilizing the only language they

---

2. *Bartels v. Iowa*, 262 U.S. 404, 409 (1923); the case was consolidated with *Bohning v. Ohio* and *Pohl v. Ohio*.

understood. The court found the law invalid "because it deprives Chinese persons—situated as they are, with their extensive and important business long established—of their liberty and property without due process of law, and denies them the equal protection of the laws."[3]

In 1970 it was determined that the Sixth Amendment's confrontation clause, made applicable to the states through the Fourteenth Amendment, requires that non-English-speaking defendants be informed of their right to simultaneous interpretation of proceedings at the government's expense. The 2d U.S. Circuit Court of Appeals determined that otherwise the trial would be a "babble of voices," with the defendant unable to understand the precise nature of the testimony against him and hampering the capacity of his counsel to conduct effective cross-examination. The court noted:

> Not only for the sake of effective cross-examination, however, but as a matter of simple humaneness, Negrón [the defendant] deserved more than to sit in total incomprehension as the trial proceeded. Particularly inappropriate in this nation where many languages are spoken is a callousness to the crippling language handicap of a newcomer to its shores, whose life and freedom the state by its criminal processes chooses to put in jeopardy. [*U.S.* ex rel. *Negrón v. New York; see pp. 238–40.*]

At least one federal district court has recognized a constitutional right to bilingual education. In the case of *Serna v. Portales Municipal Schools,* the plaintiffs were Spanish-surnamed minors represented by their parents. They claimed that unlawful discrimination against them resulted from the defendant's educational program tailored to educate a middle-class child from an English-speaking family without regard for the educational needs of the child from an environment where Spanish is the predominant language. The trial court found that the school district had violated the equal protection rights of these children and ordered, among other remedies, that it provide bilingual instruction and seek funding under the federal and state bilingual education acts for that instructional program.[4] The 10th U.S. Circuit Court of Appeals found that the district court had reached the correct result and affirmed the remedial steps ordered, but it did not reach the constitutional issue of equal protection. Rather, the court chose to follow the approach adopted by the Supreme Court in *Lau v. Nichols (see pp. 251–55).*

In the *Lau* case, Chinese-speaking plaintiffs alleged that the San Francisco public schools had denied them an education because the

3. *Yu Cong Eng v. Trinidad,* 271 U.S. 500, 524–25, 528 (1926).
4. 351 F.Supp. 1279 (D. N.M. 1972), *aff'd,* 499 F.2d 1147 (10th Cir. 1974).

only classes offered were in the English language. The *Lau* decision found a deprivation of statutory rights under Title VI of the Civil Rights Act of 1964 and the guidelines of the U.S. Department of Health, Education, and Welfare that required school systems to take remedial steps to rectify language deficiency problems.[5] In *Serna* the 10th Circuit adopted the *Lau* approach and affirmed the court-ordered bilingual education plan on statutory grounds, noting the damage suffered by children whose language rights were not respected. This damage included feelings of inadequacy and lowered self-esteem which developed when Spanish-surnamed children came to school and found that their language and culture were totally rejected and that only English was acceptable. The child who goes to a school where he finds no evidence of his language, culture, and ethnic group withdraws and does not participate. Such children often demonstrate both academic and emotional disorders, feel frustrated, and express their frustration through lack of attendance or lack of school involvement. Their frustrations are further reflected in hostile behavior, discipline problems, and eventually dropping out of school.[6]

A tavern's policy against the speaking of "foreign" languages at the bar was held to be unlawful racial discrimination against Mexican Americans in *Hernández v. Erlenbusch*. In disposing of the argument that the English-only rule was justified because non-Spanish-speaking customers were "irritated" by the speaking of the Spanish language, the court stated:

> Just as the Constitution forbids banishing blacks to the back of the bus so as not to arouse the racial animosity of the preferred white passengers, it also forbids ordering Spanish-speaking patrons to the "back booth or out" to avoid antagonizing English-speaking beer drinkers. The lame justification that a discriminatory policy helps preserve the peace is as unacceptable in barrooms as it was in buses. Catering to prejudice out of fear of provoking greater prejudice only perpetuates racism. Courts faithful to the Fourteenth Amendment will not permit, either by camouflage or cavalier treatment, equal protection to be so profaned.[7]

5. 42 U.S.C. §2000d; Office for Civil Rights notice, 35 Fed. Reg. 11595, stating that "where inability to speak and understand the English language excludes national origin minority group children from effective participation in the educational program offered by a school district, the district must take affirmative steps to rectify the language deficiency in order to open its instructional program to these students."

6. 499 F.2d 1150. Teaching the Spanish-speaking child exclusively in English communicates a powerful message to the child that he or she is a second-class citizen; see *U.S. v. Texas*, 506 F.Supp. 405 (E.D. Tex. 1981), *rev'd on other grounds*, 680 F.2d 356, 372 (5th Cir. 1982).

7. 368 F.Supp. 752, 755–56 (D. Ore. 1973).

In addition to the recognition of a constitutional "right to language" in the contexts noted above, there may be a First Amendment right to receive broadcast programming in languages other than English.[8] Federal statutes (and accompanying regulations) also provide a guarantee of the exercise of language rights in a number of contexts, including education, court interpreters, employment, and voting rights. Various state constitutional provisions and statutes also afford recognition of language rights. State courts have invalidated default judgments taken against non-English-speaking litigants and have declared contract provisions unconscionable where a person's lack of English fluency precluded equality of bargaining power.[9]

While the reader at this point might conclude that the contours of a generic "language right" emerge from the authorities cited to this point, it is important to recognize contradicting lines of authority and the elusiveness of this right to language in a number of contexts where litigants have sought to assert it. One such area is the "right" of a bilingual worker to speak a language other than English on the job.

First, let us consider a bit of background. The federal Equal Employment Opportunity Act prohibits employment discrimination on the basis of race, color, religion, sex, or national origin. Early decisions by the U.S. Equal Employment Opportunity Commission protected language rights at the workplace under the "national origin" pigeonhole, and courts agreed that this category affords such protection.[10] Early violations, for example, involved situations where an employer fired a Spanish-surnamed employee for supposedly poor work attributed to language difficulties and for violating company rules prohibiting Spanish-language communications among employees. Courts accepted and continue to accept the proposition that employment discrimination based upon language or accent is unlawful discrimination based upon national origin.[11]

However, the scope of the right to language on the job is questionable after the decision in *García v. Gloor,* a case involving a lumber store in Brownsville, Texas. More than three-fourths of the population in the business area was Hispanic, and many of the store's customers expressed the desire to be waited on by Spanish-speaking

8. See Bill Piatt, "Linguistic Diversity on the Airwaves: Spanish Language Broadcasting and the F.C.C.," *La Raza Law Journal* 2 (1984): 101.

9. See, e.g., *Cota v. Southern Arizona Bank & Trust Co.,* 17 Ariz. App. 326, 497 P.2d 833 (1972); *Frostifresh Corp. v. Reynoso,* 52 Misc. 2d 26, 274 N.Y.S. 2d 964 (Dist. Ct. 1966), *rev'd as to damages,* 54 Misc. 2d 119, 281, N.Y.S. 2d 964 (N.Y. App. Term 1967).

10. See 29 C.F.R. §1606 (1985); *Jones v. United Gas Imp. Corp.,* 68 F.R.D. 1 (E.D. Pa. 1975).

11. *Saucedo v. Brothers Well Serv. Inc.,* 464 F.Supp. 919 (S.D. Tex. 1979); *Carino v. University of Okla. Bd. of Regents,* 750 F.2d 815 (10th Cir. 1984).

salespeople. García was hired in 1975 precisely because he was bilingual. He was instructed to use English with English-speaking customers and Spanish with Spanish-speaking customers. However, the owner imposed another language rule on García: even though three-fourths of the store's workers and customers spoke Spanish, employees were forbidden from speaking Spanish on the job unless communicating with a Spanish-speaking customer. Among the reasons given by the owner for this rule was that the English-speaking customers objected to the Spanish-speaking employees communicating in a language which they did not understand. One day García was asked a question by another Spanish-speaking clerk about an item requested by a customer, and he responded, in Spanish, that the article was not available. The owner overheard this exchange and fired García. In rejecting García's claim for relief under the Equal Employment Opportunity Act, the district court found there were "valid business reasons" for the rule. The 5th U.S. Circuit Court upheld this decision, refusing to examine critically either the validity of the "business reasons" offered or whether the business needs could be met in a less restrictive manner than the imposition of an English-only rule. The court found García's conduct to have been a deliberate violation of the rule, concluding that a language which a bilingual person elects to speak at a particular time is a matter of choice.[12]

The "right to language" has proved illusory in other areas as well. Courts have concluded that the refusal to appoint an interpreter in a civil proceeding does not violate due process, and that Spanish-speaking welfare recipients have no constitutional right to be notified in Spanish of the termination or reduction of their benefits.[13]

The confusing state of our domestic law regarding the right to language might well be illustrated by considering the curious results which follow from applying the principles elicited so far to the situation of a hypothetical Ms. Martínez. Ms. Martínez is a U.S. citizen. She works part-time and also receives public assistance for her children. She is bilingual, but her primary language, and that of her school-aged children, is Spanish. Ms. Martínez is fired from her job one day because some customers complain to her boss that she spoke Spanish to a coworker in their presence, contrary to the store's English-only rule. On the way home she stops in the tavern to drink a beer. The same customers who complained to her boss are seated in

12. 618 F.2d 264 (5th Cir. 1980), *cert. denied*, 449 U.S. 1113 (1981). Editor's note: The 9th Circuit has since taken a contrary view, striking down an English-only workplace rule in *Gutiérrez v. Municipal Court*, 838 F.2d 1031 (9th Cir. 1988) *(see pp. 277–84)*. The U.S. Supreme Court has yet to resolve the conflict.

13. *Jara v. Municipal Ct.*, 21 C.3d 181, 578 P.2d 94, 145 Cal. Rptr. 847 (1978), *cert. denied*, 439 U.S. 1067 (1979); *Guerrero v. Carleson*, 9 C.3d 808, 512 P.2d 833, 109 Cal. Rptr. 201 (1973), *cert. denied*, 414 U.S. 1137 (1974).

the bar. When Ms. Martínez begins to tell another patron of her problems, in Spanish, the customers object, this time to the tavern manager, who orders Ms. Martínez from the bar.

As it turns out, this has just not been her day. At home she learns of the status of two lawsuits filed against her several months previously by different department stores for failure to pay debts allegedly owed to them. In the first suit, Ms. Martínez had not fully understood the complaint and summons because of her language situation and had thrown them away. Now the store notifies her that it has taken a default judgment against her for failing to appear in court. Ms. Martínez did not really understand the second complaint and summons either, but tried to answer. Now, she finds, it has been set for trial in a few days. She is very worried because she knows her English is not good enough for her to understand what is going on in court and to explain her side of the story to the judge.

Poor Ms. Martínez's troubles are not finished. Her children tell her they have been thrown out of school because their English is so bad they are flunking all their subjects. The day's mail also brings word that the welfare assistance she receives for them has been terminated because she failed to provide information required last month by the welfare agency. Ms. Martínez understood neither the request nor the termination notice because they were written in English.

Consider the curious results which obtain from an application of our domestic laws to Ms. Martínez's situation. She would have a cause of action against the bar owner and its customers, and yet her employment termination for exactly the same conduct would be upheld. Is the right to speak Spanish more sacred in a bar than on the job? Regarding her consumer problems, it may be better for her to have ignored the summons and complaint rather than try to answer and appear to defend herself. Courts have set aside default judgments for a language barrier, but may not afford her an interpreter at the trial if she attempts to defend herself. Ms. Martínez would find, considering her children's situation, that the state could not deny her children an education based upon their language situation. It could, however, because of the language barrier, effectively deny them the food, shelter, and medical care necessary to sustain their lives while they try to study.

These are admittedly dramatic, oversimplified applications. They illustrate, however, that we have not thought through whether, why, and to what extent we might choose to respect language differences in this country.

Meyer v. Nebraska

Robert Meyer, a parochial school teacher in Hamilton County, Nebraska, was found guilty of violating a 1919 statute that mandated English-only instruction in all public and private schools and allowed foreign-language instruction "only after a pupil shall have attained and successfully passed the eighth grade."[14] His crime: teaching a Bible story in German to a ten-year-old child. The Nebraska Supreme Court upheld Meyer's conviction. It found:

> The salutary purpose of the statute is clear. The Legislature had seen the baneful effects of permitting foreigners, who had taken residence in this country, to rear and educate their children in the language of their native land. The result of that condition was found to be inimical to our own safety. To allow the children of foreigners, who had emigrated here, to be taught from early childhood the language of the country of their parents was . . . to educate them so that they must always think in that language, and, as a consequence, naturally inculcate in them the ideas and sentiments foreign to the best interests of this country.[15]

The U.S. Supreme Court rejected this reasoning in a seven-to-two decision. On the same constitutional grounds, it struck down similar statutes in Iowa and Ohio. Justice James C. McReynolds delivered the majority opinion on June 4, 1923.

The problem for our determination is whether the statute as construed and applied unreasonably infringes the liberty guaranteed to the plaintiff . . . by the Fourteenth Amendment: "No state . . . shall deprive any person of life, liberty or property without due process of law."

While this court has not attempted to define with exactness the liberty thus guaranteed . . . without doubt, it denotes not merely freedom from bodily restraint but also the right of the individual to contract, to engage in any of the common occupations of life, to acquire useful knowledge, to marry, establish a home and bring up children, to worship God according to the dictates of his own conscience, and

14. *Meyer v. Nebraska*, 262 U.S. 390 (1923).
15. 107 Neb. 657, 187 N.W. 100.

generally to enjoy those privileges long recognized at common law as essential to the orderly pursuit of happiness by free men. The established doctrine is that this liberty may not be interfered with, under the guise of protecting the public interest, by legislative action which is artibrary or without reasonable relation to some purpose within the competency of the state to effect. . . .

The American people have always regarded education and acquisition of knowledge as matters of supreme importance which should be diligently promoted. The Ordinance of 1787 declares: "Religion, morality and knowledge being necessary to good government and the happiness of mankind, schools and the means of education shall forever be encouraged." Corresponding to the right of control, it is the natural duty of the parent to give his children education suitable to their station in life; and nearly all the states, including Nebraska, enforce this obligation by compulsory laws.

Practically, education of the young is only possible in schools conducted by especially qualified persons who devote themselves thereto. The calling always has been regarded as useful and honorable, essential, indeed, to the public welfare. Mere knowledge of the German language cannot reasonably be regarded as harmful. Heretofore it has been commonly looked upon as helpful and desirable. Plaintiff in error taught this language in school as part of his occupation. His right thus to teach and the right of parents to engage him so to instruct their children, we think, are within the liberty of the amendment.

The challenged statute forbids the teaching in school of any subject except in English; also the teaching of any other language until the pupil has attained and successfully passed the eighth grade, which is not usually accomplished before the age of twelve. The Supreme Court of the state has held that "the so-called ancient or dead languages" are not "within the spirit or the purpose of the act."[16] Latin, Greek, Hebrew are not proscribed; but German, French, Spanish, Italian, and every other alien speech are within the ban. Evidently the Legislature has attempted materially to interfere with the calling of modern language teachers, with the opportunities of pupils to acquire knowledge, and with the power of parents to control the education of their own.

It is said the purpose of the legislation was to promote civic development by inhibiting training and education of the immature in foreign tongues and ideals before they could learn English and acquire American ideals, and "that the English language should be and become the mother tongue of all children reared in this state." It is also affirmed that the foreign born population is very large, that certain

16. *Nebraska District of Evangelical Lutheran Synod v. McKelvie*, 187 N.W. 927 (1922).

communities commonly use foreign words, follow foreign leaders, move in a foreign atmosphere, and that the children are thereby hindered from becoming citizens of the most useful type and the public safety is imperiled.

That the state may do much, go very far, indeed, in order to improve the quality of its citizens, physically, mentally and morally, is clear; but the individual has certain fundamental rights which must be respected. The protection of the Constitution extends to all, to those who speak other languages as well as to those born with English on the tongue. Perhaps it would be highly advantageous if all had ready understanding of our ordinary speech, but this cannot be coerced with methods which conflict with the Constitution—a desirable end cannot be promoted by prohibited means. . . .

The desire of the Legislature to foster a homogeneous people with American ideals prepared readily to understand current discussions of civic matters is easy to appreciate. Unfortunate experiences during the late war and aversion toward every character of truculent adversaries were certainly enough to quicken that aspiration. But the means adopted, we think, exceed the limitations upon the power of the state and conflict with rights assured to plaintiff in error. The interference is plain enough and no adequate reason therefor in time of peace and domestic tranquility has been shown.

The power of the state to compel attendance at some school and to make reasonable regulations for all schools, including a requirement that they shall give instructions in English, is not questioned. Nor has challenge been made of the state's power to prescribe a curriculum for institutions which it supports. Those matters are not within the present controversy. Our concern is with the prohibition approved by the Supreme Court. . . .

No emergency has arisen which renders knowledge by a child of some language other than English so clearly harmful as to justify its inhibition with the consequent infringement of rights long freely enjoyed. We are constrained to conclude that the statute as applied is arbitrary and without reasonable relation to any end within the competency of the state. As the statute undertakes to interfere only with teaching which involves a modern language, leaving complete freedom as to other matters, there seems no adequate foundation for the suggestion that the purpose was to protect the child's health by limiting his mental activities. It is well known that proficiency in a foreign language seldom comes to one not instructed at an early age, and experience shows that this is not injurious to the health, morals or understanding of the ordinary child. . . .

U.S. ex rel. *Negrón v. New York*

Despite the obvious injustice of trying a criminal defendant in a language that he or she cannot understand, not
until this 1970 decision was the right to an interpreter
clearly established by a federal court.[17] The case involved
Rogelio Negrón, a Puerto Rican farm laborer in Suffolk
County, N.Y., who killed a fellow worker during a drunken
brawl. Although no effort was made to translate the trial
into Spanish, Negrón's only language, the defendant was
convicted of second-degree murder and sentenced to
twenty years to life. The 2d U.S. Circuit Court of Appeals
overturned the conviction on constitutional grounds in a
decision that inspired Congress to pass the federal Court
Interpreters Act of 1978.[18] Judge Irving Kaufman delivered
the opinion on October 17, 1970.

The government does not dispute that at the time of his trial, Negrón, a
twenty-three-year-old indigent with a sixth-grade Puerto Rican education, neither spoke nor understood any English. His court-appoin-
ted lawyer, Lloyd H. Baker, spoke no Spanish. Counsel and client thus
could not communicate without the aid of a translator. Nor was Negrón able to participate in any manner in the conduct of his defense,
except for the spotty instances when the proceedings were conducted
in Spanish, or Negrón's Spanish words were translated into English,
or the English of his lawyer, the trial judge, and the witnesses
against him were gratuitously translated for Negrón into Spanish.

The times during pretrial preparation and at trial when translation
made communication possible between Negrón and his accusers, the
witnesses, and other officers of the court were spasmodic and irregu-
lar. Thus, with the aid of an interpreter, his attorney conferred with
Negrón for some twenty minutes before trial at the Suffolk County
jail. Negrón's own testimony at trial, and that of two Spanish-
speaking witnesses called by the state, was simultaneously translated
into English for the benefit of the court, prosecution, and jury by Mrs.
Elizabeth Maggipinto, an interpreter employed in behalf of the prosecution. . . . [D]uring two brief recesses in the course of Negrón's
four-day trial, Mrs. Maggipinto met with Negrón and Baker for some
ten to twenty minutes and merely summarized the testimony of those
witnesses who had already testified. . . .

To Negrón, most of the trial must have been a babble of voices.
Twelve of the state's fourteen witnesses testified against him in En-

17. *U.S.* ex rel. *Negrón v. New York*, 434 F.2d 386 (2d Cir. 1970).
18. 28 U.S.C. §1827.

glish. Apart from Mrs. Maggipinto's occasional *ex post facto* brief resumes—the detail and accuracy of which is not revealed in any record—none of this testimony was comprehensible to Negrón. Particularly damaging to Negrón's defense was the testimony of Joseph Gallardo, an investigator from the Suffolk County District Attorney's office. Gallardo testified both at the *Huntley* hearing and at trial—each time in English, although he also was able to speak Spanish. . . .

It is axiomatic that the Sixth Amendment's guarantee of a right to be confronted with adverse witnesses . . . includes the right to cross-examine those witnesses as an "essential and fundamental requirement for the kind of fair trial which is this country's constitutional goal."[19] But the right that was denied Negrón seems to us even more consequential than the right of confrontation. Considerations of fairness, the integrity of the fact-finding process, and the potency of our adversary system of justice forbid that the state should prosecute a defendant who is not present at his own trial. And it is equally imperative that every criminal defendant—if the right to be present is to have meaning—possess "sufficient present ability to consult with his lawyer with a reasonable degree of rational understanding."[20] Otherwise, "[t]he adjudication loses its character as a reasoned interaction . . . and becomes an invective against an insensible object."[21]

However astute Mrs. Maggipinto's summaries may have been, they could not do service as a means by which Negrón could understand the precise nature of the testimony against him during that period of the trial's progress when the state chose to bring it forth. Negrón's incapacity to respond to specific testimony would inevitably hamper the capacity of his counsel to conduct effective cross-examination. Not only for the sake of effective cross-examination, however, but as a matter of simple humaneness, Negrón deserved more than to sit in total incomprehension as the trial proceeded. Particularly inappropriate in this nation where many languages are spoken is a callousness to the crippling language handicap of a newcomer to its shores, whose life and freedom the state by its criminal processes chooses to put in jeopardy. . . .

The Supreme Court held . . . that when it appears that a defendant *may* not be competent to participate intelligently in his own defense because of a possible mental disability, the trial court must conduct a hearing on the defendant's mental capacity.[22] Negrón's language disability was obvious, not just a possibility, and it was as debilitating to his ability to participate in the trial as a mental disease or defect. But it was more readily "curable" than any mental disorder. The least we

19. *Pointer v. Texas*, 380 U.S. 400, 405 (1965).
20. *Dusky v. U.S.*, 362 U.S. 402 (1962).
21. Note, "Incompetency to Stand Trial," *Harvard Law Review* 81 (1969): 454, 458.
22. *Pate v. Robinson*, 383 U.S. 375, 384 (1966).

can require is that a court, put on notice of a defendant's severe language difficulty, make unmistakably clear to him that he has a right to have a competent translator assist him, at state expense if need be, throughout his trial.

Soberal-Pérez v. Heckler

Guarantees against national-origin discrimination, including unreasonable language restrictions, are not to be confused with an affirmative right of access to government by non-English-speaking citizens, according to U.S. District Judge Edward R. Neaher.[23] His decision, later upheld on appeal, dismissed a lawsuit seeking the translation of Social Security forms and proceedings into Spanish. The case involved Anibal Soberal-Pérez, a native of Puerto Rico who had resided in New York for twelve years but remained limited in English, when he sought disability benefits for mental illness in 1977. The Social Security Administration (S.S.A.) rejected his claim and notified him, in English, of his rights to appeal. Because of the language barrier, however, Soberal-Pérez was unable to understand and participate in the proceedings, and his claim was denied. He then sued S.S.A., seeking monetary damages and a reversal of its policy of declining to provide language assistance for Spanish-speaking citizens. In rejecting the suit, Judge Neaher gave considerable weight to the "official" character of English, by law and tradition, in governmental activities throughout the United States. His reasoning illustrates the potentially broad reach of Official English amendments.

Plaintiffs in this case assert a broad and fundamental attack on the constitutionality of monolingual government programs. Essentially, plaintiffs' equal protection claim contends that the Constitution requires the state and federal governments to provide foreign language services whenever "a language barrier exists between a particular group and the particular [government] benefit sought, be it a cash benefit, job, or other right." They argue that failure to supply materials in the primary language of a governmental beneficiary, in this case Spanish forms and interpreters, constitutes discrimination on the basis of national origin. While this Court appreciates the difficulty recent immigrants may initially encounter with the English language,

23. *Soberal-Peréz v. Heckler*, 549 F.Supp. 1164 (E.D. N.Y. 1982), *aff'd*, 717 F.2d 36 (2d Cir. 1983), *cert. denied*, 466 U.S. 929 (1984).

for the reasons stated below, we cannot say that the Constitution mandates a multilingual government.

The threshold determination in equal protection analysis is the governmental basis for the classification at issue. . . . A court must initially determine whether the classification "operates to the disadvantage of some suspect class or impinges upon a fundamental right." If so, the court must strictly scrutinize the governmental conduct, omitting application of the "usual presumption of validity" and requiring the government to come forward with compelling justification. If not, the classification must "be examined to determine whether it rationally furthers some legitimate, articulate [governmental] purpose and therefore does not constitute invidious discrimination."[24]

Since the Supreme Court concluded that "a noncontractual claim to receive funds from the public treasury" does not enjoy the constitutionally protected status of fundamental rights such as the right to raise one's children or the right to personal choice in matters of family life, the critical issue in this case is whether the current S.S.A. practices operate to the disadvantage of a "suspect class."[25] While there can be no question that Hispanic persons as an ethnic group constitute such a class for equal protection purposes, it is also clear that the [Supplemental Security Income] procedures alleged to be discriminatory are not on their face based upon ethnic origin. Rather, the allegedly discriminatory classification is based on language; that is, if a classification exists, it is not non-Hispanic/Hispanic, but English-speaking/non-English-speaking. While ethnic groups like Hispanics are often characterized by language, unlike race or national origin, language, per se, is not a characteristic protected by the Constitution from rational differentiation. As the district court in *Carmona v. Sheffield*[26] aptly noted:

> The breadth and scope of such a [contrary] contention is so staggering as virtually to constitute its own refutation. If adopted in as cosmopolitan a society as ours, enriched as it has been by the immigration of persons from many lands with their distinctive linguistic and cultural heritages, it would virtually cause the processes of government to grind to a halt. The conduct of official business, including the proceedings and enactments of Congress, the Courts, and administrative agencies, would become all but impossible. The application of Federal and State statutes, regula-

24. *San Antonio Independent School District v. Rodríguez*, 411 U.S. 1, 17 (1973).

25. *Weinberger v. Salfi*, 422 U.S. 749, 772 (1975); *Stanley v. Illinois*, 405 U.S. 645 (1972); *Cleveland Bd. of Ed. v. LaFleur*, 414 U.S. 632 (1974).

26. 325 F.Supp. 1341 (N.D. Cal. 1971), *aff'd*, 475 F.2d 738 (9th Cir. 1973).

tions, and proceedings would be called into serious question. . . .

In this case the valid historical basis and modern rationale for conducting governmental affairs in English is clear: the national language of the United States is English. As the Sixth Circuit noted in a case similar to this:

> Our laws are printed in English and our legislatures conduct their business in English. Some states even designate English as the official language of the state. Our national interest in English as the common language is exemplified by 8 U.S.C. §1423, which requires, in general, English language literacy as a condition to naturalization as a United States citizen.[27]

The complaint therefore simply calls the Secretary [of Health and Human Services] to task for policies and practices that have objective rationality and historical justification. Absent allegations or reasons other than a disproportionate impact, there is no basis to infer antipathy on the part of the Secretary. Consequently, the S.S.A. procedures are not subject to strict scrutiny and must be presumed racially and ethnically neutral.[28]

Once it is determined that a government action does not intentionally discriminate against a suspect class nor infringe the exercise of a fundamental right, the only question remaining is whether the legislative classification bears a rational relationship to a legitimate governmental purpose.[29] Given the universality of the English language in the affairs of government, it cannot be said that [Department of Health and Human Services] procedures are irrational. The cost in time, money, and administrative disruption are sufficient justifications under this tier of equal protection analysis. While plaintiffs may feel that such a policy is unwise or inequitable, such belief "is of course an insufficient basis on which to conclude that it is unconstitutional."[30] Such decisions must be made through the democratic processes, not by order of a federal court. . . .

27. *Frontera v. Sindell*, 522 F.2d 1215, 1220 (6th Cir. 1975).
28. *Dandridge v. Williams*, 397 U.S. 471 (1970); *Personnel Admin. v. Feeney*, 442 U.S. 256, 273 (1979).
29. *Vance v. Bradley*, 440 U.S. 93, 97 (1979).
30. *Schweiker v. Hogan*, 102 S.Ct. 2597, 2609 (1982).

The Educational Rights of Language-Minority Children

By Martha Jiménez

Martha Jiménez, a legislative policy analyst for the San Francisco Board of Supervisors, formerly served as an attorney specializing in language rights for the Mexican American Legal Defense and Educational Fund. She wrote this article for the *Source Book*.

Few people would argue with the principle that all children in the United States, regardless of race, sex, religion, or language ability, should have the right to an equal education. Yet for students with limited English skills, equal education was long interpreted to mean that schools had merely to provide the same books, curriculum, and teachers they provided to English-speaking students. If children failed to understand the language of the classroom and fell behind their peers, that was unfortunate, but it was not illegal. As long as school boards provided identical instruction to all children, they could not be accused of discriminating. Language-minority children were left to "sink or swim" in English-only classrooms, to succeed or drown in a sea of indifference. Faced with a meaningless educational experience, many of them simply dropped out of school.

Only in the past twenty-five years have policymakers, judges, and legislators come to recognize the injustice of this policy. New laws and court rulings have required schools to open up their curricula to limited-English-proficient (LEP) children. New federal programs like Title VII of the Elementary and Secondary Education Act (better known as the Bilingual Education Act) have funded innovative methods in the classroom. Meanwhile, the "new" approach of bilingual education has spread throughout the country.[31] In many cases bilingual programs were adopted voluntarily; in others they resulted from court orders, state laws, or pressure by federal civil rights authorities. Contrary to popular perceptions, however, none of these actions has

31. Instruction in languages other than English, in both public and private schools, was prevalent in colonial America and throughout the nineteenth century. But it declined sharply during the "Americanization" campaign of the early 1900s. From the World War I era until 1963, bilingual education was virtually unknown in American public schools; see James Crawford, *Bilingual Education: History, Politics, Theory, and Practice,* 2d ed. (Los Angeles: Bilingual Educational Services, 1991).

established for LEP students a universal "right" to instruction in their native language. The following pages will explore what it means to provide language-minority children with an equal educational opportunity and how equality of educational access may be legally obligated.

The Bilingual Education Act, contrary to its name, did not require school districts to implement programs of bilingual education for LEP children. What it did do was signal a national commitment of political will and financial resources to serving the needs of these students. It was enacted in 1968, at a time of growing concern about the educational neglect of Mexican American children in the Southwest, as documented by the Tucson Survey of the National Education Association *(see pp. 322–25)*. The Bilingual Education Act created a competitive grants program to help train teachers and administrators, finance research on effective teaching methods, and support educational projects. It mandated no special treatment for LEP children; rather, it has enabled schools to develop programs aimed at ensuring equal treatment. Over the years most of these Title VII grants have been reserved for school programs that use LEP children's native language. This became a source of controversy during the 1980s, leading to charges of federal intrusiveness on decisions previously left to local educators. But, in fact, the requirement for bilingual instruction applies only to districts that choose to apply for funding under the Bilingual Education Act.[32]

On a wholly separate track, meanwhile, the federal government was addressing the civil rights issue—the denial of equal educational access for LEP students as a form of national-origin discrimination. On May 25, 1970, the Office for Civil Rights (O.C.R.) of the Department of Health, Education, and Welfare sent a memorandum to school districts with "national origin-minority" enrollments exceeding 5 percent. In the memorandum, O.C.R. director J. Stanley Pottinger warned that many districts were engaging in practices that had "the effect of denying equality of educational opportunity" for Hispanics and other national origin-minority children. The memorandum informed local school officials of four basic areas of responsibility:

• *Ensuring effective participation:* Where limited English skills excluded national origin-minority children from participating effectively in school, districts had to "take affirmative steps to rectify the

32. Support for nonbilingual methods such as English-as-a-second-language tutoring, is available under other federal programs, e.g., Chapter I Compensatory Education, Migrant Education, Emergency Immigrant Education, and Indian Education; see RubyAnn M. Esquibel, "Federal Education Programs Serving Limited English Proficient Students," Congressional Research Service, April 26, 1989.

language deficiency in order to open its instructional program to these students."

• *Assigning students properly:* Districts could no longer assign language-minority students to classes for the mentally retarded "on the basis of criteria which essentially measure or evaluate English language skills." Furthermore, such students could not be denied access to college preparatory courses solely because the schools were failing to teach them English.

• *Limiting ability-grouping:* In addressing the special language needs of minority students, districts were expected to teach English "as soon as possible," rather than use ability-grouping systems that would "operate as an educational dead-end or permanent track."

• *Involving language-minority parents:* Districts were responsible for adequately informing parents of school activities called to the attention of other parents, even if that meant the information had to be "provided in a language other than English." [33]

Far more than a policy advisory, the 1970 memorandum was grounded in the Civil Rights Act of 1964. Specifically, Title VI of the Act prohibited discrimination on the basis of "race, color, or national origin" in all federally assisted programs, and it empowered federal agencies to issue rules, regulations, and other orders to carry out the law.[34] Moreover, O.C.R. had the means to enforce the policy through termination or refusal of federal grants to offending school districts. The dawn of language rights for LEP children had finally arrived.

The full import of O.C.R.'s memorandum would not become apparent for nearly four years. Indeed, when Kinney Lau and 1,800 other Chinese American children challenged the San Francisco public schools for failing to provide them an equal educational opportunity, their claims were rejected by federal district and appeals courts. Finally, in 1974, in its only decision ever rendered in this area, the U.S. Supreme Court ruled in *Lau v. Nichols* that the school district had violated the children's civil rights under Title VI (see pp. 251–55). A unanimous court found that because nothing had been done to address their lack of English skills, the Chinese-speaking students were "effectively foreclosed from any meaningful education." It continued:

> [T]here is no equality of treatment merely by providing students with the same facilities, textbooks, teachers, and curriculum; for students who do not understand English are effectively foreclosed from any meaningful education.
> Basic English skills are at the very core of what these public schools teach. Imposition of a requirement that, before a child can effectively participate in the educational

33. 35 Fed. Reg. 11595.
34. 42 U.S.C. §2000d.

program, he must already have acquired those basic skills is to make a mockery of public education. We know that those who do not understand English are certain to find their classroom experiences wholly incomprehensible and in no way meaningful.[35]

The court did not order a specific remedy because none was requested by the plaintiffs, although it did identify bilingual education and English as a second language (E.S.L.) instruction as options. Also, the decision was based on statute (Title VI) and did not "reach" the constitutional issues that had been raised. Thus it left unresolved the question of whether the Equal Protection Clause of the Fourteenth Amendment requires "affirmative steps" to provide equal access to the curriculum for language-minority students.

In an effort to clarify the significance of the *Lau* decision, the Commissioner of Education established guidelines spelling out school districts' obligations in greater detail than the 1970 memorandum. These so-called *Lau* Remedies were used by O.C.R. to determine whether districts were in compliance with Title VI as interpreted by *Lau*. For those found to be violating the law, the guidelines prescribed steps to correct the situation: procedures for evaluating the English skills of language-minority students, determining appropriate instruction for LEP children, deciding when they were ready for regular classrooms, and establishing professional standards for bilingual and E.S.L. teachers. The *Lau* Remedies went one step beyond the Supreme Court, however, in specifying a preference that elementary school children be instructed in their native language until they were able to participate in English-only classrooms. Furthermore, programs relying on E.S.L. instruction alone were deemed inappropriate unless districts could demonstrate that they were just as effective as bilingual programs. O.C.R. conducted more than 600 compliance reviews between 1975 and 1980 and negotiated *Lau* Plans, or consent agreements, with 359 school districts to remedy their violations of Title VI.[36]

Nevertheless, the tenuous status of the *Lau* Remedies (which had never gone through the formal rulemaking procedure, including publication of a proposal in the *Federal Register* and solicitation of public comments), resulted in a challenge to their legality. In response, the new U.S. Department of Education developed official *Lau* Regulations. Proposed by the Carter administration in 1980, these formal rules required school districts receiving federal funds to provide bilingual education for LEP students under most circumstances where it

35. 414 U.S. 563, 565.
36. James J. Lyons, *Legal Responsibilities of Education Agencies Serving National Origin Language Minority Students*, Mid-Atlantic Equity Center, Technical Series (Washington, D.C.: American University School of Education, 1988), p. 11.

was practical.[37] But substantial opposition within the education community delayed plans to finalize the regulations until after election day. Following Carter's defeat, one of the Reagan administration's first acts was to withdraw the *Lau* Regulations as an example of "harsh, inflexible, burdensome, unworkable, and incredibly costly" actions by the federal government.[38] Since that time, O.C.R. has operated without written guidelines for enforcing *Lau*, but has relied on an analytical framework set forth in a federal court decision, *Castañeda v. Pickard*.[39] To understand that case, it is necessary to retrace our steps to 1974.

Soon after the Supreme Court ruled in *Lau*, Congress adopted the Equal Educational Opportunities Act (E.E.O.A.).[40] Though it was primarily an anti-busing measure, the E.E.O.A. specifically barred any state from denying equal educational opportunity to an individual on account of race, color, sex, or national origin by "the failure of an educational agency to take appropriate action to overcome language barriers that impede equal participation by its students in its instructional programs."[41] For the first time, Congress had recognized the right of every language-minority student to seek redress for a school system's inequities (whether or not it received federal subsidies). Not only did the E.E.O.A. recognize a duty on behalf of educational agencies to ensure equal access to instructional programs for LEP children, but it provided aggrieved individuals with a private right of action to compel such relief, and it allowed the attorney general of the United States to sue on behalf of such an individual.[42]

The one thing the E.E.O.A. failed to do, however, was to define the term by which the full extent of a school district's responsibility would be measured. The meaning of "appropriate action" was never clarified, either in the language of the statute or in its legislative history. So it was left to the federal courts to solve this problem. The definitive precedent was set in *Castañeda v. Pickard*, a class action lawsuit by Mexican American children and their parents against the Raymondville, Texas, school system. The suit charged that the district used an ability-grouping system to segregate illegally by race and ethnicity, that it failed to hire and promote Mexican American teachers and administrators, and most significantly, that it failed to implement an adequate bilingual education program to overcome linguistic barriers.

37. That is, where there were twenty-five LEP children of the same minority language group in two consecutive elementary grades; 45 Fed. Reg. 52066.
38. Secretary of Education Terrel Bell, press release, Feb. 2, 1981.
39. 648 F.2d 989 (5th Cir. 1981).
40. 20 U.S.C. §§1701–20.
41. §1703(f).
42. §1706.

After losing at the district court level, the plaintiffs appealed to the 5th U.S. Circuit Court of Appeals, which was not so quick to absolve Raymondville of wrongdoing. It reversed the lower court with regard to ability grouping and employment discrimination. But the 5th Circuit did affirm the finding that Title VI required proof of *intent* to discriminate—always a more difficult standard to meet—and not merely a showing of discriminatory effect.[43]

What makes *Castañeda* the most significant case for language-minority children since *Lau* is not its specific outcome, but the analytical framework that it developed in determining whether the school district had met the E.E.O.A.'s requirement of "appropriate action to overcome language barriers." The appeals court set out a three-part test: theory, implementation, and results. First, was the district "pursuing a program informed by an educational theory recognized as sound by some experts in the field"? At minimum, the educational treatment had to be "deemed a legitimate experimental strategy." Second, was this program "reasonably calculated to implement effectively the educational theory adopted by the school"? To meet this criterion, the district must have adopted practices, secured the resources, and hired personnel necessary "to transform the theory into reality." Third, has the program "produce[d] results indicating that the language barriers confronting students are actually being overcome"? If not, even a treatment based on a legitimate theory and properly implemented over a period of time may "no longer constitute appropriate action."[44]

In addition, the court interpreted the E.E.O.A.'s key section, 1703(f), to impose a "duty to provide limited English speaking ability students with assistance in other areas of the curriculum where their equal participation may be impaired because of deficits incurred during participation in an agency's language remediation program." In other words, schools must compensate for the fact that children tend to fall behind in other subjects until they learn English. Otherwise, LEP students may overcome one obstacle only to face a lingering impediment to their full participation in the regular instructional program.

43. This conclusion reflected developments in federal case law since *Lau*, which had required no showing of intent. In *University of California Regents v. Bakke*, 438 U.S. 265 (1978), the Supreme Court implied that the reach of Title VI was coextensive with the Fourteenth Amendment. Since a violation of the Fourteenth Amendment guarantee of equal protection requires proof of discriminatory intent, so would a Title VI violation. Subsequent decisions by lower courts were divided on the question of whether *Bakke* implicitly overruled *Lau*. It was not until 1983 that a majority of the Supreme Court, in *Guardians Association v. Civil Service Commission of the City of New York*, 463 U.S. 582, ruled that claims under Title VI need not prove intent (still, this remains shaky legal ground, because the five justices came to this conclusion in different ways).

44. 648 F.2d 1009–10.

The influence of the *Castañeda* analysis soon extended beyond the 5th Circuit. For example, in *Keyes v. School Dist. No. 1*, a suit involving the desegregation of Denver's public schools, the parents and educators of Hispanic children intervened as plaintiffs during the remedy phase of the case to argue that the rights of LEP children had been violated. While the court declined to address their constitutional or Title VI claims, it chose to use the three-part *Castañeda* test to determine whether the school system was meeting its obligations under the E.E.O.A.

Accordingly, the court analyzed detailed evidence regarding the number of LEP students in the district, the curricula provided to students with varying degrees of English proficiency, the testing and placement of language-minority children, and the staffing, administration, and funding of programs for LEP students. It found, first, that the "transitional bilingual approach" used by the Denver schools was considered a "sound educational theory" by experts in the field. But moving to the second prong of *Castañeda* analysis, the court ruled that the district was failing to implement its programs adequately. It focused in particular on the weak qualifications of the "bilingual" teaching staff, many of whom were monolingual English speakers who, for reasons of seniority, could not be replaced with qualified teachers. Also, Denver had failed to train its E.S.L. teachers properly, or to adopt adequate means to evaluate its LEP programs, the court said. Finally, it faulted the district for "the apparent disregard of any special curriculum needs" of children who were deemed proficient in both English and Spanish, but were scoring well below average on achievement tests.[45]

Having found that the district had failed "to take reasonable action to implement" its bilingual program, the court did not proceed to the third, results-assessment phase of the *Castañeda* test. It did note, however, the high dropout rate of Hispanic students and the substandard teaching materials provided to LEP students as two strong indicators of Denver's failure to achieve the goal of equal educational opportunity. In their defense, district officials had relied heavily on the contention that they had acted in "good faith" to provide at least some help to every LEP student in the district. The court responded that this was an irrelevant argument: "[T]he affirmative obligation to take appropriate action to remove language barriers imposed by 20 U.S.C. §1703(f) does not depend upon any finding of discriminatory intent, and a failure to act is not excused by any amount of good faith." It ordered a series of changes, including development of adequate standards for evaluating the qualifications of bilingual and E.S.L. teachers, tutors, and aides; provision of remedial programs in English lit-

45. 576 F.Supp. 1503, 1516–18 (D. Colo. 1983).

eracy; and improvements in language assessment and placement of students.

Other important cases interpreting the E.E.O.A. concern the scope and reach of the statute—in other words, who is liable to be sued and on what grounds. While *Castañeda* provided a framework for judging whether school districts are meeting their obligations, other decisions have extended those obligations to state governments. In *Idaho Migrant Council v. Board of Education*, an appellate court ruled that the E.E.O.A. imposes a duty on state education agencies to supervise local school districts to ensure that they comply with the law.[46] Likewise, in *Gómez v. Illinois State Board of Education*, state officials were held accountable for their failure to set minimum standards for identifying and placing LEP students. The court rejected the state's claim of immunity under the Eleventh Amendment from E.E.O.A. lawsuits and its attempt to shift responsibility to local districts.[47] Most recently, in a settlement agreement in *LULAC et al. v. Florida Board of Education*, the state agreed to adopt regulations for school districts regarding the identification, assessment, and evaluation of LEP students; to create plans for LEP programs and advisory committees with parent involvement; and to guarantee the equal access of LEP students to state and federal categorical programs.[48]

Although *Castañeda* provided objective criteria for determining compliance with the E.E.O.A., the actual process can be highly subjective. One example is *Teresa P. v. Berkeley Unified School District*,[49] a lawsuit alleging failure to provide qualified teachers, sufficient resources, necessary monitoring systems, and adequate entry and exit procedures for LEP programs. Using the *Castañeda* analysis, the federal court found that the educational theory employed by Berkeley was pedagogically sound. And while recognizing that not all the teachers or aides had the education or skills necessary to teach LEP children, the court judged the implementation to be adequate. In doing so, it chose to rely on Berkeley's "good faith" efforts, its financial difficulties (although the district reportedly expended $1.5 million to defend this case), and the belief that it would be "highly unlikely that [Berkeley] could fill all necessary positions with fully credentialed teachers in the basic language groups." District Judge D. Lowell Jensen noted that the record supported the assumption that "good teachers are good teachers, no matter what the educational challenge may be." Finally, in analyzing the results of the district's programs, the court

46. 647 F.2d 69 (9th Cir. 1981).
47. 811 F.2d 1030, 1042–43 (7th Cir. 1987).
48. Case No. 90–1913 CIV (S.D. Fla. 1990).
49. Case No. C–87–2396-DLJ (N.D. Calif. 1989).

took the unusual step of comparing the achievement of LEP students in Berkeley with that of LEP students elsewhere in California (who may have faced similar barriers), rather than with English-proficient students.

Although the precedential value of *Teresa P.* is limited to a few school districts in northern California, opponents of bilingual education such as U.S. English have attempted to portray it as a "landmark case" repudiating native-language instruction. One California state representative sent a letter about the decision to school superintendents asserting that they would no longer have to employ certified bilingual teachers (a claim quickly refuted by California's highest education official).[50] In fact, the court's rejection of the plaintiffs' complaint, based on its interpretation of the facts in *Teresa P.*, breaks no new legal ground. In no way does it diminish LEP students' right of equal educational access under the E.E.O.A. and Title VI.

The ideological debate over whether and to what extent other languages should be used in instructing children not yet proficient in English will likely be with us for years to come. Lawsuits will continue to pit the rights of students against the limited capacities and resources of school districts. But as the court in *Keyes* noted, "There must be a change in the institutional commitment to the objective and a recognition that to assist disadvantaged children to participate in public education is to help them enter the mainstream of our social, economic, and political systems."[51] Ensuring equality of access to language-minority children must be a national commitment. We can no longer ignore that America's continued vitality depends upon the skills and abilities of all of its people. Fundamental guarantees against discrimination on the basis of race, sex, national origin, or religion should not be denied on the basis of language.

Lau v. Nichols

When children arrive in school with little or no English-speaking ability, "sink or swim" instruction is a violation of their civil rights, according to the U.S. Supreme Court in

50. Assemblyman Frank Hill, letter of April 5, 1989. In response, Bill Honig, superintendent of public instruction, noted that although state bilingual credentials "are not necessary . . . where a teacher of LEP students does not hold a [state bilingual certificate], he or she must be certified by the local school district as competent to do that job"; "Legal Advisory," May 15, 1989.
51. 576 F.Supp. 1503, 1520.

Lau v. Nichols.[52] This 1974 decision remains the major precedent regarding the educational rights of language minorities, although it is grounded in statute (Title VI of the Civil
Rights Act of 1964), rather than the U.S. Constitution. At
issue was whether school administrators may meet their
obligation to provide equal educational opportunities
merely by treating all students the same, or whether they
must offer special help for students unable to understand
English. Lower federal courts had absolved the San Francisco school district of any responsibility for minority children's "language deficiency." But a unanimous Supreme
Court disagreed. Its ruling opened a new era in federal
civil rights enforcement under the so-called *Lau* Remedies.
The decision was delivered by Justice William O. Douglas
on January 21, 1974.

This class suit brought by non-English-speaking Chinese students
against officials responsible for the operation of the San Francisco
Unified School District seeks relief against the unequal educational
opportunities which are alleged to violate, *inter alia*, the Fourteenth
Amendment. No specific remedy is urged upon us. Teaching English
to the students of Chinese ancestry who do not speak the language is
one choice. Giving instructions to this group in Chinese is another.
There may be others. Petitioners ask only that the Board of Education
be directed to apply its expertise to the problem and rectify the situation. . . . [53]

The Court of Appeals reasoned that "every student brings to the
starting line of his educational career different advantages and disadvantages caused in part by social, economic and cultural background,
created and continued completely apart from any contribution by the
school system."[54] Yet in our view the case may not be so easily decided. This is a public school system of California and §71 of the California Education Code states that "English shall be the basic language
of instruction in all schools." That section permits a school district to
determine "when and under what circumstances instruction may be
given bilingually." That section also states as "the policy of the state"
to insure "the mastery of English by all pupils in the schools." And
bilingual instruction is authorized "to the extent that it does not inter-

52. 414 U.S. 563 (1974).

53. Editor's note: Because the plaintiffs had made no request for bilingual instruction,
the court did not have to rule on whether it was the best remedy. Ultimately, however,
San Francisco school officials signed a consent decree inaugurating bilingual programs
in Cantonese, Spanish, and Tagalog, the languages spoken by 82 percent of the district's
limited-English-proficient children; the rest were provided English-as-a-second-language instruction.

54. 83 F.2d 497.

fere with the systematic, sequential, and regular instruction of all pupils in the English language."

Moreover, §8573 of the Education Code provides that no pupil shall receive a diploma of graduation from grade 12 who has not met the standards of proficiency in "English," as well as other prescribed subjects. Moreover, by §12101 of the Education Code (Supp. 1973) children between the ages of six and 16 years are (with exceptions not material here) "subject to compulsory full-time education."

Under these state-imposed standards there is no equality of treatment merely by providing students with the same facilities, textbooks, teachers, and curriculum; for students who do not understand English are effectively foreclosed from any meaningful education. Basic English skills are at the very core of what these public schools teach. Imposition of a requirement that, before a child can effectively participate in the educational program, he must already have acquired those basic skills is to make a mockery of public education. We know that those who do not understand English are certain to find their classroom experiences wholly incomprehensible and in no way meaningful.

We do not reach the Equal Protection Clause argument which has been advanced but rely solely on §601 of the Civil Rights Act of 1964[55] to reverse the Court of Appeals. That section bans discrimination based "on the ground of race, color, or national origin," in "any program or activity receiving federal financial assistance." The school district involved in this litigation receives large amounts of federal financial assistance. The Department of Health, Education, and Welfare (H.E.W.), which has authority to promulgate regulations prohibiting discrimination in federally assisted school systems, in 1968 issued one guideline that "[s]chool systems are responsible for assuring that students of a particular race, color, or national origin are not denied the opportunity to obtain the education generally obtained by other students in the system." In 1970 H.E.W. made the guidelines more specific, requiring school districts that were federally funded "to rectify the language deficiency in order to open" the instruction to students who had "linguistic deficiencies."[56] . . .

It seems obvious that the Chinese-speaking minority receive fewer benefits than the English-speaking majority from respondents' school system, which denies them a meaningful opportunity to participate in the educational program—all earmarks of the discrimination banned by the Regulations. In 1970 H.E.W. issued clarifying guidelines which include the following:

55. 42 U.S.C. §2000d.
56. 33 Fed. Reg. 4955; 35 Fed. Reg. 11595.

Where inability to speak and understand the English language excludes national origin–minority group children from effective participation in the educational program offered by a school district, the district must take affirmative steps to rectify the language deficiency in order to open its instructional program to these students.

Any ability grouping or tracking system employed by the school system to deal with the special language skill needs of national origin–minority group children must be designed to meet such language skill needs as soon as possible and must not operate as an educational deadend or permanent track.

Respondent school district contractually agreed to "comply with Title VI of the Civil Rights Act of 1964 . . . and all requirements imposed by or pursuant to the Regulation" of H.E.W. which are "issued pursuant to that title . . ." and also immediately to "take any measures necessary to effectuate this agreement."[57] The Federal Government has power to fix the terms on which its money allotments to the States shall be disbursed. Whatever the limits of that power, they have not been reached here. Senator Humphrey, during the floor debates on the Civil Rights Act of 1964, said:

Simple justice requires that public funds, to which all taxpayers of all races contribute, not be spent in any fashion which encourages, entrenches, subsidizes, or results in racial discrimination.

We accordingly reverse the judgment of the Court of Appeals and remand the case for the fashioning of appropriate relief. . . .

While concurring in the decision, Justice Harry Blackmun (joined by Chief Justice Warren Burger) added a caveat that could prove significant as school districts are confronted with increasingly diverse student populations.

Against the possibility that the Court's judgment may be interpreted too broadly, I stress the fact that the children with whom we are concerned here number about 1,800. This is a very substantial group that is being deprived of any meaningful schooling because the children cannot understand the language of the classroom. We may only guess as to why they have had no exposure to English in their preschool years. Earlier generations of American ethnic groups have overcome the language barrier by earnest parental endeavor or by the hard fact of being pushed out of the family or community nest and into the realities of broader experience.

I merely wish to make plain that when, in another case, we are confronted with a very few youngsters, or with just a single child who speaks only German or Polish or Spanish or any language other than

57. 45 C.F.R. §80.

English, I would not regard today's decision . . . as conclusive upon the issue whether the statute and the guidelines require the funded school district to provide special instruction. For me, numbers are at the heart of this case and my concurrence is to be understood accordingly.[58]

Martin Luther King Jr. Elementary School Children v. Ann Arbor School District

In 1974 Congress voted, in effect, to codify the *Lau v. Nichols* decision regarding school districts' responsibilities toward limited-English-proficient children. The Equal Educational Opportunities Act required each district "to take appropriate action to overcome language barriers that impede equal participation by its students in its instructional programs."[59] This provision, invoked on behalf of language-minority children, has resulted in a number of court orders for bilingual education.[60] In the King ruling, this principle was extended to children who speak a minority dialect of English. After hearing extensive testimony from linguists, Judge C. W. Joiner issued his "Black English" decision on July 12, 1979.[61]

A major goal of American education in general, and of King School in particular, is to train young people to communicate both orally (speaking and understanding oral speech) and in writing (reading and understanding the written word and writing so that others can understand it) in the standard vernacular of society. The art of communication among the people of the country in all aspects of people's lives is a basic building block in the development of each individual. Children need to learn to speak and understand and to read and write the language used by society to carry on its business, to develop its science, arts and culture, and to carry on its professions and govern-

58. Editor's note: The Equal Educational Opportunities Act of 1974, §1706, has undercut this objection by giving children with limited English skills an individual right of action against school districts that fail to help them overcome language barriers (*see p. 247*).

59. 20 U.S.C. §1703(f).

60. See, e.g, *Keyes v. School Dist. No. 1*, 576 F.Supp. 1503 (D. Colo. 1983).

61. *Martin Luther King Jr. Elementary School Children et al., v. Ann Arbor School District*, 473 F.Supp. 1371 (E.D. Mich. 1979).

mental functions. Therefore, a major goal of a school system is to teach reading, writing, speaking and understanding standard English.

The problem in this case revolves around the ability of the school system, King School in particular, to teach the reading of standard English to children who, it is alleged, speak "black English" as a matter of course at home and in their home community (the Green Road Housing Development). This case is not an effort on the part of the plaintiffs to require that they be taught "black English" or that their instruction throughout their schooling be in "black English" or that a dual language program be provided. . . . It is a straightforward effort to require the court to intervene on the children's behalf to require the defendant School District Board to take appropriate action to teach them to read in the standard English of the school, the commercial world, the arts, science, and professions. This action is a cry for judicial help in opening the doors to the establishment. Plaintiffs' counsel says that it is an action to keep another generation from becoming functionally illiterate. . . .

Section 1703(f) of Title 20, U.S.C. . . . is the sole remaining basis for the plaintiff's claims. The issues raised . . . are:

> 1. Whether the children have a language barrier.
> 2. Whether, if they have a language barrier, that barrier impedes their equal participation in the instructional program offered by the defendant. . . .
> 3. Whether, if there is a barrier that does so impede, the defendant Board has taken "appropriate action to overcome the language barrier."
> 4. Whether, if the defendant Board has not taken "appropriate action," this failure denies equal educational opportunity to plaintiffs "on account of race." . . .

The court heard from a number of distinguished and renowned researchers and professionals who told the court about their research and discoveries involving "black English" and how it impacts on the teaching of standard English. . . . The language of "black English" has been shown to be a distinct, definable version of English, different from standard English of the school and the general world of communications. It has definite language patterns, syntax, grammar, and history. . . . "Black English" is not a language used by the mainstream of society—black or white. It is not an acceptable method of communication in the educational world, in the commercial community, in the community of the arts and science, or among professionals. It is largely a system that is used in casual and informal communication among the poor and lesser educated.

The instruction in standard English of children who use "black English" at home by insensitive teachers who treat the children's language system as inferior can cause a barrier to learning to read and use standard English. . . . If a barrier exists because of the language used by the children in this case, it exists not because the teachers and students cannot understand each other, but because in the process of attempting to teach the students how to speak standard English the students are made somehow to feel inferior and are thereby turned off from the learning process. . . .

Research indicates that the black dialect or vernacular used at home by black students in general makes it more difficult for such children to learn to read for three reasons:

> 1. There is a lack of parental or other home support for developing reading skills in standard English, including the absence of persons in the home who read, enjoy it and profit from it.
> 2. Students experience difficulty in hearing and making certain sounds used discriminatively in standard English, but not distinguished in the home language system.
> 3. The unconscious but evident attitude of teachers toward the home language causes a psychological barrier to learning by the student. . . .

[T]he evidence suggests clearly that no matter how well intentioned the teachers are, they are not likely to be successful in overcoming the language barrier caused by their failure to take into account the home language system, unless they are helped by the defendant to recognize the existence of the language system used by the children in their home community and to use that knowledge as a way of helping the children to learn to read standard English. . . .

Although this statute is a direct congressional mandate to the federal courts to become involved in matters of this kind, this statute makes it clear that discretion is given to the judge to determine what is "appropriate." Accordingly, this court finds it appropriate to require the defendant Board to take steps to help its teachers to recognize the home language of the students and to use that knowledge in their attempts to teach reading skills in standard English. . . . It is not the intention of this court to tell educators how to educate, but only to see that this defendant carries out an obligation imposed by law to help the teachers use existing knowledge as this may bear on appropriate action to overcome language barriers. . . .

Bilingual Ballots: Their History and a Look Forward

By John Trasviña

John Trasviña is general counsel and staff director of the U.S. Senate Subcommittee on the Constitution, which has jurisdiction over the federal Voting Rights Act and the English Language Amendment. This article, which he wrote for the *Source Book,* is not intended to represent the views of subcommittee members or staff.

The right to vote in the United States has been expanded and extended since this nation's early days. Two hundred years ago, at the time the Constitution was ratified, suffrage was limited to adult, white, property-owning males. Gradually, the right to vote was extended to adult white males with less property, to all adult white males, to all adult males regardless of color, to all adults regardless of sex or color, and finally, to all citizens who have reached the age of eighteen. Most recently, barriers to voting have dropped, either on a state-by-state basis or nationally, for illiterates and for those citizens who may or may not be literate in another language, but lack fluency in English.

Each of these developments in our constitutional history has had a dramatic and positive impact on the lives of those directly affected, as well as on the nation as a whole. The right of all Americans to vote is now so ingrained in our body politic that any attempt to roll back voting rights would not be taken seriously. One of the most potent arguments against the confirmation of Robert Bork to the U.S. Supreme Court in 1987 was his criticism of the court's decisions, in *Katzenbach v. Morgan* and *Oregon v. Mitchell,* upholding a Congressional ban on literacy requirements for voting as "very bad, indeed pernicious, constitutional law."[62]

Against this backdrop comes the development of bilingual election materials and services. And yet, voting in languages other than English enjoys no similarly comfortable resting place in the national consensus. When Congress considers extending them in 1992, the bilingual provisions of the Voting Rights Act are likely to come under attack. They can withstand the scrutiny, however, because they are

62. U.S. Senate Committee on the Judiciary, Subcommittee on Separation of Powers, *The Human Life Bill: Hearing on S. 158,* 97th Cong., 1st sess. (1981), pp. 310, 313–14.

critically necessary for some citizens to exercise their fundamental right to vote.

Historically, the immigrant experience on election day was far different from that seen today. One hundred years ago, immigration from Europe to the United States was nearing its highest levels and, coincidentally, so was participation in American elections. Immigrants played a very active political role in the cities in which they settled. They were organized by machines of both parties and by bosses who brought political prominence to the Irish, the Germans, and others in cities like New York, Boston, Chicago, and San Francisco. One tactic used to mobilize immigrants was to register them to vote for partisan candidates shortly after they came ashore. In some areas U.S. citizenship was not required in local elections, and the secret ballot method (imported from Australia) was relatively new. After election day and throughout the year, precinct captains and ward healers provided loyalists access to jobs, food, and social services.

While the immigrants still struggled—the machines offered no means of easy wealth for European newcomers—Hispanic and Asian immigrants in the late 1800s lacked even this system of acculturation to American political life. The Hispanic and Asian political experience in that era is much closer to the enforced isolation of Jim Crow for African Americans in the post-Reconstruction South. "Separate but equal" schooling was the law for Hispanics in Texas and elsewhere in the Southwest. The U.S. Senate voted down naturalization for Chinese immigrants in 1870, and barriers to their citizenship remained in place until 1943. As historian William Courtney has written, "There is little question that had the Chinese been extended the privilege of citizenship and the right of franchise at that time, their lot during the ensuing thirty years of downright persecution would have been entirely different."[63]

Congress largely failed to recognize the history of electoral and other discrimination against Hispanics, Asian Americans, American Indians, and other language minorities when it enacted the Voting Rights Act of 1965. A cornerstone of the Great Society, passed in response to civil rights marches and sit-ins and the violent reactions to those efforts, the Voting Rights Act focused on electoral discrimination against African Americans in the South. The law virtually stripped the powers of local and state officials in that region to conduct and regulate elections. It authorized the attorney general of the United States to "pre-clear" changes in local and state election laws and to appoint election examiners to monitor enforcement. Also, literacy tests were banned for the five-year life of the Act.

---

63. *San Francisco's Anti-Chinese Ordinances* (San Francisco: R & E Research Associates, 1976).

The only mention of Hispanics during consideration of the Voting Rights Act came in relation to Puerto Ricans, who were described as "persons educated in American-flag schools in which the predominant classroom language was other than English." The Act thus nullified the English literacy requirement for voting contained in the New York State constitution, thus enfranchising Puerto Ricans who were literate in Spanish but not in English. In 1970, exercising its enforcement powers under the Fourteenth Amendment, Congress extended the ban on literacy tests nationwide.[64]

When the Voting Rights Act was due for reauthorization in 1975, the House and Senate Judiciary committees for the first time considered extending the Act's principles from banning racial discrimination to addressing discrimination based on language. After hearing testimony about the denial of equal educational opportunities by state and local governments—which had left many Hispanics, Asian Americans, and American Indians illiterate in English—Congress declared: "It is necessary to eliminate such discrimination by prohibiting English-only elections, and by prescribing other remedial devices."[65]

The one remedial device that has proven most controversial is bilingual voting. Previously, some local jurisdictions had attempted to provide such assistance to language minorities, but it was not always well implemented. Congressional testimony disclosed, for example, that one California county had printed Spanish-language ballots, but failed to issue adequate instructions on how to use them. In Arizona, interpreters for Navajo speakers were provided, but only sparingly. So in the 1975 Voting Rights Act amendments, Congress required that written materials and oral voter assistance be made available in languages other than English under certain circumstances: a single language-minority group must account for at least 5 percent of a jurisdiction's voting-age citizens, and (1) the English literacy rate must be below the national average, or (2) the jurisdiction must have conducted the 1972 election only in English and have attracted the participation of fewer than 50 percent of potential voters.[66] ("Language minority group" was defined to include "persons who are American

64. Congressional authority to mandate such changes in state electoral procedures was affirmed by the Supreme Court in *Katzenbach v. Morgan*, 384 U.S. 641 (1966), and *Oregon v. Mitchell*, 400 U.S. 112 (1970).

65. 2 U.S.C. §1973aa.

66. The first of these eligibility formulas, known as §203(c), is scheduled to expire on Aug. 6, 1992. If Congress fails to extend the provision, bilingual ballots will no longer be mandated in 69 jurisdictions, including all of Colorado and New Mexico and most of California. The second formula, §4(f)(4), will remain in effect until the year 2007. See U.S. Commission on Civil Rights, *A Citizen's Guide to Understanding the Voting Rights Act* (Washington, D.C.: U.S. Commission on Civil Rights, 1984), and Mexican American

Indian, Asian American, Alaskan Natives or of Spanish heritage.")
These criteria resulted in targeted coverage of more than 300 counties,
mainly in the Southwest, including jurisdictions as small as Loving
County, Texas (200 persons), and as large as Los Angeles County,
California (7 million persons).

Election officials, however, were largely unprepared and in some
cases unwilling to comply with the new requirements. The law directed them to hire bilingual polling officials and to translate written
materials into Spanish, Chinese, Japanese, Filipino, or American Indian languages. The vast majority of the counties that were required
to provide bilingual services did so in Spanish. Outside of Hawaii,
Asian language services were required only in San Francisco. While
the U.S. Department of Justice issued regulations, and while Congress had intended for the Act's requirements to be construed
broadly, limited federal supervision and training were offered to local
officials or minority communities.

Initial implementation problems made bilingual services, where
available, excessively expensive and produced antagonism toward
the new law. Spanish-bilingual voter registration forms in San Francisco were found in Chinatown, while the Chinese forms were sent to
the Hispanic Mission district. Instead of concentrating its resources
on the Hispanic voting-age population, which was then 12 percent of
the total, Los Angeles sent Spanish bilingual materials to all voters, 88
percent of whom were non-Hispanic (and in any case were likely to
know English, since they had registered under the old system). The
translations themselves were also problematic. One Los Angeles candidate, a small businessman, was identified as a shop-tending dwarf!
Some local governments spent no money on voter registration in minority communities or on public education, and then expressed surprise when no new voters stepped forward on election day to use the
bilingual ballots.

Civil rights attorneys and political scientists argued that the initial
poor record of implementation by local officials had nothing to do
with inherent difficulties in the new law, but reflected a desire to see
it fail or an indifference to the voting rights of Hispanics and Asian
Americans. These early experiences tended to discredit the bilingual
provisions of the Voting Rights Act and to hamper Congressional efforts in 1982 to extend the law for an additional ten years. Nevertheless, local election officials testified in favor of the extension, and most
horror stories about costly implementation were addressed by subsequent improvements. In Los Angeles, for example, the cost of bilin-

---

Legal Defense and Educational Fund, "Reauthorization of the Bilingual Provisions of
the Voting Rights Act," Jan. 31, 1991.

gual assistance dropped to less than 2 percent of all election costs, and in San Francisco, it amounted to 16 ten-thousandths of one percent of the city's budget.[67] But the most telling argument in support of extending the bilingual ballot provisions was the enhanced political power they brought for language minorities who had previously been excluded from the process. As measured by the increased voter participation of Hispanics and Asian Americans, and by their election to public office in record numbers, the Voting Rights Act has provided the "beginnings of a fair share" envisioned by Vilma Martínez, president of the Mexican American Legal Defense and Educational Fund, in 1975.[68]

Still, the debate over extending bilingual voting rights beyond 1992 will pit the greater Hispanic and Asian American political presence against an emboldened English Only movement, which has won electoral battles around the country. As early as 1983, San Francisco voters approved Proposition O, an advisory measure asking Congress to repeal the Act's bilingual provisions. English Only forces have targeted language assistance as wasteful and dangerous to the notion that Americans, whatever other differences they may have, must share English as the common language in which they communicate with government. Bilingual ballots are un-American, the opponents claim, because they allow non-English-speaking voters to be controlled by ethnic bosses. Similar arguments were raised when women gained the right to vote and literacy requirements were abolished— for example, that the women's votes would be controlled by their husbands or that illiterate Americans would be too uninformed to vote responsibly. Experience has proved both of these arguments wrong.

The Voting Rights Act guarantees that a non-English speaker will be able to cast an independent, informed vote. It offers, in a language that he or she can understand, the same assistance and explanatory materials that English-speaking voters receive. This removes the need for intervention by third parties, well meaning or otherwise. Similarly, with the expansion of minority language media and telecommunications today, candidates can advertise in many languages, and debates can be readily translated on radio and television and in newspapers. By no means is the non-English speaker relegated to the sta-

67. San Francisco voter information packet, "Argument in Opposition to Proposition O" (1983).

68. U.S. House Committee on the Judiciary, Subcommittee on Civil and Constitutional Rights, *Extension of the Voting Rights Act: Hearings on H.R. 939, H.R. 2148, H.R. 3247, and H.R. 3501*, 94th Cong., 1st sess. (Washington, D.C.: U.S. Government Printing Office, 1975), p. 876. See also Alan Hudson-Edwards, Carlos Astiz, and David Lopez, *Bilingual Election Services*, vol. 1, *A Handbook of Ideas for Local Election Officials*, and vol. 3, *A State of the Art Report* (Washington, D.C.: National Clearinghouse on Election Administration, Federal Election Commission, 1978, 1979).

tus of a "bossed" voter who must cast a ballot without knowing the issues.

Ironically, this information explosion in languages other than English has been used as an argument against bilingual ballots. Opponents maintain that immigrants will be discouraged from making the effort to learn English if they can function easily, even being allowed to vote, in their native language. Yet the use of a bilingual ballot on election day does not diminish the primacy of English in the United States the remaining 364 days of the year. A voter whose political interest is whetted by learning about the process in his or her home language will soon want to know more, and therefore will have an added incentive—beyond the economic and social motivations—to learn English.

Opponents also contend that only foreign-born voters are likely to need language assistance at the polls. However, since U.S. immigration laws make English literacy a condition of naturalization, this should be unnecessary, unless voters using bilingual ballots are not really U.S. citizens. If these arguments, taken together or separately, were true, Congress would be hard-pressed to justify a continuation of bilingual voting assistance. But they are not. The first Voting Rights Act of 1965 recognized that some American citizens, although born and raised in this country, lacked proficiency in English and were thus disenfranchised by English-only elections. African American citizens, not Hispanic or Asian immigrants, were the first beneficiaries of the ban on literacy tests for voting. Unequal educational opportunities had left them vulnerable to the discriminatory application of such tests. Hispanics in the Southwest and Puerto Rico had a similar historical experience. As native-born U.S. citizens who often learned little English in school, many elderly Hispanics today are unable to cast an informed vote in English. In Spanish, however, they are quite capable of exercising this right of citizenship.

The argument against bilingual ballots suffers from another misconception: that there is only one level of literacy for all contexts. To pass the naturalization test requires about a third grade level of English, while education experts generally designate fifth-grade English skills as the dividing line between functional literacy and illiteracy. Voting materials, in particular the explanations of ballot propositions, are written at levels as high as college English. So a foreign-born voter who has passed the literacy test for citizenship may lack the English skills to vote using an all-English ballot. In this case there is no contradiction between being literate for one governmental purpose but not for another.

The right to vote is fundamental because it provides a means to preserve all other rights. It is particularly important to new citizens who often must depend on the decisions of the legislative and execu-

tive branches for the protection of their civil and constitutional liberties. The Voting Rights Act has aided the evolution of a New South in
which African Americans have been able to participate in the electoral
process and to win public office as never before. The law has brought
about similar gains for Hispanics in Texas and the Southwest. Repeal-
ing the bilingual election provisions of the Voting Rights Act would
endanger that progress.

Castro v. State of California

The literacy test for voting, until it was finally abolished by
Congress, was used to disenfranchise a wide range of un-
popular minorities. In Massachusetts in the 1850s, Know-
Nothings enacted it as a deliberate (though quite futile) at-
tempt to keep Irish immigrants out of politics. Later it was
invoked against blacks in the South, Chinese in the West,
Yiddish-speaking Jews in New York, Finnish immigrants in
Wyoming, Indians in Alaska, and Mexican Americans in
California.[69] Shortly before Congress did so, the California
Supreme Court outlawed the English literacy requirement—at least when applied to voters who were literate in
Spanish—as a violation of the Equal Protection Clause of
the Fourteenth Amendment. It stopped short, however, of
mandating a bilingual electoral system. Justice Sullivan de-
livered the court's unanimous opinion on March 24, 1970.[70]

The English literacy requirement was introduced as a proposed constitutional amendment in the State Assembly in 1891. Its author was
Assemblyman A. J. Bledsoe who, five years previously, had been a
member of the vigilante Committee of Fifteen which expelled every
person of Chinese ancestry from Humboldt County. Assemblyman
Bledsoe was forthright about the purposes of his amendment . . . :

We look with alarm upon the increased immigration of the
illiterate and unassimilated elements of Europe, and believe that every agency should be invoked to preserve our
public lands from alien grasp, to shield American labor
from this destructive competition, and to protect the purity
of the ballot-box from the corrupting influences of the disturbing elements . . . from abroad. . . . If we do not take
some steps to prevent the ignorant classes, who are com-

69. Arnold H. Leibowitz, "English Literacy: Legal Sanction for Discrimination," *Notre
Dame Lawyer* 45 (Fall 1969): 34–37.

70. *Castro v. State of California*, 2 C.3d 223; 85 Cal.Rptr. 20, 466 P.2d 244.

ing here from Europe, unloading the refuse of the world upon our shores, from exercising the right of suffrage until they have acquired knowledge of our Constitution, our system of government, and our laws, it will soon come to pass that this element will direct in our politics and our institutions will be overthrown. . . . [71]

It is obvious that fear and hatred played a significant role in the passage of the literacy requirement. Perhaps a genuine desire to create an intelligent and responsible electorate was equally important for many of its supporters. We, no more than the trial court, need decide this issue. Our primary task is to determine whether the challenged provision is compatible with the demands of equal protection as they apply in contemporary society. Its historical origin, whether odious or admirable, cannot fully answer that question. . . .

We believe that California's concern that those of her citizens who are eligible to vote likewise be capable of informed decisions on matters submitted to the electorate, constitutes a "compelling" state interest. . . . The question of the validity of literacy requirements per se is not before us, however, and we intimate no opinion in the matter. The question which is raised is whether this interest necessitates that literacy, if required, be limited to literacy in *English.* . . .

At trial, the petitioners introduced evidence of a substantial network of Spanish language news media to which, as residents of Los Angeles County, they have ready access. This evidence, the accuracy of which was stipulated to by respondents, reveals that eight Spanish language newspapers are published in Los Angeles County, two of which are published daily, the remainder at weekly intervals. Nine additional Spanish language newspapers which are published elsewhere in the United States, in Mexico, or in South America also circulate in Los Angeles County. Eleven Spanish language magazines are available, two of which, *Grafica* and *La Raza*, are published in Los Angeles and are devoted primarily to discussion of national and local affairs. The nine remaining include Spanish translations of *Life (Life en Español)* and *Readers' Digest (Selecciones).* . . .

Petitioners contend on appeal, as they did in the court below, that their proof of access to 17 Spanish language newspapers and 11 Spanish language magazines was sufficient to shift to respondents the burden of producing evidence to show that the newspapers involved do *not* provide their readers with information about political candidates, events and issues. . . . We concur. In light of the evidence presented to us by this record, the facts required to be judicially noticed by us, the absence of any evidence indicating any substantial difference between the newspapers described in the stipulation of the parties and

---

71. *Sacramento Record Union,* Jan. 20, 1891.

those English language publications commonly denominated as "newspapers," we are satisfied that petitioners have demonstrated access to materials printed in Spanish which communicate substantial information on matters, not only of national, but also of state and local political concern. . . .

Elaborate educational qualifications for voters are incompatible with our commitment to full and equal participation in the political life of the nation. The state may have a compelling interest in establishing standards which tend to ensure a minimal degree of competence and capacity to become informed. It has no such interest in excluding voters who meet these standards on the ground that they do not also have access to mammoth quantities of information which the state does not and could not demand that other voters utilize. Exclusion of all who cannot read English is obviously *necessary* to accomplish the goal of creating an electorate which can read all material of political significance printed in English. While that may be a desirable state policy, it is hardly so compelling that it justifies denying the vote to a group of United States citizens who already face similar problems of discrimination and exclusion in other areas and need a political voice if they are to have any realistic hope of ameliorating the conditions in which they live. . . .

Although accorded only the briefest mention by respondents, there is another source of potential state interest in preserving the absolute quality of the English literacy requirement. We refer, not to the state's concern with standards for voter qualification, but to its professed desire to avoid the cost and administrative complexity entailed in providing a bilingual electoral system. Most significant would be the expense of translating, printing and distributing ballots, sample ballots, and ballot pamphlets (which contain texts of proposed measures, an analysis of them prepared by public counsel, and arguments in support and in opposition) in both English and Spanish. In addition, increased difficulties in the counting and reporting of returns reasonably could be anticipated. It is clear, as respondents appear to concede, that the question of constitutionality cannot turn on this issue alone. Avoidance or recoupment of administrative costs, while a valid state concern, cannot justify imposition of an otherwise improper classification, especially when, as here, it touches on "matters close to the core of our constitutional system."

Whether such a radical reconstruction of our voting procedures is constitutionally compelled, however, is a separate question. It is clear that the goal of efficient and inexpensive administration, while praiseworthy, cannot justify depriving citizens of fundamental rights. But this does not imply that the state must not only provide all qualified citizens with an equivalent opportunity to exercise their right to vote, but must also provide perfect conditions under which such right is exercised. . . . California is not required to adopt a bilingual electoral apparatus as a result of our decision today that it may no longer exclude Spanish literates from the polls. The state interest in maintaining a single language system is substantial, and the provision of ballots, notices, ballot pamphlets, etc., in Spanish is not necessary either to the formation of intelligent opinions on election issues or to the implementation of those opinions through the mechanics of balloting. . . .

Accordingly, we hold that the English literacy requirement . . . cannot be applied, consistently with the Fourteenth Amendment, to California citizens, wherever resident, who are literate in Spanish and in all other respects qualified to vote.[72] We add one final word. We cannot refrain from observing that if a contrary conclusion were compelled it would indeed be ironic that petitioners, who are the heirs of a great and gracious culture, identified with the birth of California and contributing in no small measure to its growth, should be disenfranchised in their ancestral land, despite their capacity to cast an informed vote. . . .

Puerto Rican Organization for Political Action (PROPA) v. Kusper

A state's simple Official English declaration does not justify practical restrictions on bilingual services, according to the 7th U.S. Circuit Court of Appeals.[73] Furthermore, the court found that Puerto Ricans residing in Illinois are entitled to election materials in Spanish. This is one of several decisions that prompted Congress to mandate bilingual voting materials in its 1975 amendments to the Voting Rights Act. The case involved a refusal by Chicago officials to provide bilingual voting instructions and election workers in Puerto Rican precincts during the 1972 election. The officials based this denial, in part, on the state's 1969 Official English statute (see p. 135). A U.S. district judge rejected this reasoning and issued an injunction requiring Chicago to provide bilingual voter assistance. Its ruling was af-

---

72. Editor's note: The court added that the decision would apply not only to Spanish-speakers, but "to any case in which otherwise qualified voters, literate in a language other than English, are able to make a comparable demonstration of access to sources of political information."

73. *Puerto Rico Organization for Political Action (PROPA) v. Kusper*, 490 F.2d 575 (7th Cir. 1973).

firmed by the appellate court in an opinion delivered by Judge Sprecher on December 18, 1973.

This [Official English] statute (which appears with others naming the state bird and the state song) has never been used to prevent publication of official materials in other languages. In fact, various state and city agencies publish numerous materials and provide many services in Spanish. . . . We conclude that no Illinois law prohibits defendants from giving voting assistance in Spanish. . . .

United States policy toward persons born in Puerto Rico is to make them U.S. citizens, to allow them to conduct their schools in Spanish, and to permit them unrestricted immigration to the mainland. As a result, thousands of Puerto Ricans have come to live in New York, Chicago, and other urban areas; they are eligible, as residents and U.S. citizens, to vote in elections conducted in a language many of them do not understand. Puerto Ricans are not required, as are immigrants from foreign countries, to learn English before they have the right to vote as U.S. citizens.[74] Their plight is as much a result of government policy as is the plight of Negroes trying to pass literacy tests in states which had subjected them to segregated, unequal school systems.

Congress responded to the inequities caused by literacy tests by outlawing them in states with low percentages of registrants or voters.[75] In the same act, Congress buttressed the right of Puerto Ricans to vote in the following language:

> Congress hereby declares that to secure the rights under the Fourteenth Amendment of persons educated in American-flag schools in which the predominant classroom language was other than English, it is necessary to prohibit the States from conditioning the right to vote of such persons on ability to read, write, understand, or interpret any matter in the English language. . . .

We agree with the interpretation . . . that "the right to vote" encompasses the right to an effective vote. If a person who cannot read English is entitled to oral assistance, if a Negro is entitled to correction of erroneous instructions, so a Spanish-speaking Puerto Rican is entitled to assistance in the language he can read or understand. . . .

74. 8 U.S.C. §1423.
75. Voting Rights Act of 1965, 42 U.S.C. §§1973, *et seq.*

Language Rights in the Private Sector

By Edward M. Chen

A staff attorney for the American Civil Liberties Union of Northern California and a litigator on language-rights issues, Edward M. Chen helped to organize Californians United against Proposition 63, a coalition opposed to that state's Official English initiative. He wrote this article for the *Source Book*.

Proponents of Official English argue that such laws are intended only to restrict governmental provision of language assistance, and not to affect the private sector. In their ballot argument in support of Proposition 63, leaders of U.S. English insisted, "Nothing in the amendment prohibits the use of languages other than English in unofficial situations, such as family communications, religious ceremonies or private business." Yet in the past several years, U.S. English officials have mounted organized protests against Burger King in Florida for its use of bilingual menus, spearheaded a letter-writing campaign against a California telephone company's publication of the Spanish-language Yellow Pages, and protested the issuance of Federal Communications Commission licenses to Spanish-language radio stations in the Southwest. Indeed, some English Only restrictions upon the private sector have been codified. In response to a recent influx of Chinese immigrants, several cities in southern California passed ordinances limiting the use of foreign languages on private business signs.

More insidious than these organized efforts, the English Only movement has catalyzed subtle forms of language discrimination. Well-publicized instances following passage of Official English initiatives in Colorado and Florida—the school-bus driver who reprimanded children for speaking Spanish and the supermarket clerk who was suspended for answering a fellow employee in Spanish—represent the tip of an iceberg. Since the passage of Proposition 63 in California, civil rights organizations have received numerous complaints about English-only workplace rules in hospitals, universities, the U.S. Postal Service, hotels, electronics manufacturing firms, insurance companies, banks, and even nonprofit charitable organizations.

Regardless of the stated intentions of its organizers, the Official English campaign has had consequences beyond regulating the language of governmental operations. This article explores the legal implications and responses to English Only restrictions in the private sector, especially in the workplace and in business advertising.

Employer rules that prohibit language-minority workers from speaking their native languages to fellow employees during working hours appear to be widespread.[76] Unfortunately, employees of private firms are not protected by the U.S. Constitution, which generally protects against abuses by governmental, but not private entities. Workers at firms with fifteen or more employees, however, are protected under Title VII of the federal Civil Rights Act of 1964.

Title VII outlaws employment discrimination based on race, color, religion, sex, or national origin. Specifically, it makes it unlawful to discharge, refuse to hire, or "otherwise discriminate against any individual with respect to his compensation, terms, conditions, or privileges of employment" on the basis of the forbidden criteria.[77] While the statute does not expressly prohibit discrimination on the basis of language, the Equal Employment Opportunity Commission (E.E.O.C.), the federal agency that enforces this law, has issued guidelines that define national-origin discrimination broadly to include denial of employment because of an "individual's or his ancestor's, place of origin; or because an individual has the physical, cultural or linguistic characteristics of a national origin group." The guidelines specifically recognize that an individual's primary language is an essential characteristic of national origin.[78]

In addition to addressing such issues as accent discrimination and English-proficiency requirements, the E.E.O.C. Guidelines specifically address English-only workplace rules:

> (a) *When applied at all times.* A rule requiring employees to speak only English at all times in the workplace is a burdensome term and condition of employment. The primary language of an individual is often an essential national origin characteristic. Prohibiting employees at all times, in the

76. See the incidents described in Note, "English-Only Rules and 'Innocent' Employers: Clarifying National Origin Discrimination and Disparate Impact Theory under Title VII," *Minnesota Law Review* 74 (1989): 387, 392–94.

77. Title VII further forbids an employer to "limit, segregate, or classify his employees or applicants for employment in any way which would deprive or tend to deprive any individual of employment opportunities or otherwise adversely affect his status as an employee" because of the employee's race, color, religion, sex, or national origin.

78. "E.E.O.C. Guidelines on Discrimination Because of National Origin," 29 C.F.R. §§1606.1, 1606.7 (1987).

workplace, from speaking their primary language or the language they speak most comfortably, disadvantages an individual's employment opportunities on the basis of national origin. It may also create an atmosphere of inferiority, isolation and intimidation based on national origin which could result in a discriminatory working environment. Therefore, the Commission will presume that such a rule violates Title VII and will closely scrutinize it.

(b) *When applied only at certain times.* An employer may have a rule requiring that employees speak only in English at certain times where the employer can show that the rule is justified by business necessity.[79]

These guidelines were endorsed by a federal appeals court in *Gutiérrez v. Municipal Court (see pp. 277–84)*, a decision that struck down a rule imposed by three municipal-court judges prohibiting bilingual court clerks from speaking to each other in Spanish except during breaks. The appeals court found that the English-only policy had a discriminatory impact on Hispanics and was not justified by a "business necessity." To meet the business-necessity test, the decision said that employer's justification must be "sufficiently compelling to override the discriminatory impact" and that the challenged practice "must effectively carry out the business purpose it is alleged to serve, and there must be available no acceptable less discriminatory alternative which would accomplish the purpose as well."[80]

Applying this stringent test, the appeals court rejected the employers' arguments to justify their English-only rule: (1) the need for the state and the country to have a single language system—an interest undercut by the fact that an important part of the clerks' duties was to communicate with the non-English-speaking public; (2) the need to prevent the workplace from turning into a "Tower of Babel"—a claim contradicted by the fact that the use of Spanish in communicating with the public was part of the normal press of the municipal court's business; (3) the need to promote racial harmony—an allegation unsupported by any evidence of inappropriate use of Spanish (in fact, the effect of the rule was to increase racial tension, as it made Hispanics feel belittled); (4) the need to assuage non-Spanish-speaking employees' fears and suspicions—fears judged to be based on racial prejudices, not on substantial facts; (5) the need for supervisors to monitor the work product of the clerks—a need inconsistent with the fact that the clerks were required to use their bilingual skills on the job—hence it would be more effective to employ Spanish-speaking supervisors; and (6) the fact that California is an Official English state

79. Ibid.
80. 838 F.2d 1031, 1049 (9th Cir. 1988), *vacated as moot*, 109 S.Ct. 1736 (1989).

by a recent constitutional amendment—a fact considered irrelevant by the court because it viewed Proposition 63 as "primarily a symbolic statement," which did not affect communications between coworkers in government.

The analysis in *Gutiérrez* would invalidate the vast majority of English-only workplace rules, which typically rely on one or more of the justifications raised in this case. However, that decision was taken off the books by the U.S. Supreme Court on grounds of mootness, because the plaintiff had settled the case and no longer worked at the court. As a result, the *Gutiérrez* decision is not a binding precedent, leaving other federal courts free to rule on the validity of the E.E.O.C. Guidelines.[81]

The guidelines do not suggest that English-only rules may never be imposed. The E.E.O.C.'s commentary to its guidelines indicates that a business necessity would exist, for example, "where safety requires that all communications be in English so that everyone can closely follow a particular task, such as surgery or drilling of oil wells,[82] or where a salesperson is attending to English-speaking customers." Another example is requiring a radio disc jockey to speak only English on the air because his use of Spanish may confuse listeners, thus affecting the identity of the product being marketed.[83] The employer's burden of justifying such rules, however, is a difficult one.[84]

When imposed by government on private business, English-only

81. In a case decided before the E.E.O.C. issued its guidelines, another federal appeals court ruled that English-only workplace rule was not discriminatory. In *García v. Gloor*, 618 F.2d 264 (5th Cir. 1980), *cert. denied*, 449 U.S. 1113 (1981), the court upheld an English-only rule challenged by a worker who was fired for speaking Spanish to a coworker while on duty. The court reasoned that the plaintiff was fully bilingual and thus his nonobservance of the rule was "a matter of individual preference" and thus did not constitute discrimination on the basis of national origin. The court refused to acknowledge that such a rule creates an atmosphere of racial and ethnic oppression. The validity of this decision is dubious, however, in view of the current E.E.O.C. Guidelines.

82. Still, in *Saucedo v. Brothers Well Service, Inc.*, 464 F.Supp. 919 (S.D. Tex. 1979), the court found that although requiring communications in English during a drilling operation was permissible, the company's termination of an employee for speaking Spanish in a nonsafety situation violated Title VII.

83. *Jurado v. Eleven-Fifty Corp.*, 813 F.2d 1406 (9th Cir. 1987).

84. The stringent definition of "business necessity" employed in *Gutiérrez* is now subject to some additional uncertainty as a result of a recent Supreme Court decision that apparently lessens the burden on employers in defending Title VII lawsuits. In *Wards Cove Packing Co. v. Atonio*, 109 S.Ct. 2115 (1989), the court held that a challenged practice need not be "essential" or "indispensable" to the employer's business; it need only serve "in a significant way, the legitimate employment goals of the employer." The burden is on the plaintiff to show that the asserted business justifications are not sufficient. One commentator has argued that the E.E.O.C. Guidelines remain valid even after the *Wards Cove* decision; "English Only Rules," *Minnesota Law Review* 74: 387.

rules may violate the First and Fourteenth amendments to the U.S. Constitution. The First Amendment prohibits government from abridging freedom of speech, expression, and association. It is clearly implicated when authorities directly restrain the private use of foreign languages. The Fourteenth Amendment requires that all residents be afforded equal protection of the law; that is, it prohibits overt and intentional discrimination against discrete and insular groups such as racial and national-origin minorities.

A graphic example of governmental restraints on private speech are laws restricting the use of foreign languages on business signs, such as an ordinance enacted in 1988 by Pomona, a suburb of Los Angeles. It provided: "On-premises signs of commercial or manufacturing establishments which have advertising copy in foreign alphabetical characters shall devote at least one half of the sign area to advertising copy in English alphabetical letters." The ordinance was challenged by local Asian American business owners and residents as a violation of free speech and equal protection (see pp. 284–87). A federal district court found the ordinance unconstitutional, holding that "language used is an expression of national origin, culture and ethnicity" and that, by regulating choice of language, the ordinance regulated expression of culture and national origin.[85] The court agreed with the reasoning in Gutiérrez, that

> language is an important aspect of national origin. The cultural identity of certain minority groups is tied to the use of their primary tongue. . . . Although an individual may learn English and become assimilated into American society, his primary language remains an important link to his ethnic culture and identity. The primary language not only conveys certain concepts, but is itself an affirmation of that culture.

Governmental regulation of cultural and political expression, in contrast to regulation of commercial speech, implicates fundamental values protected by the First Amendment. As such, it is unconstitutional unless the government demonstrates that the restriction is "narrowly tailored" to meet a "compelling governmental interest." In the Pomona case, the city argued that the sign regulation was necessary to facilitate the reporting of emergencies by ensuring the ready identification of commercial structures. While this was indeed a compelling interest, the court found that the ordinance was not narrowly tailored to meet it, because identification by numerical street address (as required by law) was clearly a more expedient solution. Moreover,

---

85. Asian American Business Group v. City of Pomona, 716 F.Supp. 1328 (C.D. Cal. 1989).

the court found it "curious" that the ordinance required an English-language sign naming a building where foreign alphabets were used, but not where a business had no sign, or where it was identified by small English letters, situations which would appear to be just as problematic as foreign-language signs.

First Amendment rights may also be denied where government attempts to restrict foreign language use by its employees, as in cases where a public agency imposes a speak-English-only policy. No court has yet ruled on such a constitutional claim. In _Gutiérrez_, the court invalidated an English-only rule on the basis of Title VII and thus did not have to resolve the constitutional question.

In a more recent decision, _Yniguez v. Mofford_,[86] a federal court found that Arizona's Proposition 106, an Official English measure approved in 1988 _(see pp. 287–91)_, was unconstitutional. The court recognized that, at least in some circumstances, an English-only mandate imposed on state officials and employees would violate the First Amendment. It found that the proposition was so broadly worded that it would have prohibited governmental officers and employers from using a foreign language in the performance of official duties, such as public employees officially commenting on matters of public concern, state legislators speaking to constituents, and judges performing marriage ceremonies.[87] Because the law was so "overbroad," it was unconstitutional on its face. Thus the court did not have to rule on the question of whether the First Amendment bars English-only restrictions for public employees in all circumstances (including those of the plaintiff, an insurance claims manager employed by the Arizona Department of Administration who ceased speaking Spanish while performing her job immediately after passage of Proposition 106).

Governmental restrictions on language use in the private sector may also violate the Equal Protection Clause of the Fourteenth Amendment. This provision has been interpreted as applying not only to discrimination on the basis of race (its historic impetus), but also to discrimination based on national origin, alien status, gender, and illegitimacy. The critical threshold question in equal protection

86. 730 F.Supp. 309 (D. Ariz. 1990).

87. The Official English measure, which amended Article XXVIII of the Arizona constitution, applied to all branches and agencies of state and local government and all "government officials and employees during the performance of government business." It required that, except in narrowly defined instances, the state and its officials must "act in English and in no other language." Also, it prohibited the enforcement of "any law, order, decree or policy which requires the use of a language other than English," and made invalid any government document unless written in English. Finally, the amendment permitted any person residing or doing business in Arizona to bring a lawsuit to enforce these provisions.

analysis is whether the law overtly discriminates against or is intended to discriminate on the basis of a "suspect" classification (and thus is subject to a strong presumption of unconstitutionality) or whether it discriminates on the basis of a classification which is not suspect (in which case the law is presumed to be constitutional). Where a suspect or "quasi-suspect" classification such as race or national origin is involved, the courts generally subject the challenged law to close judicial scrutiny, requiring that the law be justified by a "compelling" or "substantial" state interest and that the law be narrowly tailored to that interest. In contrast, where no suspect classification is involved, the courts will uphold the law so long as it has a rational or reasonable basis.

Although the U.S. Supreme Court has analyzed language discrimination in three cases,[88] it has not resolved the question of whether language minorities constitute a suspect class. A number of legal scholars have argued that language-based discrimination should be closely scrutinized because of its relationship to national-origin discrimination and because non-English speakers have experienced a history of bias, often lack political power and suffer economic and social disadvantages, and are readily identifiable—the traditional criteria for a suspect class that trigger special juridical protection.[89] Others have argued that language discrimination is really synonymous with, or a subset of, national-origin discrimination and thus should be deemed suspect on that basis.[90] Some courts, however, have rejected this argument. In *Soberal-Pérez v. Heckler*, a federal appellate court held that the failure to provide information in Spanish to Social Security recipients and applicants was not unconstitutional:

88. See *Yu Cong Eng v. Trinidad*, 271 U.S. 500 (1926), which struck down a Philippines territorial statute requiring businesses to keep accounting records in English, Spanish, or local Filipino dialects, but not in Chinese; *Meyer v. Nebraska*, 262 U.S. 390 (1923), which ruled unconstitutional a state law prohibiting the teaching of a foreign language (in this case, German) in private and public schools to students below the ninth grade (*see pp. 235–37*); *Lau v. Nichols*, 414 U.S. 563 (1974), which held that placing non-English-speaking students in a classroom with no special assistance and teaching them in a language that was incomprehensible to them deprived them of an equal educational opportunity under Title VI of the Civil Rights Act of 1964 (*see pp. 251–55*).

89. See Note, "Quasi-Suspect Classes and Proof of Discriminatory Intent: A New Model," *Yale Law Journal* 90 (1981): 912; Comment, "'Official English': Federal Limits on Efforts to Curtail Bilingual Services in the States," *Harvard Law Review* 100 (1987): 1345 (*for excerpts, see pp. 291–300*); and Antonio J. Califa, "Declaring English the Official Language: Prejudice Spoken Here," *Harvard Civil Rights–Civil Liberties Law Review* 24 (1989): 293.

90. The U.S. Supreme Court made that assumption in *Lau v. Nichols*. Title VII of the 1964 Civil Rights Act prohibiting employment discrimination has also been so interpreted. In the Pomona sign case, the federal district court found that because the use of foreign languages "is clearly an expression of national origin," an ordinance that restricts such expression "overtly discriminates on the basis of national origin."

> The Secretary's failure to provide forms and services in the Spanish language does not on its face make any classification with respect to Hispanics as an ethnic group. The classification is implicitly made, but it is on the basis of language, i.e., English-speaking vs. non-English-speaking individuals, and not on the basis of race, religion, or national origin. Language, by itself, does not identify members of a suspect class.[91]

Hence the level of protection the courts will afford to language-based discrimination under the Fourteenth Amendment is unresolved. In the future, a distinction might be drawn between laws which actively restrict choice of language (such as the Pomona sign ordinance) and practices which simply fail to provide assistance to language minorities (such as civil-service exams offered only in English).

Language discrimination in the private sector has arisen in many other contexts, and its legality must be examined on a case-by-case basis. Denial by regulatory agencies of broadcast licenses to Spanish-language radio stations or disapproval by a public utility commission of a telephone company's hiring of multilingual operators—actions previously sought by English Only lobbyists—would raise constitutional issues, since governmental conduct is involved. Refusal of insurance companies to write policies for non-English speakers may violate state antidiscrimination, insurance, or fair business practice laws.[92] The failure of private hospitals that receive federal funds to provide adequate translation services for non-English-speaking patients could violate Title VI of the Civil Rights Act of 1964 (which bars recipients of federal subsidies from discriminating on the basis of national origin) and the Hill-Burton Act (which requires hospitals receiving certain federal monies to serve low-income communities). In most of these instances, however, the applicable law does not expressly address language-based discrimination, and so the key legal

91. 717 F.2d 36, 41 (2d Cir. 1983), *cert. denied*, 466 U.S. 929 (1984) (*for the district court decision in this case, see pp. 240–42*). See also *Frontera v. Sindell*, 522 F.2d 1215, 1219–20 (6th Cir. 1975), in which a court applied the rational-basis test in upholding civil-service exams administered in English only; and *Carmona v. Sheffield*, 475 F.2d 738, 739 (9th Cir. 1973), in which a court held that the failure to provide information in Spanish regarding unemployment benefits did not violate equal protection under the rational-basis test.

92. For instance, in California the Unruh Civil Rights Act, Civil Code §§51, *et seq.*, prohibits discrimination by business establishments on the basis of sex, race, color, religion, ancestry, and national origin, and any other arbitrary discrimination. The California Insurance Code, §10140, prohibits discrimination on the basis of national origin (among others). The state Business and Professions Code §§17200, *et seq.*, outlaws unfair acts committed by business enterprises.

issue is whether the prohibition on national-origin discrimination extends to language discrimination.

The contours of the constitutional and statutory rights of language minorities remain to be clarified. Meanwhile, the debate over language rights and English Only legislation in the political arena will likely be reflected in the courts, as illustrated by the *Gutiérrez* case. In holding English-only workplace rules unlawful, the court extolled the societal value of language diversity, the cultural importance of language choice, and the plight of linguistic minorities who feel oppressed by such restrictions. In contrast, three judges who dissented from a decision by the full 9th U.S. Circuit Court of Appeals not to rehear the case argued that "the language a person who is multilingual elects to speak at a particular time is by definition a matter of choice." They added that speaking English on the job is primarily a matter of common courtesy and that world experience demonstrates that multiple languages pose a threat to unity and morale. Employing words which could just as easily have been penned by U.S. English *(see, e.g., p. 144)*, the dissenters wrote:

> Although the United States has become the home for people from all parts of the world, we have been spared much of the language-related agonies experienced elsewhere. A nation of immigrants, we have been willing to embrace English as our public language, preserving native tongues and dialects for private and family occasions.[93]

The polarization of views both in public debates and in the courts demonstrates that the struggle for language rights cannot be confined to any one arena. The judiciary is not immune to the English Only ideology that infects the wider society.

Gutiérrez v. Municipal Court

When it was delivered in 1988, this ruling by the 9th U.S. Circuit Court of Appeals had a dual significance.[94] It both outlawed arbitrary English-only rules in the workplace and declared that Proposition 63, California's Official English declaration was "primarily a symbolic statement." Because

93. 861 F.2d 1187, 1193 (9th Cir. 1988) *(see p. 283)*.

94. 838 F.2d 1031 (9th Cir. 1988), *en banc rehearing denied*, 861 F.2d 1187 (9th Cir. 1988), *vacated as moot*, 109 S.Ct. 1736 (1989).

the decision was vacated by the U.S. Supreme Court the following year (not on its merits, but because the plaintiff no longer had standing) *Gutiérrez* lacks precedential value. Nevertheless, it suggests how federal courts might view similar cases in the future. At issue was a speak-English-only rule for municipal court clerks in Huntington Park, California. Ironically, the clerks whose speech was most affected had been hired for their bilingual skills, which they used to translate for Spanish-speaking members of the public. At all other times, except for lunch and coffee breaks, they were required to speak English. Citing guidelines of the federal Equal Employment Opportunity Commission (E.E.O.C.), the court held the English-only policy to be illegal national-origin discrimination.

It is worth noting, however, that another federal appeals court took a conflicting view of similar issues in *García v. Gloor*, a case that predates the E.E.O.C.'s policy.[95] Also, a minority of the 9th Circuit judges questioned the reasoning of the *Gutiérrez* decision, as revealed by their comments on a procedural motion. Judge Stephen Reinhardt delivered the court's opinion in the case, on behalf of a unanimous three-judge panel, on January 27, 1988.

Few courts have evaluated the lawfulness of workplace rules restricting the use of languages other than English. Commentators generally agree, however, that language is an important aspect of national origin. The cultural identity of certain minority groups is tied to the use of their primary tongue. The mere fact that an employee is bilingual does not eliminate the relationship between his primary language and the culture that is derived from his national origin. Although an individual may learn English and become assimilated into American society, his primary language remains an important link to his ethnic culture and identity. The primary language not only conveys certain concepts, but is itself an affirmation of that culture.

From the standpoint of the Anglo-American, another person's use of a foreign language may serve to identify that individual as being of foreign extraction or as having a specific national origin. Because language and accents are identifying characteristics, rules which have a negative effect on bilinguals, individuals with accents, or non-English speakers, may be mere pretexts for intentional national origin discrimination.

Although Title VII [of the Civil Rights Act of 1964] does not specifically prohibit English-only rules, the E.E.O.C. has promulgated guidelines on the subject.[96] The E.E.O.C. recognizes that "[t]he pri-

95. 618 F.2d 264 (5th Cir. 1980), *cert. denied*, 449 U.S. 1113 (1981) *(see analyses by Bill Piatt and Edward M. Chen, pp. 232–33, 272).*

96. 29 C.F.R. §1606.7 (1987).

mary language of an individual is often an essential national origin characteristic," and that an English-only rule may "create an atmosphere of inferiority, isolation, and intimidation." Although an employer may have legitimate business reasons for requiring that communications be exclusively in English, an English-only rule is, according to the E.E.O.C., a burdensome condition of employment that is often used to mask national origin discrimination and that must be carefully scrutinized. Accordingly, the E.E.O.C. concluded that while a limited English-only rule may be permissible in some circumstances, no such rule will be deemed lawful unless the employer can show that it is justified by *business necessity* and notifies the employees "of the general circumstances when speaking only in English is required and of the consequences of violating the rule." . . .

[T]he English-only rule in the case before us is concerned primarily with intra-employee conversations, work-related and non-work-related. It is in no way limited to the sale or distribution of the employer's product and there is no contention that the employees' conversations among themselves in Spanish have any effect on those who use the courts. Yet, the prohibition on intra-employee communications in Spanish is sweeping in nature and has a direct effect on the general atmosphere and environment of the work place. . . .

[A]ppellants contend that the rule is necessary to prevent the workplace from turning into a "Tower of Babel." This claim assumes that permitting Spanish (or another language) to be spoken between employees is disruptive. Even if appellants' unspoken premise were true, the argument fails. . . . Since Spanish is already being spoken in the Clerk's office, to non-English-speaking Hispanic citizens, part of the "babel" that appellants purport to fear is necessary to the normal press of court business. Additional Spanish is unlikely to create a much greater disruption than already exists. Because the "babel" is necessary and has an apparently permanent status, its elimination in the area of intra-employee communication cannot be termed essential to the efficient operation of the Clerk's office. . . .

[A]ppellants assert that the rule is necessary to promote racial harmony. They contend that Spanish may be used to convey discriminatory or insubordinate remarks and otherwise belittle non-Spanish-speaking employees. Appellants, however, have failed to offer any evidence of the inappropriate use of Spanish. In contrast, there is evidence indicating that racial hostility has increased between Hispanics and non-Spanish-speaking employees because Hispanics feel belittled by the regulation. There is also evidence that non-Spanish-speaking employees have made racially discriminatory remarks directed at Hispanics. As the E.E.O.C. has warned, prohibiting the use of the employees' native tongue may contribute to racial tension. Appellants' argument that the English-only rule fosters racial harmony is unsupported by the evidence and is otherwise generally unpersuasive.

Appellants further contend that whatever the actual facts may be, non-Spanish-speaking employees believe that Spanish-speaking employees use Spanish to conceal the substance of their conversations and that the English-only rule is necessary to assuage non-Spanish-speaking employees' fears and suspicions. Appellants' contention is based on a single complaint allegedly made by an employee, a complaint based, at most, on suspicion. . . . However, even if there were evidence that a regulation mandating the use of English during working hours would calm some employees' fears and thereby reduce racial tension to some extent, this would not constitute a business necessity for a rule that has an adverse impact on other persons based on *their* national origin. Existing racial fears or prejudices and their effects cannot justify a racial classification.[97] . . .

Next, appellants argue that the English-only rule is required by the California Constitution. Appellants assert that [Article III,] section 6, added by the voters as a ballot initiative in 1986, requires the use of English in all official state business, and thus requires Hispanic employees to communicate in English while at work *(see pp. 133–34)*. Appellants' argument is unpersuasive. . . . While section 6 may have some concrete application to official government communications, if and when the measure is appropriately implemented by the state legislature, it appears otherwise to be primarily a symbolic statement concerning the importance of preserving, protecting, and strengthening the English language. . . .

Although the precise question of private conversations among public employees was not addressed in the ballot arguments, it appears that the distinction the proponents attempted to draw was between official communications and private affairs. While the initiative addressed, and arguably may have sought to regulate, the former subject, most if not all of the speech barred here would fall in the latter category. . . . [I]ronically, while the English-only rule at issue here totally bars *private* speech in Spanish during on-duty periods, use of the Spanish language for *official* communications is not only permitted by the government employer, but in a large number of instances is expressly mandated.[98] . . .

English-only rules generally have an adverse impact on protected

97. *Palmore v. Sidoti,* 466 U.S. 429, 433–34 (1984).
98. We also note that if the Municipal Court rule forbade communication in Spanish with the non-English-speaking public, serious questions of denial of access to the courts would be presented, and possibly other constitutional questions as well.

groups and ordinarily constitute discriminatory conditions of employment. Here, none of the justifications appellants offer for their English-only rule meets the rigorous business necessity standard.[99] . . . [W]e note that the district court's injunction is more favorable to the employer than the business necessity test permits: the injunction allows restrictions to be imposed based on public relations concerns. Public relations concerns do not constitute a business necessity. If such concerns were sufficient, a major goal of Title VII would be thwarted because employers would be free to consider public prejudices when setting employment policies. . . .

A majority of 9th Circuit judges declined to rehear the Gutiérrez *case en banc, that is, as a full court. Three dissenting judges, who favored reviewing the decision, voiced substantive objections to the panel's ruling. Their rationale was expressed in an opinion by Judge Alex Kozinski, an excerpt of which follows.*

By any rational standard, this case cries out for *en banc* reconsideration. The panel's opinion creates a square conflict with the Fifth Circuit's opinion in *García v. Gloor.* The panel also buries a prior opinion of this circuit whose holding is directly contrary.[100] Perhaps most disturbing, the panel reaches a result that severely undermines the principal goal of the Civil Rights Act of 1964, equal opportunity in the workplace. By giving employees the nearly absolute right to speak a language other than English, the panel's opinion will exacerbate ethnic tensions and force employers to establish separate supervisorial tracks for employees who choose to speak another language during working hours. This is not what the Civil Rights Act was meant to accomplish. . . .

We need not trot out a parade of horribles; this case illustrates the problem effectively enough. The case arises out of racial and ethnic tensions among the employees of the Southeast Los Angeles Municipal Court, largely between blacks and Latinos. The English-only rule was not adopted by the Municipal Court judges out of xenophobia, but in response to a "complaint from a black female employee concerning the use of the Spanish language between employees in order to conceal the substance of conversation during working hours on the work floor. . . . " The rule was also intended to assist "supervisors to understand the work conversations of their subordinates. . . . "[101]

The rule was adopted because [according to the *Los Angeles Times*] "several of the 27 full-time clerks, including Anglos, blacks, and even

99. See *Robinson v. Lorillard Corp.*, 444 F.2d 791, 798 (4th Cir. 1971).

100. *Jurado v. Eleven-Fifty Corp.*, 813 F.2d 1406 (9th Cir. 1987).

101. Declaration of Joseph Sharar, chief clerk and court administrator, Huntington Park.

some Latinos complained that a handful of Latino clerks were increasingly using Spanish to cloak their conversations and occasionally made it clear that they were discussing co-workers." One employee reported a particularly distressing incident:

> Suzanne Cook, a black employee who was among the first to complain about the use of Spanish . . . recalled a day at work when she tripped or dropped something "and the banter in Spanish really got going, and it was obvious that they were laughing at me for doing something stupid."
>
> If she had understood their jokes, she said, "it wouldn't have been a real big thing, because I would have just shot a comment back. But instead I had to keep it inside, and that was incredibly frustrating. After months of that kind of tension, I was looking for a new job." [102]

The English-only rule had broad employee support. The record contains a letter, signed by eight employees who were concerned that the rule might be overturned:

> If the [Municipal Court] Judges ruling is overturned it will have an adverse effect. Spanish is not essential when relating to fellow employees, and in many cases is used to undermine supervision and to talk about fellow employees. Feelings are hurt and tension builds. This is when employee camaraderie and morale begin to deteriorate. . . .
>
> The ruling was initially intended to create a more harmonious working atmosphere for all employees. It has now been turned into an issue of ethnic background and civil rights. In reality the *only* issue is common courtesy. [103]

The question of what authority an employer has to address language-related tensions in the workplace is one of exceptional importance. As sad experience elsewhere has shown, language can be a potent source of racial and ethnic discrimination, exacerbating geographic, cultural, religious, ethnic and class divisions. In Canada, for example, the bitter mutual resistance of French- and English-speaking citizens toward one another's language has taken on the characteristics of a racial confrontation. [104] Other examples abound: The long-standing divisions between the French-speaking Walloons

---

102. Jill Stewart, "Huntington Park Judges 'Incredulous': English-Only Rule Still Creating Uproar," *Los Angeles Times*, Southeast ed., April 11, 1985, pt. IX, pp. 1, 8.

103. Letter from Marie Williams et al., to Phil Giarrizzo, General Manager, Local 600, Service Employees International Union, Feb. 19, 1985.

104. See John Porter, "Ethnic Pluralism in Canadian Perspective," in *Ethnicity: Theory and Experience*, ed. Nathan Glazer and Daniel Patrick Moynihan (Cambridge, Mass.: Harvard University Press, 1975), p. 268.

and the Flemish-speaking population of Belgium and the "language demands" in various regions of India reflect linguistic as well as class and ethnic divisions of the most invidious sort.[105] The separatist movements by the Corsicans of France, the Basques of Spain, the Tamils of Sri Lanka, the Kurds of Turkey and Iraq, and the Sikhs of India have been reinforced and to some extent inspired by linguistic differences.[106]

Although the United States has become the home for people from all parts of the world, we have been spared much of the language-related agonies experienced elsewhere. A nation of immigrants, we have been willing to embrace English as our public language, preserving native tongues and dialects for private and family occasions. When employees bring their private language into a public workplace, this creates a difficult and sensitive problem for those around them who do not speak the language. Of course, where employees are unable to speak English, or where they are denied a benefit because they are identified with a particular language or ethnic group, the Civil Rights Act protects them; language is, for them, an immutable characteristic.[107] But where employees are perfectly capable of speaking English, it is a much closer question whether they should be entitled to converse in another language during working hours while performing work functions. The right answer will vary with the particular fact situation and ought not to be set in concrete for all employers and all employees.

As this case illustrates, having employees use a language other than English can seriously undermine workplace morale. Here, the Municipal Court judges acted in response to a legitimate complaint by a black employee about what she believed were insulting comments made in a language she could not understand. An English-only rule may not make sense in all situations; sometimes it may be counterproductive, causing more hurt feelings than it saves. But it is highly unwise to prohibit all employers everywhere from adopting such a rule, even when they have reason to believe that language is

---

105. Several commentators note that language differences have become emblems of class as well as ethnic group membership; often the dispute over dialect or language choice disguises deeper racial or religious divisions. See, e.g., Pierre L. van den Berghe, *The Ethnic Phenomenon* (New York: Praeger, 1987), p. 211 (arguing that the "real impetus to Québecois nationalism . . . has been a class conflict in linguistic disguise"); William Petersen, "Subnations of Western Europe," in Glazer and Moynihan, *Ethnicity* pp. 198–208; Jyotirindra Das Gupta, "Ethnicity, Language Demands, and National Development in India," in Glazer and Moynihan, *Ethnicity* pp. 466–86.

106. See Donald L. Horowitz, *Ethnic Groups in Conflict* (Berkeley: University of California Press, 1985).

107. See *García v. Gloor*, 618 F.2d 264, 270.

being used to exclude and isolate employees of a particular race or ethnic group. Our society is too complex, and the factual permutations far too diverse, to permit the imposition of a universal rule by judicial fiat.

The opinion gives an important insight into the types of problems we are creating for ourselves by failing to repudiate the rule the panel adopts. In response to the defendants' argument that non-Spanish-speaking supervisors will be unable to supervise employees who speak Spanish during working hours, the panel offers a facile solution: "employ Spanish-speaking supervisors." This "let them eat cake" attitude masks a very serious problem: By deciding to speak another language during working hours, employees can limit who may qualify for supervisorial positions. If fluency in a second language is the sine qua non of supervisorial status, employees who are not bilingual, including other people of color, will be effectively eliminated from consideration for these coveted positions. Given the natural competition for supervisorial posts, *Gutiérrez* may well exacerbate racial tensions. It is incomprehensible to me that this result is being reached in the name of a law designed to promote ethnic and racial harmony in the workplace. . . .

Asian American Business Group v. City of Pomona

Between 1980 and 1987 more than 100,000 Asian immigrants settled in the San Gabriel Valley suburbs east of Los Angeles, bringing rapid and visible changes.[108] Signs with Chinese, Vietnamese, and Korean characters began to sprout in local business districts. In response, some Official English advocates sought to impose legal limits on the amount of foreign languages (or Asian characters) on business signs. Such ordinances were passed, usually on public-safety grounds, in Monterey Park, Temple City, Rosemead, and San Gabriel, among other cities. Despite its relatively small Asian population, Pomona followed suit in 1988. It enacted an ordinance providing that if local businesses displayed signs featuring "foreign alphabetical characters," they must "devote at least one-half of the sign

---

108. Mark Arax, "Asian Influx Alters Life in Suburbia," *Los Angeles Times*, April 5, 1987, p. 1.

area to advertising copy in English alphabetical characters." A group of Asian business owners challenged the law as a violation of constitutional guarantees of free speech and equal protection under the First and Fourteenth amendments. U.S. District Judge Robert M. Takasugi agreed, in a decision issued on July 14, 1989.[109]

By requiring one-half of the space of a foreign alphabet sign to be devoted to English alphabetical characters, the [Pomona city] ordinance regulates the cultural expression of the sign owner. Since the language used is an expression of national origin, culture, and ethnicity, regulation of the sign language is regulation of content. A person's primary language is an important part of, and flows from, his/her national origin. . . . Choice of language is a form of expression as real as the textual message conveyed. It is an expression of culture.

Speech is not commercial merely because it proposes a transaction or because there is an economic motivation.[110] Although the signs regulated by the ordinance have a commercial aspect to them, it is not that aspect that the ordinance regulates. It is the aspect of expression of culture and national origin that is being regulated. As a regulation of noncommercial speech, the ordinance must meet the standard of strict scrutiny—it must serve a compelling governmental interest and be narrowly tailored to meet the interest.[111]

The governmental interest cited by [the City of Pomona] is the ready identification of commercial structures to facilitate the reporting of emergencies. Defendant City argues that if a person telephoning the police or fire department to report an emergency cannot read the sign identifying the location of the emergency, the response will be delayed. This is a compelling state interest.

It appears that the ordinance is not narrowly tailored to further the defendant City's stated interest. An undisputed portion of the ordinance requires that addresses be posted in Arabic numerals. Identification by street address would appear to be the most expedient way in which to report the location of an emergency. Requiring "advertising copy in English alphabetical characters" would not necessarily insure the posting of a sign that would be helpful in reporting the location. . . .

The defendant City does not require any business or commercial establishment to have a sign on the premises stating the name of the establishment. If that is the case and if, as defendants argue, street address is insufficient identification for reporting a location in an

---

109. *Asian American Business Group v. City of Pomona*, 716 F.Supp. 1328 (C.D. Cal. 1989).

110. *Bolger v. Youngs Drug Products Corp.*, 463 U.S. 60, 66–67 (1982).

111. *Pacific Gas & Electric v. California P.U.C.*, 475 U.S. 1, 19 (1986).

emergency, it is very curious that defendant City has chosen to require only establishments having foreign alphabet signs to post a sign naming their buildings. Such a limitation renders the ordinance equally limited in its effectiveness in furthering the stated government interest and, as such, casts suspicion on the genuineness of said stated interest.

The ordinance fails the "narrowly tailored" test for another reason: It takes one-half of all signs written in foreign characters without regard to the size and location of the sign or the amount of space necessary to identify the building. There is no reason suggested for seizing such a large portion of the signs nor an explanation provided as to why the ordinance was not drafted to limit the space taken to that necessary to identify the building. . . . [This requirement] is clearly more extensive than necessary to serve the stated interest. Whether a regulation of commercial or noncommercial speech, the ordinance violates the freedom of speech. . . .

Although an equal protection claim must generally show intent to discriminate, a showing of intent is unnecessary if the law has an overtly discriminatory classification on its face.[112] The subject ordinance expressly discriminates against sign owners who use foreign alphabetical characters in their signs. . . . [T]he use of foreign languages is clearly an expression of national origin. As such, the ordinance overtly discriminates on the basis of national origin.

There are two independent reasons for applying the strict scrutiny test to this equal protection claim: First, the ordinance burdens the freedom of expression, a fundamental interest, in that it seizes one-half of the sign space; and second, the ordinance discriminates based on a suspect classification—national origin.[113] Of course, the ordinance does not expressly refer to national origin; instead it refers to use of foreign alphabetical characters. If this were not sufficient to label it national origin discrimination and, hence, a suspect classification triggering the application of strict scrutiny, cities could avoid such heightened scrutiny by passing discriminatory laws that merely restrict those who speak foreign languages.

"To withstand strict scrutiny a statute must be precisely tailored to serve a compelling state interest."[114] This is the same test as the "narrowly tailored" test applied to the plaintiff's [freedom of] speech claim and yields the same result—a finding of unconstitutionality. Furthermore, focusing on the distinction/discrimination made by the ordinance and examining its relationship to stated government inter-

112. *Wayte v. U.S.*, 470 U.S. 598, 608 n.10 (1985).
113. *Hoffman v. U.S.*, 767 F.2d 1431, 1434–35 (9th Cir. 1985).
114. Ibid.

est results in the conclusion that although the distinction/discrimination (singling out business establishments having foreign characters on their signs) may have a rational relationship to the stated interest (facilitating the reporting of emergencies), that relationship is not strong enough to justify the discrimination where, as here, there are many other nondiscriminatory ways to more effectively further the stated interest, such as requiring all buildings to have identifying signs. . . .

Yniguez v. Mofford

Arizona's Proposition 106, passed by the voters on November 8, 1988, was the most restrictive Official English measure ever enacted at the state level. It added a new Article XXVIII to the state constitution that imposed, with a few exceptions, the sweeping policy: "This State and all political subdivisions of this State shall act in English and in no other language" *(see pp. 132–33).* María-Kelly F. Yniguez, an insurance-claims manager employed by Arizona's Risk Management Divsion, and Jaime P. Gutiérrez, a state senator from Tucson, challenged the measure as a violation of the First Amendment of the U.S. Constitution.[115]

Even though Article XXVIII is explicit by comparison with other Official English amendments, this case illustrates the potential for disputes about the legal reach of such measures. Acting on a broad interpretation, Yniguez refrained from speaking any language other than English during working hours, fearing she would violate the law and risk punishment by continuing to communicate in Spanish, when necessary, with members of the public. Gutiérrez did not stop addressing his constituents in Spanish, but questioned whether the practice conflicted with his oath to obey the state constitution. On the other hand, Arizona's Attorney General, Bob Corbin, issued an official opinion that Article XXVIII "does not prohibit the use of a language other than English to facilitate the delivery of governmental services."[116] This seemed to settle the matter, to the satisfaction of most Arizonans on both sides of the issue.

---

115. *Yniguez v. Mofford,* 730 F.Supp. 309 (D. Ariz. 1990).
116. Attorney General Opinion I89–009, Jan. 24, 1989.

But a federal court took the plaintiffs' complaint seriously, regarding their interpretation of Article XXVIII to be reasonable. On February 6, 1990, U.S. District Judge Paul G. Rosenblatt struck down the Official English amendment as unconstitutionally "overbroad"—that is, as prohibiting speech protected under the First Amendment far beyond the means necessary to achieve a legitimate state purpose. Also, in a significant procedural ruling, the court removed Corbin and another state official as defendants in the case. Governor Rose Mofford, a staunch opponent of Proposition 106, chose not to appeal the decision. But in July 1991, Arizonans for Official English won the right to do so.

In order to determine whether Article XXVIII reaches a substantial amount of constitutionally protected conduct, the court must first determine what the Article means, which is a matter of substantial dispute between the parties. The plaintiffs' position is that Article XXVIII is a blanket prohibition on the use of any language other than English in the state workplace, whereas the defendants' position is that Article XXVIII does not reach that broadly because it is merely a directive for state and local governmental entities to act in English when acting in their sovereign capacities. For the purposes of the instant action, the court finds from Article XXVIII's plain language that it is a prohibition on the use of any language other than English by all officers and employees of all political subdivisions in Arizona while performing their official duties, save to the extent that they may be allowed to use a foreign language by the limited exceptions contained in §3(2) of Article XXVIII. Given this interpretation of the Article, an interpretation obviously not binding on state authorities, the court concludes that there is a realistic danger of, and a substantial potential for, the unconstitutional application of Article XXVIII.

The court's determination of Article XXVIII's facial validity is not dependent upon Yniguez having a First Amendment right to speak a language of her choice during the performance of her duties, a "right" which the defendants assert does not exist. All the court need find, and all that it does find in this regard, is that Article XXVIII is so broad as to inhibit the constitutionally protected speech of third parties. While public employees, as a general proposition, enjoy less First Amendment protection than private citizens because governmental entities have a significant interest as employers in regulating the speech of their employees so as to promote the efficiency of public services,[117] a state may not apply stricter First Amendment standards to its legislators than it may to private citizens,[118] nor may a state re-

117. *Pickering v. Bd. of Ed. of H.S. Dist. 205, Ill.*, 391 U.S. 563, 568 (1968).
118. *Bond v. Floyd*, 385 U.S. 116, 132–33 (1966).

quire that its officers and employees relinquish rights guaranteed them by the First Amendment as a condition of public employment.[119] The sweeping language of Article XXVIII has such a prohibited effect, however. When read at its full literal breadth, Article XXVIII would force Arizona governmental officers and employees whose use of a non-English language in the performance of their official duties is protected by the First Amendment, such as state legislators speaking to constituents in a language other than English, state employees officially commenting on matters of public concern in a language other than English, and state judges performing marriage ceremonies in a language other than English, to either violate their sworn oaths to obey the state constitution, and thereby subject themselves to potential sanctions and private suits, or to curtail their free speech rights.

Although the plaintiffs have not argued that Article XXVIII is unconstitutionally vague, vagueness affects the overbreadth analysis because, in determining whether Article XXVIII is so overbroad as to deter others from engaging in otherwise protected expression, the court has to evaluate the ambiguous as well as the unambiguous scope of the article.[120] While the defendants' assertion that the examples of Article XXVIII's unconstitutional reach proffered by the plaintiffs are too extreme to demonstrate the Article's facial unconstitutionality because they represent situations which plainly do not come within the rational parameters of Article XXVIII may be correct, the defendants' assertion only emphasizes Article XXVIII's potential for chilling First Amendment rights. If those affected by Article XXVIII are unclear as to its coverage, the result will be that they will "'steer far wider of the unlawful zone' . . . than if the boundaries of the forbidden areas were clearly marked."[121] Yniguez's self-imposed decision to refrain from speaking Spanish while performing her job, a decision vociferously criticized as unfounded by the defendants, is but a product of her legitimate sensitivity to the perils posed by the Article's language and her desire to restrict her conduct to that which is unquestionably safe. A law which reasonably results in such restrictions is unconstitutionally overbroad.

In determining the facial constitutionality of Article XXVIII, the court must also consider any authoritative limiting construction placed on the enactment by Arizona state courts or enforcement agencies,[122] because a state law cannot be facially invalidated as overbroad

---

119. *Abood v. Detroit Bd. of Ed.*, 431 U.S. 209, 234 (1977).

120. *Village of Hoffman Estates v. Flipside, Hoffman Estates, Inc.*, 455 U.S. 489, 494 n.6 (1982).

121. See *Baggett v. Bullitt*, 377 U.S. 360, 372, 373 (1964).

122. *Broadrick v. Oklahoma*, 413 U.S. 601, 618 (1973).

if it is readily susceptible to a narrowing construction that would make it constitutional. As the Supreme Court has noted, the key to the application of this principle is that the state law must be "readily susceptible" of the limitation proffered by the state court or agency because a federal court lacks the power itself to rewrite a state law to conform it to constitutional requirements.[123]

No Arizona state court has as yet construed or interpreted Article XXVIII. The Arizona Attorney General has, however, construed Article XXVIII in a narrow fashion in a formal opinion, I89–009, an opinion which the defendants argue resolves the overbreadth issue in this action. . . .

The gist of the Attorney General's interpretation of Article XXVIII is that the English-only requirement applies solely to official acts of the state governmental entities and does not prohibit the use of languages other than English that are reasonably necessary to facilitate the day-to-day operation of government. The Attorney General's belief that Article XXVIII is directed only towards sovereign governmental acts centers upon §3(1)(a) of Article XXVIII, which provides, with a few limited exceptions, that the "State and all political subdivisions of this State shall act in English and in no other language." The Attorney General's interpretation of what "to act" means, however, in effect ignores §1(3)(a)(iv) of Article XXVIII, which states that the Article applies to "all government officials and employees during the performance of government business." The various levels of legislative, executive, and judicial branches of government in Arizona affected by Article XXVIII perform business in a whole variety of ways that do not rise to the level of "sovereign" acts, as the Attorney General apparently uses that term. The manner in which the term "act" is used in §3(2) of the Article, the subsection setting forth the exceptions to the ban on the use of non-English languages, is illustrative of the unreasonableness of the Attorney General's limitation on the meaning of "act." Under the provisions of §3(2)(c), for example, a governmental entity within Arizona "may act in a language other than English" to teach a student a foreign language as part of an educational curriculum. While the teaching of a foreign language by a public school teacher comes within the definition of performing government business, it does not come within the definition of performing a sovereign act. The Attorney General's restrictive interpretation of Article XXVIII is in effect a "remarkable job of plastic surgery upon the face of the ordinance,"[124] and one which this court cannot accept.

The defendants have not proffered any other limiting construction

123. *Virginia v. American Booksellers Assn.*, 484 U.S. 383, 397 (1988).
124. *Shuttlesworth v. City of Birmingham*, 394 U.S. 147, 153 (1969).

of Article XXVIII and the court is unable to discern any construction to which the Article is fairly subject that would limit its application in such a way as to render unnecessary or substantially modify the federal constitutional questions. . . .

Language Minorities and the Equal Protection Clause

By *The Harvard Law Review*

This article is excerpted from an unsigned comment, "'Official English': Federal Limits on Efforts to Curtail Bilingual Services in the States," *Harvard Law Review* 100, no. 6 (April 1987): 1345–62.

The use of Official English declarations to force the withdrawal of bilingual programs may violate not only federal statutes, but also the Equal Protection Clause of the Fourteenth Amendment. As a symbolic gesture, a state's declaration of English as its official language violates no constitutional norms; a common language is a goal that all can share. Constitutional concerns do arise, however, if litigants seek to use the declaration to bar bilingual programs. When these services are withdrawn, the effect falls exclusively on a distinct and identifiable group: those who speak little or no English. Even though the provision of services to all in English ostensibly treats all groups similarly, the actual impact is unequal: Non-English speakers are deprived of services in a language that they can understand. Courts therefore must decide whether the Constitution permits these declarations to be so broadly interpreted as to have this legal effect.

The Equal Protection Clause generally permits states to take actions that treat some groups differently from others as long as the action is rationally related to the achievement of a valid public purpose. Under these circumstances judges will defer to a legislature's judgment.[125] Laws that classify on the basis of race or national origin, however, have rarely served legitimate governmental ends, and the Supreme

---

125. See, e.g., *Personnel Admin. v. Feeney,* 442 U.S. 256, 272 (1979): "The calculus of effects, the manner in which a particular law reverberates in a society, is a legislative and not a judicial responsibility."

Court has thus deemed these classifications "suspect."[126] Courts will uphold differential treatment of members of a suspect class only if the state's action can withstand strict scrutiny—that is, only if it has been "precisely tailored to serve a compelling government interest."[127] The Supreme Court has found other legislative classifications, such as those based on gender and illegitimacy, to be "quasi-suspect," for they sometimes are a valid basis for different treatment, but more often are employed for improper purposes and violate contemporary notions of equality.[128] For these classifications a court will apply "intermediate" scrutiny, inquiring into whether the state action is *substantially* related to legitimate or even *important* governmental objectives.[129]

A strong argument can be made for treating language minorities as a quasi-suspect class. Courts have so far been unwilling to deem language minorities a quasi-suspect class for equal protection analysis when parties claim an affirmative right to governmental accommodation.[130] However, courts have not yet confronted the question whether a language-based classification, such as a blanket Official English declaration, may be employed to force a withdrawal of existing services. These Official English movements mark a qualitative shift in the modern treatment of language minorities. For the first time since the advent of "suspect class" analysis, non-English speakers have become the focus of antipathy. This shift provides impetus for applying heightened scrutiny to states' language policies.[131]

In determining whether a particular legislative classification is suspect or quasi-suspect, courts inquire into whether the group affected by the classification is an easily identifiable group that has suffered a history of discrimination, mistreatment, or political powerlessness.[132] Language minorities clearly are such groups. Congress has recog-

126. See, e.g., *Bolling v. Sharpe*, 347 U.S. 497, 499 (1954): "Classifications based solely upon race . . . are contrary to our traditions and hence constitutionally suspect"; and *Hernández v. Texas*, 347 U.S. 475, 477–80 (1954), holding that Mexicans form a "distinct class" for equal protection purposes.

127. *Plyler v. Doe*, 457 U.S. 202, 217 (1982).

128. See, e.g., the plurality opinion in *Lalli v. Lalli*, 439 U.S. 259, 265 (1978); and *Craig v. Boren*, 429 U.S. 190, 197 (1976).

129. See, e.g., *Mississippi Univ. for Women v. Hogan*, 458 U.S. 718, 724 (1982).

130. See, e.g., *Soberal-Pérez v. Heckler*, 717 F.2d 36, 41 (2d Cir. 1983), *cert. denied*, 466 U.S. 929 (1984), rejecting plaintiff's challenge to English-only Social Security notices and proceedings; *Guadalupe Organization v. Tempe Elementary School District No. 3*, 587 F.2d 1022 (9th Cir. 1978), rejecting plaintiffs' claim to a constitutional and statutory right to bilingual education; and *Frontera v. Sindell*, 522 F.2d 1215, 1219–20 (6th Cir. 1975), rejecting plaintiff's challenge to English-only civil service exams.

131. As the Supreme Court has noted, "prejudices are not static"; *Hernández v. Texas*, 347 U.S. 478. As new groups become the targets of prejudice, courts may have to examine more carefully legislative classifications involving such groups.

132. See *San Antonio Independent School District v. Rodríguez*, 411 U.S. 1, 28 (1973).

nized that discrimination against this country's language minorities is "pervasive and national in scope" and that it affects "almost every facet of life."[133] The powerlessness of non-English speakers in the political sphere is further heightened by the simple fact that a disproportionate number of them are not citizens and cannot vote.

An additional indication of "suspectness" is the immutability of the characteristic forming the basis of the discrimination. Admittedly, a person's language is not "immutable" as that term is used in the context of race, gender, or national origin. As one court has noted, however, for many who speak only one language, the practical reality is that "language might as well be an immutable characteristic like skin color, sex or place of birth."[134] For adults in particular, especially those with limited financial resources, learning a new language may be extremely difficult or impossible. The immutability of a trait suggests that courts should guard vigilantly against that trait's becoming the basis of discriminatory state actions.

As a separate basis for finding that language-related classifications implicate suspect criteria, courts might determine that such classifications in fact discriminate on the basis of national origin. Litigants have argued that no factor is more intimately tied to a person's ethnic or national identity than is language. To be sure, most members of national-origin minorities do speak English; language is thus a poorly suited proxy for discrimination against these groups. Yet litigants may be able to demonstrate that Official English rules have in fact been adopted in order to lash out at broader trends in immigration and thus reflect discrimination on the basis of national origin.

In *Olagues v. Russoniello*, the 9th U.S. Circuit Court of Appeals relied on each of the factors mentioned above—a history of mistreatment, political powerlessness, immutability, and strong links to national origin—in applying strict scrutiny to a U.S. attorney's investigation of voting fraud that singled out for special inquiry Spanish-speaking and Chinese-speaking voters who requested bilingual ballots.[135]

---

133. 42 U.S.C. §1973b(f)(1); Senate Rep. no. 295, 94th Cong., 1st sess. (1975), p. 29.

134. *García v. Gloor*, 618 F.2d 264, 270 (5th Cir. 1980), *cert. denied*, 449 U.S. 1113 (1981).

135. 797 F.2d 1511, 1520–21 (9th Cir. 1986) (*en banc*), *vacated as moot*, 108 S.Ct. 52 (1987). The court distinguished its holding from other cases rejecting the application of strict scrutiny to language minorities by noting that the discrimination at issue in those cases involved "a general classification of English-speaking versus non-English-speaking individuals." In the case at hand, the discrimination was more specific; it fell only on Spanish-speaking and Chinese-speaking immigrants. But if heightened scrutiny is justified when specific language minorities are singled out, it should surely be justified when there is discrimination against non-English-speaking people in general. The invidiousness of language distinctions is not diluted when the discrimination is more broadly based. In the end the court concluded by narrowing its holding to a suspect class defined by three characteristics: "foreign-born voter, recently registered voter, and bilingual ballot voter."

Throughout its analysis the court focused on the manner in which language-based classifications meet these criteria. Although it did not ultimately identify Spanish speakers or Chinese speakers as a suspect or quasi-suspect class, the decision provides a persuasive rationale for such a finding in future cases. A court may reasonably find, in the famous words of *Carolene Products*, that non-English-speaking people do form "discrete and insular minorities" who cannot depend on "the operation of those political processes ordinarily to be relied upon to protect minorities." [136]

In order to establish a violation of the Equal Protection Clause, litigants must demonstrate that state decisionmakers *intended* to single out a group for different treatment. [137] In cases in which state action is "facially discriminatory"—when groups are *explicitly* singled out for differential treatment—further evidence of intent is unnecessary. For example, a state's gender-based design is evident when it prohibits the sale of beer to males under the age of twenty-one and to females under the age of eighteen. [138]

136. *U.S. v. Carolene Products Co.*, 304 U.S. 144, 153 n.4 (1938) (*dictum*). State action may also trigger strict scrutiny when it infringes a fundamental right; see, e.g., *Shapiro v. Thompson*, 394 U.S. 618 (1969), involving the right to interstate travel. For example, the Supreme Court has held voting to be a fundamental right when there is an election; see, e.g., *Reynolds v. Sims*, 377 U.S. 533 (1964); thus any infringement of equal access to that right based upon language should trigger strict scrutiny, quite independent of any "suspect" quality of the class disadvantaged. See Note, "The Constitutional Future of the All-English Ballot," *Pacific Law Journal* 16 (1985): 1029.

137. See *Village of Arlington Heights v. Metropolitan Housing Development Corp.*, 429 U.S. 252, 265 (1977), and *Washington v. Davis*, 426 U.S. 229, 242 (1976). To establish intentional discrimination, a party need not show that the challenged action rested solely on invidious purposes. In *Village of Arlington Heights*, the court noted: "Rarely can it be said that . . . a particular purpose was the 'dominant' or 'primary' one." But the party must demonstrate that "the decisionmaker . . . selected or reaffirmed a particular course of action at least in part 'because of,' not merely 'in spite of,' its adverse effects upon an identifiable group"; *Personnel Admin. v. Feeney*, 442 U.S. 279.

Two subsequent Supreme Court cases show how the intent requirement may be met in the case of race. In *Rogers v. Lodge*, 458 U.S. 613 (1982), the Court upheld a finding that a county's at-large voting system, although not originally adopted to deny blacks equal access to the political process, had been maintained for this invidious purpose. In *Hunter v. Underwood*, 105 S.Ct. 1916, 1921–22 (1985), the Court found that the intent requirement was satisfied by an Alabama constitutional provision disenfranchising persons convicted of crimes involving "moral turpitude," because it was aimed at blacks and had been adopted at a constitutional convention convened to reestablish white supremacy in the state.

The analysis of intent is especially difficult in cases such as California's adoption of Proposition 63, its Official English amendment, where state action is the product of a popular referendum. See Sager, "Insular Majorities Unabated: *Warth v. Seldin* and *City of Eastlake v. Forest City Enterprises, Inc.*," *Harvard Law Review* 91 (1978): 1373, 1421. In these cases voters are the relevant decisionmakers, and their motivations are particularly varied and difficult to discern.

138. See *Craig v. Boren*, 429 U.S. 190 (1976).

A showing of intent becomes more critical and more difficult, however, in cases where allegedly discriminatory state action does not evidence discriminatory intent on its face—that is, where a policy makes no explicit reference to a suspect characteristic, but where the impact of the policy falls disproportionately on a suspect or quasi-suspect class. This is the situation when Official English declarations are used to deprive language minorities of services in their own language. A policy of monolingualism does not explicitly "classify" persons: all are given "equal" services (in English), and no distinctions are overtly drawn between individuals. Yet the adverse effects of this "equal" treatment fall disproportionately on language minorities.[139] Indeed, the disparate impact falls with perfect fit upon the disadvantaged class, because language ability is precisely the characteristic that defines the quasi-suspect class. Yet before applying heightened scrutiny, a court must nevertheless make a finding that decisionmakers pursued an English-only policy at least in part *because of* its effects upon those who do not speak English.

It is useful in these circumstances to focus on the substantive goals of the Equal Protection Clause—specifically, its prohibition of official implementation of private biases through the law.[140] Only if language minorities can show evidence of an actual intent to affect them adversely—that is, if they can show that decisionmakers enacted Official English declarations "at least in part 'because of,' not merely 'in spite of,' [the act's] adverse effects upon an identifiable group"[141]— will heightened scrutiny be appropriate. If, by contrast, litigants cannot show that Official English declarations were adopted (or that officials failed to pursue bilingual policies in the first place) for the *purpose* of affecting non-English-speaking persons, their cases will not satisfy the threshold requirement for heightened scrutiny.[142]

In fact, a strong case can be made for the proposition that the designs of English Only advocates satisfy the intent requirement. Official English supporters have openly set out to withdraw bilingual services, with the avowed purpose of affecting non-English speakers. Both in their symbolic and practical effects, Official English declarations seek to remind those who do not speak the language that they must learn it; the withdrawal of services, according to English Only

---

139. See *Lau v. Nichols*, 414 U.S. 563, 566 (1974), which notes that "there is no equality of treatment merely by providing students with the same facilities, textbooks, teachers, and curriculum; for students who do not understand English are effectively foreclosed from any meaningful education" *(see p. 253)*.

140. See *Palmore v. Sidoti*, 466 U.S. 429, 433 (1984).

141. *Personnel Admin. v. Feeney*, 442 U.S. 279.

142. Cf. *Feeney*, in which the Supreme Court held that a state's hiring preference for veterans, which had the effect of excluding almost all women, was valid because it was not pursued with an intent to exclude women.

advocates, will underscore this message.[143] This motive distinguishes the English Only movement from the general distribution of materials solely in English. In the former situation, a court that accepts language minorities as a quasi-suspect class will move on to apply heightened scrutiny to the movement's intentional attempt to affect non-English speakers. In the latter situation, by contrast, where there is no design to disadvantage those who do not understand the language, the state action fails to meet the threshold intent requirement.

Because it contains this requirement of intent, the Equal Protection Clause does not mandate that all government business be conducted in a multitude of languages. Surely there is no intent to discriminate against language minorities through, for example, the publication of the *Congressional Record* solely in English. Even if non-English speakers are genuinely disadvantaged, the Constitution does not proscribe such actions.

If a court declines to characterize language minorities as a quasi-suspect class, it may choose instead to focus on the disproportionate impact of an Official English declaration on national-origin minorities. Under this theory, however, proof of intent will be more difficult: there is no readily apparent intent to disadvantage these groups either on the face of the declarations or in the official legislative histories.

Many quite different sentiments motivate the Official English movement, however, including those that would satisfy the discriminatory intent requirement. The emotionally charged political debate preceding California's adoption of its Official English amendment provides the most striking example. Although the narrow issue was language, the debate encompassed the broader issue of immigration into the state.[144] Intolerance for and impatience with non-English speakers provide some portion of the support for the movement nationwide. To at least some extent, then, Official English pronouncements seem to reflect xenophobia. As one commentator has noted, "It

143. See statement of Senator Jeremiah Denton (R-Ala.), U.S. Senate, Committee on the Judiciary, Subcommittee on the Constitution, *The English Language Amendment: Hearing on S.J. Res. 167*, 98th Cong., 2d sess. (June 12, 1984), pp. 9–11.

144. See, e.g., Frank del Olmo, "Se Habla Ingles: Prop. 63, a Cruel Joke, Could Cost Us Dearly," *Los Angeles Times*, Aug. 28, 1986, pt. II, p. 5. Polled in a 1983 survey, 88 percent of the English-speaking residents of southern California described the immigration situation there as "very or somewhat serious," and nearly two-thirds believed that an increasing proportion of residents would have limited English-language skills. Almost 70 percent of respondents predicted that this increase in non-English speakers would negatively affect ethnic relations; Tracy Ann Goodis and Thomas J. Espenshade, "Los Angeles Rides the Wave," *American Demographics*, Sept. 1986, pp. 46–48. Senator Pete Wilson, a supporter of California's Proposition 63, linked support for the movement to growing hostility toward immigrants; *Los Angeles Times*, Aug. 21, 1986, pt. I, p. 23.

can help to make fears [of non-Anglos] tidy and manageable if one talks in an apparently rational manner about . . . safeguarding the nation's language."[145] But courts should not allow this tidiness to obscure the sentiments that may underlie the English Only movement. If a court identifies the movement's motivation as "a bare . . . desire to harm a politically unpopular group,"[146] it should invalidate any attempt to use an Official English declaration to dismantle bilingual programs.

If courts deem language minorities a quasi-suspect class, they should apply heightened scrutiny to broad interpretations of an Official English declaration. Under heightened scrutiny courts should assess the importance to the state of the publicly declared goals of Official English advocates and the extent to which the declarations, if given broad legal force, are substantially related to the achievement of these goals. It is a canon of statutory interpretation that a court should, if possible, interpret a statute so that it does not conflict with the Constitution.[147] If a court determines that giving an Official English declaration practical legal effect would put the declaration at odds with the Constitution—if it finds that striking down a state's bilingual programs would serve ends that are not sufficiently important or that the means proposed are not substantially related to these ends—it should refrain from so construing the pronouncement.

Proponents of Official English measures have argued that if schooling and government services are available only in English, non-English speakers, who would otherwise have insufficient incentives to acquire English, will be spurred to learn the language. A court must first assess the importance of this asserted goal. One may argue that this forced "Americanization" violates traditional notions of tolerance and liberty in our pluralistic society, thereby failing to satisfy even the minimum requirement that acts have valid public purposes. Courts have, however, generally found that a government has at least a "legitimate" interest in encouraging its citizens to speak a common tongue.[148] Nevertheless, given the fact that a linguistically diverse America has flourished for centuries, it is doubtful that enforced monolingualism is a truly important, as opposed to merely legitimate, state interest.

Even if litigants are able to establish the importance of compelling non-English speakers to learn English, a court must determine

---

145. Tom McArthur, "Comment: Worried About Something Else," *International Journal of the Sociology of Language* 60 (1986): 87, 91.

146. *U.S. Dept. of Agriculture v. Moreno*, 413 U.S. 528, 534 (1973).

147. *Presser v. Illinois*, 116 U.S. 252, 269 (1886).

148. See, e.g., *Guadalupe Organization v. Tempe Elementary School District No. 3*, 587 F.2d 1022.

whether allowing an Official English declaration to eliminate bilingual services is substantially related to fostering this goal. Given the overwhelming social and economic incentives that already exist to learn English, the deprivation of bilingual services seems at most a small added incentive. The means used are also overbroad: a denial of bilingual services affects *all* non-English speakers, including those who are already trying to learn the language, as well as those who are simply too old or otherwise unable to become proficient in a second language. By contrast, if acquisition of English-speaking skills is the end, government provision of language instruction would address the perceived problem more directly. The existence of such less restrictive alternatives calls into question the genuineness of the asserted connection between the goal of encouraging English proficiency and the means of denying bilingual services.

English Only proponents also argue that state governments should not have to bear the fiscal and administrative burdens of dealing with individuals in more than one language. Courts have accepted the validity of a state's desire to economize, but they prohibit a state from achieving these savings "by invidious distinctions between classes of its citizens."[149] Thus, the denial of bilingual services should not be viewed as an acceptable method of economizing.

In determining what legal effect to give an Official English declaration, a court will face a choice between interpreting the declaration broadly, thereby permitting the denial of bilingual services, or narrowly, thereby limiting its effects to the domain of symbolism. Applying heightened scrutiny, a court should find that a broad interpretation would conflict with the federal Constitution. It should therefore choose to interpret the declaration narrowly, rejecting challenges to existing bilingual services.[150]

In a democracy fair representation of groups in the political process is necessary in order to assure fair results. In a series of cases beginning in 1967, the Supreme Court has consistently invalidated measures passed by popular referendum that seek to intervene in the political process and to overturn or preclude the adoption of laws that benefit suspect classes. The Court has held that efforts to single out particular

149. See, e.g., *Shapiro v. Thompson*, 394 U.S. 633; but see also *Carmona v. Sheffield*, 475 F.2d 738–39 (9th Cir. 1973).

150. This result may obtain even if a court chooses to use the minimum rationality test. There is arguably not even a rational relationship between the movement's goal of encouraging social unity and its political struggles over the supremacy of English. Rather, the political movement represents "mere negative attitudes, or fear, unsubstantiated by factors which are properly cognizable" in a judicial proceeding; *City of Cleburne v. Cleburne Living Center*, 105 S.Ct. 3249, 3259 (1985), a case which involved prejudice against the mentally ill.

unpopular groups for special burdens in the political process violate the Equal Protection Clause and cannot stand. Thus, Official English declarations that would operate to prevent legislatures from establishing or maintaining programs to serve the needs of language minorities may be invalid because they place such an unfair burden on these groups in the political process.

In *Reitman v. Mulkey*, the Court confronted circumstances similar to those surrounding the passage of Proposition 63 in California. In that case the California legislature had enacted several statutes prohibiting racial discrimination in housing. In 1964, pursuant to an initiative and referendum, voters amended their state constitution to overturn and preclude reenactment of these antidiscrimination laws. The Supreme Court invalidated the provision on the ground that it involved the state in private discrimination.[151] Similarly, in *Hunter v. Erickson*, the Akron city council had passed an antidiscrimination ordinance. Akron voters then amended the city charter to require the approval of a majority of voters for any ordinance regulating the disposition of property on the basis of race, color, religion, national origin, or ancestry. The Supreme Court struck down this amendment, holding that it "place[d] special burdens on racial minorities within the governmental process." Justice Harlan, in concurrence, found that this provision had "the clear purpose of making it more difficult for certain racial and religious minorities to achieve legislation that is in their interest."[152] Finally, in *Washington v. Seattle School District No. 1*, the Seattle school board had operated a program of busing to desegregate its schools, and the Court struck down a statewide initiative designed to eliminate the use of mandatory busing for this purpose.[153]

In each of these cases, the Supreme Court rejected popularly approved provisions that "subtly distort[ed] governmental processes in such a way as to place special burdens on the ability of minority groups to achieve beneficial legislation."[154] If a court finds that a given state's Official English declaration is designed to impair the ability of language minorities to pursue their interests in the political process, it too should invalidate the declaration insofar as it "seriously curtail[s] the operation of those political processes ordinarily to be relied upon to protect minorities."[155] Courts should not permit such decla-

---

151. 387 U.S. 369, 379–81 (1967).
152. 393 U.S. 385–86, 391, 395 (1969).
153. 458 U.S. 457 (1982).
154. Ibid., p. 467.
155. Ibid., p. 486; quoting *U.S. v. Carolene Products Co.*, 304 U.S. 153 n.4 (*dictum*). Although the Supreme Court has explicitly reaffirmed the power of a state simply to repeal or modify its laws, that power will not vindicate the erection of "comparative structural burden[s]"; ibid., pp. 475 n.17, 483.

rations to obstruct the provision of bilingual services for which language minorities lobby successfully in state legislatures.

By its own account, the Official English movement seeks to stimulate debate on the sensitive issue of language and to promote social unity through a common tongue. In fact, however, the movement makes language the rallying point for simmering intolerance, frustration, fear, and distrust. State declarations of an official language invite legal challenges to bilingual services and programs. Thus, courts may soon have to determine how far these declarations can go to mandate monolingualism by barring legislatures from accommodating the needs of non-English speakers. Courts should find that the presence of established federal programs and the Equal Protection Clause of the Fourteenth Amendment prohibit state action limiting the rights of language minorities. If they do so, these declarations will have no practical impact; they will simply stand as hollow symbols of our generation's xenophobia.

Hernández v. New York

While racial discrimination in jury selection is a violation of the Equal Protection Clause, excluding bilingual jurors is not necessarily unconstitutional, according to the U.S. Supreme Court.[156] The case involved Dionisio Hernández, convicted of attempted murder in Brooklyn, New York. At his trial the prosecutor had used peremptory challenges to disqualify bilingual jurors, citing their hesitation when asked whether they could disregard direct testimony in Spanish and heed only the English translation of the court interpreter. Hernández's lawyer protested that this was a ruse to keep Latinos off the jury who might be sympathetic to his client. But the trial judge accepted the prosecutor's "race-neutral" explanation. So did the Supreme Court, in a six-to-three decision, but not without some caveats. The same procedure might well be unconstitutional in other circumstances, the court said. While stopping short of declaring linguistic minorities to be a "suspect class," it noted the close relationship between language and national origin for purposes of equal protection analysis. Justice Anthony Kennedy delivered the majority opinion on May 28, 1991.

156. Case No. 89–7645; argued Feb. 25, 1991, decided May 28, 1991.

Petitioner argues that Spanish-language ability bears a close relation to ethnicity, and that, as a consequence, it violates the Equal Protection Clause to exercise a peremptory challenge on the ground that a Latino potential juror speaks Spanish. He points to the high correlation between Spanish-language ability and ethnicity in New York, where the case was tried. We need not address that argument here, for the prosecutor did not rely on language ability without more, but explained that the specific responses and the demeanor of the two individuals during *voir dire* caused him to doubt their ability to defer to the official translation of Spanish-language testimony.[157] . . .

In the context of this trial, the prosecutor's frank admission that his ground for excusing these jurors related to their ability to speak and understand Spanish raised a plausible, though not a necessary, inference that language might be a pretext for what in fact were race-based peremptory challenges. This was not a case where by some rare coincidence a juror happened to speak the same language as a key witness, in a community where few others spoke that tongue. If it were, the explanation that the juror could have undue influence on jury deliberations might be accepted without concern that a racial generalization had come into play. But this trial took place in a community with a substantial Latino population, and petitioner and other interested parties were members of that ethnic group. It would be common knowledge in the locality that a significant percentage of the Latino population speaks fluent Spanish, and that many consider it their preferred language, the one chosen for personal communication, the one selected for speaking with the most precision and power, the one used to define the self.

157. Respondent cites *U.S. v. Pérez*, 658 F.2d 654 (9th Cir. 1981), which illustrates the sort of problems that may arise where a juror fails to accept the official translation of foreign-language testimony. In *Pérez*, the following interchange occurred:

> *Dorothy Kim (Juror No. 8):* Your Honor, is it proper to ask the interpreter a question? I'm uncertain about the word La Vado [sic]. You say that is a bar.
> *The Court:* The Court cannot permit jurors to ask questions directly. If you want to phrase your question to me—
> *Dorothy Kim:* I understood it to be a restroom. I could better believe they would meet in a restroom rather than a public bar if he is undercover.
> *The Court:* These are matters for you to consider. If you have any misunderstanding of what the witness testified to, tell the Court now what you didn't understand and we'll place the—
> *Dorothy Kim:* I understand the word La Vado [sic]—I thought it meant restroom. She translates it as bar.
> *Ms. Ianziti:* In the first place, the jurors are not to listen to the Spanish but to the English. I am a certified court interpreter.
> *Dorothy Kim:* You're an idiot.

Upon further questioning, "the witness indicated that none of the conversations in issue occurred in the restroom." The juror later explained that she had said, "it's an idiom" rather than "you're an idiot," but she was nevertheless dismissed from the jury.

The trial judge can consider these and other factors when deciding whether a prosecutor intended to discriminate. For example, though petitioner did not suggest the alternative to the trial court here, Spanish-speaking jurors could be permitted to advise the judge in a discreet way of any concerns with the translation during the course of trial. A prosecutor's persistence in the desire to exclude Spanish-speaking jurors despite this measure could be taken into account in determining whether to accept a race-neutral explanation for the challenge. . . .

We discern no clear error in the state trial court's determination that the prosecutor did not discriminate on the basis of the ethnicity of Latino jurors. We have said that "[w]here there are two permissible views of the evidence, the factfinder's choice between them cannot be clearly erroneous."[158] The trial court took a permissible view of the evidence in crediting the prosecutor's explanation. Apart from the prosecutor's demeanor, which of course we have no opportunity to review, the court could have relied on the facts that the prosecutor defended his use of peremptory challenges without being asked to do so by the judge, that he did not know which jurors were Latinos, and that the ethnicity of the victims and prosecution witnesses tended to undercut any motive to exclude Latinos from the jury. Any of these factors could be taken as evidence of the prosecutor's sincerity. . . .

Language permits an individual to express both a personal identity and membership in a community, and those who share a common language may interact in ways more intimate than those without this bond. Bilinguals, in a sense, inhabit two communities, and serve to bring them closer. Indeed, some scholarly comment suggests that people proficient in two languages may not at times think in one language to the exclusion of the other. The analogy is that of a high-hurdler, who combines the ability to sprint and to jump to accomplish a third feat with characteristics of its own, rather than two separate functions.[159] This is not to say that the cognitive processes and reactions of those who speak two languages are susceptible of easy generalization, for even the term "bilingual" does not describe a uniform category. It is a simple word for a more complex phenomenon with many distinct categories and subdivisions.

Our decision today does not imply that exclusion of bilinguals from jury service is wise, or even that it is constitutional in all cases. It is a harsh paradox that one may become proficient enough in English to participate in trial,[160] only to encounter disqualification because he

158. *Anderson v. Bessemer City*, 470 U.S. 564, 574 (1985).

159. François Grosjean, "The Bilingual as a Competent but Specific Speaker-Hearer," *Journal of Multilingual and Multicultural Development* 6 (1985): 467.

160. See, e.g., U.S.C. §§1865(b)(2),(3) (English-language ability required for federal jury service).

knows a second language as well. As the Court observed in a somewhat related context: "Mere knowledge of [a foreign] language cannot reasonably be regarded as harmful. Heretofore it has been commonly looked upon as helpful and desirable."[161]

Just as shared differences can serve to foster community, language differences can be a source of division. Language elicits a response from others, ranging from admiration and respect, to distance and alienation, to ridicule and scorn. Reactions of the latter type all too often result from or initiate racial hostility. In holding that a race-neutral reason for a peremptory challenge means a reason other than race, we do not resolve the more difficult question of the breadth with which the concept of race should be defined for equal protection purposes. We would face a quite different case if the prosecutor had justified his peremptory challenges with the explanation that he did not want Spanish-speaking jurors. It may well be, for certain ethnic groups and in some communities, that proficiency in a particular language, like skin color, should be treated as a surrogate for race under an equal protection analysis.[162] And, as we make clear, a policy of striking down all who speak a given language, without regard to the particular circumstances of the trial or the individual responses of the jurors, may be found by the trial judge to be a pretext for racial discrimination. But that case is not before us. . . .

Bilingual Public Services in California

By the American Civil Liberties Union of Northern California

Thus far, Official English measures have yet to produce a wholesale termination of government-sponsored bilingual programs. For example, Proposition 63 has had little, if any, direct impact on those provided by the state of California. But opponents warn that some proposed versions of a federal English Language Amendment would have sweeping consequences. A wide variety of programs could be eliminated, including many benefiting the public at large. Some essential services might not be spared even under

161. *Meyer v. Nebraska*, 262 U.S. 390, 400 (1923).
162. Cf. *Yu Cong Eng v. Trinidad*, 271 U.S. 500 (1926) (law prohibiting keeping business records in other than specified languages violated equal protection rights of Chinese businessmen); *Meyer v. Nebraska* (striking down law prohibiting grade schools from teaching languages other than English).

versions of the amendment that exempt public health and safety. What, specifically, is at stake? Some answers are provided by this survey of California laws regarding assistance for non-English and limited-English speakers, who comprise approximately 6 percent of the state's population. The survey omits bilingual programs offered by local agencies (along with any assessment of the adequacy of state efforts). It was compiled by Rachel Shigekane, a legal intern for the American Civil Liberties Union of Northern California.

General

The *Dymally-Alatorre Act*[163] requires all state agencies that provide information or render services to the public, if a substantial proportion of their clients are non-English speakers, to employ a sufficient number of qualified bilingual persons in public contact positions. Further, any materials explaining the agency's services must be translated into languages spoken by a substantial number of clients. For these provisions to become effective, non-English speakers must represent at least 5 percent of those served by any local office or facility.

The *State Personnel Board* is responsible for implementing and monitoring compliance with the Dymally-Alatorre Act.[164] In addition, the board administers bilingual examinations and certifies bilingual state employees, who are entitled to a pay differential. All state agencies are required to conduct an annual survey and to report to the board on (1) the number of public contact positions in each of its local offices; (2) the number of bilingual employees in these positions and the languages they speak; and (3) the number of non-English-speaking contacts.[165] The board summarizes these agency reports as part of its annual evaluation to the Legislature on compliance with the Dymally-Alatorre Act.[166]

According to the Annual Statewide Language Survey Report conducted in 1987–88, 9,406,895 public contacts were made by fifty-four participating state agencies. Of these, 927,981 or 9.9 percent were with limited- or non-English-speaking people. The demand for bilingual assistance was greatest in the following languages: Spanish, Cantonese, Vietnamese, Tagalog, Korean, and American Sign Language (in that order). Twenty-seven state agencies maintained a total of 4,431 bilingual positions. Of these, 85 percent were designated bi-

163. Cal. Gov't Code §7290.
164. Cal. Gov't Code §7299.2.
165. Cal. Gov't Code §7299.4.
166. Cal. Gov't Code §7299.6.

lingual in Spanish, 3 percent in Cantonese, 2 percent in Tagalog, 2 percent in Vietnamese, and 5 percent in other languages. Despite a 31 percent increase in the number of bilingual positions since 1984–85, the survey revealed vacancies in 1,327 positions. The shortages were especially acute in Spanish and American Sign Language.

Social, Health, and Emergency Services

Informational pamphlets used for educating employers and employees of their responsibilities regarding *unemployment benefits* and *disability insurance* and for advising employees of their basic rights and obligations under the state *workers compensation* program must be printed in both English and Spanish.[167] The Office of Benefits Determination must make available in English and Spanish all forms and notices regarding application for and receipt of compensation owed to injured workers.[168]

All applications and public information regarding *food stamps* must be available in each county in English and Spanish, and may be provided in other non-English languages at the discretion of the director.[169] Pamphlets describing types of and eligibility for *public assistance* offered by the Department of Social Services must be available in both English and Spanish.[170] In addition, the Department of Social Services has established units to combat discrimination on the basis of race or language and to provide a range of translation services.

Informed consent forms for purposes of physician reimbursement under the *Medi-Cal program* must be printed in both English and Spanish and must be understandable to Medi-Cal beneficiaries.[171] *Department of Health pamphlets* regarding types of available medical care also must be printed in both English and Spanish.[172]

The Department of Mental Health Services must translate the Statutory Patients' Bill of Rights, the regulatory Patients' Bill of Rights for skilled *nursing facilities* and, if appropriate, the regulatory Patients' Bill for intermediate care facilities into Spanish, Chinese, and any other language spoken by more than one percent of the state's nursing home population.[173] The department's Office of Human Rights produces *publications on the rights of the mentally disabled* that are translated into Spanish, Japanese, Chinese, Korean, Samoan, and Vietnamese. Signs regarding these rights must be displayed prominently

---

167. Cal. Unemployment Insurance Code §316; Cal. Labor Code §139.
168. Cal. Labor Code §124.
169. Cal. Welfare and Institutions Code §18915.
170. Cal. Welfare and Institutions Code §10607.
171. Cal. Welfare and Institutions Code §14191.
172. Cal. Welfare and Institutions Code §10746.
173. Cal. Health and Safety Code §1599.74.

in both English and Spanish in all facilities.[174] Additionally, Atascadero and Metropolitan State hospitals hire *bilingual-bicultural clinical staff* to provide culturally and linguistically sensitive therapy for members of the Spanish-speaking community.

All applications, forms, and informational materials regarding *emergency and disaster relief*, distributed out of the state's Emergency Operations Account or through grants by the Department of Social Services, must be available in English and the predominant non-English language in the disaster area. Moreover, bilingual staff who reflect the demographics of the disaster area must be available to assist applicants.[175] Where at least 5 percent of the population speaks a language other than English according to the latest U.S. census, the *Emergency Telephone System* must have the appropriate bilingual operators.[176]

The *Department of Rehabilitation* and its contracting agencies must provide special language assistance as needed by the handicapped clients they serve.[177] The *Department of the Aging* offers translation services, for example, in its Adult Day Health Care programs, in which 40 percent of staff members are bilingual in such languages as Spanish, Japanese, Tagalog, Vietnamese, Laotian, and Hmong. The *Department of Alcohol and Drug Programs* provides publications in Spanish, Chinese, and Tagalog on the dangers of smoking, drug abuse, and alcoholism.

The Department of Veterans Affairs, which provides services and *information to veterans* concerning their benefits, dependent assistance, and low-interest loans, participates in *La voz del Vetrano de California*, a Spanish-language radio program. It also runs advertisements in Spanish-language newspapers regarding veteran home-loan programs.

Employment

The Fair Employment and Housing Act (F.E.H.A.) prohibits discrimination based on race, religious creed, color, national origin, ancestry, physical handicap, medical condition, marital status, or sex of any person in the areas of employment and housing.[178] Discrimination based on language has been considered a form of national-origin discrimination. The Department of Fair Employment and Housing,

---

174. Cal. Welfare and Institutions Code §4503.
175. Cal. Gov't Code §8690.6 (inoperative as of Jan. 30, 1993); Cal. Welfare and Institutions Code §13600.
176. Cal. Welfare and Institutions Code §53112.
177. Cal. Welfare and Institutions Code §19013.5.
178. Cal. Gov't Code §§12900–96.

the state agency charged with enforcing the F.E.H.A., distributes Spanish-language posters and pamphlets describing the law and the agency's activities.

During *union representation elections* the Agricultural Labor Relations Board is required to make the election ballots available in both Spanish and English, as well as in other languages requested by the union.[179] *Farm labor contractors* must make available in Spanish and in English their rate of compensation received from the grower and the rate of compensation to be paid to the farmworkers.[180] Notices forbidding child farm labor without legal permits must appear in both English and Spanish.[181]

All notices, posters, and other informational materials regarding *occupational safety and health* are required to be printed in both English and Spanish.[182] Qualifying tests for tunnel and mine safety representatives must be administered in languages other than English when there is sufficient interest in these positions among non-English speakers.[183]

The Department of Industrial Relations is expected to translate complaint forms regarding *wage claim violations* into non-English languages and to provide interpreters at hearings and interviews, as appropriate.[184]

The Employment Development Department employs more than 1,200 bilingual employees in public contact positions, who administer *unemployment insurance, job-referral programs, and disability benefits.* Also, the department's Monitor-Advocate Office informs seasonal farmworkers of their rights under state and federal labor laws. Its central Translation Unit produces operational forms, informational pamphlets, handbooks, and signs, as well as correspondence in various languages.

Local Private Industry Councils (PICs) oversee *job training and job placement* by community-based organizations, which employ bilingual and bicultural staff. For example, the San Francisco PIC contracts with nonprofit groups that provide clerical, white-collar, and construction job training in Cantonese and Spanish; computer and clerical English-as-a-second-language classes in Tagalog, Korean, and Spanish; and job placement in Spanish. The California Conservation Corps, which provides job training and employment to adolescents and young adults—for example, as summer firefighters—employs

179. Cal. Labor Code §1156.3.
180. Cal. Labor Code §1695.
181. Cal. Education Code §49140.
182. Cal. Labor Code §6328.
183. Cal. Labor Code §7998.
184. Cal. Labor Code §105.

staff and recruits corps members who are fluent in Spanish, Vietnamese, and American Sign Language.

Housing

The Housing and Community Development Office of the California Department of Housing, which administers grants to assist in construction or rehabilitation of *housing for agricultural workers* and their families, is required to provide bilingual services and publications. In enforcing standards for farmworker housing under the Employee Housing Act, the office must use a staff that is, to the extent feasible, bilingual in Spanish and English.[185] The *Housing Finance Agency*, which provides mortgage loans to nonprofit sponsors of rental and cooperative housing developments for low- and moderate-income families, must provide for bilingual services and publications as necessary.[186]

The Department of Economic Opportunity, whose goal is to reduce poverty by encouraging self-sufficiency, sponsors a *Home Energy Assistance Project* to assist low-income persons with energy conservation techniques, such as weatherization. This project employs bilingual Spanish and Vietnamese staff and prints its application form in both English and Spanish.

Education

The Early Intervention for School Success Program, enacted in 1977 to train school personnel to identify *developmental disabilities* and to provide appropriate instruction for students with special needs, uses screening instruments in English, Spanish, Laotian, Vietnamese, and Cambodian to test language, auditory, visual, fine-motor, and gross-motor skills.[187] The Master Plan for Special Education requires that a program be developed to certify bilingual-bicultural personnel to assess limited- or non-English-speaking pupils for *placement in special education* programs.[188]

Motor Vehicle Licensing

Copies of *motor vehicle laws* must be printed in Spanish, as needed to meet demand.[189] Since 13 percent of its contacts are with non-En-

185. Cal. Health and Safety Code §§50517.5, 17956.
186. Cal. Health and Safety Code §51200.
187. Cal. Education Code §54685.9.
188. Cal. Educational Code §56362.7.
189. Cal. Vehicle Code §1652.2.

glish speakers, the Department of Motor Vehicles employs more than 1,200 bilingual employees in its 169 field offices, who are certified in languages ranging from Arabic to Vietnamese. Oral driver's license exams and road-sign tests are administered in twenty-three different languages. The department's Multilingual Programs Office translates and publishes handbooks, pamphlets, forms, and correspondence into languages other than English, covering such topics as drinking and driving, accident liability, and the operation of motorcycles, trucks, and school buses.

Consumer and Environmental Programs

The *Department of Real Estate* prints mortgage loan disclosure statements and information booklets in Spanish and employs Spanish bilingual staff. The *Department of Insurance* translates some publications into Spanish and Chinese, including pamphlets on purchasing cars and car insurance.

The *Department of Consumer Affairs*, which oversees business licensing, investigates consumer complaints, and enforces consumer protection laws, employs bilingual Spanish, Cantonese, Vietnamese, and Japanese staff in public contact positions. The department also publishes brochures in Spanish. It relies on interpreters and translators from the State Personnel Board when administering a license examination in a language other than English.

The Department of Conservation sponsors a statewide *recycling program*, staffed by bilingual Spanish employees and using Spanish-language billboards. The *Department of Water Resources* prints brochures describing various water projects, energy plants, reservations, and recreational areas in both Spanish and Chinese. The *Department of Fish and Game* has used a bilingual Vietnamese-English video to explain California's hunting and fishing laws.

In state pest-control efforts, *notification of aerial spraying* must be provided in both English and Spanish in areas where Hispanics account for more than 5 percent of the persons affected.[190]

Taxation

In counties whose residents are at least 10 percent Hispanic, *property tax forms* and instructions must be provided in both English and Spanish; bilingual forms may be provided elsewhere at the discretion of the county assessor.[191] The Franchise Tax Board employs bilin-

190. Cal. Food and Agricultural Code §5777.
191. Cal. Revenue and Taxation Code §255.8.

gual workers and also translates posters and forms into Chinese and Spanish.

Voting

Upon request, the County Clerk must provide a copy of the sample ballot and the voter's pamphlet containing the written statements of each candidate in Spanish and other languages.[192] The Precinct Board must *post a facsimile of the ballot* in English, Spanish, and other languages in a conspicuous location near the polling place, or *provide printed ballots in languages other than English*, in precincts where the number of voting-age residents of a minority language group represents at least 3 percent of the population, or where interested citizens make it known to the Secretary of State that language assistance is necessary.[193] In such cases the county clerk must also make reasonable efforts to recruit *election officials who are bilingual* in the area's predominant minority language.[194]

Due Process

A non-English-speaking person who is charged with a crime has the right to an interpreter throughout a *criminal proceeding*.[195] When a witness is incapable of hearing, understanding, or communicating in the English language, an interpreter must be provided.[196] Further, approximately seventy state agencies, including the Agricultural Labor Relations Board, the Fish and Game Commission, and the Bureau of Repair Services, must provide *language assistance at adjudicatory hearings*.[197]

At *parole and clemency hearings* of the Board of Prison Terms, limited- and non-English-speaking prisoners and witnesses are entitled to an interpreter. The board also publishes Spanish-language forms and pamphlets regarding a request for interpreter, the rights of prisoners and parolees at hearings, a glossary of legal terms frequently used, and letters to subpoena witnesses. *The Department of Corrections* employs bilingual employees to serve as interpreters in custody, medical, and clerical positions, and translates rules and regulations, medical examinations, and correctional officer recruitment information. It also

192. Cal. Election Code §10012.
193. Cal. Election Code §14203 (a), (b).
194. Cal. Election Code §1634.
195. Cal. Const. Art. I, §14.
196. Cal. Evidence Code §752.
197. Cal. Gov't Code §11501.5.

distributes information in Spanish on the spread, prevention, and treatment of the *AIDS virus.*

In civil courts, notice of regulations to proceed *in forma pauperis* must be posted near the filing clerk's counter in both English and Spanish.[198] The bold heading that appears on a *court summons* advising that the recipient has been sued must appear in both English and Spanish.[199] In ex parte *protective orders in domestic violence cases,* a section describing the temporary nature of the order and the right to seek its extension, must be written in both English and Spanish.[200] Pamphlets explaining the nature of *guardianship of a minor* and the guardian's rights and obligations must be published in English and Spanish using language easily understood by a person not trained in the law.[201]

The Legislature has recognized the need to provide equal justice under the law to all Californians and to accommodate the special needs of non-English speakers in their relations with the judicial system. Accordingly, it has instructed the Judicial Council to survey these language needs and to work with the State Personnel Board in developing programs to certify competent *court interpreters.*[202]

198. Rules of Court R985, Deering 1990.
199. Cal. Code of Civil Procedure §412.20.
200. Cal. Code of Civil Procedure §546.
201. Cal. Gov't Code §68511.1.
202. Cal. Gov't Code §§68560–61.

PART FIVE

Language Diversity and Education

How should American schools respond to the growing number of children who arrive each year speaking little or no English? Today there is general agreement that these students need some kind of special help. For anyone with lingering doubts, the old "sink or swim" treatment has been outlawed by the U.S. Supreme Court. But setting aside the legalities, many pedagogical questions remain: What are the most promising methods in teaching language-minority children? Need they involve bilingual instruction? Or are there workable alternatives that use only English? Is it more important to keep children from falling behind academically while they learn English or to prepare them for "mainstream" classes as quickly as possible? Should schools develop students' native-language skills or concentrate on intensive English instruction? Does research support the superiority of one approach over another, or is it premature to judge?

There are also practical concerns. It would be problematic enough if all limited-English-proficient (LEP) students spoke the same minority language. But with immigration on the rise, as many as eighty languages are represented in some school districts—exacerbating the difficulties of recruiting qualified teachers, assessing student skills, and communicating with parents. Besides the language barrier, children from immigrant and refugee homes are often "at risk" because of poverty, neglect, crime, and other factors that affect school performance. They are more likely to need remedial classes or special education. Meanwhile, resources are stretched thin as state and federal governments cut back on education spending. Regardless of what educational theorists prescribe, local school boards operate under real-world constraints. They tend to ask: What is the best *affordable* alternative in teaching LEP children? How can legal obligations be met and minority communities be appeased without disrupting the bureaucracy or provoking resistance from teachers?

Debate over these questions is further complicated—some would say, obfuscated—by politics. However unfortunate, the politicization of educational decision-making is hard to avoid, in this field more than most. Often bilingual education becomes a stage for acting out larger conflicts. Opponents charge that legislators support the program less for its pedagogical merits than as a way to appease ethnic voting blocs and to provide jobs for Hispanics. Proponents respond that such critics are inspired by racial and ethnic hostility or, at best, put a higher priority on quick assimilation than on the welfare of language-minority students.

Public support for bilingual education has declined since the 1960s because many Americans see it as a diversion from English instruction. They worry that immigrants—Spanish speakers, in particular— are no longer making the effort to learn the national tongue. That impression is erroneous but understandable, as Siobhan Nicolau and Rafael Valdivieso explain. Sociolinguistic research shows that immigrants are acquiring English, if anything, more rapidly today than at the turn of the century. By the second generation in this country, Hispanics tend to speak English as their *usual* language; by the third generation, as their *only* language. And yet, owing to immigration and fertility rates, the number of Spanish speakers continues to increase. Moreover, Hispanics are perhaps more likely to maintain their bilingualism than earlier groups of newcomers (although melting pot mythology, not hard data, is the main basis for comparison). Spanish and other languages are certainly more likely to be heard in the formerly pristine domains of anglophone Americans. Hence the misconception that newcomers are failing to learn English, which has led in turn to a political backlash against bilingual education. Ironically, a program designed to foster assimilation is now perceived as obstructing it.

Coexisting with the contradiction between politics and pedagogy are differences over ends and means: What should the schools be teaching LEP children, and how should it be taught? Such questions were left unresolved by the Bilingual Education Act of 1968. Senator Ralph Yarborough, the chief sponsor of the law, conceived it primarily as a poverty program for Mexican Americans and Puerto Ricans. (Before final passage the bill was broadened to include other language groups.) Its goal was to remedy the high rates of school failure and the resulting lack of economic opportunity for these groups. Whether bilingual education would stress the transition to English or the maintenance of other languages was a question for local educators to decide.

In testimony on the bill, both of these aims were endorsed, but the main focus was on what *not* to do for LEP students. Bruce Gaarder explains the long-term damage, intellectual and psychological, that resulted from the sink-or-swim method. Interrupting cognitive development during the time children spent learning English (often imperfectly) left many of them permanently behind in school. Rejecting their native tongue as substandard, and even punishing students for speaking it, left *them* feeling rejected and substandard, as Rubén Salazar describes. Bilingual schooling was promoted as an antidote to the poisonous effects of educational neglect.

With little practical experience to guide them, early programs developed by trial and error. But soon critics began to demand results. If bilingual was better—the preferred remedy when federal authorities found districts violating the *Lau* decision—where was the evidence to support it? Noel Epstein asserts that nonbilingual approaches may be equally effective and deserve to be tried. Also, he charges that many bilingual educators are less eager to hasten assimilation and English acquisition than to preserve ethnic languages and cultures. Should the latter function, previously left to private and parochial schools, now be assumed by the taxpayers? Appearing in 1977, Epstein's monograph reshaped the policy discussion. The burden of proof began to shift from traditional educators who had failed LEP students with all-English instruction to innovators who had promised better outcomes from bilingual approaches.

Either way, insists Richard Rodríguez, the hard choices of assimilation cannot be evaded. Notwithstanding his own painful experience with sink-or-swim education, Rodríguez objects that bilingual education postpones the task of learning English. Moreover, he believes that it offers "a linguistic solution to a social dilemma," holding out the false hope that minority children can live comfortably in two worlds.

José Cárdenas exposes the fallacies behind these and similar criticisms, for example, that bilingual programs are failing to teach English, that children will suffer if not moved quickly into all-English classes, or that "simple English" is all students need for academic pursuits. By now, the existence of successful bilingual programs should have refuted such misinformed attacks; yet they continue to circulate widely. To Cárdenas, the critics' refusal seriously to consider the rationale for native-language instruction suggests that hidden prejudices are at work.

Former secretary of education William Bennett is one opponent who has no hesitation about articulating a broader agenda. Since a common language is essential to American democracy, he says, "we should not be bashful about proclaiming fluency in this language as our educational goal." Bennett characterizes bilingual education—or, at least, the federal preference for bilingual education—as a failure, alleging that it has slighted English in favor of "cultural pride." He argues that research on the effectiveness of bilingual programs remains inconclusive and that therefore funding should be available to explore English-only alternatives.

James J. Lyons responds that no one quarrels with the goal of English acquisition as necessary (though hardly sufficient) in educating a LEP child. Yet Bennett's fixation on English threatens to interfere with an equally important goal of the Bilingual Education Act: overall academic achievement. Research is increasingly documenting the superiority of bilingual approaches, not only in teaching other subjects, but—paradoxically—in teaching English as well. Stephen Krashen explains that what counts in second-language acquisition is the quality, not the quantity, of exposure. That is, we acquire language only to the extent we understand it. Well-designed bilingual programs provide factual context and develop native-language skills, both of which help to make English "input" comprehensible. As Lily Wong Fillmore points out, ineffective bilingual programs are numerous. Still, they should not discredit the concept of dual-language instruction—only the educators who sabotage it.

Children receive other benefits from bilingual instruction, as well. Robert Bunge elaborates the role of language in affirming Native American identity, values, and a spiritual orientation toward the natural world. The Bilingual Education Act has provided an important impetus to reviving Indian tongues that are threatened with extinction.

An interesting parallel to the bilingual education debate may be found in the world of deaf education. As Ceil Lucas explains, the doctrine of "oralism"—the emphasis on teaching children to speak and sign in English—long outweighed other considerations. Denied full access to the tools of a natural language, deaf students' intellectual development has suffered. But there has been a significant exception: the deaf children of deaf parents, who grow up as native "speakers" of American Sign Language and fare much better academically. Now that A.S.L. is beginning to gain acceptance in deaf education, however, its use is threatened by the English Only movement.

Official English proponents cite many social and political pitfalls associated with bilingualism. But according to Catherine Snow and Kenji Hakuta, they never calculate "the costs of monolingualism." English immersion programs, and even transitional bilingual education, tend to produce the same monolingual result. Without much thought, schools are depriving children of bilingual skills that the country (not to mention the individuals) could use. Meanwhile, Americans complain about the dismal state of foreign language teaching. A more rational alternative, Snow and Hakuta suggest, would be "two-way" bilingual education. This approach conserves LEP children's mother tongue while teaching them English and at the same time provides English speakers an opportunity to learn a second language. Two decades of experimentation with such programs has shown they can produce fluent bilinguals at no cost to academic achievement. Still, they have been slow to catch on in the United States.

Spanish Language Shift: Educational Implications

By Siobhan Nicolau and Rafael Valdivieso

Siobhan Nicolau is president and Rafael Valdivieso is vice
president for program and research of the Hispanic Policy
Development Project. This article first appeared as "The
Veltman Report: What It Says, What It Means," an introduction to Calvin Veltman, *The Future of the Spanish Language in the United States* (New York and Washington, D.C.:
Hispanic Policy Development Project, 1988), pp. i–ix.

The assumptions of the national media, reflecting the belief of many
Americans that Hispanics are reluctant to learn English or to acknowledge its central place in our economy, are unwarranted and unfounded. Hispanics accept English as the primary language of the nation and recognize that its acquisition is of critical importance to their
success in the United States. Moreover, virtually all Hispanic parents
are staunch supporters of solid English instruction.

The Veltman Report should reassure the nation that its Hispanic
residents and citizens are learning English and using English. They
are fulfilling the terms of the immigrants' unwritten social contract—
they are adapting to the language and customs of their adopted land.
Like all other immigrants before them, they are moving through a
language shift process which spans three generations. The first generation generally continues to speak Spanish, although most immigrants also speak English on a regular basis. Most of their children
generally speak English, although they continue to speak Spanish as
a second language. Most of their grandchildren will not speak Spanish on any regular basis, if at all.

Yet the myth that Hispanics do not (will not) speak English persists
and is driving an ever-widening wedge between Hispanic and non-
Hispanic citizens and residents. Moreover, broad dissemination of
the myth is promoting the very suspicions and ethnic tensions that
obstruct the adaptation process of Hispanic immigrants, and reduce
the opportunities of native-born Hispanics to participate fully in the
economic, political, and social lives of their communities. The perpetuation of the myth spawns misconceptions that send a message of
rejection to Hispanics: "We don't trust you—we don't like you—we

317

don't think you can fit in—you are too different—and *there seem to be far too many of you."*

Almost every wave of immigrants that washed over our shores met with similar rejection. The clear evidence of the solid adaptation of Italian, Irish, Polish, Hungarian, Ukrainian, Asian, and Jewish people—all initially deemed hopelessly, indeed dangerously unsuitable for citizenship—does not diminish the high levels of stress that many Americans continue to experience whenever a significant number of newcomers appear upon the scene.

Those of us who live and work in Hispanic communities have firsthand and personal knowledge of the steady shift from Spanish to English, but our experiences cannot be accepted as more than informed opinion or anecdotal evidence. The Hispanic Policy Development Project commissioned Dr. Calvin Veltman to back up informed opinion with a scientific analysis of how Hispanics are learning and using the English language.[1] His report analyzes the latest reliable language data collected by the U.S. Census Bureau, including the 1980 national census. Population projections, however, are based on data derived from the 1976 Survey of Income and Education because it contains the best available language data for both mother tongue and current language use. The population model used by Dr. Veltman is similar to that prepared by the Census Bureau, but adds language practice and language mobility factors.

Hispanic immigrants are learning and using English very rapidly after their arrival in the United States. Dr. Veltman has previously suggested in his book, *Language Shift in the United States,*[2] that Hispanic immigrants are assimilating English more rapidly than previous waves of immigrants. In the present study he shows that how fast individuals learn English and how much English they speak at any given time are related to (1) how long they have been in the United States and (2) how old they were when they arrived.

The Veltman Report tells us that *by the time they have been in the country for fifteen years, some 75 percent of all Hispanic immigrants are speaking English on a regular daily basis.* Belying the popular belief that the presence of large concentrations of Hispanics in one place will delay acquisition of English, the data show that Hispanics in urban centers learn English more rapidly than those who live in rural environments. This may well reflect the need for greater verbal skills in many urban jobs; language choices the world over have historically been tied to utility and trade. First-generation Hispanic immigrants do not,

1. Editor's note: Calvin Veltman is professor of urban studies at the Université du Québec à Montréal and author of numerous studies on language loyalty and language shift in the United States and Canada.
2. The Hague: Mouton, 1983.

however, become English monolinguals. Language is not something that can be thrown or bleached away. Almost all Hispanic immigrants remain lifetime bilinguals. They use different languages in different situations with different people in different settings. However, *more than half the immigrants who arrived in the United States before they were fourteen have made English their usual, everyday language,* relegating Spanish to the status of a second language. A small number, in fact, no longer speak Spanish at all.

The children of first-generation immigrant parents become fluent English speakers. Most of them have some knowledge of their parents' native language as well, because they heard it early in their lives in their homes and in their neighborhoods. Nonetheless, *seven out of ten children of Hispanic immigrant parents become English speakers for all practical purposes, and their children—the third generation—have English as their mother tongue.* Because of ongoing immigration, bilingualism may persist longer among Hispanics than it did among other immigrant groups, particularly in certain geographical areas. Immigration, however, does not delay the acquisition of English by the native born or by the immigrants themselves. And if all immigration were halted, Spanish would not long survive in any significant manner in any area of the United States.

In 1976 there were 10.5 million persons in the United States who could speak Spanish. Approximately 4.5 million of this number were predominantly Spanish-speaking; the remainder preferred English, including more than 2 million who reportedly did not speak Spanish on a daily basis. At this same point in time, there were in the United States more than 3 million additional persons of Hispanic ancestry who were English monolinguals, not speaking Spanish at all. Using a model that projects a net increase in Hispanic immigration at the rate of 250,000 per year and birthrates of approximately 3.0 children for women who did not speak English well and 2.4 for those who could, we arrive at the following conclusions:

• The Spanish-speaking group, both monolingual Spanish speakers and bilinguals—individuals who speak both Spanish and English—will total 16.6 million by the year 2001.

• By the year 2001, however, an additional 4.4 million persons of Hispanic ancestry will have abandoned Spanish and become English monolinguals.

• The maintenance of Spanish language use depends on the continuous arrival of new Hispanic immigrants. Any interruption in the immigrant stream would stabilize the size of the Spanish-speaking population for approximately fifteen years, after which a progressively more rapid decline would set in.

As we look at the large numbers of Hispanic individuals who are concentrated in a relatively small number of markets—individuals who are in the process of learning English and shifting from one language to another—it becomes clear that there are reasons, both practical and humane, for the provision of basic services and public announcements in both Spanish and English. Because language shift is not accomplished overnight, it is appropriate that basic services and helping institutions speak to Hispanic immigrants and young children in a language they can understand. Furthermore, many Spanish monolinguals are elderly. It is both practical and compassionate to offer them services in their own language. It is not only appropriate; it is a policy that is worthy of a great nation which is confident in its power to attract and integrate new citizens.

Failure to provide such services blocks rather than hastens the adaptation of non-English or limited-English speakers. If we believe that it is important that Hispanics participate in our society and shoulder the responsibilities of good citizenship, then we must make it possible for them to do so. The newly arrived who are welcomed in their own language are likely to accustom themselves more rapidly to our ways and to the English language. Isolating groups and individuals by denying them transitional services in a language they can understand slows their integration into the mainstream.

At the same time there is a desperate need for the provision of increased opportunities for individuals to learn English. In addition to the lack of adequate programming for school children, there is a huge, unmet adult need. At present, there are long lists of adult Hispanics in a number of cities, notably Los Angeles and New York, who are waiting to enroll in English classes.

As a result of immigration, the population increase from Spanish-speaking countries is likely to average 250,000 a year for the foreseeable future. We know that immigrant children, as well as the native-born children of immigrant parents, enter school speaking Spanish. It appears, then, that the best interests of the nation and these children are served by programs that teach English and simultaneously develop basic reading and computation skills in Spanish. At present, less than a quarter of the Hispanic children who need language assistance are enrolled in transitional bilingual education or other programs designed to expedite language shift and teach basic skills. As a result, we find that at least 25 percent of Hispanic youngsters fall behind and are overage for their grade level on entering high school. We have learned that doing poorly and being older than one's classroom peers contributes directly to cumulative Hispanic dropout rates of 45 to 50 percent during the high school years. An additional 25 percent of Hispanic students who enter high school graduate without sufficient skills to enter today's labor market.

Given data which show that a large amount of human resources are being squandered through the undereducation of Hispanic youth, anything which would help such children do well in school, and stay in school, would be desirable. Since we now know that both immigrants and their children adapt very rapidly to English, and even make it their preferred language, we should not stand in the way of bilingual education programs which have proved themselves effective tools to promote educational attainment. Hispanics are concentrated in the metropolitan areas of five states—California, Texas, Illinois, New York, and Florida. In some areas they will become the majority of the entry-level workforce. Their lack of educational preparedness is of increasing concern to business, industry, and government, particularly in light of the structural changes in the economy that require higher skills for entry-level employment. The manufacturing and manual labor jobs that historically were filled by immigrants, providing an upward-mobility ladder for their children, are disappearing. The growing mismatch between the skills Hispanics *require* and the skills Hispanics *acquire* calls for an increased emphasis on both education and job preparation.

Educators, job trainers, and policymakers alike have virtually ignored the long-range need for literate English-Spanish bilingual professionals to service international trade and diplomacy. It is projected that there will be 550 million Spanish-speaking consumers in Latin America by the turn of the century. The economic well-being and the diplomatic standing of the United States would be served by a conscious effort to conserve and foster a large bilingual pool of *literate* Spanish speakers. Data from the federal Center for Education Statistics show that only 4 percent of Hispanics take the three years of Spanish that is a minimum required to be able to write properly in a language. Both educators and professional trainers might well focus attention on the preparation of individuals for bilingual employment opportunities.

Shifting from one language to another is a process. Although the Veltman Report documents extensive language shift within ten years of arrival in the United States, nobody does it overnight. It is not accomplished without effort; think of the legions of people we all know who bemoan the fact that they took *years* of French, or Spanish, or German and still can't speak a word of it. We should not be impatient with new Americans who are struggling to acquire fluency in what is for them a foreign language. And we should not be surprised or dismayed by the fact that they tend to communicate with their children in the language they can handle.

Parental responsibility is a weighty matter that involves the transmission of complicated values, discipline, knowledge, self-esteem, and affection. It requires communicating with a sophistication, subtlety, and nuance not available in a half-mastered language. Second, a child's development of language—the ability to deal with language logic and structure—is a mysterious, interactive process that requires babies and toddlers to hear language and to engage constantly in conversations. It is unreasonable to imagine that parents can converse easily in languages they are in the process of learning. If children were exposed only to their parents' halting English from birth to age six, they would arrive in school with an underdeveloped sense of how language works and what it does. It is far preferable that they come to school with language development in Spanish, and then transfer that understanding from Spanish to English. This is the point, frequently misunderstood, of *transitional* bilingual education.

The vast majority of U.S. Hispanics voluntarily arrived within our borders prepared to make a place for themselves in a pluralistic, English-speaking society. They do not scorn English, nor do they threaten it. Hispanics in the United States are following the U.S. immigrants' historical three-generation pattern of abandoning the ancestral tongue, despite a demonstrated need for literate Spanish speakers. It may well be that we are looking at Hispanics and language in the wrong way. In light of demographic changes and shifts in the structure of international markets, the national interest may best be served by preserving the valuable Spanish-language resources we now are allowing to wither away.

Introducing the Bilingual Education Act

By Senator Ralph Yarborough

The Tucson Survey of 1965–66, conducted by the National Education Association, publicized the educational plight of Mexican American children in the Southwest. Typically, students were subjected to sink-or-swim schooling in a language and culture foreign to them and, often, were punished for speaking their native Spanish. Moreover, the stigma of limited English proficiency was compounded by the stigma of poverty. Many of these children were dropping out of school; many who remained were judged to be failing. But the Tucson Survey concluded that it was the schools that were failing the children, by ignoring or inadequately addressing the language barrier. There must be a better way, the N.E.A. believed, and it held a series of conferences to explore the alternative of bilingual education. Attending one of these gatherings, Senator Ralph Yarborough, a Texas Democrat, became intrigued by the idea of instructing children in their native language while they were learning English. On returning to Washington, he sponsored legislation to provide federal aid for schools experimenting with bilingual approaches. What follow are excerpts from Senator Yarborough's speech on January 17, 1967, in which he introduced legislation that became the Bilingual Education Act.

In the Southwestern part of the United States—bordered by my state of Texas on the east, California on the west, and reaching to Colorado in the north—there exists, as in the rest of the country, a folklore that we have achieved equality of economic opportunity, that everyone has an equal chance to succeed. The reality lurking under this belief is that for a group of 3,465,000 persons, 12 percent of the population of the Southwestern states, equality of economic opportunity awaits the future. It is a myth, and not a reality, today for the Mexican Americans of the Southwest.

The Spanish-speaking people of the United States at one time greatly outnumbered the English-speaking people in the area. By 1790 the white population had reached 23,000 and was practically all Spanish. But by 1848 all the land in the Southwest—except for a strip later added by the Gadsden Purchase—had been acquired by the United States, and the one-time majority of Spanish-speaking people became a minority in the face of the influx of English-speaking people who flocked to the land. With minority status came economic disadvantage. And exploitation. And discrimination. But throughout all these years, the Mexican American people have lived their lives with patience and courage. Equality of opportunity has not been theirs, yet they have been good citizens, good parents, have fought for democracy in our wars, and lived their lives as best they could.

I believe the time has come when we can no longer ignore the fact that 12 percent of the people of the Southwestern United States do not have equal access with the rest of the population to economic advancement. The time has come when we must do something about the poor schooling, low health standards, job discrimination, and the many other artificial barriers that stand in the way of the advancement of the Mexican American people along the road to economic equality.

The most promising area for progress is in the field of education. Here Mexican Americans have been the victims of the cruelest form of discrimination. Little children, many of whom enter school knowing no English and speaking only Spanish are denied the use of their language. Spanish is forbidden to them, and they are required to struggle along as best they can in English, a language understood dimly by most and not at all by many.

Thus the Mexican American child is wrongly led to believe from his first day of school that there is something wrong with him, because of his language. This misbelief soon spreads to the image he has of his culture, of the history of his people, and of his people themselves. This is a subtle and cruel form of discrimination because it indelibly imprints upon the consciousness of young children an attitude which they will carry with them all the days of their lives. Its effects can be perceived by looking at the dropout rates among Mexican American children. Among adults twenty-five and over, Mexican Americans in 1960 had an average of 7.1 years of schooling as compared to the 12.1 years for Anglos, and 9 years for nonwhites.

The time for action is upon us. I am introducing today the Bilingual American Education Act. Its declaration of policy reads as follows:

> In recognition of the special educational needs of the large numbers of students in the United States whose mother tongue is Spanish and to whom English is a foreign language, Congress hereby declares it to be the policy of the United States to provide financial assistance to local educational agencies to develop and carry out new and imaginative elementary and secondary school programs designed to meet these educational needs.

In addition to Mexican American students, those of Puerto Rican descent would be eligible.[3] Activities such as bilingual educational programs, the teaching of Spanish as the native language, the teaching of English as a second language, programs designed to impart to Spanish-speaking students a knowledge of and pride in their ancestral culture and language, efforts to attract and retain as teachers promising individuals of Mexican or Puerto Rican descent, efforts to establish closer cooperation between the school and the home,

3. Editor's note: Before final passage, the scope of Yarborough's bill was broadened to authorize aid to instructional programs serving any group of "children of limited-English-speaking ability"—not just Spanish speakers—who came largely from households receiving welfare payments or earning less than $3,000 per year; P.L. 90–247 (Jan. 2, 1968). In 1974 the poverty criterion was essentially dropped. Also, a requirement was added that all programs receiving federal aid must feature some form of native-language instruction (although, as a practical matter, no _nonbilingual_ project had ever been funded under the Bilingual Education Act). A decade later this provision of the law would prove controversial. See Arnold H. Leibowitz, _The Bilingual Education Act: A Legislative Analysis_ (Rosslyn, Va.: National Clearinghouse for Bilingual Education, [1980]).

and other activities which meet the purposes of the bill, could be carried out.

This is not a general aid bill to all schools with Mexican American students. Rather, it is a bill which will enable many schools to make the large expenditures required to substantially revamp their courses. These schools will be able to experiment, try new things, blaze new trails, and demonstrate to other schools what might be done. Compared to the minor shot in the arm which most schools are receiving from Title I of the Elementary and Secondary Education Act, the Bilingual American Education Act will be a major transfusion of new blood. Schools which are selected for the program will receive the resources they need to do a real job. And I hope that the example they set will influence other schools to follow their lead.

The existence within our borders of a sizable group of people who speak the same language and share many of the same traditions and much of the outlook of the countries of Latin America has considerable relevance to our future Latin American foreign policy. If America stands for anything, it is for the principle that we have something of relevance to say to so many of the nations on earth precisely because we are made up of immigrants from those nations. So, in our dealings with Latin American nations, how much more sensible it would be to make better use of the Americans who speak Spanish as a native language and who understand from within the outlook of our southern neighbors. We have a magnificent opportunity to do a very sensible thing—to enable naturally bilingual children to grow up speaking both good Spanish and good English, and thereby to be in a position to go forth confidently to deal with the world, rather than retreat in embarrassment from a world which speaks a language which they can understand only imperfectly.

Teaching in the Mother Tongue

By A. Bruce Gaarder

A. Bruce Gaarder was chief of the Modern Language Section, U.S. Office of Education, when he gave the following testimony in support of the Bilingual Education Act. His views are representative of the linguistic and pedagogical arguments advanced at a time of limited experience, but growing interest, in alternatives to sink-or-swim instruction. (Notwithstanding arguments over details of the legislation, in 1967 there was virtually no opposition to federal support for bilingual education.) Gaarder's remarks are excerpted from U.S. Senate, Committee on Labor and Public Welfare, Special Subcommittee on Bilingual Education, *Hearings on S. 428*, 90th Congress, 1st Session (May 18, 1967), pp. 50–54.

Bilingualism can be either a great asset or a great liability. In our schools millions of youngsters have been cheated or damaged or both by well-intentioned, but ill-informed educational policies which have made of their bilingualism an ugly disadvantage in their lives. The object of this testimony is to show the nature of the damage that has been done and suggest how it can be remedied in the future.

Bilingual education means the use of both English and another language—usually the child's mother tongue—as mediums of instruction in the schools. It is not "foreign language teaching," but rather the use of each language to teach all of the school curriculum (except, of course, the other language itself). There are five main reasons which support bilingual education. The first three apply to the child's years in the elementary school:

> 1. Children who enter school with less competence in English than monolingual English-speaking children will probably become retarded in their school work to the extent of their deficiency in English. On the other hand, the bilingual child's conceptual development and acquisition of other experience and information could proceed at a normal rate if the mother tongue were used as an alternate medium of instruction. Retardation is not likely if there is only one or very few non-English-speaking children in an entire school. It is almost inevitable if the non-English language is spoken by large groups of children.
> 2. Non-English-speaking children come from non-English-speaking homes. The use of the child's mother tongue by some of the teachers and as a school language is necessary if there is to be a strong, mutually reinforcing relationship between the home and the school.
> 3. Language is the most important exteriorization or manifestation of the self, of the human personality. If the school, the all-powerful school, rejects the mother tongue of an entire group of children, it can be expected to affect seriously and adversely those children's concept of their parents, their homes, and themselves.

The two other reasons apply when the bilingual child becomes an adult:

4. If he has not achieved reasonable literacy in his mother tongue—ability to read, write, and speak it accurately—it will be virtually useless to him for any technical or professional work where language matters. Thus, his unique potential career advantage, his bilingualism, will have been destroyed.

5. Our people's native competence in Spanish and French and Czech and all the other languages and the cultural heritage each language transmits are a national resource that we need badly and must conserve by every reasonable means.

There is a vast body of writing by educators who believe that bilingualism is a handicap. The evidence seems at first glance to be obvious and incontrovertible. There is a clear, direct-chain relationship between language competence, formal education, and economic status among Americans whose mother tongue is not English. The children speak Spanish, or Navajo, or French, and they do poorly in school. Therefore (so goes the argument), their bilingualism is to blame. Many researchers have established a decided correlation between bilingualism and low marks on intelligence tests, but what no research has shown is that bilingualism, per se, is a *cause* of low performance on intelligence tests. On the contrary, studies which have attempted to take into account all of the factors which enter the relationship show that it is not the fact of bilingualism, but *how* and *to what extent* and *under what conditions* the two languages are taught that make the difference. (If this were not true, how could one explain the fact that the governing and intellectual elite in all countries have sought to give their children bilingual or even multilingual education?) Much of the literature on bilingual education does not deal at all with bilingual education. Rather, it shows the unfortunate results when the child's mother tongue is ignored, deplored, or otherwise degraded.

Two McGill University psychologists, Elizabeth Peal and Wallace Lambert, have shown that if the bilingualism is "balanced," that is, if there has been something like equal, normal literacy developed in the two languages, bilingual ten-year-olds in Montreal are markedly superior to monolinguals on verbal and nonverbal tests of intelligence and appear to have greater mental flexibility, a superiority in concept formation, and a more diversified set of mental abilities.[4] It is their judgment that there is no evidence that the supposed "handicap" of

4. Editor's note: The methodology of this study, "The Relation of Bilingualism to Intelligence," *Psychological Monographs* 76 (1962), has come under criticism; see Kenji Hakuta, *Mirror of Language* (New York: Basic Books, 1986), pp. 35–41. Hakuta's own research, however, provides evidence of a link between "balanced" bilingualism and nonverbal intelligence.

bilingualism is *caused* by bilingualism, per se, and that "it would be more fruitful to seek that cause in the inadequacy of the measuring instrument and in other variables such as socioeconomic status, attitude toward the two languages, and educational policy and practice regarding the teaching of both languages."

There is an educational axiom, accepted virtually everywhere else in the world, that *the best medium for teaching a child is his mother tongue.* What happens when the mother tongue is so used? A recent study made in Chiapas, Mexico, by Dr. Nancy Modiano for the New York University School of Education shows the results that can be expected. The Modiano research examined the hypothesis (implicit in current educational policies throughout the United States) that children of linguistic minorities learn to read with greater comprehension when all reading instruction is offered through a second language than when they learn to read first in their mother tongue.[5]

The investigation involved all students attending twenty-six schools in three Indian *municipios* in Chiapas. All students were native speakers of either Tzeltal or Tzotzil, two of the indigenous languages of Mexico. Thirteen were federal or state schools in which all reading instruction was offered in Spanish. Thirteen were National Indian Institute schools in which literacy was developed in the mother tongue prior to being attempted in Spanish. The purpose of the study was to determine which group of schools produced the greater measure of literacy in the national language, Spanish. Two indications of reading comprehension were obtained. First, all teachers were asked to designate "all of your students who are able to understand what they read in Spanish." Approximately 20 percent of the students in the all-Spanish schools and approximately 37 percent of the students in the bilingual schools were nominated by their teachers as being able to understand what they read in Spanish. Second, a carefully devised group reading comprehension test was administered to all of the selected children. The children's average score in state and federal schools was 41.59; in the bilingual Institute schools it was 50.30. Within each of the three *municipios*, mean scores in the Institute schools were higher than in federal and state schools. Thus, not only did the teachers using the bilingual approach nominate more of their students for testing, but their judgment was confirmed by the fact that their students scored significantly higher on the group test of reading comprehension.[6]

5. Nancy Modiano, "A Comparative Study of Two Approaches to the Teaching of Reading in the National Language" (Ph.D. diss., New York University, 1966).

6. In the first comparison, the difference favored the bilingual approach beyond the .001 level of probability; in the second, the difference between means was significant at the .01 level.

The establishment of bilingual education programs in our schools could be expected to increase and improve, rather than lessen, emphasis on the proper teaching of English to children who speak another mother tongue. Under our present policy, which supports the ethnocentric illusion that English is not a "foreign" language for anyone in this country, it is almost always taught as if the bilingual child already knew English. Our failure to recognize the mother tongue, and thus to present English *as a second language*, helps to produce "functional illiteracy" in almost three out of every four Spanish speakers in Texas.

In a bilingual education program, English would be taught from the child's first day in school, but his concept development, his acquisition of information and experience—in sum, his total *education*—would not depend on his imperfect knowledge of English. Bilingual education permits making a clear distinction between education and language, that is, between the content of education and the vehicle through which it is acquired.

Aquí No Se Habla Español

By Rubén Salazar

Rubén Salazar (1928–70), news director of KMEX-TV in Los Angeles and a columnist for the *Los Angeles Times*, was killed by police while covering the Chicano Moratorium on August 29, 1970. This article is excerpted from a monograph he authored for the U.S. Commission on Civil Rights, *Stranger in One's Land* (Washington, D.C.: U.S. Government Printing Office, 1970). It summarizes the findings of a Commission hearing held in San Antonio, Texas, in December 1968.

You know it almost from the beginning: speaking Spanish makes you different. Your mother, father, brothers, sisters, and friends all speak Spanish. But the bus driver, the teacher, the policeman, the store clerk, the man who comes to collect the rent—all the people who are doing important things—do not. Then the day comes when your teacher—who has taught you the importance of many things—tells you that speaking Spanish is wrong. You go home, kiss your mother, and say a few words to her in Spanish. You go to the window and look out and your mother asks you what's the matter?

Nada, mama, you answer, because you don't know what is wrong.

Howard A. Glickstein, acting staff director of the Commission on Civil Rights asked witness Edgar Lozano, a San Antonio high school student, whether he has ever been punished for speaking Spanish at school. Yes, in grammar, in junior high, and in senior high schools, he answers. "They took a stick to me," says Edgar. "It really stayed in your mind. Some things, they don't go away as easy as others."

Edgar relates with some bitterness and anger the times he was beaten by teachers for speaking Spanish at school after "getting a lecture about, if you want to be an American, you have got to speak English." Glickstein tries to ask Edgar another question, and the boy, this time more sad than angry, interrupts and says:

> I mean, how would you like for somebody to come up to you and tell you what you speak is a dirty language? You know, what your mother speaks is a dirty language. You know, that is the only thing I ever heard at home. A teacher comes up to you and tells you, "No, no. You know that is a filthy language, nothing but bad words and bad thoughts in that language." I mean, they are telling you that your language is bad. . . . Your mother and father speak a bad language, you speak a bad language. I mean you communicate with dirty words, and nasty ideas. . . . That really stuck to my mind.

Edgar, like many Mexican Americans before him, had been scarred with the insults of an Anglo world which rejects everything except carbon copies of what it has decreed to be "American." You start being different and you end up being labeled as un-American. An Anglo-oriented school in a Mexican American barrio can do things to the teachers, too. Bad communication can sorely twist the always sensitive relation between teacher and pupil.

Under questioning from David Rubin, the Commission's acting general counsel, W. Dain Higdon, principal of San Antonio's Hawthorne Junior High School, 65 percent Mexican American, asserted that he felt there was something in the background or characteristics of the Mexican Americans which inhibits high achievement. Mexicans or Mexican Americans, Higdon told the Commission, have a "philosophical concept" in dealing with life which says *lo que Dios quiera,* "what God wishes." An Anglo, on the other hand, says "in God we trust," not "this is how it shall be and you are limited," Higdon continued. "Whenever some situation befalls me [as an Anglo], I say it is my fault. Whenever some situation befalls a Mexican American, he may say it is his fault, but more generally and from a heritage standpoint, he would be inclined to say, *lo que Dios quiera.*"

> Rubin: Would it be fair to say that you feel there are genetic factors involved which account for the differences in achievements, that mixture of genes causes differences in people?
> Higdon: Well, when you were in my office, I made that statement to you and I will stick by it. . . .

The Mexican American child learns early that he is different. Then he learns that speaking Spanish prevents his becoming a good American. It's at this time, perhaps, when he most needs sensitive guidance. Yet, how do some teachers see the role of their profession?

> Rubin: Did you state in an interview with me and another staff member that the obligations of the teacher were first to complete paperwork and secondly to maintain discipline?
> Higdon: Yes, sir, I did.
> Rubin: And thirdly, to teach?
> Higdon: Yes, sir.

What can a school, in which teacher and student speak not only different languages, but are also on different emotional wave lengths, do to a Mexican American child? This kind of school, Dr. Jack Forbes of Berkeley's Far West Laboratory for Educational Research and Development, told the Commission,

> tends to lead to a great deal of alienation, a great deal of hostility; it tends to lead also to a great deal of confusion, where the child comes out of that school really not knowing who he is, not knowing what he should be proud of, not knowing what language he should speak other than English, being in doubt as to whether he should completely accept what Anglo people have been telling him and forget his Mexican identity, or whether he should listen to what his parents and perhaps other people have said and be proud of his Mexican identity.

Distortion of or deletion of Mexicans' contribution to the Southwest in history books can inhibit a Mexican American child from the beginning of his schooling. State Senator Joe Bernal of Texas told the Commission that the "schools have not given us any reason to be proud" of being Mexican Americans. People running the schools "have tried to take away our language," the senator continued, and so Mexican American children very early are made to feel ashamed of the Spanish language and of being Mexican.

The children start building up defenses such as insisting on being called "Latin" or "Hispano" or "Spanish American" because, said Bernal, "they want no reference made to being Mexican." One of the reasons for this, he told the Commission, is that "it has been inculcated" in the minds of grammar school children that the Mexican "is no good," by means of, for instance, overly and distortedly emphasizing the Battle of the Alamo and ignoring all contributions made by Mexicans in the Southwest.

To be Spanish, of course, is something else. Spanish has a European connotation and Europe is the motherland. Carey McWilliams in his *North from Mexico* explains that

> the Hispanic heritage of the Southwest has two parts: the Spanish and the Mexican-Indian. Originally one heritage, unified in time, they have long since been polarized. Carefully distinguished from the Mexican, the Spanish heritage is now enshrined throughout the Southwest. It has become the sacred or templar tradition of which the Mexican-Indian inheritance is the secular or profane counterpart. . . .

Aurelio Manuel Montemayor, who taught in San Felipe High School at Del Rio, Texas, explained to the Commission how in his view all this is ignored in the school curriculum. Quoting from a state-approved textbook, Montemayor said the book related how "the first comers to America were mainly Anglo-Saxons, but soon came the Dutchmen, Swedes, Germans, Frenchmen, Africans, then the great nineteenth-century period of immigration added to our already melting pot. Then later on, it [the textbook] said, the Spaniards came."

"So my students," continued Montemayor, "had no idea where they came from" and wondered whether "they were part of American society." This frustrated Montemayor so much that he told his students, "let's see if we can write our own textbook." He instructed them to write papers on the subject, Who Am I? "They told me in their words," Montemayor said, "that they were inferior to the standards of this country. That no matter how much they tried, they could never be blonds and blue-eyed."

While this part of the hearing was intended to probe into the educational problems of Mexican Americans in the Southwest, something just as important emerged from the testimony: the Anglo children (and, for that matter, the Negroes) had been cheated also—they had not been permitted to take advantage of the Southwest's cultural and language heritage. This became clear when Harold C. Brantley, superintendent of the United Consolidated School District of Webb County, Texas, explained his district's bilingual program.

It should be noted that the United States' first full-fledged bilingual program in public schools was not initiated in the Southwest, where its need had been apparent for generations, but in Florida—following the Cuban crisis. It was in Florida that Brantley got some ideas for the bilingual program in his school district. The philosophy behind his approach, Brantley told the Commission, was that "I don't feel like a kid's ability to speak Spanish is a detriment. I think that it is an asset. . . . It is merely our responsibility as educators to turn this asset that these kids bring to us, where it not only becomes an asset to them, but can become an asset to the little blue-eyed, blond-haired Anglo."

Brantley's district is made up of the larger part of the rural area of Webb County—some 2,400 square miles—and does not include the county's largest city, Laredo. The district has 987 students, 47 percent of them Mexican American and 53 percent Anglo. Without waiting for more research, specialized teachers, bilingual instructional materials, or substantial financial resources, Brantley in 1964 persuaded his staff, Anglo and Mexican American parents, and the Texas Education Agency to begin a bilingual program in his bicultural district. Today, in the district's three elementary schools, instruction is 50 percent in Spanish and 50 percent in English in the first through the fifth grades.

"I am not a linguist," Brantley explained to the Commission. "My sole service is creating [an] atmosphere where things can happen." Brantley said his program does not ignore the fact that it is very important for schools to facilitate Mexican American children "getting into the mainstream of the dominant culture and the dominant language of the country." By the same token, he continued: "We also try to stress to that child who comes from this other culture, speaking this other language [that] we want to provide him with the opportunity to improve upon his knowledge of his culture and his ability to function in his vernacular."

As for the Anglo child, Brantley said, his district tries "to create an atmosphere in the classroom where the children who come to us from the dominant culture, speaking the dominant language . . . recognize that here this little kid [Mexican American] has got something that [the Anglo] doesn't have, and that he ought to be interested in getting what this little kid can teach him." Warming to his subject, Brantley asked the Commission: "Now, can you begin to see what this does for the stature of this little kid that comes from this other culture with this other language? Where he is made to feel like he can do something that somebody can't do, and that he has something that this other little kid wants to learn about?" The Commission understood.

Affirmative Ethnicity

By Noel Epstein

Noel Epstein was an education writer for the _Washington
Post_ when he authored this early and influential critique of
federal policy on bilingual education. The Bilingual Education Act (also known as Title VII of the Elementary and
Secondary Education Act of 1965) was passed in 1968 and
reauthorized in 1974 with virtually no opposition. But by
1977 the climate had changed, with the federal Office for
Civil Rights aggressively enforcing the Supreme Court's
ruling in _Lau v. Nichols_ and requiring school districts to
adopt bilingual programs as a remedy for past civil rights
violations _(see pp. 245–47 and 251–55)_. Epstein questioned
the rationale for preferring bilingual education over other
instructional approaches. Also, he struck a sensitive nerve
on Capitol Hill with his criticism of minority-language
"maintenance" programs. The following year Congress
voted to terminate their eligibility for federal aid, restricting support to "transitional" bilingual programs. This article is excerpted from _Language, Ethnicity, and the Schools:
Policy Alternatives for Bilingual-Bicultural Education_ (Washington, D.C.: Institute for Educational Leadership, 1977).

A good deal of American social policy is based on what might be
called the Columbus Complex. This is the urge to sail off in a new
direction in the belief that, at some point, we are bound to bump into
something. The exploring spirit is, of course, a critical element of the
human drama, always to be encouraged. But problems arise when we
are unsure about which way we are headed or why.

This has long been the problem of the federal government's "bilingual-bicultural education" policy, which has been struggling to go in
two sharply different directions at the same time. Congress, the Department of Health, Education, and Welfare, and the courts have
sought to aim their efforts at low-achieving students who have little
or no command of English. Since enactment of the Bilingual Education Act of 1968, the U.S. Office of Education has been exploring ways
to help these pupils, concentrating on a technique known as _transi-
tional bilingual education_. The goal of this approach is to help students
keep up with reading, math, and other subjects in their native
tongues while they are taught enough English to transfer to regular

classrooms. After nearly nine years and more than half a billion dollars in federal funds, however, the government has not demonstrated
whether such instruction makes much difference in the students'
achievement, in their acquisition of English, or in their attitudes toward school.

This does not mean that the transitional bilingual technique itself
can be judged a failure. The uncertain results may in part reflect the
fact that bilingual projects have been poorly implemented, that qualified teachers and adequate curricula have been in short supply, and
that relatively little attention has been paid to project evaluations and
even less to seriously controlled research on individual projects. On
the other hand, the evidence never has given reason to believe that
bilingual instruction could "solve" the educational problems of these
children, many of whom have been falling badly behind in school or
dropping out altogether. The question is whether, to some undetermined degree, it can help, and whether other approaches would be
equally promising. There is as yet no answer.

Despite this uncertainty, Congress has rapidly expanded its commitment to bilingual education and also to bicultural instruction, in
which students are taught about their own ethnic groups. The Bilingual Education Act is funding 425 bilingual-bicultural projects in 68
languages and dialects in fiscal year 1977; about 80 percent of the projects are in Spanish, by far the most widely used non-English language
in the nation. As the General Accounting Office reported in 1976, this
effort, originally designed as an experiment, "has taken on the characteristics of an educational service program," even though the Office
of Education "has made little progress in achieving the program's
goals of identifying effective educational approaches, training bilingual education teachers, and developing suitable materials."

Separately, the Health, Education, and Welfare Department's Office
for Civil Rights (O.C.R.) has identified 334 school districts which may
have to begin bilingual-bicultural classes for students with English
language deficiencies or face a potential loss of all their federal school
aid. The O.C.R. policy is difficult to explain. This is not only because
of the absence of reliable evidence that such instruction would make
much difference in the students' achievement, but also because there
is no federal legal requirement for schools to provide bilingual or bicultural education.

The O.C.R. position stems from an interpretation of civil rights law
which was upheld by the Supreme Court in a 1974 ruling, *Lau v. Nichols*. The court affirmed that schools must do something special for
these pupils. But it neither required bilingual education as the remedy, nor favored it over other approaches, and it did not deal at all
with bicultural instruction. O.C.R. nevertheless has told school dis-

tricts that if they are found in violation of *Lau*, they must provide bilingual-bicultural education for the bulk of the affected students—unless the school districts can prove that another approach would be "effective to cure the violation."[7] If the national government has spent more than half a billion dollars without demonstrating the effectiveness of bilingual-bicultural education, it seems fair to ask how a local school district can be expected to prove that another approach would be effective.

A more fundamental question raised by both congressional and O.C.R. policies is whether they are indeed carefully aimed at or reaching the target students. Definitions of eligible children under both policies are broad enough to include many pupils who actually are proficient in English, though they may also speak another language. Students have been admitted to bilingual programs based on their surnames, Census Bureau data, and other grounds which do not necessarily measure a pupil's proficiency in speaking, understanding, reading, and writing English. A federally sponsored study of thirty-eight bilingual projects for Hispanic Americans, in fact, reported that teachers judged about 70 percent of their pupils to be dominant in English, not Spanish, for test-taking purposes. While teacher judgments are not considered accurate measures of language dominance—the actual figure could be lower or higher—no generally accepted and validated tests have been developed to compare pupil proficiency in speaking, understanding, reading, and writing different languages. This is another hindrance to effective bilingual policy. It is self-evident, however, that using limited funds for children who are sufficiently fluent in English to learn in that language takes these resources from pupils who cannot learn in English and who therefore are most in need.

It is also clear that bilingual-bicultural advocates *want* to provide such instruction to students who are proficient in English. They oppose using the native language only temporarily as a bridge into English instruction. Rather, they long have sought to give equal importance to the mother tongue and culture, pressing for what are called language and cultural "maintenance" programs. In these, students

7. Editor's note: After O.C.R.'s informal *Lau* Remedies were challenged in federal court, the Department of Health, Education, and Welfare agreed to go through the formal process of rulemaking to clarify school districts' obligations toward language-minority children. Issued in early 1981, the *Lau* Regulations would have mandated bilingual instruction in cases where a sufficient number of limited-English-proficient spoke the same minority language. But the regulations were withdrawn by the incoming Reagan administration. No revised version was ever issued, leaving O.C.R. to rely on court precedents such as *Castañeda v. Pickard* in its efforts to enforce civil rights law (see pp. 247–50).

continue to learn partly in their native tongue and about their ethnic group, even if they can function in the English curriculum. Many social and educational justifications have been given for this second, sharply different approach to bilingual-bicultural education. But beneath almost all of them is the idea that the federal government should finance and promote pupil attachments to their ethnic languages and histories while the students also go through the normal process of learning the common English language and the common national history. This approach reflects a philosophy which might be called *affirmative ethnicity.*

This philosophy has stirred continuous debate within the government, and it long has woven its way in and out of federal policy. In Congress the issue of whether Washington could finance maintenance programs was left ambiguous when the Bilingual Education Act authorization was renewed in 1974. In projects funded under the Act, there clearly have been maintenance efforts at least through elementary school, as evidenced both by the large numbers of English-dominant students reported in such classrooms and by the overwhelming determination of project directors to maintain the pupils' mother tongues and cultures. In civil rights enforcement, O.C.R. has told school districts that it is "acceptable" to correct the students' English deficiencies by also maintaining their native languages and cultures. And in the city involved in the Supreme Court's *Lau* decision, San Francisco, a consent decree has resulted in a court order to implement a language and cultural maintenance program.

Beyond the fact that money spent for these purposes takes limited resources from children who are most in need, the maintenance movement has raised profound social issues. Separating students temporarily in basic skills classes in the native language until they can learn English, for example, can be justified on both compensatory education and civil rights grounds. But keeping students and teachers segregated to maintain the native language and culture cannot be so justified, and the evidence indicates that most maintenance efforts are highly segregated. This is distressing observers both inside and outside the bilingual movement. They worry variously about educational consequences, social separation, and the possibility that the maintenance movement might lead to bitter linguistic politics.

An irony of the drive for maintenance programs is that, if they were to succeed, they would be just as likely to help erode native languages and cultures in this country as to nourish them. If students with English difficulties were to become well educated in English, as well as in their native tongues, most probably would find English the more useful language in our 96 percent English-speaking society, and there would likely be a steady attrition in use of the native tongue. That has been the pattern in this country and elsewhere. Transitional programs, of course, would have the same effect, only sooner and more surely. This obviously is a premature concern at this time, given the absence of reliable evidence that bilingual programs produce students who are well educated in English or in the native language. But some scholars within the movement have been warning that only strenuous efforts to reinforce cultural and language "pluralism" in the wider community can protect the ethnic language and culture from erosion. Concepts of such societal "pluralism" range all the way from bilingualism in local newspapers and television to a possible need for an Official Languages Act on the Canadian model to recognize Spanish as an official language of this country.

Some observers doubt that Hispanic Americans are that committed to protecting their language and cultures, seeing them as more determined to increase their economic and political power and prestige. There is no question that bilingual-bicultural policy has been governed in large measure by the quest of discriminated-against minority groups, and particularly Hispanic Americans, for more power, prestige, and jobs. The policy, in fact, has become perhaps the largest federally funded expression in this country of the ethnic political wave that has been sweeping the globe. Where it ultimately will lead politically, socially, economically, educationally, or culturally is unclear. At this point the policy is still seeking to go in two different directions, and in either case it has raised questions about how deeply Washington should be involved in determining the most socially sensitive aspects of the local school curriculum, language, and history, and about how united or divided ethnic group members themselves are on the many issues involved. One state-funded bilingual program in Chicago, for example, set Greek American parents bitterly against each other.

The basic task before policymakers is to clarify the policy's direction. If the federal government is seeking to discover the best ways to help students who are disadvantaged in English and who are doing poorly in school, a number of alternative courses are available to Congress, the executive branch, and the courts. The first, for all three branches, would be tight definitions of eligible children to ensure that resources reach those who are most in need. This would require a generally accepted definition of the degree of English proficiency needed to learn in English. It also would require written and oral language dominance tests to determine whether a student is better equipped to learn in the native language or English. These tests could be developed under the Bilingual Education Act. Much, in fact, depends upon what is done under that statute.

This law, it has been suggested, originally was needed to force school districts to stop neglecting or abusing children who had little or no command of English. If that was the case, the Supreme Court's *Lau* decision ended that need; schools now *must* provide special instruction to these pupils. The problem is that it cannot be said with confidence what kinds of instruction would offer the most educational opportunity to different students. If the Bilingual Education Act program had concentrated research on this question, some important answers might have emerged by now. But instead, the program has provided discretionary grants to hundreds of local projects in the hope that local evaluations would turn up models which others could emulate—a good example of the Columbus Complex at work. Most of the local evaluations have been of little or no use. Logic suggests— and the Office of Education has proposed—that what is needed is carefully controlled "planned variation" research. The object of such research is not to discover whether a single educational technique "works," but to compare the benefits of different approaches.

The available evidence indicates that, in addition to transitional bilingual instruction, two other approaches deserve careful testing. One would be special, sensitively applied English "immersion" programs. Special immersion techniques—far different from merely putting students in a "sink or swim" situation—have proved successful for English-speaking students in Canada and in two United States schools. Beginning in kindergarten, the students have been taught in a language which initially was foreign to them, with their native tongue later introduced as a separate subject. In basic skills the students have generally done as well as or better than English speakers learning in English; they also have acquired a near-native command of the second language and have done as well in the English language itself as those learning in English. Several researchers have indicated that similar techniques could be sensitively applied to children who speak a minority language, and there appears to be no reason why they should not be tested.[8]

The second approach calls for the curriculum to be made compatible with a student's language, culture, race, and socioeconomic class.

8. Editor's note: The researchers who designed and evaluated Canada's French immersion programs, an "additive" approach aimed at cultivating bilingualism, have vehemently opposed the use of immersion as a "subtractive" strategy for making monolingual English speakers out of language-minority students in the United States. See Wallace E. Lambert, "An Overview of Issues in Immersion Education," in *Studies on Immersion Education: A Collection for United States Educators* (Sacramento: California State Office of Bilingual Bicultural Education, 1984); and G. Richard Tucker, "Implications of Canadian Research for Promoting a Language Competent American Society," in Joshua A. Fishman et al., *The Fergusonian Impact*, vol. 2, *Sociolinguistics and the Sociology of Language* (Berlin: Mouton de Gruyter, 1986).

Considerable sentiment in the bilingual-bicultural movement has centered on this and related theories, and the ideas should be tested to determine the effect on pupil achievement and on the acquisition of English.

O.C.R. and the courts essentially are in the same position of not having reliable evidence about which approaches can provide the most educational opportunity. In addition, O.C.R. has a limited compliance staff, and the courts have been wary of becoming involved in curriculum decisions. This suggests similar alternatives for both of them. One would be to require affected school districts to offer a variety of approaches and allow individual parents to choose from among them. Parents and their children, after all, are the ones directly affected. Until reliable evidence is available, individual parent choice would appear to provide a greater degree of fairness than the imposition of one technique or another by government. The alternative techniques would have to be carefully explained to the parents. The options offered would have to include assessments of local resources available to meet each choice. Experience suggests that badly implemented bilingual programs, like badly implemented programs of any kind, can provide a poorer quality education than that of the more traditional school program.

The picture changes sharply if language and cultural maintenance programs are the goal. In this case limited resources would not be concentrated on children who cannot function effectively in English. The federal government would assume a responsibility to maintain other languages and cultures regardless of a student's degree of fluency in English.

Going in this direction raises many issues, all of which deserve extensive and careful debate. For one thing, advocates would have to clarify what they mean by "maintenance" programs. Among the many reasons given for such efforts, supporters have argued that it makes no sense to ignore the native language abilities of these pupils once they learn English—and then require them to study language as a subject in later grades. This is an important point. But if developing and maintaining literacy in the native language is the goal, that would not require giving the native tongue the kind of equal status in the curriculum envisioned by many bilingual-bicultural supporters. It could be accomplished by continuing to teach these pupils one or two classes in the native language for the rest of their school careers. Moreover, any federal funds needed for this purpose, as well as for second-language "immersion" programs for English-speaking children, could be legislated separately or be provided under the National Defense Education Act if that statute should be extended again.[9]

This approach would define maintenance programs as a way of sustaining and building valuable national language resources, opening other worlds to all. It would raise no serious social or political issues. It would be administratively feasible. And it would not divert any Bilingual Education Act funds from children who cannot learn in English.

Bilingual backers, however, have not been content with the idea of maintenance programs as a way to build language resources. They have stressed their views of language "pluralism" and cultural "democracy," pressing for federal financing and promotion of ethnic identities through more extensive use of the native language and culture in the schools. This does raise social, political, and other issues, and they would have to be thoroughly examined. The central issue would not be the unquestioned importance of ethnicity in individuals' lives, any more than it would be the unquestioned importance of religion in individuals' lives. Nor would it be about the right or the desirability of groups to maintain their languages and cultures. The question would be the federal role. Is it a federal responsibility to finance and promote student attachments to their ethnic languages and cultures, jobs long left to families, religious groups, ethnic organizations, private schools, ethnic publications, and others?

Would this lead to better or worse relations between groups? In addition to the racial and ethnic segregation found in many bilingual programs, there has been a sharp rivalry among groups for limited federal funds distributed on the basis of ethnicity. Would it result in better or worse relations *within* groups? There are as many cultural, class, ideological, religious, and other divisions within groups as there are between them. Would it promote ethnic "conformity" rather than cultural "democracy," as some critics suggest? One bilingual supporter has assailed discrimination by Spanish-speaking educators against children who speak some of the many different Spanish dialects used in this country. Would it result in a poorer quality education for these pupils and a neglect of the English skills they need to compete in the job market? Another scholar within the movement found this to be the case in maintenance programs he visited in the Northeast. Would language become a major point of cleavage in state and local politics in many areas, in educational institutions, job qualifications, and general social relations? One critic believes this possibility

9. Editor's note: This 1958 law, passed in the wake of *Sputnik*, authorized the first federal subsidies to support foreign language instruction.

must be seriously considered. Should the government role be to promote teaching of "each about every" rather than "you about yours"? That has long been a goal of educators and integrationists who have sought to foster greater respect and tolerance across groups.

Why is it the federal role to reinforce ethnic identities? Bilingual-bicultural supporters have offered a variety of reasons. Many advance claims of historical justice for groups that were conquered or that have suffered from severe discrimination in American society. Other advocates believe that maintenance programs would improve the general academic performance of students from these groups. This view rests on psychological benefits, on making students feel greater pride and acceptance and thereby increasing their eagerness to learn. There is scarcely any research evidence to support this view, but it is a strongly held article of faith among many bilingual-bicultural supporters.

Still others do not necessarily rely on historical justice claims or on beliefs about general education benefits. They support federal financing of maintenance programs in large part for the "enrichment" they believe these would provide to the society and to protect ethnic languages and cultures from erosion. The question is whether the potential benefits outweigh the potential costs. Would the result be more harmony or more discord in American society? What would we ultimately bump into?

An Educator's Rationale for Native-Language Instruction

By José A. Cárdenas

José A. Cárdenas is director of the Intercultural Development Research Association in San Antonio, Texas. This article originally appeared as "The Role of Native Language Instruction in Bilingual Education," *I.D.R.A. Newsletter*, January 1984, pp. 1–6.

There are few public issues today which produce such a range of diverse reactions as does bilingual education. Proponents for bilingual educational programs are strong and loud in their demands for it;

opponents are equally adamant against it. The reasons for support or opposition are so varied that one tends to lose sight of a pedagogical rationale in the heat of emotional, patriotic, racial, and other arguments. Criticisms of bilingual education stem from every type of person and every conceivable reason. Noel Epstein coined a new phrase, "affirmative ethnicity," to voice his opposition. Others criticize the violation of the official national language (there is none in this country), the dangers of language-minority separatism, unwillingness to learn and speak the English language, and the undesirable need for a crutch in the American and English-language culture. One even hears the perennial resurrection of the discredited "interference theory" (if they are allowed to speak their native language, it will interfere with the learning of English).

An uninformed observer would venture that part of the problem is the failure of proponents of bilingual education to present an adequate rationale, but such a viewpoint would be extremely naive. The rationale has been presented again and again in educational articles, in the media, in court decisions, and in legislation. The fact is that opponents of bilingual education seldom seem to go beyond the title in the formulation of negative responses. Opponents of bilingual education seldom use an accurate definition, a fair description, or factual information. In most cases the emotional response overshadows all rational considerations. Yet it would be remiss to allow those who peruse press releases, news coverage, and letters to the editor to form negative concepts on the basis of information presented solely by opponents of bilingual education. For that reason I am again presenting some arguments in favor of bilingual education and the educational reasons for the temporary use of native-language instruction.

Bilingual education came into favor as an alternative program in the late 1960s. Persons not around the educational scene in those days, and persons who were around but have short memories, need to be informed or reminded of the educational scenario at the advent of bilingual education. My first contact with second-language development occurred much earlier than that, in the middle 1930s. I was placed in an all-English first grade without an adequate knowledge of the English language. I still remember it, not as an uncomfortable, unpleasant, or challenging situation, but rather as a traumatic, disconcerting, terrorizing experience. This type of educational methodology can best be described as a sink-or-swim approach. A student either learned the English language fast and swam, or he failed to do so and sank. A recent newspaper article points out that some of us swam. That is true, but demographic evidence shows that over 80 percent sank. Furthermore, of the few that did not sink, many of them never really learned to swim; they just stayed in the water, not sinking, but unable to swim out.

It is interesting to note that those who swam grew up, almost without exception, in homes with strong language capability. Though this capability was usually in a language other than English, an unusually good language ability was present during the developmental years. This is as true for language-minority persons in the past who grew up to become congressmen, mayors, educators, and successful businessmen, as it is today for the Korean or Vietnamese children who are graduating as valedictorians. The common denominator invariably is extensive competence in some language.

Another personally significant event occurred in the 1950s, when I worked as a teacher, supervisor, and principal in Texas public schools. The performance of limited-English-proficient children in classes I taught constituted another traumatic experience. These children, who in any other way would be classified as normal, were unable to perform the most basic classroom activities. I joined the thousands of other teachers who experienced the frustration that, in spite of dedication, commitment, caring, and hard work, the instruction of language-minority children did not produce the same type of performance we took for granted with nonminority children.

Another memory pertains to the implementation of English-as-a-second-language programs in the early 1960s. The main difference between this approach and the earlier sink-or-swim approach was that a concerted effort was made at introducing the English language in a structured, nonthreatening context. As a result of this approach, the trauma of an early transition to a new language was reduced, though it is difficult to claim that this new methodology was clearly successful. Though the approach was vastly superior, it was evident that the child would suffer from cognitive discontinuity as basic and content learning were deferred until the student demonstrated a certain level of English language mastery. Although this became common educational practice, children in such programs were commonly one calendar year behind their English-speaking counterparts, and the development deficit tended to grow rather than to diminish in subsequent years.

By 1966 the frustrations associated with the instruction of limited-English-proficient children were intolerable for many. Language-minority students were dropping out of school at rates higher than 80 percent. Their performance as measured by standardized tests indicated achievement levels at an average of two grade levels below expectancy norms, and the English language programs had not met the anticipated promise. In addition, the civil rights movement had awakened the interests of minorities regarding the education of their children. Students and parents alike were demanding improved educational opportunities, while educators were at their wit's end in trying to cope with the growing pressures.

The compensatory education programs of the late 1960s and early 1970s did little for language-minority children. This was to have been expected, because such programs seldom went beyond giving students more of the inadequate approaches of the 1950s. The same methodologies which ill-served them six hours a day for nine months a year were extended for a couple of hours a day and the remaining three months of the year.

Thus it was that a group of concerned educators began to speak about alternative teaching strategies. One such program which surfaced at the time was a bilingual approach for the teaching of limited-English-proficient children. It is not sufficient to say that the bilingual approach was "accepted" in the late 1960s. It was welcomed, it was embraced, it was grasped as the proverbial straw which could prevent the continued drowning of limited-English-proficient children in the dark waters of our elementary and secondary schools. The traditional all-English approach, which is now being widely recommended as a new "alternative," was so bad that anything different was worth trying.

The original concept of utilizing a child's native language for instructional purposes while English was being learned was based primarily on the need for continued learning as the child moved from one language to another. Limited familiarity with the new language made it tenuous to attempt to develop reading skills without assurance that a sufficient mastery of English enabled the child to understand what was being read. The same was true in the acquisition of mathematical concepts and learning in the various content fields.

A second consideration was the need to diminish the alienation which children frequently faced when pushed into an unfamiliar language situation. Not only will use of the native language lessen the trauma of this transition, but it does much to develop or maintain a positive concept of self. The advent of bilingual programs indicated to the language minority child a new sense of acceptance. The school appeared to be saying: "I accept your language; therefore, I accept you. I accept your heritage, your culture, your family, your ethnicity." In contrast to previous school experiences, the language-minority child received a feeling of acceptance, worth, and self-esteem seldom experienced before.

I have seen several recent newspaper items which state that a positive self-concept should be the outcome of successful learning. In reality, there is a cyclic relationship between input and outcome. A negative self-concept is detrimental to learning, which in turn strengthens the negative self-concept, and so on. This produces a cumulative deficit phenomenon which leads children caught in this cycle to do worse and worse in school. On the other hand, a positive concept of self contributes to successful performance, which leads to an improved self-concept and more successful performance.

There is a third reason for the use of a native language in bilingual programs that received little recognition in the past, but now looms as the most important consideration. The use of language is imperative to the intellectual development of the child. The extent to which a person develops an intellectual capacity is very much dependent on the extent of language acquisition. This is not the same as the amount which an individual learns, but rather the amount of capability for learning which is developed.

Bruce Gaarder, an early advocate of bilingual education in the middle 1960s, used an effective analogy to illustrate this point. He compared the use of language to a window through which a person interacts with the environment. This "window" of language provides the experiences which produce learning. The bigger the window, the wider the panorama with which the child interacts; conversely, the smaller the window, the smaller the panorama. Gaarder then proceeded to compare submersion into an all-English curriculum to the closing of the window, eliminating the interaction of the child with the environment, thereby precluding any learning. Gaarder would relate the minority language to a blue window and the English language to a rose window. The language-minority child who had used the blue window for communicating with the environment would be placed in a closed room and would be told, "From now on, you may no longer use this blue window. You will learn to use the rose window in communicating with your environment." Thereupon, the blue window would be covered, and the child would stare at a blank wall. Occasionally, a child would say, "I don't see any rose window," and the school would respond, "that's because we haven't built it yet, but keep looking at the blank wall, and we will eventually place a rose window there." Staring at a blank wall does little to develop any learning, or the capacity for learning. Bilingual programs allow for continued learning, as well as the continued increase in the capacity for learning, as the transition to a new language is being made.

For some undetermined reasons, commentators on the education of language-minority children frequently appear obsessed with the concept of immediate transition to an all-English-language curriculum. Though the school should be concerned with the immediate and extensive development of English language usage, there are dangers in discontinuing the use of the native language too soon. One hears educators and laypersons recommending that the school should discontinue the utilization of the native language as soon as the child has a basic understanding of English. The danger in this practice is that a basic understanding of English is frequently determined by measures of the child's ability to communicate in social situations, which is far from the level of language utilization needed for learning activities.

A Hispanic member of the Texas University Coordinating Board expressed opposition to bilingual education on the basis that it can become a crutch for Hispanic children. Well, crutches are very useful implements when there is a need for them. Crutches can provide support until such time as the body overcomes trauma and can function without them. It is true that the use of crutches can be overextended beyond the time of need, but if one were to err in determining the time of need, most orthopedic specialists would likely prefer that the error be in favor of overuse rather than underuse. That same is true for native-language utilization.

The use of the native language does not preclude the learning of English; on the contrary, research shows that it enhances it. Therefore, rather than risk premature restriction of native-language use and the accompanying loss of language and communication capability, I would recommend continuation of native-language utilization until there is complete assurance of sufficient English-language mastery.

Each person at any point in time has a quantity of language which has been acquired over the years. This quantity of language has a close and cyclic relationship with intellect. People with high intelligence have a large language capacity; people with large language capacity develop high intelligence. A small portion of this language is rather superficial; that is, it is apparent, readily available, and commonly used in everyday social situations, such as, "I am fine, thank you. How are you?" Each person also has a much larger quantity of language which is more sophisticated, technical, and not commonly used in social situations. The relationship between these two types of language has been described as analogous to an iceberg where only the tip can be seen above the water, leaving the larger bulk well-hidden below the water line.

In learning situations the learner continuously uses language for discovery. In fact, the individual's entire language capacity may be utilized. Determining language development and the capacity for its use in learning on the basis of a working command of the superficial social aspects of language may be detrimental to the learner. The ability to communicate in a social situation does not guarantee the existence of the sophisticated, technical language necessary for coping with the learning situation.

Educators believe that at least six years of language development are desirable to allow children to acquire a minimal language reservoir before starting to learn basic skills in the first grade. Research shows that language-minority children may require several years in building the same minimal language reservoir before being able to cope with an all-English curriculum. Failure to allow sufficient language development before the transition will result in the child's being unable to cope with anything but the most shallow levels of learning and will affect the future capacity for learning.

The Miracle Worker is the story of Helen Keller's early life and her tutor's attempts to teach her the concept of language. Having a total loss of sight and hearing, Keller is living an animal-like existence, not even cognizant of the existence of language with which she can communicate with her outer world. The climax of the movie occurs when she realizes that the hand movements which her teacher has been trying to teach her constitute a method of interpersonal communication. In that scene we see Helen Keller leave her minimally human existence by acquiring the power of language and her transformation into an eager and voracious learner. The placement of a language-minority child into an all-English curriculum before sufficient English language mastery is like running *The Miracle Worker* in reverse. We take an eager and voracious learner and remove the power of language, thereby sentencing the child to an animal-like existence until such time as he or she acquires sufficient fluency in a different language.

The emerging science of language development substantiates this contention. As educators discover more and more about the role of language in the intellectual development of children, the rationale of bilingual education becomes stronger and stronger. Not only can we prevent academic retardation and negative self-concepts through the use of native-language instruction, but the whole future capability for learning can be effectively enhanced.

If the pedagogical evidence is so overwhelming, why is there so much opposition to bilingual education and the use of the native language in the classroom? The answer to this question cannot and does not rest in pedagogy. Without exception, all experts in language development and second-language acquisition concur regarding the advantages of native-language utilization. The reason must lie elsewhere. After reviewing scores of criticisms on the use of native-language instruction in bilingual education programs, I have concluded that they generally fall into three areas: emotional, misinformational, or attitudinal.

Emotional reactions range from Noel Epstein's "affirmative ethnicity" to the religious objection of Ma Ferguson: "If English was good enough for Jesus Christ, it ought to be good enough for the children of Texas." Unfortunately, there is little that can be done to diffuse these strong emotional reactions. If a true-blue American patriot feels it is un-American to speak a language other than English, there is little ground for rational argument. When I ask the question, "Which is less patriotic—to allow a child to develop his intellect using a language other than English or to allow a child to grow up deficient in all language and reasoning skills because of an English language limitation needlessly imposed?" the common response has been to perpetuate the limitation. It is no small wonder that so much of the implementation of bilingual education programs has come about as a result of equal protection litigation and civil rights legislation rather than because of public support.

If negative emotional responses are the main source of criticisms of bilingual programs, then misinformation must rank as a close second. The public media have consistently failed to give extensive coverage to what they perceive as educational, and therefore not very newsworthy, material. On the other hand, criticisms of bilingual education are considered controversial, interesting, and are given top coverage. A recent report on the shortcomings of bilingual education received front-page headlines in several prominent newspapers. But criticisms of the scandalous methodology used in the study received little or no coverage; if reported in the print media, the story was usually found in the back pages close to the classified ads.

It is not unusual for an article criticizing bilingual education to state or imply that native language is being used in lieu of English language acquisition. This is simply not so. An emotional writer in the *San Antonio Light* states: "In many instances, according to reliable published reports, [the] teachers [of limited-English-proficient children] are more dedicated to teaching them the correct and literary form of their native language than teaching them English." Again, this is not so. I have observed bilingual classrooms in at least twenty different states, and I have never seen teachers neglect the teaching of English in bilingual programs. I have reviewed hundreds of reports on bilingual programs from school districts, state education agencies, and the U.S. Department of Education and have never seen a report, let alone a reliable report, of the practice described in the article.

The emotional responses to bilingual education sometimes get so intense that they defy all reason. On two occasions I have read articles in which the writers object to the use of the phrase "English as a second language." The argument presented in both cases was that English is the greatest language on earth and therefore second to none. How does one argue with such an individual that the word "second" refers to chronological order?

The third area of criticism is a difficult subject to deal with. There are some hard-core opponents whose opposition is neither emotional nor pedagogical. Their opposition is based on past discriminatory attitudes about the place of racial and ethnic minorities and on the belief held by some that equal educational opportunity is not desirable. Some are saying that a basic command of the English language is sufficient and should be the desired educational outcome for language-minority children. They agree that it is well and good to afford these children an English-as-a second-language program which allows them to develop sufficient language and intellectual skills to understand and follow basic instructions, allows them to earn a decent living, and prevents them from becoming a social liability. But do not go so far as to develop language and intellectual skills to the point that it disrupts the social order. First thing you know, their children will be competing with our children for admission to medical schools, they will be seeking political offices, and they will be wanting managerial and supervisory positions. This attitude was manifested by the reaction of some community leaders to the introduction of Title I Migrant Education programs in the 1960s. Their viewpoint was expressed as, "If you give them so much education, they won't want to pick crops for a living."

A recent newspaper item critical of bilingual education also exemplified this attitude. The writer had visited a high school class made up of Asian immigrant children and observed that without native-language instruction the students appeared to be doing fine. She stated that they had a basic understanding of the English language and could communicate with each other in simple English. It seems to me that high school students are not supposed to be communicating in simple English; they are supposed to be communicating about algebra, geometry, physics, and social studies. They are supposed to be reaching near-adult levels of cognition, affective development, and aesthetic appreciation.

So much of the criticism of bilingual education comes from emotional responses, misinformation, and racist attitudes that one must make a conscious effort to look at criticism objectively. It is dangerous to formulate an immediate reaction without a constraining question: "Is the critic emotional, ignorant, or racist?" Yet the vast majority of criticism does fall into one or more of these basic classifications.

In spite of all the criticism being heard about the use of native-language instruction for language-minority children, I continue to be a strong advocate for this methodology. I see bilingual education as the best approach for teaching the English language without academic retardation, with the minimum development of negative concepts of self, and with the maximum development of the intellectual potential of the individual. As a professional educator who has worked with language-minority children since 1950, I have not found a better alternative. I will look into alternative approaches, although I see the current push for experimental alternative programs as more of an attempt to establish loopholes for complying with current law and regulations, rather than as serious educational experimentation. Current efforts to provide an alternative which consists of the traumatic and disastrous programs of the prebilingual era have not been, cannot be, and will not be acceptable to me. Bilingual education with native-language instruction still appears the best option for children with limited English proficiency.

The Romantic Trap of Bilingual Education

By Richard Rodríguez

Richard Rodríguez, a Mexican American writer, is best known for his 1982 autobiography, *Hunger of Memory*,[10] in which he recounts a painful struggle to learn English without bilingual education. Nevertheless, Rodríguez has become one of the most frequently quoted critics of native-language instruction. This article originally appeared as "Bilingualism, Con: Outdated and Unrealistic," *New York Times*, November 10, 1985, sec. 12, p. 83.

How shall we teach the dark-eyed child *inglés?* The debate continues much as it did two decades ago. Bilingual education belongs to the 1960s, the years of the black civil rights movement. Bilingual education became the official Hispanic demand; as a symbol, the English-only classroom was intended to be analogous to the segregated lunch counter, the locked school door. Bilingual education was endorsed by judges and, of course, by politicians well before anyone knew the an-

10. Boston: David R. Godine, 1982.

swer to the question: Does bilingual education work? Who knows? *Quién sabe?*

The official drone over bilingual education is conducted by educationists with numbers and charts. Because bilingual education was never simply a matter of pedagogy, it is too much to expect educators to resolve the matter. Proclamations concerning bilingual education are weighted at bottom with Hispanic political grievances and, too, with middle-class romanticism.

No one will say it in public; in private, Hispanics argue with me about bilingual education, and every time it comes down to memory. Everyone remembers going to that grammar school where students were slapped for speaking Spanish. Childhood memory is offered as parable; the memory is meant to compress the gringo's long history of offenses against Spanish, Hispanic culture, Hispanics.

It is no coincidence that, although all of America's ethnic groups are implicated in the policy of bilingual education, Hispanics, particularly Mexican Americans, have been its chief advocates. The English words used by Hispanics in support of bilingual education are words such as "dignity," "heritage," "culture." Bilingualism becomes a way of exacting from gringos a grudging admission of contrition—for the nineteenth-century theft of the Southwest, the relegation of Spanish to a foreign tongue, the injustice of history. At the extreme, Hispanic bilingual enthusiasts demand that public schools "maintain" a student's sense of separateness.

Hispanics may be among the last groups of Americans who still believe in the 1960s. Bilingual-education proponents still serve the romance of that decade, especially of the late sixties, when the heroic black civil rights movement grew paradoxically wedded to its opposite—the ethnic revival movement. Integration and separatism merged into twin, possible goals. With integration, the black movement inspired middle-class Americans to imitations—the Hispanic movement, the Gray Panthers, feminism, gay rights. Then there was a withdrawal, with black glamour leading a romantic retreat from the anonymous crowd. Americans came to want it both ways. They wanted in and they wanted out. Hispanics took to celebrating their diversity, joined other Americans in dancing rings around the melting pot.

More intently than most, Hispanics wanted the romance of their dual cultural allegiance backed up by the law. Bilingualism became proof that one could have it both ways, could be a full member of public America and yet also separate, privately Hispanic. "Spanish" and "English" became mythic metaphors, like country and city, describing separate islands of private and public life. Ballots, billboards, and of course, classrooms in Spanish. For nearly two decades now, middle-class Hispanics have had it their way. They have foisted a neat ideological scheme on working-class children. What they want to believe about themselves, they wait for the child to prove: that it is possible to be two, that one can assume the public language (the public life) of America, even while remaining what one was, existentially separate.

Adulthood is not so neatly balanced. The tension between public and private life is intrinsic to adulthood—certainly middle-class adulthood. Usually the city wins because the city pays. We are mass people for more of the day than we are with our intimates. No Congressional mandate or Supreme Court decision can diminish the loss.

I was talking the other day to a carpenter from Riga, in the Soviet Republic of Latvia. He has been here six years. He told me of his having to force himself to relinquish the "luxury" of reading books in Russian or Latvian so he could begin to read books in English. And the books he was able to read in English were not of a complexity to satisfy him. But he was not going back to Riga. Beyond any question of pedagogy, there is the simple fact that a language gets learned as it gets used, fills one's mouth, one's mind, with the new names for things.

The civil rights movement of the 1960s taught Americans to deal with forms of discrimination other than economic—racial, sexual. We forget class. We talk about bilingual education as an ethnic issue; we forget to notice that the program mainly touches the lives of working-class immigrant children. Foreign language acquisition is one thing for the upper-class child in a convent school learning to curtsy. Language acquisition can only seem a loss for the ghetto child, for the new language is psychologically awesome, being, as it is, the language of the bus driver and Papa's employer. The child's difficulty will turn out to be psychological more than linguistic because what he gives up are symbols of home.

I was that child! I faced the stranger's English with pain and guilt and fear. Baptized to English in school, at first I felt myself drowning—the ugly sounds forced down my throat—until slowly, slowly (held in the tender grip of my teachers), suddenly the conviction took: English was my language to use.

What I yearn for is some candor from those who speak about bilingual education. Which of its supporters dares speak of the price a child pays—the price of adulthood—to make the journey from a working-class home into a middle-class schoolroom? The real story, the silent story of the immigrant child's journey is one of embarrassments in public; silence at home; and at school the hand tentatively raised. Bilingual enthusiasts bespeak an easier world. They seek a linguistic solution to a social dilemma. They seem to want to believe that there is an easy way for the child to balance private and public, in order to believe that there is some easy way for themselves.

Ten years ago, I started writing about the ideological incantations of bilingual education. Ten years from now some newspaper may well invite me to contribute another Sunday supplement essay on the subject. The debate is going to continue. The bilingual establishment is now inside the door. Jobs are at stake. Politicians can only count heads; growing numbers of Hispanics will ensure the compliance of politicians.

Publicly, we will continue the fiction. We will solemnly address this issue as an educational question, a matter of pedagogy. But privately, Hispanics will still seek from bilingual education an admission from the gringo that Spanish has value and presence. Hispanics of middle class will continue to seek the romantic assurance of separateness. Experts will argue. Dark-eyed children will sit in the classroom. Mute.

Sink-or-Swim "Success Stories" and Bilingual Education

By Stephen D. Krashen

Stephen D. Krashen is professor of linguistics at the University of Southern California and author of *The Input Hypothesis*, *The Natural Approach* (with Tracy Terrell), and numerous other works on second-language acquisition. This article originally appeared as "Bilingual Education, Acquiring English, and the Case of Richard Rodríguez," *California Association for Bilingual Education Newsletter*, May–June 1982.

Hunger of Memory: The Education of Richard Rodríguez is a moving account of a Mexican American growing up in Sacramento, California. The book is also a criticism of bilingual education. Rodríguez's argument is not new. It is based on his own case history, his success in acquiring English, and his academic success—Rodríguez did graduate work in English literature—despite the fact that he knew little English upon entering school. Bilingual education, he claims, delays the acquisition of English:

> Without question, it would have pleased me to hear my teachers address me in Spanish when I entered the classroom. I would have felt much less afraid. I would have trusted them and responded with ease. But I would have delayed—for how long postponed?—having learned the language of public society.[11]

The fact is that it is not the intention of bilingual education to delay the acquisition of English. Few, if any bilingual educators (none that I have met) doubt the value of acquiring English and acquiring it quickly. Moreover, successful bilingual programs do, in fact, result in faster acquisition of English than "submersion" or "sink or swim" programs, even when such programs are supplemented with English as a second language (E.S.L.).

To understand why this is so, how a program that appears to provide less exposure to English actually results in faster acquisition of English, we need to take a brief look at recent progress in the field of second-language acquisition. It is now well established that language acquisition happens in only one way: when acquirers *understand* incoming messages, when they receive *comprehensible input*. Language acquisition does not result from grammar drill, repetition of patterns, or from listening to incomprehensible input or noise.

Good bilingual programs, while they may give the child less overall exposure to English, actually provide more comprehensible input in English. They do this directly in several ways. One way is via E.S.L. classes.[12] Another is by comprehensible subject-matter teaching in English.[13] When a second-language acquirer understands the language of a geography lesson, it is also a language lesson. Subject matter classes taught in the first language contribute indirectly but powerfully to the acquisition of English. First, such classes result in knowledge, knowledge that helps make English input more comprehensible. A limited-English-speaking child who has had a good math background will acquire more English and more math in the English-language math class than the limited-English-speaking child whose

---

11. *Hunger of Memory* (Boston: David R. Godine, 1982), p. 19.

12. E.S.L. classes vary in their effectiveness. Research indicates that language classes are most effective when they provide large amounts of comprehensible input; Stephen Krashen, *Principles and Practice in Second Language Acquisition* (New York: Pergamon Press, 1982). Successful methods that do this include Asher's Total Physical Response method and Terrell's Natural Approach; T. Asher, *Learning Another Language through Actions* (Los Gatos, Calif.: Sky Oaks Productions, 1981); Tracy Terrell, "The Natural Approach in Bilingual Education," in *Schooling and Language Minority Students: A Theoretical Framework* (Los Angeles: California State University, 1981), pp. 117–46.

13. Such classes require special care. Simply placing a limited-English speaker in a subject-matter class for native speakers does not ensure comprehensible input.

math background is poor. This is because the former child has more context, more background information that makes the input easier to understand. In addition, Dr. Jim Cummins of the Ontario Institute for Studies in Education argues that language skills related to academic success (the ability to argue, analyze, contrast, and so forth) can develop in either language; there is a general academic language proficiency that can be gained in either the first or second language.

Rodríguez attributes his success in English to his teachers' insistence that his parents speak English with him at home. This occurred after six months of classroom silence on his part. Weeks after the home language switch from Spanish to English, Rodríguez reports, he finally volunteered an answer in English in class. He describes in detail how this event profoundly changed his family life:

> As we children learned more and more English, we shared fewer and fewer words with our parents. Sentences needed to be spoken slowly when a child addressed his mother or father. (Often the parent wouldn't understand.) The child would need to repeat himself. (Still the parent misunderstood.) The young voice, frustrated, would end up saying, "Never mind"—the subject was closed. Dinners would be noisy with the clinking of knives and forks against dishes. My mother would smile softly between her remarks; my father at the other end of the table would chew and chew at his food, while he stared over the heads of his children.[14]

Rodríguez's acquisition of English could have occurred without this sacrifice. The silence that provoked his teacher's visit was not necessarily a symptom of nonacquisition. Children typically go through a "silent period" of several months before speaking a second language. I have hypothesized that this is often a time of active acquisition, a time during which competence is built up via input. The child's first words are not the beginning of language acquisition, but are testimony to the comprehensible input he has received during this time.

Even though Rodríguez was in a "submersion" class, and probably received little comprehensible input in class, he had several other sources of comprehensible input. He describes extra tutoring—private lessons "at the end of each school day" for a year. In addition, unlike many minority children today, Rodríguez lived in an English-speaking neighborhood; the vast majority of his classmates spoke only English. The playground is an important source of input—very often, those who "made it" without bilingual education or other spe-

14. *Hunger of Memory,* p. 23.

cial programs got their input from English-speaking friends.[15] On the other hand, it is unlikely that the use of English at home contributed much in the way of comprehensible input, according to Rodríguez's description:

> After dinner each night, the family gathered to practice our English. . . . Laughing, we would try to define words we could not pronounce. We played with strange English sounds, often over-anglicizing our pronunciations. And we filled the smiling gaps of our sentences with familiar Spanish sounds.[16]

Empirical evidence supports the probability that Rodríguez may have succeeded quite well without giving up Spanish at home. Several studies reviewed by Cummins conclude that the use of the first language at home by minority students does not prevent success in school. Some studies, in fact, suggest that the use of the majority language at home leads to poor progress. Cummins concludes that the actual language used at home is not the important factor. What is important is the quality of parent-child interaction. He concludes:

> Viewed from this perspective, encouraging minority parents to communicate in English with their children in the home can have very detrimental consequences. If parents are not comfortable in English, the quality of their interaction with their children in English is likely to be less than in [the first language].[17]

Rodríguez's cognitive development clearly did not suffer from use of English at home. He was already old enough to interact with others. But had the decision to use English been made earlier, he might have suffered intellectually. And there is no reason to assume that his use of English at home added much, if anything, to his English proficiency, given his other sources of comprehensible input.

Bilingual education is especially useful for children who do not live in English-speaking neighborhoods, who cannot get comprehensible input outside of the classroom. But it would have been helpful even for a "success story" like Rodríguez. It could have meant faster, more comfortable acquisition of English, better communication with his family, and even a richer career as a literature scholar, with two great literary traditions to learn from instead of only one.

---

15. Although Rodríguez describes himself as introverted, a heavy reader even in grade school, it is nevertheless likely that he received a significant amount of comprehensible input from school friends.

16. *Hunger of Memory,* p. 21.

17. "The Role of Primary Language Development in Promoting Educational Success for Language Minority Students," in *Schooling and Language Minority Students,* p. 33.

The Bilingual Education Act: A Failed Path

By William J. Bennett

William J. Bennett served as U.S. secretary of education from 1985 to 1988. This speech, delivered in New York City on September 26, 1985, inaugurated a high-profile campaign to "reform" bilingual education. Bennett favored the use of Bilingual Education Act funds to finance alternative, nonbilingual approaches in teaching limited-English-proficient children. But the law set aside most grants for school programs that made some use of students' native language. Bennett called for eliminating this requirement in the interest of greater "flexibility" for local educators. Congress declined to remove all restrictions, but in 1988 voted to expand support for English-only methods (up to 25 percent of program funding). Throughout his tenure, in keeping with Reagan administration policy, Secretary Bennett remained silent on the question of Official English. But in a collection of his writings published after leaving office, he chose to entitle this speech "In Defense of Our Common Language," a slogan favored by U.S. English.[18]

Our origins are diverse. Yet we live together as fellow citizens, in harmony. In America, and perhaps especially in New York, we can say, *E pluribus unum;* out of many we have become one. We cherish our particularities, and we respect our differences. Each of us is justly proud of his own ethnic heritage. But we share this pride, in common, as Americans, as American citizens. To be a citizen is to share in something common—common principles, common memories, and a common language in which to discuss our common affairs. Our common language is, of course, English. And our common task is to ensure that our non-English-speaking children learn this common language.

We entrust this task, in part, to our schools. We expect them, in this as in other respects, to prepare our youth to participate fully in the opportunities and challenges of American society. That is why we become so concerned when we discover that our schools are, in various ways, falling short of what we expect of them. We expect much of them—to impart basic skills, to help form character, to teach citizenship. And we expect our schools to help teach all of our students En-

18. William J. Bennett, *Our Children and Our Country: Improving America's Schools and Affirming the Common Culture* (New York: Simon & Schuster, 1988).

glish, the common language that will enable them to participate fully in our political, economic, and social life.

Teaching non-English-speaking children English is not a new task for this nation. It has been performed, with fair success, in communities across this nation since its beginning. But only in the mid–1960s did the federal government accept responsibility for assisting in this task. The timing was no accident. For America was then engaged in a peaceful revolution—our civil rights revolution—in which the federal government stepped in to make good on the great American promise of equal opportunity for all. And this promise extends with full force to those of our children who speak no English, or little English.

Many of these children are the sons and daughters of immigrants and refugees, who have left behind their homes, and all that was familiar to them, to come to this land of freedom and opportunity. Many of these children grow up in circumstances that are not easy, their parents struggling day to day for the sake of a brighter future for their children. Other Americans have always, in their churches and communities, done their part to help give such children a chance to achieve that brighter future. It was reasonable and proper, twenty years ago, for the federal government to step in to play a role as well.

How has our government done by these children? The answer, I am afraid, is not very well. But not from a lack of trying. We began with the best of intentions. We began with two legislative landmarks, the Civil Rights Act of 1964 and the Elementary and Secondary Education Act of 1965. But in both cases, after sound beginnings, federal policies went astray. In a now-familiar pattern of events, over the next two decades our policies gradually became confused as to purpose, and overbearing as to means. As a result, too many children have failed to become fluent in English, and have therefore failed to enjoy the opportunities they deserve. Now is the time to get our policies back on track; now is the time to deliver on the promise of equal opportunity so solemnly pledged twenty years ago.

Despite the *Lau v. Nichols* decision's endorsement of flexibility of approach *(see pp. 251–55)*, the federal government moved in another direction. In 1975 the Department of Health, Education, and Welfare (H.E.W.) began to require that educational programs for non-English-speaking students be conducted in large part *in the student's native language,* as virtually the only approved method of remedying discrimination. These regulations were never formally published, for public notice and comment. Indeed, when H.E.W. was sued and forced to publish them in August 1980, they aroused a storm of opposition, and they were withdrawn in February 1981. By that time, however, they had served as the basis of some five hundred "compliance agreements" negotiated with school districts across the nation. Because of their intrusiveness and heavy-handedness, these regulations came close to giving bilingual education a bad name. More important, by the time they were withdrawn in 1981, the evidence was becoming increasingly clear that this educational method imposed from Washington was doing very little to help students learn English.

Why did the government turn down this path? Partly because of a foolish conviction that only Washington meant well and knew best. Local school districts, it was thought, could not be trusted to devise the best means, given their own circumstances, to teach their students English. But our government made this fateful turn for another reason as well. And that was that we had lost sight of the goal of learning *English* as the key to equal educational opportunity. Indeed, H.E.W. increasingly emphasized bilingual education as a way of enhancing students' knowledge of their native language and culture. Bilingual education was no longer seen so much as a means to ensure that students learned English, or as a transitional method until students learned English. Rather, it became an emblem of cultural pride, a means of producing a positive self-image in the student.

Let us be clear: Pride in one's heritage is natural and commendable. We in the United States cherish our diversity, and local schools should be free—and more, should be encouraged—to foster the study of the languages and heritages of their students in the courses they offer. But the responsibility of the federal government must be to help ensure that local schools succeed in teaching non-English-speaking students English, so that every American enjoys access to the opportunities of American society.

The Bilingual Education Act was most recently reauthorized last year. Congress had before it yet more evidence that the mandated method of instruction in the native language was no more effective than alternative methods of special instruction using English, and in some cases the mandated method was demonstrably less so. Indeed, the English-language skills of students in bilingual education programs seemed to be no better than the skills of those who simply remained in regular classrooms where English was spoken, without *any* special help. In addition, Hispanic children, the largest subgroup of the eligible population, have continued to perform educationally far below the national average. The recent news of gains by Hispanic students in Scholastic Aptitude Test scores is welcome indeed, and is a testimony to the impressive efforts of many Hispanic parents and children. Yet we cannot take these scores as a sign that all is well. The scores of Hispanics remain unacceptably below the national average and, more important, these scores only reflect the achievement of *half* of all Hispanic children. For almost half of all Hispanic high school students in the United States drop out *before* graduation, and of these dropouts, 40 percent never reach the tenth grade. This figure is as tragically high now as it was twenty years ago.

In response to these facts, and in response to immigrants from various parts of Asia and elsewhere, for many of whom it is practically impossible for schools to provide native-language instruction, Congress last year recognized the need for programs using alternative instructional methods. These methods include English as a second language (E.S.L.) and "structured immersion," and provide special instruction *in English* to students of limited English proficiency. Congress did allow, in its 1984 reauthorization, for such alternative programs, but it limited funding for those programs to 4 percent of the total appropriation, leaving local school districts still very much constrained. And Congress unfortunately further backed away from a clear statement of the goal of learning English, by authorizing for the first time funding for programs designed simply to maintain student competence in the native language.[19]

This, then, is where we stand: After seventeen years of federal involvement and after $1.7 billion of federal funding, we have no evidence that the children whom we sought to help—that the children who deserve our help—have benefited. And we have the testimony of an original sponsor of the Bilingual Education Act, Congressman James Scheuer of New York, that the Act's "original purposes were perverted and politicized"; that instead of helping students learn English, "the English has been sort of thinned out and stretched out and in many cases banished into the mists and all of the courses tended to be taught in Spanish. That was not the original intent of the program."

What, then, are we to do? Give up on the promise of equal educational opportunity for those of our children who are not proficient in English? Our sense of what we owe our fellow Americans will not permit this. Continue down the same failed path on which we have been traveling? This is an equally bankrupt course. We ought to do more for our fellow citizens than throw good money after bad, and we ought to offer more than increasingly hollow protestations of concern and gestures of solidarity.

19. Editor's note: *Developmental*, or "maintenance," bilingual programs allow students to continue studying in their native language after they are judged to be functional in English; *transitional* bilingual programs require such students to enter "mainstream" classrooms. Both approaches were funded until 1978, when Congress restricted federal support to transitional bilingual education. The 1984 reauthorization of the Bilingual Education Act reversed this policy, specifically authorizing the Department of Education to fund developmental programs. Under Bennett, however, it rarely did so.

We intend to make good on the promise of real equal educational opportunity for all Americans. We shall therefore explore with Congress the possibility of removing the 4 percent cap on alternative instructional methods, as well as other legislative changes. We shall move, through regulatory and administrative changes, to allow greater flexibility for local school districts. And we shall take care, in the course of ensuring that the civil rights of minority-national-origin students are respected, that we do not impose a particular method of instruction. These reforms will allow local school districts to choose the sort of program, or to design the combination of programs, best suited to their particular needs. School districts serving recent immigrants who speak seventy different languages may after all need different sorts of programs from school districts whose students speak only two languages.

These reforms will allow local school districts the flexibility to adapt to local circumstances. They will also allow them to take advantage of research results which are now coming in. Let me be clear: We do not intend to prescribe one method or another. Many school districts will undoubtedly continue to pursue programs with some instruction in the native language. In some circumstances, these can be very useful in helping students keep up with their classwork until they become fluent in English. We do not intend to prescribe one method or another. But the goal of any method should be clear—fluency in English. As President Reagan has said: "Bilingual programs should serve as a bridge to full participation in the American mainstream. They should never segregate non-English-speaking students in a way that will make it harder, not easier, for them to succeed in life."

Our movement away from exclusive reliance on one method, and our endorsement of local flexibility should not be mistaken for a return to the old days of sink-or-swim. Many children in earlier generations learned English in such circumstances, but some did not, and at times the cost was high. We intend to enforce the requirement that school districts provide equal opportunity for students deficient in English by providing programs that address their needs. And we intend to continue funding programs that address the needs of school children who need to learn English. But we believe that local flexibility will serve the needs of these students far more effectively than intrusive federal regulation.

Paradoxically, we have over the last two decades become less clear about the goal—English-language literacy—at the same time as we have become more intrusive as to the method. But there ought to be no confusion or embarrassment over our goal. The rise in ethnic consciousness, the resurgence of cultural pride in recent decades, is a healthy thing. The traditions we bring with us, that our forefathers brought with them to this land, are too worthwhile to be discarded. But a sense of cultural pride cannot come at the price of proficiency in English, our common language.

As fellow citizens, we need a common language. In the United States that language is English. Our common history is written in English. Our common forefathers speak to us, through the ages, in English. This is not contradicted by the fact that it is an enduring glory of this nation to have welcomed with open arms immigrants from other lands, speaking other languages; nor by the fact that it is a feature of our free society that these languages can continue to find a place here, in the United States. But beneath the wonderful mosaic of cultures here, beyond the remarkable variety of languages, we are one people.

We are one people not by virtue of a common blood, or race, or origin. We are one people, above all, because we hold these truths to be self-evident: that all men are created equal, that they are endowed by their Creator with certain unalienable rights, and that therefore just government is by consent of the governed. And government by consent means government by discussion, by debate, by discourse, by argument. Such a common enterprise requires a common language. We should not be bashful about proclaiming fluency in this language as our educational goal. And we should not be timid in reforming our policies so as to secure it. For with this goal comes the reward of full participation in this remarkable nation of ours—"not merely a nation but a teeming nation of nations," Walt Whitman said—but still, at the end of the day, beneath all the differences of politics and color and creed, one nation, one people.

Secretary Bennett *versus* Equal Educational Opportunity

By James J. Lyons

James J. Lyons is executive director of the National Association for Bilingual Education (NABE), the major professional organization in the field. As NABE's legislative counsel, he played an influential role in drafting the 1984 reauthorization of the Bilingual Education Act. This article originally appeared as "Education Secretary Bennett on Bi-

lingual Education: Mixed Up or Malicious?" *NABE News* 9,
no. 1 (Fall 1985): 1, 14.

Secretary of Education William J. Bennett launched the Reagan administration's "initiative" on bilingual education September 26. In a
media-hyped speech to the Association for a Better New York, Bennett attacked the new Bilingual Education Act, passed by an overwhelming bipartisan majority in Congress in the fall of 1984, following three years of study, hearings, and debate. At the same time,
Bennett branded as "a failure" two decades of federal policies to help
educate language-minority students. Lost upon many listeners of the
Secretary's lengthy address was a more fundamental message: Equality of educational opportunity no longer means what it used to.
Language-minority students—native-born Americans, immigrants,
and refugees—must be satisfied with only a partial education.

Veteran Washington observers were shocked by the vehemence of
the Secretary's attack. Both prior to and immediately following the
Secretary's confirmation last February, Bennett repeatedly declined to
give his views on how the federal government should help communities across the land to educate more than 4 million language-
minority students who don't know English well enough to learn
successfully in monolingual English classrooms. Exhibiting unchar-
acteristic reticence and thoughtfulness, Mr. Bennett promised that he
would undertake a thorough examination of this complex and compelling issue. In his New York address, however, lawyer-philosopher
Bennett, who recently has taken to teaching high school American
history under the doting eye of network television, recounted the development of federal bilingual education policy. In so doing, Bennett
not only rewrote the history of bilingual education, but he redefined
the meaning of equal educational opportunity.

According to Bennett, "the responsibility of the federal government
must be to help ensure that local schools succeed in teaching non-
English-speaking students English, so that every American enjoys access to the opportunities of American society." Certainly, none of the
members of Congress who developed and voted for the new Bilingual
Education Act last year would question the importance of effectively
teaching English to language-minority students. And the Hispanic
leaders and advocates of bilingual education whom Education Department officials charge are out of touch with their constituents have
never discounted the importance of teaching English to language-
minority students.

However, no one with an ounce of sense would say that a child who
has mastered English, but who has not learned mathematics, history,
geography, civics, and the other subjects taught in school was edu-

cated or prepared for life in this society. Why Secretary Bennett, who generally champions a rigorous comprehensive education, has so narrowly set out the purpose and goal of schooling for language-minority students is anyone's guess. It may be that Bennett finally knuckled under to U.S. English, a well-financed private lobby group which opposes use of non-English languages in public education (or, for that matter, for any public purpose). What is clear is that Bennett's narrow and unworkable definition of what constitutes equal educational opportunity is central to his confused attack on federal law and policy. Secretary Bennett cited the tragic and dangerously high dropout rates of Hispanic students as proof that these laws and policies were wrong. Nowhere in his seventeen-page speech did Bennett acknowledge the fact that most Hispanic students—indeed, most students eligible for federal bilingual education services—have never attended bilingual education classes.[20]

And so, Secretary Bennett has declared that English as a second language (E.S.L.) and undefined "immersion" programs are viable alternatives to bilingual education. Yes, E.S.L. is a sound method of teaching English to non-English-language-background students, especially when carried out by bilingual school personnel. And that is exactly why the new Bilingual Education Act now requires that *every* federally funded program of bilingual education provide intensive "structured English language instruction." The trouble, however, is that E.S.L. and so-called "immersion" programs often fail to teach anything but English.

Prior to enactment of the 1968 Bilingual Education Act, language-minority students who didn't know English were universally ignored. Either they were segregated in inferior schools, or instruction was tailored to the needs of students from English language backgrounds. A majority of the parents of limited-English-proficient students today are themselves the casualties of this earlier educational neglect. Thanks to federal policy—the Bilingual Education Act and other compensatory education programs, the 1974 U.S. Supreme Court decision in *Lau v. Nichols (see pp. 251–55),* and technical assistance to help

20. Editor's note: The Bilingual Education Act creates no entitlement to federal services—only a discretionary grant program that depends on congressional appropriations. As such, the program has never been "fully funded" to reach every eligible child. From an initial appropriation of $7.5 million in 1969, its funding reached a peak of $167 million in 1980, declined to $133 million in 1986, then resumed a gradual increase, to $159 million in 1990. Besides supporting school programs, these budgets include subsidies for research and personnel training. While national estimates of the limited-English-proficient population vary, informed observers believe that only 5 to 10 percent of such students are served directly with federal funds. A larger but undetermined amount is spent by state and local governments.

school districts achieve civil rights compliance—the situation has improved. Because of federal encouragement and financial support, E.S.L. and native-language instructional methods have been developed, teachers have been trained, classroom materials have been prepared and published, evaluation instruments have been written and refined—the list goes on and on. Now, many more teachers can comprehend a student's question or even the simple plea, "I don't understand" when it is delivered in the only language the child knows.

Federal education and civil rights policies have increased the number of school personnel who can communicate with non-English-speaking students and parents. It has, if you will, opened the schoolhouse door. Moreover, the new Bilingual Education Act requires that parents receive information about the placement and progress of students in programs funded under the Act, and gives parents the right to decline placement of their children in these programs. Most important, federal bilingual education policy has made it possible for parents who don't know English to become active partners in their children's education. The principle of parent choice—championed so ardently by Secretary Bennett—is at the heart of bilingual education law and policy.

In support of his pared-down concept of equal educational opportunity, Secretary Bennett decried the "lack of flexibility" in current law. At the same time, the Secretary conveniently ignored a number of facts. He ignored the fact that more than three hundred school districts applied for supposedly "inflexible" Transitional Bilingual Education program grants this year, but that the Department of Education was able to fund just over one hundred applications. He ignored the fact that forty-eight school districts and community organizations asked for seed money to start Family English Literacy programs, but the department awarded grants to only four. And he did not tell his audience that the Reagan administration has already asked Congress to eliminate all funding for these programs next year. Unlike the other programs authorized under the Bilingual Education Act, Family English Literacy has a single objective: to teach English to parents. The law does not require *any* use of the parent's native language in these simple, straightforward English instruction programs.

Since taking office, William Bennett has traveled widely and talked loosely. Some of what he says makes sense: "Parents are the first and most influential teachers of their children; they should spend more time with their children, reading to them and teaching them to read." But Mr. Bennett's message on bilingual education, coupled with facts the Secretary knew but never disclosed, does not make sense. At best he is mixed up; at worst he is malicious.

Against Our Best Interest: The Attempt to Sabotage Bilingual Education

By Lily Wong Fillmore

Lily Wong Fillmore is professor of education at the University of California, Berkeley, and author of numerous works on the education of language-minority children. She wrote this article for the *Source Book*.

As a self-avowed advocate of bilingual education, I am often asked: "If bilingual education is as you good as you claim, why doesn't the research show it?" It seems that just about everyone believes that "research" has proven that bilingual education is ineffective and that language-minority students are better off in sink-or-swim classes than in bilingual programs. My usual response is a long-winded discourse (serves 'em right!) on what the research really does show. The short version is this: Bilingual education done well gives excellent results; bilingual education done badly gives poor results, just as one would expect. But this kind of argument rarely convinces people who have their minds made up—at least, no one has ever said to me, "Gosh, I was completely wrong about bilingual education. Thanks for setting me straight." Usually, they respond, "If it isn't being done right, why do it at all?" That counterargument has not caused me to reconsider my position on bilingual education, but it does make me reflect on why it is so often done poorly.

Over the years, I have observed many bilingual classes, and have learned to tell good programs from bad programs. Sad to say, the bad outnumber the good. This might lead people to conclude that bilingual educators do not know what they are doing or that bilingual education is too shaky a concept to be implemented reliably. Not true. There are plenty of educators who know how to do it well.[21] The problem has been a lack of commitment on the part of schools to make it work.

In every good program, the people who are involved from top to

---

21. For examples of programs that are working, as measured by student performance in English as well as other subjects, see Stephen Krashen and Douglas Biber, *On Course: Bilingual Education's Success in California* (Sacramento: California Association for Bilingual Education, 1988).

bottom believe in bilingual education and are committed to making it work. There are teachers who know the ethnic language well enough to teach in it and have developed a workable plan for using it in school. English is used in these programs in ways that allow the students to master it eventually, but not in ways that displace the native language. In good bilingual programs, the level of the curricular content is consistent with the level offered to all other students in the school. In fact, except for the language of instruction, it is essentially the same.[22]

Bad programs are something else. For one thing, they are seldom bilingual except in name. One finds, for example, "bilingual" programs in which everything is taught exclusively in English. The native language is rarely used by the teachers, except as a last resort, when they can find no other way to communicate with their students. Because the children have trouble understanding the English-language materials they are given, teachers water down their lessons until they are educationally inappropriate. In extreme cases, high-school-age students are assigned primary-grade texts on grounds that they lack the English skills to handle anything else—although they would have no trouble dealing with age-appropriate materials in their native language. These students are not receiving bilingual education, no matter what the program is called. Not unexpectedly, when their school performance is compared with that of limited-English-proficient (LEP) students in all-English programs, one finds little or no difference between them. In other words, these "bilingual" programs are doing no better than all-English programs—and that is exactly what the opponents of bilingual education want the public to believe.

Teachers and administrators who oversee ineffective programs often harbor secret doubts about the wisdom of bilingual methods— whether children will learn English if they first learn to read in another language; whether they can master important subjects like math and science in a language like Spanish; whether the use of students' native language will hinder their incorporation into an

---

22. Some people argue that the curriculum must be specially tailored to the cultural background and linguistic capabilities of the students in each bilingual program. What they are really saying is that the standard curriculum is too difficult for language-minority students and needs to be watered down. I don't buy that. If students with limited English proficiency are instructed in a language they understand, and if teachers are doing their job, there is no reason why these students would have more difficulty with the standard curriculum than anyone else. Another objection to using the standard curriculum is that it seldom represents the cultural and historical perspective of the minority groups served by the bilingual program. This may indeed be so. But in that case, what needs fixing is the standard curriculum.

English-speaking society. It's no wonder they are not committed to making these programs work.

Why are such people involved in bilingual education if they are not committed to it? I began asking that question more than fifteen years ago, not long after the U.S. Supreme Court's 1974 ruling in the *Lau v. Nichols* case and the passage of the federal Equal Educational Opportunity Act some seven months later *(see pp. 247, 251–55)*. That was when I became aware of efforts to subvert the legal mandate for school districts to provide bilingual education for LEP students. With the U.S. Office for Civil Rights policing compliance with *Lau*, and with many state legislatures adopting bilingual education laws,[23] educators throughout the country were compelled to get involved in bilingual education, whether they knew anything about it, or believed in it, or not.

Previously, the U.S. Supreme Court had outlawed school segregation by race or ethnic background. But until 1974 there had been no federal move to establish what should be taught in schools or how it ought to be done. Strictly speaking, *Lau v. Nichols* did not get into curricular or instructional issues. It only required schools to ensure that all students had access to the school's curriculum; if there were language barriers, then steps had to be taken to assist students in overcoming them. In the enforcement of *Lau*, however, bilingual education was prescribed as the most effective and appropriate means to that end. This was interpreted by many educators as an attempt by the federal government to abrogate local authority in curricular and instructional decision-making. This, in part, explains the early resistance to bilingual education, but it is not the whole story.

A decidedly mean-spirited aspect of the American psyche is also involved: an intolerance of foreigners and of foreign influences. People who don't look or act or think in the way Americans do—and most of all, who don't talk the way Americans talk—are suspect. This is ironic because Americans are among the most diverse peoples in the world. A quick look at the populace in just about any U.S. city will show us that we have not limited membership in the society to those who look, act, think, and talk the same. Nonetheless, as a people we have a hard time tolerating differences among us. Immigrants are expected to adopt American ways as soon as they can, with as little resistance as possible. The expectation is that newcomers will learn and use English immediately. There has never been much recognition of

23. California, for example, passed the Chacon-Moscone Bilingual-Bicultural Education Act in 1976 (and strengthened it in 1981). Among other things, the Act mandated bilingual classrooms in elementary schools where there were at least ten LEP children of the same language group and grade level. But the law "sunsetted" in 1987, and efforts to extend it were twice vetoed by Governor George Deukmejian.

the fact that it takes people, even children, time to learn a language, or that some cannot learn it well despite their best efforts. For many Americans, to suggest that immigrant children should learn initially through their native language, rather than be made to bite the linguistic bullet and start learning exclusively in English, seems tantamount to saying they don't have to learn English at all.

This sentiment has inspired resistance to bilingual education almost from the first. Some administrators and teachers have opposed it for ideological reasons, others simply because they did not like being told what to do. But the resistance to bilingual programs has seldom been out in the open, since there has been, and continues to be, substantial community support. A close examination of bilingual education where it has performed poorly will often show the extent to which it has been sabotaged from within by the people who were supposed to make it work.

Subversive Activity #1: Doing as little as possible.

A cheap trick used by many schools is to set up one bilingual classroom at each grade level—enough to serve, say, one out of every four children who need the program. This means that only the neediest students can be enrolled in bilingual education, namely, those who speak no English at all. Those who speak a few words are declared to have "survival-level skills" and placed in slow-track classes in English, where they do not have much trouble keeping up, despite not being able to understand the language. Those who know a little more English are declared fluent and placed in whatever regular classes have empty seats. Meanwhile, the school staff continues to perform educational triage as new LEP students show up throughout the year, fresh from the jumbo jets and Winnebagos that bring new immigrants to town. As students in the overstuffed bilingual classes learn a few words of English, they are moved out to make room for newcomers who speak none at all.

Taking the most advanced students out of their bilingual class, where presumably they have been getting the help they need, has two major effects. First, it usually sets back the prematurely "mainstreamed" students, linguistically and academically. They lack the English language skills needed to stay afloat in the sink-or-swim classrooms where they are placed, and so tend to lose the momentum they had in English while trying to adjust to a new teacher's ways. Second, the constant coming and going of students keeps the bilingual class as a whole from making academic progress. As soon as the teacher gets a group of children to the point where they understand what's going on, some of them are replaced by new students who are starting from scratch.

In evaluations of bilingual programs that have been subverted in these ways, students compare poorly with their peers who have never been in the program at all—and little wonder. The comparison students haven't been in a classroom where the instructional program is constantly disrupted by new students passing through its revolving doors. They haven't had their progress interrupted just as they were getting somewhere. They are not composed mainly of newcomers and students who learn English so slowly that no one is even tempted to mainstream them.

The do-as-little-as-you-can ploy is carried out at both the macro and the micro levels. At the macro level, we find school districts setting up bilingual education programs at the smallest possible number of school sites, thus requiring children to be bused from one end of town to another. At the micro level, we have teachers providing as little native-language instruction as possible. The teachers at one school with a do-nothing bilingual program were told that outside monitors had discovered they were teaching exclusively in English, and that now they must provide regular instruction in the LEP students' native languages. So once a week, as regular as clockwork, they gave their students fifteen minutes of Cantonese or Spanish or Vietnamese reading instruction. I don't need to explain why fifteen minutes of native language per week does not add up to bilingual education.

Subversive Activity #2: Staffing the program with the wrong people.

A bilingual program must have teachers who are proficient in the home language of the students as well as in English, and are willing to use both languages in the classroom. One sure way to cripple a bilingual program is to staff it with people who cannot speak the students' home language well enough to teach in it. This tactic might seem so lacking in subtlety that no self-respecting saboteur would stoop to it, but one can find countless examples. It works best when inappropriate teacher placements can be made plausible by using English monolinguals whose surnames or ethnic backgrounds suggest they *could* be speakers of their students' native language. Other placements may be justified on grounds that the teachers have studied the language formally (perhaps for one or two semesters, thirty years earlier). Sometimes in California, monolingual English teachers are entrusted with bilingual classrooms after signing agreements to seek certifications in Ilocano, Khmer, Hmong, or Thai, even though there is little hope they will ever become proficient in these languages. These "bilingual" teachers may indeed be qualified to be the English-speaking half of a teaching team, but they cannot possibly teach bilingually on their own.

The saboteurs seldom do things half-way, however. The teachers they assign to bilingual classes are often people who neither speak the language, nor believe it has a place in school. Some are second- or third-generation immigrants who may have faced discrimination themselves until they learned approved ways of talking and acting. But now they suffer from the more-American-than-thou syndrome: "If these people want to be Americans, they better learn English and be quick about it. We did it without help, and they can do it, too." Teachers with this kind of attitude would not teach bilingually even if they could. The saboteurs know this; they count on it.

Subversive Activity #3: Hobbling teachers so they can't function bilingually or otherwise.

This strategy is necessary when antibilingual administrators find themselves stuck with teachers who not only believe in bilingual education, but are doing it right. They look around the school for the disturbed and disturbing children—the unhappy little guys who, because of emotional or psychiatric problems, are bouncing off the walls—and assign them to the bilingual program, even though their educational needs have nothing to do with language. When such placements are questioned, the justification is often that the bilingual teachers have assistants and can therefore manage the difficult children more easily than regular teachers. Needless to say, being placed in classrooms where they do not understand the language spoken by classmates and teachers does little to help these children deal with school, no matter how many adults are present. Nor are the bilingual teachers helped to manage the already complex job of educating LEP students when given the added burden of working with emotionally disturbed children.

Another form of inappropriate placement might be described as the "close-enough" ploy. It works this way: A Portuguese-speaking child who is limited in English enrolls in a school where there is no Portuguese bilingual program. The newcomer could legitimately be placed in a mainstream classroom, while being provided tutoring and English-as-a-second-language instruction. But that would be too easy on the school's bilingual teachers. So what does our saboteur do? He puts the hapless newcomer into a Spanish or Cantonese or Vietnamese class—whichever happens to have space, on the rationale that these programs are meant to help non-English-speaking students. In one such incident, when it was pointed out that the child spoke Portuguese and not Spanish, the principal retorted, "It's close enough."

What do you do with a "Southeast Asian" bilingual class? I have seen mix-and-match classrooms that resemble miniature assemblies of the United Nations, with children from as many as eight language backgrounds and a teacher who speaks (at most) one of those languages. What kind of bilingual instruction is possible when the students speak Khmer, Vietnamese, Thai, Burmese, Laotian, Cantonese, Mandarin, and Hmong? Or when, in the case of "Native American" bilingual classes, the children speak dialects of English and a variety of Indian languages. What language are teachers going to use in such situations? Just as one might guess, they use English almost exclusively.

Subversive Activity #4: Testing students in English to make teachers look as bad as possible.

What is to be done when bilingual teachers insist on teaching the students in their own language? How do the saboteurs put the fear of God (who speaks English) into such teachers? It's easy. They test the students' academic achievement exclusively in English and tell the teachers that their performance evaluations will be based on their students' test scores. The effect on teachers is not hard to imagine. Children who are being taught to read in Spanish are unlikely to make a good showing on English reading tests. Naturally, this pressure causes even committed bilingual teachers to reconsider their use of LEP students' native language in the classroom—pushing them in the opposite direction from where research says they should be going.

According to educational experts, materials that are cognitively demanding should be taught in language the students understand, especially when the subject or skill being taught is language dependent. Reading is one such skill. Children can be taught to decode English words even if they do not know what the words mean, but no one would call this reading. To really learn to read, children must know what the decoded words and sentences mean so they can make sense of the printed materials. Reading experts say children should be taught to read initially in their dominant language. Only after achieving a level of stable reading proficiency should they be taught to read in a second language (assuming of course, that they know that language well enough to understand what they are reading).

What do teachers do when they feel compelled to teach LEP children to read in English, even though they know it is better to do so in their primary language? All too often they resort to a counterproductive practice: teaching children to read in both languages simultaneously. This is especially common in districts where reading achievement is tested in English only. Anyone who remembers the daunting task of learning to read should be able to appreciate the problems of trying to become a reader in two languages at once—especially when the learner speaks only one of them. The challenge is doubly difficult when the same set of symbols means different things in English and the child's native tongue, be it Spanish, Portuguese, French, Vietnamese or other languages which use the Roman alphabet.

Assessing the academic progress of LEP children exclusively in English encourages another counterproductive practice: the premature transition of students from bilingual to mainstream classrooms.

Rather than waiting until students have achieved stability in first-language reading, teachers often yield to the pressure to mainstream children as quickly as possible. The students' educational development is interrupted, and they are confused by having to start all over in a language they do not thoroughly understand.

Subversive Activity #5: Accentuating the negative to eliminate the positive.

The ploy here is to emphasize the obstacles to implementing bilingual education. For example: "We want to serve every LEP child, but we can't find qualified teachers. There are literally no bilingual teachers out there for us to hire. We have offered bonuses; we pay top dollar; we beat the bushes everywhere, but we can't attract teachers."

One wonders why they haven't tapped an obvious source: members of the immigrant and refugee communities. Surely, among the many people who have arrived here over the past twenty years, there must be some educated individuals who could be recruited to our teaching force. I have personally met former teachers from Vietnam, Cambodia, Hong Kong, Guatemala, El Salvador, Nicaragua, and Argentina who are working as teacher aides in schools and elsewhere as seamstresses, short-order cooks, and busboys. But, alas, the saboteurs point to insuperable obstacles that keep these immigrants from becoming classroom teachers: (1) they don't have proper teaching certificates; (2) the school systems in their home countries are not comparable to ours, so it is hard to evaluate their records; (3) they don't speak English well enough to teach bilingually; and (4) they could never pass the National Teacher Examination (or the state equivalent, for example, the CBEST in California), which is given in English, of course.

But none of these problems is insurmountable. Licensing requirements and guidelines can be modified. School districts can get help in evaluating foreign transcripts. If foreign-educated teachers had shortcomings in their preparation, they could be asked to take make-up courses before receiving full certification. And why would these teachers need perfect English to teach in a bilingual program? Why not team them with English monolingual teachers who might do the English instruction for two classes, while the foreign-educated teacher provided instruction in the native language? What about developing versions of the National Teacher Examination in other languages—Spanish, Vietnamese, or Khmer, for example? These, after all, are the languages in which there is a desperate need for teachers.

Subversive Activity #6: Balkanizing the school.

In 1987, members of the Los Angeles teachers' union approved a referendum by more than three to one, calling for the school district to abandon bilingual education. The district's administrators wisely chose to ignore this advice. Nevertheless, the referendum accomplished its intended purpose—revealing the extent to which teachers, especially in ethnically diverse districts like Los Angeles, disagree about bilingual education. This should not be surprising. The saboteurs have worked hard to isolate bilingual educators in their schools and districts and to turn other teachers against them. One way this is achieved is to make it appear that each bilingual teacher hired means one "regular" teacher put out of work. A few years ago, dropping enrollments caused schools in many communities to furlough teachers at a time when bilingual programs were expanding to serve the one group of students that was growing. While that situation has changed somewhat, many non-bilingual teachers still see themselves in competition with bilingual teachers for jobs and scarce resources.

The saboteurs make little effort to correct the mistaken notion that bilingual teachers get more than their fair share. While federal funds often enable bilingual programs to hire teaching assistants, the children in such programs need more individual attention than a lone teacher can provide. Federal funds augment whatever budget schools have available to purchase instructional equipment and materials, freeing up resources for other programs. Thus, all teachers benefit whether directly or indirectly. And they might recognize it if administrators were inclined to promote harmony rather than dissension between bilingual and nonbilingual teachers.

Never before has a change in instructional methodology engendered so much public scrutiny or opposition, overt and covert, from inside the schools. Looked at objectively, bilingual education does not constitute a big change. It requires neither a radical reorganization or restructuring of schools. It calls simply for the commonsense practice of teaching LEP students at least part of the time in a language they understand. We know that teaching them exclusively in English—while they are still in the process of learning it as a second language—puts them at risk educationally. So why hasn't bilingual education been given a better reception in American schools? Why has it inspired so many acts of subversion?

There is no organized conspiracy. Rather, there is spontaneous resistance to a change that, however small in objective terms, disturbs some fundamental American prejudices. Our zeitgeist is encoded in our national motto: *E pluribus unum*—out of many, one. But this sentiment lends itself to a dual interpretation, revealing a basic ambivalence about ourselves as a people. On the one hand, we celebrate the fact that many nations have contributed to the formation of one nation. We see our multiple origins as a source of pride and strength. On the other hand, we idealize ourselves as a single, unified people and insist on conformity to a common culture, language, and purpose. Though we are a nation of immigrants, Americans have never felt at ease with diversity. To achieve the feel (if not the sight and sound) of homogeneity, we have often shut out those who are different, or have suppressed those who cannot or will not give up their differences.

Bilingual education is seen by the public, and by too many of the educators charged with implementing it, not as giving LEP students a fighting chance to function in an otherwise all-English environment, but as freeing them from the obligation of immediate and absolute assimilation. This has been at the heart of the controversy for the past twenty years. Because bilingual education recognizes the educational validity of languages other than English and cultures other than "American," it is regarded with suspicion and treated accordingly. Only when we have eliminated this prejudice—that to be united, Americans must give up the very things that make them interesting—only then will the good bilingual programs outnumber the bad.

Language: The Psyche of a People

By Robert Bunge

Robert Bunge teaches in the Department of Modern Languages at the University of South Dakota. This article is excerpted from a paper presented at the Seventh Annual Native American Language Issues Institute, in Saskatoon, Saskatchewan, May 1987.

Language is not just another thing we do as humans; it is *the* thing we do. It is a total environment; we live in the language as a fish lives in water. It is the audible and visible manifestation of the soul of a people.

The first thing a victorious people does to a vanquished people is to disarm them—take away their weapons and take over their lands. This is bad enough, but then there follows something far worse: the theft of the psyche of the people. The English knew the Highlands of Scotland would never be "pacified" until the Gaelic language of the natives was destroyed. This suppression of Gaelic has gone on for over 400 years and continues to this day. Gaelic survives at the present time only in the most remote places of the Highlands and offshore islands of Scotland.

At the time of contact with European settlers, there were more than 600 different aboriginal languages spoken on the North American continent between the Rio Grande and the Arctic Circle. Only 300 still survive, and of these, over one-half are spoken by a handful of elderly people. This means that these systems of thought, and the worldview embodied in them, will probably not survive this century. They are moribund and, for practical purposes of communication have become functionally, if not actually, extinct.

An example of a functionally extinct language is Mandan, which is still spoken by an indeterminate handful of people, but not widely or fluently, even by the direcf descendants of Mandan speakers. An example of an actually extinct language is Anglo-Saxon, also called Old English, which died out about 1150 A.D. Various literary words have survived, but no one alive today has ever heard it from the lips of a first-language speaker of Anglo-Saxon; educated guesses can be made by linguistic analysis and reconstruction from a prototype or proto-language. Since knowledge of dead languages is confined today solely to a reading knowledge, pronunciation is a secondary and relatively unimportant consideration. This is lamentable because language, any language, is primarily spoken and only secondarily written down.

A nation's language is a system of thought and expression peculiar to that nation and is the outward expression and manifestation of that nation's view of the universe. It is the key to the psychology and philosophy of a people and is the lens through which the national and individual psyche (soul) may be understood. Through its structure, phenomenological data are strained and even altered in accord with a manner the people can comprehend and make part of their worldview.

To illustrate how languages force down a grid upon what we see and do not see, an anthropologist named Albert Heinrich conducted tests among the Eskimos of the Canadian Northwest in 1972. The test consisted of the anthropologist showing color chips to the native informants and having them name the color in the Inuit language. There were names for all colors except gray. When shown a chip of dark gray, the informants described it as "blackish"; when shown a chip of light gray, they described it as "whitish." None of them had ever heard of one word that described the condition of gray itself. So they did not "see" this color.[24]

24. "Some Notes on Central Eskimo Color Terminology," in *Language and Thought: Anthropological Issues,* ed. W. C. McCormack and Steven A. Wurm (The Hague: Mouton, 1977), pp. 49–50.

In the Lakota language, the term for green and blue is the same. For example: *wató* means greenery or green grass and green bushes, while *mahpíya tó* means blue sky. If greater precision is required, two color words are combined such as *tozí*—blue and yellow equals light green—while *canhpápizi*, the color of liver or rotten wood, equals dark green.[25]

The Lakota say English is a "thingy" language. This does not mean that English has many names for things, although that is true. It means, rather, that words in English have a concrete, absolute quality not found to the same degree in Lakota. This perceived quality gives English the rigidity of a "thing" or a physical object, while Lakota is fluid and dynamic. Words have a functional rather than an absolute meaning. The function is determined by word order. For example, *hi* means tooth or teeth when the word appears at the beginning of a sentence. *Hi mayazan* means "my tooth (or teeth) hurts me." When the word *hi* comes at the end of a sentence, it changes from a noun into a verb, from the name of a thing into an action word. *Paul ehanni hi yelo* means "Paul arrived here earlier." The European tongues, including English, do not enjoy this flexibility. "Tooth" remains "tooth," no matter where it is positioned in a sentence or phrase, and does not change to "arrives" if it comes at the end.

Language is a conceptual tool. It is the grid through which the phenomenological data of the universe are strained. It is the way we cut up experience. In the Lakota experience, it is a method of total apprehension and comprehension. It is the seal or affirmation of "Indianness," of *identity*. It is a way of "seeing" with the eye of the heart and the mind in what Scott Momaday, the Kiowa writer, calls reciprocal appropriation.[26] Among the traditional Sioux there is a saying: "The white man sees so little, he must see with only one eye." This is because the white man is taught to see only with the mind—facts—and he forgets to combine or add that imaginative and moral aspect of nature which alone makes facts meaningful and beautiful to human beings.

Take the ceremony of the sweat lodge. Even the Lakota name *iníkagapi*, which means "with it they make life," is a much more compelling and profound concept than the English term "sweat lodge," which reduces this important ritual to the level of an early sauna bath. At various points in the ceremony, cold water is poured on glowing rocks and steam results. The white man sees this procedure as a fact, but this is as far as he goes in his mind's eye. Indians also know the

25. Robert Bunge, *An American Urphilosophie* (Lanham, N.Y.: University Press of America, 1984), p. 151.
26. "Native American Attitudes to the Environment," in *Seeing with a Native Eye*, ed. Walter Holden Capps (New York: Harper Forum Books, 1970).

facts—that every time one pours cold water on hot rocks, steam results—but the native does not stop there. He applies that imaginative
and moral act of the mind which alone makes facts meaning-laden.
For the Sioux this additional element is expressed thus: *Mní ki wakáyá
inázi yeló*, "the water stands in a holy way." The spirit of the water has
released the spirit of the stones, and thus combined, they both
"stand" in a holy way to purify the participants spiritually and physically. Facts alone are often poor servants of what is true, or of what is
significant. It is seeing with the eye of the heart, which is embodied
in our native languages, that makes the facts significant.

Some people, even Indians, will tell you that the native tongues are
primitive and are no longer suitable vehicles of expression in high-
tech societies. To them I say that I have studied over twenty languages, including five Native American tongues, and I have yet to
find a "primitive" one. I have never encountered a language that was
crudely devised or incapable of expansion and growth. The Navajo
have names for all the parts of a modern automobile, not borrowed
from English, but constructed from their own native word-pool.

Language is a spiritual experience, and this is particularly true of
our native languages, not only in the ceremony of the sweat lodge,
but in an everyday sacred way of perceiving and expressing these
perceptions. The universe of discourse of the dominant European
tongues is that of an impersonal, inanimate, mechanistic, and amoral
state of affairs, while the universe of discourse of Lakota and other
Native American languages is one of a personal, animate, and moral
state of being.

There is nothing more important for native young people than to
know their native language and the tribal lore and wisdom embodied
in that language. It is the very heart of identity. Many people will tell
you that having an education is the most important thing in the
world. Important as education is, there has to be a foundation upon
which education can be built. This foundation is character, character
that can only arise from an identity and an identity one can be proud
of, undergirded by a knowledge of our ancestral wisdom and the language containing that wisdom.

The worst aspect of cultural genocide is that, once successfully cut
off from one's roots, *loss of identity* follows, the deepest calamity which
can befall a people or an individual. A good deal of this destruction
was imposed from without and beyond the power of the native
peoples to resist: the taking of native children to government boarding schools far from their country and parents, the punishment of
children for wearing native dress or for speaking their native language. Just as destructive, many parents so vividly recalled the
trouble they had at various schools that they decided it would be bet-

ter for their children if they were not taught in their native language and lore right from the beginning, thus avoiding the psychic upheaval.

Today young native people, for a variety of reasons, are abandoning their own language and culture. In the 1950s, I visited a village in which the whole population spoke the native language fluently; it was the first language of the village, the language of daily social intercourse in which people discussed the weather, birth, death, and hunting conditions. It was the language of feasting, praying, loving, and sorrowing, as the people lived through the activities, sacred and secular, of the cycle of the year. Only two people in the village spoke the European tongue of the dominant society. Twenty years later I visited that same village and the linguistic picture was completely reversed. Everyone spoke the European language and only two still spoke the native language fluently. Sometime during this period the youth of the village, young adults and teenagers, made a decision to go with the language of the larger society. This is cultural suicide.

Some people, white and Indian alike, will tell you: "You can't go back" to a more traditional time. While this statement is true, it is beside the point. It is not a question of "going back," because the traditional languages and religions still live. It is a question rather of practicing those timeless values which have served the Indian people well in the past and continue to serve in the present. The native way of life has undoubtedly changed, but so has the life of white society. Is the white man less white because he drives a car and not a buggy like his grandfather? Is an Indian less Indian because he drives a pickup and does not ride a horse any longer?

Do not let propagandists of any stripe tell you the native languages are archaic relics of a bygone age, best forgotten. Know that speaking your own tongue along with that of the dominant society is a gain rather than a loss for everyone. Remember that a people who lose their language, and the view of the universe expressed by that language, can no longer survive as a people, but only as rootless individuals. We must continue to use the tongue of the grandfathers and imbibe the wisdom contained therein, for they are the only fixed point in a changing and confusing age, the anchor of identity and meaning.

Official English: Implications for Deaf Education

By Ceil Lucas

Ceil Lucas is associate professor of linguistics at Gallaudet University in Washington, D.C. An earlier version of this article appeared as "English Only: Bad News for the Deaf Community," *EPIC Events* 31, no. 6 (January–February 1989): 3–4.

The growing debate over initiatives to make English the official language is one that cannot be ignored by the American deaf community. Deaf people stand to be very negatively affected, particularly in the areas of education and interpreting.

To fully grasp the impact of the English Only movement on deaf education, some background is required. The beginning of deaf education in the United States is traditionally set in 1817 with the founding of what is now known as the American School for the Deaf in Hartford, Connecticut. The school was founded by Thomas Hopkins Gallaudet and Laurent Clerc, a French deaf man, after Gallaudet had traveled to France and seen an innovative method of teaching deaf students to read and write French. This method involved the use of French Sign Language (the natural sign language indigenous to French deaf people) and an added set of invented signs that were used to represent certain parts of written French. Upon returning to America, Clerc and Gallaudet began to train deaf American teachers in this fashion at the American School, and these teachers, in turn, went out to teach deaf children using American Sign Language (A.S.L.).

In 1880, however, an international congress was held in Milan, Italy, where deaf educators decided that *oralism*, or the use and teaching of speech, was the best way to educate deaf children and that sign language should not be allowed as the medium of instruction. Oralism meant using a spoken language in the classroom and focusing efforts on teaching students to speak English, to the exclusion of sign language. (It should be noted that, while the French method did involve teaching students to read and write French, the intent was not to teach them to *speak* French.) While deaf education in the United States never became totally oral, many deaf teachers lost their jobs; deaf teachers who were allowed to teach sign language were restricted to working with older students, as it was feared that exposure to A.S.L. would retard children's English skills.

The focus on oralism continued in the United States until the early 1970s. By that time educators had begun to realize that strict oralism was simply not accomplishing educational objectives and that deaf students' attainment was lagging far behind that of their hearing peers. Also around this time, many educators of the deaf decided to include signing in the educational process, and an eclectic approach evolved that eventually came to be known as *total communication*. This method involves the simultaneous use of signs and spoken English, the premise being that it is important for deaf students to see English modeled on the hands. While this approach may seem attractive intuitively, in fact, the use of this *sign-supported speech* results in slow and awkward speaking and signing, often with signs omitted or incorrect signs used.

Nevertheless, sign-supported speech is still widely used in deaf education, while programs that use A.S.L. as the medium of instruction are just now being implemented. The product of oralism and total communication in deaf education is a preponderance of young adults who read on average at a fourth grade level and who often are not prepared to compete in the working world on an equal footing with their hearing peers.

One exception to this state of affairs is the increasing evidence that deaf children of deaf parents often demonstrate significantly better skills in reading and writing English than their peers who have hearing parents. Why this discrepancy? It may be explained by the fact that deaf children who have deaf parents are exposed to a natural language, A.S.L., and acquire it in a normal and natural way—in the same way that hearing children acquire a spoken language from their parents and care-givers. When these deaf children are then exposed to English in the school system, they already have a natural language base, to which English is added as a second language.

This experience contrasts with that of many deaf children, whose first exposure to any linguistic system that they can perceive (but may or may not comprehend) is to an invented sign code for a spoken language, such as Signing Exact English. During these children's early years, the "critical period" for developing language skills, they are not exposed to a natural sign language. On the other hand, it should be noted that deaf parents are extremely sensitive to the fact that their children will need English skills to function as successful adults in American society, and consequently, there is a lot of English instruction that takes place in the home—bilingually, in English and A.S.L.

Evidence for the advantages enjoyed by the deaf children of deaf parents is dramatic. In March 1988, during the nationally publicized protest at Gallaudet University (which resulted in the appointment of the university's first deaf president, instead of a hearing one with no experience in the deaf community) all four of the student leaders came from deaf families. Also, most of the children in the gifted and talented program at the Kendall Demonstration Elementary School on the Gallaudet campus are from deaf families. There appears to be a clear link between early acquisition of a natural sign language and educational achievement, including achievement in English. Thus awareness is increasing of the potential to use A.S.L. in educational settings, be it in the education of deaf children or of young adults in a university, and there are efforts to make this potential a reality.

The English Only movement gives fuel to exactly what has failed in deaf education, that is, the insistence on using English to the exclusion of A.S.L. It places in jeopardy what may be the best solution: early acquisition of A.S.L., and education through A.S.L., combined with English-as-a-second-language instruction.

Furthermore, A.S.L. is an autonomous, viable linguistic system quite independent from English, and is the preferred mode of communication for many deaf people in many situations. (It is true that contact with English has resulted in a kind of contact signing that occurs in many social situations, but this is by no means the preferred or sole mode of communication.) In this regard, English Only legislation also raises very difficult issues for the whole area of sign-language interpreting. That is, it would seem that deaf people have a right to receive information in the language of their choice and the language they understand. The situation may be of a medical, legal, educational, or personal nature. The English Language Amendment, by restricting the use of languages other than English, could have the effect of severely restricting the deaf person's right of access to information through A.S.L.

Finally, there is the issue of speaking English, as opposed to reading and writing it. Many deaf adults choose to learn to speak, in addition to learning to read and write. But *speech* and *language* are not synonymous. The issue is one of choice. The English Only outlook reinforces the traditional view that deaf children and deaf adults must be taught to speak and use English, and rules out instruction through the medium of A.S.L., a view that has led directly to the failure of deaf education. Such a course would be unnecessarily restrictive, myopic, and damaging.

The Costs of Monolingualism

By Catherine E. Snow and Kenji Hakuta

Catherine E. Snow is professor of education at the Harvard Graduate School of Education. Kenji Hakuta is professor of education at Stanford University and author of *Mirror of Language: The Debate on Bilingualism.* This article was originally published in 1989 by the Bilingual Research Group, Working Paper No. 89–06, Merrill College, University of California, Santa Cruz.

A society makes choices based on an implicit cost-benefit analysis. The assumption behind any cost-benefit analysis is, of course, that choosing a desirable course of action has consequences which are less desirable—often the need to give up an alternative choice which has its own set of benefits. The United States is currently grappling with decisions about language; members of groups like U.S. English argue that the social costs of tolerating the use of languages other than English, in terms of potential disruption and political factionalism, are unacceptable. Proponents of bilingual education argue that the social costs of low achievement by a significant minority of school children are too great.

While the proponents of U.S. English and of bilingual education can be seen as defending conflicting positions, we will argue in this paper that the conflict is apparent, not real. Furthermore, we will argue that both the proposal of U.S. English to establish English as the official national language, and the institution of bilingual education as it is typically practiced, entail additional serious costs not usually computed into the final amount of this particular societal decision—the costs of monolingualism. Perhaps some light can be shed on the consequences of either of these decisions by considering what basic psychological and linguistic research can tell us about the costs and benefits of monolingualism and bilingualism.

The classic characterization of American society is "the melting pot"—a merging of immigrant groups into a single, undifferentiated whole. A prerequisite to the melting has been acquiring English, an unsurprising requirement in a country where English is the language of government, of education, of business, and of daily life. What should surprise us is the willingness among immigrants, almost as strong as their tendency to acquire English, to lose their traditional languages. Nonetheless, the United States is, at the societal level, staunchly monolingual. Legislating monolingualism as a requirement for citizenship could hardly have been more successful in creating a monolingual society than have been the unofficial economic and social forces at work.

It may seem odd to claim that the United States is one of the most monolingual societies in the world. What of the Hispanic population of the United States, currently 9 percent and growing? What of the millions of dollars spent on bilingual education, for the benefit of students from homes where Spanish, Portuguese, Vietnamese, and Chinese, or a myriad of other languages are spoken? What of the French-speaking communities in Louisiana and in northern New England? What of the Chinatowns in Boston, New York, and San Francisco and the Japanese communities in California? What of the immigrant communities of Cubans, Southeast Asians, Haitians, and Central Americans, all maintaining ties with their traditional languages? These groups look like cases of bilingualism within the melting pot.

Demographic studies, both current and historical, however, tell us that stable bilingualism is not characteristic of these groups. Only the old folks, the very young, and the recent arrivals, in general, speak these other languages; the school children and young adults have often switched to "dominance" in English. Once the parents' generation becomes more comfortable in English—something that can happen in the course of the second generation—then the third generation is monolingual in English. This shift from bilingualism to monolingualism can be seen even in the current groups of immigrants to whom bilingual education services are widely available.

There is an unfortunate tendency to believe that this linguistic laissez-faire toward English monolingualism is the natural state, even perhaps the morally correct one, and that attempting to change its course would inflict large costs elsewhere. It is therefore important to understand the psychological and societal forces underlying this shift, for it has been the source of frustration and perplexity to many educators and policymakers who understand that monolingualism is costly both to the monolingual individual and to society. The rapid shift into English means that children who could have learned fluent Spanish or Chinese or Portuguese from their mothers and grandmothers are instead struggling to learn it, and often succeeding poorly, in high school foreign language classes.

Aside from the communication gap that is created across generations of immigrants by this shift, there are many other costs associated with the melting pot's shift into monolingual English. Costs to society include:

- *Educational costs.* We need to devote teachers, school time, and part of the educational budget to foreign language training. American schools are notoriously poor in this field, and the resultant levels of fluency and correctness among foreign language students are much lower than among children who have learned these languages at home.
- *Economic costs.* American multinational businesses that compete abroad are severely hampered by the low numbers of Americans competent in languages other than English.
- *National security costs.* Millions of dollars are spent annually training foreign-service personnel, military personnel, and spies in foreign languages.

Costs to the individual include:

- *Time and effort.* It takes time, effort, commitment, motivation, and hard work to learn a foreign language in high school, and much less effort just to maintain a language already learned at home.
- *Cognitive costs.* There is some evidence suggesting that monolingual children are missing out on an opportunity to develop an early appreciation of language that results in better ability to perform well on tasks requiring linguistic and cognitive flexibility.

These are only some of the costs. They can be minimized by efforts to maintain the natural linguistic resources of bilingual youngsters, rather than standing by and tolerating the shift into monolingualism. So why does this shift occur? Why do people who can speak two languages tend to shift into the exclusive use of one? Is this shift inevitable, or are there certain circumstances that deflect this shift? Some answers to these questions can be found in the nature of bilingualism and the nature of language proficiency.

Strange as it may seem, there is no general consensus on the definition of language proficiency. Though there are many ways that people assess language, without a definition of proficiency it is difficult to know exactly what those assessment techniques are measuring. Those who study bilingualism are rather like four-year-old children just taught how to use a ruler—they can measure length, width, and height, but have no idea how to compute volume.

Typical approaches to assessing bilingual proficiency involve doing things like counting the errors made in the second language. This sort of approach is clearly inadequate; we know someone who speaks perfectly error-free Spanish, but can only carry on conversations about how much things cost and what size they are; we know someone else whose Spanish is chock full of errors, but who can talk about a wide variety of topics with anyone from a Puerto Rican taxi driver to the professor of Romance languages at the university. Which of these has higher proficiency in Spanish? Clearly, a notion of proficiency that is based on getting communicative tasks accomplished has a certain merit, but we cannot totally ignore matters of correctness, either.

We favor a notion of proficiency very like that proposed by François Grosjean in his book *Life with Two Languages: An Introduction to Bilingualism*.[27] Grosjean assesses bilingualism functionally. Think of a chart of the tasks one faces in a given month: shopping, going to restaurants, talking and writing notes to your children's teachers, helping children with homework, having professional conversations, attending professional lectures, giving talks, writing letters, reading and writing reports, watching television, having family dinner-table conversations, keeping a diary, negotiating with plumbers, babysitters, gardeners, or repairmen, and so forth. Grosjean suggests that if any of these tasks is accomplished in a second language, you are a bilingual. The more tasks you can perform in either of two languages, the more proficient a bilingual you are.

But, of course, no one does all those things every day in two languages. In fact, for any particular bilingual, certain spheres of life (perhaps home and friendship) are in one language, while other spheres (perhaps work and public encounters) are in another. Furthermore, one's ability to function in any of those spheres in either language may wax and wane with circumstance and need. What this means is that, even for adults, proficiency in a language is not stable. Knowledge of a language and skills in using it are more like dancing the lead in *Giselle* than like the traditional notion of riding a bicycle. Not only are practice and conditioning crucial to being able to perform, but someone who has not played the role in a long while may even forget some of the steps! Attrition of language skills, even of *first* language skills when they are long unused, is a common phenomenon, now beginning to be documented by a number of researchers. We need to know much more about the circumstances that promote or prevent such attrition.

The fact that one's proficiency in a language, even a native language, can decline suggests that languages have to be used to be maintained. Thus, there is a personal cost to bilingualism: the psychological energy needed to keep using both the languages or to risk losing proficiency in one. It may be this cost, among others, that is reflected in the demographic trends toward monolingualism in the society.

There is another psychological cost for a bilingual individual who has to interact in an only partially bilingual society: the threat to hu-

27. Cambridge, Mass.: Harvard University Press, 1982.

man relationships, to self-image, and to personal identity associated with every choice of which language to use. The reason why language choice for the bilingual can be so difficult may be explained by one of the basic principles of social psychology—the convergence principle. The convergence principle states that we tend to shift our language style toward that of persons we like and admire. In everyday monolingual conversations between speakers of slightly different dialects or generations, one can see examples of the convergence principle at work, as the northerner starts shifting into a slight drawl with a southern friend or a grandparent adopts a grandchild's baby-talk words.

Consider the case of the perfectly bilingual Mexican American whose children start to speak English among themselves and eventually to their parents. The adults can stubbornly go on speaking Spanish, which their children understand, to maintain the children's proficiency in Spanish. But conversations where one partner speaks Spanish and the other speaks English are hard to keep going for long, as the convergence principle predicts. Not surprisingly, the parents typically give in, with the result that the children end up monolingual English speakers. Such parents can talk about the conflict—they would like their children to speak Spanish—but they do not want to sacrifice the familial intimacy, the freedom from conflict, and the convenience associated with acceding to their children's preferences. Costs to the family are reduced, but the children (and the society) pay the resultant costs associated with monolingualism.

Why do the children in such a family gravitate to English monolingualism? English, because it is the language of prestige and the majority culture; monolingualism, because for the child, as much as for the adult, maintaining two languages is harder than learning, maintaining, and using just one. In fact, the loss of one language under the influence of the other, a problem for adults, is particularly acute for children. Learning a second language takes so much energy for young children that it is difficult to maintain the first language at the same time without extensive support. The child who is still learning the first language, as five- and six-year-olds certainly are, is particularly susceptible to stagnation and decline. Becoming bilingual as a child is sure to involve some costs: perhaps a cost to the first language; certainly the cost of a period of inadequacy, discomfort, and low proficiency in the second language; and perhaps the cost of being judged a poor student because the assessment of intelligence and aptitude is made based on performance in a language not yet fully mastered.

How long, then, does it actually take to learn a language for a child or an adult? Anyone who has studied a foreign language knows it's a

painful process that can take a lot of time, effort, and willingness to
risk feeling foolish in public. There is a myth that such is not the case
for children, that "kids just pick up languages with no trouble." In
fact, however, kids have *more* trouble than adults. If we take objective
measures of how long it takes children and adults under similar circumstances to learn a second language, the adults are much faster.
Children may appear to learn faster because they can function without knowing much, or because they pick up crucial social expressions
quickly, or because their accents are better. But their knowledge of
vocabulary, syntax, morphology, and discourse rules is much inferior
to that of teenagers and adults after a similar interval of exposure to
the second language. Moreover, the speed of second-language learning depends on many factors, including motivation, aptitude, and
the setting in which the learning takes place.

And so, although there is a general belief that children just pick up
a language and absorb it with no effort, in fact, it turns out that learning a language is hard for young children, hard enough that they will
avoid it if possible and will take quite a long time accomplishing it if
they cannot avoid it. Young children, as much as older ones, feel the
"cost" of personal discomfort, social isolation, and lowered self-
esteem associated with speaking the language of their interactants
poorly.

Oddly enough, some researchers have suggested that there is a
personal cost associated with becoming too fluent and proficient a
speaker of a second language as well, especially for adolescents and
adults in a submersion situation. This cost derives from the fact that
one expresses cultural identity through language. One's way of
speaking conveys personal information about ethnicity, geographical
origin, social class, age, political leanings, and many other aspects of
the self. This presentation of the self is, of course, different in another
language. Fluent bilinguals often report having different personalities
in their two languages, and studies have suggested that bilinguals
show different responses in projective psychological tests, such as the
Thematic Apperception Test, depending on which language is used.

The adult who learns a second language so well that he can "pass"
as a native speaker is, in a sense, in a very risky situation. He is in
danger of losing the identity that is well established in the first language, because he is being treated as a native of the second culture.
Furthermore, since he is *not* really a native in the second culture, he
is liable to make errors, both of self-presentation and in understanding others, that would be forgiven in a second-language speaker, but
are not even recognized in a supposed native. One of the authors, for
example, picked up and started using in Dutch an expression learned
from some neighbors which turned out to be a sociolinguistic

"marker" for a working-class dialect. People who were inclined to accept the speaker as a native of the Netherlands would have made a serious error in judging social class and educational background. Protection against such misinterpretation is provided by an accent, a clear marker of "the foreigner," whose misuse of such expressions can be taken as an error or a joke. For the other author, who sounds like a native speaker of English, such protection was unavailable shortly after coming to the United States. He went into a delicatessen and ordered what he now calls "roast beef on hard," but with the last two words reversed, much to the shock of the butcher. It would have been more graceful with a thick accent.

Perhaps the greatest cost of bilingualism feared by Americans with a belief in the melting pot is not the cost to the individual, but the price paid by society as a whole. It is often felt that bilingualism costs too much at the societal level, where different language-based ethnic groups might weaken the status of English and cause the splintering of the nation. Those with such misgivings are worried that the United States might follow the footsteps of officially bilingual countries such as Canada and Belgium, where tensions among the linguistic groups abound. However, most political scientists who have studied the relationship between language and politics seem to agree that language is rarely the *causal* agent of such conflicts. Although language differences may serve as the focal point of the controversies, they usually just mirror the tensions already existent. Indeed, one can point to officially multilingual countries such as Switzerland, where there is very little conflict among the language groups. The crucial characteristic of tension-free bilingual nations is the expectation that it is normal for all citizens to be bilingual. In contrast, in tension-ridden bilingual nations, bilingualism at the individual level is considered abnormal.

How does the current status of bilingual education fit into this accounting of the costs of monolingualism and bilingualism? The federal government and the overwhelming majority of state and local boards of education have a very narrow view of costs. They do not consider the costs to society of losing linguistic resources. Their concern, in tune with the times, is with the amount of money spent on bilingual education programs. Bilingual education in its present form may be one of the greatest misnomers of educational programs. What it fosters is monolingualism; bilingual classrooms are efficient revolving doors between home-language monolingualism and English monolingualism. Were it not for the name, the champion of linguistic homogeneity on American soil could not have found a better friend than transitional bilingual education.

To be sure, there have been changes in the ways in which language-minority children have been educated in American schools. The old days of sink-or-swim submersion in regular classrooms with no special help are looked upon with almost universal shame and anger for their cruelty. The bilingual initiatives that were taken in the 1960s have certainly made the transition easier for students. But the bottom line of all of these programs has been an almost single-minded interest in the extent and the efficiency of English proficiency development.

Submersion is, for society, a cheap route to second-language learning (no special teachers, classes, curriculum, or programs required). But it is costly for the individual and may have associated with it a high risk of total failure (school dropouts barely literate in either the home language or English) and of educational delay. If a society decides it is important, for example, that non-English-speaking children be as good as English-speaking age-mates in reading, arithmetic, and other content areas, then allowing the non-English speakers to be mute observers while the English speakers learn the basic school skills may produce permanent scholastic problems.

Bilingual education or English as a second language (E.S.L.) programs in American schools were designed to minimize that risk in two ways: (1) by speeding up the acquisition of English and (2) by ensuring that the basic school skills and some content-area instruction go on while English is being learned. Submersion puts the entire burden on the child. Bilingual education and E.S.L. divert some of the burden to the schools. Research suggests that, particularly for children who are at some educational risk anyway—for example, children whose parents have limited schooling; children who arrive at school without the prereading or early reading skills typical of their middle-class peers; children from homes where economic and psychological stress may prevent parents from monitoring school progress, helping with homework, or contacting teachers—the likelihood of success, both in English proficiency and in school achievement, is greater if the schools discharge that burden effectively.

Even with the support of bilingual education or E.S.L., however, young children cannot be expected to learn second languages quickly. Research by Lily Wong Fillmore and Barry McLaughlin suggests that as many as half the non-English-speaking children in bilingual programs need more than three years of help before their English is good enough to understand reading books at their grade level or to understand teachers' talk during lessons on science or math. Some children were faster, but some who were potentially good students needed as much as four or five years of help with English before they could display their skills as learners. Such children, if placed prematurely in mainstream classrooms, run the risk of being seen as slow learners, as dyslexic, as learning disabled, or as just stupid by teachers who are unaware that the students' control of English is simply inadequate. Surprisingly, such children are sometimes given I.Q. tests (based heavily on vocabulary knowledge—obviously a weak point for children who came late to English) and diagnosed as retarded on this basis! Clearly, if we are going to mainstream non-English speakers prematurely, we must at least postpone diagnosing, classifying, or grouping them based on their performance in their second language.

Bilingual education programs are doing precious little to maintain the native languages of the students. In a recent national survey of the goals of school districts with language-minority students, fewer than 10 percent of the districts cited native-language maintenance to be their goal. Furthermore, even in programs with a strong component for the development of native-language skills, students are quickly moved out into mainstream classes, often after one or two years in the program. For the majority of language-minority youngsters who go through the revolving door of bilingual education, what lies ahead is the shift to English monolingualism.

Strictly in terms of second-language acquisition, foreign language classrooms are less effective than submersion or bilingual approaches because the second language is spoken _only_ in the classroom and not in the society. The age differences in speed of acquisition noted above for submersion settings are, if anything, even more pronounced in foreign language settings. In the 1950s American schools initiated a program called foreign language in the elementary school (FLES), which was abandoned after results came out suggesting that gains made during two to three years of FLES could be matched with a few months of instruction at the high school level. However, while relatively little foreign language proficiency was acquired by FLES students, they did evidently derive from the experience some interest in foreign language study. Since the abandonment of the FLES programs, the number of students taking foreign languages in high schools has dropped precipitously. The United States is the only technologically advanced western nation in which there is no requirement for foreign language study, even for academic-track students, in high school. A current, mild return of interest in foreign languages among high school students is creating a personnel crisis, since so few trained teachers emerge from a system that postpones serious foreign language study until the university. Achieving sufficient levels of proficiency in a foreign language to teach it can take several years, even for adults. Starting at age eighteen just does not give very much time.

A novel method for foreign language instruction to elementary school children was first introduced in Canada by Wallace Lambert and associates in the Montreal school system. They taught whole classes of English-speaking children French simply by giving them a French teacher who taught the entire curriculum in French. In the beginning the children answered in English, but after a year or two were expected to use only French in the classroom. Such *immersion programs* have been tried in the United States as well. Immersion can be remarkably successful, but again, it takes several years for children to become fluent, it works faster with older than with younger children, and the levels of second-language skills achieved are rarely native-like. The primary problem with foreign language immersion programs seems to be that all the students in such programs are from the same, majority-language background. They have little or no contact with peers who speak the foreign language as natives.

There is an irony here, of course. Bilingual and E.S.L. programs were designed to get children who speak a language other than English into English classrooms as soon as possible. Because it requires effort on the child's part, and perhaps commitment and skill on the parents' part as well, to maintain and develop the native-language skill when the child is in an English-speaking classroom all day, there is a risk of losing proficiency in the home language. Even if the parents maintain bilingualism, we have seen above that their children are extremely unlikely to do so. Thus the children in our society who have the best bet at proficiency in two languages are being seduced by the school system into monolingualism in English, while the children who might be willing to work hard to achieve bilingualism are given instruction in foreign languages that is typically too little and too late to ensure adequate proficiency.

One novel method, called the *two-way bilingual program*, has been taking the best of both worlds from bilingual and foreign language education. In these programs minority students are provided the traditional form of bilingual education, that is, instruction in their native language, with gradual increments of English. The difference is that English monolingual students are placed in the same program and thus immersed in the foreign language spoken by the minority students. By the third grade, both groups of students receive equal amounts of instruction in English and in the foreign language. A major strength of two-way bilingual programs is that both groups of students act as linguistic models for each other. The chance of becoming proficiently bilingual is increased—in the case of minority students, through retention and development of their native language while acquiring English, and in the case of majority students, through exposure to real speakers of the foreign language.

Two-way programs can be found in many parts of the country, including California, New York, Michigan, and Ohio. They take advantage of the local linguistic resources, and certainly must maintain flexibility to allow for fluctuations in these resources, such as new immigration. What differentiates these two-way programs from transitional bilingual education is their philosophy that the costs of monolingualism are far greater than the costs associated with bilingualism.

Perhaps it is inevitable that educators debate methodology when they are really debating politics. The current attack on bilingual education is seen as yet another example of a conservative administration's lack of commitment to minority programs and is counterattacked accordingly. What is truly saddening is that this political furor obscures any discussion of the costs or the benefits of bilingualism. Indeed, most proponents as well as opponents of bilingual education share the same long-term objective, which is English monolingualism. Program-evaluation research, difficult though it is to do and interpret, seems to show that bilingual education does work to teach English, but certainly not to create bilinguals.

Learning a second language is a tough task for children and adults everywhere in the world. Within the United States it is especially hard because of the remoteness of most Americans from any place where other languages are actually used. Americans lack the expectation that everyone will be bilingual. In fact, bilingualism is associated in this country with the lower classes and the immigrants, not with the educated elite. This association may be one of the reasons why we have defined the melting pot as monolingual rather than multilingual. As with any such choice, there are real costs involved.

PART SIX

International Perspectives on Language Politics

Do language differences inevitably spell political trouble? There is a widespread assumption that a nation cannot accommodate more than one language without paying a social price. The fear of balkanization—that bilingualism will divide and disrupt, fostering tribal loyalties and misunderstanding between groups—has generated much support for Official English. Many Americans look at bilingual Canada and see a country at war with itself. While language tensions are not yet acute in the United States, they reason, we would be wise to avoid policies that might encourage a similar situation here.

International analogies have played a starring role in the Official English debate. Unfortunately, they have been stock characters in a rather simple-minded melodrama. Consider, for example, the analysis of Senator Steve Symms, an Idaho Republican and a sponsor of the English Language Amendment. He blames Canada's troubles on the 1867 British North America Act, which gave coequal status (in principle) to the English and French languages. "More than a hundred years later," Symms explains, "the Canadian people suffer from a tragic split as a result of this legislated language difference." Presumably, bilingualism would have withered away without legal sanction. The senator goes on to warn: "Countless hundreds of thousands have lost their lives in the language riots of India. Real potential exists for a similar situation to be replayed in the United States."[1] By means of such fantasies, Symms reduces language diversity to an internal security threat. (Logically, his argument should extend to religious diversity, a larger factor in India's social turmoil since independence.)

One need not succumb to paranoia, however, to draw negative conclusions about bilingualism elsewhere. No American who has visited Quebec envies the seemingly pointless bickering between anglophones and francophones. Few of us would reject the advantages of a common language, spoken almost universally within our borders. Babel is a curse we can do without, and the experience of other nations may provide some guidance in avoiding it. But skimming superficial lessons can be dangerous—in particular, the conclusion that language differences are at the root of complex social and economic

1. *Congressional Record*, 98th Cong., 1st sess., Sept. 21, 1983, p. S12643.

conflicts. The Babel legend reverses cause and effect, explains Einar Haugen. Speech distances are the result of social distances rather than vice versa. "Language is not a problem unless it is used as a basis for discrimination," he argues. Yet that is precisely the impact of legislating conformity. However tempting in the interest of efficiency, such policies can end up widening divisions instead of bridging them.

Ronald Inglehart and Margaret Woodward analyze language conflicts as a function of ethnic inequality—or more precisely, as resulting from a blockage of social mobility for members of subject groups with rising expectations. Such conflicts are not universal, but historical phenomena. In static and stratified societies—feudal ones, for example—language differences pose few political problems because the masses are excluded from political discourse (the elites can always hire translators). By contrast, industrialism brings economic opportunities, the migration of rural populations to the cities, the expansion of public education and literacy, and the centralization of government—changes that inspire projects to standardize communication and incite competition among national groups. As a practical medium and a "marker" of ethnicity, language becomes a predictable source of tension. And so, as Inglehart and Woodward observe, language-based animosities tend to "take on a life of their own," though they are spawned by larger social contradictions.

Canada's language politics are impossible to appreciate without a grasp of its history as a union of two founding nationalities. From the outset, however, ethnic equality was purely theoretical. The lowly status of French not only reflected, but also enhanced the economic and political advantage of English speakers, even in Quebec. Language discrimination, by design and by neglect, created a mutual estrangement over time and loosened the bonds of the Canadian federation. Moves toward reform in the 1960s, toward applying at long last the principle of official bilingualism, came too late to stem Québecois nationalism and separatism. Jonathan Lemco describes the backlash of francophones, who have developed their own system of language discrimination within the province of Quebec. Enacted in 1977, Bill 101 has established a French Only regime affecting most phases of government, education, and business. With the understandable aim of defending French against the encroachments of English, the policy has trampled the civil liberties of Quebec's anglophone minority and exacerbated ethnic mistrust.

Language diversity has both costs and benefits, explain economists David E. Bloom and Gilles Grenier. While a Babel of tongues can lower productivity, language skills are also a form of human capital. Their worth is affected not only by the forces of supply and demand, but by social and political variables. For example, research has shown that French-speaking ability is an increasingly valuable asset for Canadian workers, no doubt as a result of official bilingualism, while in the United States there has been a corresponding decline in the value of Spanish. Limited English skills seem to be a growing disadvantage in the American labor market

Still, the European model of "one nation = one language" is the world exception rather than the rule, argues Gregory Guy. Even where one language dominates, the vast majority of nation-states remain linguistically diverse. While this creates a range of complications, governmental responses are generally more pluralist than the nostrums of the Parti Québecois or U.S. English. Official recognition of minority tongues is regarded not only as a question of fairness, but as an opportunity to exploit valuable resources. Australia, with its mix of immigrant and indigenous languages and its English-speaking-majority, more closely resembles the U.S. situation than any other. Rather than focus on the negative example of Canada, Americans might do well to study Australia's resource-oriented National Policy on Languages.

Harold Isaacs, in describing the language problems of emerging nations, also illustrates the problems of generalizing about language conflicts. A powerful myth, which recurs with slight variations in many cultures, the Tower of Babel story crystallizes fears and frustrations about human diversity. As a political factor, however, language may be crucial at one juncture and irrelevant at another. Moreover, its capacities are contradictory. It may be used to fragment and polarize, to serve tribalism and class domination, to unleash bloody strife. But it is also dynamic and flexible, a planning tool for uniting postcolonial peoples, promoting development, and enhancing democracy. Paradoxically, language is an immutable feature of human identity, yet at the same time our most versatile and creative instrument.

The Curse of Babel

By Einar Haugen

Einar Haugen is professor of Scandinavian languages and linguistics at Harvard University and author of *The Norwegian Language in America: A Study in Bilingual Behavior,* among other works. This article is reprinted from *Daedalus* 102 (Summer 1973): 47–57.

There is, in Genesis, an intriguing tale about the origin of language diversity, well known as the Tower of Babel story, which will serve me as the text of my discourse. We are told, in the King James Version, that "the whole earth was of one language, and of one speech." But then pride fills the hearts of men, so that they are misled into trying to build "a city and a tower, whose top may reach unto heaven." The Lord Jehovah comes down to earth and decides to punish this presumption, perhaps worried that men might usurp His omnipotence, for "now nothing will be restrained from them, which they have imagined to do." In His infinite wisdom He proceeds to "confound their language, that they may not understand one another's speech." They are no longer able to cooperate in the building of their tower, and are "scattered abroad upon the face of all the earth." [2]

Similar stories are known from other cultures, but among the Hebrews the story was associated with the name of Babylon, which, by a false etymology, was understood to derive from a verb *bālal* meaning "to confuse." Babylon, as the capital of the Babylonian and Assyrian empires, was a big and sinful city in the eyes of the rural and severely religious Hebrews. The story not only explained why the towers of Babylon had crumbled, but more important, it answered the question thoughtful men and women must have asked everywhere: why is it that all men have languages, but all so different? In the multilingual Near East the natural answer was: the diversity was a curse laid upon men for their sinful pride.

Those of us who love languages and have devoted our lives to learning and teaching them, and who find in language a source of novel delights and subtle experience, find it hard to put ourselves in the right frame of mind to understand the conception of language diversity as a curse. Yet we need only find ourselves in a country, say Hungary, where every sign looks like an abracadabra, and speakers

2. Genesis 11:1–9.

399

shrug their shoulders at our efforts to communicate, to sense some of the terror of isolation that underlies the Hebrew view. As linguists, however, we are entitled to offer one basic correction to the Hebrew tale: men were not scattered abroad because they could not understand one another's speech. They could not understand one another *because they were scattered;* in the story cause and effect have been turned around. When men are separated by barriers of time and distance, their languages deviate in regular, if sometimes astonishing, ways.

The reason for this is clear: language is man's most distinctive and significant type of social behavior, and is, like all social behavior, learned anew by every child. The child not only can, he *must* learn whatever language is spoken around him. In learning it, however, he never learns it exactly like those from whom he heard it. His "creative imitation" (as we may call it) is not identical with its model, since it is not turned out in a factory, but is a piece of human craftsmanship. The gift of language is certainly innate and instinctive, but human speech differs from the music of birds precisely by being diverse and relatively idiosyncratic. What keeps it from being totally idiosyncratic is that each act of communication forces the communicators to monitor their expression by the response of those they are trying to reach. When one group ceases to communicate with another, the groups drift apart and develop their idiosyncracies, which linguists call *idiolects*, and as these accumulate, they grow into dialects, and languages, and language families.

The historical and social parallel between linguistic and biological inheritance has often obscured the fundamental difference between them. Races and languages have been confounded to the detriment of both, leading to a type of linguistic racism which is the true curse of Babel. Linguists know better, but they are not without fault in having developed a terminology that speaks of "language families" and "mother tongues," the "generation of dialects" and the "descent of words." These are all metaphors that can be drastically misleading, for there is nothing at all in language that is identical with biological descent. *There are no genes in language,* aside from the universal human gift of tongues. When linguists say that English is "descended" from Germanic and Germanic from Indo-European, they are only saying that there has been an unbroken transmission of speech habits all the way back to that tribe of conquerors who issued from the Caucasus or wherever, some five or six thousand years ago, and succeeded in imposing their language on most of Europe, on much of western Asia, and eventually on America, Australia, and other parts of the world. At every step of the way there were children who learned the language of the elders in their own way, and there were adults who learned and unlearned their languages to meet the demands put upon them by social and political necessity. There are no genes; there is only learning.

That *learning* is the key to every language problem is so obvious as to be almost a truism. But there is one condition of learning that I have observed over and over in various societies, without having heard of research upon it. This is the cross-fire of mutual criticism and correction within a close-knit social group. As children we have all felt the taunts that were directed at us when we deviated from the valid norms of speech. Children are cruel in applying laughter and ridicule to those who speak "differently." As they grow older, they become aware that linguistic deviation is an index to social distance. As adolescents they discover the difference between upper and lower class, the significance of belonging on this side or the other side of the tracks, and the speech mannerisms of the current peer-group hero as opposed to those of their obsolescing parents. As adults they have internalized these norms to the point that they register automatically, not that somebody's language is deviant, but that a speaker is "vulgar," or "stuck-up," or "foreign," and behave toward him according to these identifications. Wherever such identifications lead to antagonism or prejudice, to the exclusion of outsiders, or to the denigration of individuals, there I would find an example of the curse of Babel.

The gradual drifting apart of languages and dialects is a natural and inevitable consequence of the drifting apart of mankind. The Hebrew legend was surely right in assuming that all men were once of "one language and of one speech"; I cannot find any other hypothesis adequate to account for the basic similarities of all known natural languages. Insofar as mankind is *one* and language is man's chief distinction from the animals, polygenesis of language is hard to imagine. The further back we go in the known history of languages in the last four thousand years, the less difference we find among them. If we cannot yet find the ultimate point at which the so-called families or proto-languages diverged, this is presumably due to the enormous length of time that has passed. In this sense the Tower of Babel is a profound symbol for man's ultimate unity and for his common descent as a talking animal. The tower is the hypothetical point at which all the converging threads of today's and yesterday's languages meet, one which we can probably never know, and which is therefore best expressed in symbolic terms.

In their efforts to remove God's curse, men have resorted to various policies, ranging from neighborly tolerance to rigid isolation, from eager acceptance of a new language to brutal suppression of its speakers. Out of this crucible of language contact has come a class of speakers who can manage more than one language, the multilinguals or polyglots. To simplify our expression we shall call them all "bilinguals" and define them as "users of more than one language." To use a language does not necessarily entail mastering all its skills or its entire range: often it is enough, for example, to understand it when spoken, or to read it when written.

There is a vigorous flurry of interest these days in bilinguals and bilingualism. Linguists, sociologists, and educators have been mobilized to implement the federal Bilingual Education Act of 1968, which recognizes for the first time in American history that "the use of a child's mother tongue can have a beneficial effect upon his education." Black English and Chicano Spanish have emerged as valid and highly productive subjects of study by linguists. Ethnic groups are being urged to maintain their identity by teaching their native tongue to their children. Bilingual schools have been established in a number of communities where large blocs of non-English speakers live. Some degree of training in the native languages of these speakers has been introduced into the early grades in the hope of reducing the children's sense of alienation in an English-speaking world. To be sure, its goals go no further than to produce what is called "transitional bilingualism," a step on the way to integration into the English-speaking world. And it is hardly less discriminatory than earlier policies, since it does not provide for advanced training in these languages and does not give their communities any hope of continuing to exist as ethnic identities within our countries. There is no change in the official policy of Anglo-conformity, only a passing toleration of "linguistic pluralism." Nevertheless, even this is a great step forward and should be encouraged.

We are hardly unique in the world in having such problems. What is unique is that in our time a great many populations which speak minority languages are refusing to accept the status of second-class citizens in the countries they inhabit. Such a refusal could not arise as long as most peoples were locally bound as hewers of wood and drawers of water. We rarely hear of language problems arising in the Middle Ages or in the Czarist empire; only when governments instituted universal school systems, which in Europe was in the eighteenth century, did language become an explosive issue. The schools brought into age-old local communities a force for linguistically homogenizing the population; they were a kind of mold imposed on the people by a previously tolerant or indifferent government. The school became an instrument for "mobilizing" the population, in Karl Deutsch's happy phrase,[3] so that it could participate in national life, opening opportunities and imposing responsibilities that had never

3. *Nationalism and Social Communication* (Cambridge, Mass.: M.I.T. Press, 1953).

before been imagined. But this mobilization also had the effect of plugging the entire population into a network of communication that was expected to function fast and efficiently, which it could not do unless one language rather than many was spoken. Translation is slow and costly, and interference between codes results in loss of information; the obvious solution was to insist on one government, one language.

To illustrate the resulting problems and to offer a parallel with our own situation, let me take you to a remote corner of Sweden, the province of Norrbotten, at the top of the Gulf of Bothnia. Sweden, like the other Scandinavian countries, is often viewed as a highly homogeneous society with a successful social policy that ensures equality and prosperity for all. When Sweden has been touted to Americans as a model of the "middle way" between capitalism and communism, one deprecatory reply has been that, after all, Sweden is a small and homogeneous country, and has no problems of the magnitude of those facing America.

Norrbotten is a province a little bigger than Maine, with a population a little less than Alaska's and at the same latitude. It is located squarely on the Arctic Circle, a good 500 miles north of Stockholm, the capital. It is separated from Norway on the west by high barren mountains, from Finland on the east only by the Torne River. From sea to mountain there is virtually nothing but forest and tundra, with some agricultural valleys as one approaches the sea, and a few coastal towns, the largest being Luleå with 32,000 inhabitants. Inland is Sweden's most important mining town, Kiruna, the heart of her steel industry. In this remote district there exist within a population of a quarter of a million people no less than three kinds of bilingual problems. Each of these has called forth some of the same passions and concerns that such situations arouse elsewhere in the world.

First are the Lapps. They speak dialects of the language used by Lapps in various parts of northern Sweden, Finland, Russia, and Norway. Lappish is a Finno-Ugric language, related to but mutually incomprehensible with Finnish. The Lapps constitute a very small proportion of Norrbotten, possibly only 1.5 percent or something over 3,000 persons, a third of all the Lapps in Sweden. They are the aboriginal inhabitants, not only of this region, but of much of northern Norway and Sweden and all of Finland. They were a nomadic people of hunters and fishermen, who step by step were forced back from the more desirable lands, until they were left with territory that proved to be suitable only for reindeer herding. Even this occupation, traditional since the sixteenth century, is threatened today, and many Lapps have abandoned their native heath for occupations in urban centers and more southerly climes. As late as 1913 a nomad school system was devised by Sweden, in which the children were taught Swedish, with Lappish used chiefly for religious training. By now many have drifted off into urban areas and have slowly been climbing the ladder of Swedish life, a few succeeding to the extent of going to a university. The jobs most of them have found, however, have been positions as kitchen maids, shop assistants, office clerks, nurses, or teachers, railway workers, unskilled laborers, miners, or builders' workmen. The Lapps were dominated, gradually pushed north-wards, and even partially assimilated by the Finns, who were their superiors, being cattle breeders and culturally dominant. They had not been fully Christianized until the eighteenth century, but in the second half of the nineteenth century many of them were converted by a lay religious movement known as Laestadianism, which is ec-static and primitive in its expression. Finnish became the language of this Christian revival, a sacred language with which most Lapps were familiar even if they did not speak it. In addition, although Finnish was not their own language, they felt at home with it because it was related.

We are told by Nils Erik Hansegård, a Swedish scholar with a Lap-pish wife, that

> some of the Lapps are proud of their Lappish descent, oth-ers are ashamed of it and try to conceal it. Some of them value their Lappish mother tongue highly, others would care little or nothing if it should disappear—and there are many attitudes in between. . . . Some Lapps are firmly convinced of the superiority of Swedish in comparison with Lappish (and Finnish) as a means of communication, as a cultural instrument and as a logical symbol.[4]

Lapps who have found nonagricultural occupations have taken over "manners, customs, views, opinions, values, or other cultural ele-ments from the Swedes."[5] Their Lappish language shows a growing number of Swedish loan-words, and even among themselves they switch from one language to the other, often without pause in the middle of a sentence. Fifty or sixty years ago, Swedish was repre-sented in the area only by a few civil servants, including clergymen and teachers, but today there has been a large influx of Swedes from other parts of the country. The residents are impressed on every hand by the usefulness of Swedish and the uselessness of their native tongue. "Some parents speak Swedish on purpose to their children,

---

4. *Recent Finnish Loanwords in Jukkasjärvi Lappish* (Uppsala: Acta Universitatis Upsa-liensis, 1967), p. 84.

5. Ibid., p. 55.

but often the fact that Swedish has become the language of the children seems to be due to the fact that Swedish is the language spoken by their playmates."[6]

While the Lapps mostly live in the backwoods and mountain areas, the Finns of Norrbotten occupy one large agricultural area, the west bank of the Torne River. When Finland was separated from Sweden in 1809 after the Russian defeat of the Swedish armies, the border was arbitrarily drawn at the Torne River, without regard to the fact that several thousand speakers of Finnish lived on the west bank. Today it is estimated that 40,000 speakers of Finnish live there, in partial isolation from their kinsmen across the border on the other side of the river. Before the separation, the two areas were one continuous community, speaking the same dialect of Finnish and sharing all cultural conventions. Today, more than a century and a half later, there are marked differences. The Swedish community is more prosperous, more urbanized, and more modern. Their Finnish is a daily language, used for home purposes and out of touch with that of Finland, since they do not learn to read or write modern Finnish in their schools, but only Swedish, a situation that has existed since schools were instituted in the nineteenth century. The Swedish government feared that Finland's Russian masters would demand that it hand over the incredibly rich ore fields of Norrbotten on the plea that the inhabitants were Finnish. So they proceeded to enforce Swedish as the language of school and government, completing the process by 1920, and not until 1970 did it once again become possible to study Finnish as a subject in the lower grades. In 1945, 72 percent of the school beginners spoke only Finnish; twenty years later this was reduced to 14 percent. The proportion of bilinguals has grown from 21 percent to 57 percent, while the number of monolingual Swedes has multiplied from 7 percent to 29 percent.

The trend is unmistakable. A study by a Finnish research team found that, in spite of the obvious value of knowing both languages, there was marked discrimination against those who did.[7] Only 22 percent of the Finnish-speaking children went on beyond grade schools, compared to 46 percent of those who came from Swedish-speaking homes. The positions of social importance, the decision-making jobs, are nearly all in the hands of Swedish speakers. Bilingual Finnish speakers tend to be limited to agriculture and manual occupations. They feel themselves to be inadequate both in Finnish and in Swedish. In other parts of Sweden, they claim to have suffered

6. Ibid., p. 84.
7. Magdalena Jaakkola, "Språk och sociala möjligheter i svenska Tornedalen," in *Studier kring gränsen i Tornedalen*, ed. E. Haavio-Mannila and K. Suolinna (Stockholm: Nordiska Rådet, 1971), pp. 110–28.

discrimination, and some have returned home rather than expose themselves by their inadequacy in Swedish. One interviewee complained that only by learning her Swedish lessons by rote could she manage to get through school. A few insisted that they were discriminated against and that Finns from the Torne Valley were met with scorn and contempt. When speaking Finnish, they constantly borrowed Swedish words to fill gaps in vocabulary left by their lack of constant contact with modern Finnish life. Hansegård, who was a high school teacher in Kiruna for ten years, emphasizes that, even so, Finnish is the mother tongue of 70 percent of the population, and he insists that every consideration of minority rights calls for a new Swedish policy here.[8] He asks for the introduction of Finnish into the lower schools, not merely as a subject, but also as a medium for at least some subjects, and that pupils be given the opportunity to continue studying it up to the point where they can make it a useful instrument for culture and contact. The Finns in Norrbotten are actually in a worse position culturally than the Lapps, for whom at least a degree of paternalistic interest has been shown.

From this account one would judge that at least the Swedes of Norrbotten should be at the top of the heap and happy with their linguistic lot. But, in fact, the language spoken by the old, established Swedish population in the area is a dialect so remote from the standard Swedish which is taught at school that at first blush other Swedes are quite baffled. The indigenous population has for centuries been so isolated from the main body of modern, bourgeois, increasingly urbanized Sweden that they have developed a Swedish dialect that is virtually a language of its own.

The author of a dissertation on the language problem of Swedish schoolchildren, Tore Österberg, was himself a teacher in the community for many years. Here are some of the episodes he describes. A teacher in the seventh grade who was teaching a famous poem written in another Swedish dialect made reference to the dialect spoken by her own pupils. The pupils "began tittering, crouched together on the benches, waved their arms defensively, and one or two made themselves comic. The class reaction, however, gradually became dumb, crushed, and repressed. The pupils—especially the girls—blushed, stammered, and—what was worse—in many cases retreated into silence."[9] A ten-year-old boy who was asked to write an essay could not remember an essential word in Standard Swedish and was too bashful to ask; so instead, he wrote nothing at all. Österberg

8. Nils Erik Hansegård, *Tvåspråkighet eller halvspråkighet?* (Stockholm: Aldus/Bonniers, 1968), p. 131.

9. Tore Österberg, *Bilingualism and the First School Language: An Educational Problem Illustrated by Results from a Swedish Dialect Area* (Umeå, 1961), p. 45.

reports that school beginners are tense and stiff in their self-expression and bring to their work a fear instilled by their parents which makes them conceal their dialect, as well as their descent from dialect speakers. Österberg performed the experiment of giving beginners reading materials written in their own dialect alongside materials in Standard Swedish. For four weeks they got intense instruction in the dialect, and for the rest of the year a gradual transition was made to Standard Swedish. He found, at the end of the year, that the experimental group could read better and assimilate more than the control group. He contends that consistent teaching along these lines would reduce the tension in the community between dialect and Standard Swedish, and ease the transition from one to the other for those whose lives will be led outside the community.

In this microcosm of Norrbotten, I see remarkable parallels to our own language problems. The *Lapps*, like our Indians, are a people driven back from their original territory by invaders, and they have been assigned to areas so infertile that the invaders do not usually molest them. They have developed occupations so strenuous or so unprofitable that they are not threatened by entrepreneurs. The *Finns*, like our Spanish speakers in the Southwest, are an established population who found themselves on the wrong side of a border and are being gradually de-ethnicized, but meanwhile are playing the role of proletariat in their new nation. The *Swedish dialect speakers* are like our West Virginia mountaineers or our ghetto blacks, who are being forced into urban areas where they find themselves discriminated against unless they change their speech. It is a layer cake with Standard Swedish on top over successive layers of rejected minorities: dialect speakers, Finns, and Lapps.

Language is not a problem unless it is used as a basis for discrimination, but it has in fact been so used as far back as we have records. The trend in Sweden, as in the United States, is clearly toward a language shift on the part of the minorities as they are more fully integrated into the national life. But this is a process that promotes cultural dislocation and social rootlessness, that deprives the minorities not only of their group identity, but even of their human dignity. Because their language is not considered valid in the larger society, they are made to feel that they are not personally adequate.

There are several ways one can look at these situations. One can take the cold-blooded, even cynical point of view that such differences in language stand in the way of progress and should be eliminated by a firm and ruthless policy of assimilation: it impedes the national machine to have a multitude of codes which interfere with one another and slow up the process of organizing the people into a homogeneous workforce. At the opposite extreme, one can wish to preserve forever such enclaves in the name of ethnic variety and the sacredness of mother tongues; local and even national romanticism has played on these chords for going on two centuries, with the result that many languages have come into being which might perhaps just as well have died.

And yet, who are we to call for linguistic genocide in the name of efficiency? Let us recall that although a language is a tool and an instrument of communication, that is not all it is. A language is also a part of one's personality, a form of behavior that has its roots in our earliest experience. Whether it is a so-called rural or ghetto dialect, or a peasant language, or a "primitive" idiom, it fulfills exactly the same needs and performs the same services in the daily lives of its speakers as does the most advanced language of culture. Every language, dialect, patois, or lingo is a structurally complete framework into which can be poured any subtlety of emotion or thought that its users are capable of experiencing. Whatever it lacks at any given time or place in the way of vocabulary and syntax can be supplied in very short order by borrowing and imitation from other languages. Any scorn for the language of others is scorn for those who use it, and as such is a form of social discrimination.

What are the solutions? The economic disadvantages of having more than one language in a country or in the world are so patent as to make an almost irresistible argument for homogenization to be used by administrators who are congenitally and professionally hostile to language minorities. Such people argue for (1) assimilation by force; (2) assimilation by precept; (3) assimilation by teaching. In any case, assimilation. Groups that refuse to assimilate must either be (1) repatriated or (2) segregated. Repatriation can be brutal and may be impossible. Segregation is contrary to the spirit of an open society. Yet it is the policy practiced by most religious communities and the ultimate justification for the existence of nations. Within a nation it is enforced by geographical separation, by economic necessity, by class differences, and by caste distinctions. There are two humanistic solutions which suggest themselves immediately to people of good will: (1) deliberately to inculcate and to promote by means of education a spirit in the general population of interest and understanding of minority peoples, and (2) to make sure that people who speak differently understand and are understood, if necessary by making them bilingual.

In principle, this is the policy that Sweden is today trying to implement, at least for the Lapps. In the law that regulates educational policy in this area since 1962 we read:

> As far as the schooling of the Lapps is concerned, they have the right to an instruction which is in all respects equal, but which does not therefore have to be identical with that which the majority receives. By virtue of being a minority group, they have certain peculiar instructional needs which society cannot overlook. They have the right to get in their schools an orientation concerning the development of their own culture and its status in the present, an orientation which does not merely aim to communicate knowledge, but also to awaken respect for and piety towards the heritage from earlier generations, as well as a feeling of solidarity with their own people.[10]

The first step in applying our best scientific knowledge to language problems is to realize that no man's speech is inferior, only different. Like Lappish, American Indian languages have not been used for atomic science, but their subtleties of expression for their users are beyond our imagination. Like Finnish in Sweden, Chicano Spanish may be the idiom of a population lost in an alien land, but in its homeland it is a language of the highest literary and scientific cultivation. Just as Norrbotten Swedish sounds strange to Swedes, ghetto or backwoods English sounds quaint or baffling to speakers of standard English; nevertheless, it follows internal laws of its own that permit its users to express anything they wish to say. Our problem is how to teach tolerance of difference and acceptance of a man for what he is, not for how he talks.

So, by a long and circuitous route, we are led back to bilingualism as the solution to the curse of Babel. Bilinguals are often unpopular, and may be looked on with distrust by monolingual neighbors, who suspect that their loyalties are divided. They are viewed as mentally handicapped by certain misguided psychologists who depend on I.Q. tests to assess human potentialities. Bilinguals do have problems of their own in keeping their languages apart. But in hundreds of situations in our world, bilingualism offers the only humane and ultimately hopeful way to bridge the communication gap and mitigate the curse of Babel.

10. Quoted in Israel Ruong, *Samerna* (Stockholm: Aldus/Bonniers, 1969), p. 157.

Language Conflicts and Political Community

By Ronald F. Inglehart and Margaret Woodward

Ronald F. Inglehart is professor of political science at the
University of Michigan, and Margaret I. Reilly (née Woodward), is professor of history at the GMI Engineering and
Management Institute in Flint, Michigan. This article is excerpted from *Comparative Studies in Society and History* 10,
no. 1 (Oct. 1967): 27–45.

Must a viable nation be made up largely of one language group?
If this is true, then there are almost insuperable difficulties in the
way of establishing a European political community. Recent events
in India, Canada, Belgium, Nigeria, and several other areas give one
cause to think that there may be some basis for drawing that conclusion.

In the Western world of the mid-nineteenth century, language became accepted as the most important single defining characteristic of
nationality. Fichte summed up a widely influential attitude when he
asserted: "Wherever a separate language is found, there is also a
separate nation which has the right to manage its affairs . . . and to
rule itself."[11] In the twentieth century this notion has had continued
prominence. The peacemakers of Versailles tended to define national
boundaries on the basis of language zone (with appropriate exceptions in favor of the victor powers), and showed an unprecedented
respect for the rights of linguistic minorities. Mussolini seemed to feel
that his claim to the south Tyrol would be valid only if the region were
populated by Italian-speaking people, and urged Italians to migrate
there.[12] Hitler later invoked the same principle against the Western
allies when, in the 1930s, he claimed the right of all German-speaking
peoples—of Austria, the Sudetenland, Alsace, and Poland—to be
united; and important elements of public opinion in the West found it
difficult to deny his claim, at least in the first two instances. Even today, De Gaulle appears to be highly skeptical of the possibility that

11. Cited in Naresh Chandra Roy, *Federalism and Linguistic States* (Calcutta: Mukho-
padhyay, 1962), p. 158.
12. Ibid.

any nation could be constructed as a federation of the various West European language groups.[13]

An examination of this question in comparative and historical perspective suggests that political separatism is not inherent in the existence of linguistic pluralism, as the foregoing position implies. On the contrary, the centrifugal force which it exerts can be strong or weak, and is largely dependent on two related situational factors:

• The level of economic and political development attained by the country in question.
• The degree to which social mobility is blocked because of membership in a given language group. This second factor is related to the first, in that it appears to be particularly critical in societies undergoing the transitional stages of early industrialization.

A political community may be viewed as a group of people living together under a common regime, with a common set of authorities to make important decisions for the group as a whole. To the extent that the regime is "legitimate," we would further specify that the people have internalized a common set of rules. Given the predominantly achievement-oriented norms which seem to be a necessary concomitant of industrial society, these rules must apply equally to the entire population—or precisely those criteria (e.g., language) which are a basis for blocking individual social mobility can become the basis for cleavage which threatens the disintegration of the political community.

Among posttribal multilingual populations where the masses are illiterate, generally unaware of national events, and have low expectations of social and economic mobility, the problem is largely irrelevant—even if such populations have a linguistically distinct elite group. In contrast, when the general population of a society is going through the early stages of social mobilization,[14] language group conflicts seem particularly likely to occur; they may develop animosities which take on a life of their own and persist beyond the situation which gave rise to them. The degree to which this happens may be significantly affected by the type of policy which the government adopts during the transitional period.

The likelihood that linguistic division will lead to political conflict is

13. See, e.g., his sarcastic reference to stateless people speaking "some kind of integrated Esperanto or Volapük"; statement of May 15, 1962, cited in Roy C. Macridis, ed., *De Gaulle: Implacable Ally* (New York: Harper & Row, 1966).

14. For a discussion of "social mobilization" as we will use the term, see Daniel Lerner, *The Passing of Traditional Society* (Glencoe, Ill.: Free Press, 1959). Cf. Karl W. Deutsch, *Nationalism and Social Communication* (New York: Wiley, 1953).

particularly great when the language cleavages are linked with the presence of a dominant group which blocks the social mobility of members of a subordinate group, at least partly on the basis of language factors. Where a dominant group holds the positions of power at the head of the major bureaucracies in a modern society and gives preference in recruitment to those who speak the dominant language, any submerged group has the options of assimilation, nonmobility, or group resistance. If an individual is overwhelmed numerically or psychologically by the dominant language, if his group is proportionally too small to maintain a self-contained community within the society, assimilation usually occurs. In contrast, if one is part of a numerous or geographically concentrated minority group, assimilation is more difficult and is more likely to seem unreasonable. If the group is numerous and mobilized, political resistance is likely.

A special case of the linkage between social mobility and linguistic pluralism among transitional populations may exist when ambitious members of minority groups see the opportunity to make careers for themselves by fanning a large potential group into consciousness of its separate identity. Language is well suited to become the basis of such a cleavage, even if awareness of group identity is at first low. Such men presumably calculate that they can rise higher at the head of a large but relatively leaderless minority group than as an assimilated member of the majority society.

In the United States, the pattern was predominantly one of assimilation. Non-English-speaking immigrant groups spoke many languages and were fairly well dispersed among the English-speaking populations. Even in the case of concentrated ethnic ghettos, usually confined to large Eastern cities, assimilation to the English-speaking group seemed to be an obvious route for eventual social mobility, one which was encouraged and facilitated by the American public school system. But in many other countries, assimilation was slow and painful, and in some cases has not occurred to this day.

In Canada, for example, the French-speaking groups have been a compact mass until the last few decades, with most of their contacts limited to other French Canadians. The distinctness of the two "races" was institutionalized by the British North America Act of 1867, which set up a federal system of government.[15] Unilingualism has been the rule ever since in the Canadian national government, in the armed forces, and in the overwhelming majority of businesses:

15. The union of the two Canadas had been attempted in 1840 with very little success. The French clung more firmly than ever to their language, religion, and outlook on life, and suspected that the British—having conquered and forcibly ruled them—were trying to destroy their identity.

one had to know English to advance beyond the menial level. The differences between the French and the British populations were multiplied by the fact that, until relatively recently, the former were largely an agrarian people, so that linguistic differences were complicated by the antagonism of farm versus commercial interests.

The situation was further aggravated by the fact that the French Canadians placed less emphasis on education than the Canadian population in general; not until World War II did a secondary education become a normal expectation for them. As a consequence of their lack of formal education, and their social and geographical isolation in Quebec, their level of mastery of English has never approached linguistic assimilation. Yet the business activity of the province is almost entirely in the hands of the English-speaking minority.[16] Describing a series of public meetings held in Quebec, an investigating commission reported: "The reiterated contrast between 'master' and 'servant' always conjured up an image of a collective personage—'the English.' . . . Basically it seemed to us that the French Canadians who attended our meetings mainly wanted to put on record their indignation at their 'economic weakness' in a province where they are in a majority."[17]

By the 1950s French Canada had developed a leadership class capable of effective political organization, and separatist activity became important. A demand for equal dignity and a resentment at the superior attitude often adopted by the dominant English minority have been associated with the competition for economic positions. Religious differences also have contributed to the problem to some extent, tending to reinforce the line of linguistic cleavage, but they seem to have been a declining factor. While the Church may well have contributed in the past to the perpetuation of the French Canadians as a distinct and compact group, they now rebel almost *in spite of* being Catholics, with separatist leaders generally being among the least church-oriented of the population.[18] Another contributing factor to the discord in Canada may be the ambition of a small French elite group whose careers are dependent upon leading their people against the English.

16. Editor's note: This situation had changed dramatically by the 1980s; *see* Jonathan Lemco, "Quebec's 'Distinctive Character' and the Question of Minority Rights," *pp.* 423–33.

17. *Preliminary Report of the Royal Commission on Bilingualism and Biculturalism* (Ottawa: Queen's Printer, 1965), pp. 73–83.

18. See Pierre Elliott Trudeau, "Some Obstacles to Democracy in Quebec," *Canadian Journal of Economics and Political Science* 24 (1955): 297–314; Arthur Malheux, "Democracy and the French Canadian," in Douglas Grant, ed., *Quebec Today* (Toronto: University of Toronto Press, 1958); and Pierre R. Amyot, "Factors Leading to Integrative or Nonintegrative Attitudes Towards Canada among French Canadians of Quebec" (Ph.D. diss., Northwestern University, 1966).

The situation in Belgium parallels that of Canada, with additional complications. In 1815 the socioeconomic elite of Belgium had become largely French-speaking, partly as a result of twenty years of French rule, and the Dutch language there "was in a bad way."[19] At this juncture, the area was handed over to William I of Orange as part of the Kingdom of the Netherlands. The king was a Dutch-speaking Calvinist, and Dutch was made the official language in all except the Walloon districts of Belgium.

Within fifteen years, however, the Catholic Belgians—both Flemish and Walloon—rebelled against their union with Holland and gained independence. The new Belgian state launched into a violent reaction against the late Dutch regime; now Dutch (or Flemish) was banned from administration, from the law courts, from the army, universities, and secondary schools, causing a tremendous hardship for the Dutch speakers included within the new state. The nineteenth century was thus a period of profound humiliation for Flanders, and every aspect of public life, including business, tended to be dominated by the French. Only in the twentieth century was Dutch again made a medium of higher education; key demands made recently by the Flemings (who constitute a majority of the population) have been for equal status for their language in government and military service. Membership in the Dutch-speaking group has a persisting connotation of lower social status.[20] Though the Flemings are now economically resurgent, past discrimination and animosity persist as a tradition influencing the present.

A change has taken place in Europe, where religion was traditionally a source of much contention and even warfare. Today, a stable political cooperation exists between Protestants and Catholics in the Netherlands and West Germany, and the Catholic churches of Italy and France seem to be moving toward depoliticization. Language now seems more important than religion as a basis of political cleavage in modern societies. But this is true only insofar as it becomes linked with differences in social mobility. In India, on the other hand, religion has remained a predominant basis of cleavage, as was manifested in the partition of Bengal and the Punjab in 1947 along religious rather than linguistic lines. Among Hindus, linguistic cleavages have frequently been complicated by caste conflicts as well.[21]

19. Pieter Geyl, *Debates with Historians* (Cleveland: World Publishing Co., 1958), p. 216. At that time a variety of dialects of Dutch were spoken in Northern Belgium, some of them mutually incomprehensible. The dialects were known as Flemish.

20. Flemish families in the Brussels region still have a tendency to learn French and "pass" as Walloons. See "Debat in Belgische Kamer Over Taalgemeenschappen," *Niewe Rotterdamse Courant*, Jan. 27, 1966. Over a period of many years, this has contributed to making Brussels—once part of the Flemish region—a largely French-speaking city.

21. Roy, *Federalism*, p. 121.

With autonomy from Britain and the secession of Pakistan, however, the foreign-native conflict largely disappeared from India, religious conflicts were partly transferred from the internal to the international sphere, and linguistic cleavages have emerged as an increasingly important basis of conflict. In some ways this conflict bears a resemblance to the separatist movements in Belgium and Canada: it seems closely related to the demands of emerging parochial elements for a share of the government jobs in competition with a cosmopolitan elite. In the absence of extensive opportunities for employment in business and industry, government jobs have been the chief avenues of upward social mobility. The elite which had administered India under the British was generally bilingual, speaking English in addition to a regional language. The less-educated masses, on the other hand, could communicate only in one of the regional languages. They were, and are, effectively excluded from office except insofar as the locus of power has been shifted to regional centers, and the medium of communication shifted from English to regional languages. Since government jobs are a chief source of social mobility, this exclusion came to be an important problem.

Widespread riots made a series of reorganizations necessary, beginning with the creation of a Telegu-speaking Andhra state in 1953, and continuing (most recently) with the agreement to set up a separate Punjabi-Sikh state in 1966. The partition of 1953 was typical of the pattern: Telegu aspirations for separate statehood were especially strong because of the dominance in the Madras government of the generally more highly educated Tamils, who had a considerably higher rate of command of English. Indian federalism seems to be a rather uneasy compromise between two forces: the need for central coordination by a national government, which necessarily communicates largely in English, against centrifugal demands to turn a maximum amount of activity over to regional linguistic states.

Let us note another interesting aspect of India's language controversies: the use of English as an official language has continued despite powerful opposition. At first glance, this might seem astonishing considering the fact that it was the language of colonial dominance, and in view of the small percentage of Indians who speak it. What has been even more adamantly opposed, however, is the adoption of Hindi as the sole national language, for this would tend to give the Hindi-speaking group preferential access to political office. Attempts to abolish the use of English and replace it with Hindi have been shelved repeatedly, in the face of bitter opposition from non-Hindi groups. The attempt to make Hindi the official language is seen as the work of Hindi imperialism: Hindi-speaking Indians from the north tend to dominate the national government. Feelings of resentment are no doubt aggravated by the fact that the coastal areas had previously been the most advanced parts of the subcontinent. These regions are largely non-Hindi, and their inhabitants experienced the disagreeable sensation of being passed up by the inhabitants of the interior. To a limited extent, another factor may be an attitude of racial superiority on the part of the fairer-skinned, and generally higher-caste, Hindi-speaking northerners. But the feeling that establishment of Hindi as the sole national language would block social mobility of the non-Hindis remains a key concern for the nonparochial minority. As expressed by a southern politician: "Be just, Hindustanis, that you may be true to your democracy and not merely exploit it by seeking to make what you possess by birth the sole passport to full Indian civilization and all its honors."[22]

Where languages are of officially equal status and where social mobility is not blocked by a dominant elite made up of one language group, upwardly motivated individuals can seek to rise as individuals. Where social mobility is blocked by the existence of one preferred language among several, language differences seem to be politically divisive. The individual must unite with others of his language for political action to raise the group as a whole, as in Belgium or Canada. On the other hand, where all major languages are on an officially equal footing, as in Switzerland, the presence of several language groups may not necessarily be divisive. Similarly, although it is far less widespread than Hindi, English is less divisive as an official language in India because all groups there are more or less equally handicapped by it. Belgium, Canada, and India have one factor in common: the conflicts have been aggravated by a situation in which social mobility tends to be blocked by the presence of a dominant language group.

One of the most important cases of language conflict in modern times has been the Austro-Hungarian Monarchy. In terms of social development, it seems to occupy a position between that of India and the two Western countries. Starting from a stable system based on an agrarian, Christian, Latin-speaking elite, it was eventually shattered by the mobilization of new elements, partly because those elements found their social mobility blocked by the existence of a dominant and alien language.

There was a time in the eighteenth century when Maria Theresa seemed capable of welding the diverse and multilingual segments of the Austrian state into one cohesive mass. Magyar appeared to be dying out at the elite level, and the Hungarian nobles were flocking to the court, marrying German princesses, and apparently ready to

22. Chakravarti Rajagopalachari, *Our Democracy* (Madras: B. G. Paul, 1957), p. 45.

cooperate with the Hapsburgs. Or at least so it seemed until Joseph II attempted to establish German as the universal language of empire (along with other sweeping reforms). Revolts broke out across the land. Resentment against the policies of the Austrians combined with the emphasis of intellectuals such as Herder on languages and folk culture to encourage linguistic separatism within the empire. The example of mass participation in politics set by the French Revolution led to aspirations for a political voice among progressively broader classes of the empire's population. Napoleon's creation of separate states for favored minorities made the idea look like a concrete possibility. Given the educational facilities of the time, mass participation necessarily implied linguistic separatism. Unlike the ruling elite, the aspiring middle classes of the ethnic minorities generally did not have instruction in the cosmopolitan language.

In the first quarter of the nineteenth century, practically every ethnic group in the empire showed signs of emerging from parochialism and demanding the restoration of real or imagined traditional privileges, laws, and languages. The Magyars were the first on the scene, the most intransigent in their demands, and the most successful. Academies, newspapers, clubs, and societies were founded, all demanding the exclusive use of Magyar within their kingdom, while political leaders led by Lajos Kossuth tirelessly stirred up the anger and pride of the people. In 1839 the Diet declared Magyar the official language of government and clergy, and in 1843 made it the exclusive language of the schools. Hungary revolted against Austria in 1848, and although brutally crushed, its people grew increasingly restive under the control of Vienna. When the humiliating defeat by Prussia in the war of 1866 forced the Hapsburgs to make a drastic change in the government, the Magyars were on hand to push through their demands.[23]

By the terms of the *Ausgleich* of 1867, the empire was divided into two parts and relabeled the Austro-Hungarian Monarchy, each half having its own government, laws, and courts, with only a vague and rather amorphous superstructure over the whole. Seton-Watson has argued that the real motive behind the Dual System was a league between the two strongest races—the Germans and the Magyars—who divided the monarchy between them and granted autonomy to the next two strongest races—the Poles and the Croats—who were to be their accomplices in holding down the remaining eight.[24] Although a

23. See R. W. Seton-Watson, *Racial Problems in Hungary* (London: A. Constable, 1908), pp. 38ff.; and Oszkár Jászi, *The Dissolution of the Habsburg Monarchy* (Chicago: University of Chicago Press, 1961).

24. Seton-Watson, *Racial Problems*, p. 137.

series of laws granted equality to all the different nationality groups and respected their languages, these laws were applied only partially in Austria and not at all in Hungary.

Language restrictions had the effect of stifling the ambitions and slowing the economic development of the subject races. In the respective halves of the monarchy, the state gave preferential treatment to Hungarians and Germans. In Hungary, government was effectively closed down to all but Magyars, and Magyar alone was spoken in her courts. "It is no exaggeration," commented Seton-Watson in 1908, "to say that the non-Magyar peasant stands like an ox before the courts of his native lands."[25] Of the state elementary schools, as of 1904–5, 91 percent were Magyar, although 48 percent of the population consisted of other nationality groups. There was not one Slovak or Ruthenian secondary school in existence at the time. Yet due to the scarcity of teachers who knew Magyar, the most important effect of "Magyarization" was not that Slovak, Croatian, or Rumanian children were forced to learn the language, but rather, that an increasing percentage of them received no education at all. From 1900 to 1906 the percentage of children not attending school rose from 18 to 24 percent.[26] Thus, one important result of Magyarization was to cut off the principal prerequisites for social mobility.

The Croat case illustrates once again how social mobility, when blocked by language barriers, contributed to the dissolution of the empire. For 700 years the Croats had enjoyed relative autonomy. Then, in the 1840s, sharp contention arose over a proposal to replace Latin with Magyar as the official instrument of administration. Croatian was not even considered as a possibility, and the only Croats involved in the decision were the upper classes—the only ones apt to know Latin. The Magyars crushed the opposition with a number of laws enforcing their own language, and overnight the conflict intensified. Practically the entire Croatian population began to develop, in reaction to the Hungarian policy, a sense of group awareness.[27] This was a pattern to be repeated, with various modifications, from one end of the empire to the other.

In the Austrian half of the monarchy, no group was more vociferous in their language demands than the Czechs. From the 1870s on, the language question was the "main issue of official Czech policy," "the permanent, unhealed wound of the national struggle."[28] A climax of sorts was reached in 1897, when several decrees were issued by Min-

25. Seton-Watson, *Racial Problems*, pp. 150–51.

26. Ibid.; see also Jaszi, *Dissolution*, pp. 279, 304ff.

27. Robert Kann, *The Multinational Empire: Nationalism and National Reform in the Habsburg Monarchy, 1848–1918* (New York: Columbia University Press, 1950), 1:239, 241.

28. Ibid., 1:199.

ister Badeni in Bohemia requiring all judges in Czech lands to conduct trials in the language of the accused, and requiring all civil servants to be bilingual. Since it was far more common for a Czech to know German than the reverse, the two laws would have established a body of Czech judges and civil servants. In this case it was the Germans who felt oppressed and who resorted to riots to have the laws repealed. German waiters refused to serve Czech customers, Germans obstructed parliament and refused to pay taxes. Badeni was forced to resign and the hated decrees were repealed, which in turn inflamed Czech extremists led by Karel Kramář, who demanded a Pan-Slav state.[29]

It is clear that language was not the sole divisive element at work within the Austro-Hungarian Monarchy. As Masaryk commented in 1907: "The national question is not only the language question. It is at the same time an economic and social question."[30] Yet as issues grew more complex and the factions jostling for power more numerous, language tended to become a symbol that summed up other conflicts. In the early phases of social mobilization and economic modernization, linguistic nationalism was seized upon by reactionary elements (such as the feudal nobility) as a means by which they might isolate themselves from cosmopolitan influences. At the same time, it was seen by a variety of upwardly aspiring groups, particularly the new middle class, as a potential vehicle for smashing through the existing lines of stratification. In general, the minority groups found themselves in a position where social mobility was blocked unless they were willing to learn the dominant language, particularly in the Hungarian half of the monarchy. Probably the most notorious example of the use of language to block the mobility of minority groups is the Railway Servant's Act of 1907. It arbitrarily decreed that all railway workers not conversant in Magyar be fired from their jobs.[31]

There is at least one other case to be discussed in our typology of motivating forces behind language-group conflicts: the occasions in which language conflicts are encouraged by political leaders to promote their special interests. Such a case can be found in the Catalan language conflict in Spain.[32]

29. See Arthur James May, *The Hapsburg Monarchy, 1867–1914* (Cambridge, Mass.: Harvard University Press, 1960), pp. 325ff.

30. Quoted by Kann, *Multinational Empire,* 1:211.

31. Language conflicts remain a potential problem in the former Austrian lands. In March 1967 President Tito of Yugoslavia "angrily warned" Croatians and Serbs to stop stirring up linguistic disputes; *New York Times,* March 27, 1967, p. 1.

32. Out of 28.6 million Spaniards in 1950, there were 5 million Catalans—a force to be reckoned with. An equally discontented group are the Basques, but as of 1950 they numbered only a half million people. Albert Dauzat, *L'Europe linguistique* (Paris: Payot, 1953), p. 155.

Since the unification of Spain, the Catalans have been an industrious and relatively prosperous people, frequently discontented with their union with the economically less progressive Castilians. Feelings that they were being exploited by the rest of Spain led to revolts in 1640 and again in 1705. By the nineteenth century their principal grievance was that the low-tariff policy of the central government in Madrid was hurting their industry. In the 1890s their resentment widened to include anger over the prospective loss of Cuba, for at that time Catalans more or less dominated the American trade. Language had very little to do with these basic economic grievances, and in fact, the Catalan language had been on the verge of dying out completely. In 1860 it was spoken only in the most remote and obscure villages,[33] while Castilian was taking hold in cities like Barcelona. The revival of the language was originally the work of a small group of intellectuals and poets, but after the defeat of the conservative forces in the Carlist War of 1876, the Church turned to the support of Catalanism. Businessmen who had grievances against Madrid joined them in a party, the *Lliga Regionalista*, led by Francisco Cambo.

Catalan nationalism flourished greatly at the turn of the century, to the dismay of the central government, and became increasingly troublesome in its demands. A climax was reached about 1917, when the Catalan industrialists united with the Socialists and other left-wing parties in open revolt against the government, demanding, among other things, a freely elected legislature. A strike was called, and in the ensuing violence, the industrialists retreated completely to form an alliance with the army and the central government. So timid had the industrialists become that they even supported Diego Primo de Rivera as dictator in 1923. He responded by terminating Catalan privileges, including the use of their language in the schools.

When the conservative Catalan leaders sold out to their principal enemies, the issue of Catalanism did not die; instead it was taken up by elements from the opposite end of the political and social spectrum. The radical extremist Colonel Macía formed a new party, the Esquerra.[34] Its motives were political and not economic, radical instead of clerical or conservative; yet it effectively represented Catalan nationalism throughout the 1920s and 1930s. It was even successful. The vote of the Catalan leftists was one of the main reasons for the fall of the monarchy and the advent of the Republic, and the Esquerra

33. Gerald Brenan, *The Spanish Labyrinth* (Cambridge: Cambridge University Press, 1962), pp. 26–28.

34. In the Basque country conservative nationalism also failed, but the people were too religious and concerned with tradition to turn to the left. Instead, extremists urged Basques to learn English or French instead of Spanish. See Raymond Carr, *Spain, 1808–1939* (Oxford: Oxford University Press, 1966), p. 556.

was rewarded by a large measure of autonomy, with Catalan declared the official language.[35]

One can see the issue of Catalanism, in which the free use of the language is an important part, taken up and discarded by political leaders of extremely varied interests as it suited their needs. Franco declared open war on the language and on Catalan nationalism, with the result that today the leftists are still its primary defenders. Ironically, the Church has now joined forces with the left, and has caused considerable trouble by demanding the right to use Catalan in services.[36]

The case of Catalonia is, in a sense, an exception to our general rule; it could hardly be described as an instance of an economically oppressed group opposing the use of an alien language which was blocking their upward mobility. In part, it seems to be an example of the role of ambitious political leaders turning to language as a device to inflame the masses against the central government. As such, it was not an isolated phenomenon, but one which was repeated in various other European countries.

One of the most obvious indications that languages, oftentimes, were not intrinsically a cause for conflict is that a good many of them were actually dying out a hundred years ago. In the eighteenth century Magyar was on the decline, and in the nineteenth, both Catalan and Gaelic seemed on the point of disappearing.[37] Yet in each case, within a generation, Magyar, Catalan, and Gaelic suddenly gained new vigor and became a cause for revolting against an alien government. In each case the dying embers of an antiquated, archaic, or primitive speech were consciously fanned by intellectuals and political leaders, at least partly to provide an audience and a constituency.

Yet whatever the role of Catalan leaders with ulterior motives for emphasizing the distinctiveness of their language, in a more general sense the Catalan case can be considered to support our main point. For the fact remains that the Catalans felt they were being oppressed and economically exploited as a group. Instead of a minority whose social mobility is blocked by lack of access to the cosmopolitan lan-

---

35. Brenan, *Spanish Labyrinth*, pp. 29–34; see also Hugh Thomas, *The Spanish Civil War* (New York: Harper & Row, 1963), p. 29.

36. Editor's note: Spain's policy toward Catalan changed again following the death of Franco. Under the autonomy granted by the Constitution of 1978, Catalan is now official (along with Castilian) in Catalonia, the Balearic Islands, and Valencia. Owing to government efforts to revive the language, Catalan is spoken by an estimated 7 million of the 10 million inhabitants of these territories. Also, it has always been the sole official tongue of the small republic of Andorra; Direcció General de Política Lingüística, *Catalan in Europe* (Barcelona: Generalitat de Catalunya, 1987).

37. Dauzat, *L'Europe*, p. 177. In 1800, 4 million Irishmen spoke Gaelic, yet by 1921 there were only 300,000.

guage, they illustrate the case of a minority with a *favored* position which is threatened by pressures toward predominance by the majority. In either case, however, members of the minority are not free to seek social mobility as individuals (the normal course, in the absence of pressures to act collectively), but are either blocked or threatened in their social status *as a group.*

In conclusion, we would advance the generalization that there is a curvilinear relationship between political/economic development and the divisive effect of linguistic pluralism.

1. At a low level of development, the masses of the population are normally inert and irrelevant to the national politics of an extensive community (that is, one in which political activity can no longer be based on face-to-face communication). Whereas it is relatively easy to provide a small ruling elite with education in a cosmopolitan language and to assimilate them into a stable allegiance to the regime, to do this on behalf of the general public requires an elaborate apparatus for public education, and a highly developed communications network.

2. Consequently, at a transitional stage—where the masses are "mobilized" but not yet assimilated—the divisive force exerted by multiple language groups will be greatest.

3. At a high level of political/economic development (e.g., contemporary Western Europe) exchanges of persons among language areas are numerous, mass media minimize the remoteness of foreign groups, and above all, most upwardly mobile individuals have the opportunity to become fluent in one or more languages.

We would argue that blockage of social mobility has been the chief motivating force behind language group conflicts, especially in transitional countries. It is of little use for predicting the limits of political community among nonmobilized populations, or in societies which are not oriented toward achievement of individual social mobility. There are ways in which the conflict can be neutralized:

• Cases in which the politically mobilized strata master a cosmopolitan language; or wherever one finds widespread bilingualism. Symmetrical bilingualism is desirable, but not necessary, and would require a highly developed educational system.

• Cases where equality exists or is granted to major language groups.

Both types of neutralization can be seen operating in Europe today. In contrast to the Belgian and Canadian cases, where action was deferred until violence had erupted, the European Community institutions give a scrupulous formal equality to the four principal languages, in staffing their bureaucracies and making documents and facilities available. Modern communications technology also lends a hand: proceedings are held with simultaneous translations in all four languages. Today, with widespread public education and increasingly achievement-oriented, technocratic societies, there are few groups in Western Europe which need feel that they as a group are being exploited and restricted. The increasing tendency toward bilingualism is impressive. A six-nation survey indicates that in 1962 a *majority* of adult Dutch and Belgians claimed to understand one or more foreign languages, as did a quarter of adult Germans and a third of the adult French.[38] A tendency toward asymmetrical bilingualism exists and will probably increase, but an intelligent awareness of the tensions which would result if one language were given preference may prevent language from becoming a serious basis of cleavage.

Quebec's "Distinctive Character" and the Question of Minority Rights

By Jonathan Lemco

Jonathan Lemco is a senior fellow at the National Planning Association in Washington, D.C., and an adjunct professor at the Canadian Studies Center of the Johns Hopkins School of Advanced International Studies. He wrote this article for the *Source Book*.

One of the most fascinating political developments in North America, and one of the least understood by the vast majority of North Americans, concerns the evolution of Quebec—a thoroughly modern, Westernized society whose majority population remains defiantly proud of its French language and culture. The roughly six million French-speaking Québecois have thus far been able to maintain their distinctive character notwithstanding the political, cultural, and economic dominance of the continent by nonfrancophones. This minority group situation, however, has prompted Quebec's leaders to pursue strategies to protect their language and culture that have proven controversial and frequently injurious to the interests of the more

38. Cited in *Sondages*, no. 1 (1963): 41.

than one million Quebecers whose native language is other than French.

The story of modern Quebec is the story of a people who regard themselves as having emerged from a relatively backward, agrarian, or urban working-class background to a modern, industrial, entrepreneurial society that can prosper economically and thrive culturally.[39] After providing a cursory overview of Quebec's political history, this paper will focus on the reasons cited to justify its restrictive language laws and on the costs and benefits thereof. Of particular concern will be the plight of the minority-language speakers in the province.

Quebec francophones (native French speakers) are a national minority-language group that represents a majority in a particular province, a situation similar to that of Hispanic groups that constitute a majority in parts of the southern and southwestern United States. One should not push this comparison too far, however, for the French language has been entrenched in Canada since the preconfederation period. Furthermore, Canadian and American political cultures are very different. To understand the plight of Quebec's francophones, a bit of background is needed.

In 1759, in the midst of the Seven Years' War, the British defeated the French on the Plains of Abraham in Quebec City. This was a momentous event in the history of Quebec, for it transferred the small French-language settlement situated along the St. Lawrence River to British control. Shrewd colonizers, the British allowed these French-speaking "habitants" to retain their language, culture, and Catholic religion so long as they swore allegiance to the British Crown. For the most part, the francophones could live their lives as before, despite their humiliating defeat. Quebec automobile license plates today bear the motto *Je me souviens*, 'I remember'. The phrase is fraught with meaning, for it is both a simple acknowledgment of historical circumstance and, more important, a declaration that the humiliation of 1759 can never be repeated. That is, francophones will never allow themselves to be threatened by outsiders (i.e., anglophones) again.

After the 1759 "Conquest," habitant society, which had always been church-dominated and culturally insular, became even more so. Relations with English-speaking Upper Canada (now called Ontario) were limited. The church discouraged its parishioners from entering the world of commerce, and so the economic elites of the colony were

---

39. For detailed histories, see William Coleman, *The Independence Movement in Quebec, 1945–1980* (Toronto: University of Toronto Press, 1984); Alain G. Gagnon and Mary Beth Montcalm, *Quebec: Beyond the Quiet Revolution* (Scarborough, Ont.: Nelson, 1989); and Ken McRoberts, *Quebec: Social Change and Political Crisis*, 3d ed. (Toronto: McClelland & Stewart, 1988).

most often English-speaking. The French Revolution of 1789 forced another rift with the outside world. To Quebec's Catholic Church, the revolution was the work of the devil, depriving the clergy of their special privileges and bringing heathens or atheists to power. Relations between France and its former North American colony would not return to normal until Charles De Gaulle's visit in the mid–1960s.

At the time of the Canadian Confederation in 1867, Quebec remained an economically underdeveloped, rather closed society by North American standards. Nevertheless, it chose to join a sovereign Canada for two reasons. First, Great Britain was in the process of dissolving its empire for predominantly economic reasons. Its colonies had grown expensive to administer and so the mother country made efforts to encourage their independence while retaining British parliamentary institutions. Second, despite Quebec's relative isolation, its political leaders shared with Ontario's elites a concern that they not be forced to become Americans.[40] After the Civil War, several "war hawks" in the U.S. Congress had actually threatened to punish the South's economic ally, Great Britain, by annexing Canada. This was thought to be an easy affair so long as the British colonies there remained divided. Whether annexation was realistic is debatable, but the threat motivated Canadian politicians to seek national union. After the creation of a Canadian nation-state, however, dialogue between English and French Canada remained restricted largely to consultation among elites. Even within Quebec, francophones and anglophones had little to do with each other.

The relative isolation of Quebec permitted a strong sense of Québecois identity to evolve. When episodes of apparent discrimination against French speakers outside the province flared up, as they did during the Riel rebellion of the 1880s, francophones inside Quebec, spurred on by their political and religious leaders and their newspapers, were enraged. Most became convinced then, as they remain today, that only in Quebec could a North American francophone be assured that his language and culture would be protected.

These views were reinforced through both world wars, during which riots ensued in Montreal and elsewhere to protest the conscription of French Canadians into an "English" conflict. Francophones were perfectly willing to defend Quebec if it were attacked, but few were prepared to fight overseas for the British king. Indeed, a referendum in 1942 revealed that 71 percent of Quebecers opposed conscription. Nevertheless, many francophones, primarily volunteers,

40. Poll data in the 1980s reveal that this is one of the few things that Canadians from coast to coast can still agree upon. Indeed, many Canadians, when asked about their sense of national identity, will insist only that they are not Americans (though usually with no hint of *anti*-Americanism).

distinguished themselves fighting for the allies during both wars. Sporadic strikes and riots against perceived English discrimination (e.g., the Thetford Mines strike and Richard riots) occurred throughout the 1950s. By contrast to almost all other nationalist movements, however, Quebec's situation has been characterized by a remarkable degree of nonviolence. Emotions have run high from time to time, but with one glaring modern exception, the October Crisis of 1970 to be discussed below, there is only the most occasional evidence of violent action.

In the early 1960s, French-speaking Québecois began to assert their political interests to an unprecedented degree. Jean Lesage was elected premier of Quebec and, along with his young natural resources minister, René Lévesque, nationalized the province's vast and profitable hydroelectric power resource and named it Hydro-Québec. Lesage declared that henceforth francophones would be *maîtres chez nous*, 'masters in our own house'. No longer would they be beholden to dominant anglophone economic interests, or discriminated against in the province where they commanded a numerical majority. This marked the beginning of the Quiet Revolution, in which Quebec francophones began to alter the economic, political, and social structure of the province.

This nonviolent revolution occurred for a number of reasons. First, Catholicism's hold on Quebec had begun to diminish. Sunday church attendance had declined, and Québecois were not entering the priesthood in the same numbers as before. Throughout much of the history of the province, young men of ability would be encouraged to become priests, notarial lawyers, or occasionally doctors. Few other professions were encouraged by the church or tolerated by nonfrancophone elites. By the early 1960s, however, this had begun to change. Rural and urban francophones aspired to more, their hopes rising with industrialization in the province and with much greater access to postsecondary education. Trade unions independent of the church became more prominent, and bureaucratic elites in Quebec City discovered they had more discretionary power than ever before.

Quebec of the 1960s was a rapidly changing place, and with increased social mobilization, French-speaking Quebecers had discovered that certain obstacles would have to be overcome for them to fully realize their potential. These included a largely unsympathetic anglophone community, a conservative church, a parochial and corrupt political leadership, and the absence of successful role models. The francophones' plight inspired some to join fledgling nationalist and separatist organizations, which maintained that only a politically sovereign Quebec could ensure that the French language and culture would be protected and promoted. Although attracting relatively few participants at first, these groups struck a responsive chord in many francophones who, though sympathetic to their goals, still questioned their ability to make a difference. The founding of the Parti Québecois under René Lévesque enhanced the legitimacy of the independence movement, but few P.Q. candidates were elected to the National Assembly (the provincial legislature) until the early 1970s.

The separatist cause experienced a major political setback in 1970. In what came to be known as the October Crisis, the British trade commissioner in Montreal, James Cross, and Quebec's justice minister, Pierre Laporte, were kidnapped. Their abductors, who called themselves Le Front de Libération du Québec, broadcast a message in which they pledged to use violent tactics if necessary to promote a free and sovereign Quebec. Soon after, Laporte was found murdered. After consulting with his cabinet and with Quebec's premier, Robert Bourassa, Prime Minister Pierre Trudeau instituted the War Measures Act in the province and prepared for the possibility of a large-scale armed insurrection. Ultimately, Cross was freed, and it was revealed that the F.L.Q. was made up of only two cells of five to seven members each.

By 1976 Bourassa's Liberal government had become enmeshed in scandals associated with the construction of the Montreal Olympics, and there was also a widespread perception that his administration had failed to manage the economy effectively. In something of an upset, the separatist P.Q. was elected to office. Its leader, Lévesque, pledged that he would take no steps to promote an independent Quebec until his government's second term. In 1980 a referendum asked Quebecers whether they would authorize provincial officials to begin negotiations with Canada's federal government toward Quebec's eventual "sovereignty-association." The wording of the question was left purposefully vague so as to maximize support for the separatist position. Sovereignty-association referred to political sovereignty combined with continued economic association with the rest of Canada. After a hard-fought campaign, the opponents of negotiations were victorious, 60 percent to 40 percent. The vast majority of anglophone Quebecers opposed the plebiscite, of course, as did the allophones (those of neither French- nor English-language background) and even a slight majority of francophones, thus depriving the nationalists of the opportunity to blame the English for their defeat. René Lévesque later said that the referendum result was the biggest disappointment of his political life.

In 1987 Prime Minister Brian Mulroney and the ten provincial premiers met at Meech Lake, Quebec, and tentatively agreed to an accord, subject to ratification by all the provincial legislatures. In return for endorsing the Canadian constitution (see pp. 433–35), which it had refused to sign in 1982, Quebec would be recognized as a "distinct society," an official statement with great symbolic meaning for francophone Quebecers. But the Meech Lake Accord collapsed with the failure of Newfoundland and Manitoba to ratify it before the deadline of June 23, 1990. With the Bourassa government threatening to take sterner measures to protect Quebec's distinctiveness, and with polls revealing that a majority of Quebecers now favored political sovereignty, it was a very difficult period for those who sought to encourage accommodation.

One of the most divisive conditions associated with the stability of any nation-state is linguistic cleavage. Canadian policymakers, in attempting to strengthen national unity, have been faced with the dilemma of how to appease francophones while not alienating anglophones. The federal government's solution has been to recognize both English and French as official languages across Canada, while also guaranteeing certain minority linguistic rights. This policy is directed at ensuring equal footing for the two official languages in the courts, the legislatures, educational institutions, provision of services, the civil service, and the private sector. Emphasis is placed on creating bilingual institutions that will in turn lead to the creation of a bilingual society—an ideal expressed by the 1969 Royal Commission on Bilingualism and Biculturalism (the Laurendeau-Dunton Commission), which laid out the blueprints for much of the federal government's language legislation.

Today, the ideal of national bilingualism is far from being a reality. Indeed, the Ottawa-Hull national capital area is the only truly bilingual part of Canada. The large majority of Canadians remain monolingual, although francophones are far more likely to speak the other language than are anglophones. The absence of bilingualism, and the perceived threat to French Canadian culture and language, prompted the Parti Québecois in 1977 to enact Bill 101, a law that defied the national bilingualism policy and made French the sole official language of Quebec (see pp. 435–45). While provincial governments in the 1960s and 1970s had enacted language legislation, never before had it been so pervasive and restrictive of other languages.

Camile Laurin, the architect of Bill 101 and the P.Q. education minister, espoused a variety of goals for the legislation: to end the economic inferiority of francophone Quebecers, to redistribute economic opportunities, to promote the assimilation of immigrants into the francophone community, and to make it clear to all concerned that Quebec was French-speaking.[41] Certainly, these concerns are under-

41. For a particularly thoughtful journalistic study of the political actors in the Parti Québecois, see Graham Fraser, P.Q.: René Levesque and the Parti Québecois in Power (Toronto: Macmillan, 1984).

standable. Outnumbered by anglophones in North America, 260 million to 6.5 million, the francophones also have the lowest birthrate on the continent and virtually no population growth, as it has been difficult to attract French-speaking immigrants to Quebec. French Canadian children are exposed to English-language media, culture, and business, and they find it very attractive. Many francophones fear, quite legitimately, that unless steps are taken to protect and promote their language and culture, it will disappear in the not-too-distant future. Also, it should be noted that some francophones have a desire to retaliate against the English in their province, viewing them, rightly or wrongly, as intruders and oppressors. Finally, francophone Quebecers have only to look at the plight of francophones in other provinces to conclude that only in Quebec can their distinctive character be protected.

Bill 101 affected almost every aspect of Quebec society, including the courts, the legislature, the civil service, education, health and social services, and private business. Government services were curtailed in the language of the anglophone minority, which numbers more than one million in the province (although English-language materials would be provided on request). The instruction of English-speaking students was to be increasingly in the French language, with anglophone public schools available only to those whose parents had been educated in English in Quebec. Street and commercial signs were required to be posted in French only, and reported violations would be investigated by government bureaucrats, commonly referred to as "language police." Most professionals would now have to pass a French language-proficiency test. Clearly, there was a complete inconsistency between the bilingual policies of Ottawa and the unilingual policies emanating from Quebec City.

Nevertheless, Bill 101 was enormously popular in the province. Many francophones began to feel that their distinctive language and culture was secure. Although Canada is a country where the protection of individual rights is considered mandatory, collective rights are regarded as almost as important in both English-Canadian and French-Canadian political culture. By world standards the francophone minority is remarkably homogeneous, and their history in Canada dates back as far as the anglophones'. Both factors contribute to their sense of cohesion and legitimacy.

Furthermore, the Canadian federal system grants so many discretionary powers to the provinces that Quebec can legally declare French its official language, play a determining role in immigration policy, and maintain separate public school systems based on religion and language. The Canadian Supreme Court and the Quebec Superior Court have ruled that much of the language legislation is unconstitutional. But the Bourassa provincial government has been able to disregard those rulings by using the "notwithstanding clause" of Canada's constitution,[42] arguing that Bill 101 was in the best interests of Quebec's distinctive character.

Following the passage of Bill 101, Minister of Education Laurin announced that a 50 percent reduction in the number of children attending English-language schools would be appropriate.[43] In fact, the reduction has been even greater. The Protestant School Board of Greater Montreal had lost 60 percent of its anglophone students by 1984, substantially more than the natural decline suffered by all schools at the end of the baby boom. Recently, the entire educational system in Quebec was thrown into turmoil by a move to abolish religious school boards (Catholic as well as Protestant) and to restructure them along linguistic lines.[44] Many anglophones strongly resisted losing the constitutional guarantee for Protestant schools without gaining in return an equally strong protection for English schools. The courts are now studying this case.

A major rationale for the educational provisions of Bill 101 was the fear that most immigrants to Quebec would choose English-Protestant schools for their children. This was perceived as a threat to French-language dominance in the province, and for good reason. Immigrants tended to concentrate in Montreal, where English was a powerful attraction. In 1972, according to the Gendron Commission, 89.3 percent of the allophone children under the jurisdiction of the Montreal Catholic School Commission were enrolled in English schools.[45] A variety of factors have been cited to explain this preference among immigrants: the relatively poor quality of French-language education, including the teaching of English as a second language; perceived prejudice against allophone children in French schools; the ethnic and religious heterogeneity of English schools;[46] the importance of English in North America; and the economic supremacy of English in Quebec.

42. This provision of the Charter of Rights and Freedoms (with a five-year time limit beginning in 1982) allows provincial legislatures to override certain sections of the charter.

43. See Joan Fraser, "The Minorities: Time for Solutions," *Language and Society,* no. 17 (March 1986): 16–18.

44. Section 93 of the British North America Act (Canada's first constitution) established the right to denominational schooling, which tended to follow linguistic lines; that is, most Catholic schools were French, and most Protestant schools were English.

45. While 52 percent of Italian children had attended French schools in 1943, by 1972 this figure had dropped to 9 percent; Government of Quebec, *Report of the Commission of Inquiry on the Position of the French Language and on Language Rights in Quebec* (Québec: Editeur Officiel du Québec, 1972).

46. E.g., Jews were defined as Protestants by Quebec law. For a discussion, see Daniel J. Elazar and Harold M. Waller, *Maintaining Consensus: The Canadian Jewish Polity in the Postwar World* (Lanham, Md.: University Press of America, 1990), pp. 11, 86–88.

Neither the place of English in the province, nor any special educational provisions for English-speaking migrants from other parts of Canada was mentioned in Bill 101. This latter omission conflicted with the right to minority education set forth in Canada's 1982 Constitution. One consequence of Quebec's language legislation is that Quebec anglophones can no longer rely, as they once did, on their economic power to ensure the protection of their rights within the province. As a result, they have become articulate proponents of administrative, legislative, and constitutional action to extend appropriate educational and other public services to linguistic minorities.

Bill 101 had important implications for business and employment in Quebec, as well. Despite promises by the P.Q. government in 1977, some jobs were lost as a result of the legislation. Section 20 of the bill, for example, created obstacles to the hiring, promotion, and transfer of English-speaking Quebecers in the public sector. Section 35 (among others) impeded access by English-speaking Quebecers to an increasingly French workplace. For a time the Office de la Langue Française proposed that some firms restrict the number of positions in which contacts outside Quebec were required, a policy that would have been particularly punitive to the tourist industry.

Most important, businesses were required to undertake "francization" programs aimed at making French the predominant language of industry and commerce. Bill 101 established the fundamental right of every Quebecer to work in French, in both the public and private sectors.[47] Every firm with over fifty employees had to prepare a francization plan covering such concerns as French communications with employees and French-language proficiency at managerial levels. Penalties would be imposed where French was not sufficiently promoted and where merchants advertised their products in languages other than French. Public administration, health and social services, professional corporations, and employees' associations were now obliged to inform and serve in French.

Francophones, now guaranteed that workplaces and schools would operate in French, could more effectively control their cultural and linguistic destiny. By the same token, however, Quebec was the only province in Canada to restrict the legal rights of a minority to work, study, and function freely in its own language. Bill 101 was possible in a society that had accepted the principle of state intervention in relation to language and had mobilized to withstand a perceived threat to its survival as a majority within Quebec. The resulting climate of fear and mistrust between the English and the French, especially in Montreal, gave rise to a worsening environment for economic

47. The law has since been amended to allow employers and employees to communicate exclusively in English if both parties agree.

investment. On the other hand, most observers would agree that Bill 101 has served to reduce, if not totally eliminate, the economic disparity between French-speaking and English-speaking Quebecers. The francization of private enterprise has also contributed to the emergence of a French-speaking entrepreneurial class.

Amid the enormous level of popular support for Quebec's language legislation, many nonfrancophones felt bitter and charged that, even when they spoke French, they were being discriminated against by the provincial bureaucracy. The *Montreal Gazette,* the leading English-language newspaper in the province, has systematically listed episodes of discrimination against Quebecers of English heritage. Alliance Quebec was organized to protect minority rights in the province. In 1989, for the first time, an anti–Bill 101, anti–Meech Lake, English-rights party, the Equality Party, won four seats in the provincial legislature. Two of the four elected members do not speak French, a frequent pattern among Quebec's anglophones—which should prove interesting, since all debates in the National Assembly are conducted in French. One could argue that denying the rights of anglophones hurts francophones as well, by limiting their exposure to English and thus their social mobility. Quebec's economy depends heavily on exports to the United States and almost all bilateral contracts are written in English. Also, English predominates in advanced technologies, where French terms often do not exist. And yet, Quebec's education department has expressed concern that children not learn a second language at too early an age for fear it would hinder their learning of French.

Since 1976, 170,000 Quebecers have emigrated, principally anglophones and often the best educated, most skilled members of Quebec society. Similarly, many individuals and businesses refuse to relocate to the province because of perceived language problems. Many corporations regard Quebec as a distribution area rather than a manufacturing center or home-office location. These circumstances do not bode well for Quebec's economic future.

Given the failure of the Meech Lake Accord, it is hard to be optimistic about the future of the Canadian polity. By 1990 Quebec nationalism was at a fever pitch, manipulated effectively by its provincial politicians. And unlike earlier periods in Quebec history, the business class of the province was no longer averse to considering the option of political sovereignty so long as the required economic arrangements could be negotiated successfully with the federal government. Canada has had a long history of resolving apparently intractable internal problems, and the current crisis might be similarly ameliorated. Nevertheless, there is no sign that most Canadians are interested in keeping Quebec in the federation. There is a wellspring of mutual suspicion and anger. Many observers suggest that a quick, amicable divorce might be best for all concerned, although separation is unlikely to ensue for at least five to ten years. That being said, Quebec's assertion of its national identity is not going to disappear, just as previously dormant nationalist movements in various parts of the world are reemerging now with a vengeance.

Canada's Charter of Rights and Freedoms

Canada's 1982 Constitution, which Quebec refused to sign, included a Charter of Rights and Freedoms that made official bilingualism binding on all provinces. According to an earlier precedent set by the Supreme Court of Canada, provincial legislatures could go beyond, but not diminish the language rights guaranteed under the constitution. The 1982 Charter established two important principles: a fundamental equality between English and French and a goal of advancing the "equality of status or use" of both languages. Also, it included a section providing for linguistic minority rights in education.[48]

16. (1) English and French are the official languages of Canada and have equality of status and equal rights and privileges as to their use in all institutions of the Parliament and government of Canada. . . .

(3) Nothing in this Charter limits the authority of Parliament or a legislature to advance the equality of status or use of English and French.

17. (1) Everyone has the right to use English or French in any debates and other proceedings of Parliament. . . .

18. (1) The statutes, records, and journals of Parliament shall be printed and published in English and French and both language versions are equally authoritative. . . .

19. (1) Either English or French may be used by any person in, or in any pleading in or process issuing from, any court established by Parliament. . . .

20. (1) Any member of the public in Canada has the right to communicate with, and to receive available services from, any head or

48. For further legal analysis, see André Tremblay, "The Language Rights," in *The Canadian Charter of Rights and Freedoms: Commentary*, ed. Walter S. Tarnopolsky and Gérald-A. Beaudoin (Toronto: Carswell Co., 1982).

central office of an institution of the Parliament or government of Canada in English or French, and has the same right with respect to any other office of any such institution where

(a) there is a significant demand for communications with and services from that office in such language; or

(b) due to the nature of the office, it is reasonable that communications with and services from that office be available in both English and French. . . .

21. Nothing in sections 16 to 20 abrogates or derogates from any right, privilege, or obligation with respect to the English and French languages, or either of them, that exists or is continued by virtue of any other provisions of the Constitution of Canada.

22. Nothing in sections 16 to 20 abrogates or derogates from any legal or customary right or privilege acquired or enjoyed either before or after the coming into force of this Charter with respect to any language that is not English or French.

Minority Language Educational Rights

23. (1) Citizens of Canada

(a) whose first language learned and still understood is that of the English or French linguistic minority population of the province in which they reside, or

(b) who have received their primary school education in Canada in English or French and reside in a province where the language in which they received that instruction is the language of the English or French linguistic minority population of the province, have the right to have their children receive primary and secondary school instruction in that language in that province.

(2) Citizens of Canada of whom any child has received or is receiving primary or secondary school instruction in English or French in Canada, have the right to have all their children receive primary and secondary school instruction in the same language.

(3) The right of citizens of Canada under subsections (1) and (2) to have their children receive primary and secondary school instruction in the language of the English or French linguistic minority population of a province

(a) applies wherever in the province the number of citizens who have such a right is sufficient to warrant the provision to them out of public funds of minority language instruction; and

(b) includes, where the number of those children so warrants, the right to have them receive that instruction in minority language educational facilities provided out of public funds.

Enforcement

24. (1) Anyone whose rights or freedoms, as guaranteed by this Charter, have been infringed or denied may apply to a court of competent jurisdiction to obtain such remedy as the court considers appropriate and just in the circumstances.

(2) Where, in proceedings under subsection (1), a court concludes that evidence was obtained in a manner that infringed or denied any rights or freedoms guaranteed by this Charter, the evidence shall be excluded if it is established that, having regard to all the circumstances, the admission of it in the proceedings would bring the administration of justice into disrepute.

General

25. The guarantee in this Charter of certain rights and freedoms shall not be construed so as to abrogate or derogate from any aboriginal, treaty, or other rights or freedoms that pertain to the aboriginal peoples of Canada including

(a) any rights or freedoms that have been recognized by the Royal Proclamation of October 7, 1763; and

(b) any rights or freedoms that may be acquired by the aboriginal peoples or Canada by way of land claims settlement.

Quebec's Bill 101: Charter of the French Language

Bill 101 passed Quebec's National Assembly on August 26, 1977, shortly after the Parti Québecois came to power in the province. Prescriptive down to the tiniest detail, the legislation was aimed at preserving a language and culture perceived to be threatened. While many would agree that Bill 101 has reversed the erosion of French and elevated the economic status of Quebec's francophones, it has done so by sharply restricting the rights of anglophones and other linguistic minorities. Although some provisions have been invalidated by Canada's Supreme Court, the law remains largely intact. In the abridged text that follows, a number of technical, administrative, and repetitive sections have been omitted.

Preamble

Whereas the French language, the distinctive language of a people that is in the majority French-speaking, is the instrument by which that people has articulated its identity;

Whereas the Assemblée Nationale du Québec recognizes that Québecers wish to see the quality and influence of the French language assured, and is resolved therefore to make of French the language of Gouvernement and the Law, as well as the normal and everyday language of work, instruction, communication, commerce and business;

Whereas the Assemblée Nationale du Québec intends in this pursuit to deal fairly and openly with the ethnic minorities, whose valuable contribution to the development of Québec it readily acknowledges;

Whereas the Assemblée Nationale du Québec recognizes the right of the Amerinds and the Inuit of Québec, the first inhabitants of this land, to preserve and develop their original language and culture;

Whereas these observations and intentions are in keeping with a new perception of the worth of national cultures in all parts of the earth, and of the obligation of every people to contribute in its special way to the international community;

Therefore, Her Majesty, with the advice and consent of the Assemblée Nationale du Québec, enacts as follows:

Title I. Status of the French Language

Chapter I. The Official Language of Québec

1. French is the official language of Québec.

Chapter II. Fundamental Language Rights

2. Every person has a right to have the civil administration, the health services and social services, the public utility firms, the professional corporations, the associations of employees and all business firms doing business in Québec communicate with him in French.

3. In deliberative assembly, every person has a right to speak in French.

4. Workers have a right to carry on their activities in French.

5. Consumers of goods and services have a right to be informed and served in French.

6. Every person eligible for instruction in Québec has a right to receive that instruction in French.

Chapter III. The Language of the Legislature and the Courts

7. French is the language of the legislature and the courts in Québec.

8. Legislative bills shall be drafted in the official language. They shall also be tabled in the Assemblée Nationale, passed and assented to in that language.

9. Only the French text of the statutes and regulations is official.

10. An English version of every legislative bill, statute and regulation shall be printed and published by the civil administration.

11. Artificial persons addressing themselves to the courts and to bodies discharging judicial or quasi-judicial functions shall do so in the official language, and shall use the official language in pleading before them unless all parties to the action agree to their pleading in English.

12. Procedural documents issued by bodies discharging judicial or quasi-judicial functions or drawn up and sent by the advocates practising before them shall be drawn up in the official language. Such documents may, however, be drawn up in another language if the natural person for whose intention they are used expressly consents thereto.

13. The judgments rendered in Québec by the courts and by bodies discharging judicial or quasi-judicial functions must be drawn up in French or be accompanied with a duly authenticated French version. Only the French version of the judgment is official.

Chapter IV. The Language of the Civil Administration

14. The Gouvernement, the government departments, the other agencies of the civil administration and the services thereof shall be designated by their French names alone.

15. The civil adminstration shall draw up and publish its texts and documents in the official language. This section does not apply to relations with persons outside Québec, to publicity and communiqués carried by news media that publish in a language other than French or to correspondence between the civil administration and natural persons when the latter address it in a language other than French. . . .

18. French is the language of written internal communications in the Gouvernement, the government departments, and the other agencies of the civil administration.

19. The notices of meeting, agendas and minutes of all deliberative assemblies in the civil administration shall be drawn up in the official language.

20. In order to be appointed, transferred or promoted to an office in the civil administration, a knowledge of the official language appropriate to the office applied for is required. . . .

22. The civil administration shall use only French in signs and posters, except where reasons of public health or safety require use of another language as well. . . .

29. Only the official language shall be used on traffic signs. The French inscription may be complemented or replaced by symbols or pictographs.

Chapter V. The Language of the Semipublic Agencies

30. The public utility firms, the professional corporations and the members of the professional corporations must arrange to make up their services in the official language. They must draw up their notices, communications and printed matter intended for the public, including public transportation tickets, in the official language. . . .

34. The professional corporations shall be designated by their French names alone.

35. The professional corporations shall not issue permits in Québec except to persons whose knowledge of the official language is appropriate to the practice of their profession. . . .

Chapter VI. The Language of Labour Relations

41. Every employer shall draw up his written communications to his staff in the official language. He shall draw up and publish his offers of employment or promotion in French.

42. Where the offer of employment regards employment in the civil administration, a semipublic agency or a firm required . . . to have a francization certificate, establish a francization committee or apply a francization programme, as the case may be, the employer publishing this offer of employment in a daily newspaper published in a language other than French must publish it simultaneously in a daily newspaper published in French, with at least equivalent display.

43. Collective agreements and the schedules to them must be drafted in the official language. . . .

45. An employer is prohibited from dismissing, laying off, demoting or transferring a member of his staff for the sole reason that he is exclusively French-speaking or that he has insufficient knowledge of a particular language other than French.

46. An employer is prohibited from making the obtaining of employment or office dependent upon the knowledge of a language other than the official language, unless the nature of the duties requires the knowledge of that other language. The burden of proof that the knowledge of the other language is necessary is on the employer, at the demand of the person or the association of employees concerned, or as the case may be, the Office de la langue française. . . .

49. Every association of employees shall use the official language in written communications with its members. It may use the language of an individual member in its correspondence with him. . . .

Chapter VII. The Language of Commerce and Business

51. Every inscription on a product, on its container or on its wrapping, or on a leaflet, brochure or card supplied with it, including the directions for use and the warranty certificates, must be drafted in French. This rule applies also to menus and wine lists. The French

inscription may be accompanied with a translation or translations, but no inscription in another language may be given greater prominence than that in French. . . .

53. Catalogues, brochures, folders and similar publications must be drawn up in French.

54. Except as provided by regulation of the Office de la langue française, it is forbidden to offer toys or games to the public which require the use of a non-French vocabulary for their operation, unless a French version of the toy or game is available on no less favourable terms on the Québec market.

55. Contracts pre-determined by one party, contracts containing printed standard clauses, and the related documents, must be drawn up in French. They may be drawn up in another language as well at the express wish of the parties. . . .

57. Application forms for employment, order forms, invoices, receipts and quittances shall be drawn up in French.

58. Except as may be provided under this act or the regulations of the Office de la langue française, signs and posters and commercial advertising shall be solely in the official language.

59. Section 58 does not apply to advertising carried in news media that publish in a language other than French, or to messages of a religious, political, ideological or humanitarian nature, if not for a profit motive.

60. Firms employing not over four persons including the employer may erect signs and posters in both French and another language in their establishments. However, the inscriptions in French must be given at least as prominent display as those in the other language. . . .

63. Firm names must be in French. . . .

67. Family names, place names, expressions formed by the artificial combination of letters, syllables or figures, and expressions taken from other languages may appear in firm names to specify them, in accordance with other acts and with the regulations of Office de la langue française. . . .

71. A non-profit organization devoted exclusively to the cultural development or to the defense of the peculiar interests of a particular ethnic group may adopt a firm name in the language of the group, provided that it adds a French version.

Chapter VIII. The Language of Instruction

72. Instruction in the kindergarten classes and in the elementary and secondary schools shall be in French, except where this chapter allows otherwise. . . .

73. In derogation of section 72, the following children, at the request of their father and mother, may receive their instruction in English:

(a) a child whose father or mother received his or her elementary instruction in English, in Québec;

(b) a child whose father or mother domiciled in Québec on 26 August 1977, received his or her elementary instruction in English outside Québec;

(c) a child who, in his last year of school in Québec before 26 August 1977, was lawfully receiving his instruction in English, in a public kindergarten class or in an elementary or secondary school;

(d) the younger brothers and sisters of a child described in paragraph (c). . . .

79. A school body not already giving instruction in English in its schools is not required to introduce it and shall not introduce it without express and prior authorization of the Ministère de' l'education. . . .

84. No secondary school leaving certificate may be issued to a student who does not have the speaking and writing knowledge of French required by the curricula of the Ministère de l'education. . . .

Chapter IX. Miscellaneous

89. Where this act does not require the use of the official language exclusively, the official language and another language may be used together.

90. Subject to section 10, anything that, by prescription of an act of Québec or an act of the British Parliament having application to Québec in a field of provincial jurisdiction, or of a regulation or an order, must be published in French and English may be published in French alone. Similarly, anything that, by prescription of an act, a regulation or an order, must be published in a French newspaper and in an English newspaper, may be published in a French newspaper alone. . . .

Title II. The Office de la Langue Française and Francization

Chapter II. The Office de la Langue Française

100. An Office de la langue française is established to define and conduct Québec policy on linguistics research and terminology and to see that the French language becomes, as soon as possible, the language of communication, work, commerce and business in the civil administration and business firms.

101. The Office is composed of five members, including a president, appointed by the Gouvernement for not more than five years. . . .

113. The Office shall:

(a) standardize and publicize the terms and expressions approved by it;

(b) establish the research programmes necessary for the application of this act;

(c) draft the regulations within its competence that are necessary for the application of this act and submit them for consideration to the Conseil de la langue française in accordance with section 188;

(d) define, by regulation, the procedure for the issue, suspension or cancellation of the francization certificate;

(e) assist in defining and preparing the francization programmes provided for by this act and oversee the application thereof;

(f) recognize, on the one hand, the municipal bodies, school bodies, health services and social services that provide services to persons who, in the majority, speak a language other than French, and, on the other hand, the departments that have charge of organizing and giving instruction in a language other than French in the school bodies.

114. The Office may:

(a) adopt regulations within its competence under this act, which shall be submitted for examination to the Conseil de la langue française;

(b) establish terminology committees and determine their composition and their terms and conditions of operation and, as may be required, delegate such committees to the departments and agencies of the civil administration;

(c) adopt internal management by-laws subject to approval by the Gouvernement;

(d) establish by by-law the services and committees necessary for the attainment of its purposes;

(e) subject to the Act respecting the Ministère des affaires intergouvernementales, make agreements with any other agency or any government to facilitate the application of this act;

(f) require every teaching institution at the college or university level to file a report on the language used in its manuals and state its observations in that respect in its annual report;

(g) assist the agencies of the civil administration, the semipublic agencies, business firms, the different associations, and individuals, in refining and enriching spoken and written French in Québec. . . .

Chapter III. The Commission de Toponymie

122. A Commission de toponymie is established at the Office de la langue française. . . .

125. The Commission shall:

(a) establish the standards and rules of spelling to be followed in place names;

(b) catalogue and preserve place names;

(c) establish and standardize geographical terminology, in cooperation with the Office;

(d) officialize place names;

(e) publicize the official geographical nomenclature of Québec;

(f) advise the Gouvernement on any question submitted by it to the Commission relating to toponymy. . . .

128. Upon the publication in the *Gazette officielle du Québec* of the names chosen or approved by the Commission, the use of such names becomes obligatory in texts and documents of the civil administration and the semipublic agencies, in traffic signs, in public signs and posters and in teaching manuals and educational and research works published in Québec and approved by the Ministère de' l'education. . . .

Chapter V. Francization of Business Firms

136. Business firms employing fifty or more employees must, from the date determined under section 152, which shall not be later than 31 December 1983, hold a francization certificate issued by the Office.

137. From 3 January 1979, any firm required to hold a francization certificate is guilty of an offence if it does not hold one.

138. A francization certificate attests that the business firm is applying a francization programme approved by the Office, or that French already enjoys the status in the firm that such programmes are designed to ensure. . . .

141. The francization programme is intended to generalize the use of French at all levels of the business firm. This implies:

(a) the knowledge of the official language on the part of management, the members of the professional corporations and the other members of the staff;

(b) an increase at all levels of the business firm, including the board of directors, in the number of persons having a good knowledge of the French language so as to generalize its use;

(c) the use of French as the language of work and as the language of internal communication;

(d) the use of French in the working documents of the business firm, especially in manuals and catalogues;

(e) the use of French in communications with clients, suppliers and the public;

(f) the use of French terminology;

(g) the use of French in advertising;

(h) appropriate policies for hiring, promotion and transfer.

142. Francization programmes must take account of the situation of persons who are near retirement or of persons who have long records of service with the business firm.

143. Francization programmes must take account of the situation relations of business firms with the exterior and of the particular case of head offices established in Québec by business firms whose activities extend outside of Québec. . . .

151. The Office may, with the approval of the Minister [responsible

for application of this act] and on condition of a notice in the *Gazette officielle du Québec*, require a business firm employing less than fifty persons to analyze its language situation and implement a francization programme. . . .

152. The Office may, by regulation, establish classes of business firms according to the nature of their activities and the number of persons they employ. For each class so established, it may fix the date on which francization certificates become exigible, set the terms on which certificates are issued and prescribe the obligations of the firms holding certificates. . . .

Title III. The Commission de Surveillance and Inquiries

158. A Commission de surveillance is established to deal with questions relating to failures to comply with this act. . . .

168. The investigation commissioners and the staff of the Commission de surveillance cannot be prosecuted for acts done in good faith in the performance of their duties.

169. The investigation commissioners shall make the inquiries provided for by this act.

170. The inspectors shall assist the investigation commissioners in the performance of their duties, verify and establish facts that may constitute offences against this act and submit reports and recommendations to the investigation commissioners on the facts established.

171. The investigation commissioners shall make an inquiry whenever they have reason to believe that this act has not been observed.

172. Business firms to which the Office has issued or is about to issue a francization certificate are subject to an inquiry where so requested by the Office.

173. Any person or group of persons may petition for an inquiry.

174. Petitions for inquiry must be in writing and be accompanied with indications of the grounds on which they are based and identification of the petitioners. The identity of a petitioner may be disclosed only with his express authorization. . . .

182. When, after an inquiry, an investigation commissioner considers that this act or the regulations hereunder have been contravened, he may put the alleged offender in default to conform within a given delay. If the investigation commissioner considers that the offence has continued beyond such delay, he shall forward the record to the Attorney-General for his consideration and, if necessary, institution by him of appropriate penal proceedings. . . .

Title IV. Conseil de la Langue Française

188. The Conseil shall:

(a) advise the Minister on the questions he submits to it relating to the situation of the French language in Québec and the interpretation or application of this act;

(b) keep a watch on language developments in Québec with respect to the status and quality of the French language and communicate its findings and conclusions to the Minister;

(c) apprise the Minister of the questions pertaining to language that in its opinion require attention or action by the Gouvernement;

(d) advise the Minister on the regulations prepared by the Office.

189. The Conseil may:

(a) receive and hear observations of and suggestions from individuals or groups on questions relating to the status and quality of the French language;

(b) with the approval of the Minister, undertake the study of any question pertaining to language and carry out or have others carry out any appropriate research;

(c) receive the observations of any agency of the civil administration or business firm on the difficulties encountered in the application of this act and report it to the Minister;

(d) inform the public on questions regarding the French language in Québec. . . .

Title V. Offences and Penalties

205. Every person who contravenes a provision of this act other than section 136 or of a regulation made under this act by the Gouvernement or by the Office de la langue française is guilty of an offence and liable, in addition to costs:

(a) for each offence, to a fine of $25 to $500 in the case of a natural person, and of $50 to $1,000 in the case of an artificial person;

(b) for any subsequent offence within two years of a first offence, to a fine of $50 to $1,000 in the case of a natural person, and of $500 to $5,000 in the case of an artificial person.

206. A business firm guilty of an offence contemplated in section 136 is liable, in addition to costs, to a fine of $100 to $2,000 for each day during which it carries on a business without a certificate. . . .

208. Any court of civil jurisdiction, on a motion by the Attorney-General, may order the removal or destruction at the expense of the defendant, within eight days of the judgment, of any poster, sign, advertisement, bill-board or illuminated sign not in conformity with this act. . . .

Title VI. Transitional and Miscellaneous Provisions

211. Every person who has complied with the requirements of section 35 of the Official Language Act (1974, chapter 6) in respect of bilingual public signs shall have until 1 September 1981 to make the required changes, in particular to change his bill-boards and illuminated signs, in order to comply with this act.

212. The Gouvernement shall entrust a minister with the application of this act. Such minister shall exercise in regard to the staff of the

Office de la langue française, that of the Commission de surveillance and that of the Conseil de la langue française the powers of a depart-ment head.

Economic Perspectives on Language: The Relative Value of Bilingualism in Canada and the United States

By David E. Bloom and Gilles Grenier

David E. Bloom is chairman of the Department of Econom-ics at Columbia University and author of numerous papers on labor and population economics. Gilles Grenier is asso-ciate professor of economics at the University of Ottawa and a specialist in the economic aspects of language. They wrote this article for the *Source Book*.

My father came over in 1894 . . . as a deserter from conscription in the Czar's army. He came from a town called Zinkov . . . about two hundred miles from Kiev. He had somewhat of an education, apparently, because he was the town clerk, the Jewish town clerk . . . in other words, the Jewish registrar of births, deaths, et cet-era.

My father was illiterate in English, so he could not get any job in this country. And he was not by nature an entrepreneur, like so many who surmounted the language. So he drove a blind horse—that's all he could afford—and hauled potatoes from what was called a commission house—[a] wholesale vendor. . . . Four o'clock in the morning he would go—he was a sort of independent contractor—and load up with potatoes and deliver them to hotels. That was his business.

So goes Arthur Goldberg's remembrance of his father, the very same Arthur Goldberg who served the United States as secretary of labor, Supreme Court justice, and United Nations ambassador.[49] It vividly illustrates the crucial role that language skills can play in de-termining economic opportunities and success, even among individ-

49. Quoted in Howard Simons, *Jewish Times* (Boston: Houghton Mifflin, 1988), pp. 73–74.

uals who are educated and undoubtedly above average in intelligence.

Stories like this make many economists' noses twitch because they raise so many perplexing questions. Why did the elder Goldberg fail to overcome his inability to read in English? Was it because he chose to live in an enclave with other English-illiterates? Why did he not enroll in English language classes? Was it because he could not afford the tuition and learning materials, or the lost income from spending several hours each week in school? Or did he doubt that these immediate costs could be justified in terms of the future benefits that a knowledge of English might confer? Did he consider the possibility that learning English might benefit others with whom he came into contact, including his children?

These questions summarize, in essence, most of the economic inquiry into the subject of language. Although this research provides few clear-cut answers to the questions raised above, it does sharpen our ability to analyze the experiences of Arthur Goldberg's father and others like him. We begin this article by reviewing the conceptual branch of the literature, then proceed to its empirical applications, with particular attention to the relative value of language skills in Canada and the United States, and conclude with some implications for language policy in both countries.

The recognition of language as an economic variable was in initiated in the seminal work of Marschak, Hocevar, and Breton and Mieszkowski and furthered by the contributions of Vaillancourt, Grenier, and Robinson.[50] At the intellectual core of these articles are four key ideas that relate to decisions, both individual and collective, about the language in which communication takes place in different contexts.

1. *Economic well-being is enhanced in the aggregate when all members of a society are able and willing to communicate in a single language.*

The efficiency of many economic activities and transactions is affected by the ability of economic agents (e.g., workers, consumers, managers) to communicate with each other. For example, a virtual requirement of most production activities that involve teamwork, su-

50. Jacob Marschak, "Economics of Language," *Behavioral Science* 10 (1965): 135–40; Toussaint Hocevar, "Equilibria in Linguistic Minority Markets," *Kyklos* 28 (1975): 337–57; Albert Breton and Peter Mieszkowski "The Economics of Bilingualism," in Wallace E. Oates, ed., *The Political Economy of Fiscal Federalism* (Lexington, Mass.: D.C. Heath & Co., 1977), pp. 261–73; François Vaillancourt, *Differences in Earnings by Language Groups in Quebec, 1970: An Economic Analysis* (Quebec: International Centre for Research on Bilingualism, 1980); Gilles Grenier, "Language as Human Capital: Theoretical Framework and Application to Spanish-Speaking Americans" (Ph.D. diss., Princeton University, 1982); Chris Robinson, "Language Choice: The Distribution of Language Skills and Earnings in a Dual-Language Economy," *Research in Labor Economics* 9 (1988): 53–90.

pervision, or the interpretation of written or verbal instructions is that workers and managers speak a language that all can understand. Similarly, a common language greatly facilitates distribution activities that involve transactions among sellers and buyers of just about any good or service. By contrast, communication in two or more languages that not everyone can understand tends to slow down workplace and marketplace activity and to create impediments to the generation of value added.

2. *Language is a kind of "human capital," which can be developed in the same way that individuals develop other productive skills.*

Individuals can acquire or improve their language abilities by attending school, conversing with others, engaging in self-study, and so forth. Although most people communicate predominantly in their mother tongue throughout their lives, it is not uncommon to learn another language. Members of linguistic minorities are particularly likely to acquire the dominant language of their society. What is significant for economists is that the development of language skills is not without costs. As noted in the case of Goldberg's father, language-learning typically requires resources to pay for instruction and materials and, perhaps more important, the commitment of time, which also has value. Since one of the most basic propositions of economic analysis is that individuals respond to pecuniary incentives, economists generally believe that individuals will seek to acquire those language skills whose expected financial benefits exceed their expected costs. The promise of various nonpecuniary benefits—for example, widening intellectual horizons or gaining social acceptance—though difficult to measure, will also influence these decisions.

3. *Leaving individuals to pursue their self-interest will not necessarily yield the most desirable outcome—from society's point of view—with respect to the acquisition of language skills.*

For example, in deciding whether to learn the dominant language of the labor market, members of linguistic minorities will consider only the benefits to themselves (e.g., a broader set of job opportunities) and not the benefits that would accrue to society from expanding the domain of the common language. Thus, from society's point of view, the individual may be led to underinvest in the acquisition of language skills. Absent other considerations, it would be proper for this type of social inefficiency to be corrected by the government through the establishment of inducements or regulations designed to encourage the acquisition of additional language skills, including those aimed at promoting the use of a single language.

4. *Nonpecuniary considerations, in particular the connection between language and cultural identity, may also influence decisions about the language used for communication.*

Individuals may place some value on having the opportunity to use a particular language, independent of its value in the production and distribution of goods and services. This point is well illustrated by the preference that most residents of Quebec have for communicating in French, a preference so strong that it has achieved powerful expression in the national politics of Canada. An implication of this fourth key idea is that government policies that discourage the use of particular mother tongues may impose costs on individuals who speak those tongues. Because the social benefits of a single common language will not necessarily outweigh these costs, economic analysis cannot justify—at a conceptual level—public policies that promote the eradication of alternative languages.

In the past few years, most of the research on the economics of language has had an empirical orientation. These efforts have been devoted almost exclusively to testing the notion that individuals' language abilities are a genuine component of their overall stock of abilities—both inherited and acquired—which are rewarded in the labor market. A typical test involves comparing the earnings of two groups of individuals that are similar in terms of labor-market characteristics such as education and experience, but different in terms of language ability. The central question is whether the group that communicates less effectively in the language of the labor market also has lower earnings. Economists interpret the magnitude of the earnings gap between two "otherwise similar" groups as an estimate of the market value of their differential language skills.

Most of the empirical research on the relationship between language skills and earnings has focused on data from Canada and the United States,[51] two countries that are interesting to compare because they are so similar in some respects and so different in others. For example, both have a capitalist economic structure, both have English as the majority language, and both have sizable immigrant populations with widely varying linguistic backgrounds. On the other hand, the two countries' major linguistic minorities have little in common; there are three important differences that deserve mention. First, Canada's French-speaking population is not an immigrant group, while the U.S. Spanish-speaking population generally is. Second, although French speakers are a minority in Canada, they are a majority in Quebec, the second most populous province. In contrast, Spanish

51. For a recent review of twenty-seven published papers on this topic, see David E. Bloom and Gilles Grenier, "The Earnings of Linguistic Minorities: French in Canada and Spanish in the United States," in Barry R. Chiswick, ed., *Immigration, Language, and Ethnicity: Canada and the United States* (Washington, D.C.: American Enterprise Institute, in press).

speakers are a minority in the United States, within each state, and in most metropolitan areas. Finally, French is an official national language in Canada, whereas Spanish is not an official language in the United States.

Empirical analyses have shown the relative economic positions of the two linguistic minorities to be similar in one important respect. Twenty years ago, in both countries, individuals whose mother tongue was not English were penalized in terms of earnings. In 1970 francophone men in Quebec earned 13 percent less than "otherwise-similar" anglophone men. In 1969 Spanish-speaking men residing in New York, Florida, Arizona, California, Colorado, New Mexico, and Texas (states with the largest proportion of Spanish speakers) earned 21 percent less than white male counterparts from English-language backgrounds. These figures suggest a strong connection between ability to communicate in the dominant language and success in the national labor market.[52]

Further support for this conclusion can be found in the contrasting earnings and employment rates between bilingual and monolingual individuals. In 1970 French-speaking males in Quebec who also spoke English earned 9 percent more than otherwise similar males who spoke only French. But among English-speaking workers in Quebec, there was no significant differential between the earnings of those who knew French and those who did not. In addition, employment of bilingual francophones in Quebec was 6 percentage points higher than among the monolingual French population. Similarly, in 1979, in the most heavily Hispanic areas of the United States, Spanish-speaking workers who knew English earned 10 percent more than comparable Spanish-speaking workers who did not, and the bilinguals enjoyed an employment-to-population ratio that was 7 percentage points higher.[53]

Since the early 1970s, however, the language-related earning trends have differed markedly between Canada and the United States. The gap between Canadian francophones and anglophones had almost disappeared by 1980, while between U.S. Spanish- and English-speaking men, it remained large and actually widened slightly. This contrast can be explained by differential supply-demand shifts in the two countries. The demand for French speakers seems to have increased in Canada (and especially in Quebec) during the 1970s, while there were relatively small changes in the supply of French speakers. In Quebec the increased demand was closely associated with the implementation of new language policies, for example, a requirement

52. Ibid.
53. Ibid.

that immigrants send their children to French-speaking schools, regulations to expand the use of French in workplaces, and restrictions on commercial signs in languages other than French *(see pp. 435–45)*. These policies tended to enhance the labor-market value of French-language skills in Quebec at a time of rapid growth in public-sector employment and large out-migration by English speakers.

Meanwhile, in the United States, the supply of Spanish speakers increased during the 1970s because of rising immigration rates, but there is little evidence of any sizable increase in the relative demand for Spanish-speaking workers. As expected, such circumstances produced no measurable increase in the labor market rewards associated with Spanish-speaking ability.

Economists have also studied the significance of language skills in the assimilation of immigrants into the labor market. Here it is generally found that immigrants who come from non-English-speaking countries fare less well in Canada and the United States—both upon arrival and in their subsequent rate of progress—than immigrants who come from English-speaking countries. There are important differences, however, among non-English-speaking immigrants of various nationalities. For example, in 1969, the average earnings of Mexican immigrants to the United States were two-thirds as high as those of comparable English-speaking immigrants. For Cuban immigrants, the corresponding proportion was three-fourths; for Asian and African immigrants, four-fifths; and non-English-speaking European immigrants earned roughly the same as immigrants from English-speaking countries.[54] This pattern highlights the importance of culture and ethnicity—in addition to language background and ability—in determining the rate of immigrants' labor market assimilation.

Although it has been well-established that language skills form a part of workers' human capital, and thereby help to determine their earning capacity, remarkably few attempts have been made to subject other basic propositions about the economics of language to empirical test. Most important, attempts to measure the magnitude of the aggregate benefits associated with communication in a single language are still in their infancy. Moreover, economists have devoted little attention to designing cost-benefit analyses to test the hypothesis that individuals are more likely to acquire new language skills when they have stronger pecuniary incentives to do so.[55] Presumably, such studies will figure prominently in the next generation of empirical research.

Linguistic divisions are a source of ongoing political debates around the world. The influx of Spanish speakers to the United States has

54. Barry R. Chiswick, "The Effect of Americanization on the Earnings of Foreign Born Men," *Journal of Political Economy* 85 (1978): 897–921.
55. But for one worthwhile contribution, see Robinson, "Language Choice."

created severe political tensions in some parts of the South and West related to the provision of bilingual public services. Canada is currently experiencing a serious constitutional crisis related to Quebec's desire to be recognized as a distinct, and possibly even a separate, society. Both situations involve societies with two major linguistic communities whose languages are on an unequal footing in practice and, in the U.S. case, in law.

In response to these language-related tensions, policies have been adopted in both countries to influence the ways in which different languages are used in each economy.[56] Such policies must contend with two contradictory pressures that are naturally present in multilingual societies. First, market forces will tend to support the emergence of a single dominant language in a multilingual society because of the efficiency gains associated with centralized communication. Second, linguistic minority individuals, who are unlikely to be influenced by societal goals and likely to prefer communicating in their mother tongue, may resist learning the dominant language. There is evidence to support the existence of both pressures. On the one hand, English has tended over time to displace French in Canada (outside Quebec) and Spanish in the United States (certainly among the children and grandchildren of immigrants). On the other hand, there is a continuing fear among linguistic minorities that their cultural identity may become less distinct, or lost entirely.

Economists can make two types of contributions to debates on language policy. First, they can help to determine whether there is any legitimate basis for government intervention to promote or discourage the utilization of particular languages. Second, they can provide guidance concerning the relative desirability of alternative intervention plans.

There are two compelling justifications for a government role in the area of language: efficiency and equity. The main efficiency argument is that accelerating the emergence of a one-language economy raises a society's level of prosperity by reducing production and transaction costs. The main equity argument is that slowing the emergence of a one-language economy improves society's distribution of economic well-being by accounting for the language abilities and preferences of linguistic minorities.

Since the efficiency argument supports policies that are fundamentally in conflict with policies supported by the equity argument, policymakers who desire to maximize social well-being must naturally

---

56. For a useful survey of language policies in these two countries in the areas of education, commercial transactions, work, and government activities, see Vaillancourt, "Language and Public Policy in Canada and the United States," in Chiswick, *Immigration, Language, and Ethnicity.*

balance the consequences of one against the other. Indeed, evaluating policies on the basis of efficiency-equity trade-offs is an age-old practice in economics. Unfortunately, in the area of language policy, economists are as yet unable to measure the quantitative strength of these two opposing influences. As a result, the process of weighing efficiency against equity must occur on policymakers' own subjective scales. Put another way, the value added of economic analysis in the development of language policy does not yet derive from a set of objective measurement techniques. Rather, it is conveyed via the power and simplicity of the conceptual framework that economic science offers for evaluating alternative policies.

Coping with Diversity: Australia and the Soviet Union

By Gregory Guy

Gregory Guy is assistant professor of linguistics at Stanford University. This paper, first presented at the Conference on Language Rights and Public Policy held at Stanford University on April 16–17, 1988, was later published as "International Perspectives on Linguistic Diversity and Language Rights," *Language Problems and Language Planning* 13, no. 1 (Spring 1989): 45–53.

An extended debate is currently underway in the United States concerning official language policy, the English Only movement, and the status of minority languages. But of course, the United States is not the first society to confront such issues. By looking at the experiences of other nations, the United States stands to gain insight and information in these matters of linguistic diversity.

We should begin by putting the issue in historical perspective. Linguistic diversity is not new: not in America or anywhere else in the world. Rather, it is as old as human history. For most of recorded time, multilingual societies have been the rule, not the exception. In fact, the only aspect of the matter that is even somewhat new is the idea that a nation *should* be linguistically homogeneous.

In the ancient world, all major states and empires were multilingual. Egypt, Persia, China, and Babylon all included among their sub-

jects speakers of dozens of languages. The Roman Empire encompassed speakers of Italic, Greek, Celtic, Basque, Semitic, Slavic, and
Germanic languages, among others. Native speakers of Latin were a
small fraction of the population of the empire. Although Latin eventually took root as a native language in many areas outside its Roman
homeland, this was never true in Greece, Britain, North Africa, or the
Middle East. The Romans never attempted to pursue a "Latin only"
policy. Nevertheless, they successfully maintained the most powerful
political entity in the world for half a millennium, despite their profound linguistic inclusiveness.

The major medieval and early modern states were also polyglot entities. The Ottoman, Russian, and Austrian empires all used an official language that was known only to a small minority of their subjects. The Napoleonic empire included half of Europe. Among
precolonial states outside Europe, we find the Incas and Aztecs, the
states of Benin and Abyssinia in Africa, the Mogul state in India, and
the empire of the Khans of China, all incorporating peoples who
spoke many different languages. After European colonial expansion
in the eighteenth and nineteenth centuries, the situation became even
more complicated. The erstwhile British and French empires were
probably the most linguistically complex political entities in history.

In the modern world the same picture still obtains. Nations like
China, India, the Soviet Union, Nigeria, and Indonesia all include
speakers of not five or ten different languages, but rather fifty or a
hundred, and not small numbers of speakers, but millions. Linguistic
diversity is therefore the normal human experience. Historically, most
human beings have lived in close contact with speakers of other languages. This fact is markedly at odds with the basic rationale underlying the English Only movement, namely, that a nation should have
just one language. Yet this monolingual ideal is fairly widespread.
Where has it come from, if monolingual nations have been so rare?

Essentially, the equation of "one nation = one language" was an
invention of the nineteenth century, a by-product of the rise of European nationalism. Amid the great social upheavals of the age of revolution, in the democratic struggles against the *anciens régimes* of Europe, language became a rallying point around which to build a new
political identity. Instead of being subjects of the Austrian kaiser or
the Ottoman sultan, people began to redefine themselves as Poles,
Hungarians, or Serbs. Similarly, in the movement to unify the many
small principalities of Germany and Italy, language served as a useful
argument in favor of the elimination of small states like Venice and
Bavaria and the creation of large modern nations that could compete
effectively with the likes of France and Britain.

The model for this ideal came primarily from what were actually

exceptional cases: England and France. These two nations had dominated Europe for centuries and were perceived as linguistically homogeneous. In point of fact, their relative homogeneity had been
achieved at considerable cost to their linguistic neighbors. The English had violently suppressed speakers of Irish and Scots Gaelic for
centuries and the Welsh somewhat less violently. Medieval France
witnessed the protracted imperialist march by a dialect that was originally confined to a small region around Paris across the territory that
now forms the French Republic, at the cost of the suppression and
eventual elimination of substantially different dialects and languages,
such as Provençal.

The monolingual model was first applied as a political principle in
the Versailles treaty, which redrew the map of Europe after World War
I. Carved out of the Eastern empires were new nations such as Poland, Romania, and Hungary, whose boundaries were ostensibly
drawn on linguistic lines. The outcome of this process is that, in the
course of the past century, a few cases of linguistically imperialist
peoples who had established relatively monolingual but powerful
states, have been promulgated as a model for the world. This monolingual model is inappropriate for the ethnically diverse United
States—a nation of immigrant and indigenous peoples who originally
spoke hundreds of different languages, a nation that has never been
monolingual.

It is also inappropriate for most other nations. Should Kenya attempt to suppress one hundred different indigenous languages in favor of English or Swahili? With such a policy it would soon dissolve
in civil war. Even the Versailles treaty could not successfully implement this ideal. The world is linguistically diverse, and no amount of
partitioning and boundary-drawing could alter this fact. So the
treaty-makers left German speakers in Czechoslovakia, Turks in Bul-
garia, Hungarians in Romania, and so on, all over Eastern Europe. In
the case of Yugoslavia, they deliberately threw in the towel, creating
a state with half a dozen different "official" languages.

Thus the most common experience of humankind has always been
one of living in linguistically diverse societies. But how have these
societies dealt with diversity? What approaches have people taken to
the practical, political, and "official" problems of multilingualism?
What are the language policies of other countries?

Former senator S. I. Hayakawa, in a brochure entitled "In Defense
of Our Common Language" (see p. 146), cites the example of several
nations in support of his view that diversity is a threat to America:
"People can live with language differences, as Switzerland has
shown. But if these differences are politicized, as in Belgium, Canada,
and Sri Lanka, a nation can be torn apart." He goes on to advocate

that English be established as "our national language by law," so as to avoid this fate in the United States. Is this an accurate picture? Is the fate of multilingual societies to be "torn apart" if they do not have an official language? And what does it mean to "politicize" linguistic differences? These are among the questions that must be addressed if we are to have a reasoned understanding of the international experience with language diversity. To approach these issues, we need to take a closer look at language policies in several countries. Let us begin by considering two rather different cases, Australia and the Soviet Union.

The language situation in Australia is similar in many respects to that in the United States, or perhaps more accurately, to the United States of seventy years ago, when higher immigration rates prevailed. Both are former colonies of England, with English as the dominant tongue. But both nations also have many other languages, spoken by immigrants as well as indigenous peoples. As in North America, English was preceded in Australia by many indigenous languages—approximately two hundred in the Australian case. Most of these aboriginal languages have died out in the face of the English onslaught, but between fifty and one hundred survive as active languages of whole communities. In addition, literally hundreds of other languages were brought to Australia by non-English-speaking immigrants.

Since World War II Australia has encouraged high rates of immigration, to the extent that about one-half the present population are first- or second-generation immigrants. A substantial portion of these postwar newcomers were not native speakers of English. They came from places like Greece, Italy, Lebanon, and Turkey, and more recently from Vietnam, the Philippines, and Malaysia. More than one million Australians (out of a total population of 14 million) regularly use a language other than English. There are at least ten languages (other than English) spoken in Australia by more than 50,000 people. As in the United States, English has long been the *de facto* national language, but it was never enshrined as the *official* language.

Language policy in Australia has undergone rapid change in the last two decades. The principal development was the emergence of a powerful movement on behalf of minority language rights. This began with an aboriginal civil rights movement in the early 1970s, in which a variety of aboriginal rights were legally established: rights to land, language, and education, and maintenance of traditional culture. Federally funded programs in support of language maintenance and development, bilingual education, and literacy in traditional tongues are now underway.

The next minority rights movement involved immigrants. The last fifteen years have seen the establishment of the principle of equal access to information and services by speakers of minority languages, through the provision of interpreting and translation services, bilingual publications, and so forth. One development that materially affected the career prospects of many immigrant children was the inclusion of their languages among the Higher School Certificate subjects. The H.S.C. examination is a combination of high-school diploma and college entrance examination, and it typically includes a language component. Traditionally, however, the only languages covered were French, German, and Latin. This yielded the paradoxical situation in which a fluent bilingual in, say, English and Croatian would score zero on foreign languages, while an Anglo-Australian child with only halting classroom French might do well. Now, however, a long list of immigrant languages is included in the H.S.C. in most states, generally including Modern Greek, Italian, Turkish, Arabic, and Serbo-Croatian, among others.

The next stage in establishing immigrant language rights was recognition of the validity of efforts to preserve and develop the linguistic and cultural heritage of these communities. Many groups have developed after-school programs for their children to acquire literacy in their native language, and these "ethnic schools" are in some ways supported by and partially integrated into the public school system. Another significant step was the creation of a public multicultural broadcasting network. Australia, like Britain, has a government-owned radio and television network, as well as commercial channels. But in the early 1980s the federal government established a parallel network to broadcast in languages other than English. This has proven to be a great cultural asset. Australians can now watch the best television and films of the entire world, in their original languages with English subtitles; even monolingual English-speaking Australians have become avid fans of soap operas from Brazil, films from Japan, and soccer from Europe.

The culmination of these developments in Australian language policy has been the discovery of linguistic diversity as a national resource. A broad recognition has emerged of the importance of competence in languages other than English for purposes of international commerce, development, investment, and diplomacy. The 1980s have seen the establishment of an official language policy that takes into account all the diverse linguistic needs of a continental-sized, ethnically varied nation. Developing this policy involved grassroots efforts, discussion documents from federal and state governments, conferences at state and national levels, and extensive hearings by the Australian Senate.

The outcome of this nationwide discussion of language issues was the promulgation in 1987 of an official *National Policy on Languages*.[57] In addition to incorporating the maintenance of minority languages, this policy establishes a national goal that every child in Australia should learn a second language. For those who do not speak English natively, this means learning English while maintaining the first language. But reciprocally, Anglo-Australians will all be encouraged to learn a language other than English. Emphasis will be placed on those languages that reflect the new ethnic diversity of Australia, and those that are important for Australian trade and tourism, such as Japanese.

Thus Australian language policy is moving in precisely the opposite direction from the one advocated by U.S. English. Australia, while encouraging everyone to learn English, is also recognizing the great value of minority languages, to the extent of providing government support for their maintenance and advancement. While some seek to move America toward a monolingual future, Australia has declared in favor of a thoroughly multilingual population.

Let us now turn to a second case, one with a very different history and tradition, but where similar issues arise. The Soviet Union faces far greater linguistic diversity than Australia or the United States. Only half of its 280 million people speak Russian. The other half are divided among over one hundred languages, including other Slavic languages, such as Ukrainian and Byelorussian; languages belonging to the Indo-European family, such as Latvian, Lithuanian, and Armenian; languages of the Finno-Ugrian family, such as Finnish and Estonian; languages of the Altaic family, such as Azerbaijani and Kazakh; and languages not related to any of these, such as Georgian and Eskimo.

How does the Soviet Union cope with linguistic diversity on such a scale? The administration of the Soviet Union is federally organized, consisting of the constituent republics and autonomous regions. Each republic uses its local indigenous language as its official language, for local education, commerce, industry, broadcasting, cultural affairs, and so on. The Russian language functions as the lingua franca for the whole Soviet Union, and children outside the Russian Republic study it as a school subject. However, they usually do their "reading, writing, and arithmetic" in Armenian, Uzbek, or whatever native tongue they speak. The separate identities of the numerous national languages and cultures are officially guaranteed.

Soviet language policy thus involves *official recognition of several dozen languages*. The policy has succeeded in keeping a great polyglot country together. In this regard, the current dispute over Nagorno-

57. By Joseph LoBianco (Canberra: Australian Government Publishing Service).

Karabakh is instructive. It has not arisen from the multilingual official policy, but rather from apparent circumventions of that policy. Armenians in Nagorno-Karabakh, which happens to be located within the Azerbaijani republic, are complaining that their language and culture have been suppressed by the Azerbaijanis (whose language is related to Turkish). Moscow has recently agreed with this complaint and proposed a solution involving official status and enhanced institutional support for the Armenian language and culture in Nagorno-Karabakh. Thus official recognition for linguistic minorities is seen as the solution, not the problem.

These two examples could be multiplied many times over. Singapore, India, Paraguay, Nigeria—all are places where government recognition and support of multiple languages is the accepted policy. On the other hand, where language is used to obstruct access to jobs, education, progress, and power, it becomes politicized and a source of conflict.[58] If Senator Hayakawa's real aim is to prevent the United States from being "torn asunder" by the politicization of linguistic differences, then the experience of other countries shows that he is going about it in exactly the wrong way. Language differences become divisive precisely when a dominant group tries to impose its language as an "official" requirement. Therefore, the officialization of English will more likely *create* language conflict than *prevent* it. The solution would be to guarantee minority language rights.

The cases that Senator Hayakawa cites in the passage above demonstrates this point. French Canadian separatism comes from two centuries of second-class citizenship in their own land. Official national bilingualism is the solution, painfully arrived at in Canada; it guarantees equality of opportunity, status, access, and legal rights to the French-speaking majority. Belgium and Sri Lanka have similar histories of one language group discriminating against another. Conflict always continues as long as the discrimination prevails. The emerging solutions in such countries are always framed in terms of linguistic tolerance and equality.

The successful example that Senator Hayakawa cites is Switzerland. Four different languages have coexisted peacefully there for several centuries. It is instructive to ask how the Swiss have managed to achieve such multilingual harmony. The answer is that all four languages have official status, and speakers of each are accorded equal rights to maintain and use their languages wherever they see fit.

There is a parallel between language and other social differences that have divided people, such as race and religion. At various times

58. *See* Ronald F. Inglehart and Margaret Woodward, "Language Conflicts and Political Community," *pp. 410–23.*

in this and other countries, racial and religious differences have been highly contentious issues, politicized and divisive. One could argue that in the 1960s this country was being "torn apart" over racial issues, with marches, demonstrations, and riots. But the solution found in those perilous times was not to make white the "official color" of the United States. Rather, it was to guarantee minority rights and equal opportunity. Similarly, the United States has not solved religious disputes by establishing an official religion, but by guaranteeing religious freedom.

Therefore, an "official language policy" for America in the spirit of the Constitution would be one that guarantees minority language rights and prohibits linguistic discrimination. This is the approach to linguistic diversity that is historically successful, while the official discrimination represented by the proposed English Language Amendment is a sure path to divisiveness and discord. The lesson to be learned from the experiences of other nations is that, when it comes to language differences, we should say, *Vive la différence!*

Australia's National Policy on Languages

By the Department of Employment, Education, and Training

This brochure, published in twenty-nine languages, summarizes a report commissioned by Australia's Minister of Education, *National Policy on Languages*, by Joseph Lo Bianco (Canberra: Australian Government Publishing Service, 1987). By 1990 the Australian government had appropriated $94 million toward implementing Lo Bianco's recommendations.

A national policy on languages is a set of nationally agreed principles which enables decision makers to make choices about language issues in a rational, comprehensive, and balanced way. A national policy on languages should form the basis for the allocation of resources for language programs to suit the interests and needs of all members of the community.

Why does Australia need a national policy on languages?

Australia is a multilingual society. While English is the first language for about 83 percent of Australians, and the language of Australia's major public and private institutions, many Australians speak some problems in Australia associated with language which can only be properly addressed through a national approach. These problems include:

- residual levels of illiteracy among native English speakers;
- poor command of English among some recent and longstanding immigrants and some aborigines;
- relative lack of skills in second languages among English-speaking Australians (even fewer study the languages of Australia's major trading partners);
- the erosion of Australia's linguistic resources through the neglect of potential for bilingualism amongst the children of families who speak a language other than English at home;
- imminent extinction of various aboriginal languages, and the accompanying loss of a significant element of Australia's cultural heritage;
- lack of sufficient emphasis on practical communication skills in university courses in some languages;
- unmet needs for interpreting and translating services for non-English speakers, including migrants, aborigines, the deaf, and tourists from overseas.

A national policy on languages would enable decision makers to:

- devise strategies for meeting the language-related requirements of international trade, economic, and diplomatic relationships;
- initiate action to alleviate and overcome problems, disabilities, inequality, and discrimination which have their origins in language;
- appreciate and support the value of languages other than English for those whose first language is not English;
- improve communication in written and spoken forms of the languages used in Australia;
- enrich Australia's cultural, artistic, and intellectual life.

The principal objective of Australia's national policy on languages is, therefore, to ensure that Australia derives maximum benefit from its rich linguistic resources.

How can this objective be achieved?
This is not an easy task which can be accomplished quickly. However, a good start would be to give all Australian residents the opportunity to learn at least two languages: English and one other. At the same time, use of languages could be fostered through the extension of a range of services in languages other than English.

What are the benefits to Australia and its people of learning a second language?

Proficiency in English and at least one other language brings significant benefits in four important areas:

• *Economics: foreign trade and vocations.* Other major English-speaking countries recognize that depending only on English in the world of business can be a major disadvantage. Australia's trade is mostly conducted with non-English-speaking countries, particularly Asian countries. The link between economics, trade, and languages is not a simple and direct one. However, there is substantial evidence that Australian economic activities, particularly in competitive situations, would benefit from the skilled use of the host countries' languages and understanding of their cultures. This can be a determining factor in gaining a competitive advantage. Other economic dimensions of languages are Australia's role as an education provider for the region (e.g., in the teaching of English as a second or foreign language) and the use of languages as an ancillary skill in servicing the Australian multilingual community.

• *External: Australia's role in the region and the world.* The Asian-Pacific region is the fastest growing economic zone in the world. Recent decades have witnessed a maturing and strengthening of Australia's relationships with its neighbours in this region. The widespread teaching of the languages of the region can contribute to the broad policy objectives of promoting optimal Australian participation in the region's affairs. To fulfil its responsibility on the world stage, Australia needs to ensure that languages of world significance, some of which may not be widely used in the Asia-Pacific region, are well-represented in Australian education.

• *Enrichment: cultural and intellectual.* Learning any second language can provide invaluable insights into ways of being human, and reveal how languages have marked the boundaries between human groups and how these groups order their social relationships. The artistic and philosophical traditions and the values and world view of all cultures are embodied in the languages which give expression to them. There is strong evidence from research that individuals who attain a high level of proficiency in two languages often gain nonlinguistic as well as linguistic benefits in their intellectual functioning. Specifically, these are higher levels of verbal intelligence, greater capacity to think divergently, and greater mental flexibility.

• *Equality: social justice and overcoming disadvantages.* Since language permeates all social life, there are inevitable correlations between social inequalities and language. In Australia lack of proficiency in Standard English correlates with lower-paid employment and lack of access to education and other services. One of the most significant contributions that Australian governments can make to overcoming disadvantages is to provide all Australian residents with the fullest access to English. Preferably such access ought to be from the basis of secure maintenance of the first language.

Who should study another language and which languages should be studied?

All Australian students should have the opportunity to study at least one language other than English through as many years as possible of the education system. However, compulsion is undesirable as it generally leads to poor learning.

There are two major emphases regarding the learning of languages other than English. The first is education in the mother tongue (or so-called "community languages") in all cases where this is possible. The second is the teaching of languages which can be justified for national reasons. Ideally, it would be desirable if all children who speak a language other than English at home had the opportunity to undertake their schooling in this language as well as English, in well-planned and integrated bilingual education programs. Where this is not possible, children should have the opportunity to study the language as a subject at a level appropriate to their pre-existing knowledge.

In practice it is simply not possible to provide all students with the chance to study all languages. Whilst it is acknowledged that all languages have value and that support should be given to all languages, limitations on resources and the need for school programs to insist on excellence require the setting of priorities. The Lo Bianco report on a national policy on languages, therefore, proposes a category of "languages of wider learning," which would balance Australia's domestic and external needs. The languages suggested for wider learning are: Arabic, French, Greek, Italian, Spanish, Chinese (Mandarin), German, Indonesian/Malay, and Japanese.

The report stresses that the teaching of *any* language desired by each school community is educationally and culturally warranted and should be encouraged. At Year 12 level, states/territories should examine as many languages as possible. The report suggests ways of increasing the number of languages taught and for diversifying the venues and the ways in which languages can be learned. However, maximum benefit from language learning can only be gained by careful planning. Planning is needed to make the best possible use of Australia's linguistic resources.

What does planning involve?

In the case of Australia, the planning of linguistic resources requires cooperation and coordination of initiatives at all levels of government, federal, state, and local, especially in education. In particular, it requires the recognition that:

- the "needs" of the nation and the community are interdependent, rather than conflicting;
- although English is currently a major world language, other languages are also growing in global importance, both in terms of economic power and number of speakers;
- the maintenance of immigrant and indigenous languages spoken in Australia may be encouraged—or discouraged—by public policy decisions.

What does Australia's policy on languages aim to do?

Australia's policy on languages recognises the nation's linguistic situation and declares national expectations on language matters publicly. It initiates action towards the achievement of these ends in a nonprescriptive way. Basically, this would be accomplished through four strategies:

- *conservation* of Australia's linguistic resources;
- *development and expansion* of these resources;
- *integration* of Australian language teaching and language use efforts with national economic, social, and cultural policies;
- *provision* of information and services in languages understood by clients.

Australia's policy on languages will direct the multilingualism of Australia in accordance with national aims, stressing national unity but rejecting imposed uniformity. It will do this by:

- asserting the primacy of English in Australia;
- advocating the widespread learning of languages in addition to English;
- promoting the continued use of languages other than English, both aboriginal and nonaboriginal, by the Australian community.

What is Australia's policy on languages based on?

Australia's policy on languages is based on six principles:

- Australian English is Australia's national language. It is the uniquely Australian way of speaking English which takes its place alongside other varieties of English. Australian English should be used with confidence in Australia and overseas.
- The social dialects of English in Australia serve valuable group identity functions for their speakers. Education must aim to enable all

Australians to add Standard Australian English to the forms of language they may already speak, so that they will not be socially or economically disadvantaged.

• There is a need for public authorities to use plain English, to reject racist and sexist language and to retain the Australian character of our environment through the continued practice of using aboriginal place names.

• Aboriginal and Torres Strait island languages, including creoles and pidgins, are legitimate forms of communication, and information about government programs and services should be made available in those languages. The very low level of awareness of these languages among most nonaborigines is deplored.

• Aboriginal people should be consulted and involved in all decision making which affects them.

• Community languages other than English, including Australian Sign Language used by the deaf, are firmly established in the Australian context and fulfill the communicative needs of large groups of Australians. These Australians are entitled to access to government services in the language they know best and to increased opportunities to continue learning their first language in addition to English.

What has the Government agreed to do?

The Government has agreed to provide $15 million in 1987–88 to fund a number of language programs. These programs form the basis of a balanced and sound national policy on languages for the benefit of all Australians. This amount will increase to $28 million in a full year. The programs to be funded in 1987–88 include:

• *English as a second language for children.* English as a second language (E.S.L.) for children is an integral part of all English language development. The Commonwealth English as a Second Language Program for new arrivals will be expanded so that students who need E.S.L. instruction will be able to participate in intensive English classes for up to twelve months.

• *Adult literacy.* The Lo Bianco report recommends that, during 1988, a concerted campaign should be implemented to improve the level of adult literacy in English.

• *Aboriginal languages.* The Commonwealth will implement a National Aboriginal Language Project (N.A.L.P.). Its aim is to provide supplementary funding for initiatives in aboriginal language education to state/territory and nongoverment education authorities or school communities for projects. This funding may be directed to bilingual education and language maintenance and development programs.

• *A language other than English for all.* An Australian Second Language Learning Program (A.S.L.L.P.) will be established to foster proficiency in languages other than English. Only programs and initiatives which stress excellence will be supported by the A.S.L.L.P. Bilingual education programs could be included.

• *Multicultural and cross-cultural supplementation programs.* As part of the Government's commitment to the development of the national policy on languages, a program will be introduced to boost multicultural and intercultural studies in tertiary education institutions. The programs will provide a foundation for the development of cross-cultural training within professional courses, the provision of in-service courses for teachers, and multicultural education programs.

• *National strategy for Asian studies.* A program to boost Asian studies in Australia will include, for example, initiatives to develop curriculum materials and tagged funding to tertiary institutions offering or extending courses in the Asian languages of major importance to Australia.

Coordination of the programs and initiatives outlined above is to be provided by an Advisory Council.

Is there anything Australia's national policy on languages will not do?

Yes. The national policy on languages will provide guidance rather than be prescriptive. Four ground rules apply:

• Legislation on any aspect of language is inappropriate and undesirable for Australia.

• Although it is desirable that in the long term, all students should acquire some proficiency in English and at least one other language, language study should not be compulsory.

• While the status of all languages used in Australia is acknowledged, the policy does not devalue English. It recognises the status of English as Australia's national language.

• A national policy on languages would not discriminate in favour of or against any group in the Australian community. While it will seek to determine a coherent set of national guidelines, groups at state/territory and local level should retain their traditional responsibility for their community and set priorities appropriate to the communities' needs within the broad framework provided by the policy.

Language As a Factor in Inter-Group Conflict

By Harold R. Isaacs

Harold R. Isaacs (1910–86) worked as a foreign correspondent for *The New York Times, Newsweek,* CBS, and other
news media before becoming professor of political science
at the Massachusetts Institute of Technology. This article is
excerpted from *Idols of the Tribe: Group Identity and Political
Change* (New York: Harper & Row, 1975), pp. 100–114.

To identify a person as being by origin a speaker of German or of
Hausa or of Chinese is to assume much about him from this single
fact alone. Much, but far from all, for among the elements that make
up the basic group identity, language is but one, and its weight,
value, and importance in relation to the other elements vary greatly
in varying situations.

Examples of this are almost without number. Attempts to revive old
tongues among the Irish and the Welsh have been much less successful than the survival of the strong sense of Irish and Welsh separateness. Command of the revived Hebrew language may have become
essential for anyone who defines his basic group identity as "Israeli,"
but it was not for centuries and is not now at all essential in the identity cluster that makes a "Jew." Some American Indians, it has been
pointed out, have held on to pieces of territory and let their ancestral
languages go; others have held on to the languages and lost the land.
Joshua Fishman cites, among many other examples, studies that
show that second- and third-generation Americans have retained
"ethnic group loyalty" long after losing the ethnic language (like
those Germans who "maintained their self-identification as Germans
in the midst of Polish or Ukrainian majorities long after completely
giving up their German mother tongue," or, one might add, like the
"Baba" Chinese in Malaya who lost the language long ago but never
lost their identity as Chinese) and others, like some American ethnic
groups, who hold on to the language long after losing anything de-
scribable as functional ethnic group loyalty.[59]

Pierre Van Den Berghe has pointed out that in South Africa all

59. Joshua A. Fishman, ed., *Readings in the Sociology of Language* (The Hague: Mouton,
1971), p. 313.

members of the Afrikaner *Volk* are Afrikaner speakers, but that all Afrikaner speakers—e.g., many of the Colored, or persons of mixed Afrikaner-black descent—are most emphatically not members of the *Volk*. Indeed, in this setting where color and physical characteristics play such a commanding role, a non-Afrikaner speaker *can* belong to the Afrikaner Nationalist Party—as "quite a number of German and a few English-speaking whites do"—whereas an Afrikaner-speaking Colored cannot.[60]

Karl Deutsch identifies language as one of the major "building blocks of nationality," at the heart of the communications system, which is the main source of the "complementarity" that makes "a people." At the same time, he stresses that it is never language alone, but always a cluster of characteristics that brings about the complemented result. He cites the experience of the Swiss, who, he suggests, "may speak four different languages and still act as one people," each Swiss having enough learned habits, symbols, memories, and other patterns in common with all the others to enable him "to communicate more effectively with other Swiss than with speakers of his own language who belong to other peoples."[61] Even in Switzerland, however, some language tensions have come into view, and although the example is a small one, it is a peculiarly telling example of how a language can serve as the forward point of the interests of one group of its speakers and be quite subordinate to other interests held by another group speaking the same language. Thus the French-speaking Catholic minority in the Swiss Jura has been pressing for the creation of a separate canton of its own, apart from the German-speaking majority, whereas "the francophones who share Protestantism with the German Béarnais are either indifferent or, in part, hostile to the demand for a separate canton."[62]

Language, in sum, is crucial to the way any individual sees the world; but it not only shapes, it is also shaped by what is seen. Language is a critical element in the making of every individual's basic group identity, but, to repeat, only as one of a cluster of critical elements that can arrange themselves in a host of different combinations. It plays its role in highly varied ways, a variety now spectacularly on view in every corner of the world where groups, tribes, nations, and cultures are trying to sort themselves out in new patterns of self-identification and relation to one another. In the new pol-

---

60. Quoted in Joshua A. Fishman et al., eds., *Language Problems of Developing Nations* (New York: Wiley, 1968), p. 216.

61. *Nationalism and Social Communication* (Cambridge, Mass.: M.I.T. Press, 1953), p. 97.

62. William Peterson, "Ethnic Structure in Western Europe," unpublished manuscript, Oct. 1972.

itics of retribalization and fragmentation that is currently such a large part of this process, the issues are often marked most clearly by conflicts over language, which serves as the most obvious and handiest sign of political, social, or group boundaries, overlying many other more deeply laid concerns. As a symbolic or triggering cause, language places high among the many reasons people have been confronting and killing one another in mounting numbers in so many parts of the globe in recent years.

Language issues of one kind or another appear now in the politics of "old" Europe and America and "new" postcolonial Asia and Africa. Old language loyalties (like Basque, Catalan, Breton, Welsh) reappear in varying intensities in countries made up of one or nearly one piece linguistically (such as Spain, France, Britain), and a new language dispute even turns up in the one-language culture of Norway. New pressures for varieties of bilingualism turn up out of the seams of racial and ethnic division opening in the English-speaking culture of the United States. Old bilingualisms generate new levels of hostility and confrontation, as in Belgium and Canada. New language strains appear even in multilingual Switzerland and again, as of old, around the edges of old irredentisms along the frontiers of Italy and Austria.

Such issues have assumed their sharpest forms in the postcolonial world, made up for the most part of countries with dozens, scores, even hundreds of distinct language communities (e.g., India, Nigeria, Philippines). In Europe long centuries of linguistic evolution led eventually to the forming of nations made up of relatively homogeneous language communities. In the colonial world—Latin America, southern Asia, Africa—colonies were forcibly put together of conglomerated and agglomerated populations speaking many tongues. At the upper levels of these societies, the language of the colonial master became the key to education, status, prestige, power, advancement, development, modernization. In postcolonial India and Africa, members of the ruling groups from different regions and countries speak to one another in the ex-metropolitan lingua franca, English or French, not in any of their local tongues. At lower social and economic levels, the requirements of the slave trade and the colonial experience produced widely used pidgin or patois or Creole tongues that drew on the power-prestige languages of the masters and on varieties of local languages and dialects, as in East Africa, the Caribbean, along the China coast, and in the lands and islands of Southeast Asia. One of these newly created languages grew into Swahili, heavily derived from Arabic, now the lingua franca of much of East Africa and the adopted national language of Tanzania; another became the pidgin English-Melanesian that some believe may become the national language of the Australian half of New Guinea, even as the new Indonesian masters of old Dutch New Guinea seek to make their language the current one in their territory.

A language, a famous linguist once said, "is a dialect with an army and a navy." With the collapse of the old colonial power system, the forming of new nations in the old colonial boundaries, and the new push and pull for power among the various population groups, the question now was who had the army and the navy, in both the literal and the cultural sense. As symbol and as substance, language issues rose to bedevil the nation-building process everywhere: how to handle the multiplicity of languages, what to choose as a national language, whether to continue to use the ex-colonial master's language, advance the use of some one or two of the country's own languages, or even to create a new one. In many cases, as in parts of India, there are strong emotional-cultural attachments to mother tongues, readily generated into political cleavages and leading to murderous violence, often on specifically linguistic issues. Some studies purport to show that elsewhere, as in parts of Africa, insistence on the primacy of particular single languages is much less strong, partly because in so many countries no single language group is clearly dominant either in numbers of speakers or in prestige. In these cases, perhaps wishfully, some believe there is a chance for what Joshua Fishman has tried to call "nationism"—a harder-headed, state-oriented, practical approach to nation-building—in place of the much more emotional, ethnic-oriented, mother-tongue bonds of Mazzini-type or European-style nationalism. Other students of the matter seem to believe that language divisions, both in themselves and in what they come to stand for, will persist and sharpen rather than decline and disappear.

The variety and complexity of the language aspects of current politics are well illustrated in the attempts that have been made by some scholars to draw up typologies that are meant to describe the situation in some reasonably coherent fashion. The difficulty of doing this is a language problem in itself, especially when it is done by linguists, the tangled and tortured actualities producing tangled and tortured terminologies.[63] In a much more usable way, Dankwart Rustow, a political scientist, has grouped types of language situations by the history and politics of the way different states were formed at different times.[64] He produces a broad and often unavoidably crude, but a lucid and workable sequence in which he locates:

63. See, e.g., Heinz Kloss, "Notes Concerning a Language-Nation Typology," in Fishman et al., *Language Problems*, pp. 69–85.

64. "Language, Modernization, and Nationhood," in Fishman et al., *Language Problems*, pp. 87–105.

• Postimperial states, meaning large traditional states that have kept their geographic identity in the modern period, for example, Japan, which also remained linguistically homogeneous, and Russia and China, both of which under Communist rule follow the old imperial policy of political and linguistic dominance by an all-powerful center.

• Postdynastic states of western Europe, which largely grew out of, or developed into, linguistically homogeneous nations, with notable exceptions in Belgium, Finland, and Switzerland, the latter becoming a model of that rare political accomplishment, a viable multilingual nation-state.

• Linguistic states of central and eastern Europe and the Middle East, in which the multivaried shapes and styles of history, politics, and nationality emerging out of the Hapsburg, Russian, and Ottoman empires are included. Here the principle of "linguistic nationality" found the going hard, whether in the characteristic multilingual fragmentation of most of this vast area on the European side, or in the relative homogeneity achieved by the spread of Arabic over its large domain.

• Countries of overseas immigration, with the varying linguistic experiences of the United States, Australia, New Zealand, Argentina, Brazil, Canada, and Israel providing the main examples.

• Postcolonial states of Asia, Africa, and Latin America in which, Rustow remarks, "the principle of linguistic nationality has fared far worse" than in all the other areas and categories. Here the large blocs of 100 million Spanish speakers and 70 million Arabic speakers are divided, often bitterly and violently, among a large number of states. In the rest of the postcolonial world, only relatively few intermediate-sized language communities and large numbers of small to tiny groups make up the great bulk of the new nations formed out of the fallen empires. More than half the new states created after 1945 have no linguistic majority, and among those that do, ironically, there are bitter political divisions, as in Korea and Vietnam. In Africa, paradoxically again, the few relatively large linguistic groups, like the Hausa speakers, are divided among several countries.

Rustow goes on to sort out a number of characteristic language situations where a distinct language is predominant throughout the country, as in western Europe, Japan, Turkey; where a single language dominates in a number of neighboring countries, as in Spanish-speaking America; where among a variety of closely related languages one serves as the official language, as in Indonesia; where among a variety of unrelated languages only one has a substantial literary tradition, as in Morocco or Peru; where a number of unrelated languages have no literary tradition, as in tropical Africa; where un-related languages have their individual literary traditions, as in India or Malaysia. From this crowded list of varieties, Rustow draws the plain general conclusion that language is never a single controlling factor and is never static. The Herder-Mazzini romantics "assumed that language is the most indelible characteristic of peoples," whereas in fact it "is a variable, dependent on political factors." Here too, it seems to me, the actuality blurs such sharp divisions: language is variable in some aspects, powerfully indelible in others.

Immensely varied language effects have come, then, out of all the different kinds of political experience over time. They appear always folded in with other elements of identity. They have come as a consequence of the rising and falling of empires and other power systems, of the massive shifts of cultural impact and influence, the huge forced or free movement of people across seas and continents over the centuries, the push and pressure and press of trade, industry, enslavement, conquest, communication, war, and revolution. To trace the single element of language in the basic identity cluster held by any individual or group of individuals, one would have to begin with the surviving—that is, the indelible—traces of the mother tongue and then go on to the added layers expressed in, or formed by, other languages acquired in each setting of time and circumstance.

The spread of European power, the colonial experience, and the great migrations during the last three or four hundred years created such layered effects in the lives of vast numbers, bringing about what is probably the greatest mixing of peoples and tongues to take place since they were scattered apart by the Great Divider at Babel. The products of this experience fill all our recent history and crowd the contemporary scene, with the heavy European stamp on people in the Americas, Asia, and Africa much more widely pressed than the Hellenic and Roman marks left on the peoples of a much smaller world long ago. Out of this has come our vast patchwork design of connected and contending cultures; of shared and conflicting systems of ideas, beliefs, and values; all the great jagged irregularities of uneven development of societies, economies, technologies separating and uniting different peoples and different parts of the world.

Hence whatever pluses may be made of this history: the belief that through all this movement has come enlargement of knowledge and with it some enhancement of human existence. But hence, too, all the crippled cultures, the besieged traditionalists, the deracinated modernists, the deformed wielders and victims of power: all the cost and confusion, the alienation and anomie, produced by what is called the modernizing process. In painful flight from all these consequences now, many people of many kinds surge to what refuge they can find or retrieve from the ruins of their many Houses of Muumbi.[65] This includes for many the languages they spoke or their fathers and mothers spoke when they still lived there. Trying to retrieve the "variables" and identify the "indelibles" of this experience is like trying to see all this history as through it were a film that can be reversed, when it is actually live action going on all around us, some of it in view, much of it still unseen and unheard.

All these dramas take place on a stage crowded with players talking to one another mostly in obscure riddles, like characters in a Pinter play. In this cast, the Nehru-like between-two-cultures type is a familiar and usually pathetic or poignant figure who moves, as Nehru never did, far and deep into the alien culture to which he can never quite belong and is driven or drawn back to the other to which he can never quite return. Often this is a matter of pieces of different worlds into which individuals divide themselves, dividing indeed by the language spoken in its different parts. This could be, and to some extent is, part of the process of creating a more universal culture, as, for example, in science, but for the individual it has been more frequently an experience deeply ribbed and tangled in complicated emotional and psychological conflicts. There are those Africans, for example, represented by the black Frenchman Leopold Senghor, or the African English speakers Julius Nyrere had in mind when he said that "at one time it was a compliment rather than an insult to call a man a 'Black European.'" Citing this remark, Ali Mazrui has argued that the British colonial African's adoption of English was actually an expression of cultural nationalism because the African was proving how wrong the European was to think that the African was mentally inferior.[66] Or Mazrui, again, depicting an African heaven in which all the African languages continue to be spoken, but are simultaneously translated for all listeners into their preferred tongues, not by any electronic machinery but by an act of will. Mazrui portrays, as a witness at a remarkably heavenly trial, a poor Ibo cobbler who had been murdered by Hausa rioters and who, under the terror of that memory, chose vainly to try to conceal his Ibo identity by speaking not in his own tongue but in halting English.[67]

65. Editor's note: Members of Kenya's dominant Kikuyu tribe swear an oath of tribal loyalty: "I shall never leave the House of Muumbi," referring to the tribe's progenitor mother and the symbolic womb in which all Kikuyu are nurtured; *Idols of the Tribe*, pp. 1–2.

66. "Some Sociopolitical Functions of English Literature in Africa," in Fishman et al., *Language Problems*, p. 184.

67. *The Trial of Christopher Okigbo* (New York: Third Press, 1972), p. 102.

Similar problems and ambiguities are attached, reports another African language specialist, to the development and use of Swahili in East Africa. Arab slavers had been around for much longer than the Europeans, but the Arabic origins and associations of this language were eagerly and pridefully appropriated as a way of acquiring higher status; for many of the same reasons, Arab forms, names, origins, and religious beliefs were adopted by a number of cults that rose among American blacks. More recently, the Arab connection in East African affairs has shifted in value from a borrowed plus to an ambivalent minus. In Zanzibar, for example, where black Africans took power from the hands of their former Arab rulers, it became the fashion to shift emphasis from the Arabic to the Bantu origins of Swahili words in order to "stress the African rather than the Arab character of the language." Tanzania's decision to make Swahili its national language, this writer says, was more "a decision of intention than of fulfillment," for while Swahili in general served as the common medium of ordinary speech among speakers of many other tribal tongues, English continued to be used at all higher levels of national activity.

This has led some East African intellectuals to fear that "having English as a medium of thought and Swahili as a medium of the masses" opens the prospect of class divisions deepened along linguistic lines. Said one African scholar: "By passively accepting English as the medium of intellectual activity, we are unwittingly placing a barrier to the intellectual development of our people. We are unconsciously inflicting the same malady that the great bulk of the so-called intellectual elite of East Africa suffers from—namely, of being almost completely incapacitated to undertake any serious thinking in our own languages. This kind of mental and spiritual stagnation is a direct but long-lasting effect of colonialism."[68]

The same strong issues appear in a different setting in Peru, where the issue of using Spanish or the Indian Quechua and Aymara languages in the Peruvian educational system has been much debated. In one such discussion, a Quechuan scholar pleaded for the teaching of literacy in the Indian mother tongue "so that the individual child will not learn an inferiority complex along with his Spanish," an experience heavily documented in studies of the Peruvian school experience. A priest replies: "This business of saying that the Castilian language is a foreign language is false. [It] is completely our own; it has survived for more than four centuries among us." A Quechua speaker replies that Quechuans who want to follow European ways take up an apprenticeship in the Spanish language and culture, "and

---

68. Lyndon Harries, "Swahili in Modern East Africa," in Fishman et al., *Language Problems*, pp. 415–29.

once they have learned 500 or 600 words, they bury Quechua within themselves and do not wish to speak it any more; they exchange a language of limitless possibilities for a restricted language which constricts their minds and diminishes them as humans instead of exalting them."[69]

The Philippines is a country in which, by some counts, about eighty languages are spoken. There are eleven principal languages, each with more than a million speakers. Tagalog, spoken in a large part of the major island of Luzon, is the language of about one-third of the total population. English, according to census figures, is spoken by as many. A version of Tagalog, called "Pilipino," has been proposed as the national language. It is still far from widely used, although the mass media, especially films, have been extending the spread of Tagalog, many of whose words, along with Spanish and English and Chinese words, have been absorbed into many of the regional languages.

Some of the Filipino experience is reflected in the view of a well-known Filipino writer who had always written in English. Under the nationalist impacts of his later years, he told me, he began trying to write in his mother tongue, Tagalog, and found himself experiencing a shift of cultural personality, which he summed up as the transfer from "active" English to "passive" Tagalog, a difference, he found, that cast different light and different meaning on every sentence he wrote. In the Filipino school system, Spanish was still regarded, in a ritualistic sort of way, as a prestige language that was required study for all, but rarely acquired as a language for actual use. English was studied by everyone from the first or third grade on, but acquired, he said, with something less than 50 percent effectiveness by the great majority; a test of university freshmen in 1963, based on American placement standards for comprehension and inference, rated them most generally at the sixth-grade level. The basic language of his students, he said, was "mix-mix," a combination of Tagalog and English similar to what has in other places been called "Spanglish" or "Franglish" or, in India, "Hinglish." In Filipino political life when it used to be free and open, politicians would speak publicly in English, informally in Tagalog or their local tongue, and most of the time in some kind of "mix-mix."

Despite various well-intentioned programs, he said, neither Tagalog nor the other Filipino languages are being studied or enriched in any systematic way, and English remains at best a partially ac-

69. Cited by Robert Armstrong, "Language Policies and Language Practices in West Africa," in Fishman et al., *Language Problems*, pp. 228–30.

—

quired language. He said: "Mix-mix—'halu-halo,' we call it—*is* the language," as indeed it has been at one early stage or another of most of the languages we now speak. But now even for the best-educated, the difference between English and the mother tongue remains one of depth of expression. Another highly placed intellectual with an impeccable command of English said: "Tagalog expresses the tones of feelings of everyday life, which English cannot do. English is academic and abstract, a way of manipulating ideas. But for the vivid, dramatic, emotional parts of my life, Tagalog serves in a way English cannot. When I make love, it's in Tagalog. We communicate best in Tagalog. Persuading my children to do something, I do it best in Tagalog. When I want to register the most, I do it in Tagalog."

Another figure who comes to mind is the middle-aging father of a family of American Jewish immigrants I met in Israel. His father had been an immigrant from Russia who lived in Brooklyn. "I remember," he said, "how ashamed I used to feel when I heard my old man speak his broken English, and I really made sure that my English wouldn't sound like that. But here I am now in the same position with *my* kids. I wonder how they feel when they hear me speak my broken Hebrew. And it's all turned around because they're the ones that speak English with an accent!" The language *he* commanded, learned on the streets and docks of his native heath where he'd worked from boyhood until his middle years, was pure Brooklynese.[70]

The feeling of inadequacy in the use of a language marks one of the many points where variabilities and indelibilities are not easily separated. Unlike the immigrant or the immigrant's son who wants and needs to be like those to whom he has come as a stranger, the Frenchman who thinks his own is the queen of all languages does not suffer from speaking other tongues with a French accent; he only suffers from hearing others speak French with non-French accents, or even hearing other Frenchmen whose accent is not Parisian. On the other hand, the immigrant carries with him his own indelible attachment to the language he knows as he knows no other. I think of the example of an Argentinian Jew who left Argentina as a youth and acquired relative fluency in several other languages in the course of building his personal and professional life in other countries for the next twenty-five years, speaking them all, however, with an accent that is unmistakably Spanish, and writing them with something less, he al-

70. A dying if not already dead language, according to a mourning writer in *The New York Times*, Aug. 16, 1972: "Brooklynese died for lack of native speakers. . . . In streets where Brooklynites once argued in unmistakable accents, the liquid sound of Black English and the musical intonation patterns of Spanish are now heard. . . . The only surviving speakers of that lovely dialect are television comedians and a small number of elderly citizens. When they pass, Brooklynese will be one with the ages."

ways feels, than impeccable accuracy. "Can you imagine what it means," he once asked me, "never, really *never*, to be at home in the language you are using?"

He occasionally revisits Argentina, where except for surviving members of his family he has virtually no pleasant associations or attachments, but where he now finds the experience of visiting unaccountably pleasurable. The pleasure, it soon appeared, came partly from regaining physical touch with some of the scenes of his childhood, but mainly from his ability to speak and hear the one language of which he felt fully and unaccentedly in command, not just Spanish but Argentinian Spanish as it is spoken in Buenos Aires. Here, if only momentarily, the indelibles displaced all the political and religious and other variables that shaped the element of language and everything else that has gone into the making of this man's basic group identity.

In Malaysia a deep cultural cleft lies between all Chinese and the Malays, and almost as deeply between those Chinese who were educated in the Chinese-language schools and those who came up in the English medium schools in the late colonial or immediate postcolonial period.

The Chinese-educated Chinese, always by far the larger part of the Chinese population until now, used to be taught in Chinese schools built and paid for by the Chinese themselves. In these schools the children of generations of Chinese in Malaya learned to "see" the world with China at its center. They studied Chinese language, history, geography, literature. In the lifetime of the present adult generation, they successfully established *kuo-yu*, the so-called Mandarin national language of China, as the common tongue of educated Chinese in the South Seas, although each regional group preserved its own dialect at home. The older Chinese-educated continued to regard China as their homeland and some version of Chinese traditional behavior as central to their way of life. During the colonial period and up to 1949, this was for the most part an unquestioned and unambiguous attachment. After 1949 there was considerable ambivalence and some conflict between the generations of old and young Chinese-educated as to which "China" they had in mind.

The English-educated were those who moved at a very early age— usually from primary first grade—into the English stream, entering missionary schools or government schools set up to help produce English-educated office workers and minor bureaucrats for European business and government needs. Prudence and foresight in many Chinese families dictated sending at least one child of the family, sometimes several, into this important stream. By the time Malayan independence came in 1957, an estimated one-quarter of the Chinese population was English-educated. These individuals acquired English as their principal language and the only one in which they discovered the world beyond their homes. Somewhere during their time in secondary school, they found themselves "thinking" in English. They no longer had enough Chinese to deal with all the new matter in their heads that had nothing to do with China at all.

Some had never known any Chinese; some so-called Baba families from much older immigrations had dropped Chinese for Malay or English many generations before. More commonly, Chinese children could still use the dialect learned at home—Hokkien, Hakka, or Cantonese—which remained good for the limited talk of personal family affairs, the kitchen, and the market, but useless for the subjects opened to them in school. These had to do with the "West" or the colonial British version thereof: history of the British Empire, literature from Shakespeare to Tennyson ("and not one step further!" said one product of the system) in the form of two or three plays laboriously read in class and a poem or two memorized. (One Chinese intellectual told me how it was not until he was sent to China for higher education—it was in 1947—that he learned for the first time of the existence of Russian, French, and American literature.) But whatever enrichment they were able to acquire thereafter, it was in English, via books, press, films, just as for the Chinese-educated it was in Chinese, also via books, press, films. The result was the acquisition of two wholly different universes. As one unhappy Baba put it, the main difference between the two was that, for one, China was still the most important place in the world; for the other, it was not.

After 1957 both groups had to cope with the pressure of the Malay rulers of the newly independent country to impose Malay as the national language of the new "Malaysia," in which the Chinese found themselves precariously located as second-class citizens. This became the source of friction and collision. In Singapore, a Chinese city which became an independent state by itself in 1965, a new experiment was launched in the form of a four-language-track educational system in which the major medium of instruction could be selected: Chinese, Malay, English, or, for the 10 percent Indian minority, Tamil. Only the curriculum was to be exactly the same in every case, aimed at creating not little Chinese, Malays, Englishmen, or Tamils, but something new, "Singaporeans."

In Malaysia generally, meanwhile, the issue of language has continued to be both an element in the fragile new politics and a complicated problem in the educational system and, indeed, throughout the society. The Chinese, whether Chinese-educated or English-educated, have to adapt to a language and a cultural/intellectual tradition that they find difficult to regard as equal or even comparable to their own. One Chinese intellectual, who felt a great stake in the new Malaysia partly because he felt so strongly opposed to the new regime in China, slapped his forehead and said with great passion: "I am doing my best, my damnedest, to convince myself: we must and will all become *Malaysians*. But in my heart, I don't know how not to be *Chinese!*" A completely Anglicized Baba who did not want his little daughter "to be left out as I was" was sending her to a special tutor to be taught not Malay but Chinese.

The Official English Movement: Reimagining America

By Geoffrey Nunberg

Geoffrey Nunberg, a researcher at the Institute for Research on Learning in Palo Alto, California, is consulting associate professor of linguistics at Stanford University and usage editor of *The American Heritage Dictionary.*

Nations are "imagined communities," in Benedict Anderson's suggestive term. "Imagined," because

> the fellow members of even the smallest nation will never know most of their fellow-members, meet them, or even hear of them, yet in the minds of each lives the image of their communion. . . . Communities are to be distinguished, not by their falsity or genuineness, but in the style in which they are imagined.[1]

There are many styles of imagining national communities, out of stories of common lineage, history, religion, or culture. But symbolically, these commonalities are often expressed in terms of a common language, particularly in the European traditions where the modern models of nationality were first formed. The connection between language and nation was a side effect of the introduction of print, which made it possible to project the common experience of the members of the community as a kind of public knowledge. Language has sometimes seemed so important as an instrument of communication that nineteenth-century nationalists came to see it as the essential ingredient of nationhood. As Fichte put it in a celebrated dictum: "Wherever a separate language is found, there is also a separate nation which has the right to manage its affairs . . . and rule itself."

But languages are not "found," like biological species with natural limits. They are imaginings, too. A linguist looking at the map of Europe in 1400 would have discerned no "languages" at all in the modern sense, but only patches of local dialects and varieties, scattered under the shadow of Latin. National languages were formed in a process of conscious creation, as a certain variety was standardized, cod-

---

1. Benedict R. O'G. Anderson, *Imagined Communities: Reflections on the Origin and Spread of Nationalism* (London: Verso, 1983), p. 15.

ified, and most important, assigned a cultural value.[2] For it is not language as such that becomes a bond of national unity, but language as the emblem of a particular conception of community. The sense of common experience shared by speakers of vernacular languages like French or Polish cannot be the same as what attaches to divinely sanctioned "truth languages" like Arabic, Hebrew, or Church Latin; the first is a community of men, the second a community of God.

Even within vernacular communities, the social role of language can be imagined and reimagined in a seemingly infinite number of ways to reflect the changing conceptions of commonality that are intended to serve as the basis for nationhood. The classic example is the Italian *questione della lingua,* or "Language Question," a debate that stretches through the entire course of modern Italian history, from Dante, Machiavelli, and Castiglione on down through Manzoni, Croce, Gramsci, and beyond. In retrospect, the issues these writers raised may seem obscure and trivial: should standard Italian be based on archaic Tuscan, modern Tuscan, or some amalgam of literary dialects? But the debate was really concerned with the social basis of Italian nationality—*Italianità*—that was conceived as the basis for an eventual Italian nation-state. As Gramsci wrote, speaking of Language Questions in their universal, rather than their specifically Italian manifestations: "Whenever the language question surfaces, in one way or another, it means that another series of problems is imposing itself: the formation and enlargement of the ruling class, the necessity . . . of reorganizing cultural hegemony."[3]

Not all questions about language are Language Questions. For one thing, language obviously plays a role in sorting out social and cultural distinctions that are unrelated to national identity. Conversely, the sense of national community can be shaped by other instruments. This is most apparent in multilingual nations like Switzerland and India. But even in essentially monolingual nations, the political basis of the state may be independent of the particular notion of community that the common language implies.

Britain, for example, has had a dominant standard language since the seventeenth century, at least. Yet the legitimacy of the British state has not rested on its claim to represent a cultural order symbolized by standard English, but rather on political institutions like Parliament, the Crown, and the body of English common law. Apart from a brief flirtation with proposals for a language academy in the early eighteenth century (a course that Joseph Priestly disparaged as "unsuit-

2. The process is often referred to with Heinz Kloss's term of *Ausbau,* or roughly, "extension." See Kloss, *Entwicklung Neuer Germanischer Kultursprachen* (Munich: Pohl, 1952).

3. Antonio Gramsci, "Note sullo studio della grammatica," in *Quaderni del Carcere,* ed. Valentino Gerrantano, vol. 3 (Turin, 1975), p. 2347.

able to the genius of a free nation"),[4] the British have not looked to the state for protection of the English language. It is true that, in practice, they have had few qualms about imposing English on colonial peoples, whether in Scotland, Ireland, or India. And beginning in the late nineteenth century, British educators made systematic efforts to associate the study of English language and literature with nationalist ideology.[5] Symbolically, however, the political apparatus of the British state has been kept separate from the linguistic and cultural order. For all the talk of "the king's English," the speech of the court (when the court spoke English at all) has not been a model of correctness since the early eighteenth century; in language, the monarch neither reigns nor rules.

In this sense, Britain offers a marked contrast to France, where the state has taken an active role in the preservation and promotion of the national language since the Académie française was established in the seventeenth century. It strikes the French as perfectly natural that government should pass laws to limit the amount of airplay given to foreign-language songs; that it should spend fully half its foreign-service budget to subsidize the teaching of the French language abroad; or that recent spelling reforms should have been announced at prime-ministerial press conferences. These may seem trivial matters, but they have a larger symbolic importance. To the extent that the legitimacy of the French state is based on an essentially cultural sense of community, its political form is flexible. France has been a liberal democracy for more than a century (apart from the Nazi occupation) and is likely to remain one. But there is little in the conception of French nationality that requires this form of government, and certainly it is imaginable that the Fifth Republic should someday be replaced by a sixth or seventh. The history of the French nation is not, like those of Britain and the United States, identified with the history of a single political regime.

The United States inherited from Britain not just its language, but its understanding of the relation between language and national identity. Initially, there were questions: Would citizens of the new nation go on speaking "English," or develop a new "American language"? Would the state take a role in standardizing the language and, by extension, the national culture? But by the time the nation was fifty years old, Americans had come to believe that they required no national language of their own, and that American identity could rest on a common commitment to the political institutions established at the nation's founding. The state was seen as neither the representative nor the guardian of an official culture.

4. Joseph Priestley, *The Rudiments of English Grammar* (London, 1761), p. vii.
5. See Brian Doyle, *English and Englishness* (London: Routledge, 1989); Tony Crowley, *Standard English and the Politics of Language* (Urbana: University of Illinois Press, 1989).

Like other aspects of the American experiment, however, the relation between cultural and political institutions has never been definitively resolved. It may be, as Rousseau argued and as recent history seems to bear out, that no nation can successfully constitute itself around a set of purely political ideals. Certainly the American system has always presupposed a rough cultural consensus as a necessary feature of political life. For the most part, that consensus has been negotiated informally. But whenever it has appeared to be threatened from without by large-scale immigration or by the absorption of groups from different cultural backgrounds, there have been movements to bring to bear the power of the state to secure the hegemony of the majority culture, in the ostensible interest of preserving political stability. As contributions to this *Source Book* demonstrate, language issues have figured in a wide variety of policy questions: immigration and naturalization, voting rights, treatment of Native Americans, statehood, civil liberties, and especially education. But only in recent years have debates over such issues given rise to a full-blown Language Question, an attempt to redefine the political basis of the American state in terms of a common culture.

In this sense, the Official English question is a new theme in the American political discourse. This may not be obvious, because the debate is often framed around specific programs—bilingual education is the most conspicuous example—that do not seem to differ qualitatively from other programs instituted to address the problems of minorities, whether English-speaking or not. Official English advocates have often explained their movement as a response to the "politicization" of these questions by "special interest groups" that are concerned more with promoting ethnic separatism or pork-barrelling for their own constituents than with helping language minorities. But the initial "politicization" of issues like bilingual education was part of the routine process of policy formulation, as enacted at the level of lobbying, Congressional testimony, behind-the-scenes maneuvering, litigation, and so forth. In the normal course of things, you would expect the opposition to these programs to take the form of the same kind of political activity—as indeed it has, down to the politics-as-usual accusations of personal ambition and venality.

But the opposition to these programs has not stopped with politics-as-usual. It has used mass-mailing techniques to establish a national political movement, with its membership drawn from groups with no particular interest in questions of immigration or minority education. It has mounted a number of successful statewide initiatives aimed at eliminating the provision of government services in languages other than English, and it has promoted boycotts to restrict the use of foreign languages in advertising, signage, and broadcasting. And in its symbolically most ambitious effort, it has called for amending the Constitution so as to declare English the official language of the United States.

This is a response calculated to move the discussion of questions of policy into the realm of symbolic politics, with the result that it becomes difficult (and somewhat irrelevant) to debate the issues on their substantive merits. Questions about the effectiveness of bilingual education can be fairly discussed in an academic forum or a legislative hearing, but not in the popular press or in thirty-second sound bites. In a state electoral campaign, voters are in no position to evaluate the claim that the country faces a "dangerous drift toward multilingualism" on the basis of the demographic evidence, or to weigh the parallels to Canada or Belgium in the light of a familiarity with the histories of those nations. This has been an understandable source of frustration to opponents of the Official English movement, especially to scholars familiar with the American minority-language situation. As the sociologist Joshua Fishman asks: "Aren't the comparisons to Sri Lanka or India not only far-fetched and erroneous, but completely removed from the reality of the U.S.A.? . . . Why are facts so useless in this discussion?" (see p. 167).

The answer is that the debate is no longer concerned with the content or effect of particular programs, but with the symbolic importance that people have come to attach to these matters. Official English advocates admit as much when they emphasize that their real goal is to "send a message" about the role of English in American life. From this point of view, it is immaterial whether the provision of interpreters for workers compensation hearings or of foreign-language nutrition information actually constitute a "disincentive" to learning English, or whether their discontinuation would work a hardship on recent immigrants. Programs like these merely happen to be high-visibility examples of government's apparent willingness to allow the public use of languages other than English for any purpose whatsoever. In fact, one suspects that most Official English advocates are not especially concerned about specific programs per se, since they will be able to achieve their symbolic goals even if bilingual services are protected by judicial intervention or legislative inaction (as has generally been the case where Official English measures have passed). The real objective of the campaign is the "message" that it intends to send.

What actually is the message? That depends, in part, on who is listening. A number of opponents of the Official English movement have stressed its immediate significance as a reaction to the perceived "demands" of immigrant groups. It is undeniable that racism and and xenophobia have played an important role in the electoral successes of the Official English movement or that some of the movement's organizers have espoused explicitly anti-Hispanic and anti-Catholic views.

Yet this cannot be the entire story. Official English has attracted wide support among people who would not ordinarily countenance openly racist or xenophobic measures. In the 1986 California election, for example, the English-language amendment to the state constitution was adopted by fully 73 percent of the electorate, including large majorities in liberal areas like Palo Alto and Marin County. Nationally, the U.S. English organization has been able to attract approximately five times as many members as the restrictionist Federation of American Immigration Reform, which shares the same founder and direct-mail fundraising apparatus (see p. 172). Apparently, many people will support English Only measures who would be squeamish about directly supporting immigration restriction. Also, it is significant that many of the national politicians who have sponsored Official English legislation—Senators Huddleston of Kentucky, Burdick of North Dakota, and Symms of Idaho; Representatives Emerson of Missouri and Smith of Nebraska—come from states in which immigration is not a pressing issue and where the scapegoating of immigrants would hardly seem to be an effective way to distract constituents from their economic problems.

So the Official English movement is really sending two messages. The first is concerned specifically with members of language-minority groups, who are understandably sensitive to its xenophobic overtones. Siobhan Nicolau and Rafael Valdivieso believe that the movement is telling Hispanics: "We don't trust you—we don't like you—we don't think you can fit in—you are too different—*and there seem to be far too many of you*" (see pp. 317–18). Already, in states where Official English initiatives have passed, they are being interpreted as a license to discriminate on the basis of language. But long after the immediate occasion for the movement has receded—after the children of the new immigrant groups have moved into the linguistic and social mainstream and established themselves as "good Americans" like generations of immigrants before them—the legacy of the Official English movement may be felt in a changed conception of American nationality itself.

Of the various "messages," this one may be hardest to perceive. Proponents of Official English claim that they seek merely to recognize a state of affairs that has existed since the founding of the nation. After two hundred years of common-law cohabitation with English, we have simply decided to make an honest woman of her, for the sake of the children. To make the English language "official," however, is not merely to acknowledge it as the language commonly used in commerce, mass communications, and public affairs. Rather, it is to invest

English with a symbolic role in national life and to endorse a cultural conception of American identity as the basis for political unity. And while the general communicative role of English in America has not changed over the past two hundred years, the cultural importance that people attach to the language has evolved considerably.

Early linguistic patriots like John Adams and Noah Webster were less concerned with the relation between the majority language and minority languages like German than with the relation between the language of Americans and the "English" from which it descended. What is significant is that the Founders viewed American political institutions not as resting on a national language or a national culture, but as giving rise to them. Noah Webster wrote:

> From the changes in civil policy, manners, arts of life, and other circumstances attending the settlement of English colonies in America, most of the language of heraldry, hawking, hunting, and especially that of the old feudal and hierarchical establishments of England will become utterly extinct in this country; much of it already forms part of the neglected rubbish of antiquity.[6]

Thus the free institutions of the new nation would naturally lead to the formation of a new and independent culture, as symbolized by a distinct language. William Thornton made much the same argument in 1793, when he told Americans:

> You have corrected the dangerous doctrines of European powers, correct now the languages you have imported . . . The AMERICAN LANGUAGE will thus be as distinct as the government, free from all the follies of unphilosophical fashion, and resting upon truth as its only regulator.[7]

The national language was to serve as the vehicle for public letters— "literature" in the broad eighteenth-century sense, which included sermons, philosophy, history, and natural science—whose success would validate the American political experiment in the eyes of the world.

Thus the emergence of a distinct national language was seen to be an effect, rather than a cause, of the success of American democratic institutions. This understanding was summed up by Tocqueville when he referred to the "influence which a democratic social condition and democratic institutions may exercise over language itself,

---

6. From the Preface to *A Compendious Dictionary of the English Language* (1806); quoted in Homer D. Babbidge, Jr., ed., *On Being American* (New York: Frederick A. Praeger, 1967), p. 134.

7. *Cadmus; or A Treatise on the Elements of Written Language* (Philadelphia, 1793), p. v.

which is the chief instrument of thought."[8] Ultimately, of course, America did develop an autonomous literary culture without any active encouragement from the state and without having to rupture its linguistic and cultural ties with Britain. That literary culture was naturally a source of national pride and an important means of consolidating national identity. But it was not regarded as the basis of national union.

The question of a national language did not emerge again until the turn of the twentieth century, when Americans found themselves confronted with the large numbers of non-English-speaking immigrants. Previously, language played a relatively minor role in nativist movements, which chiefly exploited fears that newcomers would dilute the religious and racial homogeneity of the nation. But in the first decades of this century, immigrants came to be seen as sources of political contagion. In 1919, Attorney General A. Mitchell Palmer, leader of the infamous Palmer Raids, in which more than eight thousand "radicals" were swept up and deported, could confidently assert that "fully 90 percent of Communist and anarchist agitation is traceable to aliens."[9]

One answer to the imagined threat of imported sedition was the "Americanization" campaign, a concerted effort, as John Higham writes, to "heat and stir the melting pot" *(see p. 73)*. (The other was immigration restriction, enacted in a series of laws in the early 1920s.) The most important ingredient in the Americanization program was the effort to force immigrants to move from their native tongues to English—not just by providing English instruction, but by actively discouraging the learning and use of other languages. A Nebraska law stipulated that all public meetings be conducted in English; Oregon required foreign-language periodicals to provide an English translation of their entire contents.[10] More than thirty states mandated English as the language of instruction in all schools, public and private.

These measures were based on a particular view of the relation between language and thought, in which speaking a foreign language seemed inimical to grasping the fundamental concepts of democratic society. The Nebraska Supreme Court, in upholding a state statute barring instruction in languages other than English below the ninth grade, warned against the "baneful effects" of educating children in foreign languages, which must "naturally inculcate in them the ideas

8. Alexis de Tocqueville, *Democracy in America* (New York: Vintage Books, 1990), 2:68.

9. Quoted in David H. Bennett, *The Party of Fear: From Nativist Movements to the New Right in American History* (New York: Vintage Books, 1990), p. 193.

10. John Higham, *Strangers in the Land: Patterns of American Nativism, 1860–1925*, 2d ed. (New Brunswick, N.J.: Rutgers University Press, 1988), p. 260.

and sentiments foreign to the best interests of their country" *(see p. 235)*.

The complement of such suspicions was a view of English as a kind of "chosen language," the bearer of Anglo-Saxon (or at least Anglo-American) ideals and institutions. English was turned into a kind of "truth language," like Arabic, Hebrew, and Church Latin, except that the truths for which it provided a unique means of expression were those of the secular religion of American democracy. At the New York State constitutional convention in 1916, during debate on an English-literacy requirement for voting, one delegate traced the connection between English and democratic values back to the Magna Carta (a text often mentioned in this context, though it was written in Latin): "You have got to learn our language because that is the vehicle of the thought that has been handed down from the men in whose breasts first burned the fire of freedom."[11] Theodore Roosevelt sounded a similar note when he insisted that: "We must have but one flag. We must also have but one language. That must be the language of the Declaration of Independence, of Washington's Farewell Address, of Lincoln's Gettysburg speech and second inaugural" *(see p. 85)*.

What is striking about this list is what it does not include: there is no mention of the language of Irving, Longfellow, and Emerson, much less any reference to "the language of Shakespeare," which British contemporaries would have considered obligatory. One doubts whether Webster would have approved of this list. Where are all the flowers of the literary culture that was to vindicate the American experiment in the eyes of the world? It is not that Roosevelt and his contemporaries were indifferent to literary traditions, but for them it was the political uses of English that made it an instrument of national union. The language was no longer seen as a consequence of political institutions, but as a cause of them.

This signaled a clear change in the conception of American nationality, with English as the soup stock of the melting pot. As such, Americanization was probably a more benign policy than the racially based nativism that held that immigrants were biologically incapable of adapting to American life. In the view of James J. Davis, secretary of labor under Harding and Coolidge, the earlier "Nordic" immigrants were "the beaver type that built up America, whereas the newer immigrants were rat-men trying to tear it down, and obviously rat-men could never become beavers."[12] By contrast, the proponents of Americanization put the burden of transmitting values on cultural institutions, rather than on racial descent. For example, here is Ell-

11. Quoted in Dennis Baron, *The English-Only Question: An Official Language for Americans?* (New Haven: Yale University Press, 1990), p. 59.

12. Quoted in Seymour Martin Lipset and Earl Raab, *The Politics of Unreason: Right-Wing Extremism in America, 1790–1970* (New York: Harper & Row, 1977), p. 142.

wood P. Cubberly, dean of Stanford University School of Education, describing the goals of the Americanization campaign:

> Our task is to break up [immigrant] groups or settlements, to assimilate and amalgamate these people as part of our American race, and to implant in their children, as far as can be done, the Anglo-Saxon conception of righteousness, law and order, and our popular government.[13]

While this passage may strike the modern reader as smug and condescending, it is not literally racist, at least in its historical context. Cubberly obviously believed that rat-men could be turned into beavers, if only you caught them young enough.

Taken literally, the chosen-language doctrine does not stand up under scrutiny. The Founders would have been distressed to be told that the truths they held to be "self-evident" could have been apprehended only by other English speakers; nothing could have been further from their own Enlightenment universalism. And there is a peculiarly American fallacy in the supposition that the meanings of words like *liberty* and *rights* are somehow immutably fixed by the structure of the language. It is the linguistic equivalent of the historical doctrine that Daniel Boorstin has described as "givenness": the belief that American values were defined at the outset by the Founders and continue to shape our institutions and experience in an uninterrupted chain, "so that our past merges indistinguishably into our present."[14]

But the doctrine did useful symbolic work. It implied that the features of the old-stock Protestant culture could be abstracted in universally accessible terms. As the hysteria of the war years and the early twenties abated and the flow of new immigrants was reduced to a trickle, the doctrine could be given a more temperate form. It was absorbed into the body of "invented traditions," of schoolroom rituals and folklore that shaped the patriotism of generations of Americans of both native-stock and immigrant backgrounds and, with it, an equally patriotic attachment to the English language itself. It has never been officially retired, and you may still encounter paeans to the political genius of English. But the conception of American nationality has been changing out from under it, and when later waves of immigration caused language issues to be raised again, the new case for a common language was made in very different terms.

13. Quoted in James Crawford, *Bilingual Education: History, Politics, Theory, and Practice*, 2d ed. (Los Angeles: Bilingual Educational Services, 1991).

14. Daniel Boorstin, "Why a Theory Seems Needless," in *Hidden History* (New York: Harper & Row, 1987), p. 77.

The dominant theme in the rhetoric of the Official English movement is the emphasis on English as a lingua franca, the "common bond" that unites all Americans. As former senator S. I. Hayakawa puts it, the language alone has "made a society out of the hodgepodge of nationalities, races, and colors represented in the immigrant hordes that people our nation," and has enabled Americans to draw up "the understandings and agreements that make a society possible" *(see p. 94)*.

Modern official-language advocates are careful, however, to avoid the suggestion that English has any unique virtues that make it appropriate in this role as a common bond. A U.S. English publication explains: "We hold no special brief for English. If Dutch (or French, or Spanish, or German) had become our national language, we would now be enthusiastically defending Dutch." (It is hard to imagine Noah Webster or Theodore Roosevelt passing over the special genius of English so lightly.)[15] In fact, the movement often seems eager to discharge English of any cultural responsibility whatsoever. Its arguments are cast with due homage to the sanctity of pluralism. Indeed, its advocates often rest their case on the observation that the very cultural heterogeneity of modern America makes English "no longer *a* bond, but *the* bond between all of us," in the words of Gerda Bikales, the former executive director of U.S. English *(see p. 101)*. Or, as Senator Walter Huddleston argues, a common language has enabled us "to develop a stable and cohesive society that is the envy of many fractured ones, without imposing any strict standards of homogeneity" *(see p. 104)*. Official English advocates seem to suggest that Americans need have nothing at all in common, so long as we have the means for talking about it.

Unlike the Americanizers, they no longer stress the role of English as an instrument of ideological indoctrination. The Cubans, Mexicans, Central Americans, Vietnamese, Filipinos, Chinese, Haitians, Russians, and others who have made up recent waves of arrivals are generally—and accurately—seen either as seekers after economic opportunity or as refugees from oppressive regimes of the left or right.

---

15. "Talking Points," March, 1983. A U.S. English newsletter of March 1983 does observe that English is capable of "subtle nuance and great precision of meaning" and that the language has an impressively large vocabulary (but of course the same claims might be made about the language of any developed society). It notes, too, that English is the premier language of international communications, which surely would be a good reason for choosing English as a national language if we were starting the country from scratch. But what is notable is that all of these claims involve the practical utility, real or imagined, of having English as a common language. They suggest no intrinsic tie between the genius of English and our particular conception of national identity.

Nor, in the Reagan-Bush-Gorbachev era, is there cause for concern that immigrants will add fuel to domestic radical movements or ignite labor unrest. At the most, they seem to many a bit too assertive about their rights and insufficiently enthusiastic about cultural assimilation. But then, the great mass of turn-of-the-century immigrants had no more interest in political questions than present-day immigrants do. What has changed is not the political nature of the new arrivals, but the way we perceive their differences from ourselves. So we might well ask: how have we changed, if our political unity can be threatened by unassimilated immigrants with whom we have no ideological differences?

Americans are no less patriotic than they were a century ago, but their sense of community is mediated in different ways. In 1900 it was unimaginable that there should be occasions at which all Americans could be present or that many Americans could acquire the sense of national identity that comes of frequent movement around the country. There were, of course, newspapers and books, but literacy was far from universal. So the burden of creating a sense of community was naturally laid on traditional institutions of schools, churches, and the like, which could ensure that experiences and ceremonies that ratified the national identity would be faithfully replicated from one locality to the next.

But the twentieth century brought means of replicating experience that required no institutional intervention, most notably the movies, radio, and television. Watching "The Cosby Show" or "NBC Nightly News," we can be assured that millions of other Americans are participating in the very same experience—laughing at the same jokes and finding the same reports noteworthy. More important, these media have the power to *show* Americans to one another, with such immediacy that we may be deceived into believing that the awareness of community can be created without any exercise of the imagination at all. Together with the extraordinary increase in geographical mobility and mass merchandising, the media create a vastly extended repertory of shared national experience: we view the same videos, eat at the same restaurant chains, visit the same theme parks, wait in the same gas lines, and so on.

The new mechanisms of national community are capable of imposing a high degree of cultural and ideological uniformity without explicit indoctrination, or indeed, without seeming to "impose" at all. This is what makes it possible for us to indulge in the rhetoric of "cherished diversity" and even to suppose that it is only our language that we have in common. But the pluralism that Official English advocates profess to cherish is the denatured ethnicity of third- and fourth-generation Americans, monolingual in English and disconnected from any real ties to the language and culture of their ancestors. For the most part, this "lifestyle" ethnicity is a matter of food, fashion, and festivals, which add a note of "colorfulness" that serves to "enrich"—and, in the course of things, to mask—the homogeneity of the values that regulate American middle-class life.

It could be argued that the very abundance of the common experience of national life makes linguistic unity superfluous. Benedict Anderson has suggested that new technologies make it possible to create a sense of community without a common language:

> Multilingual broadcasting can conjure up the imagined community to illiterates and populations with different mother tongues. (Here there are resemblances to the conjuring up of medieval Christendom through visual representations and bilingual literati.) . . . Nations can now be imagined without linguistic communality.[16]

This seems to be true in many states that have emerged in recent times—not just in Africa and Asia, but even in Switzerland, the last polity in Western Europe to have developed a modern sense of nationhood. In the United States, too, it is certainly easier for non-English-speaking immigrants to develop a sense of American identity today than at the turn of the century, thanks to national foreign-language media that reproduce many of the same images and programs as the English-language media, and to the ubiquitous apparatus of consumer culture.

Yet in America, the new mechanisms for establishing a sense of national community have only increased concerns about linguistic disunity. There are several reasons why this should be so. First, the new mechanisms depend on a voluntary participation in the public discourse rather than on explicit intervention by traditional institutions. This may explain why the Official English movement appears indifferent to the classes in Americanism and citizenship that played such an important part in the program of earlier assimilation movements. It is as if the schools can no longer make good Americans, but only give students a knowledge of English so that Americanization can happen to them in their free time. Then, too, the very homogeneity and ubiquity of the mechanisms of mass culture make departures from the cultural norm seem all the more aberrant. The presence of people who do not have access to this experience—or more to the point, who cannot be assumed to have such access—becomes increasingly intolerable. If our common values can command such widespread assent in the face of the apparent "diversity" of European-American life, then

16. *Imagined Communities*, p. 123.

surely it is not unreasonable to expect the members of other cultures
to conform to them.

Finally, linguistic diversity is more conspicuous than it was a century ago. To be aware of the large numbers of non-English speakers
in 1900, it was necessary to live in or near one of their communities,
whereas today it is only necessary to flip through a cable television
dial, drive past a Spanish-language billboard, or (in many states) apply for a driver's license. At a best guess, there are fewer speakers of
foreign languages in America now than there were then, in both absolute and relative numbers. But what matters symbolically is the
widespread *impression* of linguistic diversity, particularly among
people who have no actual contact with speakers of languages other
than English.

Inevitably, the effect of the new mechanisms of community has
been to make American identity increasingly a matter of cultural uniformity, as symbolized by linguistic uniformity, and to diminish the
importance of explicit ideology. This development is partially hidden
behind the rhetoric of "pluralism" and "cultural diversity," but it
emerges, as repressed concerns are wont to do, in the nightmares of
the Official English advocates, which are haunted by specters of separatism and civil strife. Hayakawa writes:

> For the first time in our history, our nation is faced with the
> possibility of the kind of linguistic division that has torn
> apart Canada in recent years; that has been a major feature
> of the unhappy history of Belgium, split into speakers of
> French and Flemish; that is at this very moment a bloody
> division between the Sinhalese and Tamil populations of
> Sri Lanka. [*See p. 99.*]

Here, too, it is notable that the line of argument has no precedent
in earlier nativist movements. Language conflicts were probably more
common on the world scene in 1920 than they are now and certainly
figured more prominently in American public consciousness during
the First World War and the debate over the League of Nations. Yet
the experience of other countries was rarely if ever mentioned in the
Americanization campaign. Not that the possibility of a multilingual
America seemed more remote then than now. Indeed, the presence of
language minorities was widely (if inaccurately) perceived as an immediate threat to political stability and prompted calls for more drastic steps than anything that the contemporary Official English movement has yet proposed. For supporters of Americanization, however,
international analogies were irrelevant. The point of establishing linguistic uniformity was not to preserve just any common culture, but
to ensure universal assent to the particular ideology associated with

English-language institutions. There was nothing that we had to learn about our national identity from comparisons with Alsace or Austria-Hungary; or, for that matter, from comparisons with mono-lingual non-English-speaking nations like France or Japan.

So why should foreign examples of language conflicts strike a responsive chord now? Not, again, because there is any actual threat to the status of English as a common language. Not even Official English advocates suggest that there is any imminent danger of separatist movements springing up in East Los Angeles or Dade County. But if the specter of civil strife is implausible, its appeal to the popular imagination is nevertheless an indication of the widespread acceptance of a changed sense of national community. If American identity is based simply on a common cultural experience, then the experience of other nations is suddenly relevant to our situation. It is notable that in the cautionary examples that Official English proponents like to invoke, particularly Canada and Belgium, the ethnic divisions are generally perceived as having no ideological significance.[17] If Quebec were to become an independent state, one assumes, it would be a liberal democracy like the rest of Canada, and like France, a secular state, despite is Catholic majority. The obvious moral is that cultural and linguistic differences alone are sufficient to divide a state—any state, including ours.

The history of American language controversies reveals a profound and troubling change in our conception of national community. For Noah Webster, the American language was a reflection of our political institutions. For Theodore Roosevelt, it was the instrument for inculcating a sense of political tradition. For proponents of the modern Official English movement, it is simply the guarantor of the cultural sameness that for them political unity seems to require. So the burden of nationality gradually shifts from political institutions to cultural commonalities, to the point where "Americanism," like "Frenchness," Italianità, and all the rest, becomes essentially a cultural matter. Not that there is anything wrong with France, Italy, or other nations; but America was supposed to be different.

Obviously, the Official English movement is not the cause of the changed sense of nationality, but neither is it merely a symptom. As I noted at the outset, language has always done the work of symbolizing cultural categories that are in themselves too deep and inchoate to

17. In point of fact, of course, the divisions in these countries owe more to long histories of social and economic inequality than to language differences per se, as the contributions to Part VI of this collection make clear; but few Americans are familiar with the details of Canadian or Belgian history, and these considerations are ignored when it comes to drawing the comparison to the American case.

be directly expressed. Even if the official-language movement is really an "official-culture movement," it could not have been formulated in such terms. We could not very well entertain a constitutional amendment that read, "The United States shall henceforth be officially constituted around such-and-such a conception of American culture." It is only when the issues are cast in terms of language that they become amenable to direct political action, and that culture can be made an official component of American identity. The great danger is in reading the debate as literally concerned with language alone—all the more because these are relatively new themes in the American political discourse, and we have no history of Language Questions to refer to. Of course, there are real questions of language at stake in all this, but they are not *merely* questions of language; they never are.

Suggestions for Further Reading

Historic Responses to Language Diversity
Baron, Dennis E. *The English-Only Question: An Official Language for Americans?* New Haven: Yale University Press, 1990.
———. *Grammar and Good Taste: Reforming the American Language*. New Haven: Yale University Press, 1982.
Cafferty, Pastora San Juan, and Rivera-Martínez, Carmen. *The Politics of Language: The Dilemma of Bilingual Education for Puerto Ricans*. Boulder, Colo.: Westview Press, 1981.
Conklin, Nancy Faires, and Lourie, Margaret A. *A Host of Tongues*. New York: Free Press, 1983.
Ferguson, Charles A., and Heath, Shirley Brice, eds. *Language in the U.S.A.* Cambridge: Cambridge University Press, 1981.
Fishman, Joshua A., et al., *Language Loyalty in the United States: The Maintenance and Perpetuation of Non-English Mother Tongues by American Ethnic and Religious Groups*. The Hague: Mouton Publishers, 1966. Rpt. New York: Arno Press, 1978.
Heath, Shirley Brice. "Language Policies." *Society*, May/June 1983, pp. 56–63.
Kloss, Heinz. *The American Bilingual Tradition*. Rowley, Mass.: Newbury House Publishers, 1977.
Read, Allen Walker. "American Projects for an Academy to Regulate Speech." *Publications of the Modern Language Association* 51, no. 4 (Dec. 1936): 1141–79.
———. "Bilingualism in the Middle Colonies, 1725–1775." *American Speech* 12 (1937): 93–99.
Sagarin, Edward, and Kelly, Robert J. "Polylingualism in the United States of America: A Multitude of Tongues." In William Beer and James E. Jacob, eds., *Language Policy and National Unity*. Totowa, N.J.: Rowman and Allanheld, 1985, pp. 20–44.
Simpson, David. *The Politics of American English, 1776–1850*. New York: Oxford University Press, 1986.
U.S. Senate, Committee on Labor and Public Welfare, Special Subcommittee on Indian Education. *Indian Education: A National Tragedy, A National Challenge*. Washington, D.C.: U.S. Government Printing Office, 1969.
Wagner, Stephen T. "Historical Background of Bilingualism and Biculturalism in the United States." In Martin Ridge, ed., *The New Bilingualism: An American Dilemma*. New Brunswick, N.J.: Transaction Books, 1981.

Wittke, Carl. *German-Americans and the World War: With Special Emphasis on Ohio's German-Language Press.* Columbus: Ohio State Archaeological and Historical Society, 1936.

The Official English Debate

Adams, Karen L., and Brink, Daniel T., eds. *Perspectives on Official English: The Campaign for English as the Official Language of the U.S.A.* Berlin: Mouton de Gruyter, 1990.

Combs, Mary Carol, and Trasviña, John. "Legal Implications of the English Language Amendment." In *The English Only Movement: An Agenda for Discrimination.* Washington, D.C.: League of United Latin American Citizens, 1986.

Daniels, Harvey A., ed. *Not Only English: Affirming America's Multilingual Heritage.* Urbana, Ill.: National Council of Teachers of English, 1990.

del Olmo, Frank. "Se Habla Ingles: Prop. 63, a Cruel Joke, Could Cost Us Dearly." *Los Angeles Times*, Aug. 28, 1986.

Fallows, James. "Viva Bilingualism: English Has Nothing To Fear." *New Republic*, Nov. 24, 1986, p. 19.

González, Roseann Duenas; Schott, Alice A.; and Vásquez, Victoria F. "The English Language Amendment: Examining Myths." *English Journal*, March 1988, pp. 24–30.

Henry, William A., III. "Against a Confusion of Tongues." *Time*, June 13, 1983, pp. 30–31.

Imhoff, Gary. "Partisans of Language." *English Today*, no. 11 (July 1987): 37–40.

Judd, Elliot L. "The English Language Amendment: A Case Study on Language and Politics." *TESOL Quarterly* 21, no. 1 (March 1987): 113–35.

Justicia y Derecho (Arizona State University) 1, no. 1 (1991). Special law journal issue on Official English.

Macías, Reynaldo F., ed. *Are English Language Amendments in the National Interest? A Policy Analysis of Proposals to Establish English as the Official Language of the United States.* Claremont, Calif.: Tomás Rivera Center, 1988.

Marshall, David F., ed. "The Question of an Official Language: Language Rights and the English Language Amendment." *International Journal of the Sociology of Language* 60 (1986).

Nunberg, Geoffrey. "An 'Official Language' for California?" *New York Times*, Oct. 2, 1986.

Schlafly, Phyllis. "Lack of English Shuts Many Doors to 'Ghettoized' Hispanics." *New York Tribune*, Feb. 21, 1986.

Smitherman, Geneva. "Toward a National Public Policy on Language." *College English* 49 (1987): 29–36.

Trasviña, John. *Official English/English Only: More Than Meets the Eye.* Washington, D.C.: National Education Association, 1988.

U.S. House of Representatives, Committee on the Judiciary, Subcommittee on Civil and Constitutional Rights. *English Language Constitutional Amendments: Hearing on H.J. Res. 13, H.J. Res. 33, H.J. Res. 60, and H.J. Res. 83.* 100th Cong., 2d sess. (May 11, 1988).

U.S. Senate, Committee on the Judiciary, Subcommittee on the Constitution.

The English Language Amendment: Hearing on S.J. Res. 167. 98th Cong., 2d sess. (June 12, 1984).

Zentella, Ana Celia. "Language Politics in the USA: The English-Only Movement." In Betty Jean Craige, ed., *Literature, Language, and Politics.* Athens: University of Georgia Press, 1988.

Language, Assimilation, and Nativism

Bikales, Gerda, and Imhoff, Gary. *A Kind of Discordant Harmony: Issues in Assimilation.* Discussion Series, no. 2. Washington, D.C.: U.S. English, 1985.

Butler, R. E. *On Creating a Hispanic America: A Nation Within a Nation?* Washington, D.C.: Council for Inter-American Security, 1985.

Castro, Richard, and Horn, Gilbert. "Hispanics Fight Their Way Past Barriers to American Dream." *Rocky Mountain News,* Oct. 1988.

Chen, Edward M., and Henderson, Wade. "New 'English-Only' Movement Reflects Old Fear of Immigrants." *Civil Liberties,* Summer–Fall 1986, pp. 8–9.

Connor, Walker, ed. *Mexican-Americans in Comparative Perspective.* Washington, D.C.: Urban Institute Press, 1985.

Dil, Anwar S., ed. *The Ecology of Language: Essays by Einar Haugen.* Stanford: Stanford University Press, 1972.

Donahue, Thomas J. "U.S. English: Its Life and Works." *International Journal of the Sociology of Language* 56 (1985): 99–112.

Dyste, Connie Diane. "Proposition 63: The California English Language Amendment." Master's thesis, University of California, Los Angeles, Graduate School of Education, 1987.

Fishman, Joshua A. "Language Maintenance." In Stephan Thernstrom, ed., *Harvard Encyclopedia of American Ethnic Groups.* Cambridge, Mass.: Harvard University Press, 1980.

Glazer, Nathan. "The Process and Problems of Language-Maintenance: An Integrative Review." In Joshua A. Fishman et al., *Language Loyalty in the United States.* New York: Arno Press, 1978.

Glazer, Nathan, and Moynihan, Daniel Patrick, eds. *Ethnicity: Theory and Experience.* Cambridge, Mass.: Harvard University Press, 1975.

Gordon, Milton M. *Assimilation in American Life: The Role of Race, Religion, and National Origins.* New York: Oxford University Press, 1964.

———. "Models of Pluralism: The New American Dilemma." *Annals of the American Academy of Political and Social Science* 454 (March 1981): 178–88.

Grosjean, François. *Life With Two Languages: An Introduction to Bilingualism.* Cambridge, Mass.: Harvard University Press, 1982.

Higham, John. *Send These to Me: Jews and Other Immigrants in Urban America.* New York: Atheneum, 1975.

Kjolseth, Rolf. "Cultural Politics of Bilingualism." *Society,* May–June 1983, pp. 40–48.

Kuropas, Myron B. "Multilingualism: A Cure for Arrogance." *Chicago Sun-Times,* Oct. 7, 1982. Rpt. in U.S. Senate, *E.L.A. Hearing.*

Lamm, Richard, and Love, John. "Apartheid, American Style: Growth of Minorities and Their Failure to Assimilate Result in Great Divide." *Rocky Mountain News,* Sept. 18, 1988.

MacKaye, Susannah. "California's Proposition 63 and Public Perceptions of Language." Master's thesis, Stanford University Department of Linguistics, 1987.

McCarthy, Kevin F., and Valdez, R. Burciaga. *Current and Future Effects of Mexican Immigration in California.* Santa Monica, Calif.: Rand Corporation, 1986.

Rodríguez, Richard. *Hunger of Memory: The Education of Richard Rodríguez.* Boston: David R. Godine, 1982.

Tarver, Heidi. "Language and Politics in the 1980s: The Story of U.S. English." *Politics and Society* 17, no. 2 (June 1989): 225–45.

Language Rights and Official English

Califa, Antonio J. "Declaring English the Official Language: Prejudice Spoken Here." *Harvard Civil Rights–Civil Liberties Law Review* 24 (1989): 293–348.

Citizens Commission on Civil Rights. "Barriers to Registration and Voting: An Agenda for Reform." National Center for Policy Alternatives, Washington, D.C., April 1988.

Dale, Charles. "Legal Analysis of H.J. Res. 169 Proposing an Amendment to the U.S. Constitution to Make English the Official Language of the United States." Congressional Research Service, June 27, 1983. Rpt. in U.S. Senate, *E.L.A. Hearing.*

del Valle, Manuel. "Language Rights and Due Process: Hispanics in the United States." *Revista de la Universidad Interamericana de Puerto Rico* 17, no. 1 (1982): 91.

Guerra, Sandra. "Voting Rights and the Constitution: The Disenfranchisement of Non-English Speaking Citizens." *Yale Law Journal* 97 (1986): 1419–37.

Leibowitz, Arnold H. *Educational Policy and Political Acceptance: The Imposition of English As the Language of Instruction in American Schools.* Washington, D.C.: Center for Applied Linguistics, 1981. Rpt. in U.S. House, *E.L.A. Hearing.*

———. "English Literacy: Legal Sanction for Discrimination." *Notre Dame Lawyer* 45, no. 7 (Fall 1969): 7–67. Rpt. in U.S. House, *E.L.A. Hearing.*

———. *Federal Recognition of the Rights of Minority Language Groups.* Arlington, Va.: National Clearinghouse for Bilingual Education, [1982].

Lexion, Valerie A. "Language Minority Voting Rights and the English Language Amendment." *Hastings Constitutional Law Quarterly* 14 (1987): 657.

Loo, Chalsa M. "The 'Biliterate' Ballot Controversy: Language Acquisition and Cultural Shift Among Immigrants." *International Migration Review* 19, no. 3 (1985): 493–515.

Lyons, James J. *Legal Responsibilities of Education Agencies Serving National Origin Language Minority Students.* Mid-Atlantic Equity Center, Technical Series. Washington, D.C.: American University School of Education, 1988.

Macías, Reynaldo F. "Choice of Language as a Human Right: Public Policy Implications in the United States." In *Bilingual Education and Public Policy,* ed. Raymond V. Padilla. Ypsilanti, Mich.: Eastern Michigan University, 1979.

Mealey, Linda M. "English-Only Rules and 'Innocent' Employers: Clarifying National Origin Discrimination and Disparate Impact Theory Under Title VII." *Minnesota Law Review* 74 (1989): 387–436.

Piatt, Bill. *¿Only English? Law and Language Policy in the United States.* Albuquerque: University of New Mexico Press, 1990.

"Quasi-Suspect Classes and Proof of Discriminatory Intent: A New Model." *Yale Law Journal* 90 (1981): 912.

Roos, Peter. "Implementation of the Federal Bilingual Educational Mandate: The *Keyes* Case as a Paradigm." *La Raza Law Journal* 1, no. 3 (1986).

Wong, Sau-ling Cynthia. "Educational Rights of Language Minorities." In Sandra Lee McKay and Sau-ling Cynthia Wong, eds., *Language Diversity: Problem or Resource?* Cambridge, Mass.: Newbury House Publishers, 1988.

Education and Linguistic Minorities

Baker, Keith A., and de Kanter, Adriana A., eds. *Bilingual Education: A Reappraisal of Federal Policy.* Lexington, Mass.: Lexington Books, 1983.

California Office of Bilingual Bicultural Education. *Beyond Language: Social and Cultural Factors in Schooling Language Minority Students.* Los Angeles: California State University, 1986.

———. *Schooling and Language Minority Students: A Theoretical Framework.* Los Angeles: California State University, 1981.

———. *Studies on Immersion Education: A Collection for United States Educators.* Sacramento: California State Department of Education, 1984.

Cazden, Courtney B., and Snow, Catherine E., eds. "English Plus: Issues in Bilingual Education." *Annals of the American Academy of Political and Social Science* 508 (March 1990).

Crawford, James. *Bilingual Education: History, Politics, Theory, and Practice.* 2d ed. Los Angeles: Bilingual Educational Services, 1991.

Cummins, Jim. *Bilingualism and Special Education.* San Diego: College Hill Press, 1984.

———. *Empowering Minority Students.* Sacramento: California Association for Bilingual Education, 1989.

Hakuta, Kenji. *Mirror of Language: The Debate on Bilingualism.* New York: Basic Books, 1986.

The Invisible Minority: Report of the N.E.A.–Tucson Survey. Washington, D.C.: National Education Association, 1966.

Krashen, Stephen D. *The Input Hypothesis: Issues and Implications.* London: Longman, 1985.

———. *Inquiries and Insights: Second Language Learning, Immersion & Bilingual Education, Literacy.* Hayward, Calif.: Alemany Press, 1985.

Krashen, Stephen D., and Biber, Douglas. *On Course: Bilingual Education's Success in California.* Sacramento: California Association for Bilingual Education, 1988.

Leibowitz, Arnold H. *The Bilingual Education Act: A Legislative Analysis.* Rosslyn, Va.: National Clearinghouse for Bilingual Education, [1980].

McLaughlin, Barry. *Second Language Acquisition in Childhood.* 2 vols. Hillsdale, N.J.: Lawrence Erlbaum Associates, 1984–85.

National Center for Education Statistics. *The Retention of Minority Languages in the United States: A Seminar on the Analytic Work of Calvin J. Veltman, May 13, 1980.* Washington, D.C.: U.S. Government Printing Office, 1980.

Ovando, Carlos J., and Collier, Virginia P. *Bilingual and E.S.L. Classrooms: Teaching in Multicultural Contexts.* New York: McGraw-Hill, 1985.

Padilla, Amado M., et al. "The English Only Movement: Myths, Reality, and Implications for Psychology." *Journal of the American Psychological Association* 46, no. 2 (Feb. 1991): 120–30.

Ruiz, Richard. "Orientations in Language Planning," *NABE Journal* 8, no. 2 (1984): 15–34. Rpt. in Sandra Lee McKay and Sau-ling Cynthia Wong, eds., *Language Diversity: Problem or Resource?* Cambridge, Mass.: Newbury House Publishers, 1988.

Simon, Paul. *The Tongue-Tied American: Confronting the Foreign Language Crisis.* New York: Continuum, 1980.

Spanish-American League Against Discrimination. "Not English Only, English *Plus!* Bilingual Education Issue Analysis." Mimeographed, Oct. 15, 1985.

Spener, David. "Transitional Bilingual Education and the Socialization of Immigrants." *Harvard Educational Review* 58, no. 2 (May 1988): 133–53.

Tucker, G. Richard. "Implications of Canadian Research for Promoting a Language Competent American Society." In Joshua A. Fishman et al., *The Fergusonian Impact*, vol. 2, *Sociolinguistics and the Sociology of Language.* Berlin: Mouton de Gruyter, 1986.

U.S. General Accounting Office. *Bilingual Education: A New Look at the Research Evidence.* GAO/PEMD–87–12BR. Washington, D.C.: U.S. Government Printing Office, 1987.

U.S. House of Representatives, Committee on Education and Labor. *Compendium of Papers on the Topic of Bilingual Education.* Serial no. 99-R, 99th Cong., 2d sess. (June 1986).

Veltman, Calvin J. *Language Shift in the United States.* Berlin: Mouton Publishers, 1983.

Willig, Ann C. "A Meta-Analysis of Selected Studies on the Effectiveness of Bilingual Education." *Review of Educational Research* 55, no. 3 (Fall 1985): 269–317.

International Experiences with Language Diversity

Anderson, Benedict R. O'G. *Imagined Communities: Reflections on the Origin and Spread of Nationalism.* London: Verso, 1983.

Blaustein, Albert P., and Epstein, Dana Blaustein. *Resolving Language Conflicts: A Study of the World's Constitutions.* Washington, D.C.: U.S. English, 1986.

Deutsch, Karl. *Nationalism and Social Communication.* Cambridge, Mass.: M.I.T. Press, 1953.

Edwards, John. *Language, Society, and Identity.* Oxford: Basil Blackwell, 1985.

Heath, Shirley Brice. *Telling Tongues: Language Policy in Mexico, Colony to Nation.* New York: Teachers College Press, 1972.

Lo Bianco, Joseph. *National Policy on Languages.* Canberra: Australian Government Publishing Service, 1987.

McRae, Kenneth D. *Conflict and Compromise in Multilingual Societies.* Vol. 1, *Switzerland.* Vol. 2, *Belgium.* Waterloo, Ont.: Wilfred Laurier Press, 1983, 1986.

Milroy, James, and Milroy, Lesley. *Authority in Language: Investigating Language Prescription and Standardisation.* London: Routledge & Kegan Paul, 1985.

Schmid, Carol L. "Quebec in the 1970s–1980s: Submerged Nation or Canadian Fringe?" *Research in Political Sociology* 2 (1986): 269–91.

Weinstein, Brian. *The Civic Tongue: The Political Consequences of Language Choices.* New York: Longman, 1983.

Yalden, Maxwell F. "The Bilingual Experience in Canada." In Martin Ridge, ed., *The New Bilingualism: An American Dilemma.* New Brunswick, N.J.: Transaction Books, 1981, pp. 71–87.

Additional Information Sources

American Civil Liberties Union of Northern California, 1663 Mission Street, Suite 460, San Francisco, Calif. 94103.

American Council on the Teaching of Foreign Languages, 579 Broadway, Hastings-on-Hudson, N.Y. 10706.

Asian Pacific American Legal Center of Southern California, 1010 South Flower Street, Suite 302, Los Angeles, Calif. 90015. Sponsors project on language rights in the workplace.

Australian Advisory Council on Languages and Multicultural Education, Department of Employment, Education, and Training, GPO Box 9880, Canberra ACT 2601, Australia. Publishes journal, *VOX.*

Center for Applied Linguistics, 1118 22d Street, N.W., Washington, D.C. 20037.

English First, 8001 Forbes Place, Suite 102, Springfield, Va. 22151.

English Plus Information Clearinghouse, 220 I Street, N.E., Suite 220, Washington, D.C. 20002. Publishes newsletter, *EPIC Events.*

Hispanic Link Weekly Report, 1420 N Street, N.W., Washington D.C. 20005.

Japanese American Citizens League, 1765 Sutter Street, San Francisco, Calif. 94115.

Joint National Committee for Languages, 300 I Street, N.E., Suite 211, Washington, D.C. 20002.

Mexican American Legal Defense and Educational Fund, 733 15th Street, N.W., Suite 920, Washington, D.C. 20005.

Multicultural Education, Training, and Advocacy (META), Inc., 524 Union Street, San Francisco, Calif. 94133.

National Association for Bilingual Education, 810 First St., N.E., Washington, D.C. 20002. Publishes newsletter.

National Association of Latino Elected and Appointed Officials, 708 G Street, S.E., Washington, D.C. 20003.

National Coalition for Language Freedom, 530 12th Street, Sacramento, Calif. 95814. Publishes newsletter.

National Council of La Raza, 810 First Street, N.E., Washington, D.C. 20002.

National Education Association, Human and Civil Rights Division, 1201 16th Street, N.W., Washington, D.C. 20036.

People for the American Way, 2000 M Street, N.W., Suite 400, Washington, D.C. 20036.

Puerto Rican Legal Defense and Education Fund, 99 Hudson Street, 14th Floor, New York, N.Y. 10013.

Teachers of English to Speakers of Other Languages, 1600 Cameron Street, Suite 300, Alexandria, Va. 22314. Publishes newsletter and journal.

U.S English, 818 Connecticut Avenue, N.W., Suite 200, Washington, D.C. 20006. Publishes newsletter, *Update.*

Copyright Acknowledgments

Index